RISK MANAGEMENT IN
THE BUSINESS ENTERPRISE

THE IRWIN SERIES IN RISK AND INSURANCE

EDITORS

EDISON L. BOWERS
The Ohio State University

DAVIS W. GREGG
The American College of Life Underwriters

RISK MANAGEMENT
IN THE
BUSINESS ENTERPRISE

by

ROBERT I. MEHR
Professor of Finance

and

BOB A. HEDGES
Associate Professor of Finance

Both of the University of Illinois

1963

RICHARD D. IRWIN, INC.
HOMEWOOD, ILLINOIS

First Printing, July, 1963

Library of Congress Catalog Card No. 63–14224

PRINTED IN THE UNITED STATES OF AMERICA

Dedicated to the memory of

Bert A. Hedges, C.L.U.,

insurance man and educator,
who was largely responsible for the beginning
of our collaborative efforts some fifteen years ago.

PREFACE

"Seven is a good handy figure in its way, picturesque, with a savour of the mythical; one might say that it is more filling to the spirit than a dull academic half-dozen." So writes the famous novelist, Thomas Mann, who somehow must have known that it would take us seven years to write this book. Of course, the past seven years were not devoted wholly to the preparation of this volume. For one thing, Professor Hedges took a year off to become a Harvard man, and for another Professor Mehr took that sabbatical so badly needed by his students.

When we undertook this project back in 1956, the concept of risk management was novel and we thought that the idea would have to be sold to our colleagues in other universities and in business. But since then a revolution has begun in education for business, and in its wake the concept of risk management has emerged as the expected savior of the curriculum in insurance: the "insurance" major has been changed to "risk and insurance;" the American Association of University Teachers of Insurance has changed its name to the American Risk and Insurance Association; and all new insurance textbooks have added the word "risk" to their itles. Even the "Irwin Series in Insurance" was changed to the "Irwin Series in Risk and Insurance." Yet all of this has come to pass without any really significant changes in most of the courses offered, the activities of the association, the content of the "new" textbooks, or, until now, the variety of books in the "Irwin Series."

Thus while the seed for this book was planted quietly in the peaceful days before the revolution, its long gestation brings it to fruition in the midst of the revolution. As a result our job now becomes one of selling *our* concept of risk management rather than one of selling *the* concept of risk management.

The term *risk management* has not been in use long enough to have an established definition. Men in top management positions who deal with risks every day in their efforts to create profits for stockholders look upon the whole of corporate management as risk management. Others take a narrow view of risk management and use the term to define the activities of the corporate insurance buyer. We take the position that risk management as a managerial function is something *more* than corporate insurance management and something *less* than all management. We believe that the function should be confined to the management of certain specific types of risks and should not encompass all risks.

Our interest in the subject stems, of course, from our interest in insurance. Insurance-oriented people have never been much concerned with "speculative" or "dynamic" risks (as distinguished from "pure" or "static" risks), and there seems to be no important reason why they should be so now. This does not mean that centralized control of speculative risk is undesirable but that the management of "pure" or "static" risks is a separate function in itself, requiring specialized skills, knowledge, and techniques.

We define risk management, therefore, as the management of those risks for which the organization, principles, and techniques appropriate to insurance management are useful. An important feature of this definition is that the word "techniques" is *plural*. Insurance is not the only technique appropriate in managing insurable risks; it is not always even the best technique. In order to handle his job effectively, the insurance manager must arrange an organized approach to his problems which utilizes principles of insurance management to select the particular technique or techniques to use on each particular insurable risk. In order for the *risk* manager to handle *his* job effectively, he must similarly use his skills and knowledge to develop and maintain an organized procedure which uses these same or similar principles to select from the same set of available techniques the one or ones to be used for each of the non-speculative risks (insurable and otherwise) faced by his business organization.

Defined in this fashion, risk management has both theoretical and practical content: on the one hand are the principles to be applied; on the other are the organized approaches to the application of these principles and the available techniques to which the principles may be applied. Formulation of the principles to be applied is the primary objective of this text. The principles offered have been deduced by the authors in the comparative security and serenity of their faculty offices. Any similarity between the guides suggested here and those (if any) actually being followed by practicing insurance managers is favorable coincidence. So far, the techniques of risk management have been given more attention and are better known than the rules for applying them. But as practicing risk managers devote more study and attention to risk management principles, these principles will necessarily be based on knowledge already found in other subject matter areas, particularly those subject matter areas which gave birth to the risk management concept in the first place. Clearly, among the most important—probably, indeed, *the* most important—of these basic subject matter areas are the fields of business finance and of probability and statistics (or actuarial science). Since the principles presented in this text are based on principles found in these two fields, it seems reasonable to expect that differences between the principles discussed here and actual business practices will diminish as time passes.

Although this book is not designed to be all things to all men, it can be more than one thing to more than one man. It can be the basic text for the introductory course in the field of risk and insurance or it can be the text for the only course that the "non-major" takes in this field. If a course in the "Principles of Insurance" is offered as the introductory course, intensive coverage of the first eleven chapters of this text along with the problem materials can be the basis for the second course, with specialized courses in life and health insurance and in property and liability insurance, following as desired. In those schools in which either facilities or philosophies limit course offerings in risk and insurance to two one-semester courses, this book combined with a basic insurance text will provide the fundamental text materials needed for a coordinated two-semester sequence with each course being self-contained and with neither having to be a prerequisite for the other. (In other words, this book is *not* a text for an insurance course of the traditional type; it is a book in risk management, and its discussion of insurance coverage and operational details is at the absolute minimum compatible with that purpose.)

Finally, this book can be useful in M.B.A. and D.B.A. programs and in executive development and other adult educational programs for businessmen interested in executive and managerial decision problems and decision-making processes.

It should be noted that, while the principles in this text are based on probability and statistics, nothing more than a nodding acquaintance with these subjects is expected of the reader. In this area, the approach is, "The risk manager, needing to know certain things, asks the company statistician, who tells him . . ." (the figures he needs to know). The sections containing probability and statistical procedures may be read faster by persons familiar with such procedures and footnotes are inserted to answer some questions such persons are likely to have, but other readers can and should ignore them. For those who would like to understand more of the procedures which are discussed, an appendix has been inserted after Chapter 4 to summarize at least the surface characteristics of the probability matters mentioned.

With respect to the other underlying field, business finance, rather more is required of the reader. Ability to read balance sheets and income statements is taken for granted, as is familiarity with the vocabulary and basic standard practices of accountancy and business finance.

Review questions have been prepared for each Chapter. We believe that use of these questions as a teaching and learning device will prove rewarding, at least that has been our experience, and that is why we prepared them. Kits of specimen policy forms available through the American Mutual Insurance Alliance, 20 North Wacker Drive, Chicago 6, Illinois, and the Insurance Information Institute, 60 John Street, New York 38, New York, can be useful to both the teaching and studying of Chapter 12 through 15.

Chapter 14 provides an index or catalogue of insurance covers. Much of that chapter perhaps will be more useful as reference material than as text material. It should be assigned and read, however, if the student is to become acquainted with these covers.

Now comes the time for the blessing. Whom do we thank and for what? Because there were no other texts in the field (1963) we had no one to emulate. We do owe a debt of gratitude to each other for patience and understanding during those critical discussions of one another's work. Only mutual respect enabled us to withstand the threats to our mental security which grew out of these discussions. And while we are on this subject we hasten to add that we will continue to re-examine our work. Its publication, however, provides us the benefit of public examination: the scrutiny of what we hope will be a large number of assayers. And this brings us to the major object of our thanks: Those who read this book critically, and, in one way or another, pass on to us their suggestions for its improvement. We fully realize that there is still much work left to be done in this fascinating and exciting field of risk management!

Also with respect to future interest in our work, we feel that special notice should be accorded to the beneficial interest which will be taken in it by the Department of Internal Revenue. This organization is worthy of special notice in this Preface because of its unique efficacy in the field of risk management: It has managed to arrange its affairs in such fashion that while it shares in such benefits as may accrue from ventures of this kind, it accepts none of the risks which these ventures involve.

Moving back to the past, and to those whose share in this project consisted of hard work and supporting effort, we wish to thank all the scholars whose works we cited in the footnotes sprinkled throughout the text. To those who recognize what seem to them to be unfootnoted products of their work, we quote from Plutarch's *Lives Sertorius* (p. 678), "It is no great wonder if in long process of time, while fortune takes her course hither and thither, numerous coincidences should spontaneously occur. If the number and variety of subjects to be wrought upon be infinite, it is all the more easy for fortune, with such an abundance of material, to effect this similarity of results." But should the footnote omission be the result of a "goof" rather than a coincidence, we apologize and offer our belated thanks.

Professor Robert N. Corley read and threw away our first draft of Chapter 7, bringing from us an initial reaction well expressed by the lines from King Henry VI: "The first thing we do, let's kill all the lawyers." We reconsidered, however, when he made us see the truth in the statement by Justice Holmes that "the life of the law has not been logic: it has been experience." We thank Professor Corley for giving us the benefit of his legal experience.

For help in reading proof, we are grateful to Gary Fish, Jane Hedges, and Margaret Mehr. For assistance in typing we especially thank Shirley Starr and Jane Hedges, and for assistance in indexing, Jane Hedges again. Finally we want to extend our most sincere appreciation to Professor William T. Beadles, who read every word of the original plus some amended manuscript and made many suggestions for its improvement in content and in style, most of which we adopted. We consider Professor Beadles, who has helped us through several editions of two other books, an indispensible member of our team. Being realists, however, we accept full responsibility for all errors that up to this point have escaped notice. But being philosophical about our shortcomings, we are not overly embarrassed by them. In particular, while we have made effort to eliminate typographical errors, proofreading is not the art on which we stake our reputations.

Robert I. Mehr
Bob A. Hedges

Urbana, Illinois
May, 1963

TABLE OF CONTENTS

PART III. ANALYZING RISK

PART IV. DEALING WITH RISKS

PART V.   INSURANCE AND RISK MANAGEMENT

PART VI.   CASES IN RISK MANAGEMENT

INDEXES

PART I

Introduction to Risk and Risk Management

The control of risk and the management of losses are the fundamental objectives of risk management in the business enterprise. The first step toward the accomplishment of these objectives is to develop an understanding of the various types of risks that business faces and to allocate the managerial responsibilities for each type of risk. After that, some fundamental rules of risk management need to be studied along with the problems of applying them. Part I consists of one chapter designed to accomplish these purposes.

Chapter 1

RISK IN BUSINESS: ITS NATURE
AND MANAGEMENT

Business cannot operate in a free society without incurring risk. From the time the decision is made to organize a business to the last distribution of funds in its liquidation, uncertainty as to its course is one of the major concerns of its owners and managers. A new business may never get off the ground, and a seasoned one may crash at any time. Risk plays such an important role in everyday business affairs that its control is a major function of business management.

NATURE OF BUSINESS RISKS

Businessmen may be said "to risk the certainty of something for the chance of something more." Chance implies only a possibility or a probability, as distinct from a certainty. Since "risk" implies chance, it is characterized by uncertainty. Only if a businessman knew exactly what was going to happen in the future to his net assets and to his net income would he be free from risk. Many factors, however, block this kind of sixth sense. In the business economy, there is much more to obscure the future than to reveal it. Conditions that make profits and losses unpredictable are the sources of risks in business. These sources may be classified as *dynamic* (speculative) and *static* (pure), and each has several subdivisions (Table 1–1). The dynamic sources are the more difficult to handle, but fortunately they are ambivalent in nature, that is, they can create profits instead of losses. The static sources, on the other hand, can only cause losses.

Dynamic or Speculative Sources of Risk

That a business will earn a profit is not a foregone conclusion. True, some operations appear to be "sure things," but even here the unexpected can happen. Costs may be estimated in advance, but a strike in a basic materials industry can cause expensive delays and produce higher prices for materials. Market demand is anticipated, but much can happen to upset the anticipation: a cold wave, a heat wave, a new threat of war, a change in government tax policy, a change in popular tastes, a new invention, or just plain human inconstancy, which causes former customers to save their money or spend it somewhere else. Changes in the behavior of the political, social, or economic environment are dynamic sources of risk, and the resulting risks are called dynamic.

TABLE 1-1

Sources of Risk

Dynamic sources (speculative risk)
    Management risks
        Marketing
        Financial
        Production
    Political
    Innovative
Static sources (pure risk)
    Sources causing physical damage to assets
    Fraud and criminal violence
    Adverse judgments at law
    Damage to property of others (causing reduced earning power)
    Death or disability of employees or owners

Of course, dynamic changes that cause one businessman's loss often produce another businessman's gain. When teen-age record buyers shift their allegiance from Croonin' Dicky Doyle to Rockin' Danny Deever, it is hard on Dicky but mighty profitable for Danny. The same cool summer that produces losses for the travel and vacation business may be a small bonanza for suppliers of garden equipment and do-it-yourself tools, and the same business whose large inventory holdings cause a big loss when prices drop reaps a windfall when prices go up.

Dynamic risks can therefore be said to be ambivalent: They offer a chance of loss, but they also offer a chance for gain. We shall call such risks *speculative*. Speculative risk bearers, who take the risks involved in the creation and operation of business firms in such an economy, are essential to its operation.

For analytical purposes, the dynamic risk may be separated into three constituents: management, political, and innovative.

Management Risk. Business executives do not have a direct line into the celestial headquarters of a guardian angel. They must reach their decisions by human, that is, fallible, means. Practically all business decisions involve an element of speculation since they are concerned with "possibly" and "probably" rather than with "is" or "is not." A wrong decision can create loss; a right decision can bring profit. The trouble is that often it is completely impossible to tell at the time the decision has to be made which choice will turn out to be the correct one. The uncertainty of the results of managerial decisions is the content of management risks. Businessmen must formulate policy with respect to production, marketing, finance, and personnel. In these areas, major and minor decisions have to be made involving such policy-making areas as what to produce, how much to produce, how to produce it, how large an inventory to carry, what marketing channels to use, how and where to advertise, how to finance fixed and working capital, how and where to recruit personnel, what pay scales to adopt, how to train personnel, how to deal with organized labor, and how to maintain the goodwill of all the types of publics with which the business deals: government, customers, community, employees, and investors. The source of management risk is, not that these decisions have to be made, but that they have to be made without all the knowledge necessary for reaching maximum profit conclusions. What might well be astute decisions based on foresight can easily appear foolish in hindsight.

The inability to judge human reactions accurately and the limitations in the expense and time that can be afforded to get all the facts make the taking of management risks essential in business.

Management risk can be divided into three categories: market, financial, and production.

Market Risks. An investment generally has to be made in inventories, buildings, fixtures, and labor in anticipation of the sale of the final product. Market risks are those elements which make it uncertain as to whether the production can be sold at a price high enough to yield a fair return on the investment. The time lapse between production commitments and the ultimate sale of the product is an important element in the market risk. More specifically, market risks consist of factors that influence either the monetary or the real demand for the good or service involved. For example, general price levels may decline after a heavy commitment has been made in fixed assets or inventories, making it impossible to dispose of the final products at a profit and perhaps requiring disposal at a loss. Fashions can change soon after an inventory is built. Fads can die overnight, leaving manufacturers and retailers with large stocks of unwanted items. New inventions can render stocks of merchandise obsolete. Unexpected competition may spring up and reduce the market share. Price wars can develop in soft markets. Population centers may shift, reducing the market potential. The size and characteristics of the firm's market are always open to fluctuation: consumption patterns change, business conditions vary, seasonal sales patterns fluctuate, and competitors improve quality, reduce cost, or enhance sales efforts. The content of market risks is not the changes themselves but the inability to predict either the extent or the time of these changes.[1]

Financial Risk. In the management of a business, the financial function is the raising and administering of funds. Careful forecasting of financial needs is essential to the successful operation of a business. Inadequate capital is frequently the principal cause of business failure. Will there be sufficient capital to operate the business on the scale necessary for success?

In arriving at decisions on financial policy, a number of questions need to be answered. For example, what is the proper division between the use of short-term and long-term funds? What is the proper distribution in the use of the many sources of short-term funds? What is the proper balance between the use of equity and long-term debt financing? How is the corporate net income best used? Should it be paid out in dividends, used to retire outstanding securities, or reinvested in business expansion? What should be the policy in granting credit? What is the proper distribution between current and fixed assets? These and many more policy decisions have to be made by those who administer the finances of a business enterprise.

If the financial manager could see clearly into the future, his job of decision making would be comparatively simple, assuming, of course, that he was properly qualified for his position in the first place. Even with all the pertinent facts at hand, managerial decisions on financial policy involve uncertainty because unexpected developments in the future might easily have dictated an entirely different policy if these developments had been known at the time the decision had to be made. The fact that so many financial decisions have to be made with an eye to the future is evidence that financial risk is widespread. It is not the fact that the future must be considered that creates the risk, but that the future is uncertain.

Production Risk. Marketing and finance are not the only areas in which the businessman needs to formulate policy. He must make decisions involving production and personnel problems.

Production risk is concerned primarily with materials, labor, and technology. Will the supply of raw materials be adequate? What are the price trends in the raw materials market? How large should the raw materials inventory be? Could other raw materials be used as effective substitutes? Would a reduction in inventory costs, brought on by simplifying products and standardizing costs, result in an improved profit position? Should the company by vertical integration acquire and manage its own sources of

---

[1] A significant degree of risk arises from the fact that even the *present* state of the market is not fully known. If the market were not dynamic, today's position, as well as tomorrow's, could eventually be learned from accretion of facts about the past. Therefore, uncertainty about the present is also a dynamic risk. Its content is inability to ascertain the extent and direction of recent changes in position.

supply? The businessman must find the best answers to these questions, but, since he is forced to deal with blind spots, he can never be absolutely sure that he has come up with the right ones.

Risk in personnel administration involves questions relating to the adequacy and dependability of the labor supply; effectiveness of training procedures; reduction of labor turnover; negotiation of satisfactory labor contracts; elimination of strikes; establishment of an equitable salary structure; improvements in labor efficiency; installation of group insurance, pension plans, and other fringe benefits; and, in general, the maintenance of smooth employer-employee relations. How to make the most efficient use of labor is not an easy problem. Labor's reaction to various managerial decisions cannot always be foreseen. The mysteries in collective bargaining are carefully guarded by both parties. When all the cards are not on the table, risk is inescapable.

An important source of production risk is that new methods of production will be found that will render old methods obsolete. Heavy investment in machinery, equipment, and materials can lose much of its value just as if it had been ravished by fire. How can the business executive tell at the time he is building or expanding his facilities whether the equipment and production processes he is using will continue to be efficient for enough years ahead to return his investment with a profit? Systematic production research will help keep the business up to date, but it cannot eliminate production risk. Even here, there is the question of how much to spend for research, how far to go in any project, and when to terminate a study.

Political Risk. Not only must businessmen make their decisions without the help of oracles, but they are also subject to important restrictions in making them. In the interests of public welfare, governments place certain limitations and prohibitions on the freedom of individual action. Businesses are told that they must do this and that they cannot do that. The regulations are not always clear, and they change from time to time. Changes in the social philosophy or merely the needs for political expediency of the government or party in power can affect business fortunes markedly. Some actions or philosophies help business in general, whereas others hurt business in general. Many more help some types of businesses but at the same time hurt others. To the extent that these local, state, national, and international political changes are unpredictable, business is faced with what can be called "political risk."

For example, the passage of a local smoke abatement law can cause a heavy increase in production costs of the local industries affected and thereby hamper their ability to compete with concerns in other localities. A teen-age curfew might be established, thus reducing the business of the local jukebox hangouts. The state university might suddenly require all students to live in university-owned dormitories, thus causing serious loss to those who profited in the field of student housing. The federal government might build a new highway that bypasses a thriving motor court, reducing the profitability of that investment. A foreign government can cause loss to American exporters by establishing trade barriers in the form of tariffs or exchange controls. Examples of political risk at all levels of government are plentiful.

Political changes or developments can cause a reduction of business profits by bringing about either a decrease in operating income or an increase in operating expenses. Government competition, wartime production controls, certain types of taxes, reduced government spending, the regulation of trade practices, and controls over public morals are examples of political developments that have brought about a decrease in income, whereas other types of taxes, minimum wage laws, safety codes, and public health standards are examples of political developments that have effected an increase in costs of operation.

Innovation Risk. The introduction of a new product with the expectation that it will meet a need apparently already evident or that the product itself will create a need on its own merit entails an uncertainty beyond that found in the production and sale of established goods and services. Will the product "catch on" as expected?

When George Westinghouse invented the air brake, orders were not rushed through. Instead, railroad executives called him a "blithering idiot" for saying he could stop a train by air. Cyrus McCormick preached the gospel of efficient harvesting for fourteen years before he sold his first hundred machines. Transcontinental airlines did not spring up overnight when Orville and Wilbur Wright built their first airplane. As one "student" put it, "until the twentieth century, there was no need for airplanes because people did not do much flying before then." Progress by innovation is risky business. The entrepreneur who risks his time and money along these lines cannot afford to be wrong often.

Static or Pure Sources of Risk

Unexpected changes in the economic productivity of a given capital investment are not the only source of business risks. A mythical businessman who estimates his market accurately, has a Midas touch in business management, and can foresee all political developments still will be faced with risk. This remaining risk is called, naturally enough, "static." It would continue to exist even in a society that had no changes in politics, tastes or habits of consumers, or level of economic activity. A major class of static risk is the risk of physical loss of, or damage to, property. Property may be physically damaged or destroyed; lost through fraud, theft, or disappearance; or taken by adverse judgments at law. Usefulness of some property may be impaired by damage to other property: Loss of one shoe renders the other useless. The usefulness of a manufacturing plant is reduced if its power plant is destroyed. Finally, losses in business value may be suffered when persons die or are injured: A particularly energetic and capable manager has more than once been the difference between a going concern and a dead one.

Static risks are seldom ambivalent in nature: If the physical plant of the business burns down, that is a loss (usually). Similarly, when prices go down, a business that holds inventory suffers a loss. On the other hand, when prices go up, the inventory holder shows a gain, even though only a "paper" one. But there is no equivalent built-in gain-making result from the experience of "no fire." "No damage by fire" can be matched in the inventory case only with "prices do not change," a condition which, of itself, makes no profit.

The ambivalent risks are denominated "speculative." The correlative term for nonambivalent risks is "pure" (signifying "unmixed").

Physical Damage to Assets. A glance at the balance sheet of a business unit will reveal a variety of assets, all subject to static risk: real property; tangible personal property, including tools and equipment, furniture and fixtures, inventories, and vehicles; cash and negotiable instruments; non-negotiable claims against others, such as leasehold rights, accounts receivable, and deferred charges; and goodwill. These assets may be damaged or destroyed directly or indirectly by "acts of God" (e.g., wind, hail, flood, earthquake, subsidence, and lightning); they may be destroyed or damaged by unintentional acts of man (e.g., fire, explosion, negligence in construction, and negligence in operation); and, finally, they may be destroyed or damaged by intentional acts of man (e.g., vandalism, riot, insurrection, war, attempted theft and the authorization of civil authority).

Loss of Possession by Fraud or Criminal Violence. One individual can obtain possession or control over the property of another by one of many illegal devices (or vices): burglary, robbery, embezzlement, forgery, misappropriation, willful abstraction, willful misapplication, confidence game, swindling, or sneak thievery. To the innocent victim, except for the faint hope that the property will be recovered and returned by law enforcement officers, a loss from any of these sources has the same effect as though the property had been physically destroyed by fire or some other peril.

Loss of Ownership through an Adverse Judgment at Law. In a perfect society, no one would be careless, and no mistakes would be made. But, unfortunately, we do not live in a perfect society. People are careless, and mistakes are made. As Pope put it, "To err is human." Frequently one man's carelessness is the cause of another man's loss. Under certain conditions, the aggrieved party is provided a legal remedy. If the person causing the loss has violated a duty and this violation is the proximate cause of the loss, the law requires that this loss be shifted from the one suffering it to the one causing it. This is the common law of negligence.

Negligence is defined as the failure to do what a reasonable man would have done or doing what a prudent man would not have done under the circumstances. The definition implies the failure to exercise care proportional to the danger involved, and it is the jury's function to determine whether or not a defendant in a negligence suit has used the standard of care expected of him. Juries appear reluctant to give the benefit of any reasonable doubt to the supposedly well-heeled business defendants in cases involving nonbusiness plaintiffs. Even if the court finds contributory negligence on the part of the injured party and fails to award damages, the defendant will suffer a loss. He must pay the cost of defense, and this expense has been aptly referred to as "the high cost of winning."

The businessman is faced with the possibility of liability claims arising from numerous sources: customers may be injured on the premises of the business; members of the public may be hit by a company automobile; the product manufactured or sold may be defective, causing bodily injury or property damage; relations with the public may produce slander, false arrest, humiliation, invasion of right of privacy, detention, or malicious prosecution; or relations with employees may produce industrial accidents or diseases. To the victim of a liability suit, the loss is just as real as though the assets used to pay the damages and other costs were destroyed by fire or were lost by theft.

Loss of Income Resulting from Damage to Property of Others. Obviously when a business suffers a loss of physical assets, it may well suffer a loss of net income until those assets are replaced and put to work. Not as obvious is the loss of net income resulting from damage to property of others. For example, if the plant of John Producer is damaged by fire, the business of Joe User may have to be shut down for lack of a substitute source of materials that heretofore had been supplied by the Producer plant. And if the plant of Joe User is destroyed or damaged by lightning, John Producer may have to curtail operations until his customer's damage is repaired and the plant put back into operation. This is especially true if Joe User is the principal buyer of the output of the Producer plant. A plant closed for repairs cannot use the products of its suppliers. If a local power plant suffers severe damage, many businesses may have to close down or curtail operations until the flow of utilities is restored. In each of these cases, net income is exposed to a loss just as real as though the business interruption were caused by damage to the physical property belonging to the business itself.

Loss of Net Income Resulting from the Death or Disability of Key Employees. An employee's continued life or good health is uncertain. Any working day may be his last. Death sometimes arrives early and unannounced, and disability has a way of catching by surprise men who have never been sick a day in their lives.

Among the personnel of a going business, usually, are men whose continued life and good health are essential to the success of that business. The untimely death or disability of one of these men can cause the business serious loss, which makes itself felt either through an increase in expenses of operations or through a decrease in gross revenue. For example, a replacement has to be trained, and that costs money. Sometimes the replacement has to be lured away from another company with an offer of a salary and fringe benefits exceeding those now carried by the position. In addition, the replacement may not be as efficient.

Formalized employee benefit plans offering a schedule of benefits for death, disability, medical expenses, and retirement help to attract and retain employees. Once these benefits are made a part of the employment contract, the employer has created an additional business risk. The trend is for business to assume more and more of its employees' financial risks. As risks that traditionally have been considered to be strictly personal are shifted to the employer, business risks asssume an even greater role in American society.

Dynamic and Static Risks and Probability

It is usual in insurance literature to note another major difference between dynamic and static risks: Static risks are subject to reduction by application of the statistical "law of large numbers," whereas dynamic risks are not.

"Risk" vs. "Uncertainty"? Following Frank Knight's analysis in the early 1920's,[2] many authors have used applicability of the law of large numbers as the defining characteristic of "risk." Knight held that, whenever a chance or rate of loss could be established, "it is possible to get rid of any real uncertainty by the expedient of grouping or 'consolidating' instances!" This, he said, was the essential characteristic of "risk." "Uncertainty" (or "true uncertainty"), on the other hand, he characterized by the notion that "in general . . . it is impossible to form a group of instances, because the situation dealt with is in a high degree unique."[3]

But not every authority has agreed with this distinction. One contemporary of Knight's, Professor C. O. Hardy, wrote:

Rather it appears probable that the cases of "statistical probability" and the cases of "true uncertainty" are essentially alike, differing only in the amount of information we happen to have at hand to deal with them, the length of time necessary to accumulate a line of cases big enough to establish a statistical frequency, or the fineness of the classification we are using. All applications of the law of averages rest on a grouping of things, unlike in many respects, into classes, on the basis of certain similarities; if cases nearly alike were infrequent, we must do our grouping on the basis of less homogeneous classes. If the classification is crude, or if the cases are not numerous, the statistical method loses its accuracy. But these cases certainly shade off into Professor Knight's "true uncertainties" by imperceptible degrees, the margin of error getting larger as the evidence grows more scanty.

---

[2] Frank H. Knight, *Risk, Uncertainty and Profit* (Boston: Houghton Mifflin Co., 1921).

[3] *Ibid.*, pp. 234, 233, respectively.

The view that the so-called "true uncertainties" are cases which would show statistical regularity, if a sufficient number of like cases were available for comparison, is confirmed by the fact noted by Professor Knight that totally unpredictable cases do show some tendency toward regularity when grouped with other similarly unpredictable data.[4]

We agree with Hardy. On the one hand, there are important, sometimes severe, limitations on the application of the law of large numbers to static risks.[5] On the other hand, today there is a significant and useful body of theory on "decision making under uncertainty" that profitably employs statistical procedures in dealing with risks (uncertainties) in many kinds of dynamic situations.[6]

The Dynamics of Static Risks. Although static risks are defined as those which would be present in a society that had no dynamic elements, they must be dealt with in societies that are fully dynamic.[7] Moreover, the dynamic elements affect the behavior of the static ones; as the society and economy change, so do the losses from fire, flood, accident, legal liability, death, and so on. Both the frequency and the severity are affected. Thus, the risk of loss from legal liability for the operation of vehicles is a "static" risk by definition (if the society were not to change anymore, this risk would still be present), but in our society the number and size of losses suffered from this "static" risk are themselves very dynamic.

Static Risks and "Pooling." While all these limitations on the differences between the statistical behavior of static risks and dynamic ones must always be carefully noted and firmly borne in mind, it is still true that the risk management device of pooling risks and applying the law of large numbers to the combined results of the pool is still one of the most effective ways of dealing with many risks. And, in general, this procedure is much less reliable when dynamic rather than static risks are the subject matter. It is easier to find a large number of rather similar exposures to a given static risk than to a dynamic one, and these exposures are more likely to be independent of one another (less likely to result simultaneously from widespread economic, political, or social conditions). And past loss experience

---

[4] Charles O. Hardy, *Risk and Risk Bearing* (Chicago: University of Chicago Press, 1923), pp. 54–55. The references from Knight are *op. cit.*, pp. 211, 225–57.

[5] See, for example, Irving Pfeffer, *Insurance and Economic Theory* (Homewood, Illinois: Richard D. Irwin, Inc., 1956), pp. 43–44, 57–70.

[6] See, for example, R. Duncan Luce and Howard Raiffa, *Games and Decisions* (New York: John Wiley & Sons, Inc., 1957), esp. chap. 13, "Industrial Decision Making under Uncertainty"; and Robert Schlaifer, *Probability and Statistics for Business Decisions* (New York: McGraw-Hill Book Co., Inc., 1959).

[7] "Static" is an unfortunate term to use in connection with something as dynamic as pure risk. Pure risk is in many ways far from static. For example, age change in houses affects the risk of fire, and age change in drivers affects the risk of automobile accident. Thus, the term "pure" appears to be a better term than "static" for the type of risk described.

from static risks is more likely to be approximately repeated in the near future (dynamic risks *are* dynamic; static risks are only partially affected by dynamic factors). Each of these characteristics of static, as compared with dynamic, risks is a feature needed for successful application of the law of large numbers.

Since, in the end, the conclusion is drawn that static risks *are* noticeably more subject to the law of large numbers, why all the preliminary discussion emphasizing the extent to which dynamic risks *are* and static risks are *not* amenable to statistical treatment? There are two reasons:

1. Risk managers who "learn" the conclusion without knowing its limitations tend to fall into two errors:
   a. On the one hand, they overestimate the statistical reliability of experience with static risks. This can be financially disastrous.
   b. On the other hand, they underestimate the usefulness of statistics and probability theory in dealing with risks ("uncertainties") that do not come close to meeting the standard requirements for statistical prediction. Thus, some useful and probably profitable risk management techniques are overlooked, particularly in connection with dynamic risks.
2. Danger also stalks the manager who "learns the rule" first and only later finds out about its important limitations. He may either:
   a. Reject the rule as one of those things which are, so it is said, "all right in theory, but just no good in practice," or
   b. Reject the limitations as contrary to his "learning."

It is hoped that the student who is introduced simultaneously to the general rule *and* its limitations will fall into none of these errors.[8]

General Observations on Dynamic and Static Risks: A Summary

Several generalizations can be made on the differences between dynamic and static risks.

1. Although both dynamic and static risks involve uncertainty, the uncertainty in dynamic risks includes the question of whether or not the results will be profitable. In static risks the uncertainty is restricted to whether or not there will be a loss. For example, when a man invests several thousand dollars in a business venture, he stands to enjoy a profit if the venture succeeds but to suffer a loss if the business fails. Adverse market changes might make his investment so unprofitable that he would lose most of his original investment. On the other hand, favorable market conditions might yield him a handsome profit. But, in the process of administering his business venture, the investor is faced with static risks that can cause losses only. His factory or store building might burn; an employee might em-

---

[8] This is not to say, of course, that he cannot invent others of his own into which to fall. Indeed, the nature of risk being what it is, it might be said that the objectives of the present book are to *help* the reader develop to the point at which his errors, while they continue to exist, are (1) usually sophisticated and (2) seldom, if ever, financially fatal.

bezzle funds; or a customer injured on the premises might sue for damages, alleging negligence on the part of the operator. Any of these occurrences can cause the investor serious loss. But if no fire occurs, if all employees prove honest, and if there are no negligence suits, the investor has not earned a profit simply by his good fortune—he is merely starting at scratch instead of with a handicap. Therefore, businessmen who assume static risks subject themselves to chances of loss without offsetting chances of gain.

2. Although statistical analysis is useful in dealing with risks (uncertainties) of any kind, static risks have certain statistical properties that make them much more amenable to the device of pooling than are dynamic risks. Even though there are changes through time, it is easier to predict next year's fire loss rate among a large group of machine shops than it is to predict the rate at which their machines will become obsolescent.

3. The growth and development of the economy depend upon the existence of an adequate number of investors and enterprisers willing and able to undertake the dynamic risks involved in the production and distribution of useful goods and services. Dynamic risk bearers as a group perform a useful social function. On the other hand, nothing generally is gained by society from the gratuitous assumption of static risks by the investor. The expenditure of large sums of money by drug firms on pharmaceutical research yields tremendous gains to society. But the assumption by these drug firms of the risk of loss to their laboratories by fire contributes nothing to society when such assumption is not necessary to the use of the laboratories.

4. In dynamic risks, individuals may suffer losses from events that result in gains to society. In static risks, when an individual suffers a loss, society usually loses too. Thus, when automobiles were invented, losses were incurred by those engaged in the horse-and-carriage business, although society in general gained (even though this latter point might possibly be questioned by anyone well acquainted with automobile accident statistics). When a government embarks on a program of public education and levies a tax to support it, it is possible that an individual taxpayer may suffer a loss, but society as a whole is expected to gain.

On the other hand, when a building is destroyed by fire, the loss in productivity is incurred by both the owner of that building and, usually, by society in general.[9] Although in a theft of the "Robin Hood" type it might be possible for the individual to suffer a static loss while society gains, that is hardly the general rule. Stolen goods probably decline in social usefulness when in the hands of thieves.

---

[9] It is not always true that society loses when a building burns. The additional investment made to rebuild, the increased income to the community resulting from the construction, the upgrading effect of reconstruction, the multiplier effect—all these in a depressed economy may well prove a social blessing. A few economists believe that more destruction is needed so that additional investment will be made.

RISK IN BUSINESS: PRINCIPLES OF MANAGEMENT

Risk is defined as "uncertainty regarding a loss." Thus, if loss is one of the possible outcomes of a given undertaking, that undertaking is said to involve an element of risk. The importance of risk in business is, in a large measure, self-evident. Existence of chances of loss would seem an obvious deterrent to business activity, for, in the abstract, risk is unattractive. No one wants to expose himself to loss unless he expects to get something out of it.

But that people hope or believe that they will get something out of taking a risk is evidenced by the large numbers of risk bearers around the country. Amateur gamblers and other thrill seekers actively seek out risk, and the great difficulties encountered in enforcing laws against gambling and rules about "do not molest the animals" are eloquent testimony to the universality of risk-taking tendencies.

Some people, unfortunately, seem to have the amateur gambler's attitude toward business management, exhibiting a regular urge "to take the big chance," "shoot the moon," or "go for broke." From an "objective" viewpoint—the viewpoint of those who study statistics rather than the gambler's psychology—the costs of these risks may greatly overbalance the gains involved.

But this is not always true. Risk taking *may* be profitable. The generalization is simple: Some risks are worth taking; others are not. As already indicated, the policy committees of big corporations regularly must consider such questions as entering new territories, producing and trying to market new products, adopting new processes, incurring new obligations, reducing assets to reduce debts, buying a subsidiary, disposing of a subsidiary, discontinuing old processes, divisions, markets, and a host of similar problems. Whether it is a matter of addition or subtraction, two questions will arise: What might we gain by it? What might we lose by it? If the loss potential appears too high (especially when compared with the potential gain), the answer to change will be "No." (Of course, there is risk in no change, too, and that fact also has to be considered. Unfortunately, this fact sometimes is overlooked in decision making.)

The problem of regular decision making is not restricted to the big corporations and their policy committees. When an individual businessman contemplates an activity for himself, he is faced with the same considerations. "Should I stay put, or move to the new shopping center?" "Should I adopt this additional line of products?" "Should I discontinue this line of merchandise or try to make it profitable by enhancing my sales effort?" "Should I arrange for more capital by taking in a partner?"

Is there any rational explanation of why risk is taken? If so, does this rationale apply with equal force to all risk takers? The purpose of this discussion is to answer these questions, first, by discussing three fundamental rules or precepts that might qualify as guides in reaching decisions involving risk situations and, second, by observing the extent of the applicability of these rules. What are the rules? Can they be applied?

Rules of Risk Management

Three precepts may be helpful in risk management: (1) don't risk more than you can afford to lose; (2) don't risk a lot for a little; and (3) consider the odds. These rules can be useful not only in business but also in personal situations.

Size of Loss. In dynamic risks, chance of loss can be thought of as merely the other side of the coin from chance of gain. On one flip of the coin, one side comes up; on another, the other. But the coin may be biased. The question is, which side comes up more frequently (and for how much money each time)? However, losses have one additional feature not possessed by gains—losses can be *irreversible.* "In the long run," a given operation might be expected to produce both losses and gains, with the anticipated balance in favor of the gains. The crucial question is: can the business survive to take advantage of a favorable long-run trend? If not, its net loss position at one point in time cannot later be changed—reversed—into a position of net gain.

For example: A wholesaler might conclude that by placing his warehouse where it has ready access to water transportation he may save, say, $150,000 a year. However, the location he has in mind involves the risk of damage from floods, which occur there on an average of once every seven years. He estimates that a single flood could cause $600,000 damage to his warehouse and its contents.

Saving of $150,000 a year for seven years would still leave $450,000 net gain above the cost of a $600,000 flood damage. This would appear to be a profitable proposition. But suppose the flood came the very first year? Could the business survive the loss and so have the chance to cover it by extra profits (lower costs) during the succeeding years? If a $600,000 uninsured loss [10] would put this wholesaler out of business, he would be suffering from an example of an irreversible loss. If, however, he could survive such a loss, savings in subsequent years would be expected to reverse its effect.[11]

---

[10] Insurance against flood losses is essentially unprocurable in connection with fixed locations. Therefore, the assumption that the loss is uninsured is realistic.

[11] An additional problem arises, of course, from the fact that an *average* of one flood every seven years is definitely not the same thing as *only* one flood in every seven years. If the 1-in-7 average is based on an experience of, say, five floods in the past thirty-five years, it is quite possible that the distribution may come out to be two in one period of five years and then no more for another nine years—or any other variant of a 1-in-7 average over time. And, of course, the future average can easily turn out to be better or worse than the past average for any number of reasons. However, these complications do not change the fundamental concept behind the irreversible loss but rather serve to make it more important.

Clearly, therefore, the potential size of loss *relative to the resources of the loss bearer* is a determining factor with regard to the importance of a risk.

Amateur gamblers are frequently warned: *Never play with more money than you can afford to lose.* This precept is perfectly applicable to the professional risk taker (and businessman) as well and is the first rule of risk management. Even if the odds are attractive, a man is not smart to risk more than he can afford to give up. The team that is one touchdown behind in the final minutes of the last quarter can better afford the risk of interception by throwing the ball than can the winning team, which should play the clock out conservatively. On the other hand, the team that is three touchdowns ahead can afford to be generous in the use of third and fourth strings during the closing minutes of the game.

Profit and Loss. Another precept of the poker table arises from the situation in which one man wins his share of pots all right, but they are always small, or, if large, contain little besides his own money. When the evening is over, such a "winner" will almost always turn out to have been a net loser. The admonition here can be phrased, "Don't risk something for nothing." Or, in this imperfect world in which "black or white" and "all or nothing" are choices seldom presented, the proper phraseology would be, *"Don't risk much for a little."* This is a second rule of risk management.

Suppose that the wholesaler in our preceding example decided that he could not stand the $600,000 loss, so gave up the idea of a warehouse at the waterfront. However, still interested in the cheapness of water transportation, he worked out another scheme. This one would involve an investment of only $50,000 (which he could afford to lose) for a forwarding station at the water's edge. Less efficient than the warehouse, this would be expected to produce a saving of only $7,500 a year. If the seven-year flood cycle held, he would save $52,500, of which, say, $40,000 would be needed to cover average flood damage. The net profit on the $50,000 investment would then be less than 3 per cent per year. Better to put the money in good bonds!

Another excellent illustration of the principle can be found in the field of automobile insurance. An example of a premium for physical damage insurance on a private passenger car can be taken as $12 for comprehensive (fire, theft, and miscellaneous) coverage. The car is insured for its "actual cash value," say, $1,600. The man who does not buy comprehensive coverage risks $1,600 for a gain of 0.75 per cent of that amount—certainly risking a great deal for a little. In concrete terms, he is taking a chance on, say, the costs of two whole vacations versus the price of two or three meals out. This certainly seems a poor exchange. It would take him two hundred years of no losses to break even.

Chance of Loss. Perhaps the most common type of error made by amateur risk managers is to give the wrong kind of consideration to the chance of loss.[12] This type of error involves either of two opposite kinds of mistakes:

On the one hand, there is a tendency to underestimate chance of loss in connection with "long shots." Adam Smith noted this tendency nearly two hundred years ago, and it was certainly not new then. Smith wrote:

> The world neither ever saw, nor ever will see, a perfectly fair lottery; or one in which the whole gain compensated the whole loss; because the undertaker would make nothing by it. In the state lotteries the tickets are really not worth the price which is paid by the original subscribers, and yet commonly sell in the market for twenty, thirty, and sometimes forty per cent advance. The vain hope of gaining some of the great prizes is the sole cause of this demand. The soberest people scarcely look upon it as folly to pay a small sum for the chance of gaining ten or twenty thousand pounds; though they know that even that small sum is perhaps twenty or thirty per cent more than the chance is worth. In a lottery in which no prize exceeded twenty pounds, though in other respects it approached much nearer to a perfectly fair one than the common state lotteries, there would not be the same demand for tickets. In order to have a better chance for some of the great prizes, some people purchase several tickets, and others, small shares in a still greater number. There is not, however, a more certain proposition in mathematics, than that the more tickets you adventure upon, the more likely you are to be a loser. Adventure upon all the tickets in the lottery, and you lose for certain; and the greater your number of tickets the nearer you approach this certainty.[13]

People seem much quicker to play against the odds if they are asked to risk a little for a lot than when they are asked to risk a lot for a little. While they are often eager to risk $1 to win $100 in face of 200 to 1 odds against them, they often are reluctant to risk $500 to win $100 even if the odds are better than 5 to 1 in their favor. The chance of a lot for a little blinds risk takers to adverse odds. Just so a chance of a little for a lot blinds risk takers to favorable odds. The explanation, of course, is found in the relative marginal utilities of the dollars risked as against the dollars to be gained. Thus the utility of a dollar is so small as compared to the utility of $100 that one is willing to risk $1 for $100 even if the odds are relatively unfair. The utility of $500 is so large when compared to the utility of $100 that one is often unwilling to risk $500 for $100 even if the odds are loaded in his favor. For this reason, people are willing to pay a small insurance premium to eliminate the possibility of a large loss even if that premium is loaded against them, as it must be to handle expenses and profit.

Unfortunately, the reverse error is common. Many persons allow smallness of chance of loss to overshadow the largeness of the loss itself. This approach produces violations of precept number one. Still, it is commonly believed that at some point the chance of loss does get too small to worry

---

[12] In this book, "chance of loss" always means the rate at which loss occurs. Thus, in matching pennies the chance of loss is one half; if one bets that the number 6 would come up when one die is rolled, the chance of loss would be $\frac{5}{6}$, and so on.

[13] Adam Smith, *The Wealth of Nations* (New York: Modern Library, 1937), Book I, chap. 10, p. 108.

about. Consider the peril of earthquakes in New England. If a significant quake should occur there, the amount of loss would be tremendous. But even the famous mythical man who regularly sells refrigerators to Eskimos would starve to death trying to sell earthquake insurance in Boston. Does this mean that there are occasions when chance of loss should overcome the rule against gambling with more than one can afford to lose?

To answer that question, consider first the following problem. Suppose that earthquake insurance were generally available at premiums strictly proportional to the chance of loss. In the eastern states the premium would be so small as to be nearly invisible. Earthquake protection added to a fire insurance policy would add perhaps a total of one cent to the cost of a five-year fire insurance policy on a $20,000 house. At such a rate, is it so clear that the best practice would be to save the penny every five years and let the earthquake insurance go?

However, as a practical matter, one cannot always handle a small chance of large loss at a cost commensurate with the odds. Because of the risks (uncertainties) involved from the insurers' point of view, premiums as low as the one suggested here are rarely offered. Consider the insurers' position, for example, if a major earthquake should occur in New York City the first year after a large amount of earthquake insurance was written there. They, too, must follow the precept: "Don't risk more than you can afford to lose!"

An alternative method of dealing with this risk is earthquake-resistive construction. But the cost of this alternative is far above that warranted by the chance of loss. (For example, one would have to take the top ninety-plus stories off the Empire State Building—a tremendous loss in site use.)

Another type of error in risk management occurs when the near-sureness of an apparent gain causes its cost to be underestimated. This is probably what underlies some of the desire for "small loss" insurance. Some people believe that the best insurance is that which is most likely to be collected. They ignore the handling costs, which on frequent small claims may equal or exceed the claims themselves. These costs must be covered in the premiums. Therefore, the man who buys more and more small-loss insurance coverage is in the same position as the man who buys more and more tickets in the lottery—he becomes surer and surer of losing.

Application of the Rules

All business management, including risk management, is an art. An "art" (in the sense used here) can be defined as the use of knowledge, science, principles, or rules to achieve a particular chosen result. The rules themselves are only one part of the story; applying them to get particular desired results is another. The successful practice of an art is a matter of properly combining talent, experience, and training. The skill required cannot be obtained overnight or away from practical situations. One cannot become a skillful doctor without experience with actual patients or a skillful pianist without playing a piano. No more can one become a skillful manager of business risks without such risks to manage.

But in the study of most arts there is a time when the artist or artisan learns about application in the abstract—a time when the fledgling doctor studies the effects of diseases and treatments by reading about them in text-books, a time when the youthful pianist learns something about music by considering the fundamental rules of acoustics, harmony, and composition. Learning to do, and to do well, is a matter of both study and practice and includes learning (*a*) what constitutes a good performance and (*b*) what are some good ways to go about producing such a performance. So it is with risk management.

The Nature of Risk Situations.   When should the art of risk management be applied? In what kinds of situations are the rules of risk management appropriate guides to action? One example involving recognition of a relatively simple, single static risk has already been illustrated in the problem of the warehouse on the waterfront. As that case was described and discussed, all the important characteristics or dimensions of the risk were assumed to be known. The size of the potential loss, how that size compared with the expected gain, and the rate at which the loss was expected to occur (i.e., the chance of loss) were all taken as given. In an actual situation, only approximations of such data would be available, and then only after considerable expenditure of time and money. Furthermore, decision in the actual case would not depend upon the flood risk alone. Many uncertainties would have to be considered simultaneously. For example, whenever decisions involve the use of public means of transportation (railroads, highways, waterways), political risks are of great importance. What is likely to be future governmental policy with regard to one means of transportation versus another? Are future subsidies, taxes, rate controls, and other regulations likely to alter the size of the differential between land and water costs and, if so, in which direction?

Management risks are involved in every situation. In the waterfront warehouse, specific problems would probably include the question of the quantity and quality of labor available at the proposed location plus the special risks involved in waterfront labor relations. Then there would be the marketing risks and perhaps some risk of innovation.

Static risks other than flood are present everywhere. Fortunately, in the practical situation, many (but not all) of them can be evaluated and handled as matters of insurance costs. This simplifies that much of the problem—and illustrates one of the benefits of the institution of insurance.

Clearly, the problem is complicated and, to the beginner, probably awesome. Yet, obviously, such decisions as where to locate a warehouse are hardly uncommon in business situations, and answers must be and are regularly obtained.

A completely different example from the warehouse, but one equally clearly involving recognition and evaluation of a risk situation, can be borrowed from Mehr and Cammack's *Principles of Insurance*. In their second chapter the authors note as follows:

. . . laws of most states prohibit the operation of trucks that contain axle-weight loads in excess of stated maximums. Some truckers, however, frequently carry weights far in excess of these maximums. They are not ignorant of the law; rather, they are taking a calculated risk. Profits from these excessive loads are so much greater than from legal loads that truckers find it to their advantage to continue hauling excessive loads and to pay the fines for the times they are caught and brought to justice by the state authorities.[14]

On its face, this is a relatively simple case with a known solution. But this is a political risk, and its possible ramifications should not be overlooked. Persistent practices of the kind described have led, in different states, to (1) increases in size of fines, especially for repeated offenses; (2) increased taxes on trucks; (3) making offenses more costly by holding up the trucks for hours pending investigation, communication, and court hearing; (4) denying overweight trucks the use of the roads, forcing the bringing in of additional vehicles and reloading.

Thus, the trucker who has estimated his risk on the basis of fines only may find himself operating in the red if the state police suddenly adopt the delaying and harassing tactics described in (3) or (4) above, or if persistent and flagrant violations arouse the ire of a legislature, with one or more of the described reactions being written into law. (Such *risk* of increased regulation, as a matter of fact, is widely considered to be one of the most effective controls that government has over business.)

Interaction among the Rules. A salient feature of risk situations is that it costs something to get information about the risk. A new product is being considered. Will it sell? A market survey may give more accurate answers than can be gotten from executives' opinions. Or perhaps a change in personnel policies is contemplated. How will employees react to it? An attitude study may help provide the answer. Suppose a new process has been invented. A pilot run may provide considerable information about possible behavior of production runs. But surveys, studies, and trial runs cost money, and, in anticipation, results are uncertain. This itself is a risk. When should such risks be undertaken? The answer depends upon:

1. The cost of the research or study relative to the financial position of the business.
2. The cost of the research compared to the saving or profit that could be made if the research results were available.
3. The probability ("odds") that the research will tell the decision makers something useful, that is, something they did not already know. Also, the prob-

---

[14] Robert I. Mehr and Emerson Cammack, *Principles of Insurance* (3d ed.; Homewood, Illinois; Richard D. Irwin, Inc., 1961), p. 26.

ability that this "something" it tells them turns out to be accurate. (Not all surveys get the right answers.)

For an illustration, consider again the decision problem with respect to placing a warehouse on the waterfront. Suppose management has at hand only rough estimates about flood frequency and costs, and suppose that on the basis of these estimates the decision is not to use the waterfront location. Now let someone (probably the man who suggested the waterfront location in the first place!) raise questions about the accuracy of the information on which the final decision has been based. Should better information be paid for? Clearly management wants to know how much various amounts of information would cost and how that cost would compare with the potential savings from waterfront warehousing.

But estimation of the potential savings from waterfront warehousing is exactly what is at issue! Expectation of net operational saving necessarily depends on expectation as to rate of flood loss, and rate of flood loss is just what the proposed study is supposed to help determine. Therefore, before the study is made, it becomes necessary to "guess" what its conclusions will be. But in the absence of the study, the decision makers have concluded that their best estimate of the situation is that flood loss potential is so high that there would be no saving. Surely their best estimate as to what the facts are must also be their best estimate as to what the study will reveal. Under the risk management principles given here, could it ever be wise to spend money on research or study to obtain further information for a decision?

The answer is "Yes," depending on what happens when the third principle is applied: What are the odds? What is the probability that the study, if completed, would lead the executives to alter their decision? After all, they are not positive of their facts. Their *best estimate* of the flood loss potential is that it is too high, but this is only an estimate and it may be wrong. So there is *some probability* that further study will lead to a different answer. The question is whether this probability is high enough to make further investigation worthwhile. What is the probability that the study will show that flood losses are low enough to make both the study and the warehouse worthwhile?

Problems in Applying the Rules.   Thinking of and answering questions such as those just described are the process of risk analysis, the first major part of the risk management function. There are two other major parts to the function: deciding what to do about the risks after they have been analyzed and then seeing that it is done. In dynamic risk situations these three steps can be said to encompass the entire management function: determining the problems, selecting among possible solutions, and seeing that the chosen solution is executed. Here we are applying this general management process to problems in pure risk. Neither process is easy, and each is full of pitfalls. Several particular pitfalls are worth special note:

The Problem of Objectivity.   Adam Smith made an observation in this area, too, which the business manager will do well to remember:

The over-weening conceit which the greater part of men have of their own abilities, is an ancient evil remarked by the philosophers and moralists of all ages. Their absurd presumption in their own good fortune, has been less taken notice of. It is, however, if possible, still more universal. There is no man living who, when in tolerable health and spirits, has not some share of it. The chance of gain is by every man more or less over-valued, and the chance of loss is by most men under-valued, and by scarce any man, who is in tolerable health and spirits, valued more than it is worth.[15]

Still, today, hundreds of new businesses are started by persons with experience neither in the particular line of trade involved nor in management techniques in general. Some people, for example, go into the restaurant business on the comforting assumption that "people must always eat." The high rate of business failures in the food service business is one of the most widely known examples of overestimation of business results. But the causes of these failures—such as the high cost of spoiled fruits and vegetables, of inexperienced or careless cutting of meats, careless buying of foods, and wasteful leftovers—are probably as equally extreme in the other direction of being poorly known. The inevitable result of overoptimism in business innovation is the tremendous mortality rate in businesses only one, two, or up to five years old.

On the other hand, it should also be noticed that there are many persons who have a built-in bias in the opposite, or pessimistic, direction. Perhaps having been "once burned," these people are "twice shy." Whatever the reason, these individuals make the opposite mistake of passing up good opportunities for gain because of too great a fear of loss. While it is often true that "a bird in hand is worth two in the bush," it is also true that "nothing ventured, nothing gained," and the overly timid man, just like the overly venturesome one, is soon left behind in the race for markets and position. Perhaps the key admonition in this area is not to be too greatly impressed with one's own one-man experience. Look around a bit, and try the broader view.[16]

The Problem of Inadequate Information. Foretelling the future is difficult enough without an added burden of having to guess about the present. The hopeful inventor who takes out his first patent may be totally unaware of the pitfalls of patent litigation. A small, inexperienced trucker may not know about the ways in which his competitors are upping their loads to get more income per dollar cost. Our wholesaler who builds his waterfront warehouse may not have heard that a downward revision of railroad freight rates is already "in the mill." Such cases of lack of information make accurate risk evaluation impossible.

Nor is all needed or useful information of the costly type (research, surveys) previously discussed. Exchange of information through trade associations and perusal of news magazines and other reports on the doings

---

[15] Smith, *op. cit.*, p. 107.

[16] Still remembering that "one man's meat may be another man's poison." Wherever one turns, there is no escape from the need for sound judgment!

of government and business are examples of ways in which risk can be reduced at small expense. Hiring of competent assistants and use of the services of outside experts (e.g., auditors, lawyers, architects) on proper occasions should be routine expenditures. In many cases, although perhaps not in all the particular examples already given, an especially effective way to get information is for the risk manager to look over the situation in person.[17]

The Problem of the Urge for Psychic Income. Part of the reason people take risk is for what economists know as "psychic income." When the risk taker is so motivated, the rules of risk management frequently are discarded. Dreams are worth something! The bootblack with a chance on the Irish Sweepstakes may well have his money's worth in thoughts of "what would happen if. . . ." But the bootblack is engaged in gambling as a consumer. The businessman who runs his business on the percentages facing the ticket buyer in a lottery is most unlikely to continue having a business to run.

The Problem of Oversight. The traffic patrolman who watches thousands of careless drivers courting death on the highway frequently asks: "Why do they do it? Why do they keep on exchanging a few minutes of seldom valuable time for broken bones, scarred faces, and the creation of widows and orphans?"

The problems here are twofold. (1) The costs are not as real in the minds of the risk takers as are the benefits: Death and disability, before they are suffered, are mere words; the feel of speed or the knowledge of the fun waiting at the beach, being a part of memorable experiences, is real. (2) Many risk takers refuse to believe that the costs are actually associated with the gains. They do not believe that accidents are the result of speed or of the particular chances that they themselves are taking.

Interestingly enough, traffic tickets are usually sufficiently close in experience to be real. Hence, traffic slows down when there is a known "speed trap" ahead or when a police car heaves into sight. Men seem quick to defer to relatively trifling but personally known and rather sure costs while ignoring the heavy but personally unknown and improbable costs. Thus, the awareness of a concrete probability of a few dollars' fine serves more to prevent risk taking on the highways than an abstract chance of death or disability.

Problem of Risk Aversion. Businessmen sometimes pass up good opportunities because of their aversion to taking what they call "unnecessary risk." The really successful businessman is not the one who seeks religiously to avoid risk but the one who knows how to keep his risk under control.

Earlier, it was suggested that people buy insurance against small losses because they overestimate the chance of loss. This is not the only reason, however. Large numbers of people who can afford a $100 loss, purchase

---

[17] See chap. 6.

$50 rather than $100 deductible collision insurance. While some do so out of ignorance of the adverse odds, others do so because of their aversion to risk. They are willing to pay something to stabilize their monthly or annual outlays. Therefore they are unwilling to expose themselves to any loss if they can purchase insurance against it.

Dealing with the Inevitable Errors. The subject at hand is, after all, *uncertainty*. If a result can be forecast with absolute accuracy, then it is not the kind of thing with which we are dealing here. Forecasting puts a probability on uncertain future events. Improbable events are only improbable, not impossible. The odds against a particular bridge player's getting a hand with no face cards or aces are nearly 274 to 1; the odds against a pat flush in a five-card poker hand for any one player are just under 504 to 1; and odds against anyone's having a pair of dice come up "seven" four times in a row are 1,295 to 1.[18]

One would properly predict the non-occurrence of any of these events in a given play of the game, but each of them happens nonetheless. The same is true of business predictions. Under uncertainty, it is inevitable that even the soundest methods of forecasting will produce results that are inaccurate for a given turn of subsequent events. Management must expect and should be prepared for these results, too. The first preparation consists of applications of rule number one: "Don't gamble with more than you can afford to lose." Then, when things do go wrong, the business and its managers will still be "in the game" to enjoy the benefits when events go right again. But, while the rule is simple, living with it calls for some degree of sophistication. "The best laid schemes o' mice and men" *do* "gang aft a-gley," and psychological as well as financial preparation is therefore important. It is necessary to face the fact that things can go wrong, and to be only wary, not frightened, of either the possibility or its outcome.

Fortunately, that is not all the preparation that can be made. The best thing to do about the inevitable errors is to try to plan so that there is some effective limit on even the most adverse of outcomes. This is done by risk and loss *control*. Methods of risk and loss control are the subject of the next three chapters.

Risk Management Principles: A Summary

Major problems to be faced in the intelligent management of business risks are (1) maintaining an objective viewpoint and seeing the whole of the risk as it really is; (2) getting complete and accurate information about the risk, including all its facets; and (3) recognizing in the beginning that some predictions will go awry and being fully prepared for that inevitability.

Having assessed the situation (including the possibilities for controlling

---

[18] In honest games, of course. Also the poker odds assume no wild cards in the deck. One joker, "wild in aces, straights, and flushes," brings the odds against the given man's pat flush down to 379 to 1.

it), management then makes its decision as to whether to take the risk on the basis of three general rules:

1. Don't risk more than you can afford to lose.
2. Don't risk a lot for a little.
3. Consider the odds.

CHAPTER SUMMARY

Businessmen face two kinds of risk: dynamic and static. Dynamic risks, often called speculative risks, arise from unexpected changes in the economic productivity of a given capital investment. They arise from market, management, and political sources and are ambivalent in nature: they can result in profit as well as loss. Static risks, often called pure risks, arise independently of the movements in the economy. They arise from loss of or damage to physical assets, loss of possession of assets by fraud or criminal violence, loss of ownership by adverse judgments at law, loss of income resulting from damage to property of others, and loss of net income owing to the death or disability of key employees. Static risks, unlike dynamic risks, can lead to losses only. Profits are not a result of assuming a static risk.

Static risks are more subject to scientific control than are dynamic risks. The growth and development of the economy, however, depend upon the existence of an adequate number of investors willing and able to assume dynamic risks. In dynamic risks, individuals might suffer a loss from a situation that results in a gain to society.

Some risks are worth taking; others are not. The difference lies in the size of potential losses, in the excess of gains over losses, and in the favorableness of the odds. Beyond this, it is a matter of knowing what the real potentials are and of being properly prepared for all of them.

REVIEW AND DISCUSSION QUESTIONS

1. It has been said that risk management is something less than all management but something more than insurance management. What would be a good workable definition of risk management?
2. What is the meaning of the word "certainty" in the statement "Businessmen may be said 'to risk the *certainty* of something for the chance of something more' "? Of what would the non-risking man be "certain"? How does the nature of this "certainty" affect the willingness of businessmen to take chances on gaining "something more"?
3. Mark Seguro is the specialist in management of static risks for the Nuts and Bolts Corporation. What is his interest in the dynamic risk problems of the Corporation? (Be as specific as possible.)
4. Is it accurate to say that static risks always involve one or more of the following types of potential losses: damage or disappearance of property, death or disability of persons?

5. In the discussion of "static or Pure Sources of Risk," two subtopics are *Loss of Income Resulting from Damage to Property of Others* and *Loss of Net Income Due to the Death or Disability of Key Employees.* Since the "income" referred to includes business *profit,* how can these loss possibilities be considered *pure* sources of risk? Can a risk be a "static" risk without being a "pure" one?

6. " 'Static' is an unfortunate term to use in connection with something as dynamic as pure risk. Pure risk is in many ways far from static." Explain why you agree or disagree with the above quotation.

7. What generalizations can be made on the differences between dynamic and static risks?

8. What is the meaning of the statement that losses can be irreversible? What is the importance of this observation to risk management?

9. Is it always possible to follow the rule "don't risk more than you can afford to lose"? Why or why not?

10. The text characterizes as "unfortunate" the tendency of some business managers to adopt a "go for broke" approach to their business operations. Do you agree with this characterization? Why or why not (that is, by what standards do you draw your conclusion)?

11. How many people would really believe, with Adam Smith, that when they purchase several tickets in a lottery they are more likely to be a loser than when they purchase only one ticket? (What do *you* really believe?) What logic would be advanced by those who disagree with Smith? Can this logic be squared with the argument Smith presented? If so, how? If not, who is right? (Are you sure?) Do these arguments really apply to purchase of insurance against small, frequent losses?

12. How would a computing machine, unaffected (presumably) by psychological factors, behave differently from human beings in managing a business? Would the machine therefore be a better manager? What standards would you use to define what is "better"? Where did you get these standards? Are you completely satisfied with them?

13. Suppose the odds were very favorable to you. Would you be willing to risk "a lot for a little" if the "lot" were no more than you could afford to lose? That is, would you choose to ignore the rule which says "Play with the odds" or to break the rule which says "Don't risk a lot for a little"? Explain your choice.

14. What is the "general management process"? What are the pitfalls involved in applying the general management process to problems in pure risk?

PART II

Methods of Handling Risk

The risk manager deals with static risks to accomplish particular ends. There are several means or methods which he may use to produce the results desired, and these means and methods are the subject of this part, which contains four chapters. The methods of risk and loss assumption are the principal subjects of Chapter 2. Chapter 3 deals with methods for reducing losses; Chapter 4 with methods for reducing risk. Insurance is, of course, an important method for reducing risk; in fact, it is so important that a separate chapter, Chapter 5, is devoted to it.

Chapter 2

METHODS OF HANDLING RISK:
RISK ASSUMPTION

It is now clear that the first problem in risk management is to decide between risks to be borne and those to be avoided. Sometimes the choice is voluntary; other times it is not. And, real-life situations being what they are, when choices are available, they are seldom simple. The question actually faced is seldom simply to bear or not to bear some single given risk, for the assumption of one risk automatically raises the problems of dealing with others. Thus, the businessman who takes on the market risks that go with the keeping of a stock of goods in inventory is immediately faced with the problems of static risks. His goods may be damaged by wind, water, or fire; they may be stolen, or their presence may cause injury for which he is sued. However, while these various risks are inseparably incurred, they are separable in treatment. Fire, windstorm, and liability are perils generally insurable; flood and perils of the market (falling prices, changes of fashion, incompetent sales personnel) are not.

In this and the following three chapters the major devices and methods for handling risks are examined in some detail. The nature, cost, and defects of each method are considered. The present chapter deals with the principal methods and devices of planned risk *bearing*. Under these methods uncertainty with regard to loss continues, but effective risk management is used to eliminate most of the disastrous effects. The next three chapters deal with risk reduction and control: the principal methods and devices by which degrees of uncertainty can be reduced.

RISK: UNCERTAINTY AND LOSS

Risk has previously been defined as "uncertainty regarding loss." Thus, risk has at least two parts: uncertainty and loss. The person, family, or business that bears its own risks (as it must, to an important degree) needs to be

31

prepared to withstand both. Therefore, this chapter on risk bearing deals with both uncertainty and loss, sometimes jointly, sometimes separately. The section headed "Risk Assumption" relates to the acceptance (or the ignoring) of both; its subsections are suggested by Figure 2-1. The section headed "Loss Prevention and Control" deals with bearing the risk (uncertainty) but reducing the effect of the loss. The last section before the chapter summary, headed "Effects of Loss Prevention and Risk Bearing," considers the interrelationship between the reduction of the effects of the loss and the practice of risk assumption.

FIGURE 2–1

METHODS AND APPROACHES IN RISK ASSUMPTION

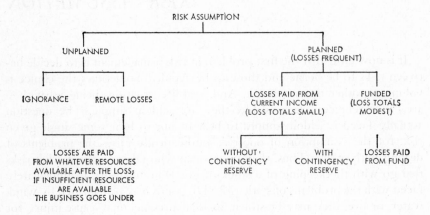

RISK ASSUMPTION

Uncertainties may be accepted and lived with, consciously or unconsciously. Acceptance may be passive or active, with or without preparation, wise or unwise. A risk taker may simply accept both uncertainty and loss as they exist, and there are occasions when this simple policy is best. Usually, however, risk acceptance should be coupled with plans for risk and loss control. But, since even the best of these plans always leave some losses and some risk uncontrolled, management of the assumed risk is inescapable.

Plan vs. No Plan

Some risks are voluntarily assumed because they are believed to carry a profit potential. Other risks are assumed because they are unavoidable. There is a third reason: some are assumed because of ignorance or indifference. The words "ignorance" and "indifference" connote the general undesirability of this approach. Yet this approach does have its place (however small).

Of all the meteors that hit the earth's atmosphere, well over 99 per cent burn up completely before they hit the ground. And over 99 per cent of those which do reach the ground are not large enough to do any significant damage. Still, several times in the history of the earth, large meteorites have hit the earth's surface and plowed up many acres of ground. A building hit by one of these meteors would suffer severe damage, probably total destruction. But the property owner who is vitally concerned about this hazard is not for this reason a better business manager than is his competitor who has never given this exposure a thought. On the contrary, in this special case the ignorant or indifferent manager has the better approach. His energies are wholly devoted to dealing with problems and events about which something can be done. He sticks to matters in which his efforts stand some chance of being productive.

But the meteor example is extreme. While it illustrates a situation in which "no plan" is the best plan, it also suggests that such cases are rather uncommon. Much more usual is the situation in which a manufacturer bears the risk that his plant will be shut down because of fire at the premises of a subcontractor. Why? Simply because he does not know that the risk exists. He has never thought of it, and no one has ever called it to his attention (and pointed out that he can buy insurance against it).

Assuming Losses on a Current Basis

All businesses have many costs that are assumed on a current basis: wages, materials and utilities used, advertising for immediate sale, and so on. No businessman considers such costs as "losses" per se. But in most plants there is a species of current costs that the management may consider "losses": Employees take hand tools home for personal use, or even sale. Poor workmanship turns materials and parts into scrap. If "loss" is defined as "unintentional decline in or disappearance of value, arising from a contingency," these may be called "losses."

But the contingency involved is not always so uncertain as to constitute a risk. A certain rate of attrition from employee pilferage, spoilage from employee or management incompetence, shoplifting in a store, and careless damage to equipment in an office can be forecast or foreseen. By definition, these are not risks. They are regular costs of operation and are properly figured in with the other costs of doing business—the costs of materials used, the wearing-out of tools and machinery, the physical deterioration of merchandise, and all the rest. No special provision is made for financial treatment of "losses" in this category.

Some true risks also produce losses that may well be treated in the same way. Suppose the balance sheet and income statement presented in Figure 2-2 belong to a retail merchandising firm. If there are two vehicles, each worth $1,750,[1] total loss of one in a collision, without any insurance, could

---

[1] For this illustration it is assumed that book value and actual value are equal, even though this is seldom true in practice. See chap. 8.

be carried as a current charge against income or surplus without upsetting results significantly. (Since the uninsured casualty would be a deductible item in calculating taxable income, only about one half of the $1,750 loss would represent reduction in net gain to surplus.)

FIGURE 2–2

JOHN JOHNSON STORE

Balance Sheet

Assets		Liabilities	
Cash	$ 50,000	Current payables	$ 80,000
Receivables	100,000	Accruals	50,000
Inventory	300,000	Installment note	100,000
Vehicles	3,500	Net Worth	
Fixtures	80,000	Capital stock	200,000
Improvements	120,000	Surplus	213,500
	$653,500		$653,500

Income Statement

Net sales	$350,000	Net before income tax	$ 73,600
Cost of merchandise	180,000	Income tax	24,300
Payroll	50,000	Net after tax	49,300
Rent	12,000	Surplus, January 1	179,200
Interest	6,000	Dividends	15,000
Depreciation	26,000	Surplus, December 31	213,500
Other expenses	2,400		

The general principle here is that, even if the occurrence of the loss is unpredictable, the business can safely plan to handle the event on a current basis if (1) the maximum size of the loss can clearly be foretold and (2) the maximum loss does not represent an amount large enough to hamper operations significantly.

Loss Characteristics. Several important loss characteristics, therefore, must be considered in the process of reaching a decision on whether to handle losses on a current basis.

Size of Possible Loss. Maximum loss is not always easy to predict. In the case of the collision loss, there may be damage not only to the truck but to its contents as well. The store's two trucks could run into each other, causing damage to both. The accident could occur on the store's premises, with resulting damage to the store building. And any collision loss may be accompanied by liability and workmen's compensation losses. And so on. Therefore, determining the maximum possible loss is a problem in itself. It constitutes the principal subject of Part III of this text and is frequently referred to through the rest of this book.

Frequency of Loss. In addition to loss severity, there is the problem of loss frequency. Johnson's store may be able to stand a single one- or two-thousand-dollar loss easily, but how about six, ten, or twenty such losses within one or two years? It is a truism in gambling that "dice have no memory." Neither do the perils that cause casualties. Property values develop no natural immunity to repeated losses. If anything, losses are more likely to recur. The conditions that resulted in any first loss (careless driving, oily waste, or poor police protection) will, if uncorrected, render a second loss quite likely.

Of course, if losses start piling up, some different method of handling or controlling the risk may have to be adopted. Ordinarily, it is cheaper to lock a barn door before a horse is stolen than to wait until afterward.

Frequent losses, however, do not always rule out the "current charge" method for handling them. The more frequent the losses, the more likely it is that the "current charge" method will continue to work. This is because frequent losses are easier to predict than are infrequent ones: they are more regular in total cost and therefore more readily susceptible to treatment as "normal" operating expense.

Other Losses. All businesses are subject to a large number and variety of risks. Many of these are dynamic and at best only partially controllable. The same assets, surplus, and income that will be called upon to carry the losses caused by some single static peril, such as fire or collision, must also absorb all the other losses that are handled on a current basis. This point is tremendously important. If fashions change, if a recession sets in, if a key employee suddenly leaves to set up a competitive store near by, the finances of the business may have all the burden they can handle without any added strain from losses that could have been handled in some way other than the "current charge" method.

Cost Considerations. Certain cost considerations also are important in weighing a possible decision to handle losses on a current basis.

Operational Costs. Clearly, the virtues of the "current charge" plan are its simplicity and low cost: few or no records to keep, no fee to a professional risk bearer, and little or no need for specialized staff personnel to handle the system. Where the losses are small and of some frequency, the costs of administrative and paper work alone may rule out any alternative plan. It is no economy to hire a $10,000-a-year man and a $3,600-a-year secretary, to provide them with equipment and office space, and have them deal only with $10,000, $20,000, or even $50,000 in losses.[2] When fire and casualty insurance companies are "hired" to handle losses, they require nearly as much to cover their operating expenses, and provide (they hope) for some profit, as is needed to pay claims (see Table 2-1.)[3]

Loss Costs. The principal disadvantage of a decision to handle losses

---

[2] They would have to reduce the $50,000 in losses by more than 25 per cent to make the described move pay off.

[3] Readers are warned against reading too much about different companies' costs and profits into Table 2-1. Analysis and comparison of companies are taken up in Chapters 16 and 17.

purely on a current basis is that the cost of the losses themselves may get out of hand. If all that is done about pilferage (whether committed by employees or outsiders) is to swallow the losses as they occur, these losses are likely to start climbing, and to keep on climbing, until some active counteraction is taken. So it is with most kinds of loss and waste. Good business practice commonly dictates that any plan for paying losses should be combined with an adequate program for preventing or controlling them. In most cases, ounces of prevention actually are worth pounds of cure.

TABLE 2–1

RANGES OF RATIOS: EXPENSES AND NET MARGINS AS RATIOS OF CLAIMS
(SELECTED LINES OF INSURANCE, 1957–61)
(In percentages)

Line of Insurance	Expenses to Claims*				Net Margins to Claims*			
	Stock Cos.		Mutuals		Stock Cos.		Mutuals†	
	Low Year	High Year	Low Year	High Year	Low Year	High Year	Low Year	High Year
Fire	93	96	85	91	(−11)	2	34	46
Inland marine	85	92	74	82	(−12)	4	14	25
Workmen's compensation	33	36	24	27	0	6	15	27
Auto collision	73	82	67	72	0	14	23	39
Auto bodily injury liability	40	43	30	34	(−18)	(−4)	(−3)	5
Burglary and theft	110	124	83	92	(−6)	7	1	16
Glass	108	118	83	93	(−12)	2	3	16
Boiler and machinery‡.........	197	222	110	207	26	39	101	299
Fidelity	111	143	54	78	3	21	21	46

* Claims adjustment expenses are included with "claims" in liability and workmen's compensation insurance, with "expenses" in other lines. See Chapters 16 and 17.
† Net margin figures for mutuals are *before* any excess premiums have been returned to policyholders as dividends.
‡ Much of the premium for boiler insurance goes for costs of inspection and other services in loss prevention.
Data in the table are based on figures in *Best's Aggregates and Averages* (1958–62 eds.; New York: Alfred M. Best Co., Inc.).

Tax Costs. Carrying one's own losses has certain income tax effects. Regardless of whether the business charges the losses off as they occur or anticipates them by means of a reserve or fund, uninsured business losses are deductible from taxable income only when and as they occur or can be ascertained.[4] Insurance premiums for business purposes (business life and business disability income insurance excepted) are deductible annually

---

[4] Internal Revenue Code, 1954, sec. 165. The rules for deduction for losses whose evaluation or ascertainment is delayed owing to the nature of the loss (e.g., embezzlement) are discussed in *Federal Taxes* (Englewood Cliffs, New Jersey: Prentice-Hall, Inc., annual), pars. 13,475 and 13,476. None of this applies to reserves for bad debt losses, which are deductible as reasonably reserved (see sec. 166). The 1954 Code originally had a sec. 462 allowing certain other reserves for future losses to be deducted, but this section lasted less than a year, and its repeal was made retroactive. (P.L. 74, sec. 1 (b), June 15, 1955.)

as incurred (that is, a single three-year premium would be deductible one third each year), even for many taxpayers who are on a cash basis.[5]

Furthermore, the amount of uninsured loss that can be deducted may be limited by the adjusted tax basis[6] of the property when that is less than the actual value lost.[7] Thus, it is easily possible that only part of the real loss may be deducted, for the rate of depreciation taken for tax purposes is commonly greater than the real economic depreciation suffered (a point the risk manager needs constantly to remember in considering potential loss values—see chap. 8). Of course, the extra depreciation has already served as a deduction against taxable income, which is why the government is not interested in letting it be deducted (again) when the loss occurs.

Naturally, too, the effective deduction of an allowable loss can be no greater than the size of the income from which it is deducted. A $200,000 loss saves just as much tax in a year in which income otherwise was $200,000 as a $300,000 loss could save. However, the law makes provision, within limits, for carrying the excess over or back to apply against income earned in later or earlier years.[8] This takes care of most cases. The net effect in the experience of one risk manager is that "the assumption of un- insured losses does not result in an overriding tax advantage or disad- vantage. Actually, it involves a calculated risk because it can be deter- mined at what point the adjusted tax base losses will equalize the premium cost of full insurance."[9]

Accounting for Losses. Two ways of charging losses off as current ex- penses are possible. One is to charge them as they occur; the other is to charge an average amount during each accounting period, setting up thereby a "reserve" against which the losses themselves are charged.

Suppose that Johnson's store (Fig. 2-1) suffered major damage to a vehicle about once every five years. The whole of a $1,750 loss can be charged against income or surplus just as it occurs—or $350 can be entered as expense each year, shown as a liability or contingency reserve, and reduced by the amounts of losses as they occur.[10] In addition to the usual advantages that an "averaging" method has for purposes of income accounting and planning budgets, the method offers special benefits in risk

---

[5] *Federal Taxes*, pars. 11,323 and 11,324.

[6] In strictly non-technical and cursory language, "adjusted tax basis" is original cost or value to the present owner plus any capital additions and less allowed depreciation. IRC, 1954, subchap. O, esp. secs. 1011–16.

[7] *Ibid.*, sec. 165 (b); *Federal Taxes*, par. 13,451.

[8] IRC, 1954, as amended, secs. 172 and 165(h). And when this subject comes up, it is time for the taxpayer to call his accountant or lawyer!

[9] Lon Vornadore, insurance manager, Weyehaeuser Timber Co., "Fire Deductibles: An Appraisal and Re-evaluation," *Problem Areas in Corporate Insurance Planning*. American Management Association, Insurance Series No. 113 (New York: The Associa- tion, 1956), p. 23.

[10] The general accountancy problems involved in starting any new reserve can be of some importance but are here left to the accountants and to accountancy textbooks.

management. *First*, an estimated "normal" rate of loss must be set up, and this suggests conscious consideration of the loss potentials of the business. *Second*, a record of how actual losses compare against the estimate is automatically included in the accounting records, thus keeping management reminded of "how it is doing" in loss anticipation and control. For this latter reason, it may be desirable to use the reserve account even for losses the incidence of which is rather uniform from one accounting period to another.

Funding for Losses

When losses are too irregular and too large to be paid for as they occur, a fund may be set up for them. The purpose of such a fund is to provide cash to cover losses without damage to working capital, present income, or surplus. The purpose of the fund is to isolate and regularize the effects of irregular drains on assets. If management desires, of course, it may also fund regular losses, for convenience, accounting control, or such other reason as may appeal. But the *need* for funding is in connection with irregular losses of important size.

Consider the flood problem discussed in chapter 1. Suppose the wholesaler calculates on the basis of one flood every seven years, costing $600,000, to be charged against earnings (before flood losses) of $9 million during the same seven years. Clearly, flood losses are a cost of doing business in the location chosen—a cost undertaken in lieu of the higher transportation costs at some other location. Each year an appropriate share of flood cost should be charged against income. *If* the once-in-seven-years forecast proves correct, the average annual charge in the six years in which there are no floods should be $100,000.[11] This amount can be taken annually, or the total can be converted to a percentage of total income (gross or net) for the period (e.g., $600,000/$9 million equals $6\frac{2}{3}$ per cent), and the percentage charged each year against income actually earned. (The choice among methods is not so much a matter of risk management in the specialized sense as it is a matter of accounting and general management procedures and purposes.)

Difficulties of Loss Funding. Some of the difficulties of the funding plan are obvious and were mentioned in chapter 1: Losses may come oftener than predicted; certainly there is no reason to believe they will hold off until a fund has been accumulated on an annual basis.

More subtle is the difficulty of hanging on to the cash needed to work the plan. Too many people confuse a contingency *reserve* with a *fund*. The

---

[11] It is better not to have a charge against the year in which the flood occurs because (1) there probably will be comparatively little income to charge it against, (2) there may by other unanticipated costs from the flood to charge off in that year, and (3) the income charge ought to match the accumulation of the fund, and there will be a disbursement, not an accumulation, of cash in the flood year.

contingency reserve is illustrated in Figure 2-3. Consider the "Balance Sheet at End of Year: Two Versions" in the figure. Each version has a "Reserve for Losses" of $5,000. But, when loss occurs, the practical effects of the two versions are quite different. In Version B, a $5,000 expenditure of cash to replace the loss property will reduce cash to three-fourths of what it was at the beginning of the year, before the loss reserve was set up. The addition of a contingency reserve as a stated "obligation" (whether in liabilities or as a segregation of surplus) has provided absolutely no guarantee that additional *money* will be available to pay for losses as needed. In Version B, the cash is gone because it has been used to acquire other kinds of assets and to pay debts. This is a common practice. A business needs a certain amount of cash "in the till" to pay current obligations: weekly payroll, regular supplies, monthly rent and utilities, and so forth. Cash for these purposes is part of *working* capital—it helps the business to produce. Cash beyond this amount is less productive. It may add nothing to current operating income.

Still, some cash beyond immediate needs can be useful, even vital, to the longevity of the business. A firm subjected to severe flood losses, or to drastic declines in the values of inventories because of sudden style shifts, has very little chance of surviving the catastrophe if it operates with only enough cash to get along under normal conditions. Additional liquid assets (cash or readily marketable bonds) may not produce much current profit for the business in "normal" years, but the lack of such extra backing is a most expensive practice when the years of crisis do arrive.

FIGURE 2–3

ACCUMULATION OF A RESERVE WITHOUT A FUND
Balance Sheet at Beginning of First Year

Assets		*Liabilities*	
Cash	$ 20,000	Current payables	$ 5,000
Receivables (net)	60,000	Accruals	15,000
Inventory	100,000	Long term	10,000
Fixed assets $85,000			
Depreciation 20,000	65,000	*Net Worth*	
		Partners' original investment .	150,000
	$245,000	Earned Surplus	65,000
			$245,000

Income Statement, First Year

Net sales	$850,000	Surplus, January 1	$ 65,000
Cost of merchandise sold.	750,000	Net earnings	24,500
Depreciation	5,000	Distributed to partners ..	10,000
Other operating expenses.	65,000	Surplus, December 31 ...	79,500
Reserve for losses	5,000*		
Interest	500		
Net earnings	$ 24,500		

FIGURE 2-3 (*Cont.*)

Balance Sheet at End of Year: Two Versions

Version A: Assuming—

    1. No net purchases or sales of assets
    2. No net repayment of debt or net borrowing
    3. No net change in lending (credit extension)

Assets			*Liabilities*	
Cash	$ 44,500		Current payables	$ 5,000
Receivables (net)	60,000		Accruals	15,000
Inventory	100,000		Long term	10,000
Fixed assets	$85,000			
Depreciation	25,000	60,000	*Net Worth*	
			Original investment	150,000
		$264,500	Reserve for losses	5,000†
			Surplus	79,500
				$264,500

Version B: Assuming—

    1. Some cash used to reduce debt (so as to reduce interest costs)
    2. Some cash invested in inventory (to support and promote increased sales)
    3. Receivables increased (also to promote sales)
    4. Fixed assets also increased (to provide for increased sales)

Assets			*Liabilities*	
Cash	$ 20,000		Current payables	$ 3,500
Receivables (net)	65,000		Accruals	15,000
Inventory	110,000		Long term	5,000
Fixed assets	$88,000			
Depreciation	25,000	63,000	*Net Worth*	
			Original investment	150,000
		$258,000	Reserve for losses	5,000†
			Surplus	79,500
				$258,000

* This could have been entered as a direct charge against surplus. The text discussion, however, has been in terms of losses as operating costs, and hence the charge here is made against income.

† Many businesses list this type of account as a liability. Here a puristic approach is used, and the item appears in net worth because at the moment it represents only an indefinite, potential claim, not a known, incurred obligation.

Psychologically, however, it is difficult to leave cash idle when it can produce immediate profits. Investment in government securities (the standard medium for getting some return on large sums while retaining a high degree of liquidity on them) may produce less than 3 per cent return. A moderately successful business can earn at least 8 per cent, and often 12 or 15 per cent, on assets actively employed in operations. The sacrifices of the additional yield that could be obtained by investing the funds in the business is the major cost of maintaining contingency funds. The lure of these additional current profits constitutes a real temptation to reduce the holding of idle cash, which, "after all, we may not need anyway."

A disadvantage of the funding process arises from the income tax rules referred to earlier. Cash drain is intensified. With an unfunded assumption of risk, cash outlay for losses occurs only when losses happen—and then some relief is offered in the form of a reduced income tax obligation. Cash used to pay insurance premiums is also partially balanced by income tax relief.[12] But cash put away to fund future losses is not partially offset by income tax relief until the losses occur.

Finally, of course, there is always the problem that the cash laid aside may not be sufficient to cover the losses that actually occur.

Advantages of Specific Funding. Despite all the problems, it seems obvious that extra money formally segregated into a special fund, with a particular announced purpose for its use, is immeasurably more likely to remain on hand until its purpose is fulfilled than is a contingency fund or account the purpose of which is vague or equivocal. In the first place, creation of a fund for a specific purpose commonly requires specific consideration and decision at the highest levels of management. This means high level recognition that the extra cash involved is indeed not superfluous. Thereafter, the very existence of the fund serves as a continuing reminder of the initial consideration of the problem and of the decision reached for its solution.

Of course, the creation and use of a fund also have the advantages associated with "loss averaging" under a contingency reserve, for example, conscious consideration and estimate of the loss potentials and automatic checking of the subsequent results against the estimate.

LOSS PREVENTION AND CONTROL

Costs and Losses

Nature and Significance of Loss Costs. An important factor in risk situations is the cost of the losses themselves. The cost of the losses must be distinguished from the cost of risk—uncertainty—concerning them. The cost of holding liquid funds, as described in the preceding section, is a cost created because it is *not known* when the loss will occur. That is a cost of risk. When the loss does occur, the fund is spent; that is the cost of loss.[13]

Under any circumstances, much of the loss cost must be borne by the business itself, whether the risk is assumed or transferred. After all, risk transferees must get enough money from the transferers to cover the losses plus operating costs if the transferees are to stay in business (and be solvent at the future date when losses occur). Furthermore, whether by choice or

---

[12] But not necessarily in the same year as premium payment. See n. 5.

[13] This is cost of risk to the individual, of course; for risk costs from the view of the whole economy see Allan H. Willett, *The Economic Theory of Risk and Insurance* (New York: Columbia University Press, 1901; reprinted Philadelphia: University of Pennsylvania Press, 1951), chaps. 3, 4, 8.

by necessity, not all the loss is insured, and the uninsured part is, of course, a direct cost to the business.

Herbert F. Morgenthaler, insurance manager for Daystrom, Inc., has put it this way:

As insurance managers, we assume the responsibility for the insurance contract. . . .

But as insurance managers, we cannot stop at this point and say we have finished the job and allow continuous recurrence of accidents and claims caused by carelessness to jeopardize our insurance contract and our employer's assets and earning power. From the standpoint of practically all corporate insurance, the claim cost of accidents will have a decided effect upon the premium paid. Regardless of the rate-making basis for the development of the premium the losses incurred because of accidents will be the most important determining factor in the cost of insurance over a period of time. Therefore, as insurance managers, we should establish a program of loss prevention to protect our interest in our contracts and effect insurance and operation economies for our company.

* * * * *

The emphasis on loss prevention controls by an insurance manager definitely affects the premium charge favorably. A stronger reason for this emphasis is that the full cost of losses is never covered by insurance. There are hidden expenses borne, by the company, that are associated with every accident and not fully realized.[14]

Indirect Costs to Individual Business. A number of indirect costs arise from losses. These costs cannot be ignored.

Work Injuries. Mr. Morgenthaler goes on to refer to the "4-for-1" ratio developed in studies reported by Heinrich.[15] These studies indicated that an employer's total costs for on-the-job injuries came to five times the amount paid to the injured worker under workmen's compensation laws, that is, that the employer's costs other than workmen's compensation payments tended to run about four times as much as the workman's compensation award.

The examples presented in support of the conclusion included the following types of costs:

Time lost by employees other than the insured person or persons
Time lost by foremen and superintendents
Property damage
Payment of forfeits for failure to complete the job on time
Loss of customers because of delays in production
Value of labor and material in connection with canceled order
Time lost by employees because supervisor was replacing injured employee instead of supervising

---

[14] Morgenthaler, "The Insurance Manager's Role in Loss Prevention," *A Critical Look at the Insurance Buyer's Role.* American Management Association Insurance Series, No. 100 (New York: The Association, 1953), p. 22.

[15] H. W. Heinrich, *Industrial Accident Prevention* (4th ed.; New York: McGraw-Hill Book Co., Inc., 1959), pp. 50 ff.

In addition to the foregoing list would be any costs of litigation over the damages or the injuries.

Beyond these costs are those of lowered quantity and quality of production arising from nervousness and poor morale on the part of uninjured workers after an accident to one of their fellows. These costs are unknown in amount but are known to exist. The general effect of work injuries was studied by the Committee on Safety and Production of the American Engineering Council. This committee concluded that "there is a positive correlation between safety and efficiency of production and, in general, the safe factory is the efficient factory."[16] Finally, in modern business, accidents mean records-keeping, and that, too, is a significant expense to an employer!

Property Losses. The indirect costs of losses other than industrial injuries, although also commonly kown to exist, have not been so thoroughly studied. However, any property damage is likely to produce a loss of income from inability to use the property, extra expenses for such items as salvage expenses and debris removal, reconstruction of records, charges for temporary replacements, overtime on payroll to expedite repairs, notices (and assurances) to customers about conditions and terms of business continuation, and a variety of miscellany. The *Fire, Casualty and Surety Bulletins*[17] report on several actual cases, including the following:

Department store:
  Direct property damage, $190,215.
  Gross income loss, $500,000.
Bank:
  Direct property damage, dollar value not stated; building a total loss.
  Extra expenses to maintain operation on a temporary basis, $193,494.
Small ($50,000 net worth) manufacturer:
  Direct property damage, not given.
  Income losses included cancellation of a $28,000 order in hand plus withdrawal of all the same buyer's future patronage, which has constituted 40 per cent of this small manufacturer's business. Total sales after fire were 55 per cent of pre-fire level.
  Other losses: Reconstruction of records to support insurance claim, $3,700; inability to prove accounts receivable, $2,000.
Large manufacturer:
  Direct property damage, $35,000,000 minimum.
  Loss of sales, $750,000,000 estimated.[18]

---

[16] American Engineering Council, *Safety and Production* (New York: Harper & Bros., 1928), p. 32. (The part of the report dealing with the committee's conclusion on this particular point is quoted in full in Heinrich, *op. cit.*, pp. 66–70.)

[17] National Underwriter Co., Cincinnati (monthly). Part of this material in the *FC & S* comes from a B.S. thesis written at Massachusetts Institute of Technology (1953?) by James Joseph Crowley. Under the title, "Indirect Fire Losses in Business," an abridgment appears in *FC & S*, Sales Section, at Losses, If-1 to 12; also in the *Quarterly of the National Fire Protection Association*, Vol. XLVII (October, 1953), pp. 139–51.

[18] *Ibid.* Specific references are, respectively, by case, Sales Section, Methods Fire and Allied, Uod-1 to 5, Ex-1 to 5; Losses, If-2 and 3, Fgm-1 and 2.

All these were fire losses, but the same kind of results follow just as easily from any major peril: tornado or hurricane, explosion, flood or tidal wave, or earthquake. Criminal takings, particularly embezzlements, have closed down more than one business completely.[19]

Social Costs. All the foregoing illustrations take no account of the losses felt by anyone except the business directly concerned. When a worker is out of a job because he is injured or his employer's plant is destroyed, he may draw workmen's or unemployment compensation benefits—but they are minimal and do not commonly cover the actual expense of supporting a family. Businesses other than the one immediately concerned may be affected. Damage to a machine in Ohio, say, may retard the construction of a dam in Utah—with consequent loss of agricultural products two years hence, when the dam's irrigation system would otherwise have been completed.

When embezzlement caused the failure of one business, a bank, the results were described as follows:

For many of the 4,500 residents of the resort village . . . the holiday season was marked by fear of economic distress—and in some cases, ruin.

Everywhere along the gaily decorated shopping streets, merchants reported sales down one-third, one-half, and even three-quarters below last year. In store after store, retailers stared out at empty streets from behind counters heavily stocked with gifts. Few people . . . this year had cash for anything but daily necessities.

* * * * *

The people . . . were demoralized and frightened.[20]

Even the national society can be affected. One fire in October, 1941, destroyed 10 per cent of the crude rubber supply in the United States. Two months later, access to the world's major sources of natural rubber was cut off, with the synthetic rubber business still in its infancy.[21] Whether waging war or peace, society always loses when productive human or property values are damaged or injured. Many of the losses involve the social costs associated with broken homes, lost opportunities for advanced education and training, the need for charity, and inhibiting effects from personal discouragement or despair.

Fortunately, it is no longer considered "good business" to ignore broad economic, social, and ethical values when making decisions within an individual business. As Ralph Blanchard says, "There is a prima-facie case for preventing (including avoiding) loss."[22]

---

[19] See, e.g., "Surety Assn. Gives Minimum of Fidelity Needed by Commercial Firms," *National Underwriter*, Vol. LX, No. 33 (August 16, 1956), p. 36, and "When a Bank Closes Its Doors," *Business Week*, December 29, 1956, pp. 71–73.

[20] "When a Bank Closes Its Doors," *op. cit.*, p. 71.

[21] "Indirect Fire Losses in Business," *op. cit.* (see n. 17), Sales Section, Losses, If-9.

[22] Albert H. Mowbray and Ralph H. Blanchard, *Insurance* (5th ed.; New York: McGraw-Hill Book Co., Inc., 1961), p. 582. (Since the quotation is from a chapter added in an edition that appeared after Dr. Mowbray's death, it is presumed to be Dr. Blanchard's.)

Loss Prevention Specialists

The art of loss prevention and control[23] is complicated and forms the subject matter of whole curricula in some schools of engineering.[24] Even the full-time risk manager[25] is unlikely to be able to learn both loss prevention and risk management techniques well; for the general management man, the case is hopeless. A staff specialist[26] in loss prevention is needed.

Obtaining Specialists. Whenever a business needs a technical specialist of any kind, three ways generally are available to obtain his services: (1) hire him—put him on the regular payroll; (2) retain him on a continuing basis, paying an annual retaining fee; or, (3) call on him when and as he is needed, paying him on a fee-per-case basis. Thus, some companies have legal or medical departments as part of their regular staff organization; others retain outside legal or medical counsel from whom they expect regular advice. Still others engage attorneys or doctors only when pertinent cases actually arise and only so long as it takes to dispose of each case.

The same three options are open in obtaining professional safety engineering. A firm of moderate to large size can profitably hire its own man or men. All except the smallest and least hazardous businesses can ordinarily gain by retaining continuing loss prevention counsel through the purchase of insurance, if not otherwise (see next topic below). The hiring of a management or engineering consultant to initiate or revitalize a loss program on a one-time basis is sometimes the most profitable approach of all.

---

[23] Some prefer to speak of "scientific" loss prevention and control (as of other forms of "scientific" management). This is well, but it must be remembered that no matter how *scientific* the practice of medicine gets, it is still the *art* of healing: "The skillful and systematic arrangement or adaptation of means for the attainment of some end," e.g., the end of curing ills or of preventing them. (Quotations from *New College Standard Dictionary* [New York: Funk and Wagnalls Co., 1947].)

[24] Even parts of it form whole curricula. The curriculum in *fire* prevention engineering at Illinois Institute of Technology is well established, while several other schools concentrate successfully on industrial accident prevention; still another available major is industrial hygiene.

[25] Here and throughout this text, the phrase "risk manager" is used to indicate that member of management who, together with his advisers (inside the company and out), has direct and primary responsibility for consideration and handling of static risks. Commonly, this function is placed in the finance division of the business. Historically, risk management is a new but growing specialty, representing an extension of the activities of professional insurance buyers. (Hence, the common titles are "insurance manager," "insurance buyer," "insurance consultant.") Naturally, many organizations are too small to warrant a full-time man in the job. The American Management Association, in a 1953 study of the organization and operation of member companies' insurance or risk departments, found the following: 85 had full-time insurance administrators; 92 had part-time, with 65 of them spending less than one-half time on it, including 39 spending less than one-fourth. But 72 of the 177 companies had annual sales of $100 million or more, only 9 had less than $5 million, and the median group was $25 to 100 million. James C. Cristy, *Corporate Insurance Manuals, Reports, and Records.* American Management Association Research Report No. 25 (New York: The Association, 1955), p. 87.

[26] "The difference between line and staff is this: Staff tells line what to do; line tells staff where to go."—Acis Jenkinson III.

Of course, there is no need for a business to limit itself to just one approach. Companies with full-time legal and medical departments still find it advantageous to go outside for particular kinds of advice or to reinforce the internal specialists. Companies with full-time safety departments still make use of the talents of outsiders who have experience with other plants in the same industry and with related operations in other industries. The outsider may on occasion have a more objective approach to the plant's safety procedures than do the people who have been directly responsible for their installation and administration. On the other hand, internal administrators are more likely to be aware of a plant's peculiar problems of production and administration and may be able to demonstrate that, in some cases, "one man's meat is another man's poison." A two-way approach gains not only from each way but also from the interplay between the two.

Insurer's Loss Prevention Services

In the field of loss prevention, the most common way of "retaining" outside counsel is by purchase of appropriate kinds of insurance. Many insurance premiums buy not only loss indemnification but also loss prevention, and the quantity and quality of prevention services received can be an important factor in deciding whether or with whom to insure. Businessmen who carry insurance against their losses find that not all insurance contracts bring equal values in loss prevention.

Factors Affecting Availability of Service. The amount of loss prevention service received from an insurer will vary according to several factors, principally the following:

1. *Kind of Insurance Coverage Purchased.* Boiler and machinery, workmen's compensation, elevator liability, automobile fleet liability, and credit insurance are lines in which much loss prevention help is commonly made available to, even urged upon, the insured. General liability and transportation insurance also are lines in which loss prevention service is often given. In other lines, much depends on the size of the policy (see below) and the severity of the loss ratio.

2. *Amount of Premium Involved.* Insurance companies are not eleemosynary institutions, not even the mutuals.[27] The continued existence of all of them depends on their ability to take in from customers (and investments) more than they pay out to policyholders, employees, and general creditors. If loss prevention expenses outrun the funds available for that activity, trouble ensues. The companies, therefore, cannot safely make a practice of spending on loss prevention for given customers sums that are much greater than the premiums received from the same customers. A saving grace is that the smaller insureds often are in such shape that great improvement in loss experience is possible for small effort expended. This

---

[27] For that matter, not even the "non-profit" "Blue Cross" and "Blue Shield" organizations; the aim of all of them is to be self-sustaining *in the market place.*

potentially favorable effect, unfortunately, is counterbalanced because the small-business manager has all his energy absorbed by the sheer struggle to keep going; his marketing, personnel, purchasing, and tax accounting problems may be all that he can handle. Even when they are not, he is less likely to have learned the importance of loss prevention to the same degree as has more experienced or better trained management. A basic truism of loss prevention is that when management cannot or will not follow through, preventive effort is wasted. Therefore, many insurers are rather reluctant to put much effort into loss prevention service for really small businesses.

3. *Insurance Company, Agency, and Broker Involved.* (*a*) Differences are found among insurance companies in the amounts of loss prevention service they are able or willing to provide. These differences are not the same in all lines of insurance: Company M may specialize in workmen's compensation, writing other lines principally as an accommodation to insureds and producers. Its service with regard to work injuries will probably be excellent, but for other losses prevention service may be essentially nil. Company N may write a great deal of transportation insurance, and pride itself on its research in the fields of packaging and of cargo salvage. Workmen's compensation, however, may be "just a headache" to Company N. Geography is a factor, too. It is one thing for a company to maintain good service when it has many important policyholders bunched in a metropolitan area; it is another thing to try to maintain such service in an area where the prevention engineers must spend half their time traveling between clients. (*b*) Some agencies and brokerage firms are large enough to maintain their own loss prevention divisions. An insured who buys enough insurance to be an attractive client for these firms naturally has an additional opportunity to obtain service.

Types of Prevention Service Available. Excluding the specialty lines of credit and title insurance, and possibly surety bonding, insurance companies cannot administer loss prevention programs for their insureds; they can only counsel. Apart from this limitation, however, the boiler and machinery insurers and most liability and workmen's compensation insurers are prepared to do a complete job of prevention engineering for any customer whose premiums (or losses!) warrant the expenditure. For small buyers, the amount spent on help is necessarily scaled down, with the amount of the reduction probably greatest in general liability and least in workmen's compensation and truckmen's liability. Safety engineering, industrial hygiene, product design—in every appropriate field, insurers are prepared to help. Notice, however, the phrase, "are prepared"; the actual doing sometimes depends upon the "who's"—who's the buyer, who's the agent or broker, who's in charge for the insuring company in the buyer's area. However, a single persistent man among these three may be able to break up inertia in the other two.

In plate glass, the service provided is, not prevention of glass breakage, but reduction of the intangible losses following it. Presumably, the value of a show window is the *show*. When the glass is out, the show is lost, but indemnity is not paid for loss of "show time." Glass insurers pride themselves on their speed of replacement, thus reducing the "show time" loss.

In surety, the bonding company's investigation of the person or firm to be bonded provides the obligee[28] with an assurance that there is no particular reason to believe in advance that the employee will not be faithful or that the construction firm will not be competent, as the case may be. (Thus, in a way, the bonding company actually enters into loss prevention administration—helping the obligee to select employees who are financially reliable and contractors who are both competent and financially reliable.) While this prevention service is still a useful device in contracting, the growth of blanket bond protection has considerably reduced its use in fidelity protection. The fidelity guarantor who covers all employees on a "blanket" basis generally "plays the averages" like an insurer and relies on long-run consistency of results over large numbers of people to protect him rather than on the old method of person-by-person investigation.

Much of the prevention work of fire insurance companies is provided as a public service and is not directly connected with the purchase of insurance.[29] Standards of design in construction, proper methods for handling ignitable and combustible materials, what constitute adequate and appropriate fire-fighting facilities and equipment—the development and dissemination of information about matters such as these are an important part of the loss prevention work of fire insurers, and the benefits are not restricted to purchasers of insurance. Anyone who wants the information may have it. The insurers' fire prevention agencies, who do not represent any particular insurer, are usually happy to be consulted for advice in planning safety features for any new piece of major construction. In other words, much of the fire prevention service of insurers can be had by anyone merely for the asking.

An insured, however, may have the additional benefits of regular inspection of his going concern, with detailed recommendations for his own particular case. Full-scale, high-grade fire loss prevention service on an indi-

---

[28] The person or organization for whom the bonded work is to be done.

[29] This is not to imply that other lines of insurance do not engage in public safety service, too. The emphasis, however, is different, since the nature of the problem is different. See, e.g., the suggested assignments under "Loss Prevention" in *C.P.C.U. Topical Outline*, Part II, "Functional Aspects of Insurance including Marketing" (Bryn Mawr, Pennsylvania: American Institute of Property and Liability Underwriters). Its topics under "Loss Prevention in Fire Insurance" are almost all concerned with such public information matters as building codes and safe construction, while for industrial acidents the list is equally preponderantly concerned with Heinrich's thesis that the only effective control is inside-the-individual-plant control. (Of course, the private automobile accident problem necessarily takes the student back into the broad "general public" approach again.)

vidual basis is a "house specialty" with certain insurance groups: the Factory Mutuals (whose founder, Zachariah Allen, established the idea), the Factory Insurance Association, and the special risk organizations, each of which specializes in the problems of a different industry (grain elevators and flour mills, petroleum processing, whisky distilling, and so on). A few independent insurers also have constructed their business around the provision of loss prevention service.

"Information on request" is the usual loss prevention service in other branches of insurance. However, insurers against theft actively concern themselves with the favorite targets of criminals, such as jewelers, furriers, long-haul trucks, and banks. Transportation insurers sometimes provide considerable aid in the problems of packaging and loading against shipping damage.

Credit insurers will, if desired, take over practically the whole administration of accounts receivable, including reduction of bad debts. Title insurers, of course, rely principally on loss prevention through title search to keep their business profitable.

General Management's Role in Loss Prevention

The fundamental loss prevention process can be stated in quite simple terms: Find the loss causes, then reduce or eliminate them. An important part of the expertise of a loss prevention specialist consists of knowing *where* to look for causes and how to recognize them when found. Then he must also know *what* to do about them—and *how* to get it done. In some ways the last is the most difficult of all. The safety engineer is fundamentally a staff, not a line, officer. He advises rather than commands. Even when he has the authority to impose some regulations, he is not likely to have fully effective means for carrying them through. It is a basic proposition in loss prevention that safe procedures must be "built in" to the production and other operational processes—and therefore necessarily must be administered by production or other "line" personnel.[30]

Non-Specialists' Knowledge. What should general and operational management know about loss prevention?

1. The costs and other deleterious effects of losses, especially as compared with the costs and energies to be used in preventing them.

2. That loss prevention *is* an integral part of operations. Safe procedures

---

[30] This theme occurs in every treatise, short or long, on loss prevention. Examples from writings already cited are Heinrich, *op. cit.*, pp. 32–49, 66–80, 85–114, 155–90, 344–75 (note how much of this basic work deals with the role of the line administrators); Morgenthaler, *op. cit.*, p. 25; and American Engineering Council, *op. cit.*, pp. 7, 32–35. On the other hand, there is no "line supervision" in the operation of a private automobile for personal use, and this makes our highway accident problem tremendously difficult to cope with; cf. Harry R. DeSilva, *Why We Have Automobile Accidents* (New York: John Wiley & Sons, Inc., 1942), esp. his chaps. 11–15 and pp. 366–67, with Heinrich's study of *industrial* accidents.

are necessarily matters of everyday operations, and are established and implemented in the same way as other operational procedures, and loss costs, in the end, are depletions of operating profits.

3. That there are two parts to loss prevention—control of frequency and control of severity—and the two are often not the same thing. Control of severity (e.g., installation of a sprinkler system to halt the spread of fire after it has started, or creation of an in-plant clinic to provide prompt treatment to injured workers) is seldom if ever a satisfactory substitute for control of frequency (e.g., using non-inflammable solvents so that sprinklers will have few fires to stop, or keeping plant and warehouse aisles clear so that fewer employees will stumble and fall and there will be fewer cuts, bruises, dislocations, and fractures to be treated).

4. That in loss prevention, as in nearly everything else, problems are often easier to avoid in the first place than to solve after they appear. Therefore, the loss prevention viewpoint should be kept in mind and always be a factor[31] in reaching final decisions whenever plans are being laid for such things as changes in plants or processes; programs for employee or management hiring, training, health, or welfare; systems of financial, accounting, or quality controls; or any action involving contractual arrangements.

5. How to make profitable use of *all* the loss prevention specialists who are or can be available. These include loss prevention engineers and risk managers, of course, but also such persons as public or private fire and police chiefs and inspectors (plant protection); maintenance supervisors, hygienists and medical personnel, financial officers, accountants and auditors (prevention of losses by embezzlements and other crimes); and legal counsel (avoidance of losses from contractual or statutory liability for acts of others). Basically, this is a matter of making effective use of staff men, and (like safety engineering and risk management) it is a big subject all by itself. The interested reader must therefore refer to books on general management and management organization. Here, only this bit of advice on the use of any kind of specialist is passed along: First, the general manager must know when he needs a specialist, and what kind he needs. (Thus, we get the inclusion of "business law" as a required subject in curricula in col-

---

31 "Be *a* factor" does not mean "be *the* (dominant) factor," except on rare occasions. Dr. Blanchard, having said that there is a prima facie case for loss prevention (n. 22), goes on to add: "Loss should be prevented *to the extent that prevention is practical.*" (*Loc. cit.*; italics added.) Dr. Willett gives us a *reductio ad absurdum* to demonstrate the point: Losses from railroad accidents could be reduced considerably if train speeds were limited to ten miles per hour (*op. cit.*, Philadelphia reprint, p. 28). Blanchard (like others) warns, however, against underestimating the value of prevention: "Not all of the savings from prevention can be measured. . . ." It is fair to cite the following as an example of a result in practice: ". . . in G.M. . . . each division, motivated largely by balancing all factors of cost, built as it pleased with no thought of an over-all protective position for company and workers alike." William B. Harris, "The Great Livonia Fire," *Fortune*, Vol. XLVIII (November, 1953), p. 178.

leges of business administration. The businessman ought to know enough about the law to know when he needs a lawyer. It is hoped that the present book, and especially the present chapter, will do something of the same with regard to safety engineers and risk managers.) Second, the general manager must be able to tell a good specialist from a bad one. (This is more difficult. However, a little further on in this work some usable guides to the selection of outside advisers in risk management are attempted. Beyond this, textbook authors can only confess that the selection of professional advisers of any kind generally proves to be another one of these famous and all too numerous problems in which there simply is no satisfactory substitute for the ability to exercise sound business judgment.)

Risk Manager's Role

Cost Control. A leading risk manager, Russell B. Gallagher, of the Philco Corporation, has called risk management a "new phase of cost control."[32] That the treasurer is the company official most often charged with the risk management function, with the controller another common choice, indicates general recognition that risk management is a matter of finance and costs.[33] The particular costs that the risk manager seeks to control are, of course, those associated with static, or pure, risks. These costs have been shown to be of two kinds: (1) The costs of *risk*: Risk costs arise because potential losses are *uncertain*, and they are incurred regardless of whether the losses materialize. That these losses *might* materialize is sufficient to produce the costs of risk. (2) The costs of *losses*: Loss costs come about when losses actually *materialize*, and they are incurred regardless of whether the frequency and severity of loss occurrence are relatively accurately predicted. That the losses do materialize produces the cost.

Furthermore, the importance of the costs of losses has been established. It follows, therefore, that the risk manager is directly and immediately interested in loss-cost control—that is, in loss prevention. Nevertheless, in

---

[32] "Risk Management: New Phase of Cost Control," *Harvard Business Review*, Vol. XXIV, No. 5 (September–October, 1952), pp. 75–98.

[33] In one study, by the American Management Association, of the practices of member companies, 48.22 per cent of the "risk managers" were in the treasurer's division; 12.50 per cent were under the secretary; 12.05 per cent under the controller; 11.16 per cent under a vice-president, 4.02 per cent under the president, with 12.05 per cent in "other" allocations. Russell B. Gallagher, *Buying and Administering Corporate Insurance*, American Management Association Research Report No. 15 (The Association, 1949), p. 101. A later study found that, of 92 *part-time* administrators, 46 spent the rest of their time in work classified as "treasurer, financial, accounting," Cristy, *op. cit.*, p. 88. Both these studies were of "insurance administrators," but wherever risk management is actually and consciously practiced as a management specialty, the insurance administrator is generally found to be the practitioner. See n. 25, and Mowbray and Blanchard, *op. cit.*, chap. 35, "Risk Management"; also the following numbers in the American Management Association Insurance Series, Nos. 100, 101 (both 1953), 102 (1954), 111 (1955), 112 (1956).

the American Management Association study of risk management organizations in member companies, it is noted that "plant protection and safety engineering are matters which the insurance administrator may control or which may be autonomous. . . . No rule of thumb, no definite theory has been indicated by the study.[34]

It has been shown that actual control of safety procedures rests with supervisory personnel in production and other operating divisions and with general management. So what is the risk manager's role?

Salesman, Policymaker, Supervisor. A survey of writings by risk managers themselves[35] indicates a strong consensus on the following points:

1. A primary function of the risk manager is to sell operating management— from the front line clear through to the top—on the need for and advantages of good loss prevention, and to help them implement it.
2. The risk manager makes, or assists in making, policy decisions on safety programs and procedures.
3. He is an active center (and not merely a repository) of usable information about hazards, losses, and safety, both as experienced and as practiced in his own company and outside of it.
4. He follows through on loss prevention policies and practices in action, checking actual performance and results.
5. In many, perhaps most, cases he has direct responsibility for at least some loss prevention work. Even when his company has a separate safety division, the risk manager may have direct charge of such areas as fire protection, safety in building design, or burglary and robbery protection. Indeed, any areas of loss prevention that are not being cared for by someone else properly become of direct concern to him; he has an obligation to ferret them out and to see that something is done about them.[36]

In sum, the risk manager's role in loss prevention is to investigate (hazards, losses, and loss prevention techniques, within his own company and elsewhere), to communicate the results of his investigations (and to do it in an intelligible and motivational form), and to follow through with a continuous checkup on the results obtained.

Insurance Agents and Loss Prevention

It should never be forgotten that agents and brokers are paid to *sell*. Some of them give some service free, but their living depends on their

---

[34] Gallagher, *op. cit.,* American Management Research Report No. 15. However, Gallagher speaks for himself in another article, and states that "both safety and fire-prevention engineers, should be brought under his [the risk manager's] control. Such a transfer will make analysis possible without the addition of personnel or duplication of activities." "Risk Management: New Phase of Cost Control," *op. cit.,* p. 85.

[35] For short bibliography see the works cited in nn. 32 and 33.

[36] For example, a common hole in loss control plans occurs with regard to checking on contractual agreements. There are two points to watch: requirements as to safety practices by the outside contractor, both as to methods of operations and as to completed results; agreements as to who is legally and financially responsible for losses resulting from damage to the property of a contracting party, from liability to third parties, and for defects in the project under contract.

getting and keeping policies on the books. However, an insurance agent or broker seeking customers sometimes finds that loss prevention services are a help in getting and keeping them.

In some instances an insurer's (or possibly agency's) loss prevention services are actually the central subject of a sale and purchase, even though the transaction bears the form of sale and purchase of a contract of insurance. For example, the prospect has to have his elevators, or his steam boiler inspected; the law says so. In many jurisdictions, the law also says that inspection by a licensed insurer meets the requirement. The customer buys the inspection and considers the insurance in the nature of lagniappe. Similarly, plate glass insurance commonly, and schedule fidelity bonds frequently, are sold with loss prevention as the principal appeal. In short, loss prevention of itself can be a salable service.

Loss prevention, however, is salable to a much wider market when its appeal lies in its ability to reduce insurance premiums, and this is its principal use to insurance agents and brokers. Thus, in Morrow and Lonergan, *Insurance Surveys*, a book on certain phases of advanced selling and service techniques for agents and brokers, the single extended discussion of loss prevention appears as only one of several topics in a chapter entitled "Securing Lower Fire Insurance Rates."[37] In recent issues of the National Underwriter Company's annual *Agent's and Buyer's Guide*, in Part II, "The Insurance Survey," the following appears:

Special Services

Probably the most important special service in connection with many risks is that of *rate engineering*. . . . A note of caution is in order, however, where an insurance man who is not experienced with rate structures attempts to give advice on this subject. It should be borne in mind that there are some buildings in which occupancies or other features have changed sufficiently since the last time the building was rated—perhaps many years ago—that a reinspection would indicate a rate increase rather than a lowered rate. Thus, for example, careless recommendation of, say, a fire door for the purpose of obtaining a lower rate might overlook the fact that the present rate does not make an appropriate charge for some existing deficiency. Without doubt, this is a field in which experience and expertness are to be much respected and sought after.[38]

Besides the emphasis on loss prevention as a means of lowering rates, two other points should be noted from the foregoing citations. One is that not all agents and brokers are qualified or willing to perform either the loss prevention or the "rate engineering" service.[39] The other is that both cita-

---

[37] Ralph E. Morrow, rev. by George E. Lonergan (3d ed.; Indianapolis: Rough Notes Co., Inc., 1951), chap. 9.

[38] (Cincinnati: National Underwriter Co., 1961), pp. 255–56.

[39] "Some agents still refuse to make any move that will lower the Fire Insurance rates upon risks which they control because of the resulting loss in commissions." Morrow and Lonergan, *op. cit.*, p. 70. These authors go on to point out that this attitude "can cost them far more commissions over a period of time. . . . It is only a question of time until some competing agent, broker or direct writing company will uncover those risks

tions refer only to fire insurance. This seems to be due to the nature of fire insurance rating. Of all the major lines, only in fire insurance does each business establishment commonly have its own rate based on its own visible hazards. Therefore, for many a businessman his fire insurance rate is one of the few insurance rates that he individually can do something about. The logical function of the agent here is (1) to call attention to the fact that something can be done, (2) to suggest some good areas in which it might most profitably be done, and (3) to help get the information and the professional advice needed to make a decision and to execute it.

Burglary and robbery is another insurance line in which the individual "average" business can to some extent control its own rates. Although businesses are rated by classes for this cover, important discounts from basic class rates are allowed for such loss preventive devices and practices as "burglar-proof" safes,[40] burglar alarms, night watch services, using guards with money messengers, and so on. Again, the insurance sales representative should call these possibilities to the insured's attention and help him find out about them. However, as most businesses spend little or nothing on burglary and robbery insurance, the opportunities for premium savings in this area are much fewer and smaller than in fire insurance.

Since most "all risk" and multiple peril[41] policies include, and hence charge for, protection against losses by fire and theft (of one kind or another), and since the rates for these policies generally either (1) specifically include the standard fire or burglary rate for the business, or (2) are set by underwriting judgment, the preceding two paragraphs apply to these contracts also.

In the other major lines of insurance, the general rule is that only the larger insureds can obtain individual rate reductions for loss preventive activities. Also, as a general rule, in all lines of insurance the largest insureds either can or must have their rates based on actual loss results (through experience or retrospective rating) rather than on the mere expectation that loss preventive devices or activities will have desirable results. In these cases, the salesman's forte is to sell the benefits of the loss prevention services that will be provided, not by himself, but by the engineers, hygienists, and other specialists employed by his companies (occa-

---

in which certain changes can be made that will materially lower their rates." This, they note, costs the agent loss of policyholder confidence and can be extremely expensive. In other words, as was remarked above in the present text, the central matter is not really loss prevention but insurance selling.

[40] Despite the terminology, no safe is really burglar-proof, just as no building is really fireproof. But in fire protection engineering, the point is made by substituting the term "fire-resistive" for the inaccurate description, "fireproof." In burglary, quite the other way: The imperfection of "burglar-proof" safes is advertised (subtly!) by the existence of safes in a still safer category, "*double* burglar-proof"; while the "X-60" and "TX-60" classes are safer than that! But none of these are burglar-proof either. (If they were, why buy burglary insurance on them at *any* discount short of 100 per cent?)

[41] "All risk" covers all perils except those specially excluded. "Multiple peril" covers a broad list of perils specifically named as included. See chap. 14.

sionally, by his agency or brokerage firm). When workmen's compensation and liability insurance premiums run into thousands, or hundreds of thousands, of dollars, and these premiums are (or can be) based on the losses that the insured actually incurs, the effectiveness of an insurer's loss prevention program is a matter of prime importance.

Controlling Loss Severity

Earlier in the discussion it was stated that "there are two parts to loss prevention[42]—control of frequency and control of severity—and the two are often not the same thing." And it was added that "the control of severity . . . is seldom if ever a satisfactory substitute for the control of frequency." Nevertheless, control of loss severity has a place of importance in risk management, and it should be examined further.

Controls Exercised before the Loss. No program to reduce loss frequency is forever perfect. That losses will eventually occur must be considered as given datum. Part of the job in controlling loss costs is to try to arrange operations so that when losses do occur, their real effects are limited in some way.

In some cases, the same procedure does tend to reduce both frequency and severity. Well-built buildings (in terms of fire protection standpoint) are less likely to incur fires; they are also less subject to damage from those fires when they do occur. Changing trip schedules so as to reduce the speeds required of vehicle drivers commonly reduces the number of accidents; slower speeds may also be conducive to reduced severity of accidents.

Separate measures, however, are also necessary. Dispersion of property will not of itself ordinarily reduce the number of fires or explosions, but it will limit the potential effects of any one of them. The desirability of this method of loss limitation (dispersion of property) is the subject of recurring conflict between good risk management and efficient production in the absence of catastrophe. The 55-million-dollar fire[43] at the General Motors transmission plant, Livonia, Michigan, well illustrates the risk

---

[42] The reader should be warned that there is considerable variety of use of terminology in this subject. Some authorities, for sound procedural as well as etymological reasons, reserve "prevention" for reduction of loss *frequency* only: Only those losses which do not happen can be truly said to have been "prevented." On the other hand, it can logically be said that, once a fire has started, if effective fire fighting keeps it within one room of a building, then this control of loss severity has *prevented* loss to the remaining rooms. Various authors describe this latter type of control as loss "protection" or "reduction." But there is no consistency among authors (sometimes not even within the work of a single author). The present text treats "prevention," "reduction," and "control" alike as general terms and, when distinction is desired, makes it by reference back to the fundamental quantities of severity and frequency.

[43] Direct loss only, total losses were in hundreds of millions, may have reached a billion dollars when all interests are considered. *Fire, Casualty and Surety Bulletins* (see n. 17), Sales Section, Losses, Fgm-1 and 2. Also, "A Fire That Changed the Course of an Industry," *Business Week*, August 22, 1953, pp. 28–30; "Major Manufacturing Losses in 1953," *Quarterly of the National Fire Protection Association*, Vol. XLVII (January, 1953), p. 237.

management side. The building was huge in order to get the maximum efficiency of a smooth, uninterrupted and continuous flow of mass production. In terms of the control of loss frequency, the design was admirable: an incombustible building with nearly all incombustible (metal and machinery) contents. Nonetheless, the factory and its contents were a nearly total loss, and, since the integrated area was large, so was the loss.[44]

An even larger area and an even greater loss would have been involved had it not been for the *one* fire wall in the total structure, separating the factory area from the offices. "Without it, Transmission probably would have lost its engineering data and Hydramatic Transmissions would have been off full production almost a year instead of four months (as it appears at this writing.)"[45]

Two years later, another multimillion-dollar industrial fire illustrated a different aspect of the dispersion problem. This fire involved the Whiting refinery of the Standard Oil Company (Indiana). After investigating the loss, Miles E. Woodworth, flammable liquids engineer of the National Fire Prevention Association, came to the following conclusions:

1. Insufficient spacing between hazard areas proved to be the primary cause of the large loss. . . . Industry must decide whether it is better to spend additional millions to secure proper plant separation or to be exposed to multi-million-dollar losses of production.

* * * * *

3. Lack of dikes and inadequate spacing between many of the banks proved to be an insurmountable fire fighting problem.
4. The desirability of having an adequate and detailed disaster plan for industrial and public fire and emergency organizations was clearly indicated. . . .
5. The refinery's own unusually complete disaster plan proved its worth in many ways.[46]

It was eight days before the last blaze was out, and the whole thing might well have been worse except for favorable weather.[47]

Although the best-known big fires of recent years have been industrial, mass concentration of values is not purely a factory problem. Mass merchandising is just as common a phenomenon as mass production, and warehouses and stores are subject to catastrophic losses. In the "large loss" reports published annually in the *Quarterly of the National Fire Protection Association*, covering fire losses of $250,000 or more each, the average property damage per large fire in store buildings was over $450,000 in 1957 (58 fires), over $462,000 in 1958 (70 fires), and over $426,000 in 1959 (82 fires). For warehouses, the figures were over $542,000 for 55 fires in 1957,

[44] One of the articles that specifically examines the question of control of severity by dispersion as raised by the fire is "GM's Fire Starts Everybody Worrying," *Business Week*, August 29, 1953, p. 31.

[45] Harris, *op. cit.*, p. 171.

[46] "Whiting Refinery Fire," *Quarterly of the National Fire Protection Association*, Vol. IL, No. 2 (October, 1955), p. 86.

[47] "Men against Fire," *National Safety News*, Vol. LXXII (October, 1955), p. 208.

over $488,000 for 39 fires in 1958, and over $734,000 for 41 fires in 1959. (The averages for large industrial fires ran from over $514,000 for 102 fires in 1959 to over $757,000 for 125 fires in 1957.)[48]

Property values do not present the only problem in concentrations of exposures. "Several years ago, almost the entire upper echelon of a manufacturing company perished in the crash of a private airplane. Shortly afterward six key men of another company barely escaped with their lives when a pleasure craft (watercraft) exploded after taking on gas."[49] Shortly after the preceding statement was published, the Phillips Petroleum Company lost five top executives from one department plus a company attorney in a private airplane crash.[50]

When one corporation calculated its possible loss if the company-owned plane should crash with eleven executives aboard, it estimated the workmen's compensation potential at $40,000, plus $780,000 in group life insurance. "The loss to the employer in knowledge and expense would have been beyond calculation in dollars-and-cents terms.[51] With these kinds of loss possibilities at stake, forestalling unnecessary placement of too many eggs in one basket is an important part of good risk management.

Controls after the Loss. Dividing up control of a company's liquid assets so that any one person has only limited access to them is one before-the-loss method of controlling the severity of embezzlement losses. Thorough, frequent, and irregular audits are an after-the-loss method of controlling the same thing; losses are generally caught before they can snowball too far. Good auditing procedures also tend to reduce loss frequency; few persons who want to take funds also want to take a good chance of being caught. Alarm systems, sprinklers, fire-fighting personnel and equipment, and medical and rehabilitation service are examples of other means of controlling the severity of various kinds of losses *after* they have happened. Encouraging and helping to plan for such services is a part of good risk management.

Salvage is also an important after-the-loss method of control. After the immediate peril has run its course, prompt appropriate action can minimize the resulting costs. Efficient salvage is a matter of engineering and of markets. The damaged property must be reconditioned; then, if the owner cannot make good use of it himself, a buyer for it must be found. Few business men have much occasion to acquire experience in salvage techniques, so most have no idea either what to do or how to do it. There is a strong tendency to overestimate the loss when the wet and smoking debris is viewed —overestimate in terms of what actually has already happened, that is. But

---

[48] For 1957's figures see *Quarterly of the National Fire Protection Association,* Vol. LI (April, 1958), pp. 224–307; for 1958 figures, Vol. LII (April, 1959), pp. 235–373; and for 1959, Vol. LIII (April, 1960), p. 343–431.

[49] Gallagher "Risk Management: New Phase of Cost Control," *op. cit.,* pp. 76–77.

[50] "Phillips Officials Die in Crash," *Oil and Gas Journal, Vol. LIV* (December 17, 1956), p. 98.

[51] Gallagher, *loc. cit.*

the overestimate rapidly will become a true estimate, or even an underestimate, if the belief that there is no salvage leads to inaction. Property left in the debris will deteriorate rapidly and soon be beyond all saving.[52]

"He who knows not, and knows that he knows not . . ." needs to find someone who knows. The major general salvage companies are owned by the insurers. In the larger cities there are independent salvors, and in ocean marine operations, salvage is an important independent business.

Closely related to salvage is the right to recover from any persons responsible for the loss. Care must be taken not to impair the value of this right.[53] This is a legal right, of course, and calls for legal counsel. Recovery on losses caused by criminal taking is a compound of salvage and legal recovery for damages: The property taken may be sought out and physically recovered (salvage), or right of recovery against the criminal's own assets may be exercised. While the latter right is not often worth much in the case of thievery by an outsider, it is useful against embezzlers, who not only may have property of their own or their employer's but also may have relatives interested in making restitution. Again, pursuit of these recoveries is generally less costly and more successful when carried on by experienced hands, such as those of insurance and surety companies.[54]

A particularly important part of "salvage" relates to saving the income and operations of the concern as well as its property. The acquisition of substitute facilities (either for the operations of the firm itself or as substitute sources of supply for vital goods and services lost because of damage at the supplier's premises) is a major, expensive operation. Planning for it before the loss can make this after-the-loss saving considerably more efficient. Duplicate facilities already in existence can even make it unnecessary.[55]

Nothing, however, gets done by itself; somebody has to do it. It may be cheaper if that "somebody" is an outsider. Thus, one supermarket decided to buy insurance against losses from bad checks, not because it could not carry the actual check losses itself—it could—but because it concluded that loss of the time its managers spent trying to effect recoveries was so large as to make the cost of insurance a net gain. In other words, it saved money by hiring the insurer's salvage service.[56]

Similarly, a business may find it worthwhile to have a traffic or shipping

[52] Prentiss B. Reed, *Adjustment of Property Losses* (2d ed.; New York: McGraw-Hill Book Co., Inc., 1953), pp. 65–69, and *passim* in chaps. 11, 12, 13.

[53] See Reed, *op. cit.*, pp. 33–37, 162–64, for a list of the possibilities of recovery and for a statement of some of the difficulties that may arise.

[54] See G. W. Crist, Jr., *Corporate Suretyship* (2d ed.; New York: McGraw-Hill Book Co., Inc., 1950), pp. 64–65, 122–23, 285, 286; Jules Backman, *Surety Rate-making* (New York: Surety Association of America, 1948), chap. 3; and William H. Rodda, *Inland Marine and Transportation Insurance* (2d ed.; Englewood Cliffs, New Jersey: Prentice-Hall, Inc., 1958), pp. 478–83.

[55] Reed, *op. cit.*, chap. 17. Cf. the quotation cited at n. 45, this chapter.

[56] Orieon M. Spaid, Actuarial Service Corporation, as reported in "Chronological Stabilization, Which Is Insurable, Desired by Corporations," *National Underwriter*, Vol. LXI, No. 29 (July 18, 1957), p. 20.

department skilled in handling claims against carriers—or it may find that costs are reduced by letting these departments concentrate on other matters, leaving the shipping losses to be covered by an insurer that pays first and recovers from the carriers later at its own discretion and expense.

Legal and Financial Controls. An important approach to controlling loss severity is one solely concerned with circumscribing the financial effects of losses so far as a given business is concerned. The most important and common device using this approach to loss control is the limited liability stock company (corporation). With this device, if losses do occur, their dollar effect on the owners can ordinarily be limited to the amount of investment in the corporation; it cannot ordinarily spread beyond that to swallow up personal assets (or investments in other businesses) too. Owners of fleets of ships have made use of this device to limit their losses from the operation of any one ship; often each ship is separately incorporated. Similar arrangements can be and are made in other lines of business.

The financial responsibility of a given individual for losses may be limited by contractual arrangement. Common carriers of all kinds use bills of lading under which their liability for cargo damage does not exceed some given number of dollars per package, pound, or ton. Bailees, such as storers of fur garments, make similar arrangements. Landlords sometimes insist on limiting their liability to their tenants. Indeed, the possibilities are almost endless.

These limitations, being financial and legal rather than physical, are really examples of risk transfer rather than of loss limitation. They limit loss severity only from the viewpoint of a particular individual or business. If the physical loss potential is not similarly limited, someone must bear the risk of the potential excess. Thus, in the case of the limited liability corporation, loss in excess of the net worth of the corporation must be borne by the corporation's creditors. In the contractual arrangements described, the excess of loss beyond the contractual limits will be borne by the shipper, the bailor, the tenant, or some other person. Therefore, in a stict sense, the use of legal and financial methods to limit the effect of loss is really an example of *risk transfer* rather than of loss prevention, and therefore it will be discussed further in the next chapter.

EFFECTS OF LOSS PREVENTION AND RISK BEARING

Clearly, loss prevention and control are not separate methods of risk handling entirely apart from risk assumption and risk transfer. The best loss prevention programs still leave losses whose incidence is uncertain. Their uncertainty must be borne or transferred, and so affects the decision to avoid, to bear, or to transfer.

It will occur to the reader that loss reduction will make a risk less undesirable. If the hazards of dangerous operations can be reduced, more people will be willing to engage in them, either for themselves or for others. Situations that would otherwise be avoided will be accepted if loss costs can be brought within the ability of a business to handle them.

As suggested earlier, what is not so obvious is that loss prevention activities, while decreasing losses, may increase the uncertainty concerning their occurrence. Losses that are frequent are generally easier to predict than losses that are infrequent. Therefore, as loss frequency is reduced, degree of risk (uncertainty) may be increased. On the other hand, when the individual losses in a series vary widely in size, loss prediction is generally much more difficult than when each of the losses falls within a limited range as to size. Therefore, an effective program that limits loss severity *may* decrease the degree of risk.

In business practice the effects of good and bad loss prevention programs appear equally contradictory. One risk manager has stated that "an effective program of loss prevention should result in a reduction in the cost of insurance, and it may justify self-insurance or non-insurance. The insurance program for a company that controls its operations and facilities through an effective loss prevention program will be quite different from that of a company where this phase of operations is still undeveloped."[57]

Two other risk managers, however, in private conversations with one of the authors, have stated that, in their companies, general management could not be interested in enforcing loss prevention and control procedures until the companies started carrying their own risks. Only then did it become completely obvious to everyone concerned that every loss represented a cost that the business had to pay out of its own assets or income. Not even retrospective rating had been able to accomplish the same thing in these particular businesses.[58]

SUMMARY

Some risks can and should be avoided. Many others must be or should be borne. Whenever a risk is borne, two aspects of it must be considered and managed: uncertainty and losses. Each element presents its own problems and involves its own costs.

Risk Assumption

Each element, uncertainty and loss, may be assumed and, in effect, forgotten and ignored. Sometimes this is the best policy. Too often it is a practice born of ignorance or indifference.

---

[57] George H. Connerat, staff assistant and insurance manager, Republic Aviation Corporation, "II. Risk Abatement," from the symposium, "Managing Corporate Risk," *Corporate Risk Management: Current Problems and Perspectives*, American Management Association, Insurance Series No. 112 (New York: The Association, 1956), p. 10.

[58] In retrospective rating, the premium is determined at the end of the insured period according to the losses that were incurred in the period. The insured is charged for his losses plus the insurer's expenses, subject to a maximum and a minimum charge.

Whenever risks are assumed, losses may be charged off against income or surplus as they occur or the charge may be regularized by the creation and maintenance of a "contingency reserve." The feasibility of any plan that does not provide for a source of *funds* for losses depends upon the possible frequency and severity of the losses that may be encountered as compared with the financial strength (solvency *and* liquidity) of the organization encountering them. If survival is a desideratum, then the worst potential loss experience with regard to losses of all kinds (static and dynamic) should be compared with the poorest (generally, the least liquid) financial position anticipated during the operation of the business.

The principal advantages of bearing risks without funding are that the method is simple and inexpensive to administer. The principal disadvantage is that the losses suffered may turn out to be most inconveniently expensive if not downright disabling. Methods that involve careful estimate of losses plus a regular review of their effects are more likely to remain successful than are less formal (more "happy-go-lucky"?) approaches. Plans that involve definite financial preparation—funds—for the preservation of liquidity are safer yet, but they involve the additional costs inherent in the maintenance of liquidity.

All risk-bearing plans can present important psychological difficulties.

Loss Prevention and Control

The costs of the losses themselves are a major part of the problem of risk. These costs may be divided into (1) direct costs, (2) indirect costs to the person or organization immediately concerned, and (3) other costs to society at large. The direct costs, or immediate cash outlays, are sometimes greatly exceeded by the indirect costs, which include loss of business, reduced employee efficiency, and other factors.[59] Other social costs are in addition to these items. Many of these costs can be controlled in only one way: prevention of the accident in the first place.

Loss prevention is a job for a variety of professionally trained specialists, including safety engineers, fire protection engineers, industrial hygienists, accounting systems specialists, and others. These specialists may be employed or otherwise engaged directly, but an important additional method of obtaining them is through the purchase of insurance. Loss prevention service is an important consideration in several lines of insurance: workmen's compensation, public liability (of all kinds), boiler and machinery, glass, credit, and title insurance; and in surety bonding. In other lines, the kind and amount of preventive services available vary with the situation;

---

[59] Note, however, that in the 4-for-1 ratio for indutrial injuries the 1 includes only payments under workmen's compensation; property damages and any other direct outlays involved are included in the 4 along with the indirect costs of loss of efficiency, sales, etc.

in particular, large-volume buyers of insurance are more likely to be offered more loss prevention help.

Ultimate success or failure of any loss prevention program depends upon the interest and follow-through of general and operational management. A risk manager's biggest job in loss prevention is to get and to keep all management personnel interested in and properly informed about it. (The risk manager's own interest arises from the fundamental nature of his job: to control all the costs associated with static risks.)

Insurance agents and brokers have an interest in loss prevention service because it helps them in their principal job, which is selling insurance. This help comes partly because insurers' loss prevention services are themselves salable items, but mostly because preventive activities usually lower the customers' insurance costs.

While the major emphasis in loss prevention is on control of loss frequency, control of loss severity can also be helpful. Severity can be controlled by certain arrangements made in advance of a loss, by the use of specialized services and salvage operations after the loss, and by legal or financial means.

Risk assumption and loss prevention are best used in combination with each other, commonly with some risk avoidance or control also applied. The employment of each method has effects important to the employment of the others.

Further consideration of use of risk-handling methods in combination will appear later in this text, after the principal methods of risk avoidance and control have been described.

REVIEW AND DISCUSSION QUESTIONS

1. Two aspects of risk are uncertainty and loss. Can the risk manager do anything about one of these aspects without affecting the other? Explain.
2. Under what conditions should a risk be assumed? Are risks ever assumed under conditions other than one of those you have just named? Explain.
3. Are all losses a result of risk? Of what importance to the risk manager is the answer to this question?
4. What conditions are necessary for successful handling of unpredictable losses on a current basis?
5. What is the meaning of the phrase "the dice have no memory"? Does this meaning have any bearing on risk management in business?
6. Explain how each of the following loss factors can influence a possible decision to handle losses on a current basis: (a) loss severity, (b) loss frequency, and (c) the possibility of dynamic loss.
7. Explain how each of the following cost factors can influence a possible decision to handle losses on a current basis: (a) administration, (b) loss, and (c) taxes.
8. Comment on the advantages of using reserve accounting in connection with the charging of losses as current expenses.

9. Under what risk assumption situations would loss funding be appropriate? What difficulties are involved in a loss funding plan?
10. Distinguish between costs of losses and costs of risks.
11. Develop the case for loss prevention. How can the risk manager assure himself of an adequate loss prevention service?
12. What factors should the risk manager consider in deciding upon the type of loss prevention service he should use?
13. Explain the types of loss prevention services offered by insurance companies. What are the important variables that govern the amount of loss prevention service that an insurer will provide the risk manager? How do you explain these variables?
14. What should be the role of each of the following interested parties in loss prevention: (a) general management, (b) the risk manager, and (c) insurance salesmen?
15. What should the non-specialist in loss prevention know about loss prevention if he is in a position either to make decision about loss prevention or to implement loss prevention decisions?
16. What are some of the measures for controlling loss severity? Do they relate in any way to the control of loss frequency?
17. Explain how loss prevention affects risk.

Chapter 3

RISK TRANSFER

In chapter 2 attention was given to *loss* reduction and control, and it was noted that losses may be reduced or controlled without any program for controlling or reducing risk. In this and the next two chapters attention is shifted to risk reduction and control. Similarly, risk may be dealt with apart from any accompanying program of loss prevention and control. But programs of loss control and risk reduction are often united through the same risk management device.

THE ENDS AND MEANS

Risk is reduced or controlled when loss (or cost) becomes more accurately predictable. The reduction of static risk is a management art that is not widely known. Its importance in sound business administration, however, cannot profitably be overlooked in this era of scientific management.

Purposes of Risk Reduction and Control

Two reasons account for management's interest in reducing risk. One is simple risk aversion; other things remaining equal, it is human nature to prefer certainty to uncertainty in economic affairs. The other reason is that risk often involves dollar costs that can be reduced or removed.

Risk aversion is a personal, individual matter. Only the managers actually in charge of a given business enterprise can determine how far it is reasonable for them to go in risk reduction on the basis of risk aversion alone. Risk costs, however, are more objective, and therefore can be discussed on a more general basis.

Identifying Cost of Risk. It is a simple matter to identify risk cost by definition. The cost of risk is the cost of *uncertainty* about loss. But how can one tell what cost is due to "uncertainty"? There are problems here, but the key question surely is, "Would this cost be incurred if the rate and incidence of future losses were certain instead of uncertain?" If the cost would be incurred even if the schedule of future losses could be written out accurately in advance, then it is clearly not a cost of uncertainty or risk. If the cost would *not* be incurred if the future losses were known, then it is reasonable to consider it a cost of risk.

For example, suppose the Orion Wholesaling Corporation operates a large fleet of automobiles and trucks. Among its risks are those of accidental damage to its trucks and their cargoes. With a given number of trucks, the corporation suffers an average annual loss of $7,500 in damage to its own property. Because of the large number of trucks in its fleet, the corporation is fairly certain to experience this loss as an annual average. But the corporation's loss experience for any given future year is still uncertain. The loss may be more than $7,500, or it may be less. How much year-to-year variance there will be is the key problem. As an aid to solving this problem, it would be helpful if some particular probability distribution could be found that (1) would be a reasonable approximation of actual experience and (2) would have useful analytic properties. Statistical studies have suggested that the probability distribution of automobile material damage losses has the characteristics of a log-normal distribution.[1] A log-normal distribution is a probability distribution in which the logarithms of the numbers, rather than the numbers themselves, are distributed in accordance with the "normal" or "bell-shaped" probability curve.[2] Assume the following two different sets of figures illustrating the distribution of the Orion Company's transportation losses over the past year. The experience in set one is more variable than that in set two, as indicated by the higher standard deviation associated with it. The variation between actual year-to-year annual losses and the given average annual loss of $7,500 is greater. Thus the risk in set one is higher than in set two where the variation, as indicated by a lower standard deviation, is less erratic.

ANNUAL LOSS RATE

	Mean	*Mode*	*Standard Deviation*
Loss Distribution I	$7,500	$6,000	$2,625
Loss Distribution II	7,500	7,000	1,650

The long-run loss costs are the same in both cases, $7,500 per year. But the costs of setting aside funds to offset the larger losses in each case are not the same. Suppose the Orion Company would like to be 99.9 per cent sure that it could handle its losses in any year without strain. Statisticians tell us that with Loss Distribution I, the company would have to be prepared to

---

[1] See Robert A. Rennie, "The Measurement of Risk," *Journal of Insurance*, Vol. XXVIII, No. 1 (March, 1961), pp. 83–91, esp. pp. 87–89.

[2] For those readers who do not know or have forgotten statistical terms and concepts, a short explanation and glossary appear in an appendix at the end of Chap. 4. If a review is needed, it will pay the technically inclined reader to check the appendix now before proceeding further.

deal with losses in any year up to $15,664.[3] With Distribution II, preparation to handle losses up to $12,069 is all that would be required. The cost (lost earnings) of holding an extra $3,595 of separate liquid assets is the cost associated with the extra risk (uncertainty) involved in Distribution I.

For another example, suppose the average annual fire loss for a group of $200,000 buildings, all similar to the single one owned by the Market Realty Agency, is $400. If the agency could be "sure" (i.e., have, say, a 99.9 per cent probability) that no single losses in any one year would exceed some figure not too far above $400 (say, $600 or $700), the agency probably would simply assume the risk of fire for the long-run loss cost of $400 per year.[4] This amount would also be the minimum possible cost if the losses could be accurately predicted. However, with much larger losses possible (in any one year the entire building could go up in smoke), prudence is likely to lead the agency to purchase fire insurance for a premium of, say, $750. The cost of risk in this event would be the difference between $750 and $400, or $350 per year.

Cost of Risk as Part of Cost of Loss. Suppose, however, the Market Realty Agency chose to ignore the large loss possibility and simply assumed the fire risk on its building on a current basis. In this case there would be no insurance cost, nor would there be any loss of income attributable to the retention of low-yielding, highly liquid resources to offset large losses. If lack of insurance or the absence of funding did not impair the agency's credit standing or cause any personal anxiety on the part of the agency's owners or managers, what then would be the cost of risk? In other words, does risk cost anything if it is ignored?

By now the distinction between the cost of loss and the cost of risk should be clear. But what may not be clear is the effect of prior preparation for loss on its cost. Without advance planning for losses, repairs and replacements may have to be financed with borrowed funds. Nothing is wrong with borrowing per se; in fact, credit often plays an important role in risk management plans. But when there are no plans, the use of credit to offset losses can be costly. In the first place, borrowing under the adverse conditions usually prevailing after a loss may be expensive. Furthermore, the excessive use of credit as a means for recovering from a loss could make it difficult or impossible to obtain additional capital when needed to finance later business opportunities. Credit following a loss may not be available, even at high rates, if the amount needed to save the business is beyond the credit worth of the firm. Under this condition, the firm would be entirely wiped out, losing its good will or "going concern" value in addition to the affected tangible assets. Would any of these additional costs (high-priced

---

[3] How the statisticians arrive at this figure is discussed in the appendix at the end of Chap. 4.

[4] This cost considers only the direct physical damage loss to the building and does not include loss of use and other consequential losses to be discussed in chaps. 6 and 7.

credit, weakened credit structure, loss of "going concern" value) have been incurred if management had known in advance that the loss was going to happen? Could these loss costs have been reduced by advance preparation for them?

Cost of risk has been defined as "cost which would not be incurred if future losses were known." If losses are higher because of their uncertainty, then by definition these losses will include some cost of risk. The cost of risk, however, is not the entire amount by which the cost of uncertain losses will exceed cost of losses that are certain. If the onset of the losses could be foreseen, usually something would be done about them, and that "something" would itself cost something. Therefore, the difference between cost under certainty and cost under uncertainty would be the *net* difference between the cost of "doing something" about the loss before it occurs and the extra cost suffered because nothing was done. Because it is not always feasible to do something effective, it may turn out that the cost of risk is zero. Even if the losses were fully known in advance, the only practicable treatment might still be simply to suffer them. Then, and only then, is the cost of risk zero.

Total Cost of Risk. We can state, in summary, a single over-all purpose or risk control: to reduce the cost of risk (as distinguished from the cost of loss). Part of the cost of risk is likely to be anxiety, something that cannot be measured in dollars and therefore will not be included in the cost comparisons to be presented later; only measurable (or approximately measurable) dollar-and-cents costs of cash laid out or income forgone will be included. If measurable costs indicate risk control to be efficient, the addition of the immeasurable costs of the disutility of risk assumption will reinforce the argument. If the measurable costs do not quite show risk control to be the least cost approach, inclusion of the psychological disutility often will turn the scales in favor of the control.

Sometimes risk control and loss control operate together, and the benefits of a program are the sum of the reduction in both types of costs. Other times, however, the two types of control can be exercised independently, and, occasionally, as we shall see later, they even work against each other. In any case, of course, the benefits of the particular program proposed must be weighed against all its costs.

Methods of Risk Reduction and Control

Risk may be avoided, assumed, transferred, or reduced. Insurance is a method of risk reduction and, usually, transfer; but it is a sufficiently important and distinctive method to warrant separate treatment. Therefore, insurance may be added to the foregoing list as a fifth method of handling risk.

Risk Avoidance and Assumption. In chapter 2 the subjects of loss avoidance and loss assumption were discussed at length. Since risk avoidance and risk assumption are accomplished by loss avoidance and loss assumption, nothing more need be said on these subjects—nothing more, that is, except, perhaps, for the rather obvious explanation of why risk avoidance and risk assumption are the same operations as loss avoidance and loss assumption. If all losses are avoided, risk (uncertainty regarding loss) is also avoided. Risk avoidance as a risk management technique means rejecting the risk in its entirety, and this, of course, avoids all losses associated with the risk. Without efforts to reduce or control them, risk assumption and loss assumption also are identical: acceptance of one is, by definition, acceptance of the other.

Risk Transfer. Risk transfer is often a useful device in risk management. One of its attractive attributes is the opportunity it affords one business to shift a risk to another at a price favorable to both parties. The value of the risk often is different in the hands of the transferor than it is in the hands of the transferee. In some cases of risk transfer, however, the price may just *appear* to favor both parties, whereas in reality it favors only one of the parties. An inequitable transfer could occur when one management group is wrong about the value of the risk transferred. The risk could be worth more or less than the price offered.

Since our concern is with how a *good* risk manager behaves in his use of risk transfer, we will not consider situations in which the risk transferor has misestimated the risk. But an important question is whether the good risk manager should transfer risks to someone else who is a poor manager of risks and who is willing to accept them at a low price simply because he underestimates the dangers and costs involved. This question presents all the same problems that come up any time one asks whether one businessman should take advantage of the mistakes or ignorance of another, plus one additional problem: A risk transferee who makes frequent or serious mistakes soon ceases to be a risk transferee. This can spell trouble for the transferor. When the transferee is no longer able to pay for losses, the transferor must bear them. Therefore, instead of being on the long end of the deal the would-be risk transferor could wind up on the short end with a transfer that boomerangs. All other considerations aside, for this reason alone a risk transferor must have some solicitude about the finances of his transferees.

Why might a risk be worth less in the hands of a transferee than in the hands of the transferor? What good reasons might a risk transferee have for accepting a risk at a price attractive to the transferor? There are several:

1. A loss that is "large" to the transferor may be small to the transferee. ("Better rent the equipment; if it goes bad, they can afford the cost of fixing it more easily than we can.")
2. The transferee may be in a much better position to prevent or reduce

losses. ("Deposit that money in the bank and let them worry about it; their vaults are a lot safer than your desk drawer.")

3. The transferee may be in a much better position to reduce or control the risk (uncertainty). ("That new operation involves a process we don't have any experience with, but there are several good shops around who work with it all the time and can give us a guaranteed cost on it. Let's let one of them handle it.")

For any one or more of these reasons, a risk transfer can be good business for both parties.

Risk Reduction and Insurance. Reduction of risk consists of reducing the uncertainty about future losses. By some means, more accurate forecasts about losses are made possible. While application of the law of large numbers through insurance is the most common means for risk reduction, it is not the only one. Means other than insurance are discussed in chapter 4; insurance (as a means of risk reduction) is the topic of chapter 5.

RISK TRANSFERS IN BUSINESS

Risk transference is usually a matter of contract. In the following discussion the more important kinds of contracts creating risk transfer are named, and attention is called to some of the ways in which they produce risk transference. The last subsection considers an important method of risk transference other than by contract. To some readers, these discussions may seem elementary, even a belaboring of the obvious. But it is a feature of this world that on many occasions nothing is less obvious than the "obvious."[5] We are continually reminded not to overlook "the forest for the trees," but the common and equally bad error of not seeing the trees for the forest slips past unnoticed.

Risk Transfer by Contracts

A general warning against risk assumption through ignorance has already been given and reiterated. Now a specific warning is given in connection with risk assumption (picking up risks) through contracts; it is an easy way to assume risks out of ignorance. In the following pages some of the common examples of contracts producing various kinds and degrees of risk transference will come to light. When the details of these transfers are brought out, they sometimes seem so obvious as to be unworthy of elaboration. That appearance is deceiving. The alleged obviousness transpires only after one has searched the contracts properly, that is, only after one has searched, knowing what to look for and where and how to find it. Perhaps the details therefore are not so much *obvious* as *patent*. *Obvious*

---

[5] Let the doubters consider Edgar Allan Poe's *The Purloined Letter* or G. K. Chesterton's *The Invisible Man*.

"implies such ease in discovering or accounting for, that it often connotes conspicuousness or little need for perspicacity in the observer," whereas *patent* "usually applies to that which is not imperceptible or obscure, such as a cause, an effect, or an imperfection, but so evident to a person knowing the material, the subject, etc., that it can be pointed out."[6]

The examples below are presented to help the reader become "a person knowing the material, the subject, etc." They further aim at showing how risk transference (and avoidance) through contract, once recognized, can be put to good use.

Construction Contracts. Moe B. Dick, who manufactures buttons, wishes to have a new plant built. Frank N. Stein is a general contractor. Moe can engage Frank on a "cost-plus" basis, or under a "firm-price" arrangement. If the agreement is cost-plus, Moe takes the chances that costs may be greater than advance estimates indicated—wages or prices of materials may rise; unexpected difficulties may be found in the site or plans; strikes, shortages of materials, or bad weather may cause cost-increasing delays. If a firm-price arrangement is made, these chances are Frank's risks. Even under a firm-price contract, a separate determination can be made as to who bears the risks of delay. Some construction contracts provide penalties if the contractor fails to meet a fixed completion date; most do not. Other subjects of special agreement are who bears the risk of physical damage to the structure during the building period (usually the contractor) and who is ultimately liable for cash losses from torts arising out of the construction. These items do not exhaust the list.

Now note the risk avoidance features common to both cost-plus and firm-price construction contracts. Moe, the manufacturer, could have acted as his own contractor. But, while he is presumably at home among many risks—problems of production, personnel administration, relations with government, marketing—he is at home with them only as they relate to buttons. And as they relate to buttons they probably keep him fully occupied. Moe wishes to avoid adding to his problems, so he avoids dealing with risks that are not familiar to him.

Frank, the contractor, not only has time and attention available to devote to construction risks, but we expect that he also knows more about such risks. If he knows more about them, his degree of risk in dealing with them is less ("other things being equal").

Of course, Moe could avoid construction risks entirely by doing without a new plant, but the potential profits in the new plant persuade him to go ahead with it. He can avoid most of the construction risks, however, by having an independent contractor build the plant. The potential losses in building it himself persuade him to engage Frank to construct it for him. These decisions having been made, his principal risk now is that he may

---

[6] *Webster's New Collegiate Dictionary* (Springfield, Massachusetts: G. and C. Merriam Co., 1951). See under "evident."

have chosen an incompetent contractor—and that risk can be largely passed on to a bonding company.[7]

Mere engagement of an independent contractor does not relieve a property owner (or any other principal on a contract) of all the risks involved. Even ignoring the risk that the building may not prove profitable when finished, several risks remain associated with the construction process itself:

1. The principal is responsible for injuries or damages that arise because of the very nature or existence of the operations specified. For example, when the plans call for an excavation directly next to a sidewalk or the foundations of a neighboring building, and injury or damage ensues simply because the digging is so close, the principal on the contract can generally be held liable. In some jurisdictions, principals can be held liable for losses to outsiders caused by defects that represent incompetence in the drawing-up of the plans. If the contracted operation constitutes a public nuisance, the principal will be liable. Property owners are commonly liable for contractors' violations of safety ordinances on the premises, regardless of whether the owner directed or was aware of the violations.

2. Although a principal does not specifically direct the work of an independent contractor,[8] direction of a general supervisory nature is relatively common. Injury or damage traceable to these supervisory acts produces an actionable claim against the principal.

Obviously, the whole matter of a principal's liability for the acts of independent contractors (and of other persons) is complex. All that is attempted here is a small introduction to the subject, principally as a warning that there are many general rules on the subject, each rule with its exceptions (and exceptions to the exceptions), and each rule with its variations among jurisdictions. The student who wishes to be more fully informed (and thus better prepared to cope with the risk) should do fuller reading elsewhere.[9] Let the non-lawyer be wary of placing too much reliance on his own knowledge, however. Reading, even studying, a few books does not make a lawyer, not even in some one branch of the law.[10]

Leases. Leases are another risk-dividing and risk-transferring contract.

---

[7] See the subject of "Suretyship" later in this chapter.

[8] If there is specific direction of the work, the status of independence is lost and the "contractor" becomes an agent or employee. Principals are directly liable for torts of employees or agents if committed while the principals' interests are being furthered (although the tort itself may not further those interests).

[9] An excellent presentation for non-lawyers is found in Reginald V. Spell's *Public Liability Hazards* (3d ed.; Indianapolis: Rough Notes Co., Inc., 1956). Mr. Spell's whole book deals with the problems of liability exposures in business. His chap. 9 specifically discusses some of the legal aspects of risk transference by contract; his chap. 14 is devoted to the liability problems of "Employers of Independent Contractors."

[10] Insurance men have been heard to complain that many lawyers do not know as much about insurance as they (the insurance men) do. This may well be true. But all too often the same shoe is found reposing smugly on the other foot.

A business that occupies leased premises, instead of owning its own, avoids some risks by means of contract. So does the landlord. In a simple lease, the landlord leaves to his tenant most of the risks that go into the operation of a business at that location.[11]

The tenant leaves to the landlord much of the risk associated with some possibilities, such as physical damage to the building or an increase in the taxes on it. Furthermore, if the commercial value of the property should decline, the tenant is stuck with the loss only until the end of his lease; the landlord has it for the life of the building (and even beyond).

However, most of these risks may be transferred by special provisions in the lease. For example, the tenant can pick up more of the landlord's risk of a decline in value by doubling the period for which the rent is fixed. But this action increases the landlord's risk of loss arising from his inability to take advantage of possible increases in the rental value of his property. Indeed, with respect to the hazard of economic changes, some lengthening of the period for which the amount of rent is fixed will increase both the chance of loss and the degree of risk for the landlord *and* his tenant. Over the longer period, there is *more chance* that changes will occur and, in general, *less ability to predict them*. Thus changes are more likely to occur over, say, a five-year period than a five-month period, and these changes generally are less predictable for five years ahead than for five months ahead. However, if the period becomes long enough (e.g., 99 years), chance of loss approaches 100 per cent (there will almost surely be adverse conditions sometime during the period) and degree of risk may be reduced with regard to cyclical changes (bad years and good ones may be expected to "average out"). But, as is most frequently the case with risk, the device (long-term leases) that reduces one risk builds up another: the risk of secular changes.

Another dichroism in the risks created by entering into a long-term lease with a fixed rent can be observed.[12] Considered from one view, a long-term lease obviously decreases the tenant's chance of being without a place to do business, and the landlord's chance of being without a tenant, during the period covered by the lease. Considered from another view, there is a small and not at all obvious increase in these same chances of loss. If either general business conditions or some specific factors affecting the one site cause a major decline in the value of property, a fixed rent that is too high may precipitate failure of the tenant's business—and do so at the very time when a successor tenant will be the hardest to find. Again the solution to one risk creates another!

---

[11] This includes most, but not all, of the tort liability involved. See Spell, *op. cit.*, chap. 19. Another good but much briefer discussion appears in C. A. Kulp, *Casualty Insurance* (3d ed.; New York: Ronald Press Co., 1956), pp. 70–74.

[12] Note that all the discussions about leases apply equally to any long-term contracts, such as contracts of supply or purchase and royalty agreements, for two examples.

This new risk, however, can be minimized. For example, the rent may be stated as a percentage of the tenant's dollar volume of sales. Such a provision reduces the tenant's chance of financial strain and ordinarily reduces his business risk in general.[13] Some of this business risk is shifted to the landlord, who accepts it in the hope and expectation that this speculative risk will produce more gain for him than loss. And, typically, the landlord's participation in the losses will be limited by a provision for a minimum amount of rent regardless of the tenant's sales volume.

Static risks as well as dynamic ones may be transferred by lease provisions. In some leases, tenants agree to take over the risks of physical damage to the building and of injuries to third parties.[14] However, in Massachusetts, New York, and some other states, statutes have been passed declaring the latter type of agreement to be against public policy and unenforceable.[15] Sometimes landlords have agreed to assume a part of the negligence risk usually borne by their tenants. A tenant is ordinarily liable, of course, for the negligence of himself, his employees, and his agents. A tenant who leases entire premises succeeds, in general, to the liability of the owner with regard to them. When tenancy is for less than the whole property, the general rule is that the landlord retains his liability for public areas and for areas used by all the tenants (e.g., lobbies, elevators, hallways, restrooms) or by himself. But again the student is warned that these are only broad statements of the general rules, which vary some from jurisdiction to jurisdiction and are subject to exceptions.[16]

At least two cases have come to light in which the landlords have assumed a part of the risk of negligence on the part of their tenants. In these instances the clauses in the leases that shifted to tenants the risk of physical damage to the building appear to have backfired. The usual wording of such clauses (see n. 14) was altered to include "fire" as an excepted cause

---

[13] The student should be aware that in some places this text says that the *chance of loss* is increased or decreased; in other places it refers to increases or decreases in the risk, that is, in the *degree of risk*. In many situations the two measures move together, but they do not always do so. The student must keep the differences between the two concepts clear in his own mind and must be particularly careful that when he thinks about these matters himself he remains aware of the distinction.

[14] Two specimen provisions of this type: (1) The tenant agrees that he "shall return said premises in as good condition as received, loss by fair wear and tear only excepted." (2) Tenant agrees "to indemnify and hold harmless [the landlord] for loss, damage or injury to persons, or property, whether of a party to this contract or of any other person or corporation, while on or about said premises, or if elsewhere this agreement shall apply if such loss, damage or injury is a result of or attributable to any operation or activity performed or thing used in connection with or as an incident to the occupancy, existence or maintenance of said premises or any part; and this agreement to indemnify and hold harmless shall apply without regard to whether said loss, damage or injury is or is not, caused by or contributed to by the negligence of either of the parties to this contract, or of both of them, or of any other person."

[15] *General Laws of Mass.*, Ch. 186, Sec. 15; New York, *Real Property Law*, Sec. 234.

[16] In Spell, *op. cit.*, chap. 19.

of loss in addition to the customary exclusion of ordinary wear and tear.[17] Fires were caused by the negligence of the tenants' employees, and the inadequately insured landlords brought the matter to court. The courts held that the contractual exceptions of the fire risk applied to these fires.[18] Despite the opinions of these courts, it may be suspected that these landlords had not intended to assume any part of the risk of their tenants' policies with respect to the hiring and supervision of personnel.[19] Thus, the importance of a thorough check of the risk transference and assumption features of all contracts is re-emphasized.

Agreements with Bailees and Carriers. Another common area of risk transfer in business arises out of placing personal property into the custody of a variety of carriers and an even wider variety of bailees.

The shipper who carries his own goods assumes his own risks (at least initially). The shipper who uses a common carrier immediately shifts many risks to the carrier. The kind and amount of risk transferred depend upon the statutes and upon the contract (bill of lading) between the carrier and the shipper. The risks shifted are principally, even exclusively, static; common carriers customarily do not accept responsibility for such losses as failure of or decline in the market, even when these losses are caused by delay in carriage. In between use of one's own vehicles and the employment of common carriers lies the practice of hiring contract carriers. Here the risk transfer is settled by the conditions of the individual contract first and by the laws of negligence second.

When personal property is voluntarily placed in the hands of another for safekeeping, processing, servicing, or other good purpose besides common carriage, a bailment exists.[20] The laws governing the relative responsibilities of the parties to a bailment generally allow a wide latitude for apportionment of these responsibilities by private contract.

---

[17] "Ordinary wear and tear" cannot cause a "loss" as defined in this book, of course, but that is the word generally used in the leases.

[18] *Goldman* v. *General Mills*, 184F (2d) 359 (1950); and *Cerny-Pickas & Co.* v. *C. R. Jahn Co.*, 7 Ill. (2d) (1955). See discussions in *Fire, Casualty and Surety Bulletins* (monthly) (Cincinnati: National Underwriter Co.), Multiple Line section, pp. F1–3 and 4; and Spell, *op. cit.*, pp. 275–79. Other states may or may not follow these precedents.

[19] We say "despite the opinions of these courts" because one of the principles of contract law is that the courts should give heed to what the parties to the contract actually intended. However, other equally good and important principles allow the courts' interpretation to differ from the landlords' (1) if what the landlords intended was not what the tenants intended, or (2) regardless of what the landlords intended, the courts found that the written contracts unambiguously said something else, or (3) if the provision was ambiguous but was part of a contract drawn solely by the landlord (a contract of adhesion, not bargained), and so should be construed strictly against him. (However, considering who the tenants were, in the cases cited, the third possibility seems unlikely.) For some discussion of the legal principles of contract interpretation, see chap. 13, below.

[20] A carrier may be a bailee. See William H. Rodda, *Inland Marine and Transportation Insurance* (2d ed.; Englewood Cliffs, New Jersey: Prentice-Hall, Inc., 1958), pp. 103–4, 301.

When a manufacturer sends his materials out to be partially processed by someone else, a bailment exists. The risk of loss to the property involved may be borne in a wide variety of ways. Suppose Moe, our button manufacturer, contracts to have Tony, an independent processor, perform a special process on certain kinds of buttons. Tony receives Moe's partly finished products, works on them, then sends them back to Moe for finishing. Title rests with Moe throughout the transaction. But suppose a fire at Tony's place destroys Moe's material. Who bears the losses? Under the regular rules, if the negligence of Tony or his men caused the damage, Tony must bear the whole loss.[21] This includes not only the value of the damaged materials (including labor and supply costs embodied therein) but also any loss of profits, wasted overhead, or other detriments that Moe is able to prove are direct results of the original damage. Besides these, of course, Tony loses the expected profit on his part of the processing and probably has other losses too. But if the fire loss occurred despite reasonable and prudent behavior on the part of Tony and his employees, Moe must bear his losses himself and Tony bears only his own.

This may be a perfectly satisfactory arrangement to Tony and Moe, or it may not be. If they do not like it, they can draw their contract otherwise. Perhaps Tony's small specialized shop is ideal for polishing certain kinds of buttons, while Moe's big plant is unable to handle efficiently the relatively small quantities involved. So Moe can save, say, 15 per cent on his costs by engaging Tony's facilities. But Tony may not be so anxious. His business is good already, and he is not properly equipped to store as many buttons as Moe wants to send. The materials may easily be lost or damaged. If they are, Tony cannot afford to pay for them. So Moe offers to relieve Tony of all the risks of loss or damage (except, probably, for any injury caused directly by poor workmanship of Tony's men).

On the other side, Tony might be the one who is anxious to have the contract. If so, he may offer to be responsible for losses in his shop whether caused by his negligence or not.

Finally, as in the previously cited cases of the leases containing the fire clauses, one of the parties may accept the responsibility for losses from some causes, while the other party remains responsible for those from other causes; the risk is then divided.

Acceptance of goods on a commission or consignment basis is another example of a business bailment situation in which a variety of arrangements with regard to risk transference and acceptance is possible. By the very process of not owning the goods, commission merchants avoid some risks. However, in many lines of business it is customary for commission merchants to accept responsibility for the physical well-being of the goods while in their hands. In other cases the static risks may be borne by

---

[21] This assumes no contributory negligence by Moe or his employees and no other intervening causes. See chap. 7.

the owners of the goods or partially by the owners and partially by the consignees.

Contracts of Sale, Supply, and Service.   Contracts concerning the distribution of goods and services also offer innumerable opportunities for risk transference. Some manufacturers and processors agree to protect their distributors against any claims arising out of the manufactured or processed products. Both producers and distributors commonly offer to consumers some guarantees against defects in items produced or handled.

In some lines of business the distributors receive agreements allowing them to return unsold items to the wholesalers or producers; in other trades the distributors have to agree to buy a certain minimum volume regardless of their actual sales. Either way, there has been an agreement or understanding as to who is to bear the risks of the market.

A common type of contract is the service or maintenance agreement in which the repairman promises protection against the occurrences of certain kinds of losses. If his promise is only to provide preventive service or maintenance and does not include payment of losses as well, then the program is one of loss prevention, not risk transference. But many sellers have tried risk acceptance schemes, some of which have fallen afoul of state insurance laws; they have been held to constitute engaging in insurance without a license. Among the many legal risk-transference service contracts that have been or are being offered are:

1. Agreements to deliver fuel on such a basis that the customer's tank or bin is never empty. (Presumably the fuel dealer will pay for frozen pipes, at least, if he slips up.)
2. Rental of equipment (data processing machines, water softeners, and vehicles, among many examples) with guarantees of maintenance and replacement as necessary.
3. Warranties of the performance of used cars.[22]
4. Some service contracts for television sets.

Contracts that have run afoul of the insurance laws have included a tire dealer's agreement to give an allowance for unused mileage if his product

---

[22] At least these used car warranties are not insurance in some states and have not yet been established to be insurance in some others. A committee of the National Association of Insurance Commissioners, which considered the question in 1958 and 1959, reached no consensus. See *Proceedings* of the National Association of Insurance Commissioners, 1958, pp. 331–32; 1959, pp. 97–99, 475–79. Subsequent meetings of the committee dealt only with reports on the progress of liquidation proceedings of several large issuers of warranties, liquidations brought on by insolvencies. *Proceedings,* 1960, pp. 167–73, 464–66; 1961, p. 270. It is of some interest to note that the subject was first listed on the committee's agenda as "The 'bonded car' warranty problem." Next year the title given it was "Auto warranty contracts." In November, 1960 (1961 *Proceedings*), however, the entry was "Automobile mechanical breakdown insurance."

A description of how one of these warranty plans operated can be found in "No Pig in a Poke," *Business Week,* December 17, 1955, p. 44.

was damaged from road hazards, including, apparently, abuse as well as use;[23] a glazier's promise to replace plate glass windows broken from any cause;[24] and a real estate company's promise to stand ready, ten or more years after a real estate sale, to buy back the property at a price agreed upon at the time of the sale.[25]

A particularly enterprising offer was that of the Griffin Fuel Company of Tacoma, Washington. It offered a guarantee that it would deliver fuel oil to customers for a ten-year period at a lower cost per BTU than could be obtained from either gas or electricity. Mr. Griffin protected himself by three provisions that would void the promise: the discovery of commercial quantities of natural gas in Washington state, the availability of nuclear power for private use, and the advent of war or price controls. He further reduced his risk taking, according to the news report, by "insuring his contracts with Lloyd's of London."[26]

A contract of service can include an agreement by one of the parties to "indemnify and hold harmless" the other. The most common example is in agreements for private sidetracks (that is, sidetracks brought in not for public use but for the particular benefit of an individual user). The earlier forms of these agreements transferred all the railroad companies' risks of physical damage and liability onto the user (just as the second example in note 14 of this chapter shifted them from the landlord to the tenant). Some few agreements resembling the earlier forms may still be in existence, but most sidetrack agreements today are worded as recommended by the National Industrial Traffic League. A reproduction of the "hold harmless" part of this agreement follows:

Whereas, the Industry desires the use of a private side track and switch located on premises at . . . and the Railroad Company is willing to permit such use upon terms and conditions hereinafter set forth:

It is understood that the movement of railroad locomotives involves some risk of fire, and the Industry assumes all responsibility for and agrees to indemnify the Railroad Company against loss or damage to the property of the Industry or to property upon its premises, regardless of railroad negligence, arising from fire caused by locomotives operated by the Railroad Company on said side track and switch connection or in its vicinity for the purpose of serving the

[23] *State ex rel. Duffy* v. *Western Auto Supply Co.*, 134 Ohio St. 163 (1938).

[24] *People* v. *Standard Plate Glass and Salvage Co.*, 156 NYS 1012 (1916). However, another glazier got away with a similar scheme because the insurance laws of his state (New Jersey) applied only to corporations, not to individuals. *Commissioner* v. *Moresh*, 122 NJL 77 (1939).

[25] *Commonwealth ex rel. Schnader* v. *Fidelity Land Value Assurance Co.*, 312 Pa. 425 (1933).

[26] See "Department Store Doldrums" *et. al, Business Week*, October 23, 1954, p. 56. The remark about "insuring" with London Lloyd's cannot necessarily be taken literally. Mr. Griffin's contract with the Underwriters at Lloyd's may not read the same as the one with his customers and may in fact be more in the nature of a bond than a contract of insurance.

same, except to the premises of the Railroad Company, to rolling stock belonging to the Railroad Company or to others, and to shipments in the course of transportation.

The Industry also agrees to indemnify and hold harmless the Railroad Company for loss, damage, or injury from any act or omission of the Industry, its employees or agents, or anyone not a party to this agreement using said side track and switch connection, their employees or agents, to the person or property of the parties hereto and their employees, and to the person or property of any other person or corporation, while on or about said side track and switch connection; and if any claim or liability other than from fire shall arise from the joint or concurring negligence of both parties hereto, or the joint or concurring negligence of anyone not a party to this agreement using said side track and switch connection and the Railroad Company, it shall be borne equally by the Industry and the Railroad Company.

In the study of risk management this agreement is of interest, not only because it is in widespread use and likely to be encountered, but also for the more general reason that it is a good example of a relatively sophisticated approach to risk transference by contract. Different risks are treated differently in it, and in no part is it a simple "all or none" affair. Thus, even with regard to the risk of fire, (1) distinction is made between fires caused by locomotives and those arising from other hazards, and (2) while much of the risk is borne by industry, the railroad retains its risks of damage to property that it owns or is transporting for others.

Drawers of risk transferring contracts of other kinds and in other circumstances could profit by the sidetrack example. From the sweeping transfer of risks in the first sidetrack agreements, experience and long negotiation have produced the present statesmanlike document. In many cases, other contractual arrangement contain risk transference provisions of the type found in sidetrack agreements of generations back rather than the ones of today. Too often it holds true that "Others' follies teach us not, Nor much their wisdom teaches."[27]

Contracts of Suretyship. When, as in the example previously given, Moe B. Dick, button manufacturer, engages Frank N. Stein, general contractor, to build a factory building, Moe relies on Frank's ability to perform according to contract specifications. If unexpected difficulties arise in performance, they are, in general, Frank's problem.[28] If the contract has been let on a fixed-cost basis, expenses associated with these difficulties are part of his problem. But if these difficulties and expenses cause Frank to default on his contract, then they become Moe's problem, and his attempt to transfer the construction risk has failed. This risk of default is transferable, however, to a third party known as a surety.

In a suretyship arrangement there are always three interests, and for

---

[27] Tennyson, *Will Waterproof's Lyrical Monologue,* st. 22.

[28] Practically every general statement of a legal rule is subject to exceptions, of course. In the present case, some few unexpected difficulties relieve a contractor of the obligation to fulfill his contract strictly according to specification.

two of them there are alternative terms of designation. One of the three parties is the surety, of course. Another party is called the obligor or principal. The third party is called the obligee or creditor.

In the example of Moe and Frank, Frank (who has agreed to do something for Moe—build him a factory) is the obligor and Moe is, of course, the obligee. Since Frank owes Moe a performance, upon completion of which Moe will owe Frank money, it seems a little confusing to refer to Moe, rather than Frank, as the "creditor." Furthermore, in discussions of the independent contractual relationship it is common to describe as the contractor's "principal" the party for whom the independent contractor is performing; therefore, to refer to the contractor himself as the "principal" with respect to the suretyship arrangement creates considerable terminological difficulty. Consequently, in this text only the terms "obligor" and "obligee" will be used with respect to the suretyship relation.

Sureties promise to provide their obligees with performance or, failing that, with indemnity for lack of performance. The obligors promise these things too, of course, but with the suretyship arrangement much of obligees' risk that obligors will not be able to perform is transferred to sureties. *The primary risk still rests with the obligors, however, and is not transferred.* If a surety suffers any cost or loss from an obligor's failure to perform or indemnify, then that surety has a legal claim against that obligor for recovery of such cost or loss.

Either individuals or corporations may act as sureties, but most important contracts of suretyship are issued by corporations that make a business of such contracts. Surety corporations are supervised by the insurance commissioners of the various states, and most such corporations also engage in the casualty insurance business. For these and other reasons, suretyship is often confused with insurance.

From the viewpoint of an obligee, there is considerable difference between having an individual act as surety and having a corporation do so. Even if the financial soundness of the two were the same—and parity of this kind is unlikely—the legal position of the obligee vis-à-vis the corporation is stronger than against the individual. The common law was traditionally solicitous of individuals who acted as sureties. Typically, suretyship promises were given as accommodations to the obligors, generally as a matter of friendship or personal good will and without any direct gain for the sureties. Therefore, traditional Anglo-Saxon law required that suretyship agreements be in writing to be enforceable and held that the writing should be strictly construed in accordance with the evident intention of the sureties bound by it,[29] and obligees were required to be

---

[29] There is some conflict as to just how the rule for interpretation of suretyship agreements should be stated, but there is general agreement that the intent and effect were that "a surety is favored in the law." See 50 Am. Jur. 922–24 (quotation from p. 922).

careful not to behave at any time in any way that might possibly injure their sureties. While these rules still are generally applied when individuals act as sureties, they have been considerably modified for professional corporate sureties.

In general, the promises of licensed corporate sureties need not be in writing; interpretation of their agreements tends to follow insurance rather than suretyship rules;[30] and acts of obligees are not considered to have voided the suretyship agreement unless the surety has in fact been injured by them. The second of these modifications means that contracts of corporate sureties are interpreted to give effect to their general sense, with ambiguities interpreted against the surety. The second and third indications together mean that only those acts of the obligee which have material effect are to be considered in determining the obligations of the surety.[31]

In the standard form of suretyship operation, the obligor arranges for the agreement with the surety. He does so only when his obligee requires such an arrangement, of course. The expenses incurred are naturally part of the total costs that determine the amount of money the obligee will be charged for performance by the obligor. The benefits to the obligee are twofold: not only risk transfer but also loss prevention. Loss prevention is accomplished because financially weak or professionally incompetent obligors cannot obtain sureties, at least not professional sureties; thus obligees who require professional suretyship protection on their contracts seldom find themselves doing business with undesirable obligors. The principal benefit to the obligor is, of course, that he gets the contract with the obligee. However, an additional benefit may be that he is kept from foolishly entering into obligations beyond his talents or resources.

Other Transfers by Contract. The variety of ways in which risks may be transferred by contract is limited only by the ingenuity of the contracting parties—or rather, perhaps, by the extent of the difference between the ingenuity of some of the parties and the ingenuousness of the others. Naturally, not all the possible ways that someone might be able to think of can be discussed here.

There are, however, some standard methods of risk transference by contract that have not yet been discussed. These have been omitted to this point because they are not in the province of the risk manager. Still, they are important ways of dealing with certain risks, and ignorance of their existence is not consonant with a claim to be an informed specialist in

---

[30] See chap. 13 for these rules with respect to insurance.

[31] The text material here is a two-paragraph summary of a complex branch of law. It therefore contains only the merest of generalizations on the subject, and generalizations in the law are commonly riddled with exceptions. However, these generalizations indicate the nature of the legal points that support the conclusion given, and that is all that is necessary or desirable here. Those who wish to pursue the subject further are referred to legal encyclopedias (the material here is based on 50 Am. Jur. 893–1148) or, better yet, to lawyers with experience in this particular field.

things having to do with risks and their control. One important standard method for dealing with certain risks is hedging. This method falls outside both the province of the professional risk manager and the purview of the present book because it is useful only in connection with dynamic risks; there is no way in which it can be applied to static risks. However, since it is an important and systematic way of transferring certain risks and many persons interested in the subject of risk management are interested in it, a short explanation of the hedging process is in order at this point.

Hedging. When compensating commitments are made on both sides of a transaction, the process is known as "hedging." A simple illustration of hedging may be found in betting transactions. A bet that Army wins over Navy can be hedged by a bet that Navy wins over Army. Whatever the outcome of the game, the hedger breaks even—what he wins on one team he loses on the other.

In the business world, the grain market provides a good illustration of hedging. Take the operations of a country grain elevator for a simple example. The operator of a grain elevator purchases grain from the local farmers for sale in the central market. The price he pays the farmer is that prevailing at the time of purchase. The price the operator will receive for the grain upon resale will depend upon the price at the central market when the grain arrives some time later. By then the price may have dropped, so the elevator operator will be unable to recover his purchase price plus the cost of handling. Of course, the price of the grain may have increased, offering the elevator operator a greater than normal profit from the transaction. The country elevator operator has no real way of knowing whether the price will be higher or lower. So far as he is concerned, the whole thing is a speculation, and a speculation of which he wants no part. All he wants is a normal business profit. He is happy to let others take the speculative profit if they will also bear the speculative losses. And there are others, called grain speculators, who are glad to accommodate the local elevator operator.

Grain speculators are in the business of buying and selling "futures"— that is, making contracts to buy or sell grain at a presently stated price for delivery at a specific future time. The wheat market, for example, is organized to deal in wheat for either present or future delivery. Prices for present delivery are called "spot prices." Prices for future delivery are quoted for March, May, July, September, and December delivery. If the speculator thinks that today's quote on July wheat, for example, is higher than the spot price for wheat will be when July comes, he will sell wheat "futures"; if he thinks today's quote is lower, he will buy wheat "futures." If he sells "futures," he can go on the market and purchase the wheat to fulfill the contract when the delivery time arrives.[32] If he has guessed right, he makes a profit; if he has guessed wrong, he suffers a loss.

[32] Or he can buy July "futures" if he wishes to wash out his short commitment before the delivery date.

At any one time, the futures market will consist of speculators on each side of the market. Some expect price declines in terms of quoted price for "futures"; others expect price increases. This army of speculators makes hedging possible.

Here is how hedging works. Assume that the country elevator operator buys wheat now being harvested. The spot price of wheat in the central market (Chicago, for example) is quoted at $2.00 a bushel. Because he must retain a margin of 20 cents for expenses and profit, the country elevator operator will pay the local farmers $1.80 a bushel for wheat delivered to his elevator. Some weeks later, when the wheat reaches Chicago, the market price may have declined. In order to protect himself against a decline in price, the local elevator operator can sell September wheat "futures" at the same time he buys the local wheat. Since prices in the "futures" markets generally move with prices in the "present delivery" markets, the dealer will find that if the price declines before his grain arrives at the central market, the price of the "futures" nearly always will have fallen by about the same amount.

Suppose he has sold "September wheat" at $2.22 a bushel. (The September price is higher to reflect the additional cost of storage between harvest time and September.) Assume that when the wheat moves to the central market the spot price has declined to $1.95 which is 5 cents less than the price on the day when the wheat was purchased. The operator will lose 5 cents off the markup on his cash purchase and sale. But the price of the September futures probably will also have declined. If this decline is by the same amount, the operator can buy September futures at $2.17, gaining 5 cents on his futures sale and purchase. The profit in the futures contracts will offset the loss in the present delivery contracts.

Most hedges will not work out so perfectly. The futures market might have declined only 4.5 cents, leaving a speculative loss of 0.5 cents. Or the futures market might have declined 5.5 cents, leaving a speculative gain of 0.5 cents. In any case, the speculative element in the country elevator's operations is drastically reduced to a point where it becomes more manageable; the elevator's normal trade profit is reasonably well protected.

The Credit Risk.   An entire group of standard methods of risk transference is available in connection with one particular type of risk: the credit risk.

A moment's reflection will show the reader that credit risks are partly static and partly dynamic. Many failures to pay are due to the dynamic risks that affect the debtors, but, even in a static economy, some debtors would default; there could still be frauds, incompetence, and overoptimism in the incurrence of debts.

Credit risks, static and dynamic, may be transferred in many ways. Suretyship itself represents a transfer of a kind of credit risk. There are forms of credit guaranty that are hardly distinguishable from suretyship:

In these, one party, called a guarantor, agrees to make good upon a debt incurred by another party, who is the principal debtor. In some forms of guaranty, the guarantor may be called upon to pay without demonstrated default on the part of the principal debtor—which is not true of suretyship.

Another form of transfer of credit risk is through a financial instrument called an "acceptance." In this instrument the debtor directs a third party, called a payer, to pay the creditor. If the payer, in writing and prior to the due date of the payment, signifies that he will accept this direction on its due date, an acceptance has been created. Thus the risk that the original debtor will not pay is transferred from the original creditor to the payer. Since payers on acceptances are generally banks or other organizations with superior financial standing, this transfer can represent considerable gain for the original creditor.

Still another way to transfer the credit risk is by sale of the claim without recourse against the original creditor. (If the claim is negotiated or sold with recourse, then the risk is not transferred, and the recipient may press his claim against the original creditor if the debtor fails to pay.)

Management of credit risks is seldom in the province of the "risk manager" of a business, however. The risks in credit are clearly a central problem in the management of credit itself, and credit management was an established specialty before the specialty of static risk management even had a name. The appearance of the newer specialty has not led anyone, professional risk managers and the present authors included, to suggest that responsibility for the handling of credit risks should be removed from the credit to the risk management office of a business.

FORMS OF BUSINESS ORGANIZATION

Transfer of risk by contract presupposes at least two separate parties to the contract. In the partnership form of business organization, such parties are brought together in the partnership contract. In the corporate form of organization, a new party is brought into being. Between the ordinary partnership and the full-fledged business corporation, a large variety of organizational forms are possible. Examples include limited and special partnerships and joint ventures, "Massachusetts" and other trusts, "mutual" financial institutions, and other types of cooperatives. There is also a miscellaneous group of benefit, fraternal, social, political, and other associations and organizations of the "non-profit" type. In each instance, the bearing of risks is affected, and there is no question but that the effect on risk is an important consideration in the decision as to what legal form of organization to use.

It is presumed that the reader knows of the broad nature of owners' liability for the debts of the ordinary unincorporated business: the sole proprietorship and the general partnership. Risk managers and other students of insurance do not often have to know much about organizations of the "in between" types,[33] and this is fortunate because the law concerning them is varied and complex. On the other hand, the effects that the corporate form of organization has on risk are common and important.

Business Corporations

One of the most important features of the common business corporation is its characteristic of limited liability. Some of the effect of this feature on risk and loss has already been noted in the discussion of loss control (chap. 2). As was noted there, however, the real effect produced is not loss control but risk transfer. The direct financial loss suffered by the owners of the corporation is limited to their investment, but that may not be the entire loss involved. In an unincorporated business, if business assets are not sufficient to cover business debts, personal assets of the owners may be called upon to make up the deficiency. Incorporation eliminates this claim (except in certain cases of fraud) and to that extent transfers the risk of insufficiency of assets from owners to creditors.

The corporate device has other important risk-shifting characteristics. Historically, the corporation has been viewed as a means for allowing the transfer of business ownership risks from the shoulders of the relatively few persons who could practicably share the ownership of an unincorporated firm to the shoulders of the many people who could participate in the ownership of a business under corporate organization. Also, the corporation has been viewed as a means by which entrepreneurs and active managers could shift risk to a separate and distinct group of business owners. Finally, the laws governing corporate organization make it relatively easy for each owner to transfer the whole of his ownership risk to someone else by the simple process of selling his shares to any available taker.

In sum, one of the most important features of the modern corporation is its amelioration of the problems of risk bearing by business owners and managers. And much of this amelioration has been effected by the creation of a whole new set of possibilities for risk transference.

Although most writers on the subject of "risk and the corporation" direct their attention principally or even wholly toward dynamic risks, the effects on static risks are the same. The practice of incorporating separately each ship in a fleet is as much a protection against libels for injury to the persons or property of others as it is against libels for operating or maintenance expenses.[34] A landlocked manufacturer can employ the same device to protect himself against catastrophic possibilities from his use of an experimental process involving large quantities of radioactive materials.

---

[33] Except, of course, with regard to them as issuers of insurance. See chap. 16.

[34] The use of the word "libel" here in its ocean marine sense represents deliberate intention to introduce the student of insurance and risk to a strange word that he ought to know.

The use of the corporate form of organization to limit effective liability for torts is one way in which risk can be transferred to others by a legal device without their direct consent. (Theoretically, they give indirect consent through their state government, which allows the corporation to be formed.) Other ways include the transfer of property into someone else's name (as transfer of assets from husband to wife to avoid the husband's creditors), the creation of a trust, and the purchase of a life insurance policy.[35]

SUMMARY

Risk itself, as distinguished from losses, may be reduced or controlled. Risk is reduced (or controlled) when accuracy of loss forecasts is improved.

Reasons for Risk Reduction and Control

The reasons for risk reduction are direct aversion to risk and reduction of risk costs. Risk aversion is an individual, psychological matter. Risk costs depend on what is (or is not) done to cope with risks. Risk costs may appear in the form of outlays (as for insurance premiums), of lost income (as when extra funds are held in liquid form), or of losses (as when losses are increased in size because of failure to prepare for them). The measure of the cost of risk is the difference between the net profit that would be received if future loss incidence could be perfectly forecast and the profit received when the same loss incidence is experienced without ability to forecast it exactly. This cost is a function of the difference between the sizes of different individual losses or of the difference between the sizes of individual losses and the long-run loss average. (One measure of this variation in loss size is the standard deviation or the variance of the loss distribution.[36] This is not the only measure, however.)

Methods of Risk Reduction and Control

The three major methods of risk reduction or control are (1) avoidance, (2) transfer, and (3) increase in accuracy of loss predictions. Insurance is a particular device for increasing accuracy of loss predictions, but it is such an important risk management device that it is not treated in the general chapter on "Risk Reduction" (chap. 4) but is accorded a separate chapter all its own (chap. 5).

Risk Transference in General. The risk control method discussed at length in the present chapter is risk transference. Risk transference may

---

[35] In most states, life insurance cash values and proceeds receive some protection against creditors' claims. See any standard life insurance text, e.g., Robert I. Mehr and Robert W. Osler, *Modern Life Insurance* (3d ed.; New York: Macmillan Co., 1961), pp. 151–56.

[36] In a probability distribution, the standard deviation is the square root of the variance.

take place because one of the parties misestimates the risk. From the viewpoint of the risk manager of the transferor, this is clearly bad if the error is his. It may also be bad if the error is his transferee's, for a transferee who accepts risks that he cannot handle solves no risk problems for the transferor. There are at least three possible reasons, however, why a risk transference may in fact be a good thing for both parties: A loss that is "large" to the transferor may be "small" to the transferee, the transferee may be better able to reduce losses, and the transferee may be in a better position to reduce or control the risk.

Risk Transference by Contract. The methods of accomplishing risk transference are limited only by the ingenuity of risk managers and their advisers. However, the principal methods in practice may be divided into (1) transference by contract (with the surety contract as a particularly important special case) and (2) transference by method of business organization. The principal types of contracts and contractual relationships in which risk transfers are accomplished are construction contracts, leases, bailments and carriage, sales of goods or services, and suretyship. Some additional types of contracts are also available with respect to transference of credit risks.

Each type of contract has its own special features with respect to the purpose and nature of the risk transference arrangements in it, and each individual example of each type can and often does have its own variation on the general approach. Summary statements about the subject are therefore too cursory to be useful. However, some warnings about possible misuse of contracts for risk transference should be borne in mind. There seems to be a general rush to contract away as much risk as possible, A trying to transfer it to B, and B to A—or, worse, A to B and C, B to C and D, C to B and D, and D to A, B, and C! One result is that it has become only too easy to acquire risks by contract, and to do so partially or totally unwittingly, without full knowledge of the responsibilities that have been taken on. Also, in the general pushing and jostling to shove responsibilities onto someone else, consideration is not always given to the most efficient or effective ways of handling some risks, with the result that responsibility for them may be handed to some party who is not in a position to handle them the way they should be handled (as by loss prevention, for example). Finally, ultimate responsibility for given risks sometimes becomes very difficult to ascertain, so that the mass of risk transference increases the contracting parties' total risk (uncertainty about loss) rather than reducing it.

However, transfer of risk by contract is a useful device and can be used to apportion risks so that the parties in the best position to bear them have them. An example of a well-thought-out set of risk transference provisions is found in the hold harmless provisions in the sidetrack agreement recommended by the National Industrial Traffic League.

A special class of risk transferring agreements are contracts of suretyship. At least three parties are involved, and one of them, known as the surety, enters the arrangement purely as a risk bearer. As a result, specialists in risk bearing—corporate surety companies—have come to dominate the surety contract field, with accompanying advantages to obligees.

Risk Transference by Incorporation. While the limited liability of the corporate form of organization is ordinarily thought of as a means of loss control, it is even more a means of risk transfer. Loss in excess of business assets is borne by the creditors of the business rather than by the owners. Other risk transfers accomplished or made possible by the device of incorporation are transfer of risk from the few who could act effectively as partners to the many who can act effectively as stockholders, transfer of innovation and developmental risks from entrepreneurs to speculators, and transfer of the ownership risk from one individual to another by the relatively simple process of selling stock shares.

To repeat, the methods of risk transfer discussed in this chapter are representative, not exhaustive.

REVIEW AND DISCUSSION QUESTIONS

1. "Other things remaining equal, it is human nature to prefer certainty to uncertainty in economic affairs." Do you agree? If not, how do you explain such things as the widespread use of insurance and the higher rates of interest commonly associated with "riskier" investments? If you agree with the quoted statement, how do you explain the popularity of gambling and the difficulty in enforcing anti-gambling laws?

2. If the average annual losses from two groups of exposures of identical amounts are equal, how can the risk in one case be greater than the risk in the other? How can the cost of this extra risk be measured?

3. How is the cost of risk measured when insurance is purchased to offset a loss?

4. Suppose that the risk is ignored, *i.e.*, the loss is neither insured nor funded. How can the cost of risk be measured?

5. Under what set of conditions would there be no measurable dollars and cents cost of risk?

6. What costs of risk are not measurable in terms of dollars and cents? How can these immeasurable costs enter into a decision involving the use of risk control methods?

7. Explain why the following statement is true: "Risk avoidance and risk assumption are the same operations as loss avoidance and loss assumption."

8. How is it possible for one business to shift a risk to another business at a price favorable to both parties?

9. Explain why the price is not favorable to both parties in all risk transfer deals. Is it good business practice to be on the long end of a risk transfer deal? Explain your answer.

10. Explain how risk assumption through ignorance can be thrust upon a businessman by the contracts he signs.

11. When a decision is made to construct a new plant, a number of risks will arise in connection with the implementation of this decision. Identify these

risks and indicate how they may be shifted to other parties. What factors should be considered in a decision to take advantage of these risk-shifting oportunities?

12. In what ways is a lease a risk-dividing and risk-shifting contract? What features of a lease should the risk manager check?

13. How is the division of risk between shipper and carrier determined when goods are transported? Should the risk manager be consulted on matters involving the moving of goods? Explain your answer.

14. How is the division of risk between bailor and bailee determined when the bailment is created for purposes other than transportation? Explain why you believe that the risk manager should or should not be consulted when a bailment is contemplated.

15. What lessons can be learned in risk management by a study of the history and development of sidetrack agreements?

16. What risk is transferred under a suretyship arrangement? What risk is not transferred?

17. What are the advantages of relying on corporate sureties rather than on individual sureties?

18. Can the hedging technique be used in the management of static risk? Explain your position.

19. Describe the risk-shifting characteristics of the corporate form of business organization.

Chapter 4

RISK REDUCTION

Methods of risk reduction cannot be understood without a clear idea of what "risk reduction" means. Risk is reduced or controlled when loss (or cost) can be predicted more accurately (chap. 3). The meaning of the word "accuracy" as used in this definition must be considered now.

ACCURACY IN LOSS FORECASTING

More than one standard is available for determining accuracy in loss forecasting. For example, one possible standard is the number of times forecasts are exactly correct. Another standard is the number of times forecasts are within a specified range of the exact amount of losses. Still other standards consider how large the differences between the forecasts and the actual results are over some period of time. In general, however, all standards for assessing the accuracy of forecasts fall into one of two classes: (1) Those standards in which *frequency of accuracy* is the prime consideration and (2) those in which over-all *size of error* is the prime consideration.

Frequency of Accuracy in Forecasts

One standard of accuracy is the percentage of times the forecasts are correct. Suppose the frequency with which a certain type of machine breaks down over a fifteen-year period shows a distribution as follows:

Number of Breakdowns in the Year	Number of Years in Which That Many Breakdowns Occur
None	One
One	Two
Two	Four
Three	Three
Four	Two
Five	Two
Six	One

Clearly, to maximize the number of times the annual forecast is correct, the best forecast is "two breakdowns." Since two breakdowns a year is the most common result, that number has the best (though only a 26.67 per cent) chance of being correct.

With many static risks, a high frequency of completely accurate forecasts is easy to obtain. Thus, one has only to predict each year that a given property will suffer no loss by fire to be completely right more than 95 per cent of the time. The same is true for other perils—burglary, explosion, liability for bodily injury, and many more.

A special application of this standard of accuracy has received a particularly large amount of attention in insurance literature. Suppose there are just two possible cases: "loss" and "no loss." The best prediction under the frequency-of-accuracy standard is to pick the more common of these two possibilities. If "no loss" has a high probability, with "loss," of course, having a correspondingly low probability, frequency of accuracy in forecasts will be high and risk will, by this standard, be low. One has only to predict "no loss" to be correct most of the time. A prediction of "loss" would be right most of the time if the situation were reversed, with "loss" having the high probability and "no loss" having the correspondingly low probability. The lowest possible frequency of accuracy in such a situation will occur when "loss" and "no loss" have the same probability—50 per cent each. From this observation comes the following kind of statement, often found in insurance textbooks: "Degree of risk is zero when probability of loss is either zero or 100 per cent. As the probability moves away from either of these two extremes, degree of risk increases until the probability of loss is 50 per cent; at this point, degree of risk is at its maximum." The conditions for this statement to be relevant, however, are restrictive and seldom occur in static risk management.

For one thing, the statement implies (and the condition is always left implicit, never made explicit) that one period with losses is just like another, that the only thing that matters is whether *some* loss occurs. Clearly, whether in the period there has been just one loss, two, three, or four does make a great deal of difference. Furthermore, usually important variations in the dollar amounts from one loss to the next are involved. For these reasons, an approach in which results are viewed as purely dichotomous— "either losses occur, or they do not"—has a range of possibilities much too limited to be generally useful to risk managers.

The frequency-of-accuracy standard for loss forecasts has an additional limitation: inapplicability to situations in which the loss possibilities are essentially continuous. Suppose that the dollar amount of a certain class of losses is to be predicted and that this amount can be any dollar-and-cents figure from zero to $100,000. Statistics collected over a number of years indicate the mode of the distribution (the figure that occurs most often) is $1,501.25, and the probability of incurring a loss of that amount is 0.4 per cent. According to these same statistics, the probability of experiencing a loss of one cent more than the mode is 0.3 per cent, and of one cent less is also 0.3 per cent. A probability of loss for any amount within the range from zero to 100,000 is calculable from these statistics. Under such circumstances, would one say that the "frequency of accuracy" of forecasts refers to the number of times the forecasts are exactly correct, down to the last penny? To do so would render the standard nonsensical. Within some range of values, a "near miss" is, in practice, every bit as good as a "hit."

Accuracy of forecasts within a loss range is considered as a separate and distinct standard from the frequency of (exact) accuracy standard because of the substantial differences in the statistical characteristics and significance of the two.

Size of Error in Forecasts

An important group of standards for accuracy in forecasts is based on the size of the difference between what the forecast predicts will happen and what actually does happen.

A common practice when considering the size of forecasting errors is to give disproportionately higher weight to large errors and disproportionately lower weight to small errors. For example, an error of $1,000 in a forecast may be considered to be *more* than ten times as bad as an error of $100; if so, the $1,000 error should be given *more* than ten times as much weight when measuring the accuracy (or lack of it) of the forecast. One popular method of increasing the weight given errors of large amounts is to measure errors by the *square* of their size; the $1,000 error is given an index number of 1,000,000 and the $100 error an index number of 10,000. Thus the larger error becomes one hundred times (instead of ten times) more important than the smaller one.

The popularity of the square of the error as an index arises from the coincidence of two circumstances: (1) In many cases, larger errors *are* disproportionately more important than smaller ones, (2) the best known and most thoroughly analyzed measure of the size of error[1] is the statistic called the *variance*.[2] The variance is based on a weighting system that takes the square of each error as the index of its size or "importance." This well-studied measure of error makes it possible to judge the accuracy of forecasts by the ability of the forecast to minimize the total of the squared errors, and it is only natural to put this measure to use for this purpose. The forecast that will minimize the total of the squared errors is the mean, or average, loss figure.

On occasion, however, the most appropriate weighting for errors is their actual size. In some situations, a $1,000 loss *is* worth exactly ten $100 losses, no more and no less. When that is the case (that is, when the total of the

---

[1] This is the phrase we are using; statisticians call it *dispersion*. For this and other statistical terms see appendix to this chap.

[2] If one prefers, he may use the *standard deviation*, which is the square root of the variance.

actual errors, rather than the total of their squares, is to be minimized), the best forecast is not the mean of the loss experience but the *median*. The median of a distribution is its middle figure: 50 per cent of all the figures in the distribution are no larger than the median *and* 50 per cent are no smaller. In some distributions (notably the "normal") the median and the mean are the same figure; in most distributions (the "log normal," for example) the mean and the median are not equal.

Of course, *neither* the square of the error nor the actual size of the error may provide a realistic index. A forecasting error of $1,000 may be more than ten times, yet not as much as one hundred times, as significant as an error of $100. Furthermore, even more important in many cases is the *direction* of the error. If the forecast is a loss of $15,000 and events prove the forecast to be wrong by $7,500, the significance of the error ordinarily is considerably different according to whether the forecast turns out to have been $7,500 *more* or $7,500 *less* than the actual loss! Clearly there are an infinite number of possibilities as to the effects of different size errors in different directions, and the long-run minimization of the bad effects calls for different "best" types of forecasts.

Examples of Measure of Size of Error. Consider again the following hypothetical distribution on a loss experience in which all losses are assumed to be the same size:

No. of Breakdowns	Probability (By Experience)
0	$\frac{1}{15}$
1	$\frac{2}{15}$
2	$\frac{4}{15}$
3	$\frac{3}{15}$
4	$\frac{2}{15}$
5	$\frac{2}{15}$
6	$\frac{1}{15}$

Maximization of frequency of accuracy in loss forecasts on this distribution calls for predicting two losses (the mode). A prediction of three losses (the median) would minimize the total size of error. In a "typical" fifteen-year period, a prediction of "three" will miss by one (up or down) six times; by two, four times; by three, twice. One times six, plus two times four, plus three times two, equals twenty, the total size of error on this forecast. Any other prediction will produce a larger total size of error. A prediction of 2.87 losses (the average rate) per year will minimize the sum of the squares of the errors at approximately 39.73.[3] Any other prediction will produce a larger total sum of the squares of the errors.

In *summary*, a forecast of the mode (two losses) would maximize the frequency of accuracy, one of the median (three losses) would minimize

---

[3] This is the *variance* of the distribution. See the appendix to this chap. for calculation of the average and variance of a probability distribution.

the total size of errors, and one of the average (2.87) would minimize the sum of the squares of the errors. Which of these forecasts is the most acceptable in the management of risks? Consider the following conditions. Suppose the extra cost of each dollar of loss in excess of the amount forecast (and prepared for) is about 25 cents. Suppose further that the extra cost of each dollar by which the forecast exceeds actual loss is only 8 cents.[4] Under these conditions none of the foregoing forecasts is the best one for the risk manager to use. The best forecast in these circumstances is the one that will minimize the sum of 8 times the error when the forecast is high plus 25 times the error when the forecast is low. A little judgment and calculus produce the answer: Given the described loss distribution and the stated effects of error, the "best" forecast to make is "four losses." With this forecast, the fifteen-year expectation is for the cost of errors to be 2.68 times the cost of one loss.[5]

Accuracy over a Range

Another possible standard for accuracy in forecasts is plainly suggested: accuracy with respect to a range. Instead of the prediction, "Loss will be X dollars," the statement is made that "Loss will be at least M dollars but not more than N dollars." Zero is often a useful value for M, in which case the statement becomes simply "Loss will not exceed N."

When considering what constitutes "accuracy" with respect to statements about loss ranges, two aspects of the forecast must be considered: the probability that the forecast will be right and the size of the range used in the prediction. The probability that the forecast will fall within a stated range is an insufficient criterion by itself. Obviously the probability that losses will fall within the range can generally be increased by increasing the range. A forecast that "the loss will not exceed one billion dollars" will have a reliability of nearly 100 per cent in nearly any risk management situation, but the prediction itself is not a useful one. Obviously the width or narrowness of the predicted range must also be considered in appraising the value of the forecast. Consequently it seems reasonable to set up the following criteria for appraising relative "accuracy" of two or more loss-range forecasts:

1. When the forecasts cover ranges of the same size, the forecast with the highest degree of reliability is the "most accurate."
2. When the forecasts all have the same degree of reliability the forecast having the smallest range is the "most accurate."

---

[4] This 8 cents represents the loss of earnings on the dollar held in liquid assets when, as things turned out, it could have been invested in higher yielding, less liquid, assets.

[5] The reader will note the implicit assumption that the "cost of one loss" does not include the extra 25-cent cost for inadequately prepared-for losses. The extra cost of unprepared-for losses is considered as an item separate (e.g., as a cost of risk) from the cost of anticipated losses (chap. 3).

The application of these criteria does not solve all the problems of evaluating forecasts. Compare the following three forecasts, each applying to a different loss exposure.

A. The loss will fall between $1,000 and $2,000.
B. The loss will fall between $500,000 and $501,000.
C. The loss will fall between $500,000 and $750,000.

Suppose each forecast has the same degree of reliability (i.e., the same probability of being right). Without question, forecast B can be considered "more accurate" than forecast C.

But when forecasts A and B are compared, question arises. Each forecast has a $1,000 maximum "error" range. The feeling that an error range of $1,000 is considerably less significant when hundreds of thousands of dollars are involved than when only one or two thousand are concerned cannot be escaped. Certainly a cost estimator who was able consistently to hit within $1,000 of a final cost figure of several thousand dollars would command a handsome income, whereas an estimator who consistently missed one- and two-thousand-dollar totals by $1,000 would have a hard time keeping his job. Yet one would like something more than a "feeling" as a basis for concluding that B is "more accurate" than A.

What about the comparative accuracy of forecasts A and C? Another measure of forecast accuracy is the relative rather than the absolute size of the loss range. In forecast A, the high figure on the range is 100 per cent greater than the low figure, whereas in forecast C the figure at the top of the range is only 50 per cent more than the figure at the lower end.[6] Are we now prepared to say that the $250,000 loss variation allowed in forecast C is necessarily of less significance or importance than the small $1,000 variation allowed by forecast A? At best, such a conclusion would seem to be a dubious proposition. A more useful measure of accuracy on a range is one that considers *both* the relative *and* the absolute size of the loss variation covered by the range. But how can this be done? Irksome as it may be to the student, no completely satisfactory solution to this problem has yet been found. And, unfortunately, none of the partially satisfactory answers is at all simple.

The best solution requires an estimation of the *real marginal cost* of the dollars involved in the range. The term "marginal cost" as used here means the additional cost incurred if the loss turns out to be the maximum rather than the minimum in the range. The modifying term *real* in the phrase is used to measure the ultimate consequences this marginal cost can have on the business and its management—such as, in some cases, the difference between continued growth and a period of stagnation, or even between survival of the business and its demise. Estimation of the real cost is itself a

---

[6] The difference between the extremes on the range gives forecast B the lowest relative loss range of the three forecasts.

difficult proposition. The nature of the real cost of losses is discussed in chapter 8, where it is considered in connection with the problem of measuring loss potential, and again in chapter 10, where it must be considered in connection with the over-all problems involved in risk management decisions. For the time being, the discussion shall rest on the simple proposition that, given two loss forecasts that (1) have the same degree of reliability and (2) involve comparable total loss figures, the forecast covering the smaller loss range is the "more accurate." Accordingly, in terms of the example, forecast B is "more accurate" than forecast C. But note that this proposition says nothing about "accuracy" as between forecast A and B, let alone as between A and C. While one may strongly suspect that B is "more accurate" than A, proof or disproof of the proposition must wait until the nature of "real costs" of loss has been examined.

One more problem, however, is left for discussion here. Suppose the probability and the range criteria of accuracy point in different directions. Suppose, for example, that forecast X, which has a 95 per cent probability of being right, involves a dollar range of losses that is narrower than the dollar range of forecast Y, but forecast Y has a 99 per cent probability of being right. Which is more "accurate," X or Y? To resolve this problem both forecasts must be reduced to at least one equal base. Either both must be brought to cover the same loss range or they must be brought to the same probability of being right. When the range is made the equal base, then the forecast with the higher probability is the more accurate; when the probability is made the equal base, then the one with the smaller range is the more accurate. As a general rule, of course, increasing the loss range covered by a forecast increases its reliability, while decreasing the loss range decreases its reliability.

ACHIEVING RISK REDUCTION

Once the risk manager becomes familiar with the standards for measuring accuracy in loss forecasting, and learns the limitations of these standards, he can apply them in selecting the most useful forecast for reducing risk in any given loss situation amenable to forecasting. He will be aware that the most useful forecast in a number of risk situations is still useless for risk reduction—the only reliable prediction of a loss range may be one that extends from all to nothing. The probabilities for any other range may be so low as to be meaningless. In such situations, the risk manager must scrap his risk reduction design and seek other methods of handling his risk.[7] It is just as important for the risk manager to be familiar with the conditions under which he cannot use forecasts to reduce his risk as it is for him

---

[7] A risk reduction plan involving transfer to an insurance company may be possible, however. See chap. 5.

to be aware of those conditions under which risk reduction is possible. There can be a great deal of false security wrapped up in ill-conceived risk reduction plans, just as there can be security in well-conceived plans.

Knowing the Best Forecast

Little reflection is necessary to realize that there are two parts to risk reduction: (1) determining what type of forecast is best in any given situation (mean, median, mode, or other figure) and (2) obtaining the greatest possible reliability for this forecast after it is made. Important to the accuracy of a forecast is the accuracy of the information upon which it is based. Consider the following annual loss distribution over a large number of years:

Amount of Loss[8]	*Percentage of Years*
$　0	5%
250	12
500	15
750	14
1,000	13
1,250	12
1,500	10
1,750	8
2,000	6
2,250	4
2,500	1

What would be the effect on the forecast if the wrong information were used? Consider a simple illustration: If the frequency-of-accuracy standard is used, but the mode of distribution is mistakenly believed to be $1,000, then a loss forecast based on this misinformation would be exactly correct only 13 per cent of the time. But if the right information were found, the loss forecast would then be $500, and this figure would be exactly correct 15 per cent of the time. Clearly, the ability to select the best forecast under any standard depends on knowledge of the facts about losses. Improving this knowledge is most likely to improve the accuracy of forecasts.

Problems in Selecting the Best Forecast. Selecting the best forecast for a loss distribution under a risk presents two problems: getting the facts about hazards and losses and knowing what these facts mean. The collection of loss experience to be used in developing a table like the one in the preceding paragraph is a problem of the first type. Deciding how accurately the assembled data on the past will foreshadow the future is a problem of the second type.

The past is not always a clear or accurate guide to the future. For one thing, the past may be only imperfectly observed. For another, conditions

---

[8] Once again, for the sake of simplicity, it is assumed that the loss distribution is discrete rather than continuous, but this assumption affects only the form, not the content, of the presentation.

change, so even perfectly observed past events are unlikely to be repeated exactly in the future. Therefore, application of judgment is commonly necessary in interpreting the past as a basis for predicting the future. It may be appropriate to read a trend into the observations. Known changes in hazards may suggest that certain specific differences between the past and the future will be encountered. Incomplete observations of past results have to be supplemented by opinion as to what really are the general underlying loss conditions. For any of these reasons, the best forecast for the future may be something different from that indicated by simply reading off some representative figure from recorded experience. Two examples may be used to illustrate the points.

Example Problem I. Suppose that the General Supply Corporation has just had a bookkeeper convicted of embezzlement. The bookkeeper had worked for the company ten years; his defalcations all occurred during the last three years of his employment. In each of the ten years that he worked he handled about $320,000 in bills and invoices, and in each of the last three years he managed to manipulate these documents so as to take a total of $8,000 of the company's money. The company's accounting system and auditing procedures have since been tightened, and a new bookkeeper has been hired. With tighter controls and a new bookkeeper, what kind of predictions can be made about losses from future defalcations? What does experience tell us? Principally, that there is a risk. Another embezzlement might occur, and if it does occur it will happen at some time or another. Whatever the probability was before, it is probably less now. Obviously, experience with one man in one company tells us neither what the loss probability was before nor what the new probability is now. Only one prediction may safely be made—most years will still be no-loss years. How many such years there are likely to be and, probably more important, how big the losses may be if (or when) they occur are for all practical purposes unknown. Therefore, the future average cost of loss is also unknown. Consequently, these statistics are of no valid use as a basis for a risk reduction program.

Example Problem II. On the other hand, accurate statistics on the same company's losses from on-the-job injuries to employees (payments required under workmen's compensation laws) may be useful for purposes of loss prediction. The problem here is to determine which statistics would be the most meaningful. Consider the following possible plans of expressing loss statistics on a year-by-year basis.

1. Total dollar losses.
2. Dollars of loss per each $100 of payroll.
3. Dollars of loss per each 1,000 labor-hours.
4. Dollars of loss per each $1,000 of production.
5. Substitute "number of accidents" for "dollars of loss" in any one of the plans given above.

6. Substitute "number of working hours lost" for "number of accidents" in plan 5.
7. Any of the foregoing types of information broken down into some pertinent categories, such as by department or by job description.

Not all these statistics are equally useful in forecasting losses. One advantage of plan 7 for prediction purposes is patent: If experience is known by department or by type of job, then adjustments can be made for changes in amount of exposure by department or in number of jobs of different types. Plans 2, 3, and 4 are better for prediction purposes than is plan 1 because adjustments can be made for changes in amount of exposure by size of payroll, man-hours worked, or volume of production.

Not so obvious, perhaps, is an advantage in plan 5 when it is used to compare the number of accidents against the total dollars lost. As was noted in chapter 2, accident frequency rates respond more readily to underlying conditions (such as loss prevention or lack of it) than do accident severity rates. Consequently, it is easier to achieve accuracy in prediction with respect to frequency than it is with respect to a combination of both frequency and severity—that is, total dollar loss. Of course, some cost-per-accident figure needs to be known and applied to a representative accident frequency figure, but the results so obtained appear to be more useful for prediction than do the dollar costs of losses taken directly.

How does plan 6 compare with the first four? Knowing the limitation of this plan requires knowledge of the workmen's compensation laws. These laws require that employees be paid not only for time lost but also for their medical expenses. The amounts of these two types of payments are by no means always related. Plan 6, therefore, omits some important information. Because of these and other considerations, workmen's compensation insurance rate makers take into consideration a number of factors: loss frequency, the average amount of lost-time payments on smaller losses, average amount of lost-time payments on larger losses, and the average amount of payments for medical expense. The final rate is a composite of these factors, with each of these items considered separately and adjusted for any changes in the statutory benefits requirements.

Thus, even if the recorded loss experience offers a fairly reliable index to future events, making the best forecast from it may be a process of some complexity, involving a considerable degree of statistical sophistication. In general, of course, the more that is known about relevant conditions in a risk situation, and the more sophistication is brought to bear in analyzing those conditions, the more accurate the predictions are likely to be.[9]

---

[9] Occasionally, increased knowledge may increase the apparent risk. Investigation may demonstrate that a proposition is not the "sure thing" that ignorance thought it was!

Risk Control through Loss Control

Many kinds of managerial controls tend to reduce risk. Materials control systems, accounting controls and audits, and product and process inspections will ordinarily reduce risk (improve prediction) if they are successful in keeping losses small. However, not all loss control systems result in risk reduction. A few examples may be used to substantiate this conclusion. Three illustrative cases for this purpose may be taken from the figures in Table 4–1. Column A represents a hypothetical loss series before loss con-

TABLE 4–1

THREE POSSIBLE LOSS SERIES, ILLUSTRATING EFFECTS OF
LOSS CONTROL ON DEGREE OF RISK

	Value of Losses with—		
Time Period	No Control of Losses (A)	All Losses Reduced 40% (B)	Maximum Loss Limited to $200 (C)
1	$ 10	$ 6	$ 10
2	20	12	20
3	5	3	5
4	300	180	200
5	5	3	5
6	50	30	50
7	250	150	200
8	15	9	15
9	40	24	40
10	25	15	25
Totals	$720	$432	$570
Averages	$ 72.0	$ 43.2	$ 57.0

trols are applied. Column B represents the series after installation of loss controls to reduce all losses, both large and small, by 40 per cent. Column C represents the same series after initiation of loss controls to set a maximum of $200 on losses.

In analyzing what happens to loss and risk costs under the conditions illustrated in Columns B and C as compared with A, an understanding of the meaning of "reduction in cost" as used here is important. If a manufacturer reduces his production and sales, he will probably reduce his total labor and sales costs. But, if the reduction is strictly in proportion to his cutback in volume, i.e., if a 40 per cent cutback in volume produces a reduction of 40 per cent in total cost of labor and sales (labor and sales costs *per unit* of production and sale remain unchanged), this change would not ordinarily be considered a reduction in labor or sales costs. The same method of measuring reductions is used in this text in connection with costs of loss and risk.

Reducing All Losses. Consider the relation between Columns A and B (Table 4–1). In B, every loss is 40 per cent less than in A. If this 40 per cent reduction is accompanied by a 40 per cent reduction in investment and sales, no reduction in either loss or risk costs as such has been accomplished; the business is simply operating on a smaller scale, with the same relative costs and profits.

But suppose the results in Column B could be accomplished simply by reducing inventory holdings by 40 per cent (possible, though not probable),[10] loss costs would then also be reduced 40 per cent. What effect would this type of loss control have on the degree of risk? The answer depends upon the standard to be used for measuring accuracy in the forecast. Remember reduction in risk is identified with increased accuracy in forecasts.

By the frequency-of-accuracy standard, the loss control would not reduce the risk; predicting the exact amount of loss would be just as difficult as ever. The mode would be reduced from $5 in Column A to $3 in Column B, and the probability of experiencing the mode would remain the same, 20 per cent.

By the size-of-error standard for measuring accuracy, the loss control would reduce the risk no matter what index of size is used. When the desire is to minimize the size of the *absolute* error, the *median* is the best forecast. In Column A, the median lies at or between $20 and $25 (either figure, or any number in between, may be used). The sum of the errors from the median over the past ten years is 610. In Column B, the median lies in the range of $12–$15. The sum of the errors from the median over the ten-year period in Column B would be 366. Thus, when the size of the losses is reduced by 40 per cent through loss control, the sum of the errors will also be reduced by 40 per cent.

When the desire is to minimize the total of *squared errors*, the mean or average is the best forecast. In Column A, the average is $72. The sum of the squared errors from the average over the past ten years amounts to 106,160. In Column B, the average is $43.20 (40 per cent less than in Column A). The sum of the squared errors from the average here is 38,217, only 36 per cent of the sum of the squared errors in Column A.[11] This represents a 64 per cent reduction in the sum of the squared errors, a substantial reduction in risk based on this method of measuring accuracy of

---

[10] A reduction of 40 per cent in inventory will not automatically reduce the sum of all losses by 40 per cent. The reduction in total inventory must somehow reduce *partial* losses as well as total ones. For example, if pilferage losses are related to value of stock on open display, then the reduction must be in stock on open display, not just in stock in storerooms or warehouses; if "very small" fires are characteristically confined to an area of, say, five or six square feet, then there must be reduction in the amount of goods in any given five or six square feet; and so on.

[11] Column B figures are 0.60 times Column A figures, and squaring gives 0.36 times as much. The sum of the squared errors in Column B is, therefore, only 36 per cent of the sum of the squared errors in Column A.

forecasts. Other indices reflecting different importance to be given to the size of error give other results. When the standard of accuracy of forecast is based on a range, Column B, as compared with Column A, (1) gives a reduction of 40 per cent in the absolute size of range for any given probability, but (2) since *every* figure is reduced 40 per cent there is no reduction in the *relative* size of ranges (that is, in the ratio between the span of a range and the figures within the range): 24–36 is the same relative span of range, for example, as 40–60. The high figures in each range are 50 per cent larger than the low figures, even though the figures within the lower range are 40 per cent under those within the higher range.

In summary, if 40 per cent reduction in inventory represents a general 40 per cent reduction in the scale of business operations, then the corresponding reduction in risk or loss costs is not a "reduction in cost." If the over-all reduction in all losses (represented by Column B as compared with Column A) is achieved simply by reducing operations, no reduction in risk occurs unless, by the standard of accuracy appropriate to the business, the error in forecasting is reduced by *more* than 40 per cent. Suppose, however, the over-all reduction in losses is accomplished without reducing the inventory but by using watchmen and guards, automatic sprinklers, better accounting controls, physical dispersion of assets, and other methods. If these loss control devices reduce all losses by 40 per cent, loss cost clearly is reduced. And if, by the standard used to measure accuracy, the error in forecasting is reduced (as has been seen, *some* reduction will be achieved under most standards), risk and risk costs also are reduced. (Of course, for the cost reductions to be worthwhile, they have to be greater than the cost of the controls used to bring them about.)

Cutting Large Losses Only. Column C (Table 4–1) is a repeat of Column A, with the largest losses held to a maximum of $200. It comes closer to representing the results that probably will be accomplished if the total amount of inventory is reduced—small losses will, in general, roll merrily on, but the maximum damage to inventory is limited by the amount of the inventory itself. Suppose the reduction in total inventory ($300 to $200) is accompanied by a corresponding reduction in the scale of the business. The exposure is reduced by one third, but in only one of the ten years is loss reduced by that much. In eight of the years there are no loss reductions at all. Losses as a percentage of value exposed, then, have gone up rather than down.

What about degree and cost of risk? Once again, by the standard of frequency of exact accuracy, forecasting is not improved. The best forecast now becomes either $5 or $200, either of which has a 20 per cent probability of being correct.

If the objective is to minimize some index on the size of error, improvement in the absolute sense is achieved by reducing the size of the inventory; the total of the absolute range of error from any forecast is reduced, and so are any direct functions based on it, such as the sum of squares. Whether there is also a relative reduction in total error depends upon the index. For example, because the median of the series is unchanged, the best forecast for minimizing total error for Column C is still any figure from 20 to 25. Whereas the sum of errors from this forecast is 610 for Column A, it is 460 for Column C, a smaller decrease than the one-third decrease in the scale of operations. On the other hand, the sum of the squares of the errors (taken from the mean) in Column A is 106,160; for Column C the sum is 53,010. The reduction here is a great deal more than one third, indeed it is more than one half.

Under the standard of accuracy over a range, there is, in general, no improvement in forecasting. Only if the range chosen includes figures of 200 or more is there any change at all. For example, the probability that losses will lie between zero and 100 remains at 80 per cent (in eight out of the ten years losses were 100 or less). On the other hand, the probability that losses will not exceed 200 is only 80 per cent in Column A, but it is 100 per cent in Column C. Where the ranges are taken as "the mean plus or minus" a given figure, a reduction in risk generally will be indicated when the maximum losses are limited as in Column C. The mean plus or minus 50 covers only 30 per cent of the experience in Column A, whereas it covers 60 per cent of the experience in Column C. Note that the change here is due to the shifting of the mean; the two years in which losses are lowered are still not brought within the range covered. When top losses are reduced enough to bring them within the forecast range, the reduction in risk (by this method of measurement) may be even greater. Suppose, for example, the largest losses had been brought down to 75 instead of 200; the new mean would be 32. A forecast range of plus or minus 50 from that mean would cover 100 per cent of the experience. In some instances it is difficult to say what the *relative* reduction in risk is under the "range of accuracy" standard; these instances include the examples given in this paragraph. Of course, if the effect illustrated in Column C is achieved simply by less physical concentration of property in one location (more dispersion) without reducing its total amount, any reduction of risk represents a real gain— offset, of course, by any additional costs created by the dispersion (increased expenses of transportation or rent, for example).

Important examples of the application of the principle illustrated in Column C are found in "stop loss" and "catastrophe reinsurance" contracts and in certain retrospective rating plans. In each of these plans, the business pays its own losses up to a certain point (such as 200 in Table 4–1); beyond that point, insurance takes over. The maximum may be on a "per loss" basis or on a "loss per year" basis. The "per loss" basis is used in most "stop loss" and "catastrophe" reinsurance agreements and in certain aspects of retrospective rating; the "loss per year" basis is utilized in some reinsurance and in the "maximum premium" feature of retrospective rating.

In summary, controls that reduce losses *may* or *may not* reduce risk. If loss controls improve the accuracy of loss forecasts, the cost of risk is reduced *if*, as a consequence, the risk manager can decrease the amount of the reserve he must hold for adverse loss fluctuations by a greater percentage than the values subject to loss are decreased. However, the risk manager should remain aware of the possibility of a reverse effect: many loss control systems only reduce the number, not the size, of large losses (few loss control systems are perfect). Since infrequent large losses are less predictable than frequent ones, loss controls may increase rather than decrease risk.

METHODS OF RISK REDUCTION

Segregation and Diversification

Segregation of assets is an important device in risk and loss control. Assets may be segregated by (1) the physical arrangement of the assets themselves or (2) the ownership arrangement of the assets. An example of segregation of the first type is found in the producing and storing of explosives, when small quantities are kept in each of many small buildings separated by bunkers. An example of segregation of the second type is found in the use of financial and legal devices, in which title to property may be placed in the names of different members of the family or in the names of separate legal entities, such as corporations or trusts formed for the purpose.

An important feature of the ability to limit losses by segregation is the possibility, in many cases, of adding the feature of *diversification*.[12] Segregation with diversification is a useful method of loss and risk control. Thus, the conservative investor tries to reduce his risk by dividing his funds among diversified investments. Complete diversification includes diversification by type of security, type of industry, companies within the industry, geographical location, time of purchase, dates of maturity, leverage position, and possibly other qualities. Diversification does not increase the in-

---

[12] It is possible, of course, to segregate without diversifying or to diversify without segregating. If a man's wife acquires a half-interest in his business under certain conditions, her interest can be beyond the reach of his creditors (and his interest beyond the reach of hers). The interest has been divided or segregated, producing some loss control, but there has been no diversification.

On the other hand, if a corporation that has been specializing in the wholesaling of dry goods diversifies by taking on a line of household appliances, all the corporation's assets are still susceptible to claims growing out of either operation. In this case there has been diversification but not full segregation. There has been some segregation of loss, of course. A decline in the value of inventory in one line will not necessarily affect the other line, for example. Also, the inability to sell one line will not necessarily affect sales in the other. On the other hand, decline in inventory value in one line or the inability to sell it may impair the working capital and credit of the business to the point where the entire business may be lost, the good line with the bad. Considerably more segregation could be had if a separate corporation were established to handle the new line. This, however, might be too cumbersome and expensive.

vestor's ability to predict what will happen to any given item in his portfolio (here his problem is loss prevention), but, by skillful planning, it may increase his ability to predict results for the portfolio as a whole.

In practice, of course, diversification sometimes increases risk. This happens when diversification gets the investor into fields in which his knowledge and ability to manage are limited. Some of the business managements that have tried to diversify their product lines or markets have found that their lack of experience in the new areas has involved them in a morass of unexpected (and expensive) difficulties.[13] Furthermore, diversifiers must guard against a tendency to aggregate rather than to segregate their assets. When things go badly in one area, there is a tendency to tap assets from other areas to try to effect a rescue. Often this turns into "throwing good money after bad." In the end, the loss is neither controlled nor limited but spreads to engulf the whole—a totally unpredicted result, of course.

Pooling of Risks

Another important arrangement to control risks is the risk pool. Risk pools use risk transfer to accomplish the effects of asset segregation. For example, instead of building two separate plants, the MNO Corporation can enter into an arrangement with the QUQ Company under which the two businesses agree to share any losses sustained at their two independent plants. This gives each company an integrated operation but a divided risk and loss exposure.

Many practical applications of the risk pool approach are possible. A more likely application than the simple, direct two-company pool just described is one in which the MNO Corporation wishes to set up some foreign operations. In many nations of the world the undertaking would be very risky.[14] Because of the risk, MNO does not like to "put all its eggs in one basket," especially if the basket is to be sent abroad. It would like an opportunity to diversify, to take its chances in more than one country, expecting that if one or two individual ventures went sour, the surviving enterprises would make up for the loss. But it may not be able to finance

---

[13] See, for example, "Polyglots—and a Touch of Babel," *Business Week*, September 21, 1957, pp. 151 ff. The article's subhead reads: "Buying up scads of unrelated companies is beginning to give some companies a touch of indigestion. But other wide diversifiers are doing nicely, and show no strain."

[14] The student should note that here is an example of the usefulness of being careful about the usage and definition of words. "Risky" is not the same as "hazardous." In this case, the undertaking may well be "hazardous," too—that is, it may involve a high chance of loss. But the statement that it is "risky" suggests that the possible range of results, between maximum possible loss and maximum possible gain, is large: The company stands to lose a great deal or to make a great deal. It is the latter possibility that makes the venture attractive. If the proposition were merely hazardous, the same attraction would not exist.

as many separate undertakings as it thinks are advisable. If the QUQ Company is in a similar situation, the two may find it advantageous to pool their resources and undertake their foreign operations jointly. By pooling, each company divides its investment among, say, six instead of three foreign ventures, and halves its losses from each failure. All this would be expected to reduce the deviations from the average rate of loss without reducing the scale of total operation. The diversification itself also reduces the risk, but discussion of this is best deferred until the "law of large numbers" is examined.

General Average. "General average" in ocean transportation is a classic example of a significant type of risk pooling.

In ocean shipping, the word "average" has a special use. It means, in effect, "partial loss." Partial losses, or "averages," are classed as "particular" or "general." Particular average is borne entirely by the interest on which it happens to fall. If part of Joe's cargo falls overboard, that is Joe's loss, just as it would have been had the cargo fallen out of his car. General average is borne "generally," that is, it is spread (pooled) among all the interests represented aboard. A general average takes place when a partial loss is incurred for the general benefit. The conditions for general average are these:

1. An imminent peril must threaten the success of the entire venture. (That is, everyone's interest is in jeopardy because the safety of the entire ship is threatened.)
2. A voluntary act must be made as part of an effort to protect the venture from the threatening peril.
3. The act must be reasonably adapted toward averting the peril or reducing its effects. ("Reasonableness" under stress is not always the same thing as "reasonableness" under conditions of calm and extended consideration.)
4. This voluntary act must be the proximate cause of the loss that is to be pooled.[15]
5. As a result of the act, the venture must be saved. (It may be badly damaged, however.)
6. The interest whose loss is to be pooled must not have been at fault in the loss.[16]

The application of these rules is partially illustrated by the following example. A vessel returning from the Far East carried, among other items, a load of copra—an oily substance. Fire broke out in the copra. Any fire on board a ship is clearly a threat to the whole venture, and the crew hastened to extinguish the fire. The water (steam) used in extinguishing

---

[15] The meaning of "proximate cause" is discussed in chaps. 7 and 15. (See Index for page reference.)

[16] Although the admiralty law and the English common law systems are different in many respects, here there is a similarity. In English and most American law, one who is in any way responsible for a loss may not collect for his own damages in the same incident. General average also bears a strong resemblance to the principle of equity, that is, to the establishment of simple justice as among the parties. In English and American equity, no recovery can be made by one who does not come into the court with "clean hands," that is, by one who was in some way at fault for the loss.

the fire caused water spots on another cargo item, raw silk. Since water spots in raw silk can neither be removed nor covered over in the finished product, the damage was serious. The imminent peril to the venture was the fire. The voluntary act against it was the using of the water or steam, and that act was certainly a reasonable means against fire. The voluntary act was clearly connected with the damage to the silk. The fire was extinguished and the venture saved. If the silk had been improperly packed and proper packing would have protected it from spotting, then the owner of the silk would not have met the no-fault requirement. If the silk were properly packed (according to the custom of the trade or the rules governing the shipment), the loss to the silk would be general average. The damage to the copra could not be general average, however, for the cause —the fire—was no voluntary act aimed at saving the venture from danger. The copra loss, therefore, was particular average.

When it is determined that a loss is general average, its amount is shared by every property interest on board (ship owners, operators, and cargo interests) in proportion to the volume of its interest when port is reached. Included in the value of this interest is right to indemnity for general average. Any shipper whose cargo was unhurt would contribute in proportion to the full value of his cargo. But the owners of the copra and the ship would make contribution according to their values after the fire had been extinguished and the voyage completed. The owner of the silk would contribute according to the value of his silk on arrival plus the amount of his general average claim.

Other Loss-sharing Devices. It is not difficult to find other arrangements similar in principle (although not in form) to general average. Remembering that labor union leaders feel strongly that benefits for individual members are dependent upon union solidarity, the principle of risk and loss sharing for the benefit of all can easily be seen in assessments against working members to aid those on strike. (The similarity to general average would be even greater if the assessment were based on wages —which are presumably union won—rather than a flat amount per capita.) The principle is even more evident in certain recent agreements among employers. For example, in 1958 the major airlines agreed that if some but not all of them were shut down by a strike, so that the lines still operating received additional revenues from traffic diverted to them, the extra profit so obtained would be shared with the struck lines.[17] From the standpoint of risk management by the airlines, this agreement is a consid-

---

[17] "Labor-troubled Carriers Sign Mutual Aid Pact . . . ," *Aviation Week*, Vol. LXIX, No. 19 (November 10, 1958), pp. 40–41; "CAB Schedules Oral Arguments . . . ," *ibid.*, No. 24 (December 15, 1958), p. 43; "Airline Mutual Aid Proposal . . . ," *ibid.*, Vol. LXX, No. 2 (January 12, 1959), pp. 39–41; "CAB Gives Tentative Approval . . . ," *ibid.*, No. 5 (February 2, 1959), pp. 40–41. See also "Strike Insurance Plan Gets Test," *Business Week*, June 28, 1958, p. 95, on employers' mutual aid pact in Hawaiian sugar industry.

erable improvement over older-style agreements in some other industries, under which the firms not struck would either (1) shut down too or (2) refuse to handle business that could be identified as having previously been handled by the struck employer.

Another example of risk reduction by pooling is the "insuring" of private atomic energy plants. The word "insuring" is put in quotation marks because the process, as it presently stands, is one of pooling and risk transfer rather than of true insurance. (As will be discussed later, the authors hold that "insurance" has certain essential characteristics that are not present in every pooling or risk transfer operation and are not present in the current atomic energy "insurance" plan.[18]) Since no one power company and no one or even a few insurance companies have felt able to carry the static risks involved in an atomic energy plant, the following system has been worked out. Most of the loss potential has been transferred from the power companies to the insurance companies; the insurers have handled the risk by setting up large pools involving nearly all American companies to share the transferred losses; and further transfer of the excess of loss beyond what insurers have felt they can handle has been accepted by the federal government.[19]

The "insuring" of jet aircraft in its initial stages offers still another example of risk reduction through pooling. A. J. Smith, president of United States Aviation Underwriters, Inc.,[20] in his testimony before the Subcommittee on Antitrust and Monopoly of the Committee on the Judiciary, United States Senate, said:

Everybody is worried about this jet program. . . . Everybody is afraid of the risk until they get it spread. . . . What they were looking for was a division of the business in order to spread the risk so that no one would be hurt out of proportion to his capacity. . . . There were many ideas advanced, a world pool for the next two or three years . . . was one alternative.[21]

Like all giant prototype risks, the jet risk was pooled and divided among many insurers both in this country and abroad.

---

[18] That the atomic risk pooling is done by insurance companies does not of itself make it insurance, any more than something done by politicians is necessarily either politic or politics—or some particular thing done in classrooms by teachers is automatically instructive or educational.

[19] United States Code, Sec. 2210 (Title 42, chap. 23, subchap. 13). Also: "Civilian Atomic Industry Gets Federal Insurance . . . ," *Business Week*, August 24, 1957, p. 124; "Atom Insurance on the Way," *ibid.*, May 26, 1956, p. 65; "Nuclear Energy Insurance," *Changing Concepts in Protection*, American Management Association Insurance Series, No. 116 (New York: The Association, 1957), pp. 10–39.

[20] This organization is a management company that handles the aviation underwriting of 62 insurance companies.

[21] Hearings before the Subcommittee on Antitrust and Monopoly of the Committee on the Judiciary, United States Senate, 85th Cong. 2d sess., *The Insurance Industry*, Part I, pp. 30, 31, and 33.

Law of Large Numbers

In pooling operations, losses are shared; in insurance operations, losses must not only be shared but also be predictable. The application of the statistical law of large numbers is essential to obtain loss predictability. The application of the law distinguishes the insurance pool from the ordinary loss-sharing pool. It must be understood at once that the application of the law of large numbers is a matter of degree, not a matter of absolute perfection. As a principle in mathematics, the "law" has several specific requirements for its application, requirements that are never fully met in the business world. In many instances it is a matter of opinion whether a given situation meets the requirements just sufficiently, or misses them just enough, to say that the "law" does, or does not, apply and that therefore the operation is, or is not, insurance. One thing is sure: Even *in* "insurance" the law applies most imperfectly.

The law of large numbers is one of the most important and useful principles in all risk management. Furthermore, while the risk reduction and control methods previously discussed have, in general, been of more use in managing speculative risks than in managing static ones, the law of large numbers has the reverse characteristic—it is, in general, much more useful for static risks than for dynamic or speculative ones.

It is important for the risk manager to understand the true nature of the law of large numbers. The law does not state what *will* happen with regard to given events. It states only what will *probably* happen. Therefore, the law of large numbers cannot tell how to remove risk; it can only help reduce it. And it helps only in certain specific ways, which often are *not* the ways the layman or novice thinks the "law of averages" (as he generally calls it) works.

The law of large numbers may be summarized: The greater the number of exposures to loss, the more the likelihood that actual loss experience will resemble the underlying rate of loss probabilities. In other words, the larger the number of units for which a loss prediction is being made, the better chance a *good prediction* has of being *reasonably correct*, provided, of course, that the situation is one which the law of large numbers fits.

To illustrate with a simple example, assume that the appearance of a six upon the roll of a regular six-sided die represents a loss. The underlying rate of loss probability is one-sixth. If six dice are thrown, the underlying rate of loss probability would produce *one loss* ($\frac{1}{6} \times 6$). If twenty-four dice are rolled, the underlying probability would produce *four losses* ($\frac{1}{6} \times 24$).

Note the italicized words "good prediction" and "reasonably correct" in the summary statement of the law of large numbers. What is a good

TABLE 4–2

SOME PROBABILITIES WITH THE ROLL OF DICE
(Individual Terms)

Exact Number of Losses*	Probability of Occurrence in:	
	6 Rolls	24 Rolls
0	0.3349	0.0126
1	0.4019	0.0604
2	0.2009	0.1389
3	0.0536	0.2037
4	0.0080	0.2140
5	0.0007	0.1711
6	†	0.1084
7		0.0557
8		0.0236
9		0.0084
10		0.0025
11		0.0006
12		0.0001
More than 12		†

° A "loss" as defined in text discussion: "the number six comes up on a die."
† Less than 0.00005.

TABLE 4–3

SOME PROBABILITIES WITH THE ROLL OF DICE
(Cumulative Terms)

Maximum Number of Losses*	6 Rolls	24 Rolls
0	0.3349	0.0126
1	0.7368	0.0730
2	0.9377	0.2119
3	0.9913	0.4156
4	0.9993	0.6296
5	0.99998	0.8007
6	1.00000	0.9091
7		0.9648
8		0.9884
9		0.9968
10		0.9993
11		0.9999
12		1.0000†

° The number six comes up on a die.
† Rounded off. The actual probability of having no more than twelve losses is 100 per cent minus a minute fraction.

prediction, and just how correct is reasonably correct? Would *one loss* be a good prediction when six dice are tossed? Would *four* losses be a good prediction when twenty-four dice are rolled? To aid in answering these questions, the tables of binomial probabilities appearing on page 109 have been prepared.[22]

A prediction of one loss in six rolls would stand a 40.19 per cent chance of being correct, whereas a prediction of four losses in twenty-four rolls would have only a 21.40 per cent chance of being correct.[23] Neither of these predictions, therefore, appears to be a good one. But take the size of range as the standard of accuracy for forecasts. The prediction, "There will be not more than three losses with six tosses," is expected to be correct 99.13 per cent of the time (Table 4–3). Such a prediction would suggest preparation for a loss rate as high as three times the underlying probability, but the prediction has a high degree of reliability. With twenty-four rolls, eight or nine losses will have to be predicted for the forecast to be equally reliable. A prediction of not more than eight losses will be expected to be correct 98.84 per cent of the time, whereas a prediction of not more than nine losses will be expected to be correct 99.68 per cent of the time. These predictions suggest preparation for loss rates of only about twice the underlying probability, which appears an improvement over the situation with only six tosses. With six throws, a prediction of losses of not more than twice the underlying probability (that is, not more than two losses) will be correct only 93.77 per cent of the time, certainly less reliable than the same relative prediction with twenty-four tosses. Thus the increase from six to twenty-four rolls enables the forecast to be improved (its relative range reduced) without reducing its reliability, or enables the reliability of the forecast to be improved without increasing its range relative to the average rate of losses. Herein lies the value of the law of large numbers in risk management.

Reduction of Business Risk with Large Numbers. Recall the rules of risk management that say, "Don't risk more than you can afford to lose" and "Consider the odds" (the latter meaning, "Stay with those propositions which show a probability of being reasonably profitable"). Increasing the number of independent exposures to loss can help the manager implement these rules.

Assume a hypothetical business engaged in the activity of sending expeditions into jungle areas to discover new sources of useful drugs. Each expedition costs $25,000. The chance that an expedition will be turned

---

[22] A table of binomial probabilities expressed in *individual* terms is one showing the probability of observing exactly *r* failures in *n* trials. The term "binomial" means "two names" and in this case the two names are "loss" and "no loss." Tables of binomial probabilities also are constructed on a *cumulative* basis to show the probability of having no more than *r* failures in a given number of independent trials. For formula, see appendix to this chap.

[23] Note that a prediction of the underlying probability has a greater chance of being correct with six rolls than with twenty-four rolls. What does this say about the law of large numbers? It says that larger numbers reduce accuracy when "frequency of exact accuracy" is the accuracy standard for forecasts, again showing the problems with this standard.

back by hostile natives or unseasonable rains before finding anything has been found to be one sixth.

With this set of facts ($25,000 exposed to a one-sixth chance of loss) the following observations may be made: The five sixths of the expeditions that are successful must return the money invested directly in each of them plus the amount lost on the unsuccessful ones if the business is to break even. However, to break even is not enough if the business is to attract and retain investors. A satisfactory profit must be possible on the entire amount devoted to the operations. On the average, then, each set of five successful expeditions must return $150,000 plus a reasonable profit. If the actual experience varies from the average in the direction of more successes, no financial strain will result. But if the variation is in the direction of more failures, then problems can arise. If the business is to continue, it must be in a position to survive losses in excess of the underlying probability of one in six.

If there is a one-sixth probability of a purely random outcome, then in six trials a range of zero to three such outcomes will cover 99.13 per cent of the experience (recall the dice discussion). Now comes the relevance of the feeling about probabilities near 100 per cent. In business, as in other practical affairs of life, 100 per cent certainty about the future cannot be achieved. One must settle for as close to it as appears necessary and practicable. Suppose that the investors in these jungle expeditions believe that 99 per cent probability is as close to certainty as is necessary. Then, taking the approximation for the actual thing, we will say: If this business is prepared for the possible outcome of as many as three failures out of six expeditions, it is fully prepared. Being prepared for a 50 per cent loss rate can mean different things to different investors. If it means being prepared to swallow losses and forget the whole thing if a 50 per cent loss rate materializes, then the following calculations apply.

Each expedition costs $25,000, so the six will require a total investment of $150,000. With *average* success, only one of the expeditions will fail. The five successful ones must return the $150,000 investment plus the profit considered reasonable with *average* success. If the investors think that, because of the hazards involved, a 25 per cent rate of return will be required to make the investment attractive with average results, then the successful ventures must return 125 per cent of $150,000, or $187,500. Each successful expedition, therefore, must gross $37,500. If only three are successful, then the total return will be only $112,500, producing a loss of $37,500, 25 per cent of the original investment. If the investor is willing to accept this loss, then he is prepared for the risk. Investors in these circumstance (Table 4–2) will have a 33.49 per cent chance of a 50 per cent profit (no losses); a 40.19 per cent chance of a 25 per cent profit (one loss); a 20.09 per cent chance of breaking even (two losses), and only a 5.36 per cent chance of a 25 per cent loss—not bad for investors who are prepared for the risk.

What would be the comparable calculations if twenty-four rather than six expeditions were dispatched? With twenty-four expeditions the chance that the number of failures will be no greater than nine is 99.6 per cent (Table 4–3). This is three times the maximum expectation of losses with six expeditions. But compare how investors in the larger number of expeditions would fare. Average results with twenty-four expeditions would produce twenty successes and four failures. For a profit of 25 per cent on average results, the twenty successful expeditions must bring in 125 per cent of the total investment made in the twenty-four expeditions: $25,000 × 24 × 125 per cent = $750,000, or, as before, an average of $37,500 per successful expedition. If only fifteen are successful (the full *maximum* expectation of nine failures is scored), the total return will be only $562,500, producing a loss of $37,500 on the $600,000 total investment (24 × $25,000).[24] This loss amounts to only 6.25 per cent of the original investment, compared with the 25 per cent loss with similar results on six expeditions. Therefore if twelve men should each invest $12,500 to raise $150,000 to finance six expeditions, they may each lose up to 25 per cent of their investment ($3,125). If the number of investors is increased to forty-eight and the number of expeditions to twenty-four, each investor may lose up to only 6.25 per cent of his investment ($781). The probability of restricting losses with twenty-four expeditions to not more than $781 is, in fact, slightly better than the probability of restricting losses to $3,125 with six expeditions. Thus, a reduction in the relative size of the range (nine is only 37.5 per cent of twenty-four, whereas three is 50 per cent of six) may be of considerable practical importance, even though, in absolute size, the range of the forecast increases.

On the other side of the coin, with twenty-four expeditions, the chance of earning a 50 per cent profit is only 1.26 per cent (Table 4–4) as compared with 33.49 per cent with six expeditions. The chance of losing 25 per cent, however, is only 0.01 per cent with twenty-four expeditions compared to 5.36 per cent with six expeditions. Thus, an increase from six to twenty-four expeditions will reduce both the large loss probabilities and the large profit probabilities, a result to be expected with a decrease in risk; the less the risk, the smaller the chance of large gains as well as of large losses.

If adequate preparations are made for the risk, average experience will yield higher profits for the larger operation than for the smaller one. The investors in the six expeditions will need $150,000 to equip the first wave of expeditions plus another $37,500 in reserve to equip the second wave if only three successes (the worst expectation) are recorded by the first group. With average experience (five successes), $187,500 worth of new drug materials will be brought back at a cost of $150,000, yielding a profit

---

[24] That the amount of loss ($37,500) is the same as with six expeditions is coincidence.

TABLE 4–4

PROFIT PROBABILITIES WITH 24 EXPEDITIONS

Percentage of Profit*	Probability Rate† (Percentage)	No. of Failures
50.00	1.26	0
43.75	6.04	1
37.50	13.89	2
31.25	20.37	3
25.00	21.40	4
18.75	17.10	5
12.50	10.84	6
6.25	5.57	7
0.00	2.36	8
−6.25	0.84	9
−12.50	0.25	10
−18.75	0.06	11
−25.00	0.01	12

* Based on the assumptions that each expedition costs $25,000 and that each successful one returns $37,500.
† Based on the binomial probability distribution where the exposures number twenty-four and the average loss rate is one sixth (Table 4–2).

of $37,500. Based on the initial investment of $187,500,[25] the net return, assuming average results, will be 20 per cent.[26] A similar computation for the sponsors of twenty-four expeditions also shows a need for a $37,500 reserve.[27] The average expectation of twenty successful expeditions for a cost of $600,000 and an income of $750,000 produces a net gain of $150,000 on the initial investment of $637,500 ($600,000 expense plus the $37,500 loss reserve). This rate of return is 23.5 per cent, 3.5 per cent more income on each dollar invested than is gained with six expeditions. The reason why only the largest business units are prone to take a chance in some ventures should now be evident. Not only has the large business more money for a larger initial investment and for absorbing larger losses; it also finds risk taking more profitable. (In the light of this discussion, the reader should appreciate why the "invention" of the limited liability joint stock corporation was so important to the development of business enterprise on the contemporary scale.)

A Static Loss Illustration. The drug expedition example deals with speculative risk and with a high chance of loss. Now consider the effects of large numbers where the chance of loss is low and where the risk is static (profits are not available to balance losses). Table 4–5 presents a set of

[25] $150,000 to equip the expeditions plus a $37,500 reserve for losses.
[26] Return earned by investing the reserve fund in liquid securities is ignored in this model to preserve its simplicity.
[27] If the worst expectation occurs, fifteen successful expeditions bring back $562,500 in value, requiring an additional $37,500 for the $600,000 needed to send out twenty-four expeditions again.

TABLE 4-5

HYPOTHETICAL ANNUAL FIRE LOSS EXPERIENCE PER
$10,000 OF CONTENTS EXPOSURE, ONE YEAR

Size Category of Loss	No. of Instances	Average Loss This Category	Total Loss This Category
No loss	149,000	$ 0	$ 0
$1–1,000	730	600	438,000
1,001–2,000	104	1,560	162,240
2,001–3,000	62	2,520	152,240
3,001–4,000	41	3,500	143,500
4,001–5,000	25	4,470	111,750
5,001–6,000	15	5,460	81,900
6,001–7,000	10	6,450	64,500
7,001–8,000	6	7,450	44,700
8,001–9,000	4	8,460	33,840
9,001–10,000	3	9,470	28,410
$1–10,000	1,000	$1,265.08	$1,265,080
$0–10,000	150,000	$ 8.43387	$1,265,080

hypothetical but realistic figures for fire losses in a superior exposure. Note (1) the infrequency of fire losses generally and (2) the still greater infrequency of fire losses of large size.

Fire loss experience not only looks considerably different from that obtained from rolling dice but also must be interpreted differently. First, look at the information readily available from Table 4–5. Past experience indicates that a business with $10,000 invested in inventory in a store similar to the model should expect an average annual fire loss of about $8.43. For $30,000 divided among three model stores the average losses would be about $25.30, and for $240,000 in twenty-four stores $202.41.

These average figures, however, mean little to the owner of just one, or three, or even twenty-four stores. The chance of a loss of $8.43 during the year in any given store, or of $25.30 in three, or $202.41 in twenty-four is minute. Indeed, the most likely experience in any given year for one, three, or twenty-four stores is for no losses to occur. For one store, a "no loss" prediction *on the average* should be right 99.3 per cent of the time (or 149 years out of 150). For three stores such a prediction should hold true 98 per cent of the time ($[149/150]^3$, more than 49 years out of 50). For twenty-four stores, a prediction of "no loss" should be correct over 85 per cent of the time. ($[149/150]^{24}$, about 6 years out of 7), again *on the average.*[28]

[28] Similarly, a prediction that a pair of dice will not come up with a double six should be right 35 times out of 36. The trouble is, the dice never remember what has happened before and occasionally come up with double sixes two or three times in a row. It is no use remonstrating with them that the odds against such repetition are 1,295 to 1 for two in a row and 46,655 to 1 for three in a row. After all, the odds are 35 to 1 against even one double six, but the number comes up anyway. So when one says that "the odds are 100,000 to 1 against" something's happening, he also says that the same event *is* expected to happen—once out of every 100,001 times, "on the average."

Loss predictability with only a few stores is also complicated by the wide variation in the size of the few losses that are experienced. The average result per loss is expected to be about $1,265 per $10,000 of contents (Table 4–5). But nearly three fourths of the fires do no more than $1,000 damage and about one sixth do more than $2,000 of damage (Table 4–5). Less than one tenth of the losses fall between $1,000 and $2,000, the bracket containing the average loss of $1,265. The "average" loss in this particular group, however, is not $1,265, but $1,560. In short, when there is a loss, a guess that it will cost something considerably different from the "average" is by far the best guess. Only by the time the store or stores have experienced many small losses and one or more large ones is there any chance of recording "average" experience. At an average rate of one loss every 7, 50, or 150 years (according to whether there are twenty-four stores, three stores, or one store), many, many years can pass before a company experiences the average dollar loss.

What Is a Large Number? Good results were possible with twenty-four jungle expeditions. With one thousand jungle expeditions, the outcome, for all practical purposes, could be predicted exactly; statistically, it would be a sure thing. But twenty-four stores were not enough to achieve stable experience in fire losses. Would fifty be sufficient? Or would it require one thousand?

With fifty stores, the chance of going a year without a fire would be $(149/150)^{50}$, or 72 per cent. But with one thousand stores, the chance of completing a full year without a fire would be $(149/150)^{1,000}$, or only 0.10 per cent—at least one fire would be practically a sure thing.

What accounts for the greater reliability in a forecast of the outcome of twenty-four jungle expeditions than in a prediction of the fire loss in twenty-four stores? Why are twenty-four jungle expeditions, but not twenty-four stores, considered to be a "large number"? The explanation lies in the difference in the rate (chance) of loss. If the frequency of fire losses were ⅙ rather than ¹⁄₁₅₀, the owner of twenty-four stores would be fairly sure of a loss in any given year. The chance of no fires would be $(\frac{5}{6})^{24}$, or 1.26 per cent. A man with fifty stores would be absolutely positive in his expectation of at least one loss because the chance of no loss would be $(\frac{5}{6})^{50}$, or approximately 0.01 per cent. Twenty-four stores, therefore, would be considered a large number if the fire loss frequency rate were ⅙, but not when it is ¹⁄₁₅₀.

Loss frequency is important in the study of risk and loss. For one thing, the more frequent are the losses, the more generally amenable are they to loss control (chap. 2). For another, loss frequency is important in determining whether or how individual and class experience can be used in making rates. And now loss frequency is shown to be important in determining what is a "large number" of exposures for statistical purposes.

What is a "large" number? The answer appears banal. A large number is one large enough to do the risk control job needed. But this banal answer is a great improvement over the all-too-common approach of letting the matter drop after noting simply, "Well, with several stores we can average out our losses." What is a realistic estimate of the maximum loss potential? What is the effect of numbers exposed on that maximum? If the number is large enough to reduce significantly the cost of risk or to enable the business to accept a risk that previously could not have been accepted, then the number is "large." In general, the size of the number needed to qualify as a "large" number becomes smaller and smaller (1) as the chance of loss becomes higher and higher[29] or (2) as the loss frequency distribution becomes more and more like the "normal" distribution and less and less like the form of distribution illustrated in Table 4–5.[30]

Applicability of the Law of Large Numbers. The presence of a "large" number of exposure units does not of itself guarantee that the law applies. Requirements for the application of the law are that (1) the rate of loss shall be predictable and (2) the occurrence of the losses shall be individually random.

Requirement of Predictability. Predictability requires (1) a base for predictions and (2) comparability between that base and the situations for which the predictions are made.[31] In dice throwing, the base for predictability is the physical nature of the dice, which leads one to predict equal possibilities for each number on a die and no possibility of standing on edge. In business situations, neither static nor dynamic risks offer this kind

---

[29] This statement will be questioned by many readers familiar with statistics and probability. "What is the difference," they will ask, "between a 20 per cent chance of loss with an 80 per cent chance of success, and an 80 per cent chance of loss with a 20 per cent chance of success? The chance of predicting losses in the first case is exactly the same as the chance of predicting successes in the second case. And, since the losses equal the trials minus the successes, predicting the one is predicting the other."

But there is a difference if, as is usual, the businessman is affected differently by an excess of losses above average than he is by an excess of successes above average. To illustrate: When six dice are thrown, the probability that number six will show on more than three dice is less than 1 per cent (Table 4–2). If the number six represents loss, the lid on its frequency is gratifying. But if the probabilities are reversed and the appearance of number six indicates success (or "no loss"), then its maximum frequency of appearance may not be as crucial as its minimum frequency of appearance. (The fewest successes to be expected is a more important figure than the most successes to be expected.) Table 4–2 is not symmetrical in this respect: The maximum frequency of appearances of number six is three, a variation of two from the average frequency of one; the minimum number of its appearances is zero, a variation of only one from the average frequency of one. Suppose a reserve is set up to prepare for the risk. If the six indicates loss, the reserve must be sufficient to cover as much as two losses above the average; but if the six represents "no loss," only one extra loss above the average need be covered. Clearly, situations are found in which the two probabilities of loss, p and $1-p$, do not produce the same effect on the range of accuracy of prediction. Thus, they do not create the same degree of risk.

[30] Forms of distribution are discussed in the appendix to this chap.

[31] In many texts these two requirements are called (1) calculable chance of loss and (2) homogeneity, although the connection between homogeneity and comparability (condition 2, above) is seldom made clear.

of base for predictions. The physical natures of wood and brick do lead one to predict that wooden buildings will suffer a higher rate of fire loss than will brick ones; and the physical nature of cleaning fluids leads to the prediction that dry cleaners will have a greater number of explosions per establishment than will shoe stores. But the physical properties of these materials are not sufficient to determine the specific fire or explosion rate for each category. In these situations, reliance is given to the assumption that "what has been, will be." Thus, if the loss rate under certain conditions has been thus-and-so (the rate indicated in Table 4-5, for example), then it will be assumed to continue at the same rate.

This assumption automatically raises two questions: (1) What has been the past rate of loss? (2) Are there any reasons why the past rate of loss should not be expected to be repeated in the future?[32] More often than not the answer to these two questions is "We do not know" or "No one knows." This kind of answer makes application of the law of large numbers rather difficult![33]

But suppose that the first question can be reasonably well answered— that fairly accurate data have been kept on a large number of past exposures to this loss and that these data are available.[34]

The answer to the second question has two parts: changing conditions and homogeneity.

Changes create dynamic risks, and dynamic risks by definition are those in which the past does not forecast the future. *Every* important risk involves at least some dynamic factors. For example, experience indicates that illness rates in prosperous times are appreciably different from illness rates in times of economic depression. Highway accident rates also change with economic conditions, and the costs of personal injuries per accident change with both economic and sociolegal conditions. Not only do the static risks of highway accidents and human illness respond to dynamic factors, but so do the static risks involving death, fire, crime, and other perils. Tornadoes, earthquakes, and volcanic eruptions perhaps are exceptions to the general rule.

The other part of the answer to the second question, "Will future loss rates be those of the past?" has to do with static characteristics of the exposures in question. Even when over-all human illness and death rates do not change appreciably, there are important differences among different

---

[32] Actually, the real question is, Is there any reason to believe that the past rate of loss *will* be repeated in the future? But this form of the question is too fundamental for practical use.

[33] A discussion of how to approach these questions properly would develop into a discussion of the scientific method, much too large a topic for investigation here.

[34] Note the reference to "*large number* of past exposures." For reliability, large numbers are needed not only to be able to apply the law to given situations but also to develop the probability figures to be applied—as everyone who has studied statistics knows, of course.

parts of the population. The rates for males, whites, the native born, high-income families, married persons, and residents of northern states are each different from the rates for females, non-whites, the alien born, low-income families, single persons, and residents of southern states. No one would use mortality rates based on experience among horses to predict mortality rates for humans; indeed, probably no one would use the mortality rates among residents of the United States to make direct mortality predictions for the inhabitants of central Africa. But many might try to use the rates for the United States as a whole to make predictions about the state of Alabama or its principal city, Birmingham. The experience from which the loss rate is computed and the situation to which it is to be applied must be comparable in order for the law of large numbers to work effectively.

If this comparability is present, no special homogeneity is needed *within* the group to which the law is applied. White groups and non-white groups in the United States have significantly different illness and death rates, but this lack of homogeneity between the two groups is of no consequence if the experience of the total population containing both of them is used as a base for predicting illness and death among the total population. Similarly, if dwelling fire insurance statistics were collected on a general mixture of frame and brick one- and two-family residences in a particular territory, the failure to distinguish between these different types of construction and occupancy would not interfere with the use of these statistics to "predict" the fire loss rate on the same mixtures of residences in this same territory. *But* a rate based on a mixture of construction and occupancy can*not* properly be used to make the predictions concerning just one ingredient of the mixture *or concerning a sample that is not representative* of the whole population whose experience was used in developing the rate. And here is where trouble with homogeneity may arise. The "mix" may change, and, if it does, there is a lack of homogeneity with the previous total experience. On the other hand, if the experience of each of the various segments of the general population is individually known (more *internal* homogeneity is achieved), changes in the over-all mix need not destroy the applicability of the experience figures. Greater homogeneity within groups helps to achieve the necessary homogeneity among groups.

Individually Random Losses. Losses must be individually random for the law of large numbers to work: No loss shall be connected with one of the other losses or with any individually foreseeable or controllable event.

To satisfy this requirement, losses first of all must be individually independent. In texts on insurance the standard statement of this requirement is that losses shall be "non-catastrophic." For emphasizing the behavior of the law of large numbers rather than the insurability of risks, a better statement is that the losses shall be discrete.

Failure to meet this requirement will not necessarily make the law inoperative; it merely applies it to a smaller number of units. Thus, in the case of the twenty-four jungle expeditions, it might be difficult to find twenty-four entirely separate jungles. "What constitutes an 'entirely separate jungle' for purposes of applying the law of large number to this particular risk?" The illustration suggested that either unseasonable rains or unusually hostile natives would be the cause of failure of an expedition. Two places are "entirely separate" from each other for the purpose of jungle expeditions, then, if they are not subject to the same set of rainstorms or inhabited by the same or allied groups of natives. If three expeditions enter areas subject to the same rainfall, then, for purposes of the law of large numbers, this is the same as though one single expedition three times as large as the others were sent into the area. No longer is twenty-four the number of expeditions for purposes of the law of large numbers. The number becomes twenty-two because three of the expeditions are merged into one exposure to loss. And the application of the law of large numbers is changed accordingly.

The need for discreteness creates a special problem applying the law of large numbers: As units are added to obtain a "large number," the task of finding entirely separate units becomes more and more difficult. Could the number of completely separate jungle expeditions, for example, be raised to one thousand? Probably not.

Another built-in difficulty is the problem of obtaining large numbers without destroying predictability. If one hundred different jungle expeditions were sent into one hundred distinctly different places, could all of them be subject to sufficiently similar conditions for the known chance of loss to hold? How far can any business go in increasing the number of its independent exposure units without having to operate under conditions with which it has had no experience?

Thus, an attempt to make use of the law of large numbers may be self-defeating; discreteness or comparability or both may be lost.

To insurance underwriters, and in insurance textbooks, the characteristic of randomness is represented by the requirement that the loss shall be accidental, at least from the viewpoint of the insured. Statisticians require randomness to establish statistical comparability between groups. Experience in which results are directed (not random) will be comparable to experience in which the results are not directed (random) only if the direction is completely ineffective: The distribution of poker hands when one dealer is stacking the deck will be similar to the distribution from unstacked hands only if someone shuffles the deck thoroughly after the dealer has stacked it!

The requirement of randomness applies only to differences between cases. The difference between the over-all distribution of hands in poker games A and B is subject to the law of large numbers if Phil, who is sitting in on both games, stacks the cards the same way in both games every time it is his turn to deal. The difference in fire loss experience between two groups of stores, one in area X and the other in area Y, will not follow the law of large numbers if 5 per cent of the store owners in area X think that arson for insurance proceeds is a legitimate way to solve their needs for cash, while only five one hundredths of 1 per cent of the owners in area Y think that way. But the law of large numbers will apply as between the two areas if 5 or any other given per cent of the owners in *both* areas are arsonists (and if, of course, other relevant factors, including economic conditions, are also similar). The insurers, however, neither have nor want to develop insurance rates for areas subject to high rates of arson. Another, more numerous class of losses not entirely fortuitous is losses arising from morale hazard. These losses are widely prevalent and are impossible to eliminate from the picture. Morale hazard may be briefly described as the loss-creating attitude of "Oh, well, let it go; it's insured." Morale hazard can be and is amenable to the law of large numbers if about the same degree of morale hazard is in both the base experience from which the loss rate is computed and the situation for which a prediction is to be made. Since morale hazard is so widespread—a touch of the larcenous heart resides in so many breasts—comparability between groups in this regard tends to be high; consequently, this non-fortuitous cause of losses can be treated on a statistical basis and insured.[35]

Some of the problems that face the insurance underwriter do not face the business manager who tries to handle his own risks with the law of large numbers. Since he is both "insurer" and "insured," the question of whether he might deliberately cause a "loss" to himself is removed. His principal problems with regard to lack of random result have to do with losses *indirectly* caused by his deliberate acts. For example, deliberate changes in his personnel policies or practices might cause an adverse change in his employees' attitudes toward company property. If so, then future loss experience with regard to employee-caused waste and pilferage will not be comparable to past experience, and there will be a variation in this loss experience not in accord with the law of large numbers.

SUMMARY

Risk reduction consists of improving, in some sense, the accuracy of loss forecasts, and there is more than one sense in which this may be done. The most common types of criteria for "accuracy" in forecasts are (1) the frequency with which forecasts are exactly accurate, (2) the long-run size of the difference between forecasts and results, and (3) the loss range over which a forecast must run in order to achieve a desired probability of having the actual loss experience covered by the forecast.

---

[35] The statistician would say that, while losses caused by morale hazard may not themselves be random, the presence of the causative factor (and of the opportunity to make anything of it) is a random proposition (in the general population) and subject to the law of large numbers.

The task of selecting the forecast that gives the greatest accuracy is not easy, regardless of the standard of accuracy used. First, the evidence of the past must be observed and properly recorded. Second, differences between past, present, and future conditions must be assessed and their effects on loss frequency and severity estimated. Past observations, particularly within a given business organization, frequently offer little or no guide to the future. However, even with imperfection in observation and in selecting forecasts, several methods of risk reduction are available, and one or more of them may be practical in a given situation.

Loss reduction may produce risk reduction. This is generally true if losses are reduced without reducing the units and values exposed to loss. (However, by some standards, loss reduction may increase risk by changing a steady rate of loss into an intermittent one.) Loss control coupled with diversification of exposures is a particularly useful device of risk control.

Diversification may be accomplished cooperatively by interchanging shares of risks, commonly called "pooling of risks." Ocean marine general average is one example of this type of pooling. "Insurance" on nuclear energy plants is, at the present time, another example.

Under certain circumstances the statistical "law of large numbers" can be applied to a pool of risks to reduce the over-all risk. The risk reduction produced by this mathematical law is only *relative* to the number of exposures involved; it is *not absolute*. Total variation in losses from the average rises as the number of exposures increases, but the total variation rises at a pace slower than the increase in the number of exposures. This result can be of considerable financial significance.

Conditions that must be met for success in the application of the law of large numbers are that (1) there must be a *large number* of (2) *independent* exposure units with (3) *random* incidence of losses whose (4) over-all long-run behavior *can be approximated* ("*predicted*") by a probability distribution with known characteristics ("parameters").[36] Among the factors that must be considered in determining whether these requirements are met are possible changes of external conditions, homogeneity (similarity) between the characteristics of groups observed and groups for which predictions are made, characteristics and effects of non-random factors, and the extent to which getting a sufficiently large number of exposures may interfere with the independence of individual units among those exposures.

To a considerable extent, chapter 4 has dealt more with questions than with answers, with problems more than with solutions. This is because one must know what the alternatives are before he can intelligently compare them. One more major method of risk reduction, insurance, has yet to be presented. It is the topic of chapter 5.

---

[36] See appendix to this chap.

REVIEW AND DISCUSSION QUESTIONS

1. What are some of the standards for assessing the accuracy of forecasts? Which of these standards is the most acceptable in the management of static risks? Explain your answer.

2. Consider again the probability distribution for machine breakdown found in in the subsection "Examples of Measure of Size of Error." Show that the forecast which minimizes cost is "four breakdowns" even when cost of losses as well as cost of risk is considered in the result. Why is this so?

3. In the same machinery breakdown case (question 2), determine the forecast with expected least cost when—
   Loss cost per breakdown is X.
   Extra cost for each breakdown in excess of forecast is 0.50 times X.
   Extra cost for each breakdown which is forecast but does not occur is 0.05 times X.

4. Suppose the standard "accuracy with respect to a range" is applied to two or more different forecasts. What criteria are available for determining whether, by this standard, one of these forecasts is more accurate than the others? What problems are encountered in applying these criteria?

5. Explain why you agree or disagree with the following statement: The most useful forecast in a number of risk situations is still useless for risk reduction.

6. Define "real marginal cost" as a general concept. State how this definition applies to risk situations. Evaluate its usefulness in risk situations.

7. Explain why the past is not always a clear or accurate guide to the future.

8. When the recorded loss experience does offer a reliable index to the future, what problems are involved in making the best forecast from this experience? Explain.

9. Under what conditions would controls that reduce losses also reduce risk? Are there any conditions under which loss reduction would *increase* risk? Explain your answers.

10. Explain how segregation of assets controls risk.

11. Diversification may either decrease or increase risk. Explain why you agree or disagree with this statement.

12. Explain how risk may be controlled through a risk pool.

13. Does spreading (pooling) the risk reduce the cost of risk? Does it reduce the risk itself? Explain your answers.

14. A statement of the law of large numbers should include the words "a good prediction" and "reasonably correct." What is the significance of these words in the application of the law of large numbers to risk management problems?

15. Use the law of large numbers to explain the following proposition: The less the risk the smaller is the chance of either large gains or large losses.

16. With reference to the law of large numbers, what is a "large number"? Upon what specific factors does the size of a "large number" depend?

17. What requirements other than the presence of a "large number" must be met in order to make the law of large numbers applicable?

18. To what extent can the past rate of loss be relied upon to be repeated in the future?

19. What is the actual role of "homogeneity" in the effective application of the law of large numbers?

20. Explain why you agree or disagree with the following statement: "An attempt to make use of the law of large numbers may be self-defeating."

21. Explain how losses with non-accidental causes (such as burglaries) can nonetheless be treated statistically as "random" events.

Appendix to Chapter 4

SOME CONCEPTS AND TERMS IN PROBABILITY THEORY

The following is a summary discussion of some of the elements of probability theory, designed to explain the terms used in the text. No discussion of the underlying philosophy or meaning of "probability" is attempted.

While this presentation is written for readers who have had little formal training in mathematics, it does require study and concentration for absorption. It is not armchair reading. Elementary algebra is used, but no calculus. For those readers who are familiar with the calculus, footnotes appear here and there, noting where calculus operations apply.[1] A glossary to define and explain the terminology used in the discussion will be found at the end of this appendix. For some students, reference to this glossary might be helpful along the way.

EXPECTED FREQUENCY OF RANDOM EVENTS

Probability theory deals with the expected behavior of "random" events. When the theory is applied to real life events, the practical meaning of a "random event" is that the causes of its occurrence are so little understood, or so difficult to observe and analyze, that whether the event occurs or does not occur appears to be a matter of pure "chance." However, probability theory is based on the idea that, while occurrence of particular events at particular times is apparently a matter of chance, there is, in general, a regularity in the occurrence of these events over an extremely large number of times. Thus, whether a coin comes up "heads" on a given toss is a matter of chance. But the number of times the coin comes up "heads" in one million tosses depends to a large degree on the construction of the coin. So convinced are we of this that, if we should toss a coin a million times and get "heads" 900,000 times, we would suspect that the coin was of an unusual nature or that the tosser was somehow controlling it rather than that this unusual result was a matter of pure chance.

---

[1] Those few readers who are familiar with both calculus and probability will find that even these notes leave the discussion incomplete and, at times, not formally correct. It is usual, in situations such as this, for the authors to hint that they do know better but have created the formal shortcomings out of intent to simplify rather than simply out of ignorance. This position the present authors hereby claim.

Probability Distributions

For our purposes, a *probability distribution* can be described as a statement of the long-run experience expected in random events. We expect the results from tossing an ordinary coin to be "heads" half the time, "tails" half the time, and "standing on edge" none of the time. This is a probability distribution; in tabular form it looks like this:

Outcome	Probability Assigned to This Outcome
Heads	.50
Tails	.50
Neither heads nor tails	.00
One of the three foregoing events	1.00

The set of figures in the "Probability Assigned to This Outcome" column is a "probability distribution," and, in common parlance, the individual figures in it are called "probabilities." A "probability" is never negative; it is always either zero or positive. Obviously, the probabilities assigned to *all the possible completely different outcomes* (e.g., "heads," "tails," "neither") must accumulate to one (1.0).[2] When all the non-zero probabilities have been stated, so that the entire quantity, 1.0, is accounted for, the events in which the associated probability is zero usually are not mentioned. Thus, in coin tossing, the outcome "neither heads nor tails" is seldom explicitly mentioned.

Possible Distributions. Nothing in probability theory requires that all probability distributions be regular in form or have neat mathematical characteristics. Fortunately, however, most random events in which we are interested do exhibit some regularity and can be represented or reasonably approximated by general formulas. Statistical work is thereby considerably simplified. Certain formulas have sound grounding in rational theory about the fundamental nature of random events and, in addition, have proved over and over again that they do, in fact, approximate much actual experience. These are the important probability distributions. They are so important and so commonly used that they have names, some of which the reader has undoubtedly heard (e.g., "binomial," "normal"). In addition, common use of these formulas has led to considerable study of their characteristics, making them even more important and easier to use. One knows

---

[2] With discrete probability distributions, "accumulate to one" means "add up to one." When the distribution is continuous, the accumulation is by the calculus operation of integration. The tossing of coins gives an example of a discrete distribution; "heads" and "tails" are separate and distinct events with no gradual blending or series of gradations between them. The time between traffic accidents at a given intersection represents a continuous distribution; the period between any two consecutive accidents may be 10.0 minutes, 426.72 minutes, 1,026.15 minutes, or any other positive real number of minutes. Time is continuous and without (natural) discreteness. (Readers who are unfamiliar with calculus may ignore this note if it confuses.)

a great deal about the nature of the occurrence of a set of random events (such as losses from static risks) just as soon as he discovers that a particular standard probability distribution approximates the behavior of the events.

CHARACTERISTICS OF PROBABILITY DISTRIBUTION

We wish to consider the individual natures of a few of the important probability distributions—particularly the ones used in this text. But we cannot do this well before we know what "the nature of a probability distribution" means. What are the characteristics by which "the nature of a distribution" is identified?

Frequencies

Each important distribution has, of course, the formula by which the probabilities in it are identified. In the most important distributions, these formulas are derived from logical reasoning rather than by experiment. The logic involved requires a good background in mathematics: in algebra and, usually, in calculus. This is not the place for presentation of this logic. Instead, the statement will simply be made that there is logic behind the formula for each of these distributions, and each formula has two salient features: (1) It states the relative probability (expected long-run frequency) of each possible outcome. (2) It provides for application of these relative probabilities over a range of basic dimensions.

For example, the results from the roll of a die and the toss of a coin are both subject to the binomial distribution for relative frequencies. But the results to be expected in each case depend on the size of two basic dimensions—one, the underlying probability of getting the particular outcome to be counted; two, the number of trials over which the count is to be made. If a die is rolled and the outcome to be counted is "the appearance of number six," the underlying probability is ⅙. But if a coin is tossed and the outcome to be counted is "the appearance of heads," the underlying probability is ½. And if the die is to be rolled five times, the expected frequencies of the given outcome are different than if the number of rolls (trials) is to be ten; similarly with the number of times the coin is to be tossed.

Therefore, the statement for expected frequencies in a binomial distribution reads: If the underlying probability of the outcome is p and the number of trials to be observed is n, then the probability assigned to the event, "the outcome will occur r times," is given by a certain mathematical formula:[3]

---

[3] Some of the logic in the derivation of this particular formula is given later, when the major features of several important probability distributions are described.

$$P(r \mid p,n) = \frac{n!}{r!(n-r)!} \, p^r \, (1-p)^{n-r}.$$

In this expression, $P(r \mid p,n)$ is read: Probability of the following event: the outcome in question will be observed exactly r times, given that the underlying probability of its occurrence is p and the number of trials over which observations are to be made is n. The mathematical symbol $n!$, read "n factorial," is a number computed as follows: Multiply together all the integers from one to n, inclusive. Thus, $n!$ equals $1x2x3x \ldots x(n-1)xn$. In addition, the following value is given: 0! (zero factorial) is defined as equal to 1. Published tables of factorial values are found in standard books on probability and statistics.

Thus, when a die is rolled twice and the probable appearance of the number six is to be considered, we have

$$n = 2 \qquad p = \tfrac{1}{6} \qquad r = 0 \text{ or } 1 \text{ or } 2$$

$$\Pr(0 \mid \tfrac{1}{6},2) = \frac{2!}{0!2!} \left(\frac{1}{6}\right)^0 \left(\frac{5}{6}\right)^2 = \frac{25}{36} \text{ (probability of no sixes).}$$

(Remember that X^0 [that is, the zero power of X] equals *one* for any value of X other than zero.)

$$\Pr(1 \mid \tfrac{1}{6},2) = \frac{2!}{1!1!} \left(\frac{1}{6}\right) \left(\frac{5}{6}\right) = \frac{10}{36} \text{ (probability of only one six).}$$

$$\Pr(2 \mid \tfrac{1}{6},2) = \frac{2!}{2!0!} \left(\frac{1}{6}\right)^2 \left(\frac{5}{6}\right)^0 = \frac{1}{36} \text{ (probability of two sixes).}$$

Similarly, the probabilities for getting "heads" when a coin is tossed three times are given by

$$n = 3 \qquad p = \tfrac{1}{2} \qquad r = 0, 1, 2, \text{ or } 3$$

$$\Pr(0 \mid \tfrac{1}{2},3) = \frac{3!}{0!3!} \left(\frac{1}{2}\right)^0 \left(\frac{1}{2}\right)^3 = \frac{1}{8} \text{ (probability of no heads).}$$

$$\Pr(1 \mid \tfrac{1}{2},3) = \frac{3!}{1!2!} \left(\frac{1}{2}\right) \left(\frac{1}{2}\right)^2 = \frac{3}{8} \text{ (probability of exactly one head).}$$

$$\Pr(2 \mid \tfrac{1}{2},3) = \frac{3!}{2!1!} \left(\frac{1}{2}\right)^2 \left(\frac{1}{2}\right) = \frac{3}{8} \text{ (probability of exactly two heads).}$$

$$\Pr(3 \mid \tfrac{1}{2},3) = \frac{3!}{3!0!} \left(\frac{1}{2}\right)^3 \left(\frac{1}{2}\right)^0 = \frac{1}{8} \text{ (probability of three heads).}$$

The formulas for other probability distributions are different, of course, but each has these salient features: It provides a statement of the probabilities to be assigned to each of all possible events, with the exact result depending upon one or more basic values (dimensions) found in the situation to which the distribution is applied. (In mathematical terminology, these basic dimensions are called "parameters.") In several distributions, these dimensions deal with the same things as they do in the binomial: a measure of the basic rate of occurrence of the outcome to be noted (its underlying probability) and some measure of the "quantity of exposure" to it. The measure of "quantity of exposure" may be "number of trials observed" (as it is in the binomial distribution), or it may be "length of time over which observations are made" (as in a distribution on frequency of fires, say, or auto accidents).

Measures of Central Tendencies

Clearly, a statement (by formula or otherwise) of "frequency"—of the probability associated with every possible event—gives a complete picture of the probability distribution in question. However, there may be many, many possible events, and the information as to all their respective probabilities may be much more than we need to know about them. Often all we want to know are the answers to such questions as: "What is the *average* result to be expected?" "Which result is the one which is most likely to occur over a given period or in a given instance?" "What is the probability that results over a given period or in a given instance will be quite different from the long-run average or the most probable result?" Certain representative characteristics of probability distributions provide either answers or guides to answers for questions like these, and the ways in which these characteristics vary from probability distribution to probability distribution are an important part of the nature of each distribution.

The most important of these characteristics fall into one of two categories: measures of central tendency and measures of dispersion. Measures that give "representative figures" for the distribution—values that are "typical" or "normal" or "long-run effects"—are measures of central tendency. Measures that deal with questions of the type, "What is the probability that results over a given period or in a given instance will be quite different from the long-run average or the most probable result?" are measures of dispersion.

The three most important measures of central tendency—"average," mode, and median—are discussed next. Measures of dispersion are then considered.

"Average." The word "average" in common speech and in the body of the present text is used to indicate what mathematicians call the "arithmetic mean" and "expectancy." In this sense, the average of the following set of numbers is 1/15 of their sum: 55/15, or 11/3.

Distribution A: 1, 2, 2, 3, 3, 3, 4, 4, 4, 4, 5, 5, 5, 5, 5.

Suppose this set of figures represented expected frequency under a probability distribution. The outcome "1" would be expected 1/15 of the time, the outcome "2" would be expected 2/15 of the time, and so on, with "5" expected 5/15 of the time. The expected sum for every fifteen observations would be 55; for thirty observations, 110; for three hundred observations, 1,100; and so on. The expected average would be 55/15 or 110/30 or 1,100/300—all equal to 11/3.

In a probability distribution, if the value of each possible event is multiplied by the probability of that event, and the resulting products are accumulated[4] for all possible events, the average is computed. For example, Distribution A can be represented by a formula: $P(X)$ equals $X/15$, where X is 0, 1, 2, 3, 4, or 5. Computing the average of this distribution by formula, one gets

$$0(0/15) + 1(1/15) + 2(2/15) + 3(3/15) + 4(4/15) + 5(5/15) = 55/15 = 11/3.$$

This average is the same regardless of the number of trials or length of time (or amount of area) observed.

Median. The median of a distribution can be described as the "middle" of it. If all the expected results are arranged in order of value, from the lowest to the highest, the middle figure (or figures) in the array is (are) the median. Technically, the lowest figure such that one-half of all the expected figures are that small or smaller is the median. Necessarily, the highest figure such that one-half of all the expected figures are that large or larger is also the median.[5]

In Distribution A there are fifteen members. The median is the middle figure (eighth from either end), which is 4. Consider the following set of figures:

Distribution B: 1, 1, 1, 2, 2, 3.

There is no single middle value; the "middle" appears to lie somewhere between 1 and 2. In such event, *both* 1 and 2 are median figures: "The median of the distribution is 1, 2."

Mode. A mode may be said to be a "peak" in a distribution. In Distribution B, 1 is the most frequent value and is the mode. In Distribution A, the mode is 5. Consider the following two distributions:

Distribution C: 1, 1, 2, 2, 3, 3, 3, 4, 4, 4, 5, 5, 6.
Distribution D: 1, 1, 1, 2, 2, 3, 3, 4, 4, 4, 5, 5, 6.

In each distribution, *two* values share the honors for "most frequent." In each case, both values are modal. However, in Distribution C, where these two values are adjacent, they are considered to constitute a single mode. Only when the modal values are separated by other, non-modal values is the distribution said to be bimodal or multimodal.

When bimodal or other multimodal distributions are encountered in real life, one should ordinarily suspect that one or more of the following things have happened: (1) The data have been improperly observed or

---

[4] That is, added (for discrete distributions) or integrated (for continuous distributions).

[5] In continuous distributions, the median figure is the one such that integration over the distribution formula from the lowest end of the distribution to the median gives the value ½. (Since integration over the entire distribution gives the value 1, it follows that integration from the median to the high end of the distribution also gives the value ½.) In a fully continuous distribution the median cannot have more than one value.

inaccurately recorded. (2) The data are artificially clustered and should be grouped or smoothed. (For example, salaries of $5,000.00 and $6,000.00 are both more common than salaries of $5,562.61. But this result is not a random event, so it is not subject to probability measures. Salary statistics should be logically grouped for statistical treatment, for example, "$15,000.00 to $15,999.99," or "$14,500.01 to $15,500.00.") (3) The inter-action of two distributions is being observed. (For example, if a set of figures on the heights of adults is found to be bimodal at about 5 feet 9 inches and 5 feet 4 inches, one should quickly suspect that a mixture of two different distributions has been observed—probably the height of adult males and the height of adult females.)

Measures of Dispersion

Consider the following two distributions:

Distribution E: 0, 5, 10, 15, 20, 20, 20, 25, 30, 35, 40.
Distribution F: 16, 16, 18, 18, 20, 20, 20, 22, 22, 24, 24.

These two distributions have the same average, median, and mode; each of these for both distributions is 20. But how well that figure 20 characterizes experience under the distribution is quite different for E as compared with F. The difference between these central measures and the actual experi-ence in E is much greater than in F, and this difference is commonly im-portant in risk situations. Indexes of this difference are called "measures of dispersion."

Range, Limits, and the "-iles." The simplest indicators of dispersion are the limits and range of a distribution. Simply to know that the range of values in Distribution E is 40, while the range in F is only 8, is itself useful. Even more useful is the knowledge that the limits in E are 0 and 40, while in F they are 16 and 24. Indeed, knowledge of the limits and the average of a distribution is sometimes all the information really needed. All necessary conclusions and policy risk management decisions may be made from in-formation such as: The annual loss experience is never less than $500 or more than $850.

More information is provided by measures known as quartiles, deciles, and percentiles. A quartile is one fourth of the distribution, a decile one tenth, a percentile 1 one hundredth. (Other divisions are possible, of course, but with the exception of thirds they are hardly ever used. Oddly, thirds are practically always called "thirds," not "terciles.") In each case, the divisions are made only after the values have been arranged in order, either lowest to highest or highest to lowest. (Unfortunately for com-munication, there is no universal agreement as to which direction to use.) Of course, exact division is not always possible. Therefore, these divisions are marked in the same way as the halves of a distribution are marked by the median. Suppose we agree to count from the lowest values toward the highest. The first quartile then starts with the lowest value and runs to the "first quartile mark."[6] And the first quartile mark is the smallest value that is as large as at least one fourth of the observations.[7] Thus, in Distribution E, above, there are eleven observations. The smallest value that is as large as at least one fourth of the observations is 10. The next smaller value, 5, is as large as only two of the observations, and two observations are less than one fourth of the total number. The value, 15, is as large as at least one fourth of the observations, but it is not the *smallest* value that meets this criterion. The second quartile mark is the smallest number that is as large as at least two fourths, that is, one half, the observations; this is the median, 20. The third quartile mark is at 30. (Three fourths of eleven observations is eight and one fourth; the smallest number of observations that includes this many is nine, and 30 is the value of the ninth smallest observation.) Similarly, the quartile marks for Distribution F are found to be 18, 20, and 22; comparison of these values with the 15, 20, and 30 of Distribution E gives a clue to the relative dispersion, or spread of values, in one distribution as compared with the other.

Percentiles are divisions too small to apply to only eleven observations, of course, but they are very useful in more populous distributions. One of the most important things to know about a loss probability distribution is that some very high fraction—99 per cent or 99.9 per cent—of all the observations are expected to be no larger than a certain number. This number is the 99th (or 99.9th) percentile mark of that distribution. The further it is away from the mean, the greater the dispersion in the distribution.

Variance and Standard Deviation. The variance of a distribution is an average. It is computed as follows:

1. Take the difference between (*a*) each value observed in the distribution and (*b*) the average of the distribution.
2. Square each of these differences.
3. Average the figures obtained in step 2. This average is the variance; its square root is the standard deviation.

The variance in Distribution E, above, is 1500/11, about 136; the variance in F is 80/11, about 7. The difference or ratio between 136 and 7 is an index of the difference between the dispersions of the two distributions. The standard deviation of E is approximately 11.7; of F, approximately 2.7. The difference or ratio between 11.7 and 2.7 is another index of the relative dispersions of these two distributions.

Just as the expected average of a probability distribution can be calculated by multiplying each value by the probability assigned to it, then

---

[6] Some writers use the phrase, "first quartile," to mean both (*a*) the range covered by the quartile (the meaning used here) and (*b*) the "mark" that indicates the limit of the quartile.

[7] If the ordering is highest to lowest, the first quartile runs from the highest value to the first quartile mark. And the mark is then the largest value that is as small as at least one fourth of the observations.

accumulating over all the resulting products, so the expected variance can be calculated by accumulating all the products of (*a*) the squared differences between values and the mean multiplied by (*b*) the probability associated with each value.[8]

Differences can be measured from figures other than the mean, of course. They can be taken from the median or the mode, for example. However, the smallest sum of *squares* of differences is obtained if the differences are taken from the arithmetic mean rather than from some other figure. For example, consider the following distribution:

Distribution G: 1, 2, 2, 3, 4, 5, 6.

The average is 23/7, the median is 3, the mode is 2. The sum of squares of differences between the values and the average of the distribution is 136/7. (The variance is 1/7 of this, or 136/49.) The sum of squares of differences taken from the median is 140/7; taken from the mode, the sum comes to 217/7.

Average Error of Forecast. It is also possible to average over some function of differences other than their squares. An obvious alternative is to use the differences themselves. However, the algebraic sum[9] of differences from a mean always comes to zero—this is one of the properties of the mean. A more useful alternative is to average the absolute amounts[10] of difference between the values and a given figure. The sum and average of a set of absolute differences are minimized if the differences are taken from the median rather than from the average or some other figure. In Distribution G, for example, the sum of absolute differences from the mean is 71/7; the sum of absolute differences from the median is 70/7; the sum of absolute differences from the mode is 77/7.

The average of absolute differences has no standard short appellation. In this text it is called "average error of forecast." This figure is commonly larger when the variance of a distribution is larger, and smaller when the variance is smaller.

SOME IMPORTANT PROBABILITY DISTRIBUTIONS

Among the most important types of probability distributions, five are used in the text of this book: binomial (also called Bernoulli), Poisson, gamma, normal, and logarithmic normal (or log normal).

---

[8] It can be shown that the variance can also be calculated as follows: Multiply the square of each value by the probability associated with the value, and accumulate the products for all values. Subtract from this result an amount equal to the square of the average of the distribution. The remaining figure is the variance.

[9] "Algebraic sum" means taking signs ("pluses" and "minuses") into account. Thus, in Distribution E, if the difference between the value 40 and the average (20) is taken to be +20, then the difference between the value 0 and the same average must be recorded as −20, and the sum of these two differences is zero.

[10] "Absolute amount" involves ignoring algebraic signs; −20 and +20 are both read as +20, and the sum of their absolute values is +40.

Binomial Distributions

Most of the characteristics and the formula of binomial distributions have already been given in this appendix. The binomial distribution applies only when no more than two distinctive outcomes are to be noted: "heads" and "tails"; "six comes up" and "six does not come up"; "loss occurs" and "loss does not occur"; or "annual loss exceeds $100,000" and "annual loss does not exceed $100,000."

There are two versions of the binomial distribution. In one, the forecasts deal with the *number* of times a given outcome will be observed; in the other, the subject matter is the *percentage* of times it will be observed. Thus, the forecast for results from 200 tosses may be "100 heads" or it may be "50 per cent heads."

The frequency formula for the first version was given earlier. It is

$$P(r\,|\,p,n) = \frac{n!}{r!\,(n-r)!}\,p^r\,(1-p)^{n-r},$$

where r is the frequency of the given outcome, n the number of trials, and p the underlying probability that the given outcome will occur on any single trial. The formula for the second version takes r as a fraction (percentage) of n, hence reads

$$P\!\left(\frac{r}{n}\Big|p,n\right) = \frac{1}{n} \cdot \frac{n!}{r!\,(n-r)!}\,p^r\,(1-p)^{n-r}$$

or

$$\frac{(n-1)!}{r!\,(n-r)!}\,p^r\,(1-p)^{n-r}.$$

The average (expectancy) of the first version is $r = pn$; of the second version, it is $r/n = p$.

Earlier we noted that one of the advantages of the standard probability distributions was that several of their characteristics were known. In addition to the average, known characteristics of the binomial are as follows:

Mode or r occurs when

$$r \leqq p(n+1) < r+1.$$

(When $p(n+1)$ is an integer, both $p(n+1)$ and $p(n+1)-1$ are the mode.)

There is no general formula for the median. It occurs variously, at $p(n-1)$, pn, or $p(n+1)$. This means that no general formula for "average error of forecast" is available either.

Variance:

$$V(r\,|\,p,n) = np(1-p).$$

$$V\!\left(\frac{r}{n}\Big|p,n\right) = \frac{p(1-p)}{n}$$

Note that the variance of r increases proportionately as n increases, while variance of r/n decreases proportionately as n decreases. Thus, sixteen times as many trials means sixteen times as much variance in r but only one sixteenth as much variance in r/n. (The standard deviation would change by a multiple of four for r and of one fourth for r/n, of course.)

Poisson and Gamma Distributions

When more than one loss is possible in a given length of time, yet total losses in the period are not large in number, the probability distributions applicable, or most nearly applicable, to the situation are Poisson and gamma. Poisson distributions deal with the probability that there will be r number of losses in t space of time. Gamma distributions deal with the probability that t length of time will pass before r losses occur. Clearly, the two distributions bear a fixed relationship to each other.

The formulas for Poisson and gamma distributions are based on three variables: (1) the number of times a given outcome will be observed, (2) the length of time over which the observations are to be made, and (3) the underlying probability of the particular outcome to be observed. These three are clearly comparable to the three variables in the binomial: (1) the number of times the outcome is observed; (2) the number of trials over which the observations are made; (3) the underlying probability. In Poisson and gamma distributions, the "underlying probability" is the average number of losses that occur in one unit of time (e.g., in one day, one month, one year).

Poisson Distributions. Letting r be the number of times the particular outcome occurs, t be the length of time observed, and a be the average number of times the outcome occurs in one unit of time, the formula for the Poisson is

$$P(r \mid a,t) = \frac{(at)^r \, e^{-at}}{r!}.$$

(The number e is the base of natural logarithms, and is approximately 2.7183.) The average of this distribution is $r = at$. The mode occurs when

$$r \leq at < r + 1.$$

(If at is an integer, both at and $at - 1$ are modal.) There is no simple formula for the median. The variance is at (equals the average).

Gamma Distributions. Gamma distributions, dealing with time, are continuous, and handling them requires calculus, so their formula is not given here. However, the following characteristics are noted.

The probability that the specified outcome (such as "a loss occurs") will happen no more than r times in period t is necessarily the probability that to get a number of occurrences greater than r will take more time than is in period t.

The average of a gamma distribution is at r/a. That is, r/a is the average length of time (t) it will take for r occurrences of the specified outcome. The mode occurs where

$$t = \frac{r-1}{a}.$$

Again, the median has no simple formula. The variance is r/a^2.

Normal Distributions

The normal distribution, which is the famous "bell-shaped curve" studied at length in every course in probability and statistics, has peculiar importance in both applied and theoretical statistics. One of the most important theorems in mathematical statistics is the "central limit theorem." This theorem states that, as more and more observations are made of the results of a probability distribution, *any* probability distribution, the results will come closer and closer to that expected for a normal distribution. This theorem justifies treatment of all kinds of probability situations as though they were subject to a normal distribution. Unfortunately, some persons apply the normal to small numbers of observations of events that are subject to other probability distributions; in such cases the approximation given by a normal curve is often much too rough for the results to have practical value.

Useful Characteristics. The formula for normal distributions has two and only two parameters: the average and the variance of the distribution. These two must be known or ascertainable before the formula can be applied. Very important in normal distributions is that these two parameters are completely independent of each other. This is unlike all the distributions previously discussed. In binomial distributions, the variance of r is its average multiplied by $(1 - p)$; since its average is pn, the value of $(1 - p)$ is already fixed when factors in the average are known. In Poisson, the variance equals the average. No such fixed relationships are present in the normal. This characteristic makes it more flexible.

Another characteristic of the normal is that it is symmetric about its average. This makes the mode and median both equal the average. Since this is one of the few distributions in which the median can be simply identified, it is also one of the few for which a formula can be given for the average error of forecast. This value is $\sqrt{2V/\pi}$, where V is the variance and π is, as usual, the ratio between the circumference and diameter of a circle (about $22/7$). As noted, the variance of a normal distribution is one of the parameters that must be given before the distribution is known.

For applied statistics, one of the most important characteristics of the normal distribution is the fixed relationship between the average and standard deviation, on the one hand, and the percentiles, on the other. The average, being the median, is always the fiftieth percentile mark. And the average plus or minus a given fraction[11] of the standard deviation always indicates the same percentile mark, no matter what values the average and the standard deviation may have.[12] Thus, the average minus two standard deviations indicates the 2.275 percentile mark (2.275 per cent of the values are at or less than the indicated value); the average plus 3.09 standard deviations shows the ninety-ninth percentile mark; and the range from one standard deviation below the average to one standard deviation above it runs from 15.87 to the 84.13 percentile mark, so covers the central 68.26 per cent of the total distribution.

The student should not make the mistake of transferring this relationship to other types of distribution, however. For example, in a binomial distribution with fifty trials and a probability of .05 of getting the given outcome, the average is 2.50 and standard deviation is approximately 1.54. This average minus twice this standard deviation gives, not the 2.275 percentile mark as in the normal, but a negative figure below the zero percentile mark in the binomial!

Limitations on Usefulness.   The normal distribution has limited usefulness in application to static risk management problems. These can be summarized by noting that it is not a good approximation of most static loss experience.

One reason the normal is not a good approximation is the probability that it gives to negative values. Unless the average of a normal distribution is at least three times the standard deviation, the normal provides for significant probability of outcomes in negative figures. "Negative losses" are seldom a useful or meaningful concept in static risks.

But even for positive values, the normal curve seldom provides an adequate approximation of static loss experience. Fundamentally, static losses are phenomena of types explained by the binomial, Poisson, gamma (and some other) distributions. Also, static losses of financial importance generally have low to extremely low loss frequency. The lower the loss frequency, the greater the number of exposure units required before a normal distribution becomes a reasonable approximation of a binomial, Poisson, gamma (or other) distribution. Since property and liability insurance companies seldom have a large enough number of exposure units to make the normal curve of a good approximation of their loss distributions, it is unlikely that the business administered by a single risk manager will have them.

---

[11] The reader should remember that *all* real numbers are fractions. Thus, the integer 3 is the fraction of $\frac{3}{1}$ or $\frac{6}{2}$ or $\frac{9}{3}$, etc.; the number 1.625 is the fraction $\frac{1625}{1000}$ or $\frac{13}{8}$; and so on.

[12] Since this relationship is both useful and fixed, it has been recorded in tables, copies of which are commonly found in books on probability or statistics. The figures given in the text are from such a table.

Logarithmic Normal Distribution

The probability distribution that assumes that the logarithms of the values observed (rather than the values themselves) are normally distributed is of considerable importance in static risks. It has most of the virtues of the normal curve and fewer limitations for this purpose.

The "log normal" distribution (as it is generally called) gives no negative values. (When the logarithm of a number is negative, the number itself is between zero and one.) And it has been found in fact to approximate some actual static loss distributions.[13]

When the logarithms of the numbers are subject to the normal distribution, most of the virtues of the normal are preserved: The flexibility obtained by the independence of the average and the variance is retained. The normal curve's fixed relationship between percentiles, on the one hand, and the average and standard deviation, on the other, continues to apply to the *logarithms* of the values and from this can be transformed to apply to the values themselves. However, the log normal distribution is *not* symmetric, and the distribution of values around its average is quite different from the distribution around the average in the normal. Thus, while the range from one standard deviation below the average to one standard deviation above the average always covers close to 68 per cent of the whole area under a normal curve, the same range in a log normal distribution encompasses a widely varying percentage of the whole, depending on what particular values the average and the standard deviation happen to have.

The Logarithmic Base. Most persons whose mathematical training stopped with college algebra think of logarithms (when they think of them at all) in terms of powers of ten. When logarithms are taken to the base ten, the logarithm of 100, which equals the second power of ten (10^2), is two; the logarithm of 1,000 (which is 10^3) is three; the logarithm of the square root of ten (which is $10^{1/2}$) is ½; and so on. However, any real number may be the base of a system of logarithms. If the base is two, then 4 (or 2^2) is the number whose logarithm is two; 8 (or 2^3) is the number whose logarithm is three; and so on. Ten is the usual base when logarithms are being used to facilitate arithmetic computations. But, for analytical work, a special number, written e, is the preferred base. The logarithmic system based on e is called the "natural" or "Napierian" system. The numerical value of e is about 2.7183.

Characteristic Values in Log Normal. Any logarithmic base may be used for a log normal distribution, but formulas and analysis are simpler if the base e is used. The following statements are therefore given using the "natural" logarithmic system. The following symbols are also used below:

---

[13] See Robert A. Rennie, "The Measurement of Risk," *Journal of Insurance,* Vol. XXVII, No. 1 (March, 1961), pp. 83–91, and sources cited therein.

A is the average, B the mode, C the median, and D the variance of the *log normal distribution; m* is the average and v is the variance of the *underlying normal distribution* (the one that applies to the *logarithms* of the values used in the log normal distribution).

The average under the log normal:

$$A = e^m \, e^{v/2}.$$

The mode of the log normal distribution:

$$B = e^m/e^v.$$

The median of the log normal distribution:

$$C = e^m.$$

(Note that the average, mode, and median are represented by three different, albeit related, values.)

Variance under the log normal:

$$D = A^2 \, (e^v - 1).$$

Although the median of the log normal is readily ascertainable, the formula for the average error of forecast from it is quite complicated and is not given here.

The easiest characteristics to observe in a distribution often are the average and the mode. Note that when these have been observed in a log normal distribution, the essential values—the average and the variance of the *underlying* normal distribution—can readily be calculated:

$$A^2B = (e^m)^3. \qquad\qquad A^2/B^2 = (e^v)^3.$$

or

$$2 \log_e A + \log_e B = 3m.$$
$$2 \log_e A - 2 \log_e B = 3v.$$

GLOSSARY

(Italicized items in definitions are themselves defined in this glossary.)

absolute amount (also, absolute sum, absolute difference, absolute value)—without "plus" or "minus" signs: The absolute value of -20 equals the absolute value of $+20$ equals 20. (See also *algebraic sum.*)

accumulate—calculate a total. For a *discrete distribution*, determine the sum; for a *continuous distribution*, take the definite integral (which gives the total area under a curve).

algebraic sum—sum including algebraic (that is, "plus" and "minus") signs: The algebraic sum of -10 and $+5$ is -5.

arithmetic mean—the sum of a set of figures, divided by the number of figures in the set. In common parlance and in this text, called the "*average.*"

average—strictly, any *measure of central tendency.* Used in this text to indicate only *arithmetic means* and *expectancies.*

base of a logarithmic system—the number whose powers are used to determine the values in a system of *logarithms.* Since the number 64 equals 2^6 or 4^3, the following statements hold for the number 64 in logarithmic systems to (a) the base 2, (*b*) the base 4: (*a*) $\log_2 64 = 6$; (*b*) $\log_4 64 = 3$. When the base is ten, indication of it is often omitted, as: $\log 100 = 2$. (See also *natural logarithms.*)

bell (or bell-shaped) curve—the graph of a *normal distribution;* hence, the distribution itself.

Bernoulli distribution—*binomial distribution.*

bimodal distribution—*multimodal distribution* with only two peaks.

binomial distribution—one of a particular class of *discrete probability distributions* in which only two different types of outcomes are noted (in general, the outcome is noted, as "a particular result did, or did not, happen"). (See body of appendix for formulas and *characteristic values.*)

central limit theorem—a theorem (and proof) that as the number of observed *random events* gets larger and larger, their behavior is more and more closely approximated by a *normal distribution.*

characteristic values (of a distribution)—in this text, the *measures of central tendency* and *measures of dispersion* in a *distribution.*

characteristics (of a distribution)—the features of a *distribution* that distinguish it from all others, notably the statement of *frequencies* under it; also the resulting *characteristic values.*

continuous distribution—a set of *values* in which there is no break, as the set of possible lengths of time between one loss and the next; opposite of *discrete distribution.*

decile and decile mark—deciles and decile marks divide a *distribution* into tenths as *percentiles* and *percentile marks* divide it into hundredths. (See "percentile" and "percentile mark.")

discrete distribution—a set of *values* in which the values are separate and distinct, as, for example, the number of employees injured in a given plant in a year. (Between the possible numbers of 5 and 6, no intermediate values, such as 5.2 or 100/19, are countenanced.) Opposite of *continuous distribution.*

dispersion—the spread of a *distribution.* (See *measures of dispersion.*)

distribution—a set of *values;* usually, a *probability distribution.*

e—the number, approximately 2.7183, that is the *base* of the *natural logarithms.*

error of forecast—the *average* of the *absolute differences* between *values* observed and values predicted. Since a forecast equal to the *median* of a distribution minimizes error of forecast, it is generally assumed that the median is the forecast made; however, other figures are possible.

event—as used in this appendix, an identifiable result or happening consisting of a particular set of *outcomes.* (The set may be, among other things, "one outcome [of the type under consideration]" or "no outcomes [of the type under consideration].")

expectancy—the *mean* of a probability distribution—with a *discrete distribution,* the *arithmetic mean* of the *values;* with a *continuous distribution,* the definite integral (over all possible values) of the product of the value times the probability assigned to it. In this text, called *"average"* or *"expected* average."

expected · · ·—a result, *value,* or other *outcome* is called "expected" in this text when an *ex ante* ("before the fact") position is under consideration. Thus "expected *error of forecast"* is the anticipated value that this error will have before actual results are known. Among the other terms so modified in the text are *frequency, average,* and *variance.*

factorial—a mathematical function on integral numbers: for the integer *n,* "*n* factorial" (written *n!*) equals the product of all the integers from 1 to *n,* inclusive. Thus, 4! equals $1 \times 2 \times 3 \times 4$, or 24. Used in the *binomial, Poisson,* and *gamma* probability distributions (among other places).

fraction—expression of a number as a ratio (e.g., 1/2, 18/10, 5/1, $\pi/14$).

frequency—as used in this text, a term used not only to indicate the actual number of times a particular *event* does or is expected to occur but also to suggest the relative *probability* assigned to the *random events* in a *probability distribution.*

gamma distribution—one of a particular set of *continuous probability distributions* generally appropriate to times or distances between *independent events* with a (presumed) fixed *underlying probability* of occurrence, such as the time between fire losses.

independent events—(See under *random events.*)

limits (of a distribution)—the highest and lowest values in a *distribution.*

logarithm—a number assigned to a particular value, based on its relationship to a fixed value called the *base of the logarithm.* If the y power of the number x is equal to the number z, then y is said to be the logarithm of z to (or with) the base x. Written: $\log_x z = y$. This means $x^y = z$.

log (logarithmic) normal distribution—a *continuous probability distribution* in which the *logarithms* of the values under the *distribution* are distributed in accordance with a *normal probability distribution.* (See body of the appendix for extended discussion, including *characteristic values.*)

mean—usually (in this text, always) either the *arithmetic mean* of a *distribution* or the expectancy of a *probability distribution.*

measures of central tendency—in a *distribution*, values that are common in or typical of the distribution, particularly the *average, median,* and *mode.* Compare *measures of dispersion.*

measures of dispersion—indexes of the general size of the difference between the *measures of central tendency* in a *distribution* and the total collection of values under the distribution; measures of the spread among the values in a distribution. Principal such measures are *variance, standard deviation, error of forecast, limits, range,* and *percentile* and other division marks.

median—the "middle" figure in a *distribution* whose *values* have been arranged in ascending or descending order. More technically, the lowest value such that at least one half of all the values in the distribution (one half of the area under a *continuous probability distribution*) are that small or smaller; *also* the highest value such that at least one half of all the values in the distribution are that large or larger. (If these two definitions give different values, the median exists at both values. Thus, the median of the distribution, 1, 2, 2, 3, 3, 4, occurs at both 2 and 3.)

mode—a "peak" in a frequency distribution. Strictly speaking, modes occur only at the value or values having the (equally) greatest *frequency* or *probability* in a *distribution.* However, in applied statistics it is often good practice to consider as "modal" every significant peak. (See *multimodal distribution.*)

multimodal distribution—a *distribution* in which two or more non-adjacent *values* are *modes.* Strictly, the values must all have the same *frequency* or *probability* to be considered modal; in practice, all marked, distinct peaks in an observed distribution should be considered as at least potentially modal, and possible causes for the multiplicity of peaks should be sought. (See discussion of modes in the body of the appendix.)

natural (or Napierian) logarithms—the set of *logarithms* in which the *base* number is e.

normal distribution—one of a particular set of *continuous probability distributions* that are symmetric about their *average*, with *mode* and *median* at the average. The graph is somewhat bell shaped. By the *central limit theorem*, all probability distributions tend toward the normal as the number of observations increases. (See body of appendix for extensive discussion.)

outcome—in this appendix, the particular *random event* that is observed to occur at a particular time.

parameter—a given value that is essential to the determination of the exact nature of a *probability distribution*. Thus, the probability that two machines will be out of production at the same time depends on the parameter, the average length of time between breakdowns on each machine.

percentile—a *range* covering 1 per cent of the *values* in a *distribution*. Percentiles are ordered and numbered either from the lowest values to the highest or from the highest to the lowest. In this text the count is from lowest to highest. (See *percentile mark*.)

percentile mark—boundary *value* of a *percentile*. The percentile mark that indicates the boundary between the first and second percentiles is called the "first percentile mark"; the mark between the fiftieth and fifty-first percentiles is the "fiftieth percentile mark" (and is also the *median* of the *distribution*); and so forth. Marks for fractional percentiles are also given, as "the 50.75 percentile mark."

pi (π)—Greek letter commonly used to denote the number equal to the ratio between the circumference and the diameter of a circle.

Poisson distribution—one of a particular set of *discrete probability distributions* that are commonly applicable to the occurrence of *independent events* whose distribution in time or space is subject to an over-all *average* density, but whose individual occurrence appears to be a matter of chance. Poisson distributions deal with the varying numbers of outcomes of a particular type that will occur or be found within the limits of a stated area or period of time. The *gamma distribution* deals with the varying areas or periods of time that must be encompassed or observed before a stated number of the events will be encountered. (See discussion in the body of the appendix.)

probability—the "real" meaning of "probability" has been a subject of hot debate for many generations. In mathematics, a "probability" is "a number assigned to each possible *outcome* in a set of *random events*, this number having the following characteristics: It is non-negative, and the sum of the probabilities of all possible different *outcomes* in a *discrete probability distribution* (the integral of these probabilities in a *continuous distribution*) equals 1.0. In applied statistics, probabilities necessarily are taken as indexes of the relative frequencies with which various outcomes are expected to occur.

probability distribution—(1) a statement (by means of a table or a formula) of the *probabilities* to be assigned to all possible *outcomes* or *values* in a situation in which these outcomes or values are to be considered *random events*. The following common probability distributions are discussed briefly in this appendix: *binomial*, *Poisson*, *gamma*, *normal*, *log normal*. (2) The set of values to which probabilities have been assigned.

quartile and quartile mark—quartiles and quartile marks divide a *distribution* into quarters as *percentiles* and *percentile marks* divide it into hundredths. (See "percentile" and "percentile mark.")

random event—an *event* or *outcome* whose causes are so little known that the appearance of a given result is considered to be purely a matter of chance, subject to the laws of probability. "Independent" random events are those which have (or are assumed to have) no cause-and-effect relationship with each other.

range—(1)the *absolute difference* between the highest and lowest *values* in a set of values. In the phrase, "range of a *distribution*," the set includes all the values in the distribution. (2) All the values encompassed between a pair of values that mark the limits of (and are themselves included in) the range so designated.

standard deviation—a *measure of dispersion* equal to the square root of the *variance* of a *distribution.*

trial—name for a discrete *unit of exposure.* A specified or specifiable occasion on which a particular *outcome* is possible. (A toss of a coin is a "trial" on which the outcome "heads" is possible.)

underlying normal distribution—a phrase used to designate the *normal distribution* to which a *log normal distribution* is related. The *logarithms* of the *values* in the log normal distribution are distributed according to the "underlying normal distribution."

underlying probability—as used in this text, a *parameter* of some *probability distributions.* This parameter specifies the average rate at which a given *outcome* is expected to occur. Thus, if the average rate at which accidents occur in a city is expected to be 120 a year, this figure gives the "underlying probability" for accident frequency in that city.

unit of exposure—measure of the opportunity for given *events* or *outcomes* to occur. Base against which *underlying probability* is measured. When units of exposure are discrete, they are commonly called *trials.* Continuous units of exposure are time and area; for example, when losses are counted "per month" or "per year," then "month" or "year" is the unit of exposure.

values (in a distribution)—numbers assigned to identify or measure the significance of an *event* or *outcome.* Sometimes values are "natural"—e.g., the number of dollars lost when a hurricane strikes, or the number of persons suffering from rabies in a year. Other times the values are arbitrary; in predictions of formal academic success, a grade of "A" may be assigned a value of four, "B" a value of three, and so on. Then forecasts may be made on the basis of assumptions about the future distributions of these assigned values.

variance—a *measure of dispersion* in a *distribution.* It is the average of the following set of numbers: the squares of the differences between the *values* in a distribution and the *average* of the distribution. Computationally, the variance is easier to find by the rule, "average of the squares (of all the values in the distribution) minus the square of the average (of the same values)."

SYMBOLS

$P(X|Y,Z)$ Symbol used in this text for *probabilities.* Read: The probability associated with the result (*event, outcome,* or *value*) X, given that the *parameters* of the distribution equal Y and Z.

$P(X)$ Same as above except that either the distribution has no *parameters* or they are, for the moment, irrelevant.

$X > Y$ X is greater than Y, that is, X minus Y is greater than zero.

$X < Y$ X is less than Y, that is, X minus Y is less than zero.

$X \geqq Y$ X is either greater than or equal to Y.

$X \leqq Y$ X is either less than or equal to Y.

$X!$ X factorial, which equals $X(X-1)(X-2) \ldots 3 \cdot 2 \cdot 1$ (unless X is zero; $0!$ is defined as equal to 1).

X^0 The zero power of X. Since
$$X^a X^b = X^{a+b},$$
then, if b equals zero, we have
$$X^a X^b = X^{a+0} = X^a.$$
Therefore $X^a X^0 = X^a.$

Unless X equals zero, this necessarily means $X^0 = 1$.

Chapter 5

THE USE OF INSURANCE

Insurance is a formal arrangement for applying the law of large numbers to risk pools. Its objective is to provide a system for reducing and sharing losses. The law of large numbers offers the basis for predicting losses and thus reducing risk, whereas the risk pool provides the mechanism for sharing losses.

WHAT IS INSURANCE?

Whether risk transfer is necessary for an operation to be called "insurance" is an open question. Authorities disagree. Those, however, who hold that a risk transfer is a necessary ingredient for insurance are faced with a self-contradictory concept if they accept the idea of "self-insurance." This text holds that risk transfer is not an indispensable ingredient to an insurance operation and that *under appropriate circumstances* "self-insurance" is a meaningful as well as useful concept.

One convincing argument in favor of recognizing self-insurance as a true insurance operation unfolds in the following example: Suppose the EZ Insurance Company is able to operate a sound business by insuring the property of only one customer, the Gigantic Manufacturing Company. Gigantic is large enough to have a sufficient number of vehicles, warehouses, stores, and plants to allow the EZ Insurance Company to predict loss rates with an adequate degree of accuracy and to underwrite them with no more than the usual amount of reinsurance protection. Now suppose that the Gigantic Manufacturing Company buys all the capital stock of the EZ Insurance Company, dissolves the insurance company, and thereafter handles all its "insurance operations" as a division of the manufacturing company. Did insurance disappear when the legal fiction of separate corporate identities was abolished? Did it disappear earlier, when the names of the stockholders on the corporate books of the insurance company were changed? Or are Gigantic's risks still being handled by insurance in spite of Gigantic's purchase and subsequent liquidation of the EZ Insurance

Company? If the operation was initially one of insurance, its essential character was not changed by the subsequent alteration of the legal form in which that operation was incased.

The conditional phrases in the two preceding paragraphs are crucial: "*Under appropriate circumstances* self-insurance is a meaningful as well as a useful procedure," and "*If the operation was initially one of insurance,* its essential character was not changed by the subsequent alteration of the legal form in which that operation was incased." In this text, a risk management device will be deemed insurance *if* (1) it applies the law of large numbers so that the requirements for future funds to cover losses are predictable with reasonable accuracy, and (2) it provides some definite method for raising these funds by levies against the units covered by the scheme. Thus, insurance involves combining the experience of different exposure units for two purposes: loss prediction and loss sharing. Loss sharing without the use of the law of large numbers is simply loss pooling, not insurance; loss prediction without loss sharing improves knowledge, but it is not insurance.

POSSIBILITIES FOR SELF-INSURANCE

The most common obstacle to self-insurance is an insufficient number of independent units to allow for predictability. Operating a risk-reduction scheme with small numbers is essentially different from operating one with large numbers (chap. 4). Despite the laboring and belaboring of this point, insurance teachers are haunted with too many classroom exchanges like this:

TEACHER: A man who has a single apartment building decides to carry his own fire risk. In terms of risk management techniques, what are the differences between setting aside a fund, equal to the value of the building, out of which to pay for fire losses, and making no preparation at all for such losses?

STUDENT: If he sets up such a fund, he is self-insuring; otherwise he is merely assuming the risk. (!)

The man who owns a thousand different buildings in scattered locations may have the possibility of self-insuring his major static risks; the man with just one, or two, or even a dozen such buildings has no possibility of self-insurance no matter what he does. Since few businesses have a thousand or even a hundred locations, self-insurance of buildings or their contents is seldom possible. The risks for which an adequate number of sufficiently independent units are most likely to be available are those of workmen's compensation, operation of vehicles, and goods in transit.

Individual Units with Some Large Loss Exposure

Even at a single factory location, each individual employee is in some ways a separate unit of exposure to work injuries: When the operator of press 63 sticks his fingers into his machine at the wrong time, the operators at presses 62 and 64 do not ordinarily lose any fingers. However, some accidents cause injury to many employees. With regard to such perils as fire, explosion, and structural collapse, individual employees are not separate or discrete exposure units; all are exposed at once.[1] Problems of this kind can be handled by reinforcing self-insurance with the purchase of commercial insurance on an excess of loss basis. (The commercial insurer pays for losses in excess of a given figure.)

Vehicles are a popular subject of self-insurance (and non-insurance), at least for physical damage to the vehicles themselves. Much of the time the units are widely scattered; the value of an individual vehicle is often small compared to the total resources of the business; and physical damage to vehicles, especially by collision, is relatively frequent. Each of these characteristics is important in making owned vehicles likely candidates for self-insurance, or even for non-insurance. But property damage *liability* losses are less frequent and are *not* limited to small dollar potential per loss. A single truck can stop a freight train and knock several cars off the track. When the dust settles, the operator of the truck may be faced with property damage claims, not only from the railroad and shippers for direct damage to their property, but also for loss of its use—loss of the use of the rail line as long as it takes to get it cleared, loss of use of the damaged freight cars while they are being repaired, loss of market for shippers whose goods never arrived, and so on. Any vehicle can cause an explosion or a fire, and claims for property damage and loss of use in these situations have no particular dollar limit.

Liability claims for bodily injury are even less frequent than liability claims for property damage (fortunately), and the dollar amounts for individual claims have climbed notoriously over the past few years. Recent examples have included a $600,000 settlement for permanent total disability of a young boy in Illinois (in lieu of appeal of a $750,000 court award); a total of $479,000 for injuries to a family in New York ($400,000 of this was for the six-year-old daughter); $206,804 (reduced from $325,000) in a case against a high school in California; and many, many others.[2] Thus, few businesses can self-insure or safely non-insure their bodily injury liability losses, whether vehicular or otherwise. Exceptions are found among the

---

[1] Thus, the largest single insurance loss in the 1947 waterfront explosion at Texas City was the workmen's compensation loss at Monsanto Chemical Company. This claim included 145 employees killed and hundreds more injured. See Fred A. Ulmer (treasurer, Monsanto Chemical Co.), "The Monsanto Chemical Company Disaster at Texas City," in *Advances in Insurance Coverage—Accident Prevention and Control*, American Management Association Insurance Series, No. 78 (New York: The Association, 1948), pp. 32–39.

[2] For an up-to-date list, with citations (usually), see *Fire, Casualty and Surety Bulletins* (monthly) (Cincinnati: National Underwriter Co., Sales Volume, Losses Pij-1 *et seq.*

metropolitan area public utilities and the major railroads. Because their losses are more frequent than are those of the usual business, they have a fairly stable loss experience (and are able to utilize fully their own claims adjustment staff). On the other hand, airlines generally purchase insurance for their public liability risk.

The successful self-insurance or non-insurance of the automobile physical damage risk is limited because the units are not always in physically separated locations. A large number of them may be concentrated in a single garage or parking area overnight and perhaps during weekends. At least some major airlines have insured their planes against physical damage on the ground even when they have not done so in the air; the value in some hangar areas at various times was so high that self-insurance was impossible and non-insurance was unwise.[3]

Goods in transit have risk characteristics similar to vehicles away from the home garage: limited values, a number of separate exposures, and some frequency of loss. But special attention must be given to this exposure. Shippers have met with financial difficulty because shipments sent out individually did not stay that way. The 1952 flood at Kansas City, which inundated the railroad marshaling yards, destroyed a large volume of shipments originating all over the country on scores of different railroads. Kansas City is one of the nation's important railheads, where cars are handed over from one railroad to another. Even worse bottlenecks are found at locations where shipments are moved from land to water transportation and vice versa. Shipments originating many days, even some weeks, apart can pile up in a given dockside area, where they are subject to loss in a single catastrophe.

Although unanticipated large losses upset self-insurance schemes, the effect is not significant unless the continuity of the business is affected or the personal finances of the business owners are seriously damaged. In considering insurance as a risk-bearing device three important points are

1. Insurance schemes do not remove all risks; unanticipated serious losses are still possible.
2. The rule "Do not gamble with more than you can afford to lose" applies to these unanticipated serious losses.
3. The rule cannot be applied unless one knows how much is being gambled.

Time of Loss. Failure to realize that losses are just as random as to time as they are as to place is an error commonly found in the thinking about self-insurance plans. If a severe loss occurs on the average of once in ten years, that one loss can occur in the first year just as well as in the tenth year. Furthermore, *every year starts a new ten-year period.* Because last year was one of the severe years does *not* mean that the next severe year

---

[3] With the advent of jet airliners, however, even individual planes have come to represent too much concentrated value ($7 million or more) to leave uninsured in the air.

is nine years, five years, or even one year off. "The dice have no memory." If the losses are random, as they must be to make a self-insurance scheme feasible, then the losses are independent of one another. The occurrence of one loss does not of itself cause the occurrence of another. By the same token, independence means also that the occurrence of one loss does *not stop* the occurrence of another.

The principle of independence can be illustrated by a hypothetical example. Suppose the annual collision rate for the Colonial Corporation's fleet of automobiles is 50. Past experience shows five-year averages to have been always remarkably close to this rate even though in individual years, taken one at a time, the rate has varied considerably. If the collision rate for the past year was 75, the expected annual collision rate for each of the next four years is theoretically unaffected. The expected rate remains at 50 per year[4] despite last year's surplus of collisions. Assuming random experience and no change in underlying conditions, it would be illogical to expect a future rate lower than 50, that is, to expect a rate in the next four years that would "average out" the whole five-year rate to the expected annual rate of 50.

The foregoing conclusion is often hard to rationalize to oneself. But consider it this way: If the wide variation in the experience for this one year *was* random, and the underlying conditions have not changed, then the drivers of the cars are neither better nor worse operators than they were before.[5] And certainly the drivers of other vehicles on the roads will not be more considerate of the Colonial fleet because of its excessive collision rate for the past year. (Unfortunately, these other drivers will not be aware of Colonial's excessive collision rate.) So driving will be as usual despite the surplus of 25 collisions. Furthermore, the forces that make for bad driving weather will not moderate their behavior simply because the fleet experienced a bad year. The natural conclusion can be only that the underlying collision rate remains at 50 per year. The rate is not influenced by either a surplus or a deficit of collisions at the beginning of any given multiyear period.

The principle of independence among losses is an important consideration in self-insurance. Suppose Colonial decides to self-insure its collision losses for the first time, with annual contributions to the self-insurance

---

[4] This assumes, of course, that there has been no permanent change in the underlying loss-causing conditions, that is, that the experience of 75 was a purely random fluctuation from the average, similar to such fluctuations in the past.

[5] Experienced underwriters and insurance agents will recognize, of course, that, if the large fluctuation was in the direction of more losses, it *was* " 'random,' and will 'average out' over all of their insureds. (After all, insurance companies are in the business of paying losses.)" A bad year, therefore, is no reason to raise rates. On the other hand, if the large fluctuation was in the direction of fewer losses, it was clearly due to "an improved program of loss prevention which can be expected to continue to produce good results in the future" and will not "average out," so that rates should now be lowered—*or so many insureds would like to have their insurers believe!*

fund equal to the cost of 50 collisions per year. If 75 collisions occur, the fund will end the first year 25 collisions in the red. There is no expectation that the experience next year or the year after will automatically produce a surplus to balance this deficit. Indeed, the chance for a deficit in the second year is just as great as was the chance for the initial deficit. Because deficits can be experienced in several consecutive years, self-insurance funds, or at least self-insurers, must have surpluses in order to be effective, just as commercial insurers need surpluses to assure their solvency.

PURCHASING COMMERCIAL INSURANCE

The reasons for purchasing commercial insurance protection boil down to one thing: Under the circumstances, the purchase of protection from a professional underwriter is the cheapest way to achieve financial safety in the face of uncertain losses. Clearly, the important question that risk managers must answer is: What are the circumstances under which the purchase of insurance is the cheapest way of achieving financial safety?

The Availability of Insurance Protection

When considering the use of insurance as a risk-bearing device, the first question to be investigated is whether the risk is insurable. Not all risks that the risk manager would like to insure can be insured. Reference has been made to the requisites of an insurable risk (chap. 4). One set of requisites is fundamental to the operation of the law of large numbers: homogeneity, randomness, discreteness, and a measurable chance of loss. Another set of requisites is important to the commercial application of the law of large numbers in the give and take between independent parties in the market place rather than in the confines of an abstract mathematical problem. To make the application of the law practical, three additional requisites generally are considered necessary:

1. The loss shall be definite (*a*) in occurrence and (*b*) in dollar amount.
2. The loss shall be serious enough to be disturbing to a large number of individual persons or businesses.
3. The cost of the insurance operation itself shall be reasonably low.

Indefinite Loss. An insurance policy is a conditional contract. The insurer's promise to pay is conditioned upon the occurrence of specified events. Since the contract is between independent parties, some objective way of determining when and how much payment is due must be available. Otherwise, too many arguments will arise over the execution of the contract for the contract to be feasible.

A few examples of the problems that can be created for the insurer by indefinite losses are:

1. A store owner keeps a running inventory on his stock. Finally, after five years, a physical inventory is taken. The quantity of goods actually on hand

comes to only 90 per cent of the value indicated by the running inventory. Has there been a "loss" (an unintentional parting with value), or is this merely another example of the inaccuracy of running inventory methods?

2. Imagine that Ed Overman has been able to purchase insurance against damage to his store building by landslide and subsidence. He has carried the insurance for six years and now discovers that his building has slid three feet downhill from its original location. A study of the evidence indicates that all the sliding had occurred before he bought the policy, but only now has the strain on the building produced any damage or need for repairs. There has been a loss, yes, but did it occur before or after the insurance was purchased?[6]

3. Joe Small is insured against illness. Joe's business is highly seasonal. After one particularly hectic but profitable season, Joe is even more tired and run down than usual. His doctor suggests a long vacation, preferably with an ocean voyage. Mrs. Small has always wanted to see Paris; Joe has always wanted to lie around on the beach at the Riviera. With an unusually profitable season behind him and the slack season ahead, Joe figures he can afford the trip. He books passage and away they go. Is Joe sick? Is he suffering a loss?

Questions like this last one bother health insurance companies considerably.

How indefinite can a loss be and still be insurable? Differences of opinion are common. For years, most insurers in the United States would not write business interruption insurance to cover loss of profits *after the physical damage had been fully repaired*.[7] Assume that an explosion in the kitchen of the S and H Restaurant did extensive damage to the premises, forcing a shutdown of operations. Three months were required to repair and rebuild the restaurant. By the time S and H reopened for business, many of its customers had developed the habit of eating at other nearby places, and were slow in returning. Pre-explosion profits, therefore, were not restored along with the restoration of the premises. Several additional months were required to redevelop the clientele. Nearly all business interruption insurance forms in this country provide payment only for profits lost up to the date the premises can be reopened for business, not thereafter. In Canada, however, a "Profits Insurance" has long been available to indemnify for profits lost within a specified time after the business can be reopened. Henry C. Klein, in the 1957 edition of his comprehensive book, *Business Interruption Isurance*, wrote:

If means were available for extending the period of coverage under all Business Interruption Insurance policy forms in the United States and Canada beyond the time required for physical rehabilitation, there would probably be little demand for the Canadian Profits forms, and many lines of business in the United States would secure a more complete and necessary coverage. If a precedent for such extension of time coverage is needed, it is at hand in the well established

---

[6] This problem is one of the reasons why insurers do not actually offer protection against subsidence and have withdrawn their offering of protection against landslide.

[7] Business interruption insurance is insurance against loss of anticipated net profits caused by the interruption of business activity following physical damage to property at a specified location.

Tuition Fees Insurance policy form and in the Louisiana Public Storage Warehouse and Pacific Coast Seasonal Stock Endorsements. As ways and means of extending the Period of Indemnity are under study as this book goes to press, manuals of Rules should be checked for possible revisions in this direction.[8]

Shortly before the present text was written, such coverage did become available as a standard form in parts of this country. To repeat, "indefiniteness of loss" is at least sometimes a matter of opinion—of different opinions at different places and times.

Indefinite Cause of Loss. William D. Winter, who was a great scholar of insurance as well as a highly successful company excutive, noted that "the original conception of insurance was not insurance against specific types of losses but against loss per se."[9] He goes on to note that this original approach has not been continued in property and liability insurance in the United States, despite the facts that

We would be appalled if life insurance companies refused to insure unless death was caused by certain named diseases. We would also be appalled if our fire departments responded only to fires caused by overheated furnaces. . . .

Such attitudes are ridiculous, and yet the insurance business in the United States has developed along an equally illogical line of reasoning to the effect that insurance companies must confine their activities to certain kinds of risks. . . .

* * * * *

. . . The development of insurance on land in this country has, from its earliest days, conformed to the theory that property should be insured against specific kinds of losses and not against loss per se. . . .[10]

The results of the described attitude have been that standard policies in this country have many exclusions and limitations aimed at delineating exactly the causative hazards and perils intended to be covered and at trying to make sure that the stated coverage applies only to those losses which are caused by these hazards and perils in an unambiguous and rather definite fashion. (Some of the difficulties that this presents are discussed in chap. 15.) These requirements have much to do with many refusals to provide coverage. Consider the example of the restaurant closed by explosion. How can the insurer be certain that the reduced business after reopening was actually due to the covered peril, explosion? For any one or more of some dozens of reasons, the business of this restaurant might have suffered a decline anyway—a decline totally unassociated with the occurrence of the explosion.

One of the most popular of physical damage coverages is the Extended Coverage endorsement attached to fire insurance policies to add coverage for additional perils: windstorm, hail, explosion, riot, smoke, damage by vehicles or aircraft. Many of the provisions in this endorsement are aimed

---

[8] (3d ed.; Indianapolis: Rough Notes Co., Inc., 1957), pp. 173–74.

[9] "The Multiple Line Concept," in *Examination of Insurance Companies* (New York: New York State Insurance Department, 1953), Vol. I, p. 529.

[10] *Ibid.*, pp. 532, 535.

at avoiding payment for losses that, though definite enough themselves, arise from causes that may be indefinite. Subsequent to a series of blizzards, roof damage is discovered in a particular building. Has this damage been caused by blizzard winds, by weight of snow on the roof, by alternate freezing and thawing of snow and ice on the roof and in the gutters after the blizzard has passed, or simply by lack of proper maintenance of the roof? Extended Coverage protection includes insurance against "windstorm," but it specifically excludes protection against "loss caused directly or indirectly by (*a*) frost or cold weather or (*b*) ice (other than hail), snowstorm, sleet, waves, tidal wave, high water or overflow, whether driven by wind or not."

Damage by water has been a particularly thorny problem in pinpointing the cause of the loss. Besides "waves, tidal wave, high water or overflow," damaging water can come from rain entering through open windows or doors or leaking in through defects in the structure; from backing-up of sewers or drains, from seepage of ground water, from broken or defective sewers or piping, or from dampness in the air (whether the water remains in the air as atmospheric humidity or is precipitated out as condensation). Regardless of the cause, the loss itself is generally definite enough. But the specific cause is often difficult to place, and the question arises whether the real cause was the presence of the water or some poor practice in containing or controlling its behavior. Since, for a variety of reasons, the companies believe it necessary to pinpoint—be definite about—the causes for which they will pay, and it is so often difficult or impossible to tell exactly which cause produced a given water damage loss, many varieties of water damage coverage are impossible, and the rest are difficult, to obtain.

Small Losses. Many people like to be able to collect from their insurance companies for every loss, regardless of its size. But one suspects that this attitude is stronger when attention is focused on losses rather than premiums. When the insurance purchase is in the contemplation stage and the question of cost to be paid versus benefits to be received is still undecided, the relatively large premium necessary for coverage of the small unimportant losses makes such protection unattractive to most people. If an insurance company is to be able to develop the large number of desirable insureds necessary to make an insurance plan workable, the coverage offered must be designed to protect against loss potentials disturbing to a large number of financially responsible, reasonable people. In general, this means protection against potentially large losses.

Uneconomic Insurance. It is axiomatic that a $1,000 insurance policy bearing a premium of $1,500 is unlikely to find purchasers. Even at a premium of $750, few sales are likely to be made, and probably then only to people who have good reason to believe that they are likely to gain on the proposition by having a loss. An insurer is unlikely to make enough money to stay in business under these circumstances.

One cause of a high premium is high chance of loss. For example, premiums on life insurance written at advanced ages are likely to be unattractive. Premiums on war risk insurance on vessels moving through an area officially blockaded by hostile powers also are likely to be too high relative to the amount of insurance involved.

On the other hand, extremely high-rate insurance sometimes is sold. When war breaks out, a rush to buy war risk coverage on vessels at sea occurs, even at high premiums. A spectacular peacetime example of the purchase of high-rate insurance occurred in January, 1952. The ship, "Flying Enterprise," was damaged in a North Atlantic storm and took on a 60-degree list. Newspapers all over the world reported on the subsequent attempt to tow her into port; when her captain stayed aboard and was joined by one man from the towing ship, news of intense human interest was made. Not so widely reported was that some of the cargo aboard was not originally insured. After the vessel was in trouble, some insurance against *total loss only* was purchased on this cargo. It was rumored that the premium was 50 per cent of the value of the cargo insured. The ship went down before reaching port, so this proved a good buy for the shippers.

Riot and civil commotion insurers have long had to quote rates applicable to imminent loss situations. For a time these rates were double the regular rate. Currently, the problem is handled by requiring that explosion insurance be purchased along with riot coverage to provide the insurer with extra premium money.[11] Probably the highest rates for standard coverage are in hail insurance on growing crops in certain areas. Hail insurance rates on growing wheat around the Kansas-Colorado border have gone as high as 25-30 per cent of the amount of insurance. Although some coverage has been purchased at these rates, most farmers have preferred to take their own chances. (At 10-15 per cent rates in some other areas, however, hail insurance has sold well.)

A high rate of loss can be caused by frequent small losses as well as by single big ones. One of the most uneconomic of all premiums is the one for automobile collision insurance with no deductible. The current manual in many territories provides that the "full coverage" premium shall be four times the premium for $50 deductible. The $50 deductible premium for certain relatively expensive cars in Chicago is (as this is being written) $62. Removing the deductible runs the premium to $248, a charge of $186 for only $50 more insurance. The high premium is simply a tactful way for insurers to say the coverage is essentially unavailable. (The tactfulness lies in arranging the premium so that the buyers will say,

---

11 Even more helpful in practice, however, has been the introduction of riot insurance as a standard coverage purchased by most insurance buyers as a part of the Extended Coverage endorsement used with fire insurance policies. The widespread use of this endorsement has done more than anything else to reduce the last minute rush to buy riot insurance in critical situations.

"No, we do not want it," rather than for the insurers to say, "No, we will not let you have it."[12]

Frequent small losses drive up the costs of losses themselves. Premiums for insurance against small losses are relatively high for another reason as well: handling costs per claim do not vary proportionately with claim size. While it does cost more to handle a $100,000 claim than a $10 one, it does not cost 10,000 times as much. The minimum cost for handling any claim is certainly $5, if it is not $10 or $15. Against a $10 claim the claims administration cost is therefore at least 50 per cent, compared to the usual run of claims expense in property insurance of 6-10 per cent of claims. Can it be worthwhile to pay an insurer $5 to write out a check for $10, especially when this $5 cost is in addition to all the other costs of sales and administration to be covered by the expense portion of the premium dollars?

Inapplicability of Law of Large Numbers.   As defined in this text, insurance is dependent upon the application of the law of large numbers. But, as noted, what is written by insurance companies under the name of insurance is not always insurance. Protection offered on atomic energy plants and that on prototype giant aircraft were offered as examples of contracts that were insurance in name only. Seldom will the risk manager care, however, whether his transfer of risk to an insurer actually constitutes an insurance operation on the part of the insurance company. The nature of the transfer becomes a matter of concern to him only when it has a possible effect on the insurer's financial stability (see chap. 16). More important to the risk manager is the use by the insurer of the inapplicability of the law of large numbers as an excuse for refusing to issue needed insurance coverage. The peril of flood, for example, has been ruled uninsurable, generally on the grounds that the exposures lack homogeneity, their loss rate is not predictable, the losses are not individually random (the peril offers a catastrophic potentiality) and the risk fails to meet the market requirement of economically feasible cost. On the other hand, not all the experts have been convinced by these arguments. William D. Winter presents a good discussion of the problems and possibilities of flood insurance in his lecture "The Multiple Line Concept."[13]

---

[12] Before and during World War II a popular form of collision insurance coverage was "80-20." Under this form the deductible was 20 per cent of the loss or a flat $50, whichever was the smaller amount. If the loss was only $2.00, say, the insurer paid 80 per cent of it and the insured stood only 20 per cent of it. Under this arrangement the companies found themselves paying for many, many small losses. Shortly after the war the companies decided to raise the premium on this form by a great deal, not really caring whether the new high price left any effective demand for the form. The insurance commissioner in Kansas, however, refused to approve the proposed rates. So the form was withdrawn and became unavailable in literal fact in Kansas instead of just in practical effect as in most other states. (Recently, however, this form has made a comeback with some companies.)

[13] Winter, *op. cit.*, pp. 551-52.

As he saw it, the two big obstacles to flood insurance were adverse selection and lack of research. However, extensive investigation by a firm of consulting engineers was sponsored by a group of major fire insurance companies, with the same old conclusion: flood losses are not insurable.[14] For one thing, the problem of adverse selection continues to arise. The authors of the present text feel strongly, however, that the really big obstacle to the development of flood insurance is lack of a strong push for the coverage by an influential number of buyers or on the part of the policymakers of any insurance company. If there were a strong drive for the coverage, underwriting research would be added to the engineering study. Since insurance is being written against earthquakes in California and hurricanes in Florida, the suspicion must remain that insurance can be written against floods in Ohio.

Thinking in this area should be conditioned somewhat by a famous letter written in 1882 by the Cincinnati general agent of a big eastern fire insurance company to Mrs. Dodds, an agent in Osage City, Kansas, explaining in condescending but quite clear terms why no self-respecting or responsible fire insurance company would ever, ever engage in such a wild speculation as the issuance of protection against the peril of windstorm. He was so shocked by the absurdity of the idea that he penned a postscript saying: "If against wind, why also not against rain, hail, crushing by snow, accidents caused by faulty construction of buildings, etc. etc. etc."[15] On the other hand, thinking should also be conditioned by the long history of failures of schemes of "insurance" against an amazing variety of the hazards that beset the human race and its possessions, from the days of the Great South Sea Bubble on.

The histories of such policies as the Jeweler's Block, Banker's Blanket Bond, Manufacturer's Output, and the recent multiple line and package policies for a wide variety of stores and offices and for residences indicate that what "could not be done" sometimes can be done. But it takes pressure from individual buyers (as with the jewelers and bankers) or from some underwriter, seeing an opportunity to seize a market (as in the case of many of the new package forms), to get something done. And, as the records show, even then the progress may be slow and halting and sprinkled with retrogressions.[16]

---

[14] American Insurance Association, *Studies of Flood and Flood Damage, 1952–1955* (New York: The Association, 1956), pp. 3–4.

[15] That the general agent, in writing this famous letter, used a typewriter, which had only recently been invented, indicated that he did not frown on *all* new ideas simply as a matter of principle. See Hawthorne Daniel, *The Hartford of Hartford* (New York: Random House, 1960), pp. 189–90.

[16] For some of the history see G. W. Crist, Jr., *Corporate Suretyship* (2d ed.; New York: McGraw-Hill Book Co., Inc., 1950), pp. 290–93 and *passim* (on Banker's and other "blanket bonds"); William H. Rodda, *Inland Marine and Transportation Insurance* (2d ed.; Englewood Cliffs, New Jersey: Prentice-Hall, Inc., 1958), pp. 222–23 (Jeweler's Block) and chaps. 3 and 5 (broad and "all-risks" coverages in general). Ex-

TO BUY OR NOT TO BUY COMMERCIAL INSURANCE?

When should insurance protection be purchased? When should some other method of risk bearing be used? Although examples of risk management decisions are presented and discussed in chapters 10 and 11, it is both useful and desirable to consider some of the characteristics of commercial insurance at this point by comparing them with alternative solutions to risk problems.

The Availability of Alternatives

Other possible solutions to risk problems should be considered and weighed along with the insurance solution. To review, these alternatives are risk assumption with or without a fund, risk avoidance, risk transfer (to someone other than an insurance company), risk reduction by self-insurance, or risk control by other means that have been described.

The practicality of risk assumption as a risk management device depends principally on the size of potential loss. As for risk avoidance, if avoidance is possible, the principal question is whether avoiding one risk will create others that are even less desirable. (Risks particularly likely to be created by a program of caution are those related to market position vis-à-vis competitors who are not so cautious.) The possibility of risk transfer hinges on finding someone willing to accept the transfer, of course, but often the real limitation is the lack of ingenuity and knowledge on the part of management of risk-shifting possibilities. Opportunities for risk control are like opportunities for control of other costs; they are almost always present, but it often takes a trained managerial mind first to find them and then to develop usable plans for exploiting them. It also takes good administrative talent to keep such plans in operation after they have been developed. What risk control plans are "usable" depends, of course, on the characteristics of the risk situation: the extent to which the risk is subject to application of the law of large numbers (self-insurance), to loss reduction without a decrease in the scale of operation, to loss dividing or loss pooling arrangements, and so on.

---

amples of recent attempts at buyer pressure can be found scattered through the insurance publications of the American Management Association and the issues of *National Insurance Buyer*. Some specific examples from the AMA Insurance Series: J. G. Reese (Consolidated Gas Electric Light and Power Co., Baltimore), "Insurance as Viewed by the Buyer," in No. 49, *The Future of Casualty and Fire Insurance* (1943), pp. 17–23; Eugene Dougherty (Anheuser-Busch, Inc.), "Evaluating Your Company's Insurance Program," in No. 81, *Development in Social Security and Workmen's Compensation* (1949), pp. 36–42; and the colloquy between an unidentified buyer and Lyle G. Wimmer (Traveler's Insurance Co.) in No. 70, *Practical Guides to Insurance Buying* (1947), p. 21.

Relative Costs

After marshaling the various risk management devices relevant to a given risk situation, the next step is to compare the costs of these devices. The more common pitfalls in comparing their costs are listed here.

1. Failing to consider all the costs, particularly in connection with either risk assumption or self-insurance:
   a. Failing to consider costs other than loss costs.
   b. Failing to consider indirect losses.
   c. Concentrating on the modal experience to the exclusion of the average and the poorest.
   d. Feeling overly optimistic as to all kinds of risk and loss costs.
2. Making inappropriate cost comparisons among risk management devices (for reasons other than those listed above) by:
   a. Comparing different measures of loss.
   b. Comparing risks of different kinds.
3. Overlooking auxiliary benefits offered by alternative risk management devices:
   a. Loss prevention.
   b. Claims adjustment.
   c. Risk management advice.

All the Costs. In a consideration of the costs of risk management devices, attention must be given to the costs of risk in addition to the costs of losses. In analyzing the costs of losses, the risk manager should be aware of two parts to these costs: the losses themselves and the cost of handling them. A final addition to costs to be considered is that ubiquitous cost, taxes, especially income taxes.

Cost of risk as distinguished from the cost of loss has already been explained, but it would not be amiss to offer another example, this time aimed at a direct comparison between two important risk management devices: risk assumption with a fund and the purchase of insurance. To be effective as risk management devices, both the amount of the fund and the face amount of the insurance obviously should be based on maximum loss potentials. The fund, of course, can be built up over a period of time, with insurance making up the deficiency during the accumulation period. In this illustration, costs after the fund has been completed will be compared with an equal amount of insurance.

While the amount of both the fund and the insurance are to be established at the maximum loss potential, loss costs under the fund and the premium costs under the insurance will depend on the average loss rate rather than on the maximum loss rate. In order to make comparisons, "loss" must be considered to mean all those loss costs that would be covered by insurance if insurance were carried. Suppose the average rate for these costs is $10,000 per year on a maximum exposure of $200,000. Where the risk is assumed and a $200,000 fund is maintained, costs are those losses and expenses actually incurred plus the investment income sacrificed by keeping $200,000 in liquid assets. No self-insurance operation is assumed here, which is to say that no assumption is made that the actual loss rate for the given business is predictable. The loss may come to any amount in any given period of time. This is the risk that has been assumed. Therefore, risk assumption may produce a large gain or a large loss when compared with insurance, all depending upon what actually happens. But, in anticipation of the unknown result and to make comparison possible, some rate must be assumed. The arithmetic average of experience is a useful one for this purpose. (See "pitfall" 1c, above.) The average earning rate of assets fully invested in the business is arbitrarily assumed to be 20 per cent before income taxes, and the average earning rate for liquid funds is assumed to be 4 per cent before taxes. Income in this business is assumed to be taxed at the rate of 50 per cent.

It is assumed that losses for the insurer have been running 54 per cent of premiums, but, because this particular firm emphasizes loss prevention, its loss experience would be expected to produce only a 50 per cent ratio of losses to premiums. In practice, an assumption of a better than average loss record is often an example of "pitfall" 1d, above. However, since a better than average loss record is sometimes the reason for seriously considering risk assumption, the illustration takes this expectation into consideration. (The business man, of course, does not have any direct interest in what loss ratio the insurer contemplates anyway; all that interests him is the rate that will be charged for his insurance. But in this illustration it is desirable to see how the various figures relate to one another.)

Now the initial estimate of the cost differential can be made.

With the fund:
Annual losses, *average* ....$ 10,000
Loss of income on $200,000
    Earning at 20% ....$ 40,000
    Earning at 4% 8,000

    Difference (earning at 16%): Gross cost of risk 32,000

    Cost of loss and risk before taxes ....$ 42,000
Less tax reduction of 50% 21,000

    Cost of loss and risk after taxes ....$ 21,000
With purchased insurance:
$10,000 losses assumed to be 50% of the premium: covering both cost of
    losses and cost of risks ....$ 20,000
Less 50% for reduction in taxes 10,000

    Cost of loss and risk after taxes ....$ 10,000

To produce the same cost with the fund as with the insurance, the fund would have to be reduced to $62,500—less than one third of the value exposed to loss. If the fund is maintained at $200,000, then the insurance alternative will be expected to be cheaper so long as money in the business earns better than 5 percentage points more than is earned with the liquid funds (i.e., if liquid funds earn 4 per cent, insurance will be cheaper than maintaining a $200,000 fund so long as the business can earn more than 9 per cent on its fully committed assets). And all this is true even though this firm's loss experience has been assumed to be better than the average on which the insurer's premium is based. Although it is not to be presumed that all cases will work out this way, it is easy to see that many will.

It is also easy to see that the most important relationship here is the one between the maximum loss (which determines the size of the fund and hence the loss-of-income cost) and the average loss rate (which determines the insurance premium). Contrary to some popular opinion, the better buys in insurance protection are those in which the average chance to collect is low, not high—which means, in general, where losses are infrequent rather than frequent. Conversely, the more frequent the losses, the more likely it is that risk assumption (or self-insurance) will turn out to be more economical than the purchase of insurance.

Note that the comparative cost figures given above were designated as an *initial* estimate of cost differential. What else needs to be considered? Have *all* the costs been included, as per directions? It was stated that the $10,000 annual average covered "all those costs that would be covered by insurance if it were carried." What other costs are there? In cases of insurance against physical damage to the insured's own property, insurers pay for little more than the losses themselves. According to the policies, the costs of ascertaining the amounts of loss and of providing the evidence for the loss are borne by the insured.[17] These costs certainly come to no less than the insured would have had to spend if he had been ascertaining the amount of the loss merely for his own benefit. They may well come to more!

When the risk involves liability for injury to the persons or property of others, the risk manager must consider possible gains accruing from a favorable difference between the costs incurred when he handles his own losses and those incurred when the insurance company handles them for

---

[17] For example, all policies based on the 1943 New York Standard Fire Insurance policy provide that when a loss occurs the insured shall "protect the property from further damage, forthwith separate the damaged and undamaged personal property, put it in the best possible order, furnish a complete inventory of the destroyed, damaged and undamaged property, showing in detail quantities, costs, actual cash value, and amount of loss claimed; and within sixty days after the loss, . . . render . . . a proof of loss . . . stating the knowledge and belief of the insured as to the following:" The various things required in connection with the proof include: "if required, verified plans and specifications of any building, fixtures or machinery destroyed or damaged." Also, the insured, "as often as may be reasonably required, shall produce for examination all books of account, bills, invoices and other vouchers, or certified copies thereof if originals be lost. . . ." All this is at the insured's expense except for actions in connection with protection of the property from further damage.

him. The insurer agrees, under the "Supplementary Payments" provision in a liability insurance policy, to

defend any suit against the insured alleging such [covered] injury . . . even if such suit is groundless . . . ; . . . make such investigation, negotiation and settlement of any claim or suit as it deems expedient; pay all premiums on [certain] bonds . . . ; pay all expenses incurred by the [insurance] company, all costs taxed against the insured in any such suit and all interest accruing after entry of judgment . . . ; reimburse the insured for all reasonable expenses, other than loss of earnings, incurred at the company's request; and the amounts so incurred, except settlements of claims and suits, are payable by the company in addition to the applicable limit of liability of this policy.[18]

This supplementary agreement can easily involve substantial sums of money. When a business carries its own liability risks, it has to pay these costs itself. The individual business might have to set up a claims adjustment organization that could not be kept employed full time at that work. The costs of handling claims, therefore, may well be higher than if these claims were settled by an insurance company because of idle capacity in the adjustment organization or because, being part-time at this job, the claims men may also be only partly trained and short on experience. The result may show up as claims handling expense, as increased loss cost, or in an indirect fashion as bad public relations with the claimants and their friends and acquaintances.

In any event, it is clear that all the important costs of loss adjustment must be remembered when cost comparisons are being made among the various available methods of dealing with a risk.

A final cost that should not be overlooked is the cost of keeping records. This is particularly important in the case of self-insurance, which, if it is really to be insurance and not just risk assumption, involves considerable records keeping and analysis. Some large businesses keep complete records on their losses (as well as on their policies and premiums) even when these losses are insured commercially. For them, risk assumption may not represent much additional office cost. But most businesses rely on their insurance companies and agents or brokers to keep track of insurance

---

[18] The quotation is excerpted from a Standard Automobile policy. Practically the same wording occurs in all "casualty" liability policies, including Workmen's Compensation and Boiler and Machinery policies. Provisions to the same effect appear in forgery coverages and in Sprinkler Leakage and Water Damage Liability covers. They do not appear, however, in the marine covers for bailees and carriers, even those that include liability coverage. As one marine form for motor carriers says, "It is the purpose of this insurance . . . to indemnify the Assured only to the amount which the Assured shall become liable to pay and shall pay in respect of the merchandise and/or goods." Nonetheless, the insurer pays any costs incurred by itself in investigation or as a result of decision to defend in court, providing that "the Assured, whenever requested, . . . shall cooperate with this Company (*except in a pecuniary way*) in all matters which this Company may deem necessary in the defense of any claim or suit or appeal from any judgment. . . ." (Quotations from a "Motor Truck Merchandise Rider—Carrier's Form." Italics added.)

matters for them. Keeping tabs on things themselves would represent considerable additional effort, and hence expense.

In group insurance—life, medical expense, or disability income—the practice is for most insured businesses to take over at least some of the bookwork from the insurer. In larger businesses, the insurance company does hardly anything more than act as a reinsurer. Its contribution to the operation is limited to receiving the employer's checks for premiums (which the employer has calculated and collected) and to accepting the claims drafts (which also have been calculated and drawn up in the employer's offices). This situation has come about because employers seem to like it that way. They would rather furnish the records work in kind than provide the cash for the insurer to do it. And group insurers' sales talks to large employers commonly emphasize the "control" that the employer can have over this kind of operation. This approach helps sell group insurance to these employers. (With small employers, however, the opposite approach often is more popular.) Self-administration of group insurance in large businesses undoubtedly has had something to do with the shift of many benefit plans to a self-insured basis.

Indirect Costs of Losses. Chapter 2 included a discussion of indirect cost (of losses) to individual businesses. One professional risk manager was quoted as saying, "There are hidden expenses borne, by the company, that are associated with every accident and not fully realized."[19] The "4-for-1" ratio for workmen's compensation was cited: Heinrich's estimate that indirect losses from work injuries ran four times as much as the direct losses. Property losses, too, involve dislocation of work schedules, interruption of sales compaigns, use of substitute goods and materials, and so on. Much of the indirect loss is not presently covered by insurance policies of any kind. This means that the business that buys "complete" insurance is still covering only part of each of its losses; plenty of risk assumption still exists. A good hard look at the static risks of most businesses will show that those managers who believe in maximum feasible risk assumption for these risks will always have their desire; there is no other course. And all this is in addition to the dynamic or speculative risks that they must bear!

Suppose a manufacturer has begun production of a new product. A great deal of money will already have been sunk into research on it: laboratory research, pilot production, market research, patent search. More money will have been spent on retooling the plant and on advance advertising promotion. Now, just as the new item begins to reach the market, a fire in a small but essential portion of the plant causes a shutdown of operations. Six months will be needed to replace the dies that have been damaged. Under "ordinary" circumstances, alternate equipment

---

[19] Cf. chap. 2, n. 14.

would have been available, and the company's credit rating would have been good. But the new product has not yet produced enough volume for additional machines to have been set up for it, so there is no alternate equipment. Extensive borrowing to launch the new product has already used up all lines of credit. Now what? Some machines are available to continue production of the old product on a small scale. But can the company postpone its entry into the market with the new item and still carry the load of interest charges and payments on its now large debt? A postponement would destroy much of the value of the company's promotional advertising and probably would impair its goodwill with its salesmen and distributors—a frightening prospect. (One is reminded of a sentence in a study of the effects of indirect losses: "Mr. Lawson, the only stockholder active in the business, was given the company as payment for six months' back salary. . . .")[20]

Because insurance companies restrict their coverage under any given policy to some particular perils, property, hazards, and losses does not mean that the excluded part of the exposure is of no consequence to the risk manager. Likewise, the fact that coverage for these excluded exposures is not offered by insurers under any policy does not mean that these exposures can be ignored when the purchase of insurance is being considered.

The Potential, Not Average, Loss. The importance of *maximum* loss potential has been and will continue to be emphasized in this book. But in real life, "averages" of one sort or another are frequently substituted for "maximums" in the minds of those who think about loss possibilities. As a rule, a business moves on year after year with only modest losses. Consequently, its owners have not experienced serious static losses. Other businesses with which the businessman is personally acquainted usually have only "average" experience, too. Big losses are reported in the newspapers, but they happen only to people in print and not to real live people known to the typical business executive.

"Oh, sure, a big loss could occur"—one bigger than any this business executive actually knows about, that is, than he himself has ever seen or than has ever been seen at first hand by someone with whom he is personally acquainted. "Why, there might even be a fire big enough to damage fixtures and inventory to the extent of, say, 30 or 40 per cent of their value, or there might be a windstorm big enough to take off the entire roof of the building! But beyond these, tales of losses are just 'scare stories,' told by insurance men out to make a few more dollars if they can." In short, here again are all those problems in applying the rules of risk management introduced in chapter 1, problems that will remain until a really big loss

---

[20] James J. Crowley, thesis for baccalaureate degree, Massachusetts Institute of Technology. Quoted in *FC & S Bulletins* (monthly) (Cincinnati: National Underwriter Co.), Sales Volume, Losses If-3.

does happen directly within the personal experience of the businessman or of one of his personal acquaintances. Nothing sells burglary insurance like a good burglary *in the neighborhood;* nothing arouses interest in fire safety in the schools like a school holocaust. (And nothing quenches interest in these things like the passage of a few months *without* another incident of the same kind!)

Big losses are uncommon, but they are not fictitious. One should be thankful for, not lulled by, good experience. Even in "Russian roulette" the odds are five to one with the players. Most of the time nothing happens, but in the long run the players will be killed. Businesses unprepared for large losses will also in the long run be killed by them. The statement, "The odds are 100-to-1 against it," means, "One time in 101 it *does* happen."

The present topic is cost comparison among methods of handling risks. The cost of suddenly being ejected from business is one of the costs that must be considered in connection with risk assumption. This cost is not readily reducible to figures, but when it is part of the loss potential, then risk avoidance, risk transfer, or the purchase of insurance surely is a less expensive risk management device.

Improper Comparisons among Costs

Even when none of the costs of risk or loss are ignored, another mistake in cost comparisons may be found; comparisons may be made on improper bases.

Comparing Different Measures of Loss. "I wouldn't buy that insurance. Why, *all* of my losses of that kind over the past ten years wouldn't even come to two years' premiums." Here the cost of the modal rate of losses (the most common annual experience, usually no losses at all) is compared with an insurance premium based on the average rate of losses. A similar error may be found when the cost of insurance is compared with the cost of risk assumption using a fund; but the insurance policy is large enough to cover most of the maximum loss potential, whereas the fund is large enough to cover only those losses that are experienced in most individual years (the mode), say a $100,000 policy versus a fund of $10,000 or $15,000.

A different kind of error in comparing different loss rates is rather common in the purchase of life and health insurance. Typically an applicant can be more easily persuaded to spend $12 annually to add $10,000 of double indemnity (coverage against death by accidental means before age sixty-five) to a $10,000 policy of life insurance, than to use the same $12 to add a few hundred dollars to his regular life insurance protection (covering death at any age from any cause). The much higher amount of insurance that can be purchased for $12 through double indemnity riders blinds the buyer to the much lower chance of loss under this rider. Death from a cause other than accidental means is far more likely than is death from accidental means. Consequently, life insurance coverage not limited to death by accidental means is worth far more than coverage with this limitation. Governed by the same type of loose thinking, many people buy loss-of-time and medical expense coverage against accident but not against illness because sickness insurance costs about four times as much as accident insurance. Again the buyers are concentrating on the direct cost comparison without paying enough attention to the associated difference in the chances of loss.

Different Risks with Different Alternatives. Innumerable opportunities for making errors by comparing risks of different kinds are present. It is probably true that the risk transferred to someone else is never quite exactly the same as the initial risk the business had before the transfer. Furthermore, as mentioned earlier, the act of transferring or avoiding one risk is almost sure to create a risk of a different kind. Complete comparability, therefore, never is found among the risks handled by different risk management devices. To make comparisons when there are inherent imperfections is one thing, but to make them when the defects in comparability are specifically identifiable, but overlooked out of ignorance or out of prejudice for or against some particular risk management device, is another. This latter class of imperfect comparison is the topic here.

Consider some common alternatives to an owner's risk of physical damage to goods in transit by common carrier. In many cases the owner has a choice, when shipping the goods, between a full-value and a released (limited-value) bill of lading. Under a released bill, if a loss occurs for which the carrier is liable, the amount of liability is limited to a value set by the bill. The risk of losses in excess of this value can be shifted by the owners to an insurance company. The lower freight rates for shipments under released bills can help offset the cost of the insurance. In many instances the transit risk may be transferred to the other party to the shipment, that is, from the shipper to the consignee or vice versa. The risk, therefore, may rest with the carrier, shipper, consignee, or insurance company.

The direct costs of each of those methods of handling the transit risk are generally ascertainable, but learning the exact risk to which of these costs applies takes some study—not much, but more than some shippers are willing to put in. Briefly, common carriers are liable for all losses except those caused by inherent defects of the goods or faults of the shipper,[21] by "acts of God," or by war; they are also liable for losses caused by their own negligence, except when the shipper is also at fault. Most transportation insurance policies insure against certain specified perils only. Included among such perils are those of the "acts of God" category (e.g., flood,

---

[21] For an excellent discussion of this point see Yoshisaku Kato, "On Inherent Defect of the Subject-Matter Insured," in *Annals of the Hitotsubashi Academy*, Vol. VIII, No. 1 (Tokyo: Hitotsubashi University).

windstorm) for which common carriers are not ordinarily liable. Also included are some of the perils for which common carriers are ordinarily liable (e.g., fire, riot). When these latter perils are covered, the insurer will pay even though the loss is one for which the carrier ordinarily would be liable.[22] The risk that can be transferred back and forth between the shipper of the goods and the consignee consists, of course, of whatever risk is not retained by the carrier. If the terms of the shipment are, for example, "f.o.b. point of shipment," then the consignee takes the ownership risk as soon as the goods are on board the carrier's vehicle. Whether the consignee accepts the risk under a full or a released bill of lading will depend on the custom of that particular trade unless his purchase agreement specifically provides to the contrary. In either case, the consignee will stand all losses when the carrier was not liable and when the cause was not traceable to an act of negligence on the part of the shipper.

Clearly, whenever these various methods of handling transportation risks are compared, the difference in the nature of the risks transferred must be considered along with the differences in costs. Only then can a meaningful comparison be made.

One more point that will be repeated again and again throughout this book: Not knowing exactly what risks are actually transferred to the insurance companies under policies purchased (let alone under the policies that could be purchased!) is one of the two most important causes of grief in the risk management of most businesses. (The other? Not knowing what risks are present that need to be insured or otherwise controlled before they destroy the business.) One who is in the habit of knowing the content of his insurance policies and other documents pertaining to risk (and that is practically all documents) does not need to read a book about them to know that the protection provisions in a bill of lading, a policy of transportation insurance, and a contract of sale and shipment are only partly similar, not nearly identical. (He may have to read several books, however, to learn exactly what the similarities and differences are!)

The use of risk transference in the handling of liability losses is increasing. Construction contracts especially, but also service and sales contracts, are being loaded with risk transference provisions by parties having superior knowledge or bargaining position. Questions have been raised as to the advisability of this procedure, even from the viewpoint of the party doing the transferring.[23] Some of these questions revolve around the

---

[22] Subject to protection of the insurer's subrogation rights against the carrier, however.

[23] "Hold Harmless Agreements: How Effective Are They?" panel discussion in *Problem Areas in Corporate Insurance Planning*, American Management Association Insurance Series, No. 113 (New York: The Association, 1956), pp. 25–48; also Anthony W. Fitzgerald, "How Harmless Is the 'Hold Harmless' Agreement?" in *The Changing Picture in Corporate Insurance*, No. 114 of the same series (1957), pp. 19–28.

problem of identifying the risks transferred and the new risks that the transfer creates.

When a business engages the services of an independent contractor, three methods are available to the business for handling the liability risk growing out of the arrangement: The business may assume the risk, it may purchase insurance on the exposure, or it may transfer (or attempt to transfer) the risk to the contractor. As between the latter two, the following problems arise in identifying the risks transferred and those retained. (The danger of improper comparison between risks again is illustrated!)

(1). Coverage under liability insurance policies is in some ways restricted by specified limitations and exclusions, even though broad policies are available. "Hold harmless" provisions transferring a principal's liability losses to his contractor are written without these limitations and exclusions, and sometimes without any limitations or exclusions at all. Just what is included under this broad, bald transfer of risk? How will the courts read it? Will they take it on its face, or will they be appalled by the attempt on the part of the principal to slough off all responsibility for his own negligence and decide that public policy requires that limitations be placed upon the transfer of risk?[24]

(2). What is the risk that the contractor will be financially unable to pay the losses transferred to him? This question is particularly appropriate for the principal to ask when he is considering whether to transfer his liability risk to an insurance company or to the contractor. Can or will the contractor adequately insure his contracted liability? Does the principal want to run the risk that the contractor may fail to carry adequate and valid coverage in a solvent company? The principal ordinarily will have more control over his own purchases of insurance than over those made by his contractor. While it is true that broader coverage is available under contractual liability insurance policies than under most other kinds of insurance, underwriters dislike to issue unlimited policies of any kind. Consequently, very broad coverage is made both difficult and expensive to buy, which brings up again the risk that the insurance protection may be inadequate or incomplete. Even when the brunt of this risk *has* been shifted to the contractor, the principal's assets still stand a chance of being involved if the contractor is in no position to handle this risk successfully.

And so it goes. While many more examples are possible, the ones given serve to illustrate the point: *The results from risk management alternatives are different, and the costs may or may not be proportional to the differ-*

---

[24] A further question, of course, asks: "If the courts do not impose limitations, is it not likely that the legislatures will?" Similar attempts at sweeping risk transfer in the past have been curbed by statutes; limitations are commonly imposed on the transfer of risk by bailees for hire, common carriers, and landlords, for examples.

ences. Discouragingly, each individual case has to be considered on its own. Encouragingly, while the single best solution may never be found, several reasonably satisfactory solutions are often available. Two main goals should be uppermost in the mind of the risk manager when he chooses among the various risk management devices: (1) the survival of the business and its place in the market despite losses arising from pure risks and (2) a reduction in the frequency and severity of the losses, regardless of who, if anyone, is reimbursing his company for them. The risk manager who achieves these goals is doing a real job of managing risks and is making a significant contribution not only to his business organization but also to the whole economy.

Auxiliary Benefits in Insurance

Loss prevention, settlement of third-party claims, and risk management advice are auxiliary benefits that an insured *may* receive with his insurance. These benefits are called "auxiliary" in insurance because they are not part of the essential nature of insurance; an insurance scheme could be undertaken for loss indemnity only, in which loss prevention services were not offered, claims were left for the insured himself to settle, and no risk management advice was available. Indeed, in coverage other than liability insurance most insureds today receive very little of these auxiliary benefits, and in liability insurance many really receive only claims service. But use of the descriptive word "auxiliary" is not to be taken as automatically deprecating the value of these additional benefits. Loss prevention is central in risk management, however auxiliary it may be in insurance, and the other two benefits mentioned can be of considerable help in achieving the central aims of risk management.

Loss Prevention and Insurance. The extent to which loss prevention services are offered to different insureds under the various insurance covers was discussed in chapter 2. It was noted that insurers' loss prevention activities for individual insureds are most prominent in workmen's compensation, bodily injury liability, steam boiler, and automobile fleet insurance, and they are likely, with some exceptions, to vary directly in proportion with the size of the insured's premium. In making comparisons between insurance and other risk management devices, the role played by loss prevention must not be overlooked.

The biggest emphasis on loss prevention and its most noteworthy results have occurred in the area of work injuries principally because many workmen's compensation insurance premiums reflect individual loss experience through various forms of merit rating.[25] With merit rating, loss prevention reduces not only the indirect costs of work injuries (production dislocations, etc.) but also the direct costs (insurance premiums).

. [25] In merit rating, an individual insured's hazards or losses affect his individual rate. See chap. 17.

Whether the insured's record in loss reduction is reflected fully or partially in his premium depends on the size of the premium and on the rating method used. In weighing insurance against other risk-bearing devices, the proper comparison for the risk manager to make is between *different* risks and loss rates—the cost of the risk and loss rate that would be expected to exist without the purchase of insurance, and the cost of the risk and loss rate expected to exist with the purchase of insurance.[26]

With the purchase of insurance, the risk manager has better assurance that the business will not suffer a crippling loss. If the insurer's loss prevention service means that fewer losses will be suffered also, there can hardly be any debate about which is the best method for achieving the risk management objectives. Thus, workmen's compensation insurance advertisements, aimed at the buying public, feature such "punch lines" as follow:

The wrong-way curves that turned out right! Or how the friendly AM man helped drop accidents to a new low, boost production 100% for an American Mutual Policyholder.

"French fried ear plugs" and "hearing histories" help Lockheed solve the problem of noise. "Wausau Story" by Dr. Roger B. Maas, Hearing Consultant for Employers Mutuals of Wausau.

New ways Liberty Mutual provides Protection in depth to safeguard your people . . . to cut workmen's compensation costs.

Insurance man with an audigage? . . . The Kemper Boiler Engineer is using a device called an audigage . . . without stopping production the Engineer guards against unsafe working pressures. . . .[27]

As always, however, there is another side to the story, as shown in two cases described by insurance consultant Dwight H. Sleeper at an insurance seminar of the American Management Association.[28] In one case, the employer with a bad loss record was a large newspaper publisher. Experience rated, his workmen's compensation rates were high. Partially to break up

---

[26] The discussion applies only, of course, to those situations in which there is a choice. Workmen's compensation laws deny such a choice to small businesses, and some states deny it to all businesses. In the latter instances, full realization on the part of risk managers that some risk management devices other than insurance could be used more advantageously might suggest to these risk managers that it would be worthwhile to try to get the law changed. The authors agree with the legislators, however, that small businesses (as defined in some reasonable and practical way) should not be allowed the choice.

[27] These four advertisements appeared, respectively, in *Newsweek*, Vol. LIV, No. 1 (July 6, 1959), p. 8; *Newsweek*, Vol. LIII, No. 12 (March 23, 1959), p. 24; *Business Week*, n.v. (May 23, 1959), p. 76; and *National Insurance Buyer*, Vol. IV, No. 3 (May, 1957), p. 19.

[28] Mr. Sleeper spoke in the discussion that followed the talk by W. J. Steidle, "Self-Insurance for the Average Company," in *Planning for Complete Insurance Coverage*, American Management Association Insurance Series, No. 55 (New York: The Association, 1944), pp. 3–11; Mr. Sleeper's remarks are on p. 11.

his experience record and get a new start on his rates, this employer dropped all workmen's compensation insurance.[29] Mr. Sleeper reported the results: "The employees were told that they would be paid the indemnities provided by the compensation law—but by the employer, not by some insurance company. . . . The employer remained a self-insurer[30] for one year. During that time the accident record fell to almost nothing." Furthermore, although the employer went back to purchasing insurance, his losses continued low.

In Mr. Sleeper's other case, a large foundry was unable to get satisfactory loss experience even with three good insurers taking turns at the job. Finally this business too dropped its regular workmen's compensation coverage, but it did retain a catastrophe loss cover, and a good safety engineer was hired. Said Mr. Sleeper: "I am not able to say whether it was the safety inspector's work or an improved employer-employee relationship (probably a little of both), but things began to improve rapidly—to such an extent that this firm, which had had a 28 per cent experience debit, has enjoyed an experience credit for the last four years."

Several things are noteworthy in these examples. One is that both employers did go back to the purchase of insurance after getting losses down. The second is that loss prevention is a matter, in the end, of employer-employee relationship. Mr. Sleeper concluded: "I don't want anybody to infer from this that I am advocating self-insurance. I am simply emphasizing the fact that when there were closer employee relationships, and the employees were definitely told that every dime of the compensation would come out of the employer's pocket, the accidents ceased."

This is an interesting phenomenon. Did the employees think to themselves, as they went through their daily routines, "Yesterday, if I stuck my hand in this machine, or fell off that ladder, or stumbled over there on that pile of materials, it cost the insurance company; but today it will cost the boss, and that's bad, so today I'll be more careful"? Or was it management, all up and down the line, which thought, "Last year when the boys got hurt, 'some insurance company' [Mr. Sleeper's choice of the adjective 'some' expresses the idea perfectly!] had to cough up for it; but this year, it's our money—it comes right out of our profits, and it will look bad in the record if it comes from my department"? An insurance buyer, in con-

---

[29] Experience rating is used only when there is consecutive recorded experience on which to base the rate; otherwise the manual rate is used, and this employer wanted to get back to the manual rate—for him, an improvement.

[30] The reader is reminded that just as there are those who say that there is no self-insurance and so call all risk assumption "non-insurance," there are those who describe any non-insurance as "self-insurance." Therefore, when the term "self-insurer" is used here, it may or may not be in accordance with the definition of the term previously presented in this text.

versation with one of the authors, told of a similar experience in a company for which he had previously worked. Experience rating or no, he just seemed unable to convince his top management that on-the-job accidents were really costing them money. So he persuaded them to carry their own risk for a while. When the losses began to come in, and he showed how they could have been avoided, the attention he needed was not long in coming.

In the same seminar, just before the remarks by Mr. Sleeper, William F. Lund, insurance buyer for United States Rubber Company, stated: "I do not believe any insurance company could be so strict as our safety department about eliminating hazards, and I doubt that any insurance company inspector could get the same cooperation—at least so quickly."[31] With doubt on the part of company management, it follows that outsiders will have to doubt it too. No results will be obtained any more effectively or quickly than management wants to obtain them. And if management itself will not implement the insurance inspectors' recommendations as surely or as fast as it will its own, then there can be no contest between the effectiveness of the two.

However, many insurance buyers and the big corporations for whom they work not only buy workmen's compensation insurance but believe that they get important benefit from having both a complete loss prevention organization of their own and the use of the insurer's organization. No universal rule is applicable to these giant businesses. For example, United States Rubber is happy with its results without insurance loss prevention service, whereas Lockheed makes use of such service. As for the less-than-giant operations, it is significant that the two companies on which Mr. Sleeper reported both went back to the purchase of insurance after they had shocked themselves adequately into taking the loss prevention problem seriously. Anyone familiar with compensation insurance operations knows that every major insurer has had hundreds of cases in which loss prevention was not taken seriously until the insurer worked, and worked hard, to put its values across. The "shock treatment" of throwing a company on its own resources to force results should be saved for only the most serious, seemingly hopeless cases that can afford it.

Everything said about loss prevention in workmen's compensation insurance applies also to bodily injury liability insurance of all kinds and to boiler insurance. Beyond these coverages, loss prevention services of insurers become much less common. A few exceptions exist: the Factory Mutuals, the Factory Insurance Association, the Oil Risks Association and some other special "pools" emphasize loss prevention and get important results with it. In other cases, loss prevention information and some aid

---

31 Sleeper, *op. cit.*, p. 11.

are available when asked for, but often no more than can be obtained from such organizations as the National Safety Council, National Fire Protection Association, and other quasi-public bodies.[32]

Some important loss prevention or loss reduction activities arise in the course of claims adjustment; these are discussed in the next section.

. *The Values of Claims Adjustment Services.*   The major objective of most insurance claims adjustment is to produce an amicable agreement between the insured and his insurer, principally by determining a dollar loss figure upon which the two can agree. Achievement of this objective represents no particular gain in favor of insurance, since, when the risk is uninsured, the problem never arises.[33] Still, in some of its aspects claims adjustment does offer important values worth weighing when the question whether to buy insurance is considered.

The ability of the insurer to prevent and reduce losses through its claims adjustment process is one of the important aspects that must be weighed in favor of insurance. The insurer naturally aims at holding losses as low as is practicable. Since the whole of any loss can never be insured, the purchaser of insurance often benefits along with the insurer from the insurer's skill in holding down losses during the adjustment process. Indeed, the insured may benefit more than the insurer. Adjusters know that insureds, unaccustomed to viewing the mess left by a fire and firemen's hoses, tend to assume that losses are total. Yet, if the remains are attacked promptly and properly, much can be saved. If machinery is dug out, disassembled, cleaned, and dried, it often can be put back to work shortly. Since most insureds do not carry business interruption insurance, this may save them more on their interruption losses than the physical damage insurer saves on the property loss. Even when interruption insurance is carried, there is the important danger that longer shutdowns will seriously reduce trade after the business is reopened. Experienced adjusters and salvage companies reduce the hazard of this loss.

Sometimes the insurer takes over the entire remains of an inventory, paying the insured in full for the loss. The insurer then waits for professional salvage efforts to produce such recovery as can be made. Meanwhile, the insured has the money to replace his stock and does not have space or personnel tied up caring for damaged goods. He is able to move right on with the job of getting back into business with new, undamaged goods. Again, his losses are reduced. Similarly, a reason often cited for the purchase of transportation insurance on goods sent by common carrier is that collections from insurers are made more quickly than are collections from carriers. Therefore, even when the loss is one for which the carrier must pay, the shipper can collect his indemnity from his insurance

---

[32] The insurance companies are important supporters of these organizations.

[33] Except perhaps between the uninsured businessman and the tax collector, but the authors have yet to see this problem advanced as a reason for buying insurance.

company, have the money with which to proceed in his business, and let the insurer wait for the payment from the carrier of the goods.

When the claims adjustment is with third parties (liability insurance and workmen's compensation), the insurer's claims adjustment process is a direct service to the insured, one he would have to provide himself or procure elsewhere if he were not insured. The efficacy of third-party claims adjustment obviously has much to do with the size of these losses. Losses may be kept lower by an insurer's full-time organization than by part-time operations of the individual business firm.

With third-party claims, the question of goodwill comes up, especially when the third party is one of the insured's employees or customers. Some managements believe that they can do a better job than the insurer in maintaining goodwill among their employees and customers in claims adjustments. Others think that their goodwill is better protected when arguments over settlement are with "some insurance company" rather than directly with the business itself. There is reason to believe that, again, some advantage usually lies with the insurers, who train and maintain a full-time, specialized claims force, better able to sell the claimants on the settlements offered, as well as better able to put up a fight when one is necessary.

In evaluating the auxiliary benefit of the service of claims adjustment, judgment, even opinion, plays an important role. Much depends on the individual case. But the following guides can be offered:

1. The benefit is auxiliary. If large loss protection is needed, that settles the issue.
2. Few businesses are, or can be, in the position to maintain their own claims adjustment organization. Thus, whatever the benefits of such an organization, they are all with the insurer.
3. This leaves just a few businesses in which there are real alternatives with regard to the benefit. These few must settle the debate individually for themselves.

Advice on Risk Management. Insurance company representatives and brokers can be extremely useful in advising the risk manager, particularly with regard to his purchases of insurance. Unfortunately, the "risk manager" who most needs help—who is also personnel manager, sales manager, office manager, plant manager, and everything else in his business—is the businessman who is least likely to find himself advised by insurance persons who are either genuinely interested in advising (distinguished from selling) or capable of it. Self-insurers can have specialists on their own staffs to help them deal with their problems, and independent advising agencies of many kinds are available for hire. Risk managers for businesses that could, but do not, self-insure frequently report that consultation with competent personnel of insurance companies, agencies, and brokerage firms is useful, even essential. They complain and warn, however, that it often takes some seeking to find competent agency or broker-age personnel. Certainly, the buyer of insurance for a small or moderate-sized business needs all the technical help he can get at any price he can afford to pay. While such help is available outside the insurance business itself, it is usually more expensive. Educational institutions and trade associations can provide some guidance at moderate cost, but beyond these the cheapest and best sources for the needed aid are likely to be insurance organizations. Two obstacles, however, are found in the effectiveness of risk management advice available from insurance companies: (1) the already mentioned problem of finding both willing and able help among agents and brokers; (2) failure on the part of most smaller businesses to appreciate and use such help when they get it. In the long run, the second obstacle is the cause of the first, a fact most discouraging to those who seek to improve the quality of the service offered by agents and brokers.

The businessman must understand and appreciate that proper management of his pure risks is a subject both important and technical, and one on which he should act accordingly. He must know enough about risk management to recognize whether his advisers on the subject are any good. In other words, he must deal with this area of management just as he is expected to deal with any other technical area, whether it be law, income tax obligations, plant or store layout and design, advertising, or anything else. He must know enough about it to know when he needs help and to be able to tell whether he has the kind of help he needs.

The Place of Auxiliary Benefits.   To reiterate, the primary function of insurance is to preserve the business by providing indemnity for losses. Through the insurance process, a definite cost (the premium) is substituted for an uncertain cost (the insured part of the loss). The indemnity function justifies the existence of the insurance business. Most of the time it is also the only justification for the purchase of insurance. There are, however, exceptions to this rule.

The *first* exception appears in those few instances in which the business has a choice between kinds of insurance: self-insurance or commercial insurance. Here auxiliary benefits may be the deciding factor.

The *second* exception is found in those few lines of insurance in which premiums are low enough for the insurance to be justified largely on the usefulness of auxiliary benefits. Plate glass insurance is an example of this exception. The loss of the pane itself is unlikely to be financially crippling. But insurers emphasize, and pride themselves on, the speed of replacement of insured panes. The reduction in the time that a store puts up an unattractive, boarded-up front, added to the indemnity feature, may make purchase of plate glass coverage worthwhile.

The *third* exception arises out of the psychological makeup of the insurance purchaser. Unreimbursed small losses simply may be so annoying to the businessman that reimbursement, even at an uneconomic price, is preferable. If the business owner can afford to indulge his tastes in this way, certainly, as the saying goes, "It's his money." A *related* and common exception is found in those situations in which individual temperament is such that the maintenance of adequate cash reserves for regular, small losses never is accomplished. The same business (or household) that finds it necessary to buy even the smaller capital items on the installment plan, and pay interest and carrying charges for the privilege, probably will find it necessary to pay for insurable losses in an analogous way: regular payments of insurance premiums, including payment of insurance sales and overhead costs, for the privilege of shifting to an insurer the responsibility of maintaining the liquid fund necessary to cover such common losses as damage to small neon signs, small thefts, disappearance of parcels in transit, and various other little losses for which insurance coverage is available.[34]

Surely even these exceptions prove the logic of the general rule!

SUMMARY

Insurance is an arrangement under which losses and risks of different physical units are pooled, and the law of large numbers is applied. Successful operation of the insurance scheme requires the presence of several factors. One is that the pool shall be adequately financed. Although this requirement applies equally to self-insurance and commercial insurance, it is in the former arrangement that violation is more likely to occur. Self-delusion as to large loss potential and as to behavior of the law of large numbers is likely to lead to underfinancing of a self-insurance scheme.

Commercial insurance operations need the presence of three additional factors to get reliability from the law of large numbers: (1) Losses must be sufficiently definite both as to their occurrence and as to their amount for an objective determination of payment due under the insurance contract; (2) losses must be large enough to encourage many people to seek insurance protection, and (3) the cost of the insurance operation must be low enough to encourage people not only to seek the protection but also actually to buy it.

When commercial insurance protection is available for a risk, the decision as to whether it should be used depends upon the availability of alternatives and on the relative costs and benefits of these alternatives. Availability of alternatives is a matter of careful and imaginative investiga-

---

[34] In household situations, the smaller hospitalization policies are excellent examples of this type of coverage in families of moderate or better means. The "medical fees" supplements on these policies go even further toward small loss coverage, so far that their purchase must be explained by the previous exception, distaste for unreimbursed losses; surely anyone who can afford the premiums for these coverages cannot need a long-term installment arrangement to pay for the limited quantity of medical fees covered under these supplements.

tion in each given case. When costs of these alternatives and insurance are compared, hidden costs must not be overlooked, and comparisons involving inconsistent assumptions or unrealistic results must not be made. Comparisons should be drawn between the best likely results from the various alternatives.

The foremost considerations in choosing among alternative risk management devices are (1) preserving the business against large losses and (2) holding down the costs of losses and risk. The order of the two statements is significant. Most important is recognizing how high the losses can run (i.e, thinking in terms of the loss unit concept) and doing something about potential maximum losses—arranging for funds to cover them and trying to reduce them. Other gains and benefits are secondary. Since commercial insurance, when it is available, is commonly the safest and most practical device for protecting against crippling losses, is generally the least expensive way of dealing with large losses, and may have useful auxiliary benefits, it is the normal choice for dealing with large loss possibilities. Its relative desirability generally becomes less, however, as the losses involved become smaller and more frequent.

REVIEW AND DISCUSSION QUESTIONS

1. What are the essential ingredients in a definition of "insurance" (according to the present text)?
2. Some authors define insurance essentially as "a systematic scheme of risk transfer, in which one party, called the 'insurer' agrees, for a fixed or determinable sum, to indemnify the other party, called the 'insured,' for losses incurred under specified conditions." What difference does it make whether this definition or the one stated in the present text is used to characterize "insurance"? Which definition appears the more useful, and why?
3. Under the definition of "insurance" given in this text, what characteristics are necessary to make self-insurance possible? What is the situation if the definition given in question 2 is used for "insurance"?
4. Under what circumstances should the risk manager purchase commercial insurance to offset his risks? Can you state a general rule to which there should be no exceptions? If not, what are the exceptions?
5. What requisites are necessary in the commercial application of the law of large numbers to make a risk commercially insurable? Explain the reasons for each of these requisites.
6. What are some of the common pitfalls that the risk manager must make an effort to avoid in comparing the costs of the various risk management devices relevant to a given risk situation?
7. Develop a set of figures to prove the following proposition: The better buys in insurance protection are those where the average chance to collect is low.
8. Why might the costs of handling liability claims be higher when handled without commercial insurance?
9. What are some of the costs that must be considered when comparing risk assumption with other risk management devices?

10. Show by example the types of mistakes that can be made in cost comparisons among applicable risk management devices arising from (1) comparing different measures of losses, (2) comparing different risks.

11. What should be the main goals in the mind of the risk manager when he chooses among the various risk management devices?

12. Describe some of the auxiliary benefits offered with insurance and show how the value of these benefits can be appraised.

13. What loss prevention or loss reduction activities arise in the course of claims adjustment by insurers? How important are these activities in weighing a decision of whether to purchase insurance for a given risk?

14. What are the obstacles found in the effectiveness of risk management advice available from insurance companies?

15. To what extent should psychological considerations enter into a decision on whether insurance should be purchased? Explain your answer.

PART III

Analyzing Risk

The management of risk requires the ability to identify loss exposures and to measure the loss potential from each of these exposures. Part III of this text includes four chapters relating to these problems of risk analysis: Two chapters are devoted to the identification of loss exposures, with one of them dealing exclusively with the complicated problem of liability exposure. The other two chapters handle the measurement of loss potential. Here the division is between measuring asset losses and measuring *net* income losses.

Chapter 6

IDENTIFYING LOSS EXPOSURES:
GENERAL

Some risk managers (and those who combine the job of risk management with other duties) make use of most of the risk management techniques discussed in Part II. Insurance, however, usually plays the major role in risk management activity. In fact, many risk managers restrict their risk management activity to insurance buying only, but a number of these do not perform even that job effectively. The result is that the insurance coverage of a business is likely to contain a number of unintended gaps that leave important losses uninsured.

The reasons for errors in insurance administration are simple: (1) The job of handling the insurance problems of a business often rests with some financial officer of the company who is untrained in the complexities of the insurance business. (2) This officer frequently shifts his responsibility to an insurance agent or broker who is untrained in the complexities of the business to be insured. The result often is an interesting collection of policies rather than an adequate program of insurance.

The key to the solution of the problem of careful and informed insurance planning is teamwork between the risk manager and the insurance agent or broker. The full acceptance of risk management as a major department of business administration and the recognition by top executives of the need for well-qualified men to operate these departments will go a long way toward reducing, and even eliminating, errors in insurance programing. The full acceptance by insurance companies (and by the regulatory authorities) of the need for higher standards of education and training for insurance agents and brokers also would help to improve the quality of the insurance service many businessmen get from their insurers.[1]

---

[1] Occasionally it is suggested that two developments will lead to improved insurance planning: the emergence of the *professional* insurance buyer and the maturing of the

Building an insurance program for any given business starts with an analysis of the enterprise itself and not with an analysis of insurance policies. The first step in analysis is to determine the loss exposures. The second step is to find out which of these loss exposures are (i.e., should be) insurable. The third step in analysis is to decide which of the insurable exposures should be insured. Only *after* completion of these steps would attention be directed to specific insurance policies, rates, and companies.

As explained in chapter 5, the insurance device may be applied only to static risks and not to all of them. Furthermore, even when the risk is insurable, some other risk-bearing device may be more appropriate. In this and the next three chapters, techniques and methods for use in determining the insurable exposures of a business are developed.

SOURCES OF INFORMATION

When one is buying a suit of clothes, a primary concern is that the suit fit, not only as to size and cut but also as to style and color. Fitting a suit to the customer is no easy task, as one can tell by observing the number of men in suits that do not adequately suit. A good job requires both a well-trained and experienced tailor and an intelligent and alert buyer.

The parallel with insurance buying is obvious. Admittedly the primary step toward the intelligent planning of a unified program of insurance is to study what the buyer needs rather than what the seller has to offer. Learning what the buyer needs is no easy task, as one can tell by observing the number of businesses with insurance programs that do not adequately insure. The job demands that the risk manager be aware of the kinds of information he will need, where he can get them, and how he will use them. Basically, he needs to know anything and everything that will help him answer two questions: (1) What are the possible events that can produce loss? (2) How much can be lost from a single event? An appreciation of the specific detailed information needed for identifying and evaluating loss exposure is an important quality in successful risk managers.

---

insurance agent and broker as a *professional* counselor. The word "professional" is used in this connection to indicate that risk management and insurance marketing can be more than merely trades, occupations, or means of livelihood. The definitions of "professional" and "profession" used by those advocating professional status for these callings follow. A *professional* is one who is skilled in the theoretic or scientific parts of a trade so that he raises his trade to the dignity of a learned profession. A *profession* is a vocation in which a professed knowledge of some department of learning is used in its application to the affairs of others or in the practice of an art founded upon it. Whether risk management and insurance marketing will reach the ranks of the learned professions, such as law and medicine, is subject to debate. Judging from the strong opposition by some companies to effective educational standards in the licensing of insurance agents, there is question as to whether all the insurance industry wants to market its product solely through professionals. The less professional aid available from the suppliers of insurance, the more the buyers need to be professional if they are to perform their jobs effectively.

The Books of Account

The balance sheet and the profit and loss statement and their supporting records provide the risk manager with important sources of information about the loss exposures of his business. In the study of this information, an accountant is a useful partner to the risk manager.

The Balance Sheet. The balance sheet is a statement of what the business owns (assets), what it owes (liabilities), and what is left for its owners (net worth). How is the balance sheet helpful to the risk manager? A systematic study of each of the asset items on a balance sheet helps the risk manager to locate loss exposures.

Among the asset items appearing on most balance sheets are cash, accounts receivable, and inventories. Assume that the balance sheet shows cash in the amount of $61,243. What must the risk manager find out about this cash? He must learn where the cash is kept: How much is in the tills? How much is in the safe? How much is in transit? How much is kept in banks? In addition, he must find out who handles this cash, including who is authorized to write checks. The balance sheet, of course, records only the amount of cash held by the company as of the time the statement is drawn; it does not show what the cash position was four, ten, or twenty-four hours before or what it will be four, ten, or twenty-four hours later. Therefore, it only suggests questions to be asked; it does not provide the answers. The answers are to be found in other records and by asking those who know—policy makers, who know what is supposed to be done, *and* workers, who know what *is* done.

Suppose that accounts receivable amount to $102,030 in the balance sheet. What important loss exposures does this item suggest to the risk manager? There appear to be two: first, losses arising from the insolvency of debtors and, second, the potential losses resulting from the destruction of account records, by fire or some other peril.

For a third example of the use of balance sheets in risk management, assume that the inventory item amounts to $297,326. Several important questions relating to this inventory will interest the risk manager. To what extent does the amount fluctuate during the year? How much was it yesterday? What is it likely to be tomorrow? How does the insurable value of the inventory compare with the accountant's value shown on the statement? Where is the inventory located, and to what extent does it shift among locations? At any given moment, how much is on the premises, in transit, in the warehouse, and in processing? How damageable are the various components of the inventory at each place?

Similar questions must be raised about each of the asset items found in the balance sheet, and each type of asset involves special problems.

The Profit and Loss Statement. The profit and loss statement is the report card for the business. It measures the success of its operations.

Specifically, it is a statement of income and expenses. How is study of the profit and loss statement helpful to the risk manager?

The profits of a business can be impaired through either of two sources: increased expenses or decreased income. Study of profit and loss figures helps the risk manager in locating exposures to expense and income loss potentials. For example, how would business profits be affected if an enforced shutdown resulted from a fire, breakdown of a machine, explosion of a boiler, breakdown of a public utility, or damage to the plant of an outside supplier or of a major customer? How would profits be affected if extra expenses were necessary to maintain operations at the same or another location because of physical damage to buildings or machinery? How would profits be affected by costs for defense and adverse judgments arising out of injuries to the persons or property of others? How would profits be affected by the death or disability of a key employee?

Study of both the balance sheet and the profit and loss statements is also important to the risk manager as an aid in deciding how large an exposure a business can safely leave uninsured.

Inspection of the Premises

The books of account do not provide all the information needed to design the insurance coverage for a business. A thorough inspection of the premises and a careful study of business operations are necessary.

The Fact Finder. A check list or "fact finder" is useful as an aid in studying the premises and operations of a business. The "fact finder" or "exposure meter," as it is sometimes called, is a useful document for directing the attention of the risk manager to information required for identifying loss exposures. The risk manager can tailor his own fact finder to fit his particular operations, or he can adapt one of those put out by insurance companies or insurance publishers. The following outline is typical of the exposure information developed with a fact finder:

I. Real Property
  A. Buildings owned
    1. Nature, use, and location
    2. Value
    3. Rental value of space used
    4. Income from space rented to others
    5. Laws and ordinances for demolition and for replacement standards
  B. Buildings rented from others
    1. Nature, use, and location
    2. Value of improvements and betterments made by tenant
    3. Total rent paid by tenant
    4. Rental income derived from subletting space to others
    5. Value of the lease (is the lease favorable?)
    6. Type of fire clause and hold harmless agreements in the lease
  C. All buildings and other real property (includes A and B above)

1. Alterations and additions in progress or contemplated
2. Boilers and pressure vessels in operation
3. Power machinery in operation (switchboards, motors, engines, generators, etc.)
4. Cold storage vaults and other special provisions for maintaining controlled temperature or humidity
5. Electric or neon signs
6. Plate or ornamental glass
7. Elevators and escalators
8. Possible fire department service charges

II. Personal Property
   A. Stock, including packaging materials (each location)
     1. Peak value and low values (month by month)
     2. Profit in finished goods on premises at any one time (for manufacturers only)
     3. Susceptibility to crime loss
     4. Values dependent on parts difficult to replace
     5. Values susceptible to damage by lack of heat or cold
     6. In-transit exposures (See III-I)
   B. Furniture and fixtures (each location)
     1. Those permanently attached to the building
     2. Unattached furniture, fixtures, machinery, office equipment
     3. Supplies and prepaid expense items
   C. Dies, patterns, and tools
   D. Personal property belonging to others
   E. Personal property in the custody of others
   F. Coins and currency (maximum amounts)
     1. Payroll cash (when)
     2. Other cash
     3. Cash in custody of each bank messenger
     4. Cash in custody of each truck driver, salesman, or collector
     5. Cash kept in safes overnight
   G. Incoming checks (maximum amounts)
     1. On premises
     2. In safes overnight
     3. In custody of each bank messenger
     4. In custody of each truck driver, salesman, or collector
   H. Bank accounts (locations, amounts, uses)
   I. Securities (maximum amounts)
     1. In safes
     2. In custody of each bank messenger
     3. In safe deposit vaults
     4. At other locations (specify)
   J. Especially valuable merchandise or other property (maximum amounts) (e.g., jewelry, furs, precious stones, fine arts, antiques, rare metals, isotopes, radium)
     1. In safes
     2. Elsewhere on premises
     3. In custody of each truck driver or salesman
     4. In safe deposit vault
     5. At other locations or in transit (specify)
   K. Valuable papers, documents, records
     1. Kind

     2. Where kept

     3. Value

  L. Accounts receivable

     1. Maximum and minimum values

     2. Where account records are kept

  M. Automobiles, airplanes, boats, teams, etc. (owned or used)

     1. Ownership

       a) Owned

       b) Non-owned

     2. Value and extent of concentration in one place at one time

III. Operations

  A. Central operation: principal products or services sold

     1. Nature of all products or services regularly sold

     2. Sources of materials and supplies used

     3. Flow of goods through plant, or steps or processes in provision of services: any bottlenecks?

     4. Extent, nature, and location of goods sold on installment or similar credit arrangements

     5. Installation, demonstration, or servicing away from premises

  B. Service for employees

     1. Operation of a plant hospital, infirmary, or first-aid station

     2. Operation of a restaurant for employees

     3. Sponsorship of employee athletic teams

  C. Operation of a beauty parlor or other service in which a malpractice hazard exists

  D. Operation of a restaurant for the general public

  E. Work let out under contract

  F. Advertising signs, vending machines, booths, etc., owned or operated away from the premises

  G. Sponsorship of outside athletic team

  H. Liability assumed under contract

     1. Sidetrack agreements

     2. Leases

     3. Hold harmless agreements with sales outlets

     4. Purchase orders

     5. Elevator or escalator maintenance agreements

     6. Easements

     7. Service agreements (for or by the corporation)

     8. Other contracts

  I. Shipments (values shipped annually and the maximum value of any one shipment, both incoming and outgoing)

     1. Own trucks

     2. Truckmen

     3. Rail

     4. Railway express

     5. Air

     6. Parcel post prepaid and C.O.D.

     7. Registered mail

     8. Inland or coastal water

     9. Foreign

    10. Other

  J. Movements of money and cash

     1. Physical movement

      2. Audits and other checkup procedures

      3. Conceptual movement (accounting cash flows, cash budget)

  K. "Time element" exposures

      1. Payroll: officers and other key persons; "ordinary" payroll[2]

      2. Net sale value of production or total net sales

      3. Cost of raw materials or merchandise

      4. Cost of heat, light, and power

      5. Trend of profits for current year; estimate for next year

      6. Maximum time required to replace facilities subject to damage

      7. Percentage of earnings that would be affected by a business interruption loss at the plant of a customer or supplier

      8. The availability and probable cost of substitute facilities to reduce loss of earnings in case of damage to present facilities

      9. If plants are interdependent, the percentage of earnings affected by a stoppage at each such plant or location, assuming damage at only one location

    10. Extent to which operations are dependent on outside sources of heat, light, or power

  L. Foreign sales and foreign operations

IV. Personnel

  A. Home-state employees

      1. Duties

      2. Use of automobiles

      3. Estimated annual payroll

  B. Employees in other states

      1. Residence state and states traveled

      2. Duties

      3. Use of automobiles

      4. Estimated annual payroll

  C. Employees required to board vessels

  D. Employees required to use or travel in aircraft

  E. Classification of employees according to duties

  F. Key men (men whose loss might seriously affect business profits)

The foregoing outline of exposure information is presented in summary form only. Each of the items may be subject to further investigation. For example, the following information on buildings owned and rented will be needed for insurance rating purposes: area of building; frontage of the property; construction with reference to floors, outside walls, roof, and the number of stories; and the nature and type of loss prevention devices installed, such as automatic sprinkler systems and burglary alarms. For elevators, it is necessary to record their location, type, use, rise, and whether they contain approved interlocks and car gate contacts.

In completing the fact finder, the risk manager should supplement his own observations by interviews with department heads and operating personnel to uncover any exposures that might develop out of special

---

[2] This is a phrase from insurance contracts and refers to that portion of payroll not containing any key or essential individuals: "ordinary" production workers, clerks, housekeeping personnel.

problems associated with the various departments. For example, with operating executives he should discuss production techniques; with research personnel, product development; with technical servicemen, products liability; with the engineers, new construction plans; and with the legal staff, various sales, purchasing, and other contracts. In summary, he must stop, look, and listen so that unusual exposures do not escape him. Trained engineers usually are welcomed companions (and often essential ones!) in any risk inspection tour. Two heads are better than one, especially when the one lacks the necessary scientific engineering knowledge.

The inspection function must not be limited to tangible property; it should also include a study of leases, mortgages, sales agreements, patent licenses, warranties on products, and all other contracts. Here an attorney is the welcomed companion. Some of the necessity for studying contracts has already been pointed out; more will become apparent as the text progresses.

The Organization Chart.   Consideration of the organization chart of the business can help systematize the study of exposures. For organizational purposes business activity may be classified into products, processes, territories, types of consumers, or management function.

For example, a breakfast food company might have a corn cereal department and a wheat cereal department, with a production manager in charge of each one. These departments can be organized on a process basis, with superintendents in charge of each of the following departments: raw materials storage, mixing and cooking, milling, tasting, cartons and containers, packaging, and inspection and testing.

A number of centralized functional departments will exist that serve all product departments. Typical functional departments are sales, production, treasurer, personnel, controller, and research. Each of these departments usually is organized on a functional basis itself. For example, the treasurer's department might include credits and collections, cashier's office, stockholders relations, investments, and insurance. A functional department also may be organized on both a customer and a territorial basis. For example, the sales department might be divided into a bulk sales and a package sales department, and into an eastern division, central division, western division, and foreign division, with a supervisor in charge of each division.

How can the organization chart of the company help the risk manager? The chart can be used advantageously in two ways:

(1) A review of the chart may reveal operations that have been overlooked in the study of the books of account and in the inspection of the facilities. For example, a study of the organization chart of the sales departments might show someone in charge of Mexican sales. These sales are the only foreign sales of the company and on the records studied by the risk manager they appear to have been lumped into the sales figures

for the southwest territory. Without a review of the organization chart, the risk manager might have overlooked this foreign exposure. The value of organization charts to the risk manager obviously depends upon the detail in which the charts are drawn. If they show the duties and responsibilities of each employee, then, of course, they can be of immeasurable value.

(2) The job of identifying loss exposures is never completed. Risk analysis is a continuous function. New exposures develop. Old ones disappear. The insurance buyer can be aided materially in his task of "keeping up" with exposures if he can encourage the operating personnel to funnel into his office all changes in products, processes, procedures, sales outlets, advertising media, machinery, size of plant, and other business activities that can affect loss exposures. The company organization chart can pinpoint for the insurance manager the personnel to whom he should look for reports on changes involving pure risk exposures.

For example, suppose the sales department negotiates a contract to provide one industrial customer with finished products amounting to 20 per cent of the total output and 25 per cent of the profit of the company. This new sales contract creates for the risk manager a new hazard to be considered, since loss of or damage to this customer's plant could cause a serious loss of profits to the risk manager's own company.[3] The sales manager should be cultivated to the point where he automatically reports this transaction to the risk manager so that necessary steps can be taken to adjust the insurance coverage. The advertising department decides to skywrite ads over the fairgrounds. The advertising manager should be trained to report this decision to the risk manager automatically so that he can arrange to cover the new exposure. The public relations director in New Orleans charters a cruise ship to entertain university students who are visiting the company as a part of a field trip. This activity needs to be reported to the risk manager so that he can be sure that he has adequate insurance coverage for the exposure.

The foregoing discussion of the nature and sources of the information needed for exposure analysis has been described in general terms and is only introductory in nature. How this information is used in specific risk management situations will be demonstrated as the discussion progresses.

THE LOSS UNIT CONCEPT

It should be re-emphasized at this point that the first criterion for the risk manager in analyzing loss exposures for insurance purposes is loss severity or the amount of the *loss potential* and not loss frequency or the *chance of loss*. That loss possibilities rather than loss probabilities are the

---

[3] And if the "special" customer also had his "special" customer, loss or damage to the facilities of this latter customer could cause loss to the risk manager's company, too.

salient considerations in selecting a risk-bearing device has already been established. The question is, if the loss does occur, could it be large or is its maximum potential amount small? Of course, what is a "large" loss or a "small" loss is a relative matter. To many college students a loss of $100 might loom large, whereas a large university could take a loss in excess of $10,000 without hardship. The important measure is the relationship of the possible loss to the free assets that the business has to meet them; the absolute amount is itself of little consequence. But, unless the maximum loss possibility from a single event has been determined, the risk manager cannot tell whether the exposure is capable of producing losses that can seriously impair the free assets of the firm.

Definition of the Loss Unit

The term "loss unit" means the aggregate of all the losses that can result from a single event. Many perils can cause losses of catastrophic proportions. For example, if a steam boiler on the premises of a department store explodes, the loss can be larger than the untrained observer would ever expect. Consideration of the number of different losses that can arise out of this single event is necessary to the estimation of its maximum loss potential. Maximum dollar amounts must be assigned to each of the following losses: damage to the boiler, damage to the store building, direct damage to the inventory and other personal property, consequential damage caused by spoilage of property from lack of power, loss of profits resulting from the interruption of business until repairs are made, workmen's compensation payments to injured employees, judgments at law for injuries to customers and other third parties, judgments at law for damages to property of others, defense and court costs relating to liability suits, and loss of the services of key men injured or killed in the explosion.

The total of the maximum amounts estimated for each of the foregoing, separably identifiable losses is not the amount of the most *probable* loss resulting from a steam boiler explosion but an estimate of the highest *possible* loss. Actual losses sustained are likely to be far less. However, to the stockholders of the department store that has just suffered the maximum possible loss, the reassurance by the risk manager (i.e., *former* risk manager) that this loss was really an exception is empty consolation. The stockholders would be more delighted to hear that the risk manager had prepared the business for such a catastrophe. The explosion of the steam boiler is itself an exception to the usual experience of the store, and so must be any event insured against,[4] so the insurance manager who ignores the exception will have no insurance to manage.

---

[4] One of the essentials of an insurable risk is that the chance of loss must be small enough that the cost of insurance is economically feasible. If loss were not the exception, the cost of insurance would be excessive in relation to the amount for which the insurance is written. A 50 per cent chance of loss would require a premium far in excess of 50 per cent of the value to be insured, since the cost of writing and administering an insurance contract approaches the amount paid out in losses.

The maximum loss potential in most cases is, of course, only an estimate of the largest possible loss. There is room for error. For one example, the values of judgments at law for injuries to customers or other third parties are difficult to estimate because two major uncertainties are present: How many can be injured, and how high can the judgments go? These questions cannot be answered definitely; at best, they are subject only to "scientific" guesses.

Fallacy in the Application of the Large Loss Principle

A common fallacy in the application of the large loss principle to risk management (especially to insurance buying) is as follows:

1. The business can safely stand a loss of X dollars.
2. Each of the following kinds of losses cannot go over X dollars.
3. Therefore the business can safely assume the risk of these losses.

The fallacy lies, of course, in assuming that no more than one of the less-than-X-dollar losses can occur in a given period. The error is usually further compounded because consideration is given only to *insurable* losses. The question asked is not "What are my risks?" but "Which insurance policies should I buy?" So the list of possible policies is examined: Tenant's improvements and betterments? Loss potential not large enough. Neon signs? Small loss. Vehicular physical damage? Books and records? Truck cargoes? Same answers. But one afternoon a windstorm hits, and the improvements and betterments *and* the neon signs *and* three vehicles *and* their cargoes *and* all the books and records are scattered over the countryside. All this in addition, of course, to the damage and injury suffered by the "large loss" exposures, which have been insured: the inventory, the furniture and fixtures, the employees, and the boss himself. Now how are company finances?

Even if *all* the items just mentioned were insured, the following losses or costs would not be covered in full.

1. The premises must be cleaned and the damage evaluated. With regard to cleaning the premises, "Debris Removal" clauses provide that "this insurance covers expenses incurred in the removal of all debris *of the property insured hereunder . . .*" (Italics added.) "The property insured hereunder" seldom includes trees and does not include the property of others blown onto the premises. It has been noted in an earlier chapter that the costs of ascertaining the amount of the damage are borne by the insured.

2. If the business owns accounts receivable and valuable papers insurance (ownership of the first of these is not common, ownership of the second is rare), there can still be uninsured loss to accounts under the loss conditions described. Accounts may become valueless because the debtors were wiped out financially by this same windstorm. (Credit insurance would cover this loss, but this coverage is not available for retail accounts.)

3. Most businesses do not carry business interruption insurance, so suffer the profit loss themselves. However, this loss is insurable and represents a large loss potential.

4. The usual forms of insurance for business deduct depreciation before making payments for damage to property. But replacements ordinarily are new property, often of a more advanced design. The difference between the insurance payment for the depreciated property and the cash outlay required for newer, more complicated replacements can represent a severe drain on cash, especially when the business is shut down. When credit is available to finance the additional cost of replacement, the cost of this credit is an uninsured expense.

5. Even if the business carries business interruption insurance (and other relevant available coverage on profits), losses of profits occurring following the lapse of the time period necessary to repair or replace the premises, using "due diligence and dispatch," are seldom covered. In the windstorm loss described there are several reasons why there might be loss of profits after the premises are repaired. Customers living in the area hit by the storm may remain short of funds for some time. Interruption of the flow of traffic from rural areas into town may continue beyond the time required to repair the buildings in town. (Bridges may be out, whole sections of road washed or ripped away.) The disability of the owner may continue to impair the efficiency of the business. (Even though he carries disability insurance, it is sure to be inadequate in amount.) Some parts of inventory may be impossible to replace fully until next season.

Even worse than the windstorm situation just described, losses from dynamic and from static risks may coincide. A long strike at a major industrial plant depletes cash in the tills of its suppliers, of retailers of all kinds in the area, of landlords, of local taxing bodies, and so on. Suppose one of the affected businesses suffers a static loss at the same time. Although the loss might not have been crippling in a "normal" period, now what? Even bank credit may not be available to help out. Local banks are also affected by the decline in cash flow in the area, and they may be strained to help those businesses still in operation. A small local firm will have difficulty in raising funds from an out-of-town source because the firm is unknown away from home. Its general credit rating will be impaired because immediate prospects for profits are dimmed by the continuation of the strike. Lenders are likely to figure that, under such pressure, only the fittest businesses can survive, and a shut-down business is not apt to be one of the fittest.

The examples illustrate the necessity of the "loss unit" concept. For survival, the risk manager must consider all possible simultaneous losses as a unit. To repeat: When the business owner in the windstorm illustration, for example, asked, "Can I stand this loss?" he should not have asked, "Can I stand the loss of my inventory?" or "Can I stand the loss of my inventory *and* my furniture and fixtures?" The proper question for him to have asked was, "Can I stand the loss that may result from damage to my inventory, my furniture and fixtures, my landlord's building, and everything else that could go at the same time?" Note carefully that the unit that must be considered includes, not just one, two, or three different categories of property at a time, but all the categories that could be involved at a single time. And the loss unit consists of more than merely the direct loss from physical damage to these properties; it contains all the other ways in which loss can be suffered from the same basic cause, including loss of income and the creation of additional expenses.

The Catastrophe Area

The catastrophe area is the range of territory over which property may be damaged or persons injured from a single event. A fire in a downtown building, for example, may lead to destruction of an entire city block. An earthquake may damage property over a wide area of the city. And practically an entire city can be destroyed by a fire in a hold of a ship, as was the case in the Texas City disaster.

Indeed, the Texas City disaster provides a significant illustration of the potential size of the catastrophe area. On April 16, 1947, a fire broke out among the 100-pound bags of ammonium nitrate fertilizer in the No. 4 hold of the 7,000-ton freighter, the "S.S. Grandcamp." Located on the waterfront about 700 feet away was a big Monsanto Chemical Company plant. Fire fighters on the boat were unsuccessful in extinguishing the blaze. Concerned over the possibility of an explosion, they decided to tow the ship into Galveston Bay. But the decision came too late. What happened is aptly described as follows by John Bainbridge in his *Biography of an Idea*:[5]

At twelve minutes after nine the *Grandcamp* blew up in a thundering roar and vanished completely. Three-hundred-pound chunks of ship's steel were blown hundreds of feet into the air.[6] A wall of oil-covered water deluged the docks. Bodies of the people who had been standing there were strewn for half a block. Then began a rapid series of deafening explosions. The Monsanto plant and most of the rest of the waterfront blew up. Refineries, gasoline, and oil tanks shot up like rockets. In the business section of the city, a mile away, the force of the blaze wreaked crazy havoc. Rows of houses were flattened; people were blown out of second-story windows; the gas, light, and water systems were knocked out. Roofs and walls of schools, theaters, and commercial buildings were blown out or puffed in. Out of the rubble of the Texas Terminal Railway Building emerged a bedraggled man carrying ten million dollars worth of insurance policies tied up in a bed sheet. Meanwhile, down at the docks, an inferno raged. The waterfront, the police said, had become "pluperfect hell." In the Monsanto plant,

---

[5] (Garden City, New York: Doubleday & Co., Inc., 1952), p. 337.

[6] Two light planes flying overhead were struck and plunged into the bay. Two miles from the pier a flying razor of steel plate slashed through a coupé and decapitated a couple in it.

buildings sagged slowly down on eight hundred workers. Trucks loaded with the dead and the dying began rumbling through the streets. . . .

Though heat from the unquenchable fires along the waterfront was blistering, firemen and squads of rescue workers wearing protective clothing and gas masks had moved into the area. They were obliterated when, at one eleven on the morning of the seventeenth, the Grandcamp's sister ship, the *High Flyer*, which had caught fire, exploded. Blown to bits, the ship, as one witness said, "mushroomed like the Bikini bomb." The explosion, which was recorded on a seismograph in Denver, rocked and raked Texas City again. Additional scores of people were killed and injured. Scarcely a single structure was left that was not ruined or badly damaged.

After three days of fire, the box score finally read: 468 dead, 100 missing, 3,500 seriously injured, and close to $100 million in property losses. No estimates of the loss of income from business interruption are available.

In considering the loss unit, the catastrophe area must be recognized. To overlook it could prove catastrophic.

LOSSES ASSOCIATED WITH A CATASTROPHE AREA

Within a catastrophe area, losses can be of three basic types: losses of property values, losses of income, and losses owing to additional expenses. As is clearly illustrated by the Texas City disaster, all three of these types of losses can result simultaneously from a given peril.

Losses of Property Values

A peril can cause either *direct* or *indirect* loss or damage to property. Measuring the maximum property losses from a single event, therefore, requires that careful attention be given to both types of property losses.

Direct Property Losses. Direct property losses are differentiated from indirect property losses principally by how the loss is caused. If the loss cause is proximate or immediate, the loss is direct. If the loss cause is remote or consequential, the loss is indirect. As the discussion progresses, the distinction between the two will become sufficiently apparent.

Direct property losses are of two types: *on premises* and *extended*. When the peril that causes the loss is activated on the same premises where the damaged or destroyed property is located, the loss is an on-premises direct property loss. If the peril that causes the loss is activated away from the premises where the damaged or destroyed property is located, the loss is an extended direct property loss.

For example, assume that a manufacturing concern has its own central power plant to generate electricity for its factory and office buildings. A fire breaks out in the power plant. Damage suffered in the power plant itself is an on-premises direct loss. Assume further that the fire in the plant causes a short circuit in the electrical wiring, with the following results:

The speed of one of the electrically powered machines used in a factory building increases so much that a fan belt is broken. The free turning fly-wheel flies off its moorings and does extensive damage to the machine, other personal property, and the building. The resulting damage is a direct loss by fire even though the damaged property was never in the range of the fire. This type of loss or damage is an example of an extended direct loss.[7] Other examples are damage caused by smoke, falling debris, and water or chemicals used to extinguish a fire—all when the fire itself is on other premises.

Indirect Property Losses. In addition to on-premises and extended direct damage losses, property may also be exposed to indirect losses. The two classes of indirect property losses commonly recognized in property insurance are (1) damage caused by a change in temperature or other en-vironmental condition and (2) damage to an integral part of a set. In the latter case, the damage to one part causes a reduction in the value of the remaining, undamaged part or parts. These indirect property losses are commonly referred to in insurance circles as consequential property losses and are part of a more general class of consequential losses. (The other members of the class are non-property losses: loss of income, loss of rents, etc.)

Suppose that lightning strikes a building containing a student cafeteria and peels off a small section of the roof. Rain enters through the exposed roof and reaches the electric wires, causing a short circuit. This disables the refrigerating equipment so that large quantities of food are spoiled be-yond use even in a student cafeteria. Damage to the roof is direct property loss by lightning, whereas damage to the food by spoilage is an indirect or consequential property damage loss caused by temperature change.[8]

---

[7] Interesting questions concerning extended losses arise when the question of cover-age under an insurance policy is involved. Here knowledge of just what peril caused the loss can be of extreme importance. In disputed cases the courts apply the *doctrine of proximate cause*, summarized as follows: "The question is not what cause was nearest in time or place to the catastrophe. The proximate cause is the efficient cause, the one that necessarily sets the other causes in operation. The causes that are merely incidental or instruments of a superior or controlling agency are not the proximate causes, and the responsible ones, though they may be nearer in time to the results. It is only when the causes are independent of each other that the nearest is, of course, to be charged with the disaster."

One court, in commenting on the doctrine of proximate cause made this realistic observation: "There is nothing absolute in the legal estimate of causation. Proximity and remoteness are relative and changing concepts. It may be said that these are vague tests, but so are most distinctions of degree. On the one hand, you have distances so great that as a matter of law the cause becomes remote; on the other hand, spaces so short that as a matter of law the cause is proximate. Between these extremes there is a borderland where juries must solve the doubt."

[8] If, in the case described above, there were direct damage insurance but not conse-quential property loss coverage, the insured might insist that the loss was a direct dam-age loss with lightning as the proximate cause, not merely an indirect or consequential loss caused by temperature change. If the insurance adjuster disagreed with this position

Businesses exposed to consequential losses arising out of temperature changes include cold storage plants, breweries, packing plants, greenhouses, creameries, bakeries, and manufacturers of precision parts.

A second type of consequential property loss results from damage or destruction of one part of a matched pair or set. The exposure is found principally in the garment trade, where separate parts of a suit are often handled at different locations. Usually, a manufacturer of men's suits cuts his cloth but contracts out to other garment firms the task of finishing the cut material into coats and pants. One garment contractor might get the coats and another the pants. Assume that a fire destroys the trousers on the contractor's premises and the identical cloth is no longer available to the manufacturer for replacement. The value of the coats will drop because there are no matching pants. The loss of the trousers is a direct loss, whereas the loss in value of the pantsless coats is an indirect or consequential loss. The manufacturer has lost his pants both literally and figuratively.

Disability or Death of Business Owners. The total disability or death of a business owner can cause a type of consequential loss often ignored by risk managers. These loss exposures are found principally in small businesses.

By definition, total disability of an owner will render him incapable of active participation in the business. If he is the driving force behind the business, his absence from the scene will have a depressing effect on the value of that business. The business or its assets may have to be sold to provide an income for the business owner and his family. When a business owner dies, his death can cause a forced sale of the business or its assets to offset estate taxes and other costs of dying. This is in addition to the necessity for arranging an income for dependent survivors.

When a going business must be disposed of in a forced sale, it may be necessary to do so at a sacrifice price. If no interested buyers are immediately available to purchase the business itself, the only way out may be to

---

and the case went into court, the court might well uphold the position of the insured. After all, lightning did cause a direct loss to the building, and the ultimate damage to the food did follow as the final occurrence in a direct chain of cause-and-effect events. How the adjuster would act and how the court would hold, however, are by no means clear. Most policies reduce the problem area by including a "consequential loss clause," which makes a specific statement as to whether the "change of temperature" and closely related perils are or are not covered. One version reads, ". . . this policy is . . . extended to cover also consequential loss . . . to stocks or merchandise covered hereunder, caused by changes in temperature or humidity resulting from damage by the perils insured against to equipment used for refrigerating, cooling, humidifying, air conditioning, heating, generating or converting power, including connections and supply or transmission lines and pipes, only when situated on the described premises." That such a clause does not settle all questions can be seen, however, by considering what was damaged by *lightning* (the peril insured against) in the example given and comparing that with the wording of the clause.

liquidate the concern and dispose of its assets. The liquidation value of a business rarely is equal to its going-concern value. Risk managers faced with the possibility of this type of consequential property loss will do well to consider it in their risk management plans.

Property Losses: A Summary.   Property losses associated with a catastrophe area are summarized in the following illustration. A fire destroys the plant of a government contractor who is working on the pants for a suit manufacturer. The walls of the building tumble, destroying power lines and severely damaging a neighboring drugstore building. The managing proprietor of the pharmacy is killed. The property losses can be outlined as follows:

A. Direct loss or damage
  1. On-premises
     a) Building
     b) Contents, including the pants of the suit manufacturer
  2. Extended
     a) Damage to the neighboring building by the falling walls
     b) Damage to the power lines and equipment by the falling walls
B. Indirect or consequential loss
  1. Loss resulting from temperature changes (food stored in a freezer at a cafeteria located some distance away spoiled because the refrigeration equipment was shut off by the power interruption)
  2. Loss resulting from destruction of one part of a matched pair or set (loss in value of the coats belonging to the suit manufacturer who has lost his pants)
  3. Loss of "going-concern value" resulting from the forced sale or liquidation of the business of the dead druggist

Net Income Losses

Although accountants will argue *ad infinitum* the question of how to allocate the net income of a business over specific periods, they invariably will agree that the net earnings of a business represent the difference between revenues and expenses.[9]

Thus either a decrease in gross revenues or an increase in total expenses might bring about a reduction in net earnings. In some situations the two may overlap, as, for example, when management incurs extra expenses in an effort to check declines in gross income. In other situations a decline in gross receipts is accompanied by a decline in total costs, leaving a correspondingly smaller decrease in net earnings.

The risk manager must be aware of contingencies that can cause revenues to be less or expenses to be more than expected. The contingencies of the market place, of course, are outside the scope of the risk manager's responsibility, but he must be aware of them. Risk managers are charged

---

[9] The term "expenses" used here is broadly defined as including all costs and taxes.

only with pure risk, while control of speculative risk is left to other management specialists.

When property is damaged or destroyed by one of the many perils to which it is exposed, the loss generally transcends that of the asset values involved. Unless that property can be replaced immediately, loss of income or extra expenses will follow. Losses of key personnel by disability or death also can cause income losses. A final source of net income loss can result from extra expenses associated with an accident or occurrence from which liability claims or suits arise.

Loss of Profits. Income earned but not yet realized may be lost. For example, losses arising from the fire that destroyed the afore-mentioned garment manufacturer's plant included damage to three types of property: finished products, goods-in-process, and raw materials. The amount of *direct property loss* to finished products and to goods-in-process is measured by the cost of raw materials plus the incurred cost of manufacture minus any salvage value. The amount of the *direct property loss* to raw materials is the cost of replacing these materials minus salvage value, if any. Damage to finished products, however, causes the garment manufacturer more than the direct property loss. He loses the anticipated profit from their sale (manufacturer's selling price minus the sum of the manufacturing and selling expenses). The expected profit from his past effort went up in smoke along with the finished goods.

Business Interruption. Business concerns must produce goods or render services in order to make sales and realize profits. A business earns its income by carrying on its day-to-day activity, whether this be manufacturing, merchandising, or servicing. Property losses, however, can interfere with the continuing operation of the business. Because some assets are quickly replaceable, their destruction will cause little or no discontinuity of the business. For example, if money or credit is available, the above-mentioned damaged food in the cafeteria freezer usually can be replaced in time to prevent an interruption of business. Because other assets cannot be promptly restored, their destruction may cause suspension of the business during the period of restoration. For example, the garment manufacturer with the fire-razed plant will lose business until his workshop can be rebuilt and his clientele reinstated. Factories are not erected overnight, and customers do not always oblige by returning to their old purchase schedules as soon as the "reopened for business" sign appears.

Business interruption losses are as real as physical damage losses, despite Izaak Walton's philosophy that "no man can lose what he never had." As will become clear in later chapters, the business interruption loss can be larger than the property damage loss that forced the shutdown. Risk managers must give careful consideration to this type of loss. The importance of planning is vividly illustrated as follows.

Consider the hypothetical case of a medium-sized factory that was swept by a damaging fire. The factory employed 10 officers, 60 clerical and sales workers, and 400 production and maintenance workers. The day after the fire, the board of directors met in an emergency session. Preliminary estimates showed that at least 105 working days would be required to restore the building, replace and repair the machinery, and replace the raw inventory material. Another 15 days would be needed to get the work in process and the finished goods inventory up to the previous levels.

The board went over each group of employees carefully and then decided to furlough without pay 350 of the production workers and 30 of the office staff. These workers would be brought back as they were required—if they were still available for employment.

Temporary quarters were hastily rented and office equipment was begged, borrowed, and bought.

The purchasing department was directed to phone suppliers and cancel or delay incoming orders. This department was asked to prepare a schedule of dates for receiving replacement supplies and inventory.

The engineering department was directed to submit a list of the necessary equipment, along with approximate costs and suggested improvements in layout and methods.

The sales manager was instructed to stop his staff from accepting orders but to keep making calls on customers so that business would be available when the firm was again ready to deliver its product.

The credit department had to make sure that the present accounts did not let their obligations slide because of the fire. The credit records had to be laboriously restored.

The personnel department was requested to keep in close touch with the furloughed employees so that a working force would be ready when needed.

The principal officers had to reassure creditors, money lenders, and important customers that this was a storm that could be weathered. The officers contacted principal suppliers to put pressure on them to cooperate in the rescheduling of orders.

The accounting department reported that sales would completely stop for 130 working days, while payments on bonded indebtedness, bank loans, payments due suppliers and other creditors, insurance, and contributions to a pension plan and salaries for the employees being retained would have to be met at approximately the present levels. It was reported that rental expense, office expense, printing, telephone, travel expense, and advertising costs would probably increase.

The risk manager of this concern presented to the board the figures that he had developed in a recent study. His report included estimates on the daily cost of maintaining the closed plant, the probable daily loss of revenue, the extra expenses that would be involved in getting the business back into operation in a reasonable time, an estimate of the time necessary to rebuild or replace the various component parts of the real property and the time necessary to replace the machinery and equipment, an estimate of the cost of modernizing and improving the plant and equipment, an estimate of the loss of profits from finished goods and work in process that was destroyed, and an estimate as to the effect of the loss of the plant on customer relations.

Because this firm was aware of the loss possibilities it faced, management had wisely taken the proper steps to see that funds would be available to use in such an emergency situation. This is a success story—the risk manager had made management aware of the amount of loss potential in such a situation, and management had made provisions to fund the loss contingency. By being forewarned, it had been able to become forearmed. When the loss occurred, the business suffered only to the extent that the risk manager had underestimated the loss potential and to the extent that management chose to discount the risk manager's recommendations.

Damage at Other Locations.　In the determination of net income losses, attention must be given to income and expense losses arising from property damage not only at the same location but also at different locations. Damage to property at one location can cause income losses at another location.

Contract of Supply.　Assume that a manufacturer has negotiated a contract for materials at a price lower than the prevailing market price. If the supplier is unable to deliver under the contract because of a fire on his premises, the manufacturer will incur a loss to the extent of the additional amount he will have to pay in the open market for the materials. Sometimes competitive sources of supply are so far away that savings in transportation costs alone make purchases from the local supplier economical. If the local supplier is unable to deliver because of a fire loss, the manufacturer has to pay the higher price, which includes transportation. These indirect losses, called *contract of supply* losses, effect a decrease in net income by increasing expenses.

Contingent Business Interruption.　In other situations damage to property at one location may cause loss at another by decreasing gross income rather than by increasing expenses. For example, suppose that the Wemakem Manufacturing Company has contracted to sell its entire output of special precision instruments to the Weusem Manufacturing Company. Weusem has no other source of supply for these parts. If the Wemakem plant or its stock of finished goods awaiting shipment is destroyed by fire, the Weusem plant may have to discontinue operations until new parts are manufactured for its use. Or, if the Weusem Manufacturing Company is forced into a temporary shutdown by a disabling fire, the Wemakem Company may have to discontinue operations until the Weusem plant is restored or until a new customer can be found. These indirect losses, called contingent business interruption losses, can also result from power interruption when a utility plant or transmission lines are damaged by fire, windstorm, or other peril.

In a vertically integrated business, where the operation of each plant is dependent upon the operations of the others, a direct damage loss at one of the locations can cause interruption losses at some or all of the others. The loss unit here resulting from a fire at one location can easily be of catastrophic proportions.

Expenses Associated with Property Damage.   Profits on finished goods, direct and contingent business interruption, and contracts of supply are not the only sources of potential *net* income losses arising from physical damage to property. After a fire, the businessman will have the expenses of clearing the premises of debris and putting the salvaged remains in order.

If the damaged building was an old one, still other outlays may have to be made. If the building did not conform to the modern building or zoning laws, and the damage has exceeded a given per cent (usually 50 per cent) of value, the laws in most jurisdictions will not allow the structure to be repaired. Instead, the building will have to be torn down.[10] A new one will have to be constructed in accordance with the building or zoning requirements. An additional loss associated with the fire damage, therefore, will be the amount by which the cost of tearing down the undamaged part of the building exceeds its salvage value, plus the amount by which the cost of constructing the new building exceeds that of repairing the old one. If the new building has greater utility, and this is reflected in operating costs, an adjustment downward in these loss figures will be necessary to reflect this gain in efficiency.

Losses Arising from Rental Situations.   Several sources of potential *net* income loss are associated with damage to rental property: some for the landlord, others for the tenant.

The Pill Building is a medical arts building owned by a private corporation that maintains its offices in the building. The building houses a number of private physicians and dentists, who occupy their own separate suites. The ground-floor space is rented to a pharmacy.

The corporate landlord has executed two types of leases among its tenants. Under one, the obligation of the tenant to pay rent is suspended during any period in which the building is untenantable. Under the other, the obligation of the tenant to pay rent continues even though the building has been temporarily rendered untenantable by fire or by some other peril. The older leases are of the first type. Those drawn after the building was remodeled and equipped especially for the practice of medicine are of the second type.

The terms of the old leases are unusually attractive to the few tenants

---

[10] In a few jurisdictions, repairs are allowed, but strict and costly standards are enforced.

still blessed with them. The monthly rent was established years ago, when dollars were more valuable; as a result, fewer of them were expected in exchange for the use of property. Consequently, the rent that was fixed under these contracts is well below the rental value of the space in the current market. These older leases, however, have a clause in the rental agreement giving the lessor corporation the right to cancel the lease if the premises become wholly untenantable because of fire damage.

The Landlord's Exposure.   Assume that a fire has ravaged the building. Aside from the direct property loss and perhaps some of the extra expense losses discussed above, what other losses will the landlord suffer as a consequence? First the landlord will lose the net rental income from those tenants whose rents are suspended during the period of untenantability. But remember that the landlord has reserved the right to cancel leases if the premises become wholly untenantable because of the fire. The gains to be made by canceling what, for the landlord, are highly unfavorable leases may more than offset the loss of rents during the suspended period —or they may not. Second, the building corporation has retained space in the Pill Building for its own offices. Loss of the use of this space will require the corporation to incur the rental expense of temporary quarters elsewhere. Furthermore, extra expenses are likely to arise in operating offices in temporary quarters.

The Tenant's Exposure.   What is a tenant likely to lose? In addition to the physical damage to his personal property (including such items as valuable papers and records, securities and currency), the tenant can lose the value of any interests he has in improvements and betterments. (Improvements and betterments are alterations on the premises made by the tenant at his expense and include such items as partitions, special lighting fixtures, and interior decorations.)

With respect to the lease arrangements, the tenants will suffer at least one other loss. One group of tenants will lose the rental value of the space for which rental payments must be continued, even though the premises are temporarily untenantable. The other group of tenants will more than likely lose their valuable leases, since the corporate landlord has the right to cancel the lease after the casualty. Because the current market value of the space exceeds the contract rent stipulated in the lease, the landlord will find it advantageous to cancel the old lease and negotiate a new one. The new lease can be negotiated either with his present tenants or with new ones. In either event, because of the fire damage to the premises, these tenants will now have to pay a higher rent. The increase in rent is an additional expense attributable to the fire and results in a lower net income to the tenants.[11]

---

[11] While a valuable lease is often thought of by the tenant as an intangible asset and its cancellation as an asset loss, it is not considered acceptable accounting practice to list intangible assets on the balance sheet unless they are specifically purchased. The profit and loss statement best reflects the existence of intangible assets.

Accounts Receivable. Direct physical damage or loss to accounts receivable records by fire, windstorm, theft, or other perils can cause loss of revenues and create additional expenses, both of which reduce net income. An example of this source of loss may be constructed from the Pill Building fire.

Physicians and dentists usually do a credit business.[12] At any one time, numerous accounts receivable are outstanding. The value of these accounts usually makes up an important part of the total business assets. If the account records of these physicians and dentists are destroyed or lost as a result of the fire damage to the building, a serious consequential loss can follow. Some patients will take advantage of the lost records and ignore their unpaid accounts. Some of these "forgetful" clients might be persuaded to pay, but only at the expense of increased collection costs. And, if the records can be reconstructed, it will cost money to do so. Furthermore, during the time it takes to re-create them, account payments will be delayed. Physicians and dentists, therefore, will lose the use of funds held up by impaired collections. Death of the physician or dentist also may reduce the willingness of patients to pay their accounts. Death nearly always causes accounts receivable losses.

Physicians and dentists maintain other valuable records, too. Case histories of patients are valuable in increasing the efficiency and maintaining the continuity of treatment, in protecting against potential allegations of malpractice, and perhaps in enhancing patients' belief that this particular medical man is "their" doctor or "their" dentist. These records are also of importance in aiding collection of accounts. Insofar as payments are to come from other persons than the patients themselves (e.g., from employers or insurance companies), records of treatment are necessary to substantiate the claim for fees, and, if both accounts receivable *and* records of treatments are destroyed, how are claims for fees going to be established against the patients themselves?

Additional Expenses of Doing Business. Some businesses by their very nature cannot afford the luxury of closing down after a fire and remaining closed until the premises again become inhabitable; to do so would be to commit business suicide. Banks, newspapers, public utilities, pharmacists, and laundries are examples of the many types of business firms whose survival depends on keeping operations continuous. An extended period of business interruption loss cannot be a part of the plans of the risk managers of these firms. Their plans must be geared to offset the additional costs that will arise in keeping the business open following a serious physical damage loss. An illustration of this source of loss may also be constructed from the Pill Building fire.

The pharmacist, physicians, and dentists cannot close up their shops

---

[12] Physicians and dentists do not like to have their services referred to as a business. Nevertheless, any professional practice must have a business side, and this end of their operation must be carried on efficiently if a successful professional practice is to be built.

and take a cruise around the world while awaiting the restoration of the building. The druggist will have to continue his prescription service at all costs or run the risk of losing an important part of his clientele permanently. Patients will continue to need the professional services of their doctors and dentists. If these doctors and dentists wish to conserve their practices, they had better be prepared to continue to offer their services. They must rent temporary quarters or use the services of other professional offices and personnel. The cost of carrying on a business or profession with emergency or substitute facilities usually is considerably higher than the cost under normal conditions.

Key Personnel Losses. In the copy of a recent advertisement appearing in *Time* and many other magazines, Merrill Lynch, Pierce, Fenner and Smith, Incorporated, tells us: "The stock market is like the sky in some ways. If you study it long enough, you get some idea of what to expect— how a company's earnings will affect the price of its stock, what various news developments may mean to certain kinds of securities, how the market will react to threats of war, new taxes, or *illness in high places.*"[13] The illness referred to here perhaps is the illness of important public figures, such as that of the President of the United States. But the illness or death of key personnel in the company itself can affect the price of the company's stock, since the level of corporate earnings is tied closely to the effectiveness of corporate management. Quality of management often is the important variable in distinguishing among corporations with consistently good, moderate, or poor earnings records.

The risk manager, therefore, cannot restrict his attention to potential capital and income losses created by property damage. He must also consider the potential income losses resulting from the disability or death of key personnel (including owners active in the business). These losses make themselves felt in one of two ways: a reduction in revenues or an increase in expenses. For example, the disability or death of a top salesman can cause a noticeable decline in sales. The disability or death of a highly successful sales or sales promotion manager may have a retarding influence on the company's growth rate and bring about a reduction in the company's share of the market. The illness or death of a key department head can adversely affect the efficiency of the department. Some inefficiency is likely to continue while a replacement is being trained. If it is necessary to go outside the company to find a qualified man for the job, the cost of replacing the department head may be costly. For a man well entrenched in his present position, a change in jobs is a gamble. To compensate him for the risks of moving, he must be offered a salary that will substantially improve his present take-home pay. Loss of key employees, therefore, is a real exposure, which should not be overlooked.

---

[13] Italics added.

A business can lose the services of its key employees by means other than disability or death. These employees can be lured away by attractive offers of other jobs. Special steps should be taken to minimize this risk. With top-level executives, higher salaries may not be sufficiently attractive because the additional compensation will be taxed at upper-bracket rates. A special deferred compensation plan, however, may help to wed the key employee to his job if severance of employment would result in forfeiture of benefits, especially if the employee has been on the job long enough to accumulate substantial benefits. The advantage to the employee of a carefully developed deferred compensation plan is tax relief. When compensation is deferred from the active years to the retirement years, it will likely be subject to a lower tax rate. The retired employee's taxable income is likely to be lower at that time. When the deferred compensation arrangements involve benefits that are uncertain as to the time and duration of their payment, these agreements create a loss exposure that could fall within the province of the risk manager's responsibilities.

Liability. Liability to others for damages caused them is another important loss exposure that must be considered by the risk manager. This exposure is so vast and requires such extensive elaboration that it is considered separately in the following chapter.

PERILS

Up to this point, attention has been directed primarily to the types of losses that may be suffered. Little reference has been made to the origin of the loss. No risk analysis is complete without consideration of the perils that produce loss.

A large variety of perils expose assets and net income to loss, and each of these perils must be identified and considered by the risk manager in analyzing his exposures. If he overlooks one of these perils, his over-all risk management plan may fall short of its objective, especially if commercial insurance plays a major role in his plan. Although the purpose of insurance is to protect the business from loss, insurance policies unfortunately have a habit of restricting coverage to certain specific causes of loss. Some of the reasons for these restrictions have already been discussed (chapter 5); others will be examined later (chaps. 14 and 15). The risk manager needs to be aware of the perils that threaten his business so that his insurance can be arranged to cover all the ones that are insurable.

Perils that threaten the assets or earning power of a business may be classified into (1) those resulting from activities of nature, (2) those attributable to human fallibility, and (3) those arising from the criminal acts of man. Because people exert some control over nature, these classes are not completely discrete. When a peril would logically fall into more than one of these classes, it will be assigned to only one class so as to avoid confusion by overlapping classifications or cross-references. The reader will be left on his own to recognize the dual nature of these perils. If any of the dual natures escapes him, nothing will be lost, however.

Activities of Nature

Some perils are independent of man's activity; they are products of nature itself, as contrasted with those of human civilization. Among these perils are windstorm, hail, lightning, rain, flood, landslide, earthquake, volcanic eruption, some sicknesses, and death. They threaten man regardless of human behavior and regardless of the stage to which society has advanced.

In surveying his exposures, the risk manager needs to give careful attention to these perils. Which ones can produce loss? What kind and how much loss can they produce? Only after careful consideration of the answer to these questions is the risk manager in a position to decide intelligently how to handle these exposures.

Human Fallibility

A number of perils arise out of man's effort to exert power over nature. "That men may err was never yet denied."[14] And when men err in their exercise of power over nature, serious losses to property and earning power may be one of the consequences. Among the perils attributable to human fallibility are fire, explosion, collision, nuclear energy, sonic boom, sprinkler leakage, war, smoke and smudge, collapse, breakdown of machinery, insolvency of debtors, mysterious disappearance, accidents and some illnesses, and negligence. The risk manager must uncover the full particulars on how these perils threaten the solvency and earnings potential of his business. Then he can decide what to do about them.

Criminal Acts of Man

A crime is an act forbidden by statute or injurious to the public welfare and punishable by law. A number of crimes result in either income loss or loss to property, or, of course, both. Punishment of the criminal, if he is caught, does not reimburse the business for the losses suffered at his hands. An effort to collect from him under civil proceedings may produce nothing but expenses, since risk managers cannot assume that they will be the targets of only affluent and easily apprehended criminals! Among the crime perils are vandalism, malicious mischief, riot and civil commotion, forgery, burglary, robbery, larceny, conversion, and embezzlement. After a careful study of these perils and how they affect his business, the risk manager is prepared to take them into consideration in formulating his over-all risk management plans.

---

[14] John Dryden, *The Hind and the Panther*, l. 61.

SUMMARY

One of the first responsibilities of the risk manager is to identify the loss exposures of his company. He should concern himself with those exposures that are capable of producing large losses and, in general, with those that have more than an infinitesimal chance of occurring.

Two basic sources of information are available to the risk manager in locating loss exposures: the books of account and a direct inspection of the physical plant operations of the business. To aid in observation and analysis, the risk manager usually will find a "fact finder" helpful. Company organization charts are also useful or essential. The aid of other managers in the business is essential.

In reviewing loss exposures, the risk manager should be aware of the interrelationship of losses. He must identify each loss unit, defined as "the aggregate of losses resulting from a single event." Each catastrophe area should be well defined in his mind so that he knows just what the loss possibilities are. Within a single catastrophe area, losses can be of three basic types: losses of property values, losses of income, and losses owing to additional expenses. The risk manager must consider each type in his risk analysis.

In studying his loss exposures, the risk manager must review the types of perils that can produce these losses. For convenience of study, these perils may be classified as to those resulting from activities of nature, human fallibility, and criminal acts.

REVIEW AND DISCUSSION QUESTIONS

1. What are the sources of information needed to answer the two questions which the risk manager must answer in analyzing his needs for insurance? How can he be sure he has covered all the sources and gotten all the information?

2. What does a balance sheet tell the risk manager about exposures to loss? What does it *not* tell him?

3. To what risk management questions do income statements give answers?

4. The fact finder in the text is long and detailed. How could it safely be shortened? Could some items be consolidated—some of the items under III. H. and I., for example? If so, which? If not, why not? What *are* the factors which determine whether it is necessary to make separate inquiry about a particular exposure

5. Write the instructions a risk manager would like to have given to the heads of operating divisions indicating what information should be reported to him *as soon as it is available.*

6. What is (are) the organization principle (principles) by which the items in the fact finder in the text are arranged or ordered? What other organizing principals might have been used? Which principle would you prefer? Why?

7. Identify all the loss units to which the asset item "cash on the business premises" belongs.

8. What is the difference between a "loss unit" and a "catastrophe area"? Of what importance are these concepts to the risk manager?

9. What is the difference between an *on-premises* direct property loss and an *extended* direct property loss? Of what importance are these concepts to the risk manager?

10. Since the dividing line between "direct" and "consequential" losses is so poorly defined, and both types of losses are parts of the same loss unit, what is the point of trying to distinguished between them?

11. Just exactly what *is* the loss suffered when a business loses "what it never had"—profits during a period of shutdown? What occurrences can cause these losses?

12. Without looking back at the chapter, list all the losses which would be suffered by the tenants of the "Pill Building" in event of severe damage to the premises. What would be the difference in these losses if the building were occupied by lawyers and a book store rather than doctors and a pharmacy? (It would then be called the "Process Building," of course.)

13. What difference is there between the exposure to loss by death or disability of a business owner, discussed under "Losses of Property Values" and death or disability of a key man, discussed under "Net Income Losses"?

14. Why does the risk manager have to identify perils? How are these perils classified in the text? How else might perils be classified?

Chapter 7

LIABILITY EXPOSURES

In the conduct of its affairs, a business owes certain legal duties to the public and to its employees. If someone suffers a loss because of the failure of the business to perform these duties, the injured party is afforded a legal remedy in the form of action for damages. The costs of defending against law suits and the amounts of compensation that must be paid to successful claimants constitute the direct losses arising from the liability exposure.

Since the misconduct of any business employee while acting within the scope of his employment can expose the business to claims for damage, risk managers will find the liability exposure one of the most difficult to control.

LEGAL BASES FOR LIABILITY CLAIMS

Two bases for legal claims for damages are possible: torts and contractual relationships. The contracts involved may be written or oral, express or implied. Claims may arise out of negotiations for contractual relationships as well as from the relationships themselves.

The word "tort" comes from the Latin *tortum*, meaning "twisted" (cf. "torture" and "tortuous"). "Tort" was commonly used as a Late Latin, Old French, and Middle English word to mean "wrong" or "injustice." Although in everyday French and English speech the word has been discarded, the law has held on to it, so that now it has only a technical legal meaning. Although William L. Prosser, a recognized authority on this branch of the law, admits that the term "tort" is incapable of precise definition, he does offer the following as a broad, vague one: ". . . . a tort is a civil wrong, other than breach of contract, for which the court will provide a remedy in the form of an action for damages."[1] As Prosser puts it, "This, of course, says nothing more than that a tort is one kind of legal wrong, for which the law will give a particular redress." Fortunately, for

---

[1] William L. Prosser, *Handbook of the Law of Torts* (St. Paul, Minnesota: West Publishing Co., 1955), p. 2.

207

the purposes of the present discussion, nothing more needs to be said. The interest of the risk manager lies not in definition but in understanding the grounds for tort action so that he can make the necessary preparations for reducing the hazard and offsetting the loss.

Claims arising from torts may be based upon one of three grounds: intentional interference, negligence, and absolute or strict liability, which is liability imposed even in the absence of intentional or negligent actions.

INTENTIONAL TORTS

If an intentional act done with the objective of accomplishing a given result causes injury to another, that act may be held to be an intentional tort. This is true even when the actor means to do good rather than harm. If the actor's conduct is "privileged," however, no tort is committed. (The question of privilege will be discussed after the types of intentional torts are introduced.)

Intentional torts can be discussed under two headings: intentional interference with the person and intentional interference with property.

Intentional Interference with the Person

Battery, assault, infliction of mental and emotional disturbance, defamation, and false imprisonment are examples of actionable intentional interference with the person.

Battery. Unpermitted, unprivileged contact with the person of another constitutes battery. This includes contact with anything connected with or associated with another, such as, for example, the clothes he is wearing, the chair in which he sits, or the package he carries in his arms. Battery exists even though no harm is done nor any hostility intended. Only the absence of an expressed or implied consent on the part of the violated person is necessary to constitute battery.

Assault. Assault is an attempt or offer to do violence to another. Assault and battery differ in that assault involves only apprehension over threatened physical contact, whereas battery involves actual physical contact. Since assault affects mental peace, failure to carry through the threat of violence does not prevent liability.

Mental Distress. Liability is also imposed for intentional acts that produce severe mental or emotional distress if the actor's conduct exceeds all bounds generally tolerated by society. However, there must be convincing evidence that the mental suffering was genuine and extreme; no damages are awarded for insults or abuses that are no more than annoyances. Serious physical illness arising from the emotional disturbance often is a prerequisite to recovery.

Defamation. Defamation is the injuring of another's reputation without good reason or justification. It takes the form of either *libel* or *slander*. Historically, libel was a written defamation, whereas slander was an oral defamation. As new forms of communication have developed, the distinction between libel and slander has become blurred. The current trend is to base the distinction on the permanence of the form of the defamation or on its harm potential. Furthermore, historically, all libel was actionable without proof of damage, whereas, in slander, proof of damage was required except when the slanderous remarks included accusation of having committed a serious crime, of having had an "odious disease," or accusations of acts incompatible with the expected conduct of a trade, business, or profession. The present trend is toward treating libel in the same manner as slander, that is, requiring proof of pecuniary damage except for the particular types of accusations mentioned above. This is not the rule everywhere, however. In a substantial number of jurisdictions the plaintiff can still be awarded a large amount as damages for purely assumed harm to his reputation, without his having had to submit proof that such harm actually was suffered. The present confusion and inconsistency in the law of libel and slander has prompted Dean Prosser to write: "Nowhere is the layman's criticism and the cry, 'Kill all the lawyers first,' more thoroughly justified."[2]

To be actionable, defamatory matter must be intentionally or negligently communicated to someone other than the defamed party. Upon establishing the intentional or negligent nature of the communication, the rule of strict liability is imposed, with no consideration given to the questions of intent or negligence insofar as the statement itself is concerned. All that is required is that the defamatory meaning be reasonably understood by others. Thus, material intentionally or negligently published but accidentally defamatory is actionable, whereas matter accidentally published but intentionally defamatory is not actionable. "Published" means "made public" and covers all forms of communication: gestures, pictures, and statues, as well as oral, printed, and written words.

False Imprisonment. False imprisonment occurs when one person's freedom of movement is intentionally restrained by another without legal justification. False imprisonment may occur even though the restraint is for only a brief period of time and there is no proof of actual damage.[3] The restraint must be intended, but there is no requirement that there be malice.[4] Thus, even when the restrainer believes the restraint to be necessary for the good of the restrained, there can be liability for false imprisonment if legal justification cannot be shown for the act.[5]

---

[2] *Ibid.*, p. 595.

[3] The restraint in movement must be total, not in merely one direction. Interference or obstruction of movement, such as results from the blocking of a highway or a refusal of admission, is not considered false imprisonment. Any action that may lie for interference of this kind ordinarily requires proof of damage.

[4] If the restraint itself is unintended, there may be liability for negligence if actual damages are sustained.

[5] False imprisonment must not be confused with malicious prosecution: the malicious institution of groundless criminal proceedings against another person.

Intentional Interference with Property

Trespass to real property, trespass to personal property, and conversion are examples of actionable intentional interferences with property.

Trespass. A wrongful entry upon land possessed by another and failure to remove an item from this land when there is an obligation to do so constitute trespass. Trespass includes invasion not only of the surface of the land but also of the area above and below it. The exact area of vertical possession allowed is a matter for the court to decide in each individual case. In the event of intentional intrusion, there can be action without proof of actual damage, and action can lie even when the trespass is in the interest of the possessor. The liability of the trespasser extends to all damages for which the trespass is the proximate cause regardless of whether it would have been reasonable for the trespasser to have anticipated such damage. (Proximate cause, however, is an abstract, undefinable term, about which courts disagree. More will be said on this point later.)

Trespass to personal property consists of intentional interference with its possession or physical condition, without legal justification. Just as in trespass to land, an innocent mistake is no defense. Unlike trespass to land, trespass to personal property generally requires proof of actual damages in order to maintain an action.

Conversion. Conversion is an intentional and unlawful interference with the personal property of others that results in depriving the owners of use and possession to such a degree that a forced sale of the property to the converter at its full value is justified. The converter need not be conscious of the conversion; he need only seriously interfere with dominion over the property. Ignorance of either the fact or the law is no defense. Return of the property also is no defense and may not be used even to reduce the damages unless consented to by the plaintiff or ordered by the court.

Conversion is accomplished (1) by taking possession of goods with the intention of exercising dominion over them adverse to the owner, as is done by a bona fide purchaser of stolen goods;[6] (2) by depriving the owner of control through an unauthorized transfer of goods, as in the misdelivery of goods by a voluntary or involuntary bailee;[7] (3) by refusing to surrender the possession of goods to one who has a right to them, as in holding goods for a charge that is clearly unreasonable;[8] (4) misusing the goods in obvious defiance of the owners, such as driving a car left to be washed; and (5)

---

[6] In the case of negotiable instruments taken in due course, an exception is made for those purchasers who rely upon them.

[7] An involuntary bailee is one who comes into possession of the goods by mistake or accident.

[8] A qualified refusal to deliver exercised for a reasonable time for a reasonable purpose (as to allow an agent to consult his principal, to determine the correct charges, or to determine the true ownership) does not constitute conversion.

damage to, destruction of, or alteration of the property as a result of intentional conduct, such as altering a fur coat so as to make it unwearable.

Privilege

The term "privilege" is used to indicate the circumstances under which liability is avoided for intentional acts that otherwise would have involved liability. The objective of privilege is to grant a person freedom to act in a manner that best serves the public good. An intentional interference with the person or property of another involves two interests: that of the interferer and that of the interferee. The question of which of these interests should have the greater legal protection is the important consideration in determining what constitutes privileged conduct. What is privileged in a given situation has to be litigated when action is brought. Intentional interference can be costly, therefore, even when the interference is privileged.

Considerations given attention in determining the existence of privilege are certain types of mistakes of facts; a reasonable assumption of consent based on conduct or custom; self-defense, defense of property, defense of others, certain actions to protect an interest from a threatened injury not caused by the wronged party, recovery of property wrongfully taken, and certain limited situations involving arrest without a warrant. A brief introduction to each of these defenses might be useful to the risk manager, but, of course, not nearly as useful as an attorney would be in situations in which one or more of these defenses are needed.

Mistakes. A mistake is privileged under a few limited conditions. While these conditions are by no means sufficiently clear for a general rule to be formulated, it does appear that a mistake is privileged when the actor must move hastily to protect what he believes to be an unmistaken right. Thus, a storekeeper is privileged to defend himself if he has sufficient reason to believe that he is being attacked, even though he is mistaken. As Dean Prosser puts it: "The boundaries of the privilege will be marked out in each situation upon the basis of the special reasons of policy and expediency bearing upon the facts."[9]

Consent. Under certain circumstances, an individual is privileged to infer consent based on the conduct of another. As the old saying goes, "Actions speak louder than words," and one's conduct toward another should be governed by what a reasonable person would assume from this conduct. Thus, if an employee holds out his arm for a flu shot and maintains silence while the company nurse administers it, he cannot successfully assert in a damage suit for battery that he did not give his express consent to the inoculation. An inference of consent is also privileged when based on sufficient custom or usage. Thus, a physician is privileged to assume consent to an emergency operation when death is impending. He cannot be ex-

---

[9] Prosser, *op. cit.*, p. 81.

pected to put off the operation until such time as he can get an expression of consent, particularly if the patient is unconscious.

Protective Acts.   One is privileged to use all the reasonable force necessary to prevent intentional or negligent interference with his person. The burden of proof of the facts giving rise to the privilege is on the actor. What is reasonable force is for the jury to determine in most cases. The court, however, may hold that the use of deadly force for self-defense is privileged only in restricted situations, chiefly when the actor is similarly threatened and has no other safe means of defense.

A person is also privileged to use force, if necessary, to protect his property. Here again, the force used must be reasonable, that is, of a kind appropriate to the defense of the property. If only the property is threatened, the defender is not privileged to use force designed to bring about death or serious injury to the offender.

An individual is privileged to use whatever force is reasonably necessary to protect another individual if that individual is privileged to defend himself. The defender is privileged to use whatever force the attacked person is privileged to use.[10] The risk that the person being defended is not privileged to defend himself must be taken by the intermeddler in most jurisdictions.

In some situations an intentional interference with the person or property of another may be privileged if the interference is both reasonable and necessary to protect a threatened injury involving a public interest. Thus, property can be jettisoned from a boat or aircraft to save the passengers, or a vehicle on the public highway can roll over contiguous land to avoid a temporary obstruction. If the interest to be protected is private rather than public, the privilege is restricted. The actor will not be held for a technical tort, but he will be held for actual damage caused. Thus, a person is privileged to trespass upon the property of another to escape danger, but he is not privileged to inflict damage to such property.[11]

When property is wrongfully taken from a person and action is promptly taken to retrieve it, the person is permitted to use reasonable force to accomplish his purpose.[12] If action is not taken immediately following the abstraction, the wronged party must look to the law for his remedy. If the owner suspects a wrongful abstraction and detains the suspect in an effort to recover the property, the suspicious owner may be held for damages arising from false arrest or from battery. Thus, a storekeeper who detains or searches a customer or employee accused of theft runs the risk of exposing

---

[10] Such defender might find himself a defendant in an action for damages for battery brought by the person defended. In *Johnson* v. *McConnel*, 15 Hun. N.Y. 293 (1878) the defendant intervened in a fight to protect the plaintiff and broke the plaintiff's leg.

[11] The owner or possessor of the property is not privileged to resist or expel the "trespasser" under these circumstances.

[12] Reasonable force does not include that which is calculated to injure the culprit seriously.

himself to liability for damages if it should turn out that no crime has been committed. This, of course, places the storekeeper in a precarious position. He must be sure of himself or allow the suspect to leave unmolested—unless, of course, he is willing to assume the risk associated with taking action.

Citizens' Arrests. Under certain circumstances a private citizen is privileged to make arrests without a warrant. Statutes and court decisions among the states vary so widely on the subject of arrest without a warrant that few if any general rules can be formulated. To avoid the risk of making an unprivileged arrest, it is important that the rules be checked for each jurisdiction. In broad, general terms it can be said that a private citizen is privileged to make arrests without a warrant to prevent the commission of a felony or breach of peace. He may be privileged even to arrest a person reasonably suspected of a felony, assuming that the felony has actually been committed. In most jurisdictions, however, the privilege to make arrests without a warrant does not extend to misdemeanors not involving a breach of peace.[13] When an arrest is privileged, reasonable force may be used. What force is reasonable must be considered in the light of the offense. Obviously, the use of deadly force would be considered reasonable in only a few situations.

Intentional Torts and the Risk Manager

The possibility of incurring liability from intentional torts may easily be overlooked by the risk manager. A number of situations can arise in which the business may find itself a defendant in an action for battery, assault, false imprisonment, defamation, trespass, or one of the other intentional torts just described. A few illustrations should be helpful in emphasizing this point.

A business may be sued for battery when one of its employees shoves an obnoxious customer around or when he literally kicks out an offensive salesman. An assault case may arise when an employee raises her hand as though she intends to slap an aggravating bill collector even though she is successful in restraining herself. A defamation case can arise when the company house organ prints a story about the encouraging medical progress of one of its employees who is a patient at a mental hospital, or when adverse gossip about a competitor's product is freely discussed. A trespass action can be instituted when goods sold on the installment plan are improperly repossessed. When a business sells goods to which it has no legal title, it may be subject to a conversion action even though it believes the title to be free and clear. When suspected shoplifters are detained, the business can be sued for false imprisonment. And when the credit manager

---

[13] A felony is defined as a serious offense, whereas a misdemeanor is an offense less serious than a felony. Felonies are usually those offenses punishable by death or imprisonment for more than one year.

threatens to ruin the credit of a slow-paying customer and this customer becomes ill as a result, the business can find itself a defendant in an action for inflicting the mental disturbance that caused the illness. The same action may result when the customer claims that an emotional illness was caused by continued hounding by the collector. Any standard casebook on torts will reveal a number of surprising as well as not so surprising actions for intentional torts against the unsuspecting businessman. Regardless of how these actions are decided, the business must be prepared to defend itself, and this will cost both time and money. The risk manager must, therefore, consider this contingency in his planning.

NEGLIGENCE

Every business is exposed to losses from claims for damages arising out of allegations of negligence. As a legal term, "negligence" is defined as "the failure to exercise that degree of care which, under the circumstances, the law requires for the protection of those interests of other persons which may be injuriously affected by the want of such care."[14] Section 282 of the *Restatement of Torts*, of the American Law Institute, defines "negligence" as conduct "which falls below the standard established by law for the protection of others against unreasonably great risk of harm." Negligence is a basis for action for an unintended tort.

Characteristics of Negligence

Negligence is an act of an unreasonable and imprudent man. It is usually a result of thoughtlessness or carelessness, but it may also be a product of poor judgment, ignorance, or stupidity. The standard by which reasonableness is measured is an external one and is based on what is expected of the individual by society rather than on what the individual himself considers reasonable or prudent. The standard requires that the conduct be reasonable in view of the risk involved. Thus, as Dean Prosser puts it: "For this reason, it is seldom possible to reduce negligence to any definite rules . . . conduct which would be proper under some circumstances becomes negligence under others."[15] If the loss potential in a given situation is not recognized by society to be great enough in terms of either frequency or severity to require regular precaution, an accident occurring from the exposure is ordinarily considered "unavoidable" and no liability is imposed.

The degree of care or duty required is also relative to the circumstances involved. For example, greater care must be taken in dealing with children than with adults, with elderly adults than with young adults, and with the mentally unsound than with the mentally sound. Furthermore, trespassers

---

[14] *The American College Dictionary* (New York: Random House, Inc., 1958), p. 813.

[15] Prosser, *op. cit.*, p. 123.

and licensees in general are entitled to less care than invitees.[16] And those invitees on the premises for the *exclusive* benefit of owners or tenants may be entitled to more care than are those who are on the premises for mutual benefits. Trespassers who are injured have no recourse against the landlord or tenant unless a trap has been set for them.

Attractive Nuisances. An important exception to the standard of care required for trespassers, however, is the doctrine of attractive nuisance. Any novel device particularly enticing to children may be judged an attractive nuisance. Examples are piles of lumber on a construction job, stores of explosives in a locked shed, and unusual machinery housed in a garage. Owners or tenants are required to give sufficient warning or protection to children who are attracted to these potentially dangerous "nuisances." The defenses that may be used against the attractive nuisance doctrine are that the injured child was old enough to be aware of the danger or that the device was common to the locality and therefore not novel. A study of court decisions, however, does not leave a defendant with a comfortable feeling with either of these defenses.

In many states the doctrine of attractive nuisance has been replaced by section 339 of the *Restatement of Torts*. Under this statute the landowner is held liable for injuries to trespassing children under the following rules: He maintains on his property a condition that can reasonably be expected to attract children who are incapable of realizing the hazards involved, and this condition has small utility to the landlord compared to the hazards involved for young children. The defenses under this section are that the landlord could not reasonably be expected to know (1) that the condition would attract children or (2) that the condition involved unreasonable dangers to children. But the most successful defense, when it has been applicable, has been the one that the utility of the condition far outweighed the hazards involved.

The Hypothetical Reasonable Man

The "reasonable man," of course, is a mythical person whose conduct varies according to the situation confronting him and according to the jury judging him. Since negligence is the failure to do what a reasonable man would do under similar circumstances, men with physical defects must take whatever precautions a reasonable man would take if he were similarly inflicted. The reasonable man is assumed to have normal intelligence and mental capacity. Only the legally insane are exempted from this assumption. As for drunkenness, a person negligently or unintentionally intoxicated will be held to the same standard of care expected of a sober man. Children are not held to the adult standard of care; they are held to the standard of care

---

[16] A trespasser is one who is on the premises without permission. A licensee is one whose permitted presence on the premises does not benefit the owner or tenant. Anyone else on the premises is an invitee.

reasonably expected of children of the same age, experience, and intelligence. Old people who have entered their "second childhood" also are held to lesser standards of care.

The reasonable man is assumed to have the minimum perception, memory, experience, and information common to the community. Certain activities in which he is engaged, however, can require him to obtain knowledge beyond the common minimum if that knowledge is necessary to protect the public. Failure to achieve this knowledge can be considered negligence. The reasonable man in a learned profession or skilled trade is assumed to have the minimum knowledge, skill, and intelligence commonly possessed by members of that profession or trade. If a person practices a profession or trade without the use of these minimum qualities, he can be held liable for malpractice if, as a consequence, harm is done. In fact, liability for malpractice was among the first of the actions for negligence to be recognized by the courts.

Elements of a Negligent Act

Before damages will be awarded one party for the alleged negligence of another, the court must be satisfied that all the elements of a negligent act were present. These elements are (1) the existence of a legal duty to protect the injured party, (2) a failure to perform that duty, (3) an injury[17] suffered by the claimant, and (4) a reasonably close causal relationship between the breach of duty and the claimant's injury.

Breach of Duty. The general nature of the legal duty involved here is to exercise that standard of care which a prudent, reasonable man would consider necessary to protect other persons against unreasonable risks. Whether this duty was owed to the injured party, and, if so, whether the duty was breached, are matters for litigation in each case. In trials before juries, questions of law are decided by the judge, questions of fact are decided by the jury. (When cases are tried without juries, the judge decides on both law and fact, of course.) The issue of negligence, however, is seldom divided into such distinct questions of law and fact: "The most common statement is that if men of reasonable intelligence may differ as to conclusions to be drawn, the issue must be left to the jury; otherwise it is for the court."[18]

The jury, in passing on facts, may tend to let "liability based . . . on a substantial probability of negligence" substitute for actual evidence of specific breach.[19] In a number of cases lay jurors unfortunately may

---

[17] In law, the word "injury" is not limited to bodily injury. The injury of which the claimant complains may have been to his person, his property, his legal rights, or his reputation.

[18] Prosser, *op. cit.*, p. 194.

[19] Louis L. Jaffe, *Insurance Law Journal*, February, 1952, p. 139.

"arrive at verdicts on the basis of their own conjectures" rather than "on the basis of the evidence actually presented to them."[20] Liability in the individual case often is justified on the ground that "it is more socially desirable for the defendant to pay the loss than the plaintiff, and that determination many times is largely influenced by the relative wealth of the parties or their ability to distribute the loss."[21] Hugh R. Gallagher writes: " 'Little man' consciousness is changing the law. The disheartening feature is the signs showing the breakdown of the idea of fault, but the real danger at present is the over-benevolence of juries and judges."[22] Gallagher is so concerned with what he considers to be a prevalence of unwarranted verdicts and ridiculous awards that he suggests the abolition of juries in civil actions and the raising of the standards for members of the judiciary. The present system, he believes, encourages gouging and chiseling.

That the determination of duty is an involved and complex question, however, must not be overlooked. For example, the courts are by no means in agreement as to whom a duty is owed. Whether a duty is owed to a person for whom no danger may have reasonably been foreseen is still controversial. Some courts say "yes"; others say "no." Frequently, the question of duty is decided on the basis of social policy, which requires the consideration of such factors as the prevention of future injuries, the moral blame involved, the capacity of the parties to bear the loss, and the ability of the parties to distribute the loss. Can one be positive that this is the wrong approach?

Liability cases will not reach the jury if, based on the facts alleged and proved by the plaintiff, the judge decides that as a matter of law the defendant is not guilty of negligence. But such cases are rare because a judge may not substitute his own opinion for that of the jury. Thus, the question of breach of duty is decided in nearly every case by untrained jurors. Because disputed questions of fact are within the sole province of the jury, the only way the judge has of expressing his disagreement is to order a new trial if he disagrees with the jury on the question of fault.

A Wrong Must Be Suffered. If damages are to be awarded, someone must have suffered a wrong as a consequence of the breach of duty. The wrong may be that of personal injury, property damage, or, in some cases, the physical consequences of a mental disturbance. Claims arising out of bodily injury may include compensation for loss of income, pain and suffering, humiliation, and other disturbances. Persons other than the injured party may suffer a wrong: an employer for the loss of the services of

---

[20] Harold S. Baile, "The Changing Concept of Your Legal Liability," *National Insurance Buyer*, Vol. II, No. 2.

[21] *Ibid.*

[22] Gallagher, "Product Liability," *Best's Insurance News*, Fire and Casualty ed., March, 1952.

an employee, or one spouse for the loss of the services of another (called loss of "consortium"). Claims arising out of property damage may include loss of use of the property as well as loss of the property itself.

As a rule, mental disturbances are not compensated in negligence cases unless accompanied by physical injury. The court in one such case held that damages to the ego were not actionable. A truck driver in an effort to avoid hitting a school bus swerved and then ran into the gasoline pumps of a roadside service station, causing fire and widespread destruction. The plaintiff, who was standing by and who was not physically injured in any way, brought action against the truck's insurer on the ground that "on seeing this holocaust and the need for someone to rush in and help rescue victims, he suddenly became overwhelmed by fear and realized for the first time in his life that he was not the omnipotent, fearless man his psyche had envisioned him to be. His post-accident awareness that this event had destroyed his self-deception image of himself precipitated great emotional and psychic tensions manifesting themselves as psychosomatic headaches, pains in legs and such, a loss of general interest, a disposition to withdraw from social and family contacts, and the like." The court held for the defendant. The Court of Appeals stated:

> As it might have appeared to the jury of lay persons, the medical theory was that the accident had made Clegg see himself as he really was, not as Clegg had thought himself to be. In short, the accident had destroyed the myth. No longer was he the brave invincible man. Now, as any other, he was a mere human, with defects and limitations and a faint heart. It was the strange case of a defendant being asked to pay for having helped Clegg by bringing him back to reality—helping him, as it were, to leave Mount Olympus to rejoin the other mortals in Baton Rouge.[23]

Proximate Cause. The breach of duty must be a proximate cause of the injury.[24] Frequently the questions of proximate cause and of duty owed are somewhat the same and are resolved on the basis of whether there is a connection between the injury suffered and a duty owed to the injured party. What was the scope of the risk? Was there a duty to someone whose injury could not reasonably have been foreseen?

An important case on this point is *Passgraf* v. *Long Island Railroad Company.*[25] The train conductor, helping aboard a passenger who was about to miss the train, caused the boarding passenger to drop a package of fireworks, which hit the rails and exploded. At the other end of the platform, some scales were upset as a result of the concussion and caused damage to the plaintiff. The jury held the railroad negligent, but the majority of the

---

[23] *Clegg* v. *Hardware Mutual Casualty Co.*, 264 Fed. (2d) 152.

[24] Because the word "proximate" means "near" Prosser thinks that it is an unfortunate choice of terms, placing emphasis on the closeness of the cause in time or space, which is no longer a significant consideration. He suggests as alternatives "legal" or "responsible" cause (*op. cit.*, p. 252).

[25] 248 N.Y. 339 (162 N.E. 99, 59 A.L.R. 1263) (1928).

higher court held that there was no liability to the plaintiff in spite of the negligent act of the defendant's servant—there was no breach of duty to this plaintiff. That is, the railroad and its employee, the conductor, had no duty for the safety of this innocent bystander in these circumstances. Therefore, the conductor's negligence was not the proximate cause of this claimant's loss. The court said that the plaintiff must "sue in her own right for a wrong personal to her, and not as the vicarious beneficiary of a breach of duty to another." The decision was a close one, 4 to 3, and although it has been accepted in the *Restatement of Torts,* the courts have been divided in its application. A number of courts in somewhat similar situations have found the causal connection sufficient to award damages to the plaintiff.

Proximate cause must not be confused with standard of care required. If the standard is met, there is no negligence; if it is not met, there is negligence. The question, then, is whether the negligence is the proximate cause of the injury. Proximate cause also must not be confused with contributory negligence. Simply because the injured person did something that contributed toward his own loss does not of itself mean that the acts of other parties cannot be the proximate cause of his damage. Contributory negligence is commonly a defense to a negligence claim, but it is not a factor in defining proximate cause.

A sure way of frustration is to attempt to define proximate cause. As Prosser says: " 'Proximate cause' cannot be reduced to absolute rules," and he quotes Street as follows: " 'It is always to be determined on the facts of each case upon mixed considerations of logic, common sense, justice, policy and precedent.' "[26] "In a philosophical sense," writes Prosser, "the consequences of an act go forward to eternity, and the causes of an event go back to the discovery of America and beyond."[27] Thus, as a practical matter, the legal or responsible cause must be limited in some manner to conform with the accepted standards of justice or social policy. These standards, of course, change through time. Important problems of determining proximate cause are those of causation, apportionment of damages among causes, unforeseeable consequences, intervening causes, and shifting responsibility. Each of these problems may be considered briefly.

The problem of causation in most cases can be handled by the *sine qua non* rule. Under this rule a person's conduct cannot be held to be the cause of the loss if that loss would have occurred anyway. However, the rule does not say that, if the loss would have occurred but for this conduct, there is liability. Consideration of other factors may preclude liability. Thus, the "but for" rule is useful only as a rule of exclusion, and then not even always. *Sine qua non* cannot always be applied when there are concurrent causes, because it can produce situations in which each party individually would

---

[26] Prosser, *op. cit.,* p. 257.
[27] *Ibid.,* p. 218.

escape liability, although jointly they are all responsible for loss to an innocent party. The "substantial factor" approach is therefore used instead; under this rule, conduct is deemed to cause the loss if it was material in bringing about that loss. Applying this rule, a loss may have more than one proximate cause. This requires apportionment of the dollar damages among the several offending parties. When an opportionment based on logic or convenience is possible, it will be made; otherwise the entire liability will be imposed upon each offender.

A negligent person usually is held liable for all the *direct* consequences of his breach of duty, even though no reasonable man would expect them to flow from his conduct. The consequence, however, may be *indirect* in the sense that there may be intervening causes. An intervening cause is one that becomes operative after the original act of negligence has transpired. If the intervening causes could reasonably have been foreseen, or if they are normal to the original risk created, they do not relieve the negligent person of liability. Thus, since a person who kindles a fire may reasonably foresee that a shift in the wind would carry the flames to his neighbor's property, he will not be relieved of damage caused by the fire. When the intervening causes are unforeseeable or abnormal, but the results are foreseeable, relief is given only in those situations in which the responsibility can be shifted to the subsequent negligent party. If, in the foregoing case, the spread of fire is caused by an abnormal increase in the wind velocity, no relief would be given because, although the cause is unforeseeable, the results are not, and there is no subsequent negligent party to whom the responsibility can be shifted. Of course, when both the causes and the results are unforeseeable, there is no negligence and hence no question of intervening causes.

The nature of the risk is the governing factor in determining how far one party may go in shifting the risk to another. An owner, for example, may shift to the tenant the responsibility for injuries arising from defects in the premises of which the owner is unaware. But, if the condition of the premises when leased is unreasonably hazardous, the landlord is not allowed to shift responsibility to the tenant. The landlord's breach of care may quite possibly be considered the proximate cause.

The Amount of Damages. If a person is held liable, the amount of damages is usually fixed by the jury under instructions from the court. Frequently liability claims are settled out of court, most often even before suits are entered. The amount of the settlement usually is based on speculation of the probable outcome of the case if it were to be taken to court.

Proof of Negligence. The burden is usually on the wronged party to prove negligence on the part of the actor. In some cases—malpractice, for example—the injured party may need expert witnesses to prove to a lay jury that the actor was guilty of a breach of duty. The burden is eased somewhat by two devices: presumption and circumstantial evidence. **Cer-**

tain facts are presumed to exist, and the burden is placed on the adverse party to give evidence to the contrary. Thus, it is presumed that when merchandise is stolen from a bailee, the bailee has been negligent, and it is presumed that a person has a desire for self-preservation.[28]

Under certain restricted conditions, when no specific evidence of negligence is available, and the facts are such that a reasonable inference of negligence would be justified, many courts will apply the common law doctrine of *res ipsa loquitur* ("the thing speaks for itself"). Under this doctrine, a prima facie case of negligence can be established and referred to the jury when (1) the alleged defective condition caused the plaintiff's injury, (2) the injury could not have occurred without the negligence of the defendant, and (3) the instrumentality causing the injury was under the control of the defendant.

To illustrate: A golfer rented a three-wheel golf cart. When the fork supporting the front wheel collapsed, the cart stopped suddenly, ejecting the golfer from the cart and injuring him. The golfer sued the golf club, predicating his case on the doctrine of *res ipsa loquitur*. The court decided for the defendant, stating that one of the basic elements of the *res ipsa loquitur* doctrine is that the instrumentality causing the injury must be under the control of the defendant.[29]

This "control" requirement *would appear* to eliminate the application of the *res ipsa loquitur* doctrine in most product liability cases because in nearly all such cases the defendant has relinquished control of the defective product. "Would appear" is used because a number of cases have been decided under the doctrine in favor of the plaintiff when the control of the instrument causing the injury did not seem to lie in the hands of the defendant. Professor Kulp points out that the ultimate consumer has been awarded damages against the manufacturer under the law of *res ipsa* "where a defective refrigerator froze the hand of a housewife to the door, knocked her unconscious, and produced serious electrical shock," and in a number of other cases in which the object was not in the exclusive control of the defendant at the time of the injury.[30]

In an address before the insurance section of the American Bar Association, Mr. Weiss said of *res ipsa* that it is "the strongest weapon in the arsenal of plaintiffs in products liability litigation."[31] How can this be true? Mr. Gallagher provides the answer when he says that the doctrine applies

after the plaintiff has shown that the agency causing the injury was exclusively within the control of the manufacturer, that the condition of such agency has not

---

[28] This latter is important in determining whether a death has been accidental or suicidal.

[29] *Hutchins* v. *Southview Golf Club, Inc.*, 243 S.W. (2d) 223 (1960).

[30] C. A. Kulp, *Casualty Insurance* (3d ed.; New York: Ronald Press, Inc., 1956), p. 76.

[31] "The Defense of Products Liability Cases," Chicago, August 24, 1943.

changed since it left the hands of the party he seeks to charge, that there was no opportunity or duty to inspect the product before using it or if there was such opportunity an examination would not have disclosed the defect, and that it was improbable that such an accident would occur without negligence.[32]

The doctrine "has been applied most successfully to canned and bottled products."[33]

Defense in Negligence Actions

Even though all the elements of a negligent act are proved to have been present, the injured party may still be defeated in his claim for damages. Certain defenses are available to the defendant that, if established, relieve him from legal responsibility for the claimant's injury.

Contributory Negligence. If the conduct of the injured party failed to meet the standard required for his own protection, and that failure contributed as a legal cause of the loss, the defense of contributory negligence may be used by the defendant in a negligence action. The standard of conduct required of a small child is much lower than that of an adult. Small children, therefore, are rarely held guilty of contributory negligence. In a number of states, statutes have been passed making children under the age of seven incapable of contributory negligence, and children between the ages of seven and fourteen presumably incapable of contributory negligence.

Assumption of Risk. Another important defense in an action for negligence is "assumption of risk." This defense is based on the argument that the plaintiff consented expressly or by implication to relieve the defendant of his duty to protect; by this consent the plaintiff accepted the chance of injury from the particular risk that produced his injury. Examples of express agreements to assume risk are found in some leases; the tenant may contract away his right to sue his landlord for the latter's negligence. Express agreements of this kind are upheld except when they are against public policy. (Contracts of hire that attempt to exempt employers from all liability to employees are held to be contrary to public policy, for example.) Consent to the assumption of the risk may be implied if the plaintiff voluntarily assumes a relationship involving obvious danger if he is aware of the risks. For example, a person who accepts a free lift in an automobile assumes the risks of a defective car and of an obviously incompetent driver unless, of course, the rider is too young and inexperienced to be aware of the risks involved.

Modifications of the Common Law of Negligence

The common law of negligence has been modified by legislation in several particular respects.

Employers' Liability. The story of work injuries and the tort law ap-

---

[32] Gallagher, *op. cit.*
[33] Kulp, *op. cit.*, p. 76

plied thereto provides some of the darkest pages in economic, social, and legal history. Consider first the effects, with respect to work injuries, of two of the tort defenses already mentioned: contributory negligence and assumption of risk. Consider the problem of the worker with respect to responsibility for his injuries. For one period of time it was essentially true that, if the worker did his job in the customary manner and in the manner in which he was told, and then was injured, it would be held that he assumed the risks involved in doing the job. On the other hand, if he did not do the job in the customary manner or the manner in which he was told and an injury resulted, it would surely be held that his deviation from usage or instructions was clearly a contributing factor in that injury and his claim would be denied under the defense of contributory negligence.

But that was not all. Employers had still a third defense available to them: the "fellow servant" rule. Under this rule, if the injury was caused by another employee of the same employer, the employer was not responsible for that negligence except in unusual cases. With the advent of the machine age, what employee ever saw his employer? From whose conduct could an employee's injury arise, in most instances, but from his own or that of some other employee?

Finally, the very concept of negligence itself was often applied in such a way as to make few recoveries possible. If the job and the shop were conducted in the manner customary to the trade or industry, then, however unsafe that customary manner might be, the employer was expected to do no more. The "reasonable man" in this instance was the general run of employer; whether the whole general run of employers might not be unreasonable, in the working conditions they supplied and the demands they made on employees, was not a question a judge in a tort case would or could have considered relevant.

The effects of the legal theories applied to employers' liability became something of a social scandal, and, as the society became slowly more enlightened, so did the makers of its law. Judges began to find ways to produce different results. (Different courts found different ways to new results.) One doctrine with some currency was called the "vice principal" rule, under which supervisory employees were held to stand in the place of the employer (principal) rather than in the position of a fellow servant. A modification used on other occasions restricted the "fellow servant" defense to those cases in which the employees involved actually worked together; this allowed recovery in instances in which one worker was injured by, say, a part made defective through negligence of workers in another, separate department of the factory. Judges began to take stricter looks at the risks that employees were said to have assumed when they took their jobs and at the standards that a "reasonable" employer was considered to believe appropriate for the safety and well-being of his employees.

Legislators are certainly not less responsible than judges to social outcries, particularly when they are voiced by persons significant in numbers, such as workers in the manufacturing industry. Modification of the common law interpretations of employers' liability appeared in statutes. Most of these modifications, like the court interpretations just noted, were aimed at limiting the fellow servant rule. (Note from the discussion previously given that this particular defense did not occur in tort law at large, but only in the law with respect to liability of employers.) But the problem had both grown and changed. Not only did complaints have to do with the amazing exemption of employers from financial responsibility for the results of injuries to their employees; they were also equally directed at the injuries themselves. Industrial accidents per se had become a scandal, right along with the tort law applying to them. Reformers were no longer looking for improvements in, or for a "tinkering" with, the law of employer negligence. They sought removal of the negligence theory entirely. Today, workmen's compensation (discussed below) has replaced employers' liability law in most industrial injury cases. But, for various reasons, including the encouragement of employers to come under compensation voluntarily, many of these same workmen's compensation laws drastically changed the law of employers' liability at the same time. Common practice was to remove the three defenses of contributory negligence, assumption of risk, and fellow servant doctrine from those employers who, given a choice, elected to stay under the employers' liability law rather than to come under the workmen's compensation law. These statutory modifications, adopted as part of the workmen's compensation laws, plus more modern judicial interpretations along the lines of modifications previously described, control employers' liability law today.

Automobile Liability. Under the common law, the operator of an automobile has a duty to exercise reasonable care for the protection of a guest and to reveal to him any defects in the vehicle that come to his knowledge.[34] More than half the states, however, have passed automobile guest statutes that modify this common law rule. This modification is one of the very few that have constricted rather than expanded the circumstances under which one person is liable for injuries or damage to others. Under guest statutes, the standard of care required of the host for the gratuitous rider is much less than ordinary. The driver is not held liable unless he has been guilty of "a conscious disregard of a known serious danger."[35] Some statutes call such conduct gross negligence, whereas others call it willful, wanton, or reckless. One of the purposes of these statutes is to protect the liability insurer from collusive automobile liability suits. Another is to satisfy a desire for justice, that is, to prevent a person from biting the hand that feeds him.

Nearly 25 per cent of the states have vicarious liability statutes holding

---

[34] A guest is defined as one who neither pays for his ride nor serves his host in any fashion. If he pays for the ride or is riding for the benefit of his host, he is called a passenger. A guest is treated as a licensee, whereas a passenger is treated as an invitee.

[35] Prosser, *op. cit.*, p. 452.

the owner of an automobile liable for the negligence of anyone driving the automobile on the public highways within the scope of the permission granted. Such statutes create an agency relationship between the owners and drivers of the automobile.

Comparative Negligence. Comparative negligence statutes are found in a few states. Some of these statutes apply only to automobile accidents and not to other actions for personal injuries. Under comparative negligence statutes the damages are apportioned between the plaintiff and the defendant on the basis of the relative fault of each. If the plaintiff's negligence is only 10 per cent, he bears 10 per cent of his own loss. This rule is the traditional one in admiralty law and probably was borrowed, at least in part, from that branch of jurisprudence.

Survival and Wrongful Death. Under common law no action could be maintained or continued after the death of either party connected with the tort.[36] Statutes have been passed in all jurisdictions modifying the common law. While some of these statutes go further than others, all of them allow the survival of causes of action for injuries to real as well as to personal tangible property. In approximately 50 per cent of the states, action for personal injury is allowed to survive. Survival action, where permitted, usually may be maintained or continued after the death of either party, plaintiff or defendant.

The common law rule meant that a person responsible for the death of another could not be held liable for the death. In the first place, the injured person's tort action died with him. In the second place, it was held that the survivors had no action for the loss of the services of the deceased. The effect, of course, was that it was better financially to kill the wronged person rather than to injure him.[37] Recognizing the senselessness of this situation, all states have passed statutes providing a remedy for wrongful deaths. A few states have only the survival acts previously mentioned; these allow the deceased's estate to prosecute any action that the deceased himself might have maintained if he had lived. Most states have "death acts," which create new causes of action for wrongful deaths. (A number of these states have the previously described type of statute, allowing the deceased's own claim to survive as well.) In most cases, the new causes of action are for losses suffered by particular surviving relatives. In a few cases, the new causes of action are for losses suffered by the deceased's estate only. When an estate collects damages, the amounts are distributed according to the plan for distribution of the rest of the estate.[38]

Damages in claims that the deceased's estate prosecutes for injuries

---

[36] One exception involved torts affecting personal property of the deceased plaintiff. Here his representative had the right of action against a living defendant but not against his estate. Contract actions, however, survived the death of either party.

[37] Legend has it that fire axes in railroad coaches were provided so that the conductors could deal effectively with the passengers who were only injured. (Prosser, *op. cit.*, p. 710, n. 9).

[38] The statutes, however, usually prohibit creditors from sharing in the award.

to the deceased himself depend on what happened to him before death—his pain and suffering, medical expenses, and loss of earnings while alive. The estate itself suffers from loss of his future earnings, cut off by his untimely death. The surviving relatives suffer loss of support and the service they reasonably could have expected to receive; their damages are generally limited to pecuniary claims only and thus do not include payment for such items as their own mental anguish or pain and suffering.

When the legislatures decided to open the gates upon claims for wrongful deaths, they also decided to protect tort feasors in these cases from what seemed possible "unlimited" claim amounts. Originally, nearly all the states set limits on the amount that could be awarded to all claimants for a single wrongful death. The typical limit was $5,000. As time went on, inflation set in, other tort claims multiplied in amount, and multiplied again. But the limits on death claims were raised either not at all or only slowly. It became true again, as it had been true so many years before, that it was cheaper to kill a man than to injure him. State after state repealed its wrongful death limit, and today only about one third of the states still have dollar limits on death claims. The limits now in effect are nearly all in the $10,000-$30,000 range. These statutes, however, have been interpreted as limiting the amount of the verdict that can be awarded for death benefit but not as prohibiting additional awards for loss of consortium and other wrongs.

Liability for the Conduct of Others

"Stupidity, ignorance, absentmindedness, and momentary and chronic carelessness are commonplace in industrial activity."[39] They are also present in commercial and professional activity. Furthermore, a person, particularly a person in business or a corporation, may be held liable without having been guilty of any wrongful conduct of his, or its, own. Important examples of vicarious liability are found in the relations between employers and their employees and independent contractors.

Acts of Employees. Under the doctrine of *respondeat superior*,[40] the employer can be held liable to injured parties for the negligent acts of his employees while they are acting in the course of employment.[41] This is true even though the employer neither knows of the act nor has given permission for it. The United States Supreme Court has ruled that the employer may be held liable even though the employee's car was being

---

[39] Donald L. MacDonald, "Risk Management in the Nuclear Age," *Proceedings of the Twelfth Annual Insurance Conferences* (Columbus: Ohio State University, 1961), p. 22.

[40] "Master is responsible."

[41] This doctrine, however, does not prevent the employer from seeking reimbursement of his liability loss from his negligent employee. For the risk manager to rely on this legal right of recovery in his risk management plans would be wishful thinking even for the most optimistic. Employees seldom have the money or the insurance coverage with which to pay.

used without the employer's knowledge and contrary to his orders.[42] In another case a factory employee used his own car to take an injured fellow employee to the hospital. On the way he struck and killed a pedestrian. The court held the employer liable because "the errand of the volunteer brought his automobile to the service of the defendant [employer] and the driver thereof being his employee was at the time of the accident acting for the defendant."[43]

Agents and Independent Contractors. In principal-agent relationships other than employer-employee relationships, the principal usually is not liable for the torts of the agent unless the agent has been given the apparent authority to commit the tort on behalf of his principal. Unlike the employer-employee relationship, the principal is not assumed to have direct control over the physical conduct of the agent.

The relationship involving independent contractors, however, presents an interesting situation. The general rule, if there is one, is that the employer does not have vicarious liability for the negligent acts of independent contractors because the employer has no control over how the work is to be done. There are strong trends away from this general rule, however, and Prosser writes that

the prediction has been made that ultimately the "general rule" will be that the employer is liable for the negligence of an independent contractor, and that he will be excused only in a limited group of cases where he is not in a position to select a responsible contractor, or the risk of any harm to others from the enterprise is obviously slight.[44]

First, it should be noted that the principal remains liable for his own acts as well as for those of his employees, of course.[45] One of his acts is selection of the contractor; he can be held liable for injuries caused by his failure to select a competent contractor. To the extent that he directs or supervises the contractor's work or provides equipment for the job, he has responsibility for the results of such direction and for any injuries arising out of defects in the equipment furnished.

In addition, property owners have certain duties for the health and safety of the general public that they are not allowed to delegate to others. Among these are a duty to keep the premises reasonably safe for business visitors and the duty of an employer to provide employees with a safe work place. The owner is also directly responsible when he hires a contractor to do inherently dangerous work; the decision to have such dangerous work performed is the principal's, and he must remain responsible for any resulting injuries. Building repairs made where the work may injure passersby are an example of inherently dangerous work; other examples are the spraying of poison and the use of explosives. In some of these cases, strict

---

[42] *Singer Mfg. Co.* v. *Rahn*, 132 U.S. 518.
[43] *Cummings* v. *Automobile Crank Shaft Co.*, 232 Mich. 158.
[44] Prosser, *op. cit.*, p. 358.
[45] *Ibid.*

liability is imposed on the owner as well as on the contractor; this type of liability (discussed below) does not depend upon negligence. In other cases, claims depend upon negligence, and the negligence is likely to be that of those actually doing the work—the contractor, subcontractors, and their employees. Yet the principal may be held liable, even though he did not direct the actual performance in which the negligence occurred.

SPECIAL CASES IN LIABILITY

There are other conditions under which one may be liable for injury to the persons or property of others. These are grouped together here under the heading, "Special Cases in Liability." The word "special" is used to indicate that the general tort rules do not control liability in these cases. "Special" is not to be taken as necessarily indicating that these cases are rare. Some of them are common causes of claims against businesses.

Wilful and Wanton Misconduct

Standing between intentional torts and negligence is a third class of torts known as wilful and wanton misconduct. While wilful and wanton misconduct borders closely on an intentional tort, it is more frequently viewed as an aggravated type of negligence. The distinction between intent and negligence is often a question of degree, and wilful and wanton misconduct differs from ordinary negligence not only in degree but also in kind and in the social attitude toward it. If a person acts with abandon in the face of great danger to others, his conduct may be considered wilful and wanton. Only when the results of his action become a substantial certainty rather than a foreseeable risk to be avoided by a reasonable man will his conduct be classed as an intentional wrong.

Wilful and wanton misconduct often is held to justify punitive damages[46] and to abrogate the defense of contributory negligence.

Strict Liability

For reasons of public policy, in some situations a person may be held liable for injuries to others when these injuries are neither intentionally nor negligently inflicted. This is called strict liability, or liability without fault, and the philosophy behind it is to shift the risk of inevitable losses to those in the best positions to control it.[47] Strict liability frequently is imposed in connection with those activities which, although socially desirable, greatly

---

[46] Punitive damages are awards to the plaintiff in excess of full compensation for injuries sustained and are made for the purpose of punishing the defendant and discouraging him and others from engaging in the conduct causing the injuries.

[47] Because of the various possible interpretations of the meaning of the concept of fault, the term "liability without fault" is said to be a poor one to use in describing strict liability.

threaten the safety of others in spite of an achievement of a high standard of care by the actor. Examples of such activity include the storage of large quantities of explosives or inflammable liquids in town, blasting operations, crop dusting operations using dangerous chemicals, drilling of oil wells in heavily populated areas, and emission of dust, smoke, or noxious gases from industrial concerns.

In most jurisdictions the keepers of animals are held strictly liable under the common law for damages resulting from the trespasses of these animals.[48] Apart from any trespasses, strict liability is imposed upon the owners and keepers of *dangerous* animals. Dangerous animals include those of species known to be dangerous (lions, wolves, tigers, etc.), even if domesticated, and those of species usually believed to be harmless (cats, dogs, horses, etc.) but individually known by their owners or keepers to have dangerous tendencies.

Special statutes have been passed imposing strict liability on railroads failing to comply with safety standards. In many states sellers of intoxicating beverages are held strictly liable to third parties injured through the intoxication of the purchaser, and manufacturers and sellers of defective foods are held strictly liable to the injured consumers. In many states strict liability is imposed on the owners or pilots of aircraft for ground damage, although the trend now is away from the strict liability rule for aircraft.

Strict liability involving neither intent nor negligence is restricted to losses that can be anticipated as consequences of the risk and foreseeable intervening causes.

Contributory negligence may not be used as a defense in cases involving strict liability, but assumption of the risk can be used. Thus if young Albert intentionally teases a lion and that lion reacts by injuring young Albert, the owner of the lion could not be held liable for the injury. This, of course, assumes that young Albert should have reasonably been expected to understand the risk involved. And if older Albert consented to the boarding of a lion on his premises, he could not expect to hold the lion's owner strictly liable if the lion took a bite of Albert in addition to a lion's share of the regular food available. But as Prosser puts it: "The plaintiff's appreciation of the risk, and his voluntary consent to encounter it, will often be a jury question, and juries frequently are reluctant to find that a true consent has been given."[49]

The defense of privilege applies to situations involving strict liability. For example, keepers of public zoos are privileged and are held only for ordinary negligence. The same is true for transporters required to move dangerous animals and explosives.

---

[48] Under case law, an exception has been made in most jurisdictions for cats and dogs. However, statutes have been enacted in many states imposing strict liability for all damage done by dogs.

[49] Prosser, *op. cit.*, p. 343.

Bailments

A special type of legal liability exposure is that created by bailments. The handling of customer's goods is an important aspect of some business operations. Dry cleaners, laundries, auto garages and other repair services, and public warehouses deal extensively with other people's property. If the customers' possessions are lost or damaged by fire, theft, or some other peril, these bailees are held liable for the customers' losses only if the loss results from negligence of the bailee or his agents.[50] In the handling of customers' property, such bailees are expected to use the care that the famous "reasonable, prudent" man would give property of his own.

Over all, the standard of care expected varies with the type of property involved and the nature of the bailment. The degree of care expected is greater in handling a fur coat than in handling a cloth coat, and a bailee who accepts bailments for profit is expected to use greater care than one who accepts bailments as a free service.[51] Common carriers are expected to use *extraordinary* care and are legally liable for nearly all losses. When a bailor can prove that his property was not returned in good condition or that it was not returned at all, negligence generally is presumed on the part of the bailee. To avoid liability, the bailee must prove that he was not negligent; he must show that he used the standard of care required of him by law. When a bailee is held liable for damages, he suffers not only the expense of the liability claim, including the cost of defense, but also the loss of processing or storage charges that he has earned on the lost or damaged property up to the time of the loss.

Within the limits of public policy and statute, the liability of a bailee can be altered in terms of the contract of bailment. Limitations found in the small print on the back of the ticket or stub received by the customer of an automobile storage garage or other public bailment service may or may not be recognized by a court as setting up an agreement enforceable in a given case of loss.

Workmen's Compensation

An important class of absolute liability is created by workmen's compensation and similar laws. These laws determine the obligations of most employers to their employees for most job-connected injuries (including some illnesses). When one of these laws applies to an injury, the employer's liability is absolute; except as noted below, his obligation is not related to the principle of negligence. Each of the fifty states and Puerto Rico has its

---

[50] As is discussed later in the chapter, the bailee may wish to reimburse his customers for losses even though he is not legally bound to do so. See also chap. 15 on this point.

[51] The greatest degree of care is expected, of course, when the bailment is primarily for the benefit of the bailee, as, for example, when one businessman borrows a power tool from another.

own workmen's compensation law. In addition there are three federally enacted laws: one for federal employees, one for longshoremen and harbor workers, and one for employees of private employers in the District of Columbia. Naturally, considerable variation among the provisions of these statutes will be found. (However, except for the persons to whom they apply, the Longshoremen's and Harbor Workers' Act and the compensation law of the District of Columbia are practically identical.)

Each law provides a method for determining what benefits shall be paid for a covered injury. Subject to provisions for maxima and minima, benefits depend on the extent of disability induced (total or partial, and amount of time for each), the exact nature of the injury (fixed schedules are usually given for certain injuries, such as amputations and death), the worker's wage rate over some given period before the injury, the number of his dependents, and the amount of his medical expenses. The maxima are set so low that compensation claims cannot run nearly as high as tort claims, and average payment per workmen's compensation claim is considerably lower than the average court award for successful claimants under tort. However, because claims are paid under workmen's compensation that would not have to be paid under the rules of tort law, the average payment *per injury* under general tort law is much lower than the average award per *successful claimant*. Whether the award per injury would be lower or higher if a revised tort system were substituted for present workmen's compensation rules is an unprovable matter subject to much debate.[52]

In studying workmen's compensation laws for the purpose of surveying the liability exposures in a business, the risk manager is primarily concerned with three points: the nature and extent of potential liability under workmen's compensation laws, the extent to which these laws still leave the business exposed to potential tort liability claims by its employees and the nature of this exposure (called "employer's liability"), and the support that workmen's compensation gives or can give to the personnel relations program of the business.

Application of Workmen's Compensation Laws. The first question to answer in surveying the workmen's compensation risk is: To which of the fifty-two laws applicable to private businesses in the United States should the risk manager look to determine his exposure? With respect to the laws of the states, Puerto Rico, and the District of Columbia, three different bases are used to establish jurisdiction for the law: the contract of hire took place in the state, the injury occurred in the state, the business of the employer is generally localized to the state.[53] Few if any states use

---

[52] For citations and a summary of major points debated see Herman Miles Somers and Anne Ramsay Somers, *Workmen's Compensation* (New York: John Wiley & Sons, Inc., 1954), esp. Appendix D.

[53] Samuel B. Horovitz, *Injury and Death under Workmen's Compensation Laws* (*Horovitz on Workmen's Compensation*) (Boston: Wright and Potter Printing Co., 1944), pp. 34 ff.

all three of these bases, but the law of each jurisdiction to which the business might be subject on account of any one of the bases must be examined to see whether jurisdiction is claimed. The federal Longshoremen's and Harbor Workers' Act applies throughout the nation to types of employment specified by the act. These employments are generally suggested by the title of the act, but the exact line between employments under this act and employments under state acts is far from clear. It is important to note that what the employee actually was doing and where he was doing it, rather than the title or general nature of his job, determine whether his injury comes under a state workmen's compensation law or the Longshoremen's Act.[54] It has been held that some injuries may come under both a state act and this federal act, although recovery can be had only under one.[55]

After determination of which laws have jurisdiction, the next problem is the extent to which these laws apply to this particular business organization. In most jurisdictions, application of the act to at least some employers is on a compulsory basis. Other employers in these jurisdictions and all employers in the remaining jurisdictions may elect whether they wish to come under the statute. (Of course, this election cannot apply to injuries over which the state does not have or does not assert jurisdiction.) Under some statutes, businesses that do not affirmatively elect "out" are automatically "in"; under more statutes, businesses that do not affirmatively elect "in" are automatically "out." Laws with some compulsory application can be considered in two classes: those in which compulsion applies to employers generally and those in which compulsion applies only to specified employments. When only certain employments are specified, they are employments that the legislature determined to be extra hazardous. Nearly all laws with compulsory features exclude agricultural labor and domestic servants from compulsory coverage.[56] Other frequent exclusions from compulsory coverage are "casual" employees (usually defined as workers "not in the usual course of the trade, business, occupation or profession of the employer"—but see discussion of construction workers, below) and all employers with fewer than a stated number of employees (the number ranges from two to fifteen under different statutes). Finally,

---

[54] See discussion and citations in Davis Tyree Ratcliffe, *Workmen's Compensation Insurance Handbook* (Jenkintown, Pennsylvania: McCombs & Co., 1952), pp. 50–57. Also Horovitz, *op. cit.*, pp. 21 ff.

[55] *Davis* v. *Department of Labor*, 317 U.S. 249 (1942).

[56] Since agriculture is one of the most hazardous of occupations, it can be seen that the concept of "extra hazardous" for purposes of compulsory application of workmen's compensation laws must be taken with some reservation—specifically with reservation for the effects of political power. Among the notorious exclusions under this reservation are those for logging in Maine and South Carolina, for turpentine production in Florida and South Carolina, and a considerable list of other operations, including sawmills and rock quarries, in South Carolina.

some statutes allow employees an election not to come under the act. Except under special circumstances, noted in the next section, election "out" by an employee must be made before occurrence of the injury to which the election is to apply.

Naturally, employments over which a state does not have or refuses to take jurisdiction are not under the compulsory features of its law. The private employments over which states do not have jurisdiction are some of those in interstate commerce and nearly all of those in maritime operations. Although state jurisdiction has been allowed to extend to interstate motor truck and aircraft operations and to some employees of interstate railroads, the federal government has retained exclusive jurisdiction over claims by most employees of interstate railroads.[57]

With respect to maritime employments, the federal government has exclusive jurisdiction over the rights of members of crews of American ships[58] wherever operating, as well as the jurisdiction previously mentioned with respect to longshoremen and harbor workers.

Tort Liability despite Workmen's Compensation. It is clear that, when an employer does not come under workmen's compensation, some other law must govern his liability for injuries suffered on the job. The applicable law is the employer's liability law, a division of tort law already discussed. In addition, an employer who is required or elects to come under the workmen's compensation law in one or more states may still have some employer's liability exposure. The risk survey should locate these exposures.

Several of these exposures have already been indicated; when there is a limitation or exclusion in the pertinent workmen's compensation law, an employer's liability exposure may arise.

Exempt Occupations. A business may be under a compensation act on a compulsory basis. But compulsion does not necessarily apply to agricultural workers, domestic servants, or casual labor. If election is not made to include these workers under the act, an employer's liability exposure exists when there are employees in any of these classes. (Some circumstances that might lead to the use of employees in these classes are considered later in the chapter.)

Occupations under Federal Employer's Liability Laws. There are two federal employers' liability laws: the Federal Employer's Liability Act (FELA), applying to most employees of interstate carriers by rail

---

[57] Federal Employer's Liability Act (45 U.S.C., Sec. 51 *et seq.*). See Horovitz, *op. cit.*, pp. 43 ff.

[58] Jurisdiction with respect to employment aboard foreign vessels lies with the foreign nations, of course, although some moves have been made to make the National Labor Relations Act (which does not deal with liability for on-the-job injury) applicable with respect to the crews on American-owned vessels of foreign registry.

(including car companies and express companies), and the Merchant Marine, or Jones, Act, applying to seamen. Businesses other than interstate carriers by rail have no exposure under FELA. Some businesses not primarily engaged in marine transportation do have exposures under the Jones Act, however. These are businesses that own or operate commercial vessels incidentally to their own operations or that own large pleasure craft for promotion, entertainment, or recreation purposes. This exposure consists of potential suits on the grounds of negligence of the employer, or of unseaworthiness of the vessel, plus absolute liability for "maintenance, care and wages" for disability (including illness) incurred during a voyage.

Employee's Election. If an employee notifies his employer, in advance of injury, that the employee elects not to come under workmen's compensation, there is an obvious employer's liability exposure. Such election is rare. However, an employee sometimes can elect after the injury. Post-injury elections exist:

1. When there has been wilful injury by the employer. (Whether this includes wilful injury by a work supervisor other than the employer appears to be an unsettled question.)
2. Under some workmen's compensation statutes when the employee was an illegally employed minor. (Most statutes that do not give such minors this election provide instead for extra amounts of workmen's compensation.)
3. In some instances, when an employee who is under workmen's compensation in State X is injured in State Y. If the injury is not automatically under workmen's compensation in State Y, and the employer has made no election to come under the compensation act of Y, laws of some states allow the employee to make claim under a tort action in Y or under workmen's compensation in X, as he prefers (i.e., sees his best interests).

Excluded Injuries. It was said in the beginning of the discussion of workmen's compensation that the laws apply to most job-connected injuries, including some illnesses. The following limitations keep this from being *all* job-connected injuries or illnesses.

1. Injuries are required to arise "out of and in the course of [covered] employment." The quoted phrase is one of the two most litigated issues in workmen's compensation.[59] Accidents that do not arise out of and in the course of employment will cause tort claims if negligence seems provable, but perhaps these should not be considered "employer's liability" cases. If the injury occurs other than out of and in the course of employment, then the claim is really brought by one who is a member of the general public at the time of the injury, whatever his relation to the defendant may be at other times, and the liability is "public liability." It is perhaps worth noting, however, that an employee can on occasion be a

---

59 The other is the extent of the disability. Somers and Somers, *op. cit.*, pp. 182–84.

member of the general public, with the privileges and rights appropriate to such status.

2. Compensation laws typically apply to "accidental" injury and, in widely varying degrees, to "occupational" disease. When an employee suffers an injury that is not "accidental" or an illness that is not subject to the local law's coverage for "occupational" disease, a tort claim will arise if the employee and his attorney think that a case can be made that the employer was at fault.

a. Definition of the word "accident" is one of the numerous knotty problems in law. Not only is the word inherently difficult to define, but what legal definition has been had for it is subject to continuing judicial reinterpretation and change.[60] A rather long discussion of some things that are and some that are not generally encompassed by the word "accident" as a legal term appears in chapter 14. Here let it simply be noted that not all bodily injuries are "accidental" or "caused by accident" in the legal sense, and those injuries that are not accidental are covered by workmen's compensation provisions only if they are classified as, or are considered to be a result of, a covered "occupational" disease.

b. As of January 1, 1958, the workmen's compensation laws of two states provided no occupational disease coverage at all, those of two more states provided limited coverage for one specified disease only, with those of the others applying over a range of diseases running from a list of six to all diseases meeting the law's general definition of when a disease is "occupational."[61] The limited coverage acts especially provide opportunities for tort liability even though an employment is covered by such an act.

Claims by Others than the Employee. Whether a claim under workmen's compensation was intended by the various legislatures to be the injured workman's exclusive legal remedy for all covered injuries (except for some special circumstances, previously noted) was a hotly debated issue in the early days of workmen's compensation. That it was so intended now appears to be a settled matter, often by legislative amendment to say so specifically.[62] Whether workmen's compensation claims are also the exclusive remedy for persons other than the injured worker is another matter, especially when these other persons received no direct payment

---

[60] Whether these *judicial* changes have also been *judicious* is a matter of conflicting opinion. In any event, this presents an example of a risk important to insurers, self-insurers, and non-insurers: the risk called "juridical."

[61] A typical definition is "a disease arising out of and in the course of employment. Ordinary diseases of life to which the general public is exposed outside of employment shall not be compensable, except where the said diseases follows [*sic*] as an incident of an occupational disease as defined in this section." *Illinois Revised Statutes*, chap. 48, sec. 172. 36, par. (d).

[62] Somers and Somers, *op. cit.*, pp. 39, 44.

themselves. The present state of affairs appears to be that the compensation remedy is probably exclusive in these cases, too, but some jurisdictions have yet to be heard from.[63]

Workmen's Compensation and Employee Relations. Payments to injured employees or their dependents clearly are significant in planning personnel relations programs. At least three points need to be considered: whether anything will be paid, how much will be paid, and the good or ill will effects engendered by the way in which the whole matter is handled. Equally clearly, the potential loss here is primarily one of goodwill rather than one of liability. In surveying the risks faced by the business, this subject is related more to the area of group insurance, deferred compensation, and pensions than to lawsuits and legal claims. However, it is convenient to include this much of the subject here: In connection with other provisions of the workmen's compensation laws, a little consideration should be given as to what these laws do for injured employees or their dependents on occasions when they do anything—which, as was originally noted, means on the vast majority of occasions in which an employee of a covered employer suffers a job-connected accidental injury or—and this depends very much on the particular state involved—contracts an occupational disease.

Even a summary of the benefits provided in the fifty-three laws that apply to private employers is too much to handle here. The figures for each state as of various dates can be found in some generally available sources. Two good, inexpensive compilations of provisions and benefits are *Analysis of Workmen's Compensation Laws,* by the Chamber of Commerce of the United States, and *State Workmen's Compensation Laws,* by the United States Bureau of Labor Standards. Each publication is revised periodically. What will be presented here is a set of guidelines to use in examining the benefits of any particular law: a list of the features that are determining with respect to what the payments will provide.

The payments under all the laws have two parts: payments for disability and provision of medical care. The amount of payment for disability

---

[63] For one summary, see *Fire, Casualty and Surety Bulletins* (monthly) (Cincinnati: National Underwriter Co.), W.C. S–1 ff., July, 1957. Part of the confusion results from the fact that in *Hitaffer* v. *Argonne Co.,* 183 Fed. (2d) 811 (1950), the United States Court of Appeals for District of Columbia held the compensation remedy not exclusive with respect to a wife's claim for loss of consortium (her husband was disabled, not killed, so she received no compensation payments herself); then, in *Smither and Co.* v. *Coles,* 242 Fed. (2d) 220 (1957), the same court reversed itself on this particular point. Several state courts have agreed with the Smither decision. But statutes vary considerably with respect to the definiteness with which they declare themselves to be exclusive remedies, and different results may yet appear under some of them. As this is being written, *Moran* v. *Nafi* is en route to the Michigan supreme court, where, according to one insurance attorney, "some of the most liberal jurists in the country are sitting." (J. L. Schueler, quoted in "WC and Liability Insurance Face Four Serious New Sources of Loss," *National Underwriter,* Vol. XL, No. 20 [May 18, 1962], p. 13.)

clearly depends, first, on the rate at which the payments are made—the amount paid per week. This depends on factors mentioned before—the employee's previous average wage (computed differently under different laws), the number of his dependents, and the nature of the loss (death or total or partial disability). These figures are subject to stated maximum and minimum rates. The next obvious question is for how long the weekly rate will be paid. Several limits are to be noted. First, the commencement of payment: waiting periods are always required before any payments are due. Usually this waiting period is in the form of a franchise deductible: After disability has continued for a stated time, no deductible applies; payments become due back to the first day of disability. How long payments will be made after they begin is subject to various kinds of limits in various states, with more than one type of limitation sometimes applying. For some types of injuries, classified as "permanent partial," a specified number of weeks is to be paid; this number may or may not be in addition to payments for any period of the "temporary total" disability arising from the same injury. For other injuries the actual duration of the disability is one limit, of course, but aggregate dollar limits or a fixed maximum number of weeks of payments, or both, are often set in addition. Death benefits may also be limited as to number of weeks or as to total number of dollars and are subject to such additional causes of cessation as children's marrying or becoming eighteen, widow's remarrying or any dependents' dying.

With respect to provision of medical care, two types of limitations appear: time and dollars. Some statutes set no limits of either type. Some other statutes are deceiving; they set limits, sometimes short in time or low in dollar amount, but the limits may be exceeded at the discretion of the state administrative authority—and the authority exercises its right with great regularity. Still other statutes set short or low limits and stick to them.

All determining factors considered, the general situation is that benefits are minimal or subminimal when compared either to costs of living or to the incurred loss of wages. This fact is important, of course, when workmen's compensation benefits are considered in connection with the overall program for employee relations, and it should be particularly borne in mind when group disability income and life insurance are being planned.

Other Compulsory Benefits for Employees

There are at least two additional sources of risk of loss through extra expenses imposed by law that require payments to be made to employees in event of specified contingencies, payments without regard to fault. One of these sources is employee unemployment; the other is employee injury not covered under workmen's compensation.

The Risk of Unemployment Benefits. At least two distinguishable sets of risks are present here: unemployment that is officially temporary and separation that is avowedly permanent.

Under "temporary" are two divisions. One contains the well-known government unemployment "insurance." The other contains the much less pervasive but almost as well-known "supplementary unemployment benefits" (SUB) negotiated by a few unions; it will include the "guaranteed annual wage" as it comes into being. A risk manager who applies his risk management techniques to a study of these exposures will find that interesting and useful things can be learned about them. For example, he might find that, with respect to unemployment "insurance," he could be helpful in one or more of three ways. He might suggest and work for improvements in the premium-rating system, which is a much debated merit rating system; he might, given the rating system, plan ways to reduce costs under it; and he might seek some transfer of risk of excessive losses under the system. Admittedly, unemployment is generally classed as an uninsurable risk, but that does not preclude there being—now or in the future— professional risk bearers who might, under some circumstances, take some of the risk at a reasonable price. And what is uninsurable under ordinary conditions and usual circumstances is not always equally uninsurable when the conditions are sufficiently manipulated and the circumstances sufficiently controlled with the possibility of successful insurance underwriting in mind.

In the second set of risks, having to do with avowedly permanent separation of employees, the obvious extra expense losses are severance payments and various payments arranged for employees deemed "technologically unemployed." It is not beyond reason that advanced static risk management techniques may be useful here, too.

The Risk of Non-occupational Injury Benefits. Four states have now adopted compulsory insurance by employers of employee disabilities not under workmen's compensation. Because of the (presently) relatively short period of disability paid for, these are sometimes referred to as "Temporary Disability Insurance" plans. Because in three of the four states private insurance may be purchased to cover liability under the plan, and the risk manager is expected to be trained and experienced in dealing with insurance companies, he may be expected to be helpful with respect to these plans. With respect to all the plans, the risk manager should be able to provide intelligence and logic useful in dealing with the plan as it stands and with the legislature as it periodically considers revision of the plan.

LIABILITY IMPOSED BY CONTRACT

A business may have legal liability exposures over and above those resulting from intentional torts, negligence, wilful or wanton misconduct, and strict liability.

Liability Assumed under Contract

A business may enter into a contract under which it agrees to assume in whole or in part the common law, or other, liability of another. When this happens, a contractual liability exposure is created. Unless the risk manager reviews all contracts made by his company, he is likely to overlook important loss exposures arising out of hold harmless or indemnification clauses. Typical contractual liability exposures are found in leases, contracts to supply goods or services, railroad switch track agreements, and permits from municipal authorities.

For example, the Prepared Potato Company leases its premises from the Wholesome Life Insurance Company. The lease requires the tenant to assume all liability to third parties for bodily injury and property damage arising not only from the operation and maintenance of the premises but also from its ownership. The Prepared Potato Company, therefore, is subject to liability under common law for its own negligence and in addition has contracted to assume the common law liability for the negligence of its landlord.

Sales contracts between manufacturers and retailers may contain clauses under which one party agrees to hold the other harmless for bodily injury and property damage claims arising out of the product involved. The Prepared Potato Company's sales contract includes a clause under which the retailer assumes all liability for bodily injury and property damage caused by the product, whether the claim is based on negligence or a violation of an implied warranty. Thus the retailer has taken over the products liability hazard. In a joint suit the retailer will be required to pay not only damages assessed against himself but also those assessed against the manufacturer.

The Prepared Potato Company has a sidetrack provided by the Western Central Railroad for use in bringing carloads of unprepared potatoes. As noted in chapter 3, the agreement under which the sidetrack is furnished usually includes a hold harmless clause in favor of the railroad. The National Industrial Traffic League has developed a standard sidetrack liability clause, which was quoted in chapter 3 and which is in wide use; this has been included in the Prepared Potato Company's switch track agreement. Under the clause, the Western Central is released from liability for damage by most fires caused by locomotives and for damages caused by the Prepared Potato Company or its employees or agents. Liability claims arising from the negligence of both the Western Central and the Prepared Potato Company and not involving fire will be borne equally. Thus, under this agreement, the Prepared Potato Company has assumed liability in excess of that imposed by law.

Many older sidetrack agreements have much more severe hold harmless clauses than the standard form; therefore, it is necessary for the risk manager to review the agreement and, if possible, induce the railroad to replace bastard agreements with the standard form.

Suppose the Prepared Potato Company engages the Abstract Concrete Company to erect a driveway for the executive clubhouse. To begin construction, a permit must be obtained from the city. This permit requires the Potato company to assume all liability for any accidents that may happen on public property in the course of construction regardless of whether the fault lies with it or with the Concrete company. The Potato company might be able to shift the risk to the Concrete company and require it to assume all liability resulting from loss or damage to third parties. In this way, the Concrete company has increased its liability exposure. But, under the permit, the Potato company must be primarily liable for all accidents and usually must post a bond to guarantee payment. Who finally bears the burden, of course, is determined by the construction contract and the common law.

Product Liability

Liability for defective products can arise on either a contractual or a tort basis. In fact, buyers have been able to recover both from the retailer for violation of contract and from the manufacturer for negligence. The basis for recovery under contract violation is breach of an expressed or implied warranty.

An express warranty is an affirmation or promise regarding the product. It is designed to induce a customer to purchase and is relied upon by the buyer in making the purchase. Whether a statement made by a seller or his representative is a warranty of fact or an expression of opinion is a matter for the court to decide. Statements made in advertisements have been held to be express warranties. An automobile manufacturer was held liable for injuries when one of its automobiles was overturned and the driver's head was punctured by jagged steel pieces welded together in the top. The court held that an express warranty was violated because the company had advertised and had distributed sales literature saying that a uni-steel top was one of the features of the car.[64]

On the other hand, a statement made by a salesman to the effect that a *secondhand* truck rim offered for sale was a good rim was held to be purely an expression of opinion, and as such was in no sense a warranty.[65]

An implied warranty is a creature of law. It is inferred from the conduct of the parties and from the facts of the transaction. Two implied product warranties are that the goods are fit for the purpose for which they are sold (purchased) and that they are merchantable.

Concerning the implied warranty of fitness, Hugh R. Gallagher says:

---

[64] *Bahlman* v. *Hudson Motor Car Co.*, 288 N.W. 309 (Mich.)
[65] *Holley* v. *Central Auto Parts et al.*, 347 S.W. 2d 341 (1961).

"Where a seller knows the purpose for which a buyer purchases the goods, and the latter relies on the skill and judgment of the seller, then if the article proves not to be reasonably fit for the particular purpose, the warranty is breached."[66] Thus, a hardware dealer was held liable when an apple orchard was damaged by an insect spray purchased for the purpose for which it was used.[67]

As to the implied warranty of merchantability, Gallagher says:

A product is of a merchantable quality if it would pass in the trade without objection under the description given, if it was of fair, average, or medium quality, if it was fit for the ordinary purpose for which such goods are used, if it was of even kind, quality, and quantity, if it was adequately packaged or contained, and if it conformed to the affirmations of fact or promises contained on the label.[68]

Thus, a grocery store was held liable when a pin, lodged in a loaf of bread, pricked the mouth of its purchaser, causing him injury.[69]

To a lesser and lesser extent the common law requirement of privity of contract has restricted the use of a warranty violation as a basis for establishing legal liability to persons other than the immediate purchaser. A warranty is a contract, and only those who are parties to it can be held for breach. The courts, however, have reasoned in cases involving medicine, food, drink, and inherently dangerous products that public policy would best be served by abating this general rule. Several lines of thought have been presented to justify awards to the ultimate consumer on grounds of breach of warranty in liability action against the manufacturer. For example, courts have held on various occasions that the warranty runs with the product from manufacturer through distributor to consumer, that the rights of the retailer against the manufacturer are assigned to the consumer, or that the producer is an insurer against harmful effects of the product he manufactures.

In a rather recent case, warranty was held to run from a *dealer* to a user with whom the dealer had had no direct contact. A hula skirt proved extraordinarily combustible, and the girl who wore it was severely burned. She had borrowed it from her aunt, who had purchased it in Hawaii. The burned girl's attorney brought suit against the *retailer* on grounds of both negligence and breach of implied warranty. When the jury found no negligence but rendered an award on the basis of implied warranty, the defendant's attorney sought a new trial on the ground that the latter finding was not in accordance with the law of sales contracts and warranties. The United States District Court held that this non-buyer consumer could recover from the seller for breach of implied warranty even though there was

---

[66] Gallagher, *op. cit.* (see n. 22 above).
[67] *Wisdon* v. *Morris Hardware Co.*, 274 P 1050 (Wash.).
[68] Gallagher, *op. cit.*
[69] *Ryan* v. *Progressive Grocery Stores*, 192 N.E. 105 (N.Y.).

no privity of contract between her and the seller. This case is of additional interest because the court took some forty pages to review and cite the law with respect to this subject matter.[70]

The law dealing with action based on breach of warranty in products liability cases has undergone such a sweeping change that Professor Kulp was prompted to write that "*Caveat venditor* (let the seller beware) . . . describes the situation of today far better than the *caveat emptor* of tradition."[71]

Professional Liability

When a physician, surgeon, attorney, accountant, beautician, dentist, or some other professional person or skilled tradesman fails to use the care required in rendering his service or performing his trade, he may be held liable in tort for his negligence if such negligence is the proximate cause of a loss to his client.[72] In these situations liability may also result from breach of contract. A physician, for example, may be held strictly liable for failure to perform under a contract to treat his patient. The basis for action is the violation of an implied warranty of his skill and ability to render the service for which he has been engaged. Thus, action in both professional and product liability cases may be based either on tort or on contract. This is true in other contractual relationships (relationships entered into voluntarily by both parties) when defective performance under the contract is a source of injury to the plaintiff.

When the wronged party has a choice of redress by action in tort or in contract, he will have to consider which type of action appears more advantageous to him. The tort remedy has the advantage of permitting higher damages but the disadvantage of requiring proof of negligence or intentional harm.[73]

VOLUNTARY PAYMENTS

In some situations, good business practice dictates compensating persons for bodily injury or property damaged even though there is no legal liability for the loss.

As pointed out earlier, bailees are liable for damage to customers' goods only if the loss is caused by the bailee's negligence. But customers often expect to be paid for a loss even though technically the bailee is not at fault. They neither understand nor appreciate the legal questions involved.

---

[70] 198 F. Supp. 78 (1961).

[71] Kulp, *op. cit.*, p. 78 (see n. 30, above).

[72] This is true whether the service is performed with or without charge.

[73] For a discussion of the advantages and disadvantages of tort and contract remedies see Prosser, *op. cit.*, pp. 483–86.

Failure to reimburse the customers, regardless of fault, might cost the bailee valuable goodwill, especially when ultimate consumers are concerned. Thus, if the Quickie Washie Laundry were struck by lightning and an ensuing fire destroyed bundles of laundry, the Godiva-like customers would be incensed if the laundry owners refused to "make good the loss." It would not help to inform the customers that the cause of the loss was an "act of God" and not the responsibility of the laundry owners. Laundries that want a spotless reputation for clean dealing will assume the loss and charge the expense to the cost of maintaining goodwill. The loss is just as real as though the laundry owners were legally liable for the damage. This type of loss exposure should not be overlooked by the risk manager.

Sometimes a customer or supplier is injured on the premises of a business under circumstances involving no legal liability. The injured party, for example, may be guilty of contributory negligence. Yet, in order to create goodwill, the management may want to pay the medical expenses involved. This is especially true when a rider in a company-owned or -operated automobile is injured and is denied legal remedy by the application of a guest statute.[74] The possibility of incurring voluntary expenses involving the bodily injury of customers or others should be reviewed by the risk manager in appraising his loss exposures.

It has already been noted that voluntary payments to employees or their dependents in the event of employee injury or death may be desirable for personnel relations purposes. Retirement is another common occasion for which voluntary payments to employees are considered useful. In connection with retirement and death benefits, and to some (and a possibly increasing) extent in connection with disability, the federal social security program should be studied. This program was omitted from the previous discussion of compulsory payments to or for employees, however, because as it is presently set up it involves neither risk for the employer nor any selection by him as to how a risk may be dealt with[75]—the two topics that are the subject of this book.

The area of voluntary payments to employees is shrinking, of course. Contractual obligations to provide various security benefits are commonly bargained for by unions, and, while union membership as a percentage of the total work force is not growing at present, the percentage of so-called "fringe" benefits that are covered or determined by bargained contracts

---

[74] Remember that under the guest statutes the at-fault party must be guilty of wilful and wanton misconduct.

[75] Note that unemployment compensation and compulsory non-occupational disability insurance plans were included because they do involve risk for the employer (with respect to what his premium may be) and because under three of the disability insurance programs the employer has a little choice as to how the risk may be dealt with (he may select among insurers).

is increasing as more and more of the bargaining turns to what are called "non-wage" provisions (a description employers are beginning to consider catachrestic).

EXAMPLES OF TORT LIABILITY LOSS

It is clear that no business can escape the possibility of incurring loss resulting from claims for damages arising out of negligence or other fault. In fact, the chance of loss is greater today than it has ever been before. Loss severity is also greater. Growth of the economy and of the individual firm, innovations and technological progress, the concentration of large numbers of people in relatively small areas of space, the higher standard of care that courts are now requiring of the prudent man, the changing concepts of liability, and more liberal verdicts have all increased the frequency or severity of liability losses. It is clearly important that the survey of exposures to liability loss overlook no potential.

To suggest the variety of problems that must be looked for, the following examples of losses are given and categorized according to the general class of hazards to which each belongs.

Property Owned or Used

A major exposure to liability claims arises from ownership or use of such property as buildings, elevators, escalators, boilers, machinery, sprinkler systems, vacant lots, outdoor signs, automobiles, watercraft, and aircraft. The legal right to own or control property carries with it the legal duty to exercise care in the maintenance and use of that property to the end that the public is protected from injury. A breach of this duty is the source of many successful liability claims against those who own or use property. For example, a store owner was held liable for damages when a window shopper slipped and fell on the store's wet vestibule floor;[76] owners of a hardware store were held liable when a customer mistook an unguarded elevator shaft in a dimly lighted building for the floor of the elevator;[77] a mercantile company had to pay damages when the hand of a small child found its way into the gears of an escalator bannister through an opening in the boxing;[78] a warehouse was held liable for damage to stored cotton when its sprinkler system sprang a leak;[79] the owner of a low-flying plane was held liable for some frightened turkeys that killed themselves by running into obstacles in their pen;[80] a moving service had to pay when a car collided with one of its vans as it was trying

---

[76] *Brody* v. *Albert Lifson and Sons, Inc.*, New Jersey Supreme Court, 4 C.C.H. (Negligence 2d) 515.

[77] *Aiken* v. *Sydney Steel Scraper Co.*, 198 S.W. 1139 (Mo.).

[78] *Hillerbrand* v. *May Mercantile Co.*, 121 S.W. 326 (Mo.).

[79] *Harper Warehouse, Inc.* v. *Henry Chanin Corp.*, 11 C.C.H. (Negligence 2d) 912.

[80] *Miller* v. *Maples*, 5 C.C.H. (Negligence 2d) 160.

to negotiate a U-turn on a highway at night;[81] and so it goes! Cases illustrating different types of negligence exposures are practically inexhaustible.

Products

Liability can arise from conditions in property conveyed to another person. The seller of the property can be held liable for losses arising from faulty, unsafe, and dangerous conditions in the premises after the property has been sold, particularly if the new owner has not been made fully aware of the full and true condition of the property.

Manufacturing, handling, or distributing products can expose a business to liability claims. Some of these claims are based on negligence; others are based on violation of contract. In the former case, a breach of care must be shown; in the latter case, a breach of warranty must be proved.

The general rule is that the manufacturer or dealer can be held liable for damages to the purchaser who suffers injury because of the defective or harmful nature of the product. Liability extends beyond the direct purchaser to the general public if the product is *inherently* dangerous or if the product is *potentially* dangerous and sufficient warning is not given to those unaware of this potential. For example, a food processor was held liable when a man broke a tooth on a metal washer while attempting to eat his prepared TV dinner,[82] and a refining company was found negligent in failing to warn of the latent dangers of its cleaning fluid.[83] In this last case, the bottle did contain a warning on its label "Do not inhale fumes. Use only in a well ventilated place," but the jury found this warning insufficient.

Concealment of known defects or misrepresentation of the product also extends the liability of manufacturers or dealers beyond the direct purchaser. Thus, an automobile dealer was held liable to a used car purchaser and his wife, who was injured when a tire blew out.[84] The salesman had told the purchaser twice that the tires were good, but an examination after the accident revealed that the blowout occurred at an old break in the tire. The court reasoned that a seller is deemed to have knowledge of a defect if it is so plain that the exercise of due care would disclose it. An automobile dealer who falsely represents a vehicle to be in good condition when he knows, or in the exercise of ordinary care should have known, that it is defective is liable not only to the purchaser but to third persons for injuries resulting from defective conditions.

In another case, illustrating the same point, a passenger riding in the right front seat of an automobile was leaning forward to deposit the ash

---

[81] *Johannessen* v. *Bekins Van and Storage Company*, No. 60831, Superior Court, Pima County, Arizona.

[82] *Campbell Soup Co., Inc.* v. *Ryan*, 10 C.C.H. (Negligence 2d) 323.

[83] *Maize* v. *Atlantic Refining Co.*, 41 A. 2d 850 (Pa.).

[84] *Johnson* v. *Beaudry Motor Co.*, 170 F. Supp. 164 U.S.D.C., Ga.

of a cigarette in the ash receptacle in the instrument panel. Just at this moment the driver had to apply his brakes suddenly to avoid hitting a car that had run a stop sign. The smoking passenger was thrown forward and struck the ashtray with his head. He sustained a cut in the cornea of his eye, which resulted in loss of vision in that eye. The cut was attributed to a sharp, jagged corner or edge on the ash receptacle. The manufacturer was held liable for the loss. The court held that proper inspection by the manufacturer would have revealed the defect. The failure to inspect was held to be a negligent act and the proximate cause of the injury.[85]

The exceptions given above appear to eclipse the general rule that product liability of manufacturers or dealers extends only to the direct purchaser and no further.

The manufacturer, wholesaler, and retailer can all be held guilty of negligence and required to pay damages for the same incident. In a recent case, a small boy fired a toy dart gun that had been given to him. When he saw that only the upper part of the dart emerged from the muzzle, he decided to look into the barrel to locate the trouble. His investigation was cut short when the remaining piece darted out, severely injuring his curious eye. The manufacturer, wholesaler, and retailer of the toy were sued for damages, and the court held all three guilty of negligence.[86]

Generally, however, the manufacturers are the ones who are held liable when product liability suits based on alleged negligence are decided for the plaintiff. Negligence on the part of the wholesaler or retailer or others handling products for resale is difficult to prove unless the product is changed or contaminated somewhere along its marketing route from manufacturer to consumer. Also, it is not easy to substantiate an allegation that the wholesaler or retailer knew the product to be defective but failed to use care by revealing the defects to the buyer.

This is not to say that it is simple to assemble specific evidence of negligence on the part of the manufacturer. Obtaining specific evidence of negligent acts committed by the manufacturer is difficult for two reasons —first, the plaintiff rarely has firsthand knowledge of the production process, and, second, those who do have this knowledge generally have the additional knowledge that their best interests are not served by testifying against the defendant.

When failure to comply with a statute controlling the manufacture, sale, or distribution of goods is the proximate cause of an injury, such failure may be taken as negligence in itself if the purpose of the statute was to protect the injured person against the harm done.[87] The legislature, through

---

[85] *Zahn* v. *Ford Motor Co.*, 164 F. Supp. 936 U.S.D.C., Minn.

[86] *Dobin* v. *Avenue Food Mart*, 345 Pac. (2d) 89.

[87] Violation of a statute may be considered negligence per se in actions involving other than product liability, also when the violation is unexcused and the statute was designed to protect the injured person against the harm done.

the statute, fixed the standard of conduct required. For example, a garage owner sold gasoline in a metal can to two men, ignoring a law restricting the amount of gasoline that can be sold other than in fuel tanks. As it turned out, these men were hired by an overinsured or underfinanced building owner to set fire to the building. Instead of burning, the gasoline exploded, killing a suspicious detective who had tailed the professional arsonists. The garage owner was held liable for damages.[88] A druggist who violates a statute by selling strychnine to a minor under age fifteen may be held liable per se if such a sale is the proximate cause of a death. Violations of the Pure Food and Drug Act constitute negligence per se in cases where the violation is the proximate cause of an injury.

As mentioned, it may not be necessary to prove acts of negligence to establish product liability because such liability can also arise from breach of contract.

Business Services

Business activity as well as the ownership and use of property and the manufacture and sale of products can expose a firm to liability losses. For example, a business can be held liable for loss or damage caused by defective installation, repair, or condition in work completed away from the premises. This liability hazard is called the *completed operations* hazard. The courts handle a large number of completed operations liability suits each year involving both bodily injury and property damage. A few recent cases follow. A contractor was held liable for damages to apartment building tenants who became seriously ill from carbon monoxide fumes arising from a faulty furnace connection.[89] A furnace company was held liable for a fire loss to a residence caused by a faulty operation of a thermostatic fan that it had installed in a home.[90] An elevator operator was awarded damages from an elevator company when the elevator plunged nine floors with its operator at the wheel, and this happened not long after the elevator company's own service man had passed upon the good condition of the elevator.[91] A power company that had improperly wired a house was held liable to the widow after the man of the house sought to do some work on the wiring and was shocked to death upon finding that moving the switch to the "off" position did not disconnect the circuit.[92]

Some Miscellaneous Exposures

Other types of activity that expose a business to liability losses arising out of negligence are the making of alterations or repairs to property

[88] *Daggett v. Keshner*, 7 N.Y. (2d) 981.
[89] *Andrews v. Del Guzzi*, 11 C.C.H. (Negligence 2d) 668.
[90] *Handy v. Holland Furnace Co.*, 11 C.C.H. (Negligence 2d) 988.
[91] *Wroblewski v. Otis Elevator*, 9 A.D.N.Y. (2d) 294.
[92] *Losh v. Ozark Border Electric Cooperative*, 10 C.C.H. (Negligence 2d) 585.

owned or used by the company; the sponsoring of athletic teams for employees or for others; the engaging in professional service, such as the operation of a beauty parlor or health service,[93] negligence in the preparation of advertising copy that might libel, slander, infringe a copyright, or violate any rights of privacy of others; and the serving of liquors to clients (or to employees at the annual Christmas party).[94] When directors of a corporation are guilty of failure to use reasonable care in supervising or directing the activities of the corporation, they can be held personally liable to stockholders and others for damages. Risk management programs should consider this liability exposure.

Nuclear Energy

The increasing use of nuclear energy represents one of the innovations that have vastly increased and complicated the liability exposure. Professor MacDonald points out that two types of losses from accidental release of radioactivity can be expected from the expanding use of radio isotopes in industry:[95] expenses to eliminate contamination and the cost of bodily injury claims. He illustrates these types of losses with the following stories:

"A researcher working alone in a laboratory spilled onto his hand a quantity of cesium 137 so small that he was unaware of the happening. His hand, nevertheless, became a few-millicuries sources of radioactivity . . . he contaminated everything he touched." These included items in the laboratory, his street clothes, his automobile, his neighbor's right hand, and many items about the house. The task of searching for the many patches of radioactivity throughout the laboratory and of retracing the researcher's steps outside the laboratory consumed many man-hours of work. Although in the end, no one was hurt by irradiation "the cost of sleuthing, decontamination, and discarded clothing and equipment totaled approximately $4,000. It could have cost much more had the researcher made a few stops on his way home."

"In the other case, a group of laboratory employees was exposed to considerable radiation when they opened a container of pellets of radioactive iridium and aluminum which had turned to dust. Before they realized what

---

[93] The exposure here, formerly known technically as a malpractice hazard, is now called the "professional liability hazard"—breach of duty by the failure of a nurse to give the patient the prescribed medicine or the failure of a lawyer to perform an act expected of him in the performance of a professional service for others in his capacity as a lawyer. As has been discussed, the professional liability hazard may arise out of breach of contract rather than breach of a standard of conduct expected of one who holds himself out to the public as a qualified expert in his field.

[94] In a number of states, liquor liability laws impose strict liability upon the sellers of alcoholic beverages. Some are concerned that these laws might be held to apply to those serving liquor as hosts. There is no clear authority on this probability, however. Nevertheless, even without the application of liquor liability statutes, servers of liquor might be held liable for negligence in serving liquor to persons already drunk.

[95] MacDonald, *op. cit.*, pp. 23–24 (see n. 39, above).

they were examining, a current of air lifted much of the dust from the box. The men claimed to have suffered cataracts, skin burns, radiation sickness, physical and mental shock, and pain and anguish. Their physicians hinted that they quite likely would develop cancer of the bladder and leukemia."

Cases involving allegations of negligence in the use of radio-isotopes have not yet been seasoned in the courts, so it is impossible to judge how much additional liability exposure is created when a firm decides to use a radiation process.[96] Until the claims attorneys have had a chance to prove their art and skill, the extent of the liability exposure in this area will remain uncertain.

SUMMARY

The liability exposure is one of the most important, if not the most important of all loss exposures faced by a business enterprise. It is capable of producing devastating losses of amounts that defy advance determination. Liability may be based either on tort or on contract. A tort has been broadly defined as one of a group of civil wrongs, other than breach of contract, for which a remedy is available through a court of law. A tort action for damages is taken to redress a wrong brought about by socially unreasonable conduct of others. This conduct may be intentional, negligent, or neither intentional nor negligent. In the latter case, liability is said to be "strict," that is, to exist without fault.

Intentional torts include interferences with the person of others through assault, battery, words causing mental disturbances (called the new tort), false imprisonment, and defamation. They also include intentional interferences with property of other through trespass and conversion.

Unintentional torts are those arising out of negligence and out of the application of rules of strict liability. Negligence is defined broadly as the failure to live up to the standard of conduct expected by society of a reasonable man in a similar situation. A person may be held vicariously liable for the negligent acts of his employees and in many cases for those of independent contractors that he engages.

Strict liability is imposed without regard to fault in cases in which one is engaged in an unusual activity involving abnormal dangers to others. Examples are found in situations involving the ownership or maintenance of animals, the sale of intoxicating beverages, industrial accidents and diseases, and the violation of certain statutes designed for the protection of the public against the specific type of injury received. The justification

---

[96] Professor MacDonald believes that the ordinary negligence law will apply, but he recognizes the possibility that commercial reactor operators may have absolute liability imposed upon them just as in the case of owners of dangerous animals. MacDonald further believes that the plaintiffs will be required to prove that their injury would not have occurred had it not been for the exposure to a particular emission of radiation (*op. cit.*, p. 28).

of strict liability is found in the social policy of placing the burden of the loss upon those best capable of bearing, reducing, or shifting it. There has been, and still is, a great deal of interest among some social reformers in extending strict liability to automobile accidents. The principal liability exposures based on contracts that risk managers need to consider are liability of others assumed under contract, product liability, and professional liability.

The primary liability exposures of business organizations are those arising out of the ownership or operation of premises, elevators, escalators, motor vehicles, aircraft, and watercraft; the manufacture and sale of products; the engaging in business operations away from the premises, including defective installations or repairs made for others; the provision of professional services; the employment of personnel; the ownership or use of animals, vacant lots, advertising signs, vending machines, and power equipment; the ownership of property rented to others; property formerly owned but sold and relinquished; the construction or demolition of structures; property of others held under bailment; and contracts to assume the liability of others.

A useful summary of public liability hazards inherent in various business operations can be found in Reginald V. Spell's *Public Liability Hazards.*[97]

REVIEW AND DISCUSSION QUESTIONS

1. Why is a term of such importance as "tort" not precisely defined in the law? (Hint: how are definitions of common law terms determined?)
2. The text mentions some ways in which business activities can produce suits for alleged intentional torts. For each type of intentional tort, describe an additional way in which a business activity might produce a claim.
3. Is liability for intentional torts an insurable hazard? Explain.
4. What is meant by the term "privilege" when used in connection with claims involving alleged intentional torts? Of what importance is this knowledge to the risk manager? Give some examples of privileged actions that are applicable to business situations.
5. Three children entered the storage yard of a construction firm. While there, they pulled a pile of sheet metal over on themselves. Two of the children were killed, the third seriously injured. On what grounds would suits against the building firm be based? Who could be plaintiffs in these suits? What defenses could the firm offer against these suits?
6. What is your definition of a "reasonable man"? Are you satisfied with this definition? Why or why not?
7. "It is more socially desirable for the defendant to pay the loss than the plaintiff when the defendant is financially more capable of doing so." Do you agree or disagree with that statement? What factors and criteria did

---

[97] (3d ed.; Indianapolis: Rough Notes Co., 1956.)

you employ in reaching your conclusion? What factors and criteria could be used to reach an opposite conclusion?

8. What must a plaintiff's attorney establish to make good a claim against the defendant in a tort suit for negligence? In a tort action between two business units, two risk managers can be involved—one who manages the plaintiff's risks and one who manages the defendant's risks. Explain how each of these risk managers might view the facts and the law differently. (Refer to each of the elements of a negligent act in answering this question.)

9. Are the jury awards in the county in which you live (or go to school) generally high, low, or about average as compared with those in other counties in the state? Why do awards vary from county to county?

10. On a bus crowded with students returning from a successful football game, high spirits and high jinks were the rule. Some student lit a firecracker with a long fuse and tossed it in the air over the crowd. When it fell toward one student, he batted it away toward another student, who in turn batted it away from himself, and so on, and so on, until it exploded and blinded a student in one eye. This student's attorney entered suit against the only two students who could be identified as having batted the firecracker. Suit was also entered against the bus company, on the grounds that their driver failed to control his passengers. Sued on the same grounds were a teacher and his wife who were the official chaperones for the jaunt. The school was also sued on the grounds that (1) the chaperones were their agents and (2) the trip had been "approved" by school officials in that they had received advance notice of it as their rules required and had sent the chaperones a standard report form to be filled out and turned in to the Dean of Women after the trip. (a) Discuss the strengths and weaknesses of the position of each of these defendants. (b) What difference, if any, would it have made if the identity of the student who lit the firecracker could have been determined?

11· "Even though all the elements of a negligent act are proved to have been present, the injured party may still be defeated in his claim for damages." Explain why you agree or disagree with the above statement.

12. The motto of the National Association of Claimants' Attorneys is "Towards the more adequate award." What *is* an "adequate award" on a liability claim?

13. The Province of Saskatchewan has applied the compensation principle to highway accidents: Fees are collected with auto licenses to provide a fund to make specified payments to persons injured on Saskatchewan highways regardless of presence or absence of any one's negligence or fault. In what ways do the arguments for workmen's compensation laws apply to highway accidents? In what ways do they not apply?

14. The liability of railroads toward most of their employees is governed by the Federal Employer's Liability Act (F.E.L.A.). This act leaves employer's liability on a tort basis (negligence must be proved to the satisfaction of the jury). However, the defenses of "assumption of risk" and "fellow servant doctrine" are not available to employers under this Act, and contributory negligence by the employee reduces but does not necessarily defeat his recovery. Railroad employees' unions have resisted suggestions that a workmen's compensation law be substituted for the present Act. Why would these unions have this attitude? Which seems to you to be the better approach —F.E.L.A. or workmen's compensation? Why (what are your criteria)?

15. The text mentions several statutory and some judicial modifications of the general tort law rules. Which of these (a) increased, (b) decreased the number of tort claims which could be successfully sustained? Which direction of change has predominated? Why? How may the exceptions be explained?

16. Which of the following changes would you consider better? (a) Removal of dollar limits from claims for wrongful death. (b) Establishment of dollar limits on claims for bodily injury other than death. Why? Do you see any reason for considering either change? Why or why not?

17. Employers have been held liable for injuries in the following circumstances: (a) An employee's job kept him driving around the city contacting customers of his employer. Driving home from his last call for the day, he injured a third party. The employer was successfully sued. (b) A salesman was at home taking a shower before attending an evening sales meeting. He slipped in the shower, and was awarded workmen's compensation benefits for his injuries. What theories of law, responsibility and justice do you find at work in these cases?

18. What rule of tort law gave rise to the (not strictly accurate) statement "Every dog is entitled to one bite"?

19. What is the difference between the liability of (a) those who have charge of the goods of others for purposes of common carriage and (b) those who have charge of such property for other business purposes? What reasons might there be for this difference?

20. Two buyers for a Denver department store make semi-annual trips to the New York markets. The compensation laws of what states might conceivably apply to injuries suffered by these buyers? Why? What provisions in the laws of these states might keep them from applying even though one of these buyers suffered an injury while within that state on a business trip?

21. Under what conditions can an employer whose operations are generally under workmen's compnsation laws be faced with a tort claim under employers' liability?

22. Shortly after a certain risk manager was first appointed to this job in a corporation engaged in heavy manufacturing, he was asked by the company's president to explain why the corporation did not carry the insurance it should have had under the Federal Longshoremen's and Harbor Workers' Act. The plain fact was that he had never heard of this Act. Apart from reading the book you presently have in hand, what procedures or sources of information would have saved this embarrassment? (To put it another way, how might one who *has* read the present text avoid missing liability under a law not mentioned herein?)

23. Of what help can the risk manager be to his company in dealing with the risks that arise from compulsory employee benefit laws?

24. One problem faced by some risk managers is that their company's legal counsel does not want nonprofessional advice on the wording or implications of clauses in contracts. How might the possibility of such a problem be avoided or minimized by the risk manager?

25. Distinguish between tort liability and contractual liability. What difference exists between the two for risk management purposes?

26. What difference does it make whether a claim for injury by a product is brought on the basis of negligence or as a suit for breach of warranty?

27. If when a factory nurse maltreats an employee his injuries would be work-

men's compensation claims for his employer, what reason is there for the company's risk manager to be concerned with a malpractice claim for the injury?

28. "In some situations, good business practice dictates compensating persons for bodily injury or property damage even though there is no legal liability for the loss." Discuss the "when's" and "why's" of these situations.

29. When a business begins to use radioactive isotopes, what difference does this action make in its need for liability insurance protection?

30. Describe a classification system that the risk manager can use in reviewing his liability exposures. Why is a classification system needed? What is the logic behind the system you have described?

Chapter 8

MEASURING LOSS POTENTIAL:
ASSETS

The risk manager not only must identify loss exposures, but also must measure how much can be lost from these exposures and the chances of losing it. What can cause loss was the subject of chapters 6 and 7; loss potentials and probabilities are the subjects of this and the following chapter.

THE OBJECTIVES

Intelligent decision making on what to do about loss exposures requires some kind of knowledge about loss potentials and loss probabilities. And when the decision is made to insure an exposure, an estimate of how much can be lost becomes fundamental in determining the amount of insurance to purchase.

What To Do about a Loss Exposure

The probability of a loss and its maximum potential are basic considerations in deciding how a loss exposure should be treated. As explained in Part III of this text, if the chance of loss is relatively high, some risk-bearing device other than insurance is indicated. The chance of loss must be relatively low if the cost of insurance is to be economically feasible. As the chance of loss increases, insurance premiums will approach the face amount of the coverage. A point will be reached somewhere, not too far beyond a 50 per cent chance of a total loss, where the premium, because of the expense loading, will exceed the amount of insurance—an uneconomic arrangement for the insured, no matter how one looks at it. The chance of loss, therefore, must be low enough to make the cost of insurance attractive.

It is possible, also, for the chance of loss to be too low to make the cost of insurance attractive. If, for example, the chance of loss is so low that the loss "could happen only once in a thousand years," the cost of the insurance might have to be much more than the actuarial value of the loss exposure—and for two reasons. The first is simple. The expense loading necessary to offset the costs of doing business, being irreducible beyond a given minimum, would bear a much greater ratio to the total premium than is customary in insurance rating.

The second reason, while equally simple, is not so obvious. And it is the more important! When the chance of loss is infinitesimal, it may well be impossible to develop a large enough group of insureds to achieve stability in loss experience. If the insurer is to apply the important rule of risk management "Don't risk a lot for a little," he will have to load the premium sufficiently to care for the irregularity of the losses. The amount of this loading, of course, will depend upon the size of the group and in many instances is likely to be large enough to make the premium unattractive.

The maximum loss potential from an exposure affects decision making in risk management in the following way. If the maximum loss potential is small when measured against net working capital, net income, and net worth of the business, some risk-handling device other than insurance is likely to be better. Premiums have to be loaded to pay underwriting and claims costs, and these costs are worth paying only when the loss protected is potentially large enough to be of concern to the risk manager.

Insurance, therefore, is an economical method of handling risk only when loss frequency is low and potential loss severity is high, subject, of course, to the following exceptions. Insurance will be purchased, regardless of the loss frequency or severity rate, when it is required by law or contract or when the risk manager wants to take advantage of some special loss prevention or loss settlement service of an insurer.

Fixing the Amount of Insurance

Frequently, mistakes are made in purchasing either too much or too little insurance. If too little insurance is purchased, the risk manager may be unconsciously assuming a risk that he had meant to cover. If too much insurance is purchased, the risk manager will be paying for some coverage that is neither needed nor collectible. Under the principle of indemnity, an insurance company is not obligated to pay more than the amount of the loss.[1]

The risk manager conceivably can have good reasons for underinsuring,[2]

---

[1] Exceptions to the application of the indemnity principle are noted at various points in this book, however.

[2] Insurance companies in many instances prefer to have their insureds overlook reasons for underinsurance and blindly accept a moral obligation to carry full insurance to value. Since most losses are partial, the underinsured buyer, in the absence of coinsurance requirements or graded rates, gains a cost advantage. In some situations insurers might like to have their insureds underinsured if this would make these insureds more conscious of loss prevention and control.

but over-insurance can rarely be explained as a conscious decision.[3] For example, the risk manager might wish to underinsure when he thinks that it is to his advantage from a cost standpoint to bear the top part of any possible but extremely improbable heavy loss or when his principal reason for buying insurance is to gain specific services from the insurer other than that of indemnity. Also, when insurance is required by law or by contract, the insured might elect to purchase only the minimum amount required, even though these requirements produce underinsurance. But for the risk manager to buy more insurance than the loss potential will support is prima facie evidence of a decision to spend his company's money unwisely.

THE PROBLEM

Lord Kelvin, the great British mathematician and physicist, said that "when you can measure what you are speaking about, and express it in numbers, you know something about it; but when you cannot express it in numbers your knowledge is of a meagre and unsatisfactory kind; it may be the beginning of knowledge, but you have scarcely, in your thoughts, advanced to the stage of science, whatever the matter may be."

The large number of variables and unknowns involved in the valuation of an exposure, however, makes the task of measuring loss probabilities and maximum loss potentials generally difficult. To be sure, frequency and severity in some loss exposures are simple to evaluate, but in others they are impossible to measure. And in between these extremes of simplicity and impossibility lies a great middle ground where only varying degrees of accuracy are obtainable under the present state of the *science* of risk management. Dr. Robert A. Rennie remarked: "The day when intuition or personal opinion can be the chief basis for evaluating risks or for determining the amounts and types of [insurance] coverages required has passed. No science ever developed very far until it began to measure quantitatively its subject matter. In the field of risk management [the] subject matter is losses and causes of losses."[4] Rennie believes that "by far the most important, and the most neglected, function of risk management is the measurement of losses."[5]

Art vs. Science in Risk Management

Dr. Rennie is justifiably concerned over the general neglect of the important risk management function of loss measurement, but he has over-

---

[3] Some insurance authorities argue that when a coinsurance clause is used overinsurance can be desirable to protect against a possible coinsurance deficiency. More efficient solutions, however, are available and will be discussed later in the text.

[4] Robert A. Rennie, "Fundamentals of Risk Management," *Proceedings of the Twelfth Annual Insurance Conferences, March 9, 10, 1961*, Ohio State University Publications, College of Commerce Conference Series, C-143 (Columbus, 1961) pp. 7–8.

[5] *Ibid.*, p. 7.

stated his case when he debases the role of intuition and personal opinion in risk management decisions. It is true that the quantitative measurement of its subject matter is basic to the development of a science, but it is also true that many subjects worthy of study cannot be treated entirely on a strictly scientific basis. In many of its aspects, risk management is an art and not a science. Those who engage in the art of risk management can only develop a body of rules for practice and nurture their faculties for applying these rules skillfully. As John Stuart Mill wrote: "To say that one should or should not do a particular thing, is in the realm of art, not science. The province of science is to predict what the result will be."[6] Risk managers have to make decisions to do or not to do particular things, but unfortunately many of these decisions have to be made with little or no ability to predict what the results will be. The management of risk by scientific formulas based on mathematics and statistics could remove much of the human element from risk management, but the statistics and formulas for these purposes are not presently available. Certainly there is room for more scientific risk management than is currently practiced but not enough to replace artful risk management.

Dr. Rennie suggests that the risk manager can obtain valuable information about his various loss exposures by comparing the loss experience of his company with the experience upon which insurance rates are based. If there is a significant difference in these experiences, that difference could be based on factors not related to chance. The risk manager armed with statistical theory and using stringent assumptions can test the hypothesis that chance is not the explanation of a typical experience in his firm. He "can also test in a similar fashion whether the difference . . . is the result of a difference between loss frequencies, the average loss cost, or both."[7] The results of these studies might suggest the self-insurance of some exposures, a plea for lower insurance rates on others, and the necessity for improved loss prevention activities in still others.

Dr. Rennie recognizes the limitations of the statistical or quantitative approach to risk management by the big *if* that he uses in the following statement: "If the frequency distributions of losses do not vary significantly over time, and the firm is of sufficient size to apply the Law of Large Numbers, statistical estimations should be an invaluable aid in measuring corporate risk probabilities."[8]

Dr. Rennie would like for risk managers and insurers to work together in measuring risk and losses and in testing results by rigorously applying statistical techniques to form valid generalizations. Speaking for an insurer, Rennie insists that "only by such careful development of data along the lines that are needed to get precise measurements of loss distribution

---

6 John Stuart Mill, *A System of Logic* (New York: Harper & Bros., 1895).
7 Rennie, *op. cit.*, p. 8.
8 *Ibid.*, p. 9.

functions can we help [risk managers] determine the magnitude of possible losses, or the probability of loss. Measurement can also determine when to use deductibles, excess coverage, and to determine the policy limits which are advisable under various circumstances."[9]

The objectivity and preciseness called for in risk management by Dr. Rennie can be achieved only in firms large enough to apply the law of large numbers, and then in these firms only to those losses whose mean value and variance are relatively stable over a period of time. Thus, in the vast majority of business firms and for many of the loss exposures in the larger firms, the risk manager will have to content himself with the art rather than the science of his profession.

Still, the risk manager has to make decisions based on loss probabilities and maximum loss potentials from given exposures. For some of these exposures, the facts and figures necessary for scientific decision making are simple to develop; for others, they are simply impossible. Yet decision making, like the show, must go on. Risk management decisions, therefore, often have to be made with too few facts for comfort. Moreover, a number of the available "facts" are based on conclusions involving circumstantial evidence. As one set of statisticians put it, "no statistician can be sure of what he has not observed. He is never quite certain of the past and is quite uncertain of the future."[10]

The Problem of Measuring Loss Probabilities

Measuring loss probabilities requires the compilation and interpretation of statistics, and involves problems in both mathematics and statistics. Although man must have certainly shown some anxiety over risk since Adam plucked his first apple, mathematicians and statisticians were not moved to study quantitative risk measurement until the seventeenth century. Even then, the pioneering studies of probability theory were concerned principally with the mathematics of gambling.[11] And, although the theory of probability has advanced beyond the boys in the back room, the use of games of chance as illustrations simplifies the explanation of the basic principles involved in probability theory.

What is the probability of throwing a seven on a roll of the dice? The game of dice requires the use of two homogeneous cubes, each having its faces marked as follows: $\boxed{\cdot}$ $\boxed{\cdot\cdot}$ $\boxed{\because}$ $\boxed{::}$ $\boxed{\therefore}$ and $\boxed{:\,:}$. When the dice

---

[9] *Ibid.*

[10] Longley-Cook and Pruitt, "Law of Large Numbers," *Best's Insurance News*, Fire and Casualty ed., May, 1953.

[11] Two important early works were Jacques Bernoulli's *Art of Conjecture* (1713) and Abraham de Moivre's *Doctrine of Chances* (1716). Among the early mathematicians studying probability was Blaise Pascal (1623–62), who is given credit by some writers for the invention of probability theory. See, for example, Oystein Ore, "Pascal and the Invention of Probability Theory," *American Mathematical Monthly*, Vol. LXVII, No. 5 (May, 1960), pp. 409–19.

are thrown, any one of the six faces on each die is just as likely to be up as any other. Since each die may reveal any one of six faces, the total number of possible combinations of the two dice is 6 × 6 or 36. Of these 36 possible combinations or outcomes, only six present pairs of figures that add up to seven: 6-1, 5-2, 4-3, 3-4, 2-5, and 1-6. The probability of throwing a 7 on any roll of the dice, therefore, is 6 in 36, or 1 in 6. The formula can be set up as follows: $P(A) = m/n$, where P is the probability, A the designated event, m the number of different outcomes corresponding to A, and n the number of equally likely different outcomes.

The extremes of probability are 1 and 0. If m (the number of different outcomes corresponding to A) is equal to n (the number of equally likely different outcomes) the probability of A is 1. If the number of outcomes corresponding to A is 0, then, of course, the probability of A will be 0 also. Thus, the probability of a certain event is 1, whereas the probability of an impossible event is 0. All other cases of probability lie between 1 and 0, the less probable ones lying closer to 0 than the more probable ones. If the probability of event A is 1 in 100, this would be expressed as 0.01. If the probability of event A is 99 in 100, the probability would be expressed as 0.99.

During the morning coffee break you flip a coin with your two companions with the understanding that the "odd" man pays for all three cups of coffee. It is agreed that if the three coins come up alike, the coins will be flipped again until a loser is found. What is the probability that this loser will be you? With three coins each having two sides, the number of possible combinations is 2 × 2 × 2, or eight. Since two of these combinations (all heads or all tails) are ruled out of the betting, the number of equally likely outcomes is six. Of these six, only in the two cases in which both your opponents throw either "heads" or "tails" can you be the "odd" man. Therefore, in the formula, m will equal 2 and n will equal 6, and the probability of A (you are the loser) will be: P (you are the loser) = 2/6 or 0.3333 . . .

The foregoing probabilities, 1 in 6 for the two thrown dice and 2 in 6 for the three flipped coins, are a priori probabilities. They are to be distinguished from a posteriori probabilities. Logic would suggest that, when dice are thrown, the probability of coming up with a seven is 0.1666. . . . There is no need for an experiment involving thousands of throws to support this conclusion. Even if a seven has appeared on eight consecutive tosses, the probability of a seven on the ninth toss is still 0.1666. . . . Dice have "neither memory, conscience, nor force" of their own and therefore "can scarcely change" their probability, in midstream or elsewhere.

But suppose we suspect that the dice are defective, so that when they are thrown any one of the six faces on each die is *not* just as likely to come up as the other. We do not know the nature of the imperfection, but we are confident that we cannot a priori say that the probability of throwing a seven is 0.1666. . . . How, then, can we determine the correct probability? Here we do need to experiment by throwing the dice thousands of times and recording the results. After the experiment is completed and the information is tabulated, we can establish an a posteriori probability, the reliability of which will depend upon the similarity of the conditions under which each of the rolls is made[12] and the size of the sample used, which in this case would be the number of times the dice are thrown. If the dice in the experiment were rolled 5,000 times, a greater degree of confidence can be placed in the probability estimate than would be reasonable if the dice were thrown only 50 times. The variation of the sample experience from the experience of the total population[13] from which it is drawn moves inversely with the size of the sample: The greater the number of observed rolls of the dice, the smaller will be the variation of the sample results from those that would be obtained with an infinite number of throws.

The number of rolls necessary to yield an acceptable level of confidence depends, to a large degree, upon the extent of the irregularities in the dice. If the dice have a strong bias in favor of a five on one cube and a four on the other, so that a nine is produced in this way about 75 per cent of the time with both 50 and 5,000 throws, then tens of thousands of throws are likely to be necessary to estimate with any credibility the chances of throwing "box cars" (double sixes) or "snake eyes" (double ones). The smaller the probability of a given event, the larger the sample necessary for a reliable estimate of probability.

Probability and the Risk Manager. Risk managers generally are concerned with a posteriori probabilities. What is the probability that the factory building will be destroyed by fire during the next fiscal period? To apply the formula $P(A) = m/n$ the risk manager will have to find statistics showing the number of factories destroyed by fire (m) out of the number of factories observed (n) for the time period considered. Suppose the probability is computed to be 1 in 100, or 0.01[14] How reliable is this estimated probability?

The reliability depends upon the size and homogeneity of the sample and upon the stability of the experience of the total population. How large the sample must be to produce a reliable estimate of probability depends upon what range of variation is acceptable. Each person must decide this question for himself. Once a decision is made on the degree of accuracy desired, probability theory can be applied to determine the size of the sample needed. Unfortunately, however, in many instances the size of

---

[12] Examples of such conditions are the resistance of the air; the touch, motion, and force of the thrower; the distance the dice are thrown; the extent of moisture in the thrower's hand; and the nature of the surface upon which the dice are thrown.

[13] The total population in this case would be an infinite number of dice rolls.

[14] The severity rate is ignored here. It is assumed that all losses are the same size.

the sample necessary to achieve the degree of confidence demanded will be greater than that which can be obtained. In this event, what should the risk manager do? Should he try to make the best use of the limited information available, or should he discard the whole idea of trying to estimate probability? Obviously, he should do the best he can with what he has and make an effort to offset deficiencies in his sample with considered personal judgment.

Probability expressed as a ratio observed from a sufficient number of repeated events is called *objective* probability. Probability expressed as a measure of personal belief is called *subjective* or *personalistic* probability. Those who insist that probability is applicable only under conditions involving adequate numbers of observed events are called *objectivists*. The objectivist would not be willing to estimate the probability of a damaging earthquake in Chicago, for example, because such an earthquake would be a unique event, and no long-run ratio can be established for it. Those who are willing to establish a probability on a subjective basis are called *personalists*. The personalist would be willing, by using various techniques, to estimate the probability of a Chicago earthquake. Given the same evidence, different reasonable personalists could come up with different probabilities for the same event. When the risk manager finds that it is impossible to assemble samples large enough to yield a respectable degree of reliability for objective probabilities, some reliance will have to be placed on personalistic probabilities.

Even objective probabilities will have to be adjusted to correct for lack of homogeneity in the sample. The observed factories will not all be identical either to each other or to the factory whose fire loss probability is being estimated. Some will be situated in towns with above or below average fire protection facilities. The uses to which the factory buildings are put will vary, with some occupancies being more hazardous than others. Furthermore, some factory buildings will be located in hazardous neighborhoods, whereas others will be located in the open country, where there is no chance of fire spreading from a neighboring plant. Factory buildings also will differ as to their size, style, layout, and construction materials, all of which affect the probability of loss by fire. In addition, loss prevention will be practiced more carefully by some companies than by others and this too will affect the fire loss probabilities among the various factory buildings in the sample. The 0.01 loss probability, therefore, will have to be adjusted to reflect this lack of homogeneity.

If the factory building whose fire loss probability is being estimated is located in a better than average fire protection town, has a non-hazardous occupancy, is situated in a non-hazardous neighborhood, is well constructed of fire-resistive materials, and is the beneficiary of a well-conceived and well-executed fire prevention program, the loss probability will have to be adjusted downward from the 0.01 base. If the situation is reversed, that is, if the factory building is below average, the probability estimate will have to be adjusted upward.

Finally, changing conditions often make it necessary to adjust probability estimates. Society is not static. Tomorrow's losses are not always accurately indicated by yesterday's losses. Economic conditions can affect fire loss frequency and severity. The 0.01 probability estimate might need correction to reflect cyclical and secular changes.

Risk managers usually have to rely on insurance companies and rating organizations for the statistics necessary for computing loss probabilities. Insurance rate makers adjust the raw data to reflect the lack of homogeneity in their sample and to give recognition to trends. Published insurance rates can be used by risk managers to indicate in a rough way the loss probabilities facing them in each of their exposures. Two actuaries, describing the insurance rate-making process, have written: "The process can hardly be described step-by-step. The rate maker does an excellent job, so long as he is not asked to set out in too much detail exactly how he comes to his final rate."[15] The risk manager, in using insurance rates to measure his loss probabilities, will have to use his own judgment in adjusting these rates to reflect any differences that appear to distinguish his exposures from the average.

What does a 0.01 probability of losing a factory building by fire mean to the risk manager whose company owns only one such structure? Clearly, this building will either burn or escape fire loss. The 0.01 probability means that, if a large number of factory buildings similar to his were exposed to fire loss, the burning rate for the period would be about 1 in 100, on the average. Furthermore, the larger the number of factory buildings exposed, the greater the chance that the burning rate will approximate the average of 1 in 100. Of what value are loss probability rates to a risk manager who has only a few such exposures? Obviously, he cannot successfully use them to predict his own actual losses unless he has thousands of such exposures. Then why should he care about the probable number of losses out of a given number of exposures?

As previously mentioned, knowledge of probability rates can become useful as an *aid* in making risk management decisions. For example, with a fire loss probability rate of 0.01 and an average insurable loss cost of $20 per $100 of exposure, the expected average rate of insurable loss would be 20 cents for each $100 of value exposed. The rate charged by a fire insurer on this exposure, however, would exceed 20 cents per $100 because the rate would have to be loaded to offset the insurer's expenses, to build a contingency fund as a buffer against risk, and to provide a margin for profit. If the rate is quoted at 40 cents per $100 of exposure, the fire insurance premium on a $200,000 factory building would amount to $800. The loss probability of 0.01 indicates an average loss cost for the exposure

---

[15] Longley-Cook and Pruitt, *op. cit.*

of only $400. The risk manager, therefore, must pay $400 more for his insurance than is indicated by the expected rate of loss. Thus the charge for insurance is justifiably called a premium.[16]

Will the risk manager be willing to pay a premium of $400 more than the average loss indemnified by the insurance company? The answer to this question depends upon what he expects to get for this $400.

First of all, the risk manager may expect more from his insurer than indemnity. Insurers and their agents provide rating, loss prevention, and claim services that may be worth something to the insured.

Furthermore, the indemnity paid by the insurer may prevent a loss much greater than the amount of indemnity paid. Destruction of most of a $200,000 factory may mean a loss of far more than $200,000 if the loss is not insured. A company without a factory and without the finances to re-build may be a company permanently out of business. Under these circumstances, stockholders will lose a great deal more than the $200,000 physical property. Shares of stock in an active business frequently have a market value in excess of the book value of the tangible assets, but this excess disappears or is drastically reduced when there is forced liquidation. And not only do the owners lose their going-concern value with the demise of the company; also lost are the jobs of the risk manager and all the other people on the payroll, with consequent losses of seniority, pension credits, and relocation costs. If a cash payment from the insurer can prevent all this additional loss, the worth of the insurance protection to the insured company (i.e., to its owners and managers) is considerably in excess of the expected average amount of *insurable* loss, that is, the amount of loss for which the insurance company will actually pay indemnity.

Finally, insurance offers intangible values of a purely psychological nature. In the first place, elimination of worry concerning the financial consequences of a possible loss is worth something even though this loss possibility is never realized. In the second place, the purchase of insurance can reduce the psychological cost of regret. Suppose the risk manager insures the $200,000 factory against loss by fire, and no fire occurs. The risk manager might look back and regret having purchased the insurance, for, as it turned out, he did not need the coverage. On the other hand, suppose the risk manager decides not to purchase fire insurance on the factory and it is completely destroyed by fire. He might then look back and regret

---

[16] The use of the word "premium" to denote the charge for insurance protection may be traced back to the bottomry and respondentia contracts of the Middle Ages. Under a bottomry contract, a shipowner would pledge his ship as collateral for a loan with the understanding that the loan would not have to be repaid if the ship were lost or destroyed at sea. For this type of loan, that is, one forgiving the debt upon loss of the collateral, the borrower had to pay a premium over the going rate of interest. The premium was to compensate the lender for accepting the risk. When the collateral for these loans was the cargo, the agreements were called respondentia contracts. Bottomry and respondentia contracts are said to be the earliest forms of risk-shifting devices regularly used in the commercial world and the forerunners of modern insurance contracts.

not having purchased insurance, for, as it turned out, he would have bene-fited by the coverage. The choice is between a large probability of a $800 regret and a small probability of a "$200,000-plus" regret.[17]

How much the elimination of worry and the reduction of the maximum possible regret are worth is something the risk manager must decide for himself. One consideration, however, cannot escape notice: It is far more painful to the risk manager to have to explain to his "boss" after a loss why that loss was not insured than for him to explain before a loss why insur-ance was purchased. The first type of explanation could well be his last, at least as far as that company is concerned.

The Problem of Measuring Maximum Loss Potential

"The problem" of measuring maximum loss potential is really two problems. One problem is estimating the value of the maximum total loss that may be incurred (e.g., demise of the business); the other is estimating the amount of resources that the business will need to have after loss or damage to preserve or restore its financial soundness. Thus, in the case of the $200,000 factory, just discussed, the first of these figures is the estimate of the loss suffered if the business does indeed go under. The second of these figures is the estimate of the amount of physical damage, unavoidable loss of profits, and other immediate costs and losses that the business must be able to make good on if it is *not* to go under. The first of these estimates tells the risk manager: "If you do not insure (or make other provision for losses), this is how much the business stands to lose." The second estimate tells him: "This is how much money you will need to have from insurance (and other sources) if the loss indicated by the first estimate is to be avoided." Overly simplified, these estimates may be interpreted as saying, in a given case: "The maximum physical damage that this factory can suffer is estimated at $200,000. The maximum loss that this $200,000 damage would cause is $400,000 (the value of the business). Therefore, the amount of loss to be concerned about is $400,000. The amount of insurance that will take care of this loss is $200,000."[18]

This and the next chapter are entitled, respectively, "Measuring Loss Potential: Assets," and "Measuring Loss Potential: Income and Expenses." The loss potentials discussed in both chapters are those of the *second* of the two types just discussed: the potential amount of physical damage, costs, and other losses that the business must be able to make good on if it is not to suffer serious financial strain. This type of estimate is needed to determine how much reserve cash, insurance, or other dollar resources

---

[17] It would be $200,000 plus all the other costs associated with the loss that insurance would have eliminated for the insured, *less* the $800 cost of insurance.

[18] The "oversimplification" in this example consists of assuming that the estimate as to the amount of resources needed is measured solely by the physical damage to the tangible property. As will be seen, this amount is actually only a starting point.

the business will need to have if it is to meet static risk contingencies. Throughout these two chapters, then, such words and phrases as "loss" and "loss potential" are to be read as referring to loss measured in this way (except, of course, when the context clearly indicates that a different meaning is intended).

With some exposures, the task of ascertaining maximum loss (in the sense just described) is simple. For example, currency, negotiable securities, and other negotiable property present few problems for valuation. The loss potential in ownership of a dollar bill is one dollar. The loss of a $1,000 coupon 2½ per cent Treasury bond of 1967-72 represents loss of whatever the market says such a bond is worth, and it takes that amount to indemnify the loser. On the other hand, the problem of measuring the potential direct loss from a liability exposure is practically insurmountable. How much does a department store stand to be charged when its watertower works loose and crashes upon a milling mob of Christmas shoppers? "It depends"—and upon so many variables that a reasonable answer seems impossible.

LOSSES MEASURED BY DECLINES IN ASSET VALUES

A detailed approach to a study of the problems of measuring direct loss potential may be divided into three broad areas: (1) losses measured by declines in asset values, (2) losses measured by declines in income, and (3) losses measured by the development of additional expenses. As the discussion progresses, it will become apparent that these classes are not mutually exclusive. The total maximum loss from a single occurrence often will involve two or even all three of these measures simultaneously.

Assets of a typical business are varied but usually include cash; receivables; inventories; fixtures, equipment, and supplies; machinery; buildings; and means of transportation. For each asset a value must be established that will accurately measure the maximum loss that will be incurred by the owner if that asset is lost or destroyed: the amount by which the owner will be damnified. Many different bases of asset value are available: sales price, reproduction cost, liquidation price, book value, replacement cost, assessed valuation, condemnation value, and so on. On different occasions, different ones of these are appropriate to use in measuring the amount by which the asset loser is damnified. Since indemnification is compensation for damnification (the first word means, literally, "undamnification"), the two are the same: that amount of cash which, if paid to the sufferer of the loss, leaves him with neither financial gain nor loss from the transaction.

Non-tangible Assets

Broadly considered, business property may be of two types: personal and real. Personal property can be classified into tangible and non-tangible.

Technically, non-tangible property can be further segregated into classes: (1) intangibles and (2) other non-physical assets. The latter class is necessary, since the accountants' definition of "intangible assets" is not broad enough to include currency, claims against other parties, and valuable papers.

Cash. Once all the cash items have been located (as discussed in a preceding chapter), evaluating the loss potential in each given item is usually simple. Each one dollar bill is worth one dollar—except of course, when it is numismatic property or when problems of foreign exchange enter the picture! Numismatics will not show up in a balance sheet as a cash item, but deposits in foreign banks may, and the risk manager must decide in what currency it is relevant to measure their loss.

Securities. The value of negotiable instruments is their current market price. Here we are presented with a clear example of two important bases for measuring value: sales price and replacement cost. Should the value of the marketable negotiable security include brokers' fees and other transfer costs? If the realizable sales price, net of sales cost, is taken as the measure of indemnity, then we are dealing with the "actual cash value," as many insurance policies put it, and, financially, the loser receives neither loss nor gain—on a *liquidating* basis. But the liquidation is involuntary, and what was had before the loss was not cash but securities. Securities earn income, and they may produce capital gains (or losses, of course). If the loser is to be left exactly where he was before, the securities themselves must be replaced, not turned into cash. And to replace them takes more money than can be netted from a sale of such securities. Since only a relatively small difference is involved here,[19] this evaluation principle is not greatly important in this particular case.[20] But in other cases the difference is large and application of the principle is important, as will be seen later.

Similarly, in non-negotiable securities the loss potential also is the cost of replacing the lost or stolen property. When a non-negotiable security is lost or stolen, the issuing corporation usually will reissue the security upon receipt of (1) an affidavit as to the circumstances of the loss and (2) a lost instrument bond as surety for indemnification against loss resulting from

---

[19] Capital gains tax, which could make a large difference between net return from a sale and net cost to replace in the ordinary case, is not relevant here because we are dealing with an involuntary conversion and replacement. When the market for the securities is thin, however, there may be a wide spread between the "bid" and "asked" prices for the security. Here the liquidating value may be several points below the replacement value.

[20] Insurance policies that particularly apply to securities specify the base to be used. The Registered Mail policy commonly provides for payment equal to the cost to replace "on an available market." The standard provision in the Money and Securities Broad Form coverage is for payments for securities to be limited to "the actual cash value thereof at the close of business on the business day next preceding the day on which the loss was discovered." These two quotations point up another problem in valuation: value as of when? When there can be considerable fluctuation in value from time to time, the date of the loss or the evaluation can make an important difference. This problem is considered further below.

the issuance of the duplicate.[21] The loss potential in non-negotiable securities, therefore, is usually the cost of the bond plus other expenses involved in the reissue. Typically, this cost is about 20 per cent of the value of the security.[22]

Accounts Receivable. Two types of losses arise out of the disappearance or destruction of accounts receivable records: direct and consequential. Of the two, consequential losses usually are the more serious.

The direct loss is the cost of replacing the destroyed books. It consists of the cost of new blank books plus the cost of re-entering the information in them *from the same or similar sources as were used in making the original records.*[23] Research and other labor in *reconstructing the original sources* is *not* considered direct loss.

Consequential losses are of two kinds: (1) the expenses of re-collecting or reconstructing the information to be transcribed into the new receivable records and (2) the inability to collect receivables because of the destroyed records. Included in the consequential loss are the interest charges on funds borrowed to offset impaired collections and any extra collection expenses incurred that are traceable to the damaged records.

While the risk manager is interested in establishing his maximum loss potentials, he wants to establish them on a minimum basis, that is, he wants to know the most he can lose if he handles his incurred losses on the most economical basis available. Thus, if the cost of reconstruction of the figures in the accounts is less than the value of the accounts themselves, the maximum real loss potential is the cost of reconstruction, not the value of the accounts. On the other hand, if the figures cannot be reproduced, or if reproduction of them would cost more than could be collected from the accounts, then the maximum real loss potential is the amount that becomes uncollectible because of the destruction of the records. This amount is the total of the accounts less two items: (1) the amount that would be collectible, for various reasons, even if the books of account were destroyed and (2) the amount that would represent "bad debts" even if the records remained intact.[24]

The values of receivables fluctuate from time to time. Not only do they

---

21 The lost instrument bond protects the issuing corporation against the cost of defending against a claim made by anyone holding the original instrument, and promises indemnification of the issuing corporation if the holder successfully establishes his title to the certificate.

22 The face amount and the premium for insurance on non-negotiable securities are based on the market value of the securities. But the premium *rate* is based on the value of potential claims, which typically are based on replacement costs as described. This is a major reason for the lower rate when insurance is to apply only to non-negotiable, and not to negotiable, securities.

23 As many insurance forms say, the cost in *transcribing* or *copying.*

24 Once again, insurance amounts and premiums are based on the amounts of the accounts themselves, not on the actual loss potential. Rates are markedly reduced if duplicate records make reconstruction simple and inexpensive. With duplicate records, however, the risk manager may well feel that the potential size of his loss is too small to make the purchase of insurance worthwhile at any rate.

show monthly and seasonal variations; they are also highly responsive to cyclical and secular changes in business. The balance sheet figure as of, say, June 30, may be a poor indication of the maximum loss potential if damage to the books should occur on December 29. The time factor, therefore, is important in measuring maximum loss potential where receivables are concerned.

Valuable Papers and Other Records. In order to comply with the laws of the state and federal governments and to maintain a sound system of internal control, businesses must keep a large number of records. In addition to customary current accounting, financial, and statistical records, such valuable papers as books, maps, films, drawings, computer programs, abstracts, deeds, mortgage documents, photographs, or manuscripts may be held by the business and exposed to loss. The task of establishing the loss potential in these valuable papers requires that they first be divided into two groups: (1) items that can be replaced with others of like kind and quality and (2) items that are irreplaceable.

Items often found in the first category are financial records, drawings, blueprints, and legal documents. Their loss potential is the cost of replacement from available records. These costs include both material and labor.

Items in the second category may be classified into two types as far as the problem of measuring loss potential is concerned. One group consists of items directly concerned with profit making. Examples are files of negatives belonging to commercial portrait photographers and architects' files of plans of buildings they have designed. In these and other cases, some future business is expected to flow from these files. Some percentage of the photographers' customers will order additional prints to be made from the negatives on file; some of the architects' buildings will be remodeled or redesigned, and the presence of the old plans will give the original architect an advantage in bidding for the job, or at least he will be offered the chance to receive a fee for reproducing the original drawings for use by others. The photographer probably can use some sort of average reorder rate to estimate the value of his negatives. The evaluation problem for the architect, however, is much more difficult. The values of old building plans will depend on the likelihood of particular buildings being remodeled and the complexity of the problems in remodeling each of them.

In any event, the proper basis for estimating the loss potentials of valuable papers like these is the net future profit that may be expected from them. Of course, if the profit is to be realized at some considerable time in the future, the amount should be discounted to arrive at the present value.

The second general category of irreplaceable papers consists of those items whose value is primarily historical. This category is actually just one part of the general group of objects with artistic, historical, or "collectors' item" interest. The characteristics of these items and the problems in evaluating them are discussed later under the heading "Property of

Special Value." In general, if there is any true value in these items, it can be established on the basis of a market price. Whether the item is a rare stamp, the original copy of the corporation's 100-year-old charter, or an oil painting by an established artist, the fundamental question in measuring the value of these items is what a dealer or other expert in the subject matter estimates the object might have fetched in a sale to a museum or other collector.

Intangible Assets. Intangible assets include such items as copyrights, franchises, leases and leaseholds, licenses, patents, trade-marks, trade names, brand names, and a host of items that can be included under the term "goodwill" or "going-concern value." The actual physical evidences of these items, such as contracts, certificates, or other supporting documents, are not the intangible assets but are conveniently handled under the heading of "valuable papers" for loss analysis purposes. Intangible assets themselves are immaterial, that is, in themselves, they possess no physical substance. Their value is derived from the contribution they make to the superior earning power of the company through either higher earnings or lower costs. They represent competitive advantages of the business enterprise, some of which are limited in duration (patents) and others of which have indefinite life (brand names).

Some intangible assets, such as patents and brand names, have a value apart from the business. They have an independent marketability. Other intangibles, such as "goodwill" and "going-concern value" have value only while the business is a going concern. They have no value apart from the business. Their value cannot be realized by sale without selling the entire business.

How are intangible assets handled in evaluating maximum loss potential? How is "goodwill" protected? The answer lies partly in a risk management program designed to insulate the fixed and working capital of the business from serious loss so that the business will be financially able to resume operations after a property or liability loss and remain in a position to realize fully the value of their intangibles.

Certain specific intangibles, however, call for special risk management treatment: key personnel, leases, and patents. Goodwill also calls for special treatment: the need to continue operation uninterrupted after a loss to preserve going concern value and the need to pay claims (property and medical) of customers and others when there is no liability to do so. But, since the losses involved with these intangibles and goodwill items are measured principally in terms of lower gross income or higher expenses, their treatment is deferred to chapter 9, which deals with the problems of measuring income and expense loss potentials.

Tangible Personal Property

Because of the way insurers group tangible personal property owned by the business, risk managers lump this property into several groups and assign a total value to each group. Notable exceptions are heavy mobile machinery, means of transportation, and certain other types of property of high individual value. In these cases, each item is separately handled with a value individually assigned to it. Dies, patterns, heirlooms, stamp collections, rare books and manuscripts, and works of art are examples of property that must be handled separately, particularly when these items are to be insured, because they must usually be insured under valued policy forms. Since these items are difficult or impossible to replace and since their values are subject to wide margins of differences among competent appraisers, it is deemed proper for the insurer and the insured to agree upon their value at the time the contract is written. The amount of insurance written on the item is held to be its value for loss adjustment purposes.

A useful classification of tangible personal property for insurance purposes involves six categories: (1) equipment, fixtures, and supplies; (2) machinery; (3) inventory; (4) property of special value; (5) mobile property; and (6) property in transit.

Equipment, Fixtures, and Supplies. Showcases, counters, signs, lighting equipment, office furniture, filing cases, typewriters, building maintenance and service equipment, and tenant-owned awnings are examples of equipment and fixtures. Stationery, printed forms, and stamps are examples of office supplies; other supplies include fuel, lubricants, packing and packaging materials, stocks of small and short-lived parts for equipment and machinery, and cleaning materials. The basis for measuring loss potential in these classes of property normally is *the estimated cost of replacement new less physical and economic depreciation.* (While physical depreciation on supplies ordinarily is zero, these supplies are subject to obsolescence—"economic depreciation"—on occasion.)

In the case of fixtures, equipment, and supplies, *loss potential* is not identical with economic value. Economic value has reference to efficiency in exchange and is measured by the amount of money that the article could command in the market. Economic value is frequently a matter of established fact rather than opinion, since the price established in the market is a clear-cut measure. Sound value for measuring maximum loss potential of fixtures, equipment, and supplies is based on the use value of the property, that is, the benefits to be received by its owner from its use. Use value frequently is greater than market value. Furniture, for example, has greater value to its owner than it would have in the secondhand market. In case of its loss, the furniture owner would be damnified to the extent of its use value; his loss would not be limited to its secondhand market value. Use value, however, generally represents only an educated opinion, and there are likely to be as many different "sound" values as there are opinions, and all the opinions might be "sound"!

The principal problem of valuation here is not one of estimating the cost of replacement but one of determining the amount of depreciation. The extent of depreciation depends upon the type of article, its age, and its physical condition. The rate of depreciation on heavy items, such as shelves and showcases, is likely to be slow, whereas the rate of depreciation on floor coverings is likely to be fast. Equipment subject to obsolescence will depreciate rapidly regardless of its physical condition. But, as noted, rarely will any depreciation allowance be appropriate for up-to-date stationery supplies.

The risk manager cannot rely upon the accountant's book value in establishing loss potentials, since balance sheets are not expressed in terms either of replacement costs or of use values. Instead, he must prepare an accurate property record for his own purposes. This record should show in detail the nature and location of all the property owned. An appraisal must be made of the cost of replacing each item. Some items will be standard, for which current market prices are available; others will be of a specialized nature requiring an analysis of the various elements of costs involved. For standard items, price quotations from established firms or from catalogs furnish a relatively accurate valuation figure when increased by transportation and installation charges. For specialized items, the valuation results are not nearly so well defined. The valuation technique is much like that used by contractors in preparing a bid. First, prices are estimated for labor and material, and then an amount is added for overhead. The estimates of material costs should be made on the basis of the type of material currently used, and the fabrication methods assumed in estimating labor costs should be those standard at the time that the estimates are made. If the same productive capacity can be furnished at a lower cost by using modern facilities rather than reproducing the existing ones, the estimated costs of replacement should be that of the modern facilities reduced by the discounted value of the savings in production costs for the life expectancy of the present facilities. In other words, *replacement* costs, not *reproduction* costs, are the measure of loss. Although estimates for labor and material are likely to vary to some extent, the widest variations are likely to be found among overhead loadings. The result is a final valuation figure that is more subjective than objective.

After the cost of replacement has been reached, the next step is to allow for depreciation. The accountant's figure for depreciation is of no use for measuring loss potential. Accountants view depreciation as a systematic method of distributing the cost of a capital asset over its estimated useful life. The concept is one of cost allocation and not asset valuation. And its application is heavily modified by income tax considerations! For purposes of measuring loss potential, the concept of depreciation is strictly one of evaluation. It measures the reduction in value brought about by both the physical deterioration of the property and its obsolescence. The determination of the amount of depreciation of an asset is based on its age, condition, maintenance and repairs, serviceability, utility, and even the probability of its future obsolescence.

The use of the concept of depreciation is gradually giving way in insurance to the concept of betterment, that is, the improvement resulting from the substitution of new for old by repair or replacement, and this newer concept is equally useful in risk management for estimating loss potential. The simple fact that new materials are substituted for old when damaged property is repaired or replaced does not necessarily mean that the repaired or replaced property automatically becomes more valuable than it was before the loss. A deduction for betterment is proper only if the repairs or replacement enhance the value of the property. Actually, in some cases the repaired property might be even less valuable than before the loss, making it necessary to add for "worsement" rather than deducting for "betterment." This latter interpretation, unfortunately, is seldom, if ever, reflected in insurance claim checks.

It should be obvious that the amount of depreciation or betterment is not capable of precise measurement. The amount established will vary among the depreciation estimates, giving a subjective flavor to the results. Nevertheless, if the risk manager uses realistic valuation figures in measuring loss potential, he will arrive at a reasonable valuation figure. Then, if the loss is insured, he will not be frustrated in his claim negotiations with reputable insurance companies in spite of the subjective nature of his figures.

If the business occupies premises as a tenant rather than as an owner, the risk manager might lump an additional class of property in with his fixtures, equipment, and supplies: improvements and betterments.[25] Tenants' improvements and betterments include such items permanently added to the buildings as show windows, partitions, store fronts, floors, ceilings, panels, and decorations. They are added by the tenant to increase the benefits that he expects to receive from the leased property. When the improvements become part of the building, they belong to the landlord. The tenant's interest in betterments, therefore, is not a property interest but a use interest, the nature of which is based on the terms of his lease.[26] The method of evaluating this exposure involves principles unlike those used by the tenant in establishing the loss potential for his own property. Since the problem of evaluating tenant's improvements and betterments is similar to the problem of evaluating a leasehold interest, further discussion of im-

---

25 Actually, there seems to be no necessity in the use of the customary double term, since "improvements" and "betterments" here are synonymous: an improvement is a betterment, and a betterment is an improvement.

26 Under some land leases, the lessee agrees to construct a building on the leased land and then turn possession of the building over to the lessor when the lease expires. Furthermore, the lessee obligates himself to repair or replace the building in the event that it is destroyed. Under such a lease, the lessee's insurable interest in the building obviously is more than a use interest. It becomes a liability interest the value of which is measured by the cost of replacing the building less depreciation.

provements and betterments is deferred until chapter 9, in which lease-hold interests are discussed.

It is important, however, to distinguish between a tenant's betterments and his trade fixtures. In the absence of special agreements to the contrary, trade fixtures belong to the tenant, whereas improvements belong to the landlord. Bowling alleys, for example, while rather firmly attached to the building, are, by custom and agreement, generally classified as trade fixtures rather than as betterments. Trade fixtures are, in general, those fixtures common or essential to and peculiar to the tenant's particular line of business. He needs them for his occupancy, but a successor in another line of business not only does not need them but is likely to find them positive obstacles to his efficient use of the premises. Walk-in refrigerators and freezers and theatrical seats and equipment are other examples of trade fixtures that to the uninformed might appear to be betterments. However, what are trade fixtures and what are betterments in any given instance depends on the customs of the trade (as interpreted by the courts in the area) and on the terms of the particular lease. In the event of doubt, pro-fessional legal advice should be obtained.

Machinery. Included in the machinery classification are such items as refrigerating and heating equipment, air conditioners, engines, flywheels, turbines, switchboards and other electrical apparatus, electrical machinery, equipment employed in the production, distribution, storage, control, or use of power. Although these items are included in the broad category of "equipment, fixtures, and supplies" in estimating the maximum potential loss of that class of property, they must also be handled individually, and for two reasons. In the *first* place, some different considerations are im-portant in evaluating machinery, and, in the *second* place, machinery is subject to losses from perils not generally affecting other equipment. These perils are the sudden and accidental breakdown of machinery and damage by electricity (other than by lightning).[27] Losses produced by these perils are mostly limited (though not always) to the value of the machinery itself. If these perils are to be covered by insurance, they must be spe-cifically insured.

The value of machinery is figured at replacement cost less depreciation, just as is the value of all other equipment. Two considerations, however, stand out as being of particular importance: the effect of obsolescence on the rate of depreciation and the effect of expenses of delivery and installa-tion on the replacement cost.

Machine users know from experience that inventions of new and more efficient machines, methods, materials, and products can cause existing machinery to suffer large losses overnight. Depreciation brought on by

---

27 It should be remembered that fire, allied lines, and inland marine insurance policies nearly always contain an "Electrical Apparatus" clause under which damage to elec-trical equipment by artificial electricity (i.e., not lightning) is excluded unless some insured peril ensues, and then only damage done by the insured peril is covered.

obsolescence is an important factor—and an unpredictable one—in measuring machinery loss potential and cannot be taken lightly.

Physical depreciation is more readily anticipated than is obsolescence. It arises from normal wear and tear, metal fatigue, rust, and corrosion. The use of the right oil and grease in the right places at the right time will extend the physical life of the machine for some years. Some machines, however, depreciate heavily regardless of the care accorded them, particularly those that operate with noise and shock. Metal parts subject to stresses are likely to experience metal fatigue, and pipes, tanks, and boilers are exposed to rust and corrosion. Machinery in regular use tends to depreciate more slowly than idle machinery, since more losses are produced by rust than by friction. Thus, in measuring the maximum potential machinery loss, the risk manager must consider the use to which the machines are put and the care that they receive from the plant manager.

The second consideration of particular concern in evaluating machinery is the importance of including the delivery and installation costs in the replacement cost figures. Replacement cost for *any* property must be taken to mean replacement in the same place. If the manufacturer's catalog price is f.o.b. point of shipment, costs of freight, insurance, and handling en route to the buyer must be added to arrive at true loss potential. This is true of all kinds of property, but with machinery, particularly heavy machinery, actual installation of the replacement in working position can be an expensive process, and overlooking it may produce an important underestimation of the value of the machine installed.

Loss Potential. It has already been noted that machinery is subject to certain perils not generally affecting other equipment, and so loss potential from these perils is pretty much limited to values of machinery. If, for example, an electrical machine arcs or otherwise suffers a burnout, damage is likely to be limited to the machine. But this is not always true, and the actual loss unit for each machine, or class of machine, needs to be carefully considered. For example, some types of machinery are leased rather than purchased. If the owner agrees to assume responsibility for loss or damage to the machine, then the lessee does not have to include the value of the machine in his valuation of fixtures, equipment, and supplies. But he cannot ignore the machinery altogether because mechanical breakdown of a machine is a peril that can cause losses or damage to other property that he owns or for which he is legally liable. This is likely to be true of such breakdown as the disintegration of flywheels or other rotating parts, leakage of contaminants, or the rupture of pressure vessels.

In considering the maximum potential loss unit arising from a breakdown of machinery, the risk manager can apply the rule of proximate cause to take many of the losses caused by machinery breakdown out of that category. If the breakdown causes fire or explosion, the subsequent loss may be considered a fire or explosion loss rather than a breakdown loss.

And, if the breakdown itself results from fire, explosion, or some other identifiable and distinct peril, the entire loss may be considered as part of the loss unit of such identifiable and distinct peril. The logical bases for this approach are that (1) insurance companies treat such losses in this way[28] and (2) it is much easier for the risk manager to conceive of total loss potential in terms of the destructiveness of fire and explosion, for example, than in terms of losses caused by machinery breakdown.

Nevertheless, the breakdown of some types of machinery and equipment is likely to cause loss to other property independently of any other peril. For instance, the breakdown of power, lighting, heating, or refrigerating equipment can cause spoilage. Flowers in a greenhouse or food in a cold storage locker, for example, could deteriorate if an accident to the power equipment shuts off heat or refrigeration. Although consequential loss exposures such as these are handled separately when insured, that is, they are generally covered under separate insuring agreements, the valuation procedures to be used in measuring their loss potential are no different from that used in evaluating direct loss. Obviously, a side of beef spoiled by lack of refrigeration represents the same loss as a side of beef burned in a fire. Therefore, whatever is the value of the property as a part of a stock of merchandise, that same value applies in measuring loss potential for the consequential loss exposure.

Merchandise Inventory.   Stocks of merchandise are held by retailers, wholesalers, and manufacturers. Valuation problems are in some ways different for the retailer and wholesaler than for the manufacturer.

Wholesalers and Retailers.   As a general rule, wholesalers and retailers can replace damaged and destroyed stock rather quickly. Because of this, the cost of replacing the stock usually is the proper measure of loss potential. All costs of replacing, however, must be considered and not just simply the invoice price of the goods. This means the inclusion of freight costs and taxes, if any; the costs of processing at the point of delivery, such as the costs of tagging and marking, and setting up the necessary display, and, if the goods are imported, all duties paid.[29]

---

[28] Thus, the electrical apparatus clause previously noted provides that the fire insurance will pay for fire loss ensuing from electrical damage, while court interpretations provide that, when fire is the first proximate cause, the entire loss shall be laid against the fire insurance. Conversely, the standard boiler and machinery policy states that it will "pay for loss on the property of the Assured directly damaged . . . excluding (a) loss from fire concomitant with or following an Accident or from the use of water or other means to extinguish fire, (b) loss from an Accident caused directly or indirectly by fire or from use of water or other means to extinguish fire, (c) loss from a combustion explosion outside the Object concomitant with or following an Accident. . . ." (These exclusions, however, do not appear in the liability insuring agreements; indeed, the bodily injury insuring agreement does not even require that the injury be "directly" caused by the insured "Accident.")

[29] If the merchandise is stored in a bonded warehouse, the duty need not be paid until the merchandise is removed or until the expiration of a given time limit, *whichever is first to occur.* The duty, therefore, should not be added to the invoice price in arriv-

Depreciation can be a factor in valuation of merchandise because some goods may be shopworn or damaged in some other way. The amount that should be allowed for depreciation is, of course, subjective. Much depends upon the types of merchandise handled. When there is a high rate of turnover on stock (as in a bakery, for example), depreciation would be negligible, but when there is a low rate of stock turnover (as in a furniture store, for instance), depreciation would more than likely be of some importance. Furthermore, merchandise that has been in stock for an abnormally long period of time will require an allowance for depreciation, especially when it is of the type that cannot or, more important, would not be replaced by the merchant. Style changes leading to obsolescence are an important factor in evaluating fashion goods, of course. And the time of year that the valuation takes place is also important. The unit value of many of the items left in the inventory of a summer resort store on September 5 is considerably less than the value of the same items on the preceding June 5.

Manufacturers. Manufacturers' inventories are of three types: raw materials, goods in process of manufacture, and finished products. In general, the basic valuation rule applying to all three classes of stock is the cost of replacement, just as with the wholesalers and retailers. However, methods of measuring the replacement cost of manufacturers' inventories and those of wholesalers and retailers are in some ways different. In the first place, the usual allowances for depreciation are not made for raw materials and goods in process. In the second place, unusual attention is given to selling prices in establishing the loss potential for finished goods.

The stage of manufacture determines the maximum loss potential of a manufacturer's stock. The maximum loss potential of raw materials is the cost of their replacement. In the case of staples, like wheat or cotton sold on organized exchanges, these exchange prices plus transportation and handling costs fix the maximum loss potential.[30] Items like crude oil are valued at their market price less the customary trade discount plus transportation and handling costs. The maximum loss potential for goods-in-process is the value of the raw material used plus the cost of manufacture to the stage reached at time of loss. Finished goods basically have a maximum loss potential equal to their replacement cost. This includes the cost of the raw materials and the manufacturing cost. Occasionally, finished goods

---

ing at loss potential of in-bond goods, for, if the duty has been paid, it will be refunded by the federal government following a loss.

[30] Note that this method of measuring loss potential is for processors who receive raw materials *from* the general market. The value of staples en route *to* the general market (e.g., grain in country elevators or cream in collecting stations) is the established market price *less* the transportation and handling costs necessary to get it to the central market. In other words, in many cases, one man's "finished produce" is another man's "raw material."

and even goods-in-process are standardized and can be replaced in the open market. In this event, the valuation method is the same as for raw materials.

In a number of cases, replacement value is not a true measure of the loss of finished goods. For example, a canner of fruits and vegetables contracts with his growers in advance of the canning season. If fire destroys his finished product, he will not be able to replenish his output this season. The result is that the canner has lost more than raw materials plus costs of manufacture. He has lost the accrued profit from his operations for one full season, a profit that is irrecoverable. Therefore, in measuring maximum loss potential, the canner should value his inventory at its cash selling price (wholesale, not retail) less unincurred selling costs. In this way he includes the anticipated profit on the canned goods.

A manufacturer of seasonal goods like Santa Claus suits will find a loss of anticipated profits if his inventory is destroyed at the beginning of the season. In this case selling price less unincurred selling costs should also be the basis of measuring maximum loss potential.

The use of selling price less unincurred selling expenses as the measure of maximum potential loss should not be restricted to manufacturers involved in seasonal operations. Any manufacturer with a large stock of finished goods that cannot be quickly reproduced should use this basis.

Property of Special Value. Many businesses own some assets that have the following characteristics: (1) high value concentrated in a compact space or in a single unit and (2) ready susceptibility to damage, either in general or from particular perils. Many, probably most, of the assets that have these characteristics also have a third; (3) they are difficult or impossible to replace, hence difficult to value. Risk managers find it useful to handle these assets in a separate category—that of property of special value.

As was mentioned in the discussion of valuable papers, examples of items that belong in this category are "a rare stamp, the original copy of the corporation's 100-year-old charter, or an oil painting by an established artist"—that is, items of special rarity, historic, or artistic value. In addition, the category contains such items as special machines and tools, patterns, models, and dies. Also, inventories of furs, jewelry, gems, or precious metals are usually in the "special value" category because of their high value coupled with high susceptibility to the peril of theft. Similarly, so is radium, which offers the additional hazard of being easily misplaced.[31]

---

[31] It can be seen from these examples that money and securities are actually cases of "special value" property, too, but they are such common cases that it is customary to consider them all by themselves, as has been done here. And, in general, money and securities do not have the evaluation problems found in the other special value properties (although most jewelry, furs, and precious metals are not particularly difficult to evaluate, either).

In evaluating these items, the following general characteristics prevail. (1) The large value in relatively small packages makes it worthwhile to give extra attention to these items. (2) Special susceptibility to damage or loss makes it necessary to take these important values separately and consider what particular perils besides the usual or general ones can produce large losses to them. (3) Where there are special problems involved in their evaluation, specific attention and care must be given and, frequently, expert professional advice obtained.

The special susceptibility of some of these items to the theft peril has been noted. Rare, antiquarian, or artistic items are additionally subject to severe damage by vandalism and by sheer accident. Precision tools, dies, etc., can be completely ruined by relatively little physical damage if such damage interferes with precision. Even rapid changes in temperature can seriously impair or destroy the usefulness of some precision items.

Readily Replaceable vs. Irreplaceable. As with valuable papers, the "special value" items must be separated as between the replaceable and the irreplaceable. At one extreme are most furs, jewelry, and other high-value inventory items. Here the evaluation is the same as for other inventory. At the other extreme are gems such as the Hope diamond, an original painting by da Vinci, Rubens, or van Gogh, and that 100-year-old charter. When an item is irreplaceable, "replacement cost" obviously cannot be used to measure its value. When "value in use" is esthetic or otherwise subjective, measurement becomes a matter of opinion. In these cases, therefore, the usual recourse is an attempt to determine "value in exchange," that is, the market value. But when an item is unique, or nearly so, no regular market can be maintained in it, so how can one discover what the market value is?

When the Gopher City Bank acquired an example of a local artist's work thirty years ago, it paid his then going price of $200. But if the local boy has since made good and acquired an international reputation, what is this picture worth? Other pictures of his have been marketed, but they are not the same as this one.[32] Here is where recourse must be had to the expert, who will attempt to say what this particular item might have brought if it had been put on the market.

The evaluation of items in which their owners have a deep personal interest is especially difficult. The formal portraits of the founders, probably done by an artist long since forgotten, may well be of little or no value to anyone outside the business concern managed by their heirs. The 100-year-old original charter will have some general historical value, but

---

[32] The artist's father, a big depositor, had "encouraged" the bank to purchase the picture. The bank's painting, therefore, is from the artist's dependency, or "rosy glasses," period. Not very many examples from that early period remain extant. Does the imperfection of the young artist's technique, or does the scarcity of examples of his happy early years, have the greater bearing on the value of this picture as compared to what is being paid for his later ones?

not as much, probably, as it has in the eyes of the managers of the corporation that it chartered. Sentimental attachment, sometimes erroneously called sentimental value, is not measurable in dollars. Attempting to measure it in money is something like trying to establish "heart balm" and "pain and suffering" in monetary terms. The judiciary system and plaintiffs' attorneys may believe it feasible to do so, but underwriters and the present authors are more skeptical and advise the risk manager not to try.[33] Let him merely conclude that the sentimental items are "very valuable" and try to protect them against loss or damage without measuring what their loss or destruction might actually "cost." At least he can be certain that the company's continued existence does not depend upon them.

In between the readily replaceable special items, such as jewelry, furs, and radium, and the totally irreplaceable ones, such as original paintings and historical documents, comes a group of items difficult but not impossible to replace. Models, patterns, and dies typically fall in this group. These items commonly have the additional characteristic of little physical depreciation (from normal use, apart from casualties) but overnight obsolescence. Reproduction cost of models, patterns, and dies is typically high, and the process of reproduction is time consuming. Since there is so little physical depreciation, items worth reproducing are worth the full cost of reproduction. But items not worth reproducing are likely to be worth exactly nothing. Old items often are kept on hand because they have been used many times in the past and *might* be useful in the future. But if it has been five years since a particular item has been active, what is its true future value? Has it been kept just because no one has taken the initiative and trouble to get rid of it? (Indeed, many dies are so much harder to destroy than to store that they may be kept indefinitely.)

If a die or pattern is in active use, it may actually be worth a great deal more than its cost of reproduction. For the duplicate, which may take months to produce, cannot make money for the business in the meanwhile, and a profitable operation may be curtailed or even shut down for lack of the necessary dies and patterns.

Early in this chapter, losses were classified into those measured by declines in asset values, those measured by declines in income, and those measured by the creation of additional expenses, and it was noted that "these classes are not mutually exclusive." The value of patterns and dies as assets cannot depend upon the market value; there is no market. The value depends entirely upon the contribution to the net earnings of the business. The only reason for reproducing the asset is to reduce the income loss. If the reproduction cannot be accomplished in time to diminish the income loss by more than the cost of reproduction, then the pattern or die

---

[33] Indeed, if the "sentimental" interest can be expressed in dollars and cents, one would immediately question whether the "sentiment" was real.

will not be reproduced. If damage to the item does not cause loss to income, there will be no reproduction either. In other words, the actual loss is the decline in income; the expenses and time involved in reproducing the asset serve, however, to set a maximum on what that income loss can be.

Mobile Property, Property in Transit. The next category of tangible personal property to be considered is the group connected with transportation. This group merits separate consideration because it has its own loss units and is subject to special hazards not ordinarily associated with property remaining on the premises. And, of course, mobile equipment and goods in transit take special policies and coverages when they are insured.[34]

Automobiles and Aircraft. Actually, automobiles and aircraft offer no new principles of evaluation. Private passenger automobiles, light trucks, and light aircraft are generally best evaluated on the basis of the cost to replace with equipment of similar condition and age in the current market. (And, as every automobile dealer knows, "Blue Book" and "Red Book" values are at best only a guide to the actual market values.) The market in heavier trucks and aircraft is too imperfect to serve as a useful guide to value, so replacement cost new less depreciation is the common base. Obsolescence can be an important factor, especially in the largest aircraft, but this is a problem only for airlines and not for businesses in general. Since nearly all automobile and aircraft physical damage insurance is written with "actual cash value" as the stated face amount of the policy, evaluation is not really necessary for insurance purposes. But, naturally, the values of the equipment should be known, at least approximately, so that an intelligent decision can be made as to whether to buy insurance on it.

A special problem arises when the sum of the cost of replacement (repair) parts in an old airplane comes to more than the market value of the plane. This can happen because the installation of new parts involves labor as well as material costs yet ordinarily does not constitute an over-all betterment in the value of the airplane. The same problem arises with older automobiles, of course. (But if the automobile is old enough to be a genuine antique or collector's item, then it should be treated under the category of "special value" property.)

Watercraft. Small watercraft are subject to the same valuation rules as automobiles. The evaluation of ocean and Great Lakes vessels is a technical specialty all its own—as is nearly everything else about ocean marine transportation and insurance. The evaluation of ships, indeed, is like the

---

[34] The special insurance divisions for these items are marine insurance plus automobile and aviation insurance. Actually, automobile and aviation insurance on property are species of marine insurance, but they are such important species that insurers have given them special categories all their own. Marine insurance also includes coverage on "instrumentalities of transportation, communication, and navigation," most of which are not mobile.

evaluation of "special value" property ashore in just about every way. Present are the same characteristics of large value in a single unit, of subjection to special hazards ("perils of the sea"), and of difficulty of replacement. Models, patterns, and dies were discussed under "special value" property as prime examples of items difficult but not impossible to replace. Ships, having this same feature, are subject to the same discussion.

With ships, however, two different features appear. One is that there is a market for them, which makes evaluation a little easier. The market for ships is generally based on buyers' estimates of the profit-earning potential of particular vessels. The second different feature about ships makes their evaluation more difficult. While not subject to as sudden technological obsolescence as are patterns and dies, ships are plagued by what might be called "temporary" or "cyclical obsolescence." In times of slow trade, the earning power of a vessel may not warrant the cost of replacement or even of extensive repair. In such times, economic factors have already caused the loss of some part of the value of the vessel and only the remaining value—a capitalization of earning power, in effect—represents the existing loss potential.

On the other hand, trade may pick up. When trade is booming, the current value of an existing vessel may be far above the cost of replacement less depreciation; indeed, it may be above the cost of replacement even without deduction for replacement. The existing vessel can earn *now;* it will be months before a replacement can be built, and during those months many dollars of earnings will be lost. And by the time the new ship is ready for use, the boom in trade may be over. The whole problem is complicated, of course, because good and bad times alternate in irregular fashion. After all, if the ship is lost in bad times, the immediate damnification may be small, but also lost is the presence of a ship all ready to go just as soon as conditions begin to improve. This potential is worth something, but estimating its value in dollars may call for the help of a crystal ball.

Unlike patterns and dies, ships are subject to considerable physical depreciation. Therefore, as with aircraft and automobiles, complete ships can have considerably less value than the cost of replacing their component parts.

Once again, it is best to hire the services of experts to estimate the value of these unique items. This estimate will approximate market values, in general, which are principally based on the expected profitability of operating the vessel.

Other Mobile Property. The maximum loss potential of road-building, earth-moving and other heavy mobile equipment of contractors is measured by the same methods used in evaluating other machinery. The reasons for establishing a special category for this property are to be sure that it will be noticed as part of a loss unit (how much is in a given place—on a given job—at a given time) and to take notice of the special perils to which it is subject (landslide, flood, collapse of bridges, for example), which do not ordinarily threaten machinery remaining on a particular set of premises.

Property in Transit. In general, the same methods would be used to measure the maximum loss potential for property in transit as would be used for that property if it were not in transit. There are a few special factors to be taken into consideration for property in transit. One is whether expenditure for shipping costs would be lost along with the property. For example, in ocean shipping it is customary to prepay the freight. If the cargo is lost, so is the payment for freight.

A second point to watch is the difference between invoice figures and full value. The invoice figures may be subject to discounts; they may or may not include such items as freight, insurance, and taxes.

A third point for consideration is whether the value lost is to be computed as of the point of destination or the point of origin. In ocean marine insurance on cargoes, particularly staples, it is customary to consider value as of point of destination. This means that the value of the asset is computed to include not only the expenses of shipping but also the possible profit in the process. (Once again we can see how asset, income, and expense losses cannot always be conveniently separated.)

Property in transit is considered separately also—for the same reasons that mobile equipment is considered separately. It should be remembered that the loss unit containing property in transit will also contain the conveying vehicle, if that is at risk for the same party as is the cargo. Furthermore, it is often possible for more than one separate shipment to be subject to one single catastrophic loss away from the shipper's premises. Thus, a single major flood in the rail marshaling yards at Kansas City destroyed several railroad car or truck loads of property for many shippers. And, when transshipping is required before property reaches its destination, considerable values can pile up in warehouses at transshipping points, particularly at ports. This fact cannot be ignored by the risk manager when he considers the loss unit.

Plants and Animals. Living things present special risk problems because, being alive, they are subject to loss by death or disease. Horses or livestock will, on many occasions, be considered properly among the "mobile property." Plants in the ground are part of real property, and the reader will find additional discussion of them later, under that topic. Such living property as thoroughbred racing horses, champion livestock, or plants of comparable distinction is best treated as "special value" property.

Otherwise, living property is best valued at replacement cost for property of like kind. The modifying phrase, "of like kind," which includes similarity in such qualities as health, age, and usefulness, stands in lieu of the usual allowance for depreciation.

Real Property

Real property consists of the land and all things permanently attached thereto. Land itself generally is not considered to be subject to static risk, although this is not strictly true; earthquake, landslide, flood, and some explosions can cause land some damage. In most situations, the principal real property other than land consists of buildings. Additional real property involving significant values includes things grown on the land and structures other than buildings.

Buildings. The insurable value of a building is its actual cash value at the time of loss. This seems simple, but is it? Enough cases have gone to court to develop a general rule that actual cash value usually means replacement cost new less observed depreciation.[35] This rule suggests two steps in establishing building values for the purpose of measuring maximum loss potentials: (1) measuring the replacement cost of the structure and (2) measuring the amount of observed depreciation. The application of this generally accepted rule would create few difficulties if depreciation could be measured by a foolproof scientific formula capable of mathematical application.

The Cost of Replacement. Of what value are the property account books in determining the cost of replacement? Unfortunately, they are of no value, and for several reasons. In the first place, these accounts typically reflect only the original investment in the property. They do not reflect subsequent changes in price levels, either up or down. Furthermore, subsequent property improvements, such as partitions, balconies, and wiring, may be charged to expenses and never enter the property account. And, too, property accounts sometimes include costs that are not, and do not have to be, incurred again when the building is lost—such items as the cost of surveying the land and architect's fees. Finally, the property accounts include items that are undamageable from most perils and therefore should not be included in considering the loss potential in most cases: foundations, underground wires and pipes, walks, curbs, pavements, excavations, and footings.

If the books of account are no guide to cost of replacement, then how can these costs be ascertained? What about original cost adjusted by one of the published construction cost indexes? First, for the reasons given above, original cost is not much help, and, second, the various published

---

[35] The term "replacement cost" is now in vogue, having been substituted for the term "reproduction cost," which was used for years. The change in terms reflects the realization that it is sometimes impossible or undesirable to reproduce buildings with the same materials and by the same methods of construction. Nevertheless, the replacement structure considered for purposes of evaluation should be of the same style, quality, and function and should include the same type of equipment as the existing structure.

indexes vary so much among themselves that it becomes an almost impossible task to justify one index over the other. Thus, such a method is exposed to double error: error in original cost basis and error in the selection of cost index.

Can the unit measurement method be used? For example, charts are published indicating square-foot or cubic-foot unit value of buildings in given locations. By multiplying the unit value by the number of units in the building, the cost of reproduction can be ascertained. The problem in using this method is that all buildings are not identical. They vary as to shape, size, design, trim, and quality of workmanship. The unit cost formula does not take these variations into consideration. Buildings containing the same number of square or cubic feet frequently have widely differing values. For certain smaller buildings of standardized use, and built by current construction methods, this approach is useful—especially in the hands of experienced persons who can and will recognize features of the building that the per unit rate does not contemplate and then make allowance accordingly. Buildings for which this approach is useful are principally small and medium-sized houses but also include the smaller and simpler commercial structures without many built-in fixtures.

The most accurate approach to building evaluation is to have a complete survey made by competent persons. Such persons can, by detailed physical inspection plus study of any plans available, develop a complete list of labor and material costs, including allowances for the builder's profits and overhead. These estimates can then be adjusted where appropriate for any differences between reproduction and replacement costs, and with current prices, delivery, and installation costs for such fixtures and machinery as heating, air conditioning, elevators and escalators, and so on, as are presently found in the structure.

Each of the parts of the structure and each of the fixtures and attached machinery then, must be considered for depreciation.

Depreciation.   Depreciation is a measure of the penalties to be assessed against the cost of the new replacement so as to reflect the value of the actual structure under consideration. It represents value that has disappeared from the building. It is, however, not simply a matter of the chronological age of the building. In fact, three factors account for depreciation: physical deterioration of the building, economic obsolescence of the structure, and economic deterioration of the location. All three of these factors are important in measuring the cost of replacement new less depreciation.[36]

The causes of *physical deterioration* are wear and tear, general decay, corrosion, and exposure to the elements. Some properties resist these causes better than others do. The quality of materials, soundness of original con-

---

[36] Robert O. Harvey, "Observations on the Cost Approach," *Appraisal Journal* (October, 1953), pp. 514–18.

struction, and extent and nature of subsequent maintenance determine, to a large extent, the rate of physical depreciation. It becomes readily apparent that no rule of thumb using arbitrary percentages can be applied to determine accurately the amount of physical deterioration for various buildings. Instead, each building presents a special case in itself and, therefore, must be handled individually.

Experienced appraisers can determine reasoned estimates of the expected physical life of each separate segment of a given structure based on the materials used in it, the architectural plans employed, the degree of skill in construction workmanship, and the love and care it has received. The basis for fixing the penalty to be charged for physical deterioration is the cost of repairing or replacing each of the deteriorated items necessary to make the structure like new. The life span of each individual item and its cost of replacement can be measured. For example, if the interior of the building needs painting once every five years, the penalty for physical deterioration would be 20 per cent of the current cost of painting for each year since the last coat of paint was applied.

Most buildings suffer *economic obsolescence;* they get out of date, just as textbooks do. New designs, new materials, improvements in architectural designs, and new construction methods have operated to reduce the relative attractiveness of old buildings. In addition, new inventions or discoveries have taken their toll of losses in the usefulness of various buildings. Thus, television has rendered obsolete a number of movie houses, just as movie houses, years earlier, had made many of the old "opera houses" obsolete. Both technological changes and changes in social attitudes and customs account for economic obsolescence.

Economic obsolescence may be curable or incurable. The cost of remodeling a present building to conform to current standards (of efficiency, safety, and aesthetics) measures the penalty to be assessed for curable obsolescence. Incurable obsolescence usually results from poor functional design, unattractive architecture, or improper relation of the building to its site. The penalty to be assessed for incurable obsolescence is the difference between the net income (cost of operation and maintenance) of the present building and that of the ideal one, capitalized at an appropriate rate of interest for the remaining life of the building.

Closely akin to obsolescence is *locational deterioration,* which may be defined as the improper location of the building in terms of the functions it is to perform.[37] Buildings designed for commercial uses are more susceptible to locational deterioration than are buildings designed for industrial use. The measure of the penalty for locational deterioration is the difference between the future economic life of the building if it were

---

[37] It is more charitable to call this problem one of "deterioration," of course. Actually, it can exist from the day that construction of the building was begun or that decision was made to put that building on that site.

in the proper location and the building in the location under appraisal.

Depreciation is one of those topics upon which many books and innumerable articles have been written. The discussion here is merely an introduction to, or rather a warning about, the complexities of the subject.

Other Structures. Perhaps the principal reason for making a separate category of structures other than buildings is to be sure that the risk manager does not overlook these structures. There is no limit to the variety of forms such structures can take. Among the better known forms are bridges, tunnels, television and radio towers, neon and other automatic signs, storage tanks, smokestacks, fences, and outdoor equipment for handling materials. Piers, wharves, docks, and retaining walls are also in this category.

Evaluation of these miscellaneous structures is a cross between evaluating machinery and equipment and evaluating real property. Their own nature is generally that of machines and equipment but when they are attached to the land so as not to be readily removable, site factors enter in, as they do with buildings.

Many structures have special problems with regard to perils. High structures (suspension bridges, television and radio towers, smokestacks) are heavily subject to wind damage. High steelwork (towers, bridges) and electrical lines are susceptible to ice. Bridges are subject to flood and ice damage from below. Wind, hail, and vandalism are particular problems with neon and other automatic signs.

On the other hand, some structures are relatively impervious. This is particularly true of low structures made of masonry—walks, curbs, drives—and underground installations—sewers, conduits. Like land, they are subject to earthquake, landslide, flood, and explosion loss; also to problems of settling and subsidence.

It is important to remember that evaluations of total property value include the land and all structures and that, when estimating maximum loss potential for most purposes, the value of the land and relatively impervious structures should be subtracted from the total.

Crops and Landscaping. Growing things attached to the land are part of the real property. Since they may be severed from the land, or grown in pots or tubs, they can also be personal property. As personal property, they offer no particular difficulty except that, while growing, they are susceptible to many special perils, such as insects and improper growing conditions.

Growing crops are a class of property of no concern to most business risk managers. But more and more businesses of all kinds are investing heavily in landscaping—trees, shrubs, plants, and lawns. Landscaping values, even when large, are frequently overlooked in evaluating loss potentials. Even if the risk of their loss is going to be assumed, it should be done so knowingly, not through oversight.

The value of landscaping is, in general, the cost of replacement. Healthy plants are not subject to depreciation except for loss of situs value. Diseased or already damaged plants, of course, are not worth full replacement value and may even have a negative worth—the cost of removing them.

Trees are a particular problem in evaluating loss potential. Badly damaged trees must be removed before they can be replaced, and removal of a large tree is an expensive process. Even removal of fallen debris (following a severe wind or ice storm, for example) presents an expense. This is important to remember because debris removal provisions in insurance policies provide coverage only for "expenses incurred in the removal of all *debris of the property insured hereunder . . .*" (italics added). "Property insured hereunder" seldom includes trees.

EVALUATORS AND APPRAISERS

Who is to do all the foregoing evaluating and appraising? The risk manager?

A senator has said that "no one has enough experience to be a United States Senator." By this he meant that the Senate deals with much too widely varied problems in much too little time for any one senator to have the background necessary to be expert in all, or even a great part, of them. The same thing is true of business management and even of specialized parts of business management, such as the management of static risks. The senator, the general manager, and the special department manager all must make recourse to the same type of source: the man or men who make a specialty of the individual matter directly in question.

Experts outside the Business

Fortunately, there are experts in every field of evaluation or appraisal. Some do evaluating or appraising on a full-time basis. Many others do it only incidentally to their main job, but their main job is such that expertise in evaluation or appraisal of certain things is essential in it. For example, professional evaluation of jewelry is done by jewelers. Depending upon the occasion, the evaluator may be a retail jeweler, a wholesaler, a manufacturing jeweler, or a broker. In any of these occupations some knowledge of gems and their values is a trade necessity. Of course, the usual local retail jeweler would be a poor estimator on the British crown jewels, but he will generally be quite competent on the average individual's ring—a type he deals with regularly. Within some trades or occupations, of course, one must be more discriminating than in others in the choice of an evaluator. Not all "antique dealers," for example, are really familiar with genuine antiques! But some are.

Experts inside the Business Concern

Many experts are available to the risk manager among colleagues in his own organization. They are necessarily experts in matters concerning their own inventories—raw materials, goods in process, and finished products.[38] Among them probably will be experts in many kinds of machines and equipment the business uses. These experts should be used in evaluating such items. But two things must be remembered: (1) familiarity with the use of an item does not always involve or require familiarity with evaluation of it, and (2) there is more than one value to be familiar with, and the risk manager must make clear just which value he wants.

As an example of the first, the business may be a department store. There are, or had better be, people in it who are completely familiar with the present market in their products, which styles are current and which have suddenly gone out of date, which way prices have moved in the past week, what percentage of the current stock will have to be marked down to be moved, which items could be replaced in time to catch their seasonal market, and which ones, if destroyed, would mean total loss for this year's season.

But suppose the store also has a pneumatic tube system, which hundreds of employees use every day. The building engineer knows how to keep it running when the trouble is not serious. The accountants have studied the system with an eye to minimizing operating costs, embezzlement, and credit losses by its use. But the basic system is eighteen years old. Which of these people can be expected to know its actual value today? The accountants can say how much loss of its use would add to costs of operation. But who would be able to say (1) how long it would take to replace the system, (2) how much it would cost to replace it, and (3) how much should be taken from replacement cost as allowance for the system's physical deterioration and obsolescence?

In factories some machines are standardized and wear out with some frequency. The plant's engineers are likely to be able to evaluate these at current prices. But suppose the plant has, say, a single 20-ton press constructed and installed eighteen years ago when the present building was built. How much would one like it cost today? Would it be replaced with one just like it? Probably not. How much allowance should be made for the difference in cost between a newer, more efficient machine and the present usable, but less efficient, one? What about additional cost to install a machine of this size inside a building already built? With only one machine like it in the plant, and that one not recently purchased, the plant's own people are likely to need the help of outside specialists in determining its present value.

Does the business include any real experts in the construction or repair of stationary boilers and associated steam systems? Or in elevators, escalators, and their machinery? Probably not.

The second thing to be remembered in using "inside experts" is to be

---

[38] But if they are not, probably the best thing for the risk manager to do is to get, not an appraisal, but another job.

sure that they understand exactly what is wanted. For example, if the accountants keep a "LIFO" inventory,[39] they know what current, or near-current, per unit costs are. They will also know the total book value they have for inventory, but this value is based on old prices. They may also know how many units are involved in the inventory. The risk manager wants to know the "value" of the inventory, but not as the accountants have calculated it. He wants from the accountants (or purchasing department and inventory control) the current costs per unit and the total number of units of different kinds, and not what the financial statements say is the "value."

Similarly, with regard to shipments that go out at the company's risk, the maximum invoice value may not be exactly what the risk manager wants from the shipping department. What he really wants to know is the actual loss if something happens to that shipment. To know this, he needs to know what discounts, if any, the invoice amount is subject to; the cost of prepaid freight, if not included in the invoice; and, of course, some routing facts to help him determine how much total exposure to loss there is likely to be at one time in one place away from the plant.

Full-Time Professional Appraisers

Without any question, the most accurate and usual information about the value of real property and of personal property in use is obtained from full-time professional appraisal organizations. The figures obtained from competent organizations of this kind are the most accurate representations of value that can be obtained by any means. They are also the most useful, being detailed and organized with insurance and loss problems prominently and consciously in mind. Furthermore, complete appraisal service includes not only the original survey and report but also the installation of a system to keep the evaluation up to date.

The principal deterrent to use of appraisal organizations undoubtedly is cost. The amount of work to be done is considerable, and it must be done by highly skilled technical people, principally professional engineers. The costs of their appraisals have been thoroughly justified in the many actual instances in which (1) they have uncovered values far beyond what were known or believed to exist[40] and (2) the existence of their figures has pro-

---

[39] "LIFO" stands for "last in, first out." Under this method of accounting for inventory, when an item is removed from inventory its cost is taken to be that of the most recent addition to inventory. That is, for price and cost purposes, the last unit added to the inventory is assumed to be the first one next taken out.

[40] And done so before the loss, contrasted with so many disastrous cases in which they were discovered after the loss. The authors know of one case, for example, in which the building was insured for $64,100. Use of a "cost per cubic foot construction index" indicated a value of $70,500. A leading appraisal firm was called in and reported a figure of $338,066. When this high figure was challenged by the managers of the building, the appraising engineers proceeded to establish it detail by detail, point by point.

vided a clear base for insurance claims after the loss, usually speeding up the loss adjustment and getting cash into the hands of the business days, even weeks, earlier.[41] In the few cases in which the matter has gone to court, the existence of figures from a competent, disinterested party has weighed heavily in the courts' opinions.

The use of outside, professional appraisers in the cases of "special value" property and ships has already been thoroughly discussed.

Insurance Representatives

A significant amount of property appraisal is done by insurance agents and company representatives. Some of them know what they are doing. Some companies make it a point to train at least some of their field men[42] in appraisal techniques, and some subsequently acquire considerable experience. Larger agencies sometimes have professional appraisers available who are experienced with the kinds of property commonly insured by the agency or commonly found in the territory. Use of trained and experienced men representing insurance agencies or companies is perfectly acceptable provided they are trained and experienced in dealing with the kind of property to be appraised.[43]

Appraisal, Art or Science?

Professor Harvey, writing in the *University of Illinois Law Forum* had this to say about appraisals: "In summary, the valuation methods are orderly processes for combining disorderly and imperfect information. The methods are used to help in the formation of an opinion, but the methods do not give 'the answer.' Value estimates must be treated as hypotheses, and never should be treated as precise or absolute and provable, as one might prove an answer to a mathematical problem."[44]

SUMMARY

Loss probability and maximum loss potential are essential considerations for the risk manager in determining how a given loss exposure is to be

---

[41] The reader, now introduced to the manifold problems in evaluating property when it is whole and present for examination, will appreciate that evaluating it after it has been reduced to ash and rubble, or has disappeared, can easily be a slow process, no matter how anxious the insurer may be to give (and the insured to receive) fast claims service.

[42] Strictly, "field men" are insurance company representatives who deal directly with the companies' sales agents to help them with technical problems. Loosely—as used here—any insurance company representative who operates in the "field," that is, out among the agents and insureds, is a "field man."

[43] When company or agency representatives make the appraisal, the question arises as to whether the insurer is bound by the appraisal (as an act of its representative) when a claim arises. In general, companies do not intend to be so bound, so, in general, risk managers should not rely on the estimate of the agent or field man as the bounden word of the claims department.

[44] R. O. Harvey, "Valuation of Mortgage Security," *University of Illinois Law Forum*, Vol. 1957 (Fall), pp. 412–19. Quotation from p. 415.

handled. The task of measuring loss probability, however, is not easy. Some help may be obtained from insurance statistics, but these will need to be modified to reflect the differences between the particular loss probability to be measured and the sample from which the statistics are obtained. A good deal of individual judgment will invariably enter the picture, so the final probability figure arrived at will in some measure be a subjective one.

The task of measuring maximum loss severity also presents some difficulties. The problems for the risk manager in measuring maximum loss potentials in asset values are those of arriving at the cost of their replacement and of determining the amount of depreciation to be charged against the replacement cost new. The latter problem is the more troublesome one.

With respect to each asset, the risk manager must be prepared to answer the following fundamental question: "How much would be lost if the asset were to be wiped out?" The valuation methods to be used will vary among assets. With some assets, like cash and securities, the answer is simple. With others, like heavy machinery, the answer is complex. In a number of instances the risk manager will be able to obtain the data needed for reasonable valuation estimates from various internal managerial and technical personnel. In others, outside experts will have to be consulted. In either event, the final valuation figure arrived at will be a "best estimate," and, the better the estimate is, the more effective the risk manager can be on his job.

REVIEW AND DISCUSSION QUESTIONS

1. What effect do loss probability and potential size of loss have on the desirability of purchasing insurance? Why?
2. What is the significance of inability to obtain all the information a risk manager really needs in dealing with risks in a scientific manner? What difference would it make to his operations if all the needed information were available?
3. (a) Under what conditions would the risk manager wish to underinsure a given exposure? (b) How do the insurers view underinsurance on the part of their insureds? Why? (c) Illustrate a situation in which the insurer might require underinsurance. Illustrate a situation under which an insurer might prohibit underinsurance. (If you do not happen to know enough about insurance to pick these illustrations with ease, then see if you can reason them out based on the theory indicated in the answer to the (b) part of this question.)
4. How would you draw a distinction between the art of risk management and the science of risk management? Is such a distinction useful? Why or why not?
5. What is the difference between *a priori* and *a posteriori* probability estimation? What important factors affect the reliability of each method of estimation? What does all this man to the risk manager?
6. Of what use to the risk manager is subjective probability as opposed to objective probability?

7. Of what use is objective loss probability to the risk manager even when he knows what it is?

8. What is the rule of "minimize the maximum regret"? Is it a good rule to use in purchasing insurance? Why or why not?

9. Leaving out all psychological considerations, why might insurance still be worth more to the insured than the actuarial value of the insurance claim?

10. Why are there two (at least two!) ways of measuring losses? Are both ways needed, or can one be substituted for the other? Why or why not?

11. What characteristics about assets are significant in classifying them for the purpose of estimating loss potentials? (For example, why are such assets as money and securities placed in the general class called "nontangible" which also includes intangible assets?)

12. What effect does irreproduceability of an asset have on loss potential with respect to it? Is this effect the same for all types of nontangible assets (e.g., the same for a historical document as for an important accounting record)? Is it the same for tangible assets as for nontangible assets?

13. Why may there be a difference between "use value" and "market value" of a tangible asset? Which value should be used in estimating loss potential, and why? How does the definition of "loss potential" affect your answer?

14. What is the role of each of the following in estimates of loss potential: original cost, book value, depreciation, obsolescence, replacement cost, reproduction cost, betterment?

15. A common method of classifying owned tangible personal property for insurance purposes is to divide it between (a) personal property in use and (b) personal property held for sale. In what ways is this classification logical for purposes of measuring loss potential? Is any further clasification or subclassification really necessary for owned tangible personal property? Explain.

16. When estimating potential losses from damage to inventories, in what ways are the problems of manufacturers and merchandisers (a) different, (b) alike? Why should inventories held by merchandising businesses be evaluated at cost, like manufacturers' raw materials and goods in process, rather than at sales value, like manufacturers' finished goods?

17. It has been suggested that custom-built production machinery should be considered as part of the class "property of special value." Do you agree, or disagree, with this recommendation? Justify your position.

18. Why should the risk manager consider "mobile property" and property in transit in separate categories from other tangible personal property? (How many *different kinds* of reasons are there for considering these classifications separately?)

19. Should land values be considered by the risk manager in measuring the loss potential of real property? What about landscaping?

20. The risk manager of the Abracadabra Production Corporation has a new handbook of construction cost indexes. What obstacles still stand between him and a reasonably accurate appraisal of the corporation's real property? Describe fully the nature of the problems presented by each of these "obstacles."

21. What factors should be considered in the selection and use of persons to appraise property? Be specific.

Chapter 9

MEASURING LOSS POTENTIAL:
EXPENSES AND INCOME

Business profits depend upon the level of expenses and gross earnings. Any contingency resulting in an increase in expenses or a decrease in gross income naturally will have an adverse effect on profits. Expenses and income exposures, therefore, cannot be ignored by risk managers. In fact, protection against these exposures may be more important than the preservation of asset values.

In his efforts to measure loss potential from expense and income exposures, the risk manager is likely to encounter many more unkowns than he finds in his attempts to estimate loss potential from exposure of asset values. In fact, the degree to which estimates and guesswork play a part in fixing dollar amounts of some potential expense and income losses are frightening, especially to the timid soul who feels he should be able to measure these exposures to the exact dollar.

EXPENSES

A number of contingencies result either in added expenses or in a loss of prepaid expenses, sometimes in both.

Leasehold Interest

One source of expense losses is the cancellation of a valuable lease after a fire or other peril has caused damage to the leased property.

A lease gives the tenant the right to use property in accordance with the terms of the contract. From this agreement the tenant derives a valuable measure of security. In addition, a lease may have an independent value measured in terms of dollars. The tenant has a lease with an independent value if the rent he has contracted to pay is less than the property would command on the current market. Leases frequently include clauses that

293

provide for cancellation if the leased structure suffers a certain minimum amount of physical damage by fire or other peril. The cancellation may be automatic or at the option of either party to the contract. A customary minimum damage figure is 50 per cent. If the lease is silent on the subject, cancellation rights are governed by the local real estate laws, which in most jurisdictions make provision for cancellation under a minimum set of circumstances.

When a lease valuable to the tenant is subject to cancellation by the landlord, the loss to the tenant may be one or both of two types: (1) increased expenses brought on by higher rents and (2) loss of prepaid expenses incurred to acquire the lease or to improve the property for the tenant's use.

Increased Expenses. Upon cancellation of a valuable lease after a fire, the tenant will find that when he resumes business his rental expense is likely to be increased. If he renegotiates a lease with his landlord for the same premises, the new rent will surely be more in line with the current market. And, if he has to look elsewhere for comparable replacement facilities, he undoubtedly will have to pay more rent for them than he is currently paying. Of course, it is possible that less valuable facilities could be found that would do equally well for the type of operation involved. Only if this latter situation is true would it be possible to hold the rent expense at or near the present level.

How can the risk manager measure the loss potential involved in the cancellation of a favorable lease? To evaluate the leasehold interest exposure, four separate kinds of information are needed: (1) the contract rental price established in the lease, (2) the number of years remaining under the lease, (3) the current market rental value of property equally satisfactory for the type of operation involved, and (4) the rate of interest appropriate for use in computing the present value of the excess of the current market value of the property over the contract rental. Since the first two of these items are a matter of record, they need no further discussion. The last two, however, do require some additional attention.

Rental Value of Equivalent Property. The value of a lease is measured in part by the difference between the contract rent and the rent the property could command in the current market. Presumably, if the property is worth $2,000 a month on the current market and the lease requires a rent of only $1,500, the tenant could sublet and enjoy a monthly profit of $500 until his lease expires. It would seem to follow, therefore, that if the lease is cancelled by the landlord after a fire, the tenant has suffered a loss equal to the present value of $500 a month for the unexpired term of the lease. But that is not necessarily the case. In the first place, under the terms of his lease the tenant might not be allowed to sublet. In the second place, if he had the right to sublet, he might not want to take advantage of it. Instead, he might prefer to concentrate his time and energy on the everyday problems of his own business rather than on those of the real estate business. Also, a move to a new location to realize the cash value of a favorable lease each time one shows up would be an inconvenient and expensive operation and most certainly a questionable business practice.

What, then, determines the tenant's loss if his lease is cancelled? The loss would be made up of two items: (1) the difference between the rent now being paid and what would have to be paid for equally satisfactory premises, this difference being discounted for the unexpired term of the lease, and (2) all the costs associated with moving and becoming established at a new location.

Thus, the first question to be answered is: What would it cost the business to rent equally suitable quarters upon cancellation of its present lease? Local realtors who specialize in commercial properties will be able to provide a satisfactory answer to this question. It must be remembered, however, that the local realtors' answers of today do not govern the rental values of tomorrow. The real estate market is by no means static. The rental value of any property can change shortly after an inquiry has been made. Thus, if the loss potentials from lease cancellations are to be kept up to date, trends in the real estate market must be watched and valuations adjusted accordingly.

What costs are associated with moving and becoming established at a new location? The physical costs of moving are obvious. Not so obvious are the costs of announcing the change to customers, the loss of business during the period of transition, the loss of efficiency during the period of adjustment, and a possible loss of trained personnel who, because of personal reasons, are not willing to work at the new location.

The Discounting Process. When a lease is cancelled, the loss is so many dollars a month for the unexpired term of the lease. For example, if the contract rent under a lease with 60 months of unexpired term is $2,500 a month and comparable substitute facilities could be leased in today's market for $3,000 a month, the loss would amount to $500 a month for 60 months. The total loss over the 60 months would amount to $30,000 ($500 x 60). The value today of $500 a month for 60 months, however, will be less than $30,000. How much less depends, of course, upon the interest rate used in the discounting process: the higher the interest rate used, the greater will be the discount and the lower will be the current value of the loss. For example, if the interest rate assumed is 3½ per cent the discount would be $2,399 and the present value $27,601. If a 2 per cent rate is used, the discount would be $1,414 and the present value would be $28,586. A 4 per cent rate would yield a discount of $2,803 and a present value of $27,197.

Because the amount of the loss is affected by the interest rate assumed, a realistic rate must be selected if an accurate measure of the loss is to be approached. The appropriate interest rate would be one reflecting the current yield on safe and liquid investments. Liquidity is necessary because part of the investment would have to be liquidated each month to offset the monthly increase in rent, in this case $500 monthly for 60 months. If a 4 per cent rate is used, an initial investment of $27,197 would allow a withdrawal of $500 a month without exhausting the fund until the end of the 60 months.

Just as local realtors can be helpful in establishing rental values of comparable facilities, local bankers can be helpful in selecting the interest rate to use in the discounting process. Interest rates, like rental values, are subject to change. Trends in the money market, therefore, must be watched and valuations adjusted to reflect changes if the estimated loss potential is to be kept up to date.

Obviously, *ceteris paribus*, the loss potential is one that decreases in amount, that is, it becomes less and less with the passage of each month. If it is assumed that 4 per cent remains the current interest rate and that $3,000 remains the current rental value of equivalent property, then the loss potential will decline each month as follows:

Unexpired Months	Loss Potential
60	$27,197
59	26,786
58	26,373
3	1,490
2	995
1	498

Equally obvious is that *ceteris paribus* may not be assumed. Variations that are likely to occur in both interest rates and current rental values will require an adjustment up or down in the loss potential from that indicated in the foregoing tabulation.

Prepaid Expenses. It is sometimes necessary for a business tenant to pay a bonus to acquire a lease; this bonus usually is not refunded if the landlord exercises his privilege of cancelling the lease after a serious fire. Also, under some leases the tenant is asked to pay rent in advance. A common arrangement is to require payment of the rent for the final year at the inception of the lease. Again the common practice is *not* to refund the advanced payments if the lease is cancelled.

When bonuses or advanced rental payments are required, how much does the tenant lose upon cancellation of his lease? For example, how much would a tenant lose if his 20-year lease is cancelled 5 years after he had paid a $20,000 cash bonus? This bonus, when prorated over the term of the lease (20 years), would be equivalent to an additional annual rental of $1,470.[1] When the lease is cancelled, 15 years of unexpired term is lost

---

[1] This is, of course, a standard problem in the mathematics of finance. What is the 20-year installment payment equivalent to a present lump sum payment of $20,000, assuming interest at 4 per cent? (Or what annual payment will amortize a 20-year loan of $20,000 at 4 per cent interest?) There is a formula, but tables of answers are found in many places. Such a table shows that, at 4 per cent interest, the present value of $1 per year, for 20 years is approximately $13.5903. Twenty thousand divided by $13.5903 gives $1,470 (to the nearest $10).

and with it 15 years of rent prepayments at the rate of $1,470 annually. The discounted value of these payments (again using 4 per cent) is $16,344.

For another example, how much would the tenant lose if his 30-year lease is cancelled 10 years after he has paid $12,000 as rent in advance for the last year? Assuming a 4 per cent rate of interest, this $12,000 payment in advance is equivalent to the payment of an additional $480 a year for all but the last year of the lease. If the lease is cancelled at the end of the tenth year and this prepayment is not refunded, the loss to the tenant is the capital sum of $12,000. No discounting is necessary because the loss of interest on this sum for the years that the lease was in force should be considered as extra rent.[2]

In the two examples given above the losses to the tenants were said to be $16,344 and $12,000, respectively. The facts considered so far bear out these conclusions, but one additional fact might make it necessary to adjust these figures. What will it cost the tenant to lease equivalent replacement facilities?

Assume that the tenant who paid $20,000 bonus pays an additional contract rent of $1,000 a month. He finds that to lease equivalent premises would now cost $1,200 a month. Thus, when the 20-year lease is cancelled at the end of 5 years, he loses the discounted value of $200 a month for 15 years, the unexpired portion of the lease. At 4 per cent this amounts to $27,171. It will be recalled that the pro rata value of the bonus was $16,344. Which of these two figures represents the effective loss to the tenant, $27,171 or $16,344? Or is the measure of loss the sum of the two? A moment's reflection will reveal that the tenant's effective loss will be $27,171, for that figure represents the present value of the extra cost of similar quarters. If he gets similar quarters, he has what he had before; therefore, he is indemnified. Of course, the full costs of moving and getting established at the new location must be added to the rental figure. However, if upon cancellation of his lease the tenant decides to discontinue business rather than to continue at a new location, then the $16,344 will measure the loss, for the loss then becomes one of prepaid rent.

What about the tenant whose 30-year lease is cancelled 10 years after he has prepaid the last year's rent of $12,000? Suppose he finds that he can lease equivalent quarters for $1,300 a month, or $300 a month more than he is currently paying. Since the lease has 20 years yet to run, the tenant's loss from cancellation amounts to $300 a month discounted for 20 years. Using a 4 per cent interest rate, this amounts to $49,817. It will be recalled that the loss on the prepaid rent to be forfeited was the full $12,000.

---

[2] Another way of looking at it: When the lease is cancelled, the tenant loses the value of his prepayment. What is that value? It is the use of the money (the $12,000) before it is due for rent plus the money itself when it becomes due as rent in the twentieth year. Suppose the tenant should receive $12,000 in cash upon cancellation of the lease. He would then lose neither the money nor its subsequent use. The amount of $12,000, therefore, must be the measure of his loss.

Which of these two figures represents the tenant's loss, $49,817 or $12,000, or is the measure of the loss the total of the two? Or is the effective loss some other figure? Here a moment's reflection will reveal that the tenant's effective loss will be some other figure. The $480 annual interest earned on the advanced payment of the $12,000 was included as additional rent under the cancelled lease. This means that in all but the last year the monthly rent differential to be paid under the new lease is about $40 less than the $300 used in the calculation given above. If the current lease remained in force, the tenant would pay $1,000 a month for the next 19 years, and nothing for the twentieth year, since that rent had been paid. Under the proposed substitute lease the tenant would pay $1,300 a month for the next 20 years. The question is how much more the rental cost will be under the substitute lease than under the original lease. The present value of $1,000 a month for the next 19 years at 4 per cent amounts to $160,481.50. The present value of $1,300 a month for the next 20 years at 4 per cent amounts to $215,874.75. The difference is $55,393.25, and this amount represents the loss that the tenant will suffer if his lease is cancelled. To this figure, of course, must be added the full cost of moving to and establishing himself in the new location. If the tenant decides to discontinue his business after his lease is cancelled rather than move to a new location, his effective loss will be $12,000, the amount of the un-refundable prepaid rent.

Improvements and Betterments

In order to adapt leased property to their own special uses, tenants frequently find it necessary to invest large sums of money in improvements and betterments. For example, they may add partitions, build balconies, put in new store fronts, or construct shelving and showcases.

Improvements, broadly speaking, are of two types: (1) those which by law, contract, or custom are removable by the tenant when the lease is terminated and (2) those which become a permanent part of the building structure and cannot be removed by the tenant upon termination of the lease.

Removable Improvements. The first category of property usually is composed of trade fixtures. The tenant is allowed to disassemble them and cart them off when he vacates the premises. Does this fact assure the tenant of no loss on his investment in improvements and betterments if his lease should be cancelled after a fire? This question, of course, assumes that the improvements and betterments are undamaged by the fire. In that event, the question of whether there is a loss depends upon what can be done with the disassembled improvements and betterments. If the tenant can use these improvements in his new quarters, then of course he has suffered no loss except the cost of moving them. But if they are not adaptable or needed in his new quarters, these improvements and betterments represent a loss. The loss is measured by the actual cash value[3] of the improvements less their salvage value.

For example, assume the tenant has an original investment of $4,000 in undamaged improvements and betterments. Suppose his 25-year lease is cancelled after 5 years. What is the loss on his undamaged improvements and betterments if he retains ownership of them? If he can use them in his new quarters, there is no loss except the cost of moving them. But if he cannot use them, his loss is figured as follows: cost of replacing improvements and betterments estimated at current prices as $4,500, less $1,500 estimated depreciation for the 5 years, minus $800 estimated salvage value, leaving a total of $2,200.

Of course, the fire that destroys the leasehold interest may also destroy the improvements and betterments. What, then, is the tenant's loss, assuming that the improvements and betterments were of the type in which the tenant retained ownership? The loss here would be the actual cash value of the improvements, that is, their current replacement cost new less depreciation.

Irremovable Improvements. When improvements become a permanent part of the building structure and cannot be removed upon expiration of the lease, the terms of the lease have an important bearing on how the tenant's potential loss exposure is to be measured. Because the tenant's interest in these improvements and betterments is a usufruct rather than a proprietary interest, damage to these improvements by fire or other peril can cause the tenant no property loss. To an important extent, the tenant's loss is governed by the terms of the lease.

If the landlord restores the improvements voluntarily, the tenant suffers the tenant will suffer no specific improvements and betterments loss because he will not be permanently deprived of their use. He will, of course, suffer loss of use of the premises until the restoration is completed, but this will be a part of his business interruption loss. When the landlord is obligated to replace the improvements and betterments, the tenant's only exposure is the chance that the landlord might not be able to fulfill his obligation. This exposure can be easily eliminated by requiring adequate insurance properly written to safeguard the tenant's right to restoration.

If the landlord restores the improvements voluntarily, the tenant suffers no loss. But, in measuring his loss potential, the tenant cannot rely on what the landlord might do. He has to know what the landlord will and can do. If the landlord will not contract to replace the improvements and reinforce an agreement to do so with financial safeguards for the tenant, the tenant must measure his loss exposure on the assumption that he will have to restore the improvements himself or that they will not be restored at all.

If the tenant assumes the obligation to restore the building if damaged or

---

[3] Actual cash value is the current cost of replacement new less depreciation.

destroyed by fire or some other peril, he again has no specific improvements and betterments exposure. Since the improvements are part of the building, they are included in measuring the loss potential for his liability under the lease. The amount of this liability is the cost of replacing the damaged property without allowance for depreciation. Depreciation is ignored because the tenant's liability is to restore the building and not to indemnify the landlord for the actual cash value of the loss.

If the lease is silent on the restoration of improvements and betterments, and the landlord is unwilling to assume the obligation for their replacement, the tenant may want to assume this obligation himself on a voluntary basis. After all, the same considerations that compelled the tenant to install the improvements in the first instance may still be present. If this is true, the tenant's maximum loss potential is the full cost of replacing the improvements, again without allowance for depreciation, since new must be substituted for old.

If the landlord is not willing to restore the improvements, the tenant might decide to do without them, move to a new location, or even go out of business. What then would be the measure of his loss? The loss in this case would be a function both of the original cost of the improvements and of the unexpired term of the lease. The original cost of the improvements would include not only the cost of the new additions themselves but also the cost of tearing out the old to make way for the new. When the improvements are not to be restored, the tenant's investment in them may be viewed as a prepaid expense similar to prepaid rent, to be amortized over the term of the lease. Thus, if a total loss occurs to improvements at the end of the fifth year of a 20-year lease, the tenant's loss will be 75 per cent of his original investment in these improvements. Theoretically, he has already recovered 25 per cent of his investment through the use of these improvements for a period equal to one quarter of the term of the lease.

What is the tenant's loss if a fire destroys a part of the building containing the improvements but spares the improvements themselves? If the damage to the building is insufficient to cancel the lease, the tenant will suffer no specific improvements and betterments loss. But if the damage is sufficiently to cancel the lease, the tenant may suffer an improvement and betterments loss even though these improvements are left undamaged. Here again the tenant can measure his loss by prorating the amount of his investment over the unexpired term of the lease. This, presumably, covers the value of the tenant's usufruct interest in the improvements for the unexpired term of the lease.

The pro rata method of measuring loss potential from the improvements and betterments exposure is, of course, open to question. The tenant might expect the greatest value from his investment in improvements and betterments to accrue during the later years of his lease, after he has established himself in business at the new location. The pro rata method evaluates the usufruct interest at a level amount each year. When use of the pro rata method is obviously contrary to reality, the risk manager will need to devise a method of estimating his loss exposure that will be more in keeping with the hard facts of real life situations. Perhaps the investment in improvements and betterments is not expected to pay off until after the third year of the lease. If this is true, then a total and permanent loss of the use of these improvements at any time during the first three years will represent a total loss of the full investment made in them by the tenant. How the investment should be amortized over the remaining term of the lease depends upon the rate at which the investment is expected to become fully productive.

Rental Expense

Some tenants have leases (usually long term) requiring them to continue rent payments even though the building becomes untenantable following a fire or other peril. These leases create for the tenant a loss exposure technically called rental value; he loses the value of the use of the property, its rental value, during the restoration period.[4]

The usual procedure is for the tenant to include the rental value exposure as a part of his business interruption exposure. But in some situations this will not hold true. If the rental property is an office or a warehouse, the tenant's business may not be interrupted if such property becomes untenantable. Temporary facilities usually can be leased to fill in until the property is restored. In these cases, the tenant's maximum potential loss from the rental value exposure is the product of (*a*) the monthly rent for the untenantable property less non-continuing expenses *times* (*b*) the number of months necessary to restore the property without undue delay. The probable restoration period can be estimated with the help of contractors. In measuring the maximum potential loss, it will be necessary to assume a total loss of the building and to make reasonable allowances for adverse conditions in rebuilding the structure.

The rental value exposure on these cases, however, is not likely to be a true measure of the tenant's loss. A more realistic measure of the loss would be the additional expenses of moving into, operating in, and moving out of temporary quarters plus the rent paid for the substitute facilities. If the substitute facilities are less expensive, the loss might well be less than the rental value exposure unless moving costs and additional operating expenses more than consume the difference. More than likely, however, the cost of the substitute facilities plus moving costs and additional operat-

---

[4] While the common law does not discharge the tenant from the obligation of paying the agreed-upon rent if the property is damaged or destroyed, statutes have been passed in most states granting relief to the tenant when there has been no express written agreement to the contrary.

ing expenses will exceed the rental value exposure. In this event, the loss will be greater than the rental value exposure.

When the tenant has a rental value exposure that does not also present a business interruption exposure, the logical approach is to lump the exposure into a broader classification, called "extra expense," and evaluate the whole class together.

Extra Expense

Some types of business enterprises would find it suicidal to close down during repairs following a fire or other loss. They must continue in operation regardless of the expense. The additional cost of operating with temporary facilities may be heavy enough not only to wipe away operating profits but also to create operating deficits. The problem of evaluating the extra expense exposure is not easy. In fact, it is impossible to arrive at an exact figure. A reasonable approximation can be developed by the risk manager, however, by breaking down the extra expenses into their component parts. Then an estimate can be made for each of the extra expenses that might be incurred in continuing the business after a fire or other loss.

Some of the items to be considered are the rental cost of temporary premises, the cost of new equipment, the cost of moving in and out of the temporary premises, the expense of cleaning premises at the temporary location, the cost of telephone installations at temporary premises, extra traveling expenses, bonuses for quick service in readying the new premises, and the cost of heat, light, and power at the new location. The risk manager may uncover other potential extra expenses as he analyzes the problem. For example, there might be additional telephone and telegraph charges, additional advertising costs, and perhaps additional expenses for skilled labor. From the total extra expenses developed, the risk manager must subtract the expenses that will not continue at the original location. The total amount of extra expenses to be incurred will depend also upon how long it will take to ready the original premises for reoccupancy. Therefore, an estimate of the time it will take to rebuild in the event of a total loss assumes an important role in measuring the maximum extra expense loss potential.

Liability

No perfect method has yet been developed for measuring the maximum potential dollar loss a given business can suffer from its liability exposure. Who can say how many injuries can arise at the maximum from the tortious actions of a business or through the violation of warranties? Furthermore, who can say how much at the maximum any one injury will cost? Only one statement about the maximum loss potential from liability can be made with full confidence: the maximum the business can lose is the business itself.[5] One who accepts any other conclusion would have to do so with much less confidence.

For a liability loss to force a business into receivership, that loss need not be equal to the net worth of the company. It can fall far short of this amount. A business severely weakened financially by the unsuccessful defense of a liability suit may never recover. Even the successful defense of a suit may take its toll because substantial costs may be incurred in winning the case.

How much of a liability loss a business can survive depends, of course, on a number of considerations, chiefly financial: its cash position and cash flow; its acid test and current ratios; its turnover of assets, receivables, and inventory; its operating and equity ratios; number of times its fixed charges are earned; its present and potential credit lines; and the caliber of its management.

How high a liability loss can a million-dollar business survive over a given period? Is it $250,000, $500,000, $750,000, or some other amount? Whatever the amount suggested for this measure, it is at best an estimate based on the considerations mentioned above and includes the shadows on either side. Obviously, if one estimates the figure at $500,000, he cannot say categorically that the business can stand a loss of $500,000 but not one of $510,000 or even $550,000. In fact, a loss of $490,000 or even $450,000 may prove to be more than the business can handle.

Of what importance is it to the risk manager to have an estimate of how small an accumulation of liability losses over a given period can be responsible for shoving a business into receivership? Suppose this estimate is $200,-000 for a $500,000 business. Ignoring the qualification made above, losses accumulating to $199,000 would register as losses of $199,000, but losses accumulating to $200,000 or more would be equivalent to losses of $500,-000, the value of the business. A $200,000 liability loss, therefore, would have the same effect as a $500,000 or $1,000,000 liability loss. It would represent a total loss. This is true, of course, only when the business is not insured against liability losses.

If the business owns liability insurance, then X dollars of losses in *excess* of the policy limits register as X dollars of losses if these excess claim accumulations remain under $200,000. Excess claim accumulations of $200,000 or more will result in a total loss of $500,000.

While the maximum potential loss is $500,000, it should be obvious that this figure does not set the policy limits necessary for full protection under a liability insurance contract. If the business has a liability insurance policy with per accident limits of $500,000,[6] the business is protected

---

[5] And if the business is unincorporated, the maximum loss is expanded to include the non-business property of its owners.

[6] See chap. 15 for a discussion of the methods of expressing policy limits under liability insurance policies.

against a total loss only if the claims arising from the accident amount to less than $700,000. The policy simply increases the maximum loss that the business can sustain short of bankruptcy by $500,000 per accident plus the cost of defense.[7] Liability claims amounting to $700,000 or more would create a total loss—a loss of $500,000. Thus, all that the risk manager knows so far about his liability exposure is that if his applicable insurance is $200,-000 or more below the amount of the liability claims against him, he will suffer a total loss of $500,000. And that is too little to know for comfort. How much liability insurance would he need if he is to be (nearly) certain that he will not come up $200,000 short? The risk manager cannot answer this question with precision. The only way he could be certain that he has purchased an adequate amount of liability insurance would be for him to buy a policy without limits. But, unfortunately, liability insurance underwriting has not yet advanced in this country to the stage at which unlimited policies are written.

The risk manager, therefore, is forced to select limits for his liability coverages. He can transfer the risk of liability losses for amounts up to these limits, but he is forced to assume the risk of losses beyond these limits. In effect, he must assume the risk of choosing inadequate limits. Of course, the higher the limits he selects, the less the chance that he will be underinsured. But limits that are too high cause the insured to pay premiums for unnecessary coverage. Sometimes when the risk manager is quoted a premium for what he believes to be "very comfortable" limits, he is shocked by it into taking something less. Underwriters, too, are sometimes shocked by applications for unusually high limits and respond by offering lower limits. The risk manager does not always find it easy to get limits as high as he might like to have.

Now back to the basic question: How can the risk manager decide on how much liability insurance to carry? About all he can do is study the statistics on liability claims incurred by other companies in his industry and by other business firms of all types located in his community. These statistics will show that the size of awards is increasing. In setting his limits, the risk manager will want to take into consideration the tendency of the courts to make higher and higher awards. In projecting a trend, he will find it useful to study the extent of the litigation delays in his jurisdiction. Awards arising from incidents occurring today may not be made for several years after suit is filed. This means that the trend has to be projected for several years beyond the policy period.

When the risk manager assembles his figures and constructs his trends, he can spread them out on his desk, muse and meditate over them, and then cross his fingers and pick his policy limits. He will not be as sure of

---

[7] Liability insurance policies pay the cost of defending the case in court and the cost of negotiating out-of-court settlements. These costs are payable in addition to the applicable limits of the policy.

his decision as he would like to be, but he knows he has given it the old college try. Of course, if someone else has a better idea, he would be both willing and eager to listen to it. (And so would the authors of this text, for that matter.)

INCOME

Earnings are the lifeblood of a business. The two basic contributors to business earnings are capital and people. Losses to income caused by damage to assets can far exceed the damage to the assets themselves. Illness or death of key personnel also can cause serious loss to the business. The nature of these losses has been discussed (chap. 6). The amount that can be lost is the subject for discussion here.

Business Interruption Losses

When a business cannot fully perform the operations for which it was established, a loss of earnings is normally expected. An accurate measurement of what this loss might be is obviously impossible because of the dynamic nature of the business structure. The limitations within accounting systems are an important barrier to completely accurate measurement of income and expense items when these items are considered *ex post*, that is, at the end of the period for which net earnings are measured. When these items are considered *ex ante*, that is, at the beginning of the period for which they are to be measured, then a different set of problems is encountered—problems of basing estimates on the data of past periods modified by such dynamic considerations as future business conditions; innovations; changes in tastes and preferences; changes within the social structure; competitive situations; changes in costs; trends; and a host of other indeterminate items that must be weighed at some point in the calculations. If projections for the future are based solely on the past, without modification, then these projections are based on the false premise that there will be no change in the strength of the forces that shape and determine the magnitude of income and expense items.

However, some practical approach to the measurement of maximum business interruption loss potential from static risk is necessary. The first step is to review the accounting records ordinarily kept by business firms regardless of their inadequacy. The profit and loss statement shows sales, other income, the costs of doing business, and profits. Profits from different transactions are gathered together to make up the income stream. The risk manager must know the composition of this stream and the relative importance of each item in it so that he can investigate how certain material damage losses would affect over-all profits. For instance, the risk manager might find that direct damage to tangible assets would not affect investment income or interest income on financed accounts receivable but that damage to one of the manufacturing processes would bring sales to a halt as soon as inventory was exhausted. On further study he might learn that some of his firm's manufacturing processes could be subcontracted rather easily and that the major business interruption loss if this particular processing section were destroyed would be the excess of the subcontractor's price over his firm's costs for the same work. Thorough knowledge of the income stream will help the risk manager to protect the maximum potential revenue loss arising from business interruption.

The risk manager must also be familiar with the expenses of the business, and to what extent, if any, they can be cut following a temporary shutdown of the business. Each dollar that can be cut from expenses means a dollar more of profit (or a dollar less in losses). Thus, the management able to cut expenses after a business interruption loss is protecting the residual profit of the business. But management must not overlook long-range considerations in determining the extent to which expenses can be reduced. The discharge of a top salesman might not be wise, even though the firm could not deliver any orders for several months.

Expenses of a business can be classified as fixed or variable. Fixed expenses are those that continue whether the business is functioning or not. Even though a business is shut down, interest on borrowed money must be paid, and periodic payments on principal must be continued as scheduled. Land lease payments are not normally cancelled, even in the face of the destruction of the improvements on leased land. Often advertising contracts provide no relief when business is interrupted. Many insurance premiums, such as those on vehicles, on undestroyed property, and on some liability exposures, are not materially lessened by an interruption of business. Premiums on pension plans, group life insurance on the more important employees, and various business life insurance plans are normally payable even in the face of a shutdown. Some sinking funds or stock retirement agreements are not abrogated by business interruption. Taxes must be paid on real and personal property, past sales, past payrolls, and income, even though the income stream has been materially lessened. Depreciation on undamaged and partially damaged property goes on at about the same rate if depreciation is considered a function of time, regardless of whether the property is being used productively. A given amount of managerial supervision, clerical help, and custodial workers will be found to be indispensable in most cases. Some public utility services, such as light, water, heat, and telephone service, will normally be consumed. The test of a fixed expense is whether that expense continues even though production ceases or the business is temporarily closed.

Variable expenses are those that vary with the productivity, output, or activity of the business. For instance, if a factory is closed, there are no longer manufacturing expenses, such as ordinary labor payroll, raw material, freight, or supervision. If a department store is closed, expenses for sales clerks, packaging, delivery, incoming freight, cleaning services, or the exchange of merchandise are no longer incurred. Elevator operators would not be needed, the credit department would have no new charges to process, the expenses of the lunch counter would be eliminated, and there would be less need for heat, light, and airconditioning. No window trimmers would be needed. Tailors would not be needed to alter newly purchased clothes. The calls for appliance repair under existing guarantees could be channeled to a repair shop.

None of the fixed expenses may be avoided by the risk manager. They will continue whether the business is open or closed. Technically, all the variable expenses are avoidable if the business closes, but few managements would make such a sharp break. Valuable, highly skilled, loyal employees may be permanently lost if they are laid off. If the outside sales force is disbanded, the relationships built up with past and present customers would be seriously disturbed. Managements are interested in bringing the business back into profitable operation as soon as possible, and it may prove penny wise and pound foolish to cut expenses to the minimum. Perhaps the risk manager may foresee increased sales conservation expenses as contacts are maintained with customers by phone, letter, and personal call. The risk manager must know top management's policy on the kinds and amounts of variable expense that will be continued in the event of an interruption. After top management has decided what expenses will be continued and for how long, the risk manager is in a position to determine some concrete estimate of the daily loss involved when the business is interrupted. Various schedules can be prepared showing the loss value of partial as well as complete interruption. The effect of the loss of any one of various locations, or even of divisions within one location, can be considered and evaluated. Then losses involving combinations of locations and divisions can be estimated.

Management may well have different ideas in determining which expenses will be continued for long periods of interruptions and which ones will be continued only if the interruption will be for a short period. For example, personnel retained during a short shutdown may be far different from that retained through a lengthy shutdown.

Research programs provide particularly vexatious problems to the risk manager. In the event of interruption of earnings, it may be necessary to curtail all research on new products and methods. An accurate measurement of the loss associated with the stoppage of a research program is practically impossible, since research efforts do not normally result in a smooth flow of innovations that can be put to productive use by the firm. A partially completed research project that is abandoned before completion, or, at least, fruition, seldom produces other than a loss. Interruption of the business and its research efforts might give the researchers of competitors the time necessary to develop a new process that will capture the market. Reliable formulas for measuring the potential loss arising from interruption of extensive research activity cannot be developed. So many individual factors must be considered that the imagination of the risk manager may be exhausted in their contemplation. But it is axiomatic that considered calculations, even though not entirely accurate, nearly always are worth more than no calculations at all.

After determining what kinds of expenses would be continued and for how long, the risk manager must turn his attention to physical factors present in the business. He must find out whether there are bottlenecks where small physical damage losses can bring about major business interruptions. Knowledge of the complexities of rebuilding the various sectors of the organization and of the time periods necessary to replace inventory, tools, equipment, fixtures, and raw material is essential. Attention must be given to the extra amount of time likely to be required to replace these items in the event of a catastrophe. The availability of difficult-to-replace items and the importance of these items to the operation of the business need investigation. For instance, a company depending on its electronic data processing equipment for all its accounting records, including sales, purchases, and inventory, might be seriously handicapped by damage to the equipment, but, if it were necessary, the business could operate successfully without the services of the machine. Either some rental service could be relied upon or the accountants could devise a non-machine record system that would allow operations to be continued until the machine was repaired or replaced. This same business that could struggle along without its data processing equipment might be completely shut down for an extended period if a particular die were destroyed.

When fire or some other peril interrupts a business, the maximum potential loss during the interrupted period can be estimated, if not accurately measured, in advance of the damage. Losses that continue after the business is resumed may also be estimated, but perhaps a great deal less closely. Consider, for example, a firm showing a profit but facing a great deal of price competition. If the firm is forced to close for six months after a serious fire, the potential loss of net earnings during the period of shutdown can be estimated on the basis of expected changes in gross income and expenses. But what about the period following resumption of business? When this firm is to be closed for repairs over a six-month period, its principal customers very likely will shift to rival firms. Thus, when business is resumed, the firm will, in many ways, have to begin all over to develop markets and outlets for its product or service. A price cut below the existing competitive levels may be necessary to recapture old and attract new customers, thus lowering the income flow into the firm. The interruption may have necessitated the discontinuance of a successful advertising campaign because of the impossibility of fulfilling sales orders. Perhaps the firm, during its six-month enforced layoff, lost many skillful workers to competitors or other business concerns. The replacement of skilled or supervisory workers may be expensive. The "hiring-in price" for new employees frequently is higher than the "keeping-in price" for comparable employees already on the staff. Many firms have a definite policy against hiring competitors' employees, but so-called "body-snatching" may be the best solution if capable personnel has to be recruited quickly. A shutdown, besides bringing about many serious problems in personnel and customer relations, may disturb other valuable relationships of the firm, such as those with money lenders and public officials.

One other category of business interruption loss is the contingent loss discussed in chapter 6. The measurement of contingent business interruption losses involves estimation by the risk manager of the possible loss from the various contingencies involved. Looking *ex post* at a series of profit and loss statements may show that it is possible to arrive at the amount of profit lost from a contingent business interruption, but it is much more difficult to determine the amount *ex ante*.

In summary, the measurement of direct business interruption losses is relatively simple, once management decides on a policy of expense reduction after a loss and once the risk manager determines what effect the various loss possibilities will have on the income of the business. Extended and contingent business interruption losses are estimated in the same way, the primary difference lying in the complexity of the assumptions that the risk manager must make.

Business Interruption Work Sheet. In developing estimates of his maximum business interruption loss potential, the risk manager can use a simple work sheet (p. 310). He will, of course, want to enlist the aid of the company accountant in ascertaining the figures needed for this work sheet. If business is irregularly spread throughout the year, that is, if much of the business is concentrated over a few months, he will want a monthly as well as an annual breakdown on his data.

The maximum business interruption loss potential developed on the work sheet is divided into two parts: the amount lost during the period the business is actually shutdown (item I); and the amount lost during the period following the reopening of the business until the level of earnings reaches its before-loss projection (item J). Although these items are not capable of exact measurement, they can be reasonably estimated and kept up to date by frequent checks at regular intervals.

In the final analysis, the measurement of loss during the shutdown period is made up of two items: loss of unabatable expenses, which would have been earned were it not for the shutdown, and loss of net profits for the period it takes to restore the damaged property. If there are no net profits, the maximum potential loss will be the unabatable expenses that would have been earned if the business were to have continued to operate.

The measure of a business interruption loss is simply the difference be-

The Work Sheet
(Figures on Annual Basis)

Items	Actual Values for Past Year	Estimated Values for Coming Year
A. Total annual net sales value of production from manufacturing operations; and total annual net sales from merchandising or non-manufacturing operations (gross sales less discounts, returns, bad accounts, and prepaid freight, if included in sales)..........	$........	$.......
B. *Add* other earnings (if any) derived from operation of the business:		
1. Cash discounts received...........	....	....
2. Commission or rents from leased departments	....	....
3.	....	....
C. Total (A + B)	$........	$........
D. *Deduct only cost of:*		
1. Raw stock from which production is derived	$........	$........
2. Materials and supplies consumed directly in the conversion of raw stock into finished stock or in supplying the services(s) sold by the insured	....	....
3. Merchandise sold, including packaging materials therefor	....	....
4. Service(s) purchased from outsiders (not employees of the insured) for resale which do not continue under contract	....	....
5. Total deductions	$........	$........
E. Gross earnings (C − D)	$........	$........
F. Deduct expenses that will not continue:		
1. Heat, light, and power	$........	$........
2. Ordinary payroll	....	....
3. Insurance premiums	....	....
4. Taxes	....	....
5.	....	....
Total deductions	$........	$........
G. Annual business interruption loss exposure (E − F)	....	....
H. Estimated maximum period of suspension likely under the most adverse conditions (expressed in fractions of a year)		....
I. Estimated maximum loss potential during the period of suspension (G × H) (adjust for seasonal businesses)		....
J. Estimated maximum potential loss from the lag after restoration		....
K. Maximum business interruption loss potential (I + J)		....

tween what the profit and loss statement reflects for the period of the shutdown and what it would have reflected were there no shutdown. The loss may be traceable to two sources: reduction of sales or production, or increased cost of producing or selling. For example, assume that the maximum potential shutdown period following a serious fire or other peril is six months, during which period the business would have to produce $500,000 of marketable goods in the absence of the fire. If materials, labor, power, and other variable manufacturing expenses amount to $300,-000, then $200,000 is available for salaries, interest, taxes, other general charges, and profit. The maximum business interruption loss during the period of shutdown in this case would be $200,000 less general expenses that can be saved because of the interruption. If these abatable charges amount to $75,000, the maximum business interruption loss potential during the suspension period would be $125,000.

If the business of the above firm is spread evenly over the year, the work sheet would show the following totals: item E, $400,000; item F, $150,000; item G, $250,000; item H, 50 per cent; and item I, $125,000. Items J and K will be considered later.

The foregoing calculations assume that the business is evenly spread over the year so that any six-month period of operations would produce the same results. If this assumption is not true, then item I will have to be adjusted to reflect the largest possible loss than can occur during a six-month period. For example, if $250,000 would be lost if the business were interrupted for a year (item G), but 80 per cent of this amount would be lost if the business were interrupted for the first half of the year, the maximum loss potential would be $200,000 rather than $125,000. Each elapsing month, of course, would vary the maximum loss potential, reducing it until it reached its lowest amount on July 1 and then raising it until it hit its highest amount again on January 1.

The risk manager must consider fluctuations not only from month to month but also from year to year in estimating maximum loss potential. If next year's business is expected to surpass this year's business, then the maximum loss potential on October 1 will exceed that on April 1, even though both dates include only three months of maximum production during the six-month maximum shutdown period. If a decline is expected, then the reverse is true. If stable business is expected, then the maximum potential loss would be expected to be the same on both these dates.

Vital to the estimate of the maximum business interruption loss potential is the maximum period of suspension likely in the event of serious damage to physical assets (item H). The important question is: How long will it take to restore the premises for business after a loss? The length of this period may be underestimated if serious attention is not given to all adverse possibilities. Damage occurring during the winter months can take much longer to repair than similar damage happening in the spring or summer months. In addition to weather, strikes may also delay the restoration of the building or its equipment. Some of the equipment or inventories may have to be imported, which can create delays. Also, the damaged stock may be available only during a given season, and if the loss occurs at the end of that season, an entire year of business will be lost.

It may be possible to reduce the period of business suspension—and perhaps the maximum loss potential as a consequence—by paying premium prices for prompt delivery of materials and by paying extra wages for overtime labor. Business interruption may be avoided entirely by making emergency installations or repairs, by entering into special contracts, or by some other method that will allow the business to continue operating following a major loss. Instead of suffering a business interruption loss, such a business might experience an increased cost of production or selling. The increased cost would be in lieu of a business interruption loss. For example, a business may find it possible (and profitable) to avoid interruption by contracting with other firms for use of their idle capacity to provide production facilities until its own can be restored. Or perhaps a new location is available where the business can operate temporarily, although at a higher cost. If the extra costs of operating under adverse conditions are less than the loss sustained by a shutdown, the maximum potential business interruption loss is limited to these additional expenses (plus, of course, the loss of any profits resulting if the temporary operations have to be on a reduced scale). An extended loss following resumption of the business after an enforced shutdown (item I) might well be the deciding factor making operation under adverse conditions less costly than a shutdown. Some time might be needed after the physical reopening of the business for the business to return to normal. For example, the shutdown may be the cause of the cancellation of a number of contracts that would extend far beyond the maximum suspension period. Restoration of the clientele frequently will take time following the restoration of the property. Some businesses cannot afford a business interruption loss and must therefore make plans to continue operations regardless of costs. Their exposure is one of extra expenses, as discussed earlier. But when the business has a clear choice of operating or closing down, and can make the choice on the basis of the relative costs involved, the exposure is a business interruption exposure, and the maximum loss potential should be measured on the basis described in these paragraphs.

Loss of Key Men

The risk manager may note several employees in his company who contribute substantially to the profits of the business. Some of them may be irreplaceable; others may be replaceable, but only after a lapse of a considerable period of time; and still others may be replaceable, but at a sizable increase in cost. The resignation, disability, or death of any one of these key men can adversely affect the net earnings of the business. The question the risk manager must answer is: How much will earnings be affected? Usually, the answer is largely arbitrary, but several factors can be considered and weighed in reaching an "educated guess." Judgment will play the principal role in determining the maximum loss potential resulting from the loss of a key man. And good judgment frequently is a product of experience.

The factors to consider in arriving at the maximum key man loss potential are those which help to measure how termination of the key man's services will affect business income and expenses now and in the future. The following is a list of questions for which the risk manager must find reasonable or acceptable answers if he is to determine the loss potential in this area.

1. What portion of the company's income is traceable to the *superior* ability of the key man?
2. How long will it take to find a replacement for the key man?
3. What will it cost to find a replacement for the key man?
4. How much salary and other benefits will be necessary to attract a suitable replacement for the key man?
5. How much will it cost to train the replacement?
6. What will be the cost of the mistakes made by the replacement during the adjustment period?
7. How long will it take to bring the replacement up to his maximum efficiency?
8. When operating at maximum efficiency, how will the replacement compare with the key man?
9. How will the productivity of the replacement compare with that of the key man during the orientation period?
10. How much investment (in research, for example) would be lost if the key man's service were terminated?

The answers to many of these questions often cannot be found, not even by those as intimately familiar with the business as the risk manager is or ought to be. Who, for example, can say with any degree of confidence, except in the most obvious cases, how much of a company's profit is attributable to the superior ability of a key man? Furthermore, who can say with any authority what the cost of mistakes will be during the replacement's adjustment period, or how the productivity of the replacement will compare with that of the key man, or even how long it will take the replacement to reach his maximum efficiency? Yet these and the other questions have to be answered if the maximum key man loss potential is to be measured accurately.

What does the risk manager do when he is faced with the problem of making an appraisal of the key man exposure if the data necessary for an accurate appraisal are unavailable? The answer is simply that he makes an inaccurate appraisal based on whatever facts he can muster and on his intuitive judgment. Just as many different independent valuations will be produced as there are independent appraisers, and these valuations may vary widely. Who is to say which one is the best so long as all appraisers are equally competent? Appraisals of tangible property also frequently represent only the best guesses of the appraisers. In appraising the value of a producing oil well, for example, the appraiser faces the unanswerable questions of how long, and at what rate, the well will produce. The appraisal must of necessity be based on speculation, just as must the appraisal of the value of the key man to the business. The ten questions listed will serve as a guide to the factors that must be considered in appraising the value of the key man. Some of these questions may be simple to answer (2, 3, 4, 5, and 10, for example), but the others may be difficult or impossible to answer. The impossible ones, nevertheless, will call to the risk manager's attention the areas in which speculation is necessary. The risk manager will have to come up with some kinds of answers, even if they are not as accurate as he would like to have them.

SUMMARY

Any contingency resulting in an increase in expenses or a decrease in gross income will have an adverse effect on profits. Expense and income exposures, therefore, cannot be ignored by risk managers.

Expense exposures include leasehold interests, improvement and betterments, rental expenses, extra expenses, and liability. Income exposures include business interruption and loss of key men.

In his efforts to measure loss potential from expense and income exposures, the risk manager is likely to encounter many more unknowns than he finds in his attempts to measure loss potential from exposure of asset values. Intelligent guesswork plays a large part in measuring some of these loss potentials.

REVIEW AND DISCUSSION QUESTIONS

1. Detail the similarities between the method of measuring a tenant's loss from cancellation of a valuable lease and the method of measuring the loss when a negotiable security is stolen (see Chapter 8).
2. "T" and "W" are new tenants in different properties. Each has just signed a lease which reflects the current rate of charges for rental property. Each lease is for twenty years and calls for an annual payment of $5,000. In addition, "T" is investing $10,000 in nonremovable improvements to the property which he occupies. "W" has paid his landlord an extra $10,000 in return for the landlord's agreement to provide the improvements which "W" needs. If each lease is automatically canceled in event of damage amounting to 50 per cent of the value of the leased property, what are these tenants' current loss potentials with respect to their interests in the leased real property? (Remember, damage may amount to more or less than 50 per cent of the property value.)

3. Can a tenant have both a leasehold and a rent (or rental value) *loss* at the same time? Illustrate your answer with examples showing the possible variations on the tenant's loss exposure with respect to leased property. Which cases present a leasehold *exposure*, which a rent or rental value *exposure*, and which present both? (Note the difference between a *loss* and an *exposure* to loss.)

4. K. C. Stangle has estimated his potential loss from interruption of his business on account of physical damage at his premises. Should he estimate in addition his loss potential from (a) cancellation of his lease, (b) loss of rent paid to his landlord in event of noncancellation of his lease? Explain.

5. Despite all the difficulties, risk managers do have to decide how much liability insurance their businesses should carry. Consider some particular business you know in each of the following classes: a drugstore; a shoe store; a dry cleaner; a filling station; a movie theater; a department store; a wholesaler of some kind or kinds of hard goods; a manufacturer; an insurance agent. What dollar amount of insurance against liability on account of (a) vehicles, (b) premises, (c) products sold or services rendered do you think each of these specific businesses should carry? Itemize the factors that entered into your judgment. What *facts* that you do not now know should be known in making this decision? Where or how are these facts to be found?

6. There is evidence that some business managers believe that the proper objective of risk management is to help stabilize the net earnings of the business. The objective stated in this text is merely to preserve the existence of the business entity. The risk manager's estimate of the amount of money needed in event of a business interruption loss will ordinarily vary according to which of these two objectives is chosen. In what ways will this estimate vary acording to choice of objective? That is, what specific things will need to be included in the list of items to be covered given one objective that would not need to be in the list if the other objective were given?

7. Which of the following potential losses appears to you the most difficult to set a dollar value on: liability, business interruption, keyman? Justify your answer. (Note: your justification certainly should include all the elements which enter into the estimation of each of these potential losses, with a consideration of the ways in which each element may be handled, as well as the difficulties in handling it.) In which of these three do you consider that error in loss estimation would have the most serious results? In which case would error be least serious? Why?

8. Estimate, as nearly as you can, the amount of business interruption potential in one or more of the cases in Chapter 18.

PART IV

Dealing with Risks

Risk management involves decision-making processes. The appropriate techniques must be selected for dealing with each nonspeculative risk. The fundamental objective of risk management is to make a before-the-loss arrangement for an effective after-the-loss balance between resources needed and resources available. To accomplish this objective, the risk manager must understand not only the principles to be applied but also how to apply them. Part IV contains two chapters on risk management decisions. One deals with the principles and the other with the application of these principles.

Chapter 10

RISK MANAGEMENT DECISIONS:
PRINCIPLES

A set of rules for risk management was presented in chapter 1. Devices for implementing these rules were described in chapters 2, 3, 4, and 5. The risk situations to which the devices may be applied were analyzed in chapters 6, 7, 8, and 9. How to apply the rules to decide which device to use in a particular situation is the core of the risk management problem. The present chapter deals with identifying and stating the problem; the next with approaches to its solution.

RULES OF RISK MANAGEMENT: A RESTATEMENT

The rules of risk management can be restated and in the process reduced to include only two fundamental considerations: (1) size of potential loss and (2) profit potential. The size of the potential loss must bear a reasonable relationship to the resources of the loss bearer, and the benefits of "risk taking must bear a reasonable" relationship to the cost. The first consideration includes the precept "Don't risk more than you can afford to lose," whereas the second includes the precepts "Don't risk much for little" and "Consider the odds."

To be in a position to apply these rules, the risk manager must prepare himself to undertake three important tasks, none of which is simple and clear cut. (1) He must be able to estimate the maximum loss potential from his exposures, (2) he must be able to measure the resources he has available to meet the potential, and (3) he must be able to develop a means of measuring both the benefits and the costs of alternative risk-bearing devices for a given risk situation. The risk manager recognizes that the costs of the various risk-management devices are not always consonant with their benefits, and that sound risk management requires him to use the ones that maximize benefits in relation to cost. The most profitable (or least unprofitable) risk-management device might prove to be any one of the gamut from complete risk avoidance to full risk assumption. For example, the most efficient way to handle a risk situation might be to avoid it altogether by withdrawing from the activity that creates it, such as eliminating a product from a given line of merchandise if it creates a serious products liability risk. On the other hand, the most profitable solution might be risk transfer, risk reduction, or risk assumption. The decision is the risk manager's[1] and is no easy one to make. Some of the problems complicating the decision can now be examined.

THE CHARACTER OF A LARGE LOSS

Two quantities are involved in deciding whether a potential loss can be large: the potential amount of the loss itself and the amount of resources available to meet it. In measuring potential losses against resources, three specifications about these losses become important: how much, when, and what kind. The problems of determining "how much" were examined in chapters 8 and 9. It remains now to examine the questions of "when" and "what kind."

For purposes of illustration, consider that the maximum potential loss from an explosion of the compressor in the cold storage locker at "Distributors Produce Company" is estimated as follows on the basis of the techniques developed in chapters 8 and 9.

Cash ....$	200
Receivables (cost of reconstruction of records)	200
Inventory	23,000
Equipment, machinery, furnishings	30,000
Expenses during shutdown	12,300
Workmen's compensation	150,000
Other liability for injury	300,000
Liability for property damage	50,000
Loss of expected profits	2,500
Total ....$	568,300

In addition to the dollar amounts involved, certain additional characteristics about each of the items in this list are important for the risk manager to study. How soon after the loss will the offsetting resources be needed? Is the loss one of a type that requires replacement? Are there hidden losses inherent in the list that require more resources for replacement than the amount of the values destroyed?

The "When" of Loss Payments

Consider for a moment the composition of the explosion loss as illustrated in the tabulation given above. Some of the loss will be spread over a period of time, whereas the rest will be felt almost immediately after the

---

[1] The final decision itself may be made at a higher level of the management hierarchy, but the responsibility for the recommendations rests with the risk manager.

onset of the loss. For example, the entire $150,000 of resources needed to provide for payments of potential workmen's compensation benefits may not have to be available all at once. Disability benefits under workmen's compensation laws usually are paid to workmen in weekly installments over the period of disability. Medical expenses compensable under the laws are not payable until incurred and then only when the bills are presented for collection. On the other hand, some death benefits are payable almost immediately, and in many states the employer may be required, by the proper authority, to pay out the estimated present value of deferred benefits, either as a lump-sum settlement to the insured or as a deposit with a responsible financial institution to guarantee payment of the required future benefits.

The $23,000 needed to offset the potential loss of inventory and the $30,000 required to meet the potential loss of equipment, machinery, and furnishings cannot be spread into the future like some of the $150,000 necessary for potential workmen's compensation losses. These amounts are not variable as to time of payment. The inventory must be replaced promptly, and so must the equipment, machinery, and fixtures. Of course, if the Distributors Produce Company happened to be overstocked at the time of the loss, all the damaged inventory would not need replacing right away, and, if the company had excessive equipment, machinery, and fixtures, some of these items might never need replacing. The $12,300 of resources that must be available for potential expenses arising during the shutdown period will be needed as these expenses are incurred and become payable. These expenses will be spread over the period of the shutdown.

In measuring potential loss against resources, the risk manager should consider when, after the loss, its incidence will be felt.

Losses of Different Kinds

Another important consideration in measuring potential loss against resources is the kind of loss that might be suffered. For example, the problems associated with the potential loss of $2,500 of expected profits are different from those associated with the $23,000 potential inventory loss or the $50,000 of potential property damage claims. The necessity for having funds for the replacement of essential assets or to pay obligations to others may be considerably greater than the need to offset net revenue or profit that fails to materialize. Ability to cover the needs for actual cash outlay at least allows the organization to maintain its previous financial position, and this *may* be enough to ensure its survival. (Note that the italicized word is "may," not "will." The reason for this choice of words will soon become apparent.)

The kind of loss must also be viewed to determine whether the resources required to offset such loss amount to more than the destroyed values. The usual measure of value destroyed by physical damage to tangible property (e.g., inventory, equipment) is the smaller of two figures:

(*a*) the difference between the actual cash value of the property before and after the loss and (*b*) the cost to repair or replace the property with (as insurance policies put it) "material of like kind and quality." But these measures often fail to show the amount of resources actually needed after a loss. Two examples, one dealing with replacement and the other with repair, may be used to illustrate this point.

Case 1: Replacement. Assume that the damaged refrigeration unit at Distributors Produce Company was obsolescent and inefficient. Units like it are not made any more. The newer style, more efficient units now available cost less to operate than the old one and can therefore produce more profit.

Suppose the values destroyed were, according to the usual measures, as follows:

Actual cash value, old unit................$25,000
Less salvage 5,000

Difference in values, before and after loss. . $20,000   Cost of repair.........$27,000

The value destroyed is $20,000, the lesser of the two bases for measurement. But the Produce Company has only two courses of action after the loss, neither of which calls for resources of only $20,000, the actual cash value less salvage of the property destroyed. The company can spend $27,000 for repairs or lay out $65,000 for a new unit. With $5,000 available from salvage on the old unit, other resources equal to $60,000 must be available if replacement is to be made.

The company is likely to reject the repair alternative. In the first place, the remaining useful life of the repaired equipment would be so short that the $27,000 of capital outlay could not be recovered before the equipment would have to be scrapped. In the second place, new equipment would be much more efficient, thus reducing costs and increasing profits. Replacement then becomes the logical choice, and this course of action will require that $60,000 in resources be available to offset the $20,000 in destroyed value.

Case 2: Repair. Even when the logical choice is to make the repairs, a similar problem can arise. Suppose that for $35,000 gross outlay the old equipment can be rebuilt with new parts so that it becomes more efficient than before and has a longer useful life. If the added profit potential derived from the increase in efficiency and longevity of the rebuilt equipment is at least as great as the added cost of renovation (i.e., the excess of the cost of complete renovation over the cost of simple repair), the extra cost represents a fair purchase: equivalent value received for value paid. A fair purchase is hardly a "loss" in any usual sense. But the extra resources needed to make the purchase must be found, nonetheless, before renovation can be considered a way to recover from the described physical damage loss.

Interim Summary. In short, the size of "loss" that the risk manager must consider in deciding which risk management devices to use must be modified to reflect the amount of *outlay* that will be required to recover from that loss, whether that outlay is purely for "loss" in the usual sense (physical damage, extra expenses) or covers some other kind of outgo that is not, properly speaking, a "loss" at all but an exchange of assets.

Conversely, it has also been noted that a loss *not* involving outlays may be a kind of loss that can be given quite separate treatment from other types of loss that make up the over-all "size of loss" totals. This second point bears further examination.

Need for Profit Replacement. Some cash income is necessary to cover obligations maturing before the business recovers from the loss. Some of these obligations will have been taken on before the loss, others will be incurred concurrently with the loss, and still others will arise after the loss but before the business is able to resume full operations. Cash income beyond the amounts necessary to handle these items represents an addition to net profits. Sometimes these added profits represent free and uncommitted funds, the loss of which will cause distress and inconvenience but will not damage the future of the business. In appraising the importance of the loss of expected profits, the risk manager must consider what would actually happen if these expected profits were lost to the business. How, for example, would a $2,500 loss of expected profits affect the Distributors Produce Company?

While the net profit from the business may be a free surplus item so far as the business itself is concerned, it may be essential as a source of personal income to the owners. Thus, although the Distributors Produce Company may be able to survive for at least a while on an even balance of cash income and outgo, the families of the owners may find the absence of surplus funds more than merely an annoyance if they have formed the habit of eating.

In addition, it is also quite possible that current (as well as long-run) net income is vital to the business itself. Suppose, for example, that the explosion of the compressor in the cold storage locker at Distributors Produce Company occurs on March 15. The date of the loss can be a significant consideration. It can affect not only the amount and mixture of assets exposed to damage but also the consequences of an income loss. On March 15 the current inventory of the Produce company is moderate, with peak value to come seven to nine weeks later. The company is counting on the net profit from sales over the next several weeks to provide part of the cash needed to build the inventory to its peak. If Distributors Produce Company is to hold its own—maintain its market as well as its financial position—this cash must be available. A loss of expected net profits at this time, therefore, deals a serious blow to the business if adequate resources are not available to offset the loss.

In many businesses, a large percentage of the annual profits will be lost if serious physical damage is experienced near the beginning of a major sales season. These profits ordinarily will be needed to provide working capital for the coming year and to keep up with necessary replacement of capital equipment. Thus the fundamental point again makes its appearance: In risk management planning, the concept of size of loss is not restricted to the amount of values lost and the expenses associated with the loss. The concept is extended to include the amount (and timing) of outlays required to prevent financial damage from and following the loss, even though some of these outlays do not represent loss in the strict sense. To put the matter yet another way, risk managers, like other financial managers, cannot afford to limit their attention to balance sheets and income statements; they must realize that cash flows and cash budgets can be even more significant.

The Loss Figures Restated

The loss statement presented earlier for Distributors Produce Company may now be revised and expanded to show the amounts and timing of the outlays involved. In the restatement the maximum amount of resources needed to offset the potential loss from the explosion is divided into three periods: (1) the maximum amount potentially needed during the first four weeks after the loss, (2) the maximum amount potentially needed during the second four weeks following the loss, and (3) the maximum amount potentially required at the end of the first eight weeks to fund fully the unpaid portion of the loss. The figures used represent a breakdown and reorganization of those presented on page 320 plus the additional outlays suggested in the text material that followed.

Period 1: First four weeks after loss

Items	Maximum Amount of Resources Potentially Needed
Wages and salaries	
Executive and administrative	$ 3,000
Clerical	1,000
Warehousemen	150
Workmen's compensation	1,800
Notices to customers and suppliers (including advertising)	400
Utilities and supplies	150
Liabilities previously incurred, now due	1,200
Total, first four weeks	$ 7,700

Period 2: Second four weeks

Items	Maximum Amount of Resources Potentially Needed
Wages and salaries	
Executive and administrative	$ 3,000
Clerical	2,000

Warehousemen and drivers 1,850
Workmen's compensation 1,800
Maintaining contacts with customers and suppliers (including advertising) 600
Utilities and supplies 150
Repairs and replacement
    Fixed assets 45,000
    Inventory (for May–June) 35,000

      Total potentially needed for second four weeks ...... $ 89,400

Period 3: Maximum potential resources required at end of eight weeks to fund unpaid claims fully and to finance resumption of business activity

Items	Maximum Amount of Resources Potentially Needed
Reserve for workmen's compensation	$146,400
Reserve for liability claims, including costs	350,000
Minimum net quick assets needed to finance day-to-day operations upon resumption of the business[2]	20,000
Total potentially needed at end of eight weeks	$516,400

Summary of resources needed to offset the *maximum potential* loss resulting from a compressor explosion

Maximum amount potentially needed first four weeks .... $ 7,700
Maximum amount potentially needed second four weeks 89,400
Maximum amount potentially needed at end of eight weeks 516,400
    Total resources required to offset maximum potential
    loss $613,500

We now have both the size and the timing of the maximum *potential outlay* that would have to be made following the loss. We are not sure that the loss will happen, of course, nor that if it does it will require an outlay of the maximum amount. Actually, we rather suspect that the loss will never occur, and that, if it does, the resources needed to offset it will be less than maximum. But, since the risk manager's job is to prepare for the worst, he must decide how the loss is to be met if the unexpected materializes. Where will he find the resources to offset the maximum potential loss if these resources should be needed?

RESOURCES AVAILABLE

Resources available to the business for covering losses may be classified into three categories: (1) resources within the business itself plus any additional resources that the owners are willing and able to provide, (2)

---

[2] Quick assets are cash and accounts receivable. The $20,000 of resources required for quick assets in this case will be almost entirely cash. The business will have been shut down for eight weeks, so most, if not all, of its previously collectible accounts receivable will have been paid. As the business resumes operations, some of this cash will be turned into new receivables, leaving the total quick asset position undamaged, unless, of course, the ratio of cash to receivables drops to a dangerously low level.

credit resources, and (3) claims against others growing out of the loss. Insurance claims fall in the third category, of course, as do claims against any other risk transferees. Also in the third category are liability claims against others for their negligence in causing the loss.

Resources within the Business

The business will still own some useful resources after the loss. Not all of the property will be directly affected by the loss. For example, cash in the bank is not destroyed by physical damage at the business premises, and the business premises are seldom physically impaired by defalcations or forgeries that destroy the bank account. In addition, damaged items often have a salvage value, that is, an after-the-loss cash value. In addition to any asset values that remain, there may be some continuing income. Partial operations may be carried on, and income-producing investments held will not suspend dividend and interest payments. Finally, in some cases the owners of the business may be willing and able to contribute additional assets toward the rehabilitation of the business.

Consider again the explosion loss at the Distributors Produce Company. Reference to the previous loss estimate shows that little damage is anticipated to cash or accounts receivable. In order to determine the resources available from these items, it is necessary to have the before-loss value of these assets. Also needed for figuring the resources available from within the business is the salvage value of assets to be replaced. The salvage value for assets to be repaired is accounted for by including only the net repair cost in the loss tabulations.

Here is a summary of the cash generated within the business:

Cash on hand before loss	$ 7,500	
Less loss	200	
Cash available		$ 7,300
Receivables before loss	$15,000	
Less allowances[3]	150	
Cash recoverable		14,850
Salvage values		
Inventory	$ 2,000	
Fixed assets	500	
Cash recoverable		2,500
Operating or other revenue, first eight weeks.		None
Additional available from owners		None
Total cash generated by business		$24,650

How to offset the difference between the maximum potential loss of $613,500 and the $24,650 available from within the business is the risk man-

---

[3] These do *not* include cost of restoration of account books. That cost is covered by the "wages and salaries" items shown earlier.

ager's problem. If he should suffer the maximum potential loss and therefore need this $588,850, where would he get it? Successful risk managers know that their plans must be made in advance of losses if these losses are to be handled efficiently.

Credit Resources

It is not necessary to pay cash for every purchase. If a business with a foreseeably profitable future wants to buy several thousands of dollars worth of new equipment, there are several organizations (including most sellers) who are happy to provide credit toward much of the purchase price.

Limitations on the Credit Resources. The phrase "a business with a foreseeably profitable future" provides an important limitation on the reliability of credit resources for covering outlays after a loss. The availability of this resource depends to a great degree on the values remaining in the business following the disaster. There is indeed some truth in the old saying, "In order to get credit you must first prove that you don't need it." Credit resources can be of significance in a risk management program if such a program is otherwise carefully arranged so that when credit is needed, credit will be available. Thus the risk manager must have plans that will assure the business a foreseeable profitable future before he can rely on credit to provide resources potentially needed after a loss. In planning for the possible use of credit resources as an offset to potential losses, the risk manager will be interested in the before-loss use of credit by the business. This information will serve not only as a guide to the amount and terms of credit likely to be available after the loss but also as a basis for measuring the probable credit position of the business following the loss. If the business overuses its credit resources, the risk manager's after-loss problem is made doubly difficult. Each credit dollar already employed may both (1) decrease the amount of credit available and (2) increase the amount of cash needed after the loss.[4]

Another limiting consideration in the use of credit resources may be cost. Of course, if no loss occurs, these resources will not have to be used, and consequently there will be no cost associated with them. And this is one advantage of relying on credit rather than arranging in advance for insurance funds or maintaining an excessive financial surplus to offset losses. Insurance costs money, irrespective of whether there is a loss, and so does the overemployment of capital within the business.

But if a loss does occur, the use of credit resources will cost more than insurance, and under normal circumstances will also cost more than using free assets retained in the business. When credit is used to help finance

---

[4] Of course, if the credit is renewable, or one form of credit can easily be exchanged for another, the effect is merely single: Each dollar of credit already outstanding merely means one less dollar available from credit sources for covering extra outlays created by losses.

extra outlays created by losses (e.g., repair or replacement of property, third-party liability claims, operating expenses in excess of revenue), the business may not be restored to its before-loss financial position. Both principal and interest must be repaid, and the payment of these obligations may reduce the net income and the cash position of the company to a point considerably below before-loss levels.

Favorable Use of Credit Resources. The use of credit for after-loss outlays does not always impair the earnings and cash position of the business. There are notable exceptions. For one example, consider the following illustrative model:

Some equipment owned by the business is damaged by fire. The business is insured for this loss up to the actual cash value of the equipment. In replacing the damaged equipment, the owner has a choice. He may spend the insurance money to purchase used equipment of the same type, or he may apply the insurance proceeds as a down payment on new and more efficient equipment. In the latter case he borrows the money for the balance of the purchase price under a loan amortized for a period equal to the remaining useful lifetime of the old equipment.

Here are the important basic data concerning both the used and the new equipment.

Used equipment:

Book value	$15,000	Annual depreciation charge	$ 1,250
Cash value	30,000	Annual operating cost	17,450
Remaining useful life	10 years	Gross annual revenue	23,000
Salvage value after 10 years	$ 2,500		

New equipment:

Purchase price	$45,000	Annual depreciation charge	$ 1,800[5]
Useful life	15 years	Annual operating costs	16,000[6]
Salvage value after 15 years	$ 3,000	Gross annual revenue	23,000

Suppose the owner decides to replace his damaged equipment with used equipment. How will this decision affect the net income and cash position of his business over the ten-year useful lifetime of this equipment? The following tabulation unveils the picture in summary form.

---

[5] The business will have only $30,000 of its own assets invested in the new equipment; the $15,000 of remaining book value in old equipment and the $15,000 invested in the new equipment (difference between insurance proceeds of $30,000 for cash value of old equipment and $45,000 new purchase price). With $3,000 salvage value at the end of 15 years, $27,000 is to be charged off at $1,800 a year (straight-line method).

[6] Note the following relationship between operating costs and market values of old and new equipment: If the business pays $45,000 for the new equipment, it has annual operating expenses of $16,000 and an annual depreciation of $2,800 ($45,000 less $3,000, divided by 15). With $23,000 of gross revenue the net revenue would amount to $4,200, or 9⅓ per cent of capital invested. If the business buys the old equipment for $30,000, it will have an annual depreciation of $2,750 over 10 years plus operating expenses of $17,450. These leave $2,800 net annual revenue—which again is 9⅓ per cent of $30,000 investment. This nicely balanced relationship, of course, explains why the cash value of the old equipment *is* $30,000.

Replace Now with Used Equipment

A. Earnings over 10 years:

Gross earnings on equipment		$230,000
Less: Operating cost	$174,500	
Depreciation	12,500	187,000
Net before income tax		43,000
Net after applying a 52 per cent income tax rate		20,640

B. Changes in cash and equity positions between the beginning and end of the 10-year period

Cash receipts:

Insurance proceeds	$ 30,000	
Gross earnings	230,000	
Salvage at the end of ten years	2,500	262,500

Cash disbursements:

Replacement (used equipment)	$ 30,000	
Operating cost	174,500	
Income taxes	22,306	
New equipment purchase at the end of 10 years	45,000	271,860
Net *loss* of cash		9,360
Net *increase*, book value of equipment owned		30,000[7]
Total contribution to equity		20,640[8]

Replace Now with New Equipment

A. Earnings over 10 years:

Gross earnings on equipment		$230,000
Less: Operating cost	$160,000	
Depreciation	18,000	
Interest	5,380	183,380
Net before tax		46,620
Net after applying a 52 per cent income tax rate		22,378

B. Changes in cash and equity positions between the beginning and end of the 10-year period

Cash receipts:

Insurance	$ 30,000	
Gross earnings	230,000	260,000

Cash disbursements:

New equipment (purchase price)	$ 45,000	
Interest	5,380	
Operating cost	160,000	
52 per cent tax	24,242	234,622
Net *production* of cash		25,378
Net *decrease*, book value of equipment owned		3,000[7]
Total contribution of equity		22,378[8]

---

[7] Before the loss the business shows $15,000 as the book value for the equipment. When used equipment is purchased, it is completely written off in ten years, and then $45,000 of new equipment is acquired, showing a net increase of $30,000. When new equipment is purchased, it comes in at $30,000 and is depreciated down to a book value of $12,000, showing a net decrease of $3,000 from the original $15,000.

[8] In each situation, no liabilities are outstanding against the equipment either at the

The comparative figures speak for themselves. By replacing the damaged equipment with new rather than with used equipment, the business will earn $1,738 more profit over the ten-year remaining expected lifetime of the used equipment. The business will also improve its equity position by $1,738. Its cash position will be better by $16,738 (a $7,378 cash increase with the new equipment, as against a $9,360 cash decrease with the old).

The Timing of Conversion. If, as the foregoing figures show, both the net earnings and the cash position of the business are improved in this particular situation by purchasing new equipment, why wait for the loss to make the shift? Perhaps the risk manager should suggest immediate replacement as a wise move for operating management, without waiting for a loss to occur. If he does, the suggestion may meet with agreement. Management, however, should not conclude anything until the following highly pertinent points are considered:

1. Changeover involves shutting down, and shutting down involves loss of revenue without a major reduction in costs. In the risk manager's analysis, the economics of shutdown have not been considered because a shutdown is one of the consequences of the loss for which he is planning. There will be a shutdown whether replacement is made with used or new equipment.

2. The $30,000 "cash value" used by the insurance company to indemnify the owner for the total loss of his equipment is based on the cost of replacing with similar equipment and is more than the cash that could be realized on a pre-loss *sale* of such equipment. Included in "cost to replace" are the expenses of getting the used machines out of one plant and into another: costs of dismantling, transporting, and resetting. A seller of used machines will net $30,000 *less* these costs. Because the insurance company will pay more after the loss than the owners could realize from a before-loss sale, a changeover before a loss will require additional credit financing. In comparison with an after-loss changeover, net earnings on the new equipment would be reduced by the amount of the interest payable on the increased debt. Furthermore, net cash gain over the period would be reduced both by the smaller amount collected for the present equipment and by the lower net earnings brought about by the cost of additional financing.

3. Finally, an important factor in voluntary conversion from old to new equipment is management's estimate of the relative rates of obsolescence in the present equipment as compared with new equipment. Such estimations are a major problem in the management of dynamic risks, that is to say, in general operational management, and are a whole subject matter to themselves. But, in involuntary conversion, comparative rates of obsolescence may be academic. The old equipment is gone, and no choice can be made to continue using it.[9]

---

beginning or at the end of the period, since the loan used to purchase the new equipment is to be amortized over the ten-year period. Since these relevant liability figures are the same for both dates, net contributions to (or depletions from) equity will equal the total net contributions to (or depletions from) assets.

[9] Income tax considerations might make a before-loss conversion attractive that otherwise might appear unattractive. The amount by which the selling price of the old equipment exceeds its book value will be taxable as a capital gain. The amount reported as a capital gain will be added into the depreciation base on the new equipment and will eventually be recovered in depreciation allowances. For each dollar turned into depreciation allowances, 52 cents in income tax is saved, as against the 25 cents paid on long-

Thus, there can be many reasons (and by no means have all of them been mentioned) why the best solution to a problem in static risk management may not be the best solution to what appears to be the same problem merely transferred to a dynamic risk setting. Perforce, the reverse statement is also true and constitutes one of the reasons why specialists in static risk management are useful.

Thus, the net earnings position of the business may, under certain circumstances, be improved by the use of credit to purchase more efficient assets after a loss, even when a change would not be profitable before the loss.

After-loss gains illustrated by the model used here do not always occur. A different set of assumed facts could reveal an entirely different picture, one in which replacement with used equipment would yield the most efficient solution. The use of credit to provide funds for outlays that do *not* improve operating efficiency (and do not merely renew existing credits) causes added expense by way of additional interest payments. It also still leaves the need to provide, sooner or later, cash with which to repay the loan.

In summary, a conclusion on the use of credit as a risk management device may be stated as follows: As a general rule, recourse to credit as means of arranging for resources to cover loss costs and expenses frequently means simply (1) delaying the need for cash, while at the same time (2) increasing the quantity of it needed. This reduces the advantage of credit as a risk management device, in most cases, to its attractiveness as a cost-free method of risk bearing if no losses develop, an advantage that must be taken into consideration when weighing the relative costs of the other risk-bearing techniques.

Claims against Others on Account of Loss

Resources are made available by others on account of claims arising against them growing out of the loss. These resources may be classified into two major groups, each with two major subdivisions. The two major groups are (1) claims on account of statutory or common law liability imposed on others and (2) claims on account of risk transference agreements. The first group may be further divided into (*a*) contingent liability and (*b*) absolute liability; and the second group into (*a*) risk transfers other than commercial insurance and (*b*) commercial insurance.

---

term capital gains; this puts 27 cents in the treasury and into the equity of the business for each dollar involved. The additional bill for interest would not all be borne by the business, either—generally, 52 cents of each interest dollar would also be provided by the government through a reduction in income tax payments. This approach to the tax problem is *also available* when the replacement is initiated by loss. The difference between insurance proceeds and book value on depreciable assets can, at the insured's option, be treated as a taxable capital gain. The purchase price of the new equipment can then be used as a tax base.

Liability Claims against Others. Whether one person may be held liable to another for damages arising out of a loss depends upon the responsibility placed by the law on the parties involved.

Contingent Liability. When liability is contingent, the injured party must prove that the loss was caused in some particular way before another person can be held liable for it. Clearly, claims that depend upon how the loss is caused, that is, upon whether it can be traced to acts of negligence or violations of specific laws on the part of others, offer little in the way of a resource upon which a risk manager can safely lay his plans. Moreover, even when such claims arise, there may be delay in collection; full-dress court trials are, at best, months and, at worst, years in being settled.

Absolute Liability Imposed by Law. For some loss exposures, liability on the part of another is absolute, that is, the claimant need prove only that the loss occurred. The important claims based on absolute liability imposed by law have the appearance of risk transfer by contract. Indeed, for risk management purposes there is no difference between the two classes except that the liability exists even without specific contractual reference to it. Thus, a bill of lading does not have to say that the common carrier shall be liable for damage from unknown causes for this liability to exist, for the statutes say it does. But, for there to be absolute liability under these circumstances, a contract of carriage by a common carrier does have to exist, so there is some contractual base for the liability. This and other examples of the same type of liability were therefore discussed, properly, in chapter 3 under the general heading of "Risk Transfer by Contracts." The risk manager can count on these transfers at least to the extent that (1) absolute liability is imposed and (2) the liable party is capable of paying the claims against him. However, there is a third limiting factor on this resource: the time of payment. The funds may be forthcoming, but not as fast as the damaged business needs them.

It should be noted that in some of these contracts it is possible for the agreement specifically to relieve the other party of at least some of the liability imposed on him by law. Obviously, the risk manager needs to know about any such agreements. Indeed, he should be consulted about them before they are made. The fees paid for benefits received under these contracts will generally reflect the onerousness of the liability requirements imposed by them.

Risk Transference Agreements. The observations made concerning claims against third parties under conditions of absolute liability apply also to claims in which the liability is imposed by specific contract provision. To illustrate: In a particular real case, contracts between the owner and each of the contractors on a certain construction job required the contractors to hold the owner harmless for any liability arising in connection with the work, even if negligence of the owner was involved. The contractors were required to carry insurance covering this liability. It would appear, therefore, that the owner was fully protected against loss from his liability exposure arising from the construction job. He had transferred it to the contractors and their insurers. But there are risks in risk transference. In this case the owner was successfully sued by an employee of one of the contractors. It turned out that the contractor's insurance had been written on a form that did not provide the required coverage.[10] A complicated suit resulted, involving the owner, the improperly insured contractor, his insurer, and still another contractor on the same job. Clearly, this risk transference agreement left something to be desired as a source of funds for the owner to cover his liability loss. Even though the insurance company whose agent issued the defective policy was eventually required to pay the loss, this requirement did not come until four years after the owner had lost the original liability suit brought by the injured employee.[11] No class of risk transference contracts is immune to unanticipated limitations and delays.

When risk transference provisions are placed in a contract by specific agreement between the parties, the particularly relevant factors to consider are (1) legal enforceability of the transfer provisions, (2) the relative abilities of the parties to manage the risks and absorb the losses, and (3) the price that has to be paid for the transfer. These problems create difficulties in the risk management process. The process involves three steps: (1) determining what static risks are faced, (2) judging the best methods for dealing with them, and (3) seeing that the methods chosen are properly applied. Transfer of a risk by specific provisions in particular contracts may or may not be the best way to accomplish these three steps.

1. *Determining what risks are faced under transfer is sometimes difficult.* It is getting more and more fashionable for negotiators and drafters of contracts to aim at transferring all possible static risks (particularly all possible risks of public liability) away from their clients and onto the shoulders of others. Too often these contracts contain ambiguities, conflicts, and confusion among their different provisions, with the result that the risk transfer enforced by the courts may be different from what the parties had in mind. And, occasionally, certain transfers are held unenforceable because they violate public policy or statutes with respect to the imposition of legal responsibility for torts. Furthermore, when several parties to a contract try simultaneously to rid themselves of the same or related risks, the ultimate effect can be difficult to determine. Risks or parts of risk may be transferred and retransferred until it is impossible to tell who has finally ended up with what risk without an extensive time- and money-consuming period of negotiation and litigation. The risk manager, therefore, must ascertain and evaluate not only what static risks are present but also what

---

[10] This suggests that the owner should have obtained and received insurance certificates (including specifications of coverage) from all his contractors, as mentioned later in this chapter.

[11] *Hully* v. *Aluminum Co. of America,* 8 CCH Fire and Casualty 1163.

juridical risks are involved. What will the courts think the contracts say? Can the contracts really be made to say what is meant?

Then there are also the *financial risks*, the uncertainties concerning the abilities of the risk transferees to pay when major losses strike. Have they taken on, in this and other contracts, more than they can handle?

In summary, injudicious use of risk transference can complicate the problem of ascertaining just what risks the business actually does face.

2. *Transferring a particular risk by means of a particular contractual provision is not necessarily the safest or most efficient way of dealing with it.* As noted, the ability of the risk transferee to pay off may be subject to question, especially if he has acquired other risks by similar transfers. Construction companies, in particular, are a common target for "hold harmless" clauses; yet, as a group they are also subject to sudden and severe financial strains in the ordinary conduct of their own business. One wonders whether there is always wisdom in such extensive compounding of risks.

As a general practice, of course, risk transferees must receive enough benefits from their contracts to cover the risks assumed under them. But what are fair benefits for the risk transferees may not always be reasonable for the risk transferor to offer. Risk transfer may not be the most efficient way for the risk manager to handle a given risk. Moreover, transferring the risk may render impracticable, or even preclude, the handling of it in a more efficient way. Not only may the risk transferee be unable to pay for the large losses under a risk; he may also be unable to do anything effective about reducing either the losses or the risk. These limitations on the efficacy of risk transfer apply particularly when the negligence hazard is among the exposures transferred. A transfer of the risk of loss arising out of actionable negligence may violate the fundamental general management principle of keeping responsibility and authority in the same hands. When liability for the negligence of one's own employees is transferred, the incentive to control such negligence is divorced from the authority to do so. The transferor retains the authority, whereas the transferee acquires the incentive.

Commercial liability insurance has not escaped criticism as a potentially dangerous instrument in this way. In the early days of liability insurance, question was raised as to whether the coverage might not be contrary to public policy because it reduced the incentive for carefulness. The courts decided that the major feature of the insurance—to insure that tort feasors would be able to pay claims made against them—was a genuine benefit to injured parties and hence in support of public policy toward tort liability.

In addition, the loss-of-incentive argument does not necessarily apply to every liability risk transfer. Some such effect undoubtedly exists among some liability insureds, but the extent to which transference of risk under liability insurance policies has induced laxity in loss prevention is unknown. Experience in workmen's compensation insurance and in experience-rated liability insurance lines suggests that the significant problem is not that risk transference makes the transferor more lax but that it does not encourage him to be any less lax. He does not get any worse, but he does not get any better either. Good loss prevention programs involve much time and effort on the part of management and at least some (sometimes considerable) direct expense. It is harder for a risk manager to justify, and for an operating manager to get excited about, a loss prevention program when someone else is paying the visible penalty for its absence and will reap the most visible gains from installation. One is reminded of the reports about corporations in which accident prevention programs made little progress until workmen's compensation insurance coverage was dropped and work injury claims had to be paid directly out of the corporations' own treasuries.[12]

3. *Risk transference may complicate the administration of the risk management program.* Compared to the other difficulties already discussed, the administrative complications of risk transference are minor. One problem is the maintenance of sufficient liaison with the legal and other departments of the business to supervise and coordinate the drawing of the contracts. Obviously, all contracts must be consistently drawn in a fashion to carry out the risk transference policies established.

A second administrative problem is the checking of transferees to be sure that they have complied with their agreements to provide financial guarantees or assurances. In this connection, the risk manager must see that these guarantees and assurances are received and that they are in order. Principal among these guarantees and assurances are surety bonds and insurance policies that offer evidence that the resources of a commercial surety or insurance company are available in addition to those of the transferee to pay the loss if one should occur. In checking the surety and insurance contracts, the risk manager will have to satisfy himself that these contracts are with sound and reputable companies and have been drawn, insofar as possible, to cover the range of risks that the risk transferee has accepted.

A final administrative problem associated with risk transference arises after the loss. The risk manager will have to take the necessary steps to make a claim against the risk transferee when a loss occurs. And, in troublesome cases, he will have to press for enforcement of his claim.

Useful and Efficient Risk Transference. By now, the following ideal conditions under which risk transference *is* useful should be apparent:

1. The allocation of risks as between transferors and transferees should be clear and unambiguous.
2. The risk transferees should be able and willing to meet all their financial obligations promptly.
3. Each transferee should have significant authority for risk and loss reduction and control and make the best use of this authority.

---

[12] Page 168, above.

4. The risks can be transferred on a basis at least as efficient (i.e., as inexpensive or as profitable) as other equally safe methods of risk bearing.

5. The risk can be transferred at a price attractive to both the transferor and the transferee. To repeat an observation from chapter 3: In the properly managed risk transfer, both parties are pleased with the transaction.

Commercial Insurance

The purchase of commercial insurance has much to commend it as a source of funds to cover loss. As a general rule, funds are received more rapidly from insurance than from any other source except cash held by the business. Of all the methods of risk transfer, commercial insurance comes closest to meeting the ideal conditions for risk transfer summarized above. Commercial insurance generally can adequately satisfy the following requirements:

1. There shall be as little ambiguity as possible about what risks have been transferred and what have not.

2. There shall be little doubt about the ability and willingness of the transferee to meet his obligations when called upon.

3. The transferee shall have and use some significant ability for risk or loss reduction. (Insurance inherently reduces risk, and some insurance operations aid significantly in loss prevention.)

The ability to transfer the risk at a price attractive to both the transferor and the transferee was one of the ideal conditions set up for risk transference. One of the limitations on commercial insurance as a risk-bearing device can be price; sometimes the premium asked by the insurer for accepting the risk is more than the prospective insured believes the transfer is worth. Another limitation on the usefulness of insurance is its availability. For some exposures, insurance simply is not available. Price and availability of insurance, of course, are closely connected—insurance is available as long as the insurer can charge what he thinks the exposure is worth. (Problems of cost and availability of insurance are discussed again in chapters 16 and 17.)

Increasing the Relative Amount of Resources

The *relative* amount of resources available to meet losses may be increased by the simple technique of reducing the amount of resources potentially needed to offset losses. To accomplish this feat, the risk manager must find ways of reducing the size of the maximum potential loss. If it is true that "a penny saved is a penny earned," it follows that any measure taken to control the size of losses may be considered an alternative resource for meeting losses.

OBJECTIVE OF RISK MANAGEMENT

It is time now to consider carefully the objective of sound risk management.

Limitations on the Rules of Risk Management

So far, the discussion has proceeded on the basis of the set of risk management "rules" presented in the first chapter: avoid large losses, play with the odds, and don't venture much for little. Implied in the discussion is that the objective of risk management is to preserve the business against the adverse effects of loss as economically as possible. While the objective is logical and the rules are sound, applying the rules to achieve the objective presents some limitations: some large losses are unavoidable, and the cost of protecting against others may be uneconomical.

Some Large Losses Are Unavoidable. Potential large losses from dynamic risks are unavoidable. Innovations, political changes, and economic disturbances, for example, are capable of causing losses that few businesses can withstand. Some large loss potential from static risks is equally unavoidable. Damage by meteors has been mentioned as an example. However remote the probability of damage by a meteor, it is something more than zero. Other perils expose business assets and income to severe losses that cannot be avoided or shifted to insurers or other risk transferees. Examination of "all risks" insurance policies shows the following perils regularly excluded from coverage:[13]

I. "Natural" water perils
   Flood, including both rising water and run-off (surface water, "flash flood")
   Waves and tides, including tidal waves
   Ground or subsurface water
II. Earth or soil movement
   Landslide
   Subsidence
   Soil collapse
III. War, revolt, rebellion

Not all these perils can be avoided and seldom can they be transferred.

Not only are assets subject to large losses from unavoidable and nontransferable static risks; income is also exposed. For example, persistently severe or unseasonable weather can cause major income losses to many kinds of businesses. These losses are hardly avoidable and seldom insurable. Even with insurable perils (e.g., fire, windstorm, explosion), not all potential income loss is insurable. For example, business interruption insurance will indemnify for a loss of income over a given period of time. Customarily, the period is limited to the time required to repair or replace the damaged property with the exercise of due diligence and dispatch. Loss

---

[13] The list is taken from "all risks" coverages that apply to property at specified locations. Omitted are exclusions for which other standard forms of coverage (e.g., boiler explosion, earthquake) are available. Except for war, it is common for these exclusions to provide that if certain other perils (e.g., fire) contribute to the loss along with the excluded peril, that part of the loss attributable to the named, non-excluded peril is covered by the policy.

of customers that has carried over beyond that period then has to be borne by the insured. Some newer forms extend the period of coverage beyond the physical restoration period to cover the losses sustained during the time the business is trying to re-establish itself. But, when important customers shift their trade to other sources of supply during a shutdown and do not shift back after the business reopens, the business may fail; at least one study found several instances in which this was the actual outcome of severe fire loss.[14]

Major losses can also arise from certain liability exposures that are generally uninsurable. Liability policies typically cover only liability losses on account of bodily injury or property damage. Many contracts require that the bodily injury or property damage be caused by accident.[15] But liability can exist for personal injury involving neither bodily injury nor property damage. Claims for libel, slander, or false arrest are in this category; so are claims based on such grounds as infringement of rights to a trade name, process, or market. Many claims are made for property damage involving no accident but caused by improper deliberate acts constituting a nuisance or professional incompetence.[16] Any of these claims can be large enough to be ruinous. Transference of the risk of claims of all these types, while possible in some businesses, is not possible for every business. Avoidance and loss prevention are useful for these exposures, but they cannot be counted upon to be perfect. Violations of the rights of others can be unintentional and unforeseeable even by the most conscientious management.

Therefore, to state that the objective of risk management is the avoidance of the large losses is to set up an objective that is unattainable.

Economy vs. Avoidance of Large Losses. Possible conflict among the rules of risk management was described in chapter 1. There it was suggested that whether insurance against damage by meteors would be worth buying would depend upon the rates charged. The conflict was between avoiding large losses and playing with the odds. Consider the same conflict in making decisions with respect to liability insurance.

As mentioned in chapter 9, setting limits in liability insurance is a major practical problem for professional risk managers. At a recent meeting of insurance buyers one of the speakers, the insurance buyer (or risk manager) for a large food chain, emphasized the need for "adequate" liability insurance limits. He ignored the problem of how to determine these limits, however, until forced to do so in the question period following his prepared address. His reply was essentially as follows: "First you sit back and you

---

[14] James Joseph Crowley, "Indirect Fire Losses in Business," *Quarterly of the National Fire Protection Association*, Vol. XLVII (October, 1953), pp. 139–51.

[15] Some policies require that only the property damage, not the bodily injury, be caused by accident.

[16] The topics in this paragraph were discussed in some detail in chap. 7.

dream up all those fantastic, horrible things that just might possibly happen to you, and you set your limits accordingly. Then the premium bills come in and you come back down out of the clouds."

A few months later at a similar meeting, another insurance buyer told about a chemical company that carried four million dollars of products liability insurance. The question presented was: Should it carry any more? No case was known in which more than four million of such coverage had ever been needed, but there was serious question as to whether past experience in this area represented a reliable guide to the future. Continuous innovations in the chemical industry and in this company constantly present new and vaster possibilities for liability claims. But, since another millions dollars of products liability coverage would cost several thousand dollars in annual premium, this company simply concluded *ad hoc* that the problematical benefits were not worth such an expenditure. And, if they were, what about the next million of coverage beyond that, and then of even another million? Where is the stopping point? It appears that eventually the cost of additional "large loss" coverage must exceed the anticipated benefits. Therefore, if the insurance buyer is to "play with the odds" (i.e., not pay more than a risk is worth), he is going to have to take *some* chance of having an unavoided large loss.

As for the third rule, "Do not venture much for a little," its role in the problem is ambiguous even when considered solely by itself. Giving up an extra million of coverage in order to save some thousands in premiums could be considered "venturing much for a little." On the other hand, over a period of years those thousands in annual premiums will themselves add up to a million or more. If they add up fast enough and losses are few enough(and if the business survives[17]), then the purchase of insurance may be the action that "ventures a lot for a little."

Proper Objective of Risk Management

What, then, is the proper objective of risk management? What useful and logical goal can be set up that can be both practical and internally consistent?

Profitability and contribution to the general welfare are two general criteria for the effectiveness of management of any kind. The thesis of classical economics was that, under the aegis of competition, accomplish-

---

[17] "If the business survives" is a complicating but necessary proviso. Its significance is reduced, however, because two types of situations are common when premiums approach losses in size: (*a*) The would-be insured who cannot afford the losses also cannot afford the premiums, and (*b*) the insured who can afford the premiums usually can afford the losses. The complicated cases, however, are those in which the business can afford the premium but not the loss. It must be understood, however, that the words "can afford" are essentially relative in the construction of any budget. They reflect the thinking of the budget maker on the relative importance he assigns to the various alternative uses of funds.

ment of the first of these objectives would result in the fulfillment of the second. Today, economists are convinced that the competitive conditions necessary for these dual and automatic results do not, in fact, exist. Furthermore, many students of economics doubt that it is either possible or desirable to bring about these conditions. This text, of course, is not the place to delve into this general problem, yet some acceptable fundamental objective of management must be postulated.

The following statement of objective is adopted as being both accurate and adaptive to nearly all philosophies. *The objective of management, including risk management, is to maximize the productive efficiency of the enterprise.*

Meaning of "Productive Efficiency." Much of the adaptability of the foregoing statement of objective lies in the multitude of possible interpretations of the phrase "productive efficiency." Clearly it refers to the relationship between the "value" of what is "produced" and the "cost" of "producing" it. But there are many ways to measure value and cost, and there are many opinions as to the meaning of the terms "produce" and "production." For example, some would include "production" of health and morale among employees as part of the "value produced," whereas others would not count any value for workers' health or morale unless it showed up as greater efficiency on the job. Neither mental stress nor peace of mind on the part of management is ordinarily explicitly considered in calculations of "cost" and "value produced" in an organization—except in discussions specifically dealing with the "costs" of risk and the "values" of risk control.

The usefulness of stating the objective of risk management as "maximization of productive efficiency" is its independence of any particulars regarding what "costs" and what values or benefits are or should be used to measure efficiency; it is even independent of that particular "cost" which is called "the onerousness, or disutility, of risk." Therefore, generalizations about risk management appropriate to achieving this objective are applicable regardless of the costs or benefits considered in a given situation; they can be independent even of questions relating to the undesirability of risk per se.

While generalizations regarding method and approach do not depend upon a particular attitude toward "cost" and "value," all possible attitudes toward costs and values are not equally useful, desirable, or acceptable in approaching any particular problem. Hence this text must necessarily concentrate its attention on those particular costs and benefits commonly useful, desirable, and appropriate in making risk management decisions.

Measuring Uncertain Quantities. It is difficult to measure the efficiency of a particular risk management policy even after "costs" and "benefits" have been defined. One source of difficulty is the uncertainty as to the nature and timing of the costs and benefits. Consider the following elementary example.

Joe Oldgard is a man who does not like to take chances. At each coffee break, Joe pays for his own coffee. Bill Newcomer and Al Gone, on the other hand, like "a bit of fun" for their money. At each coffee break they match coins to see who will buy the coffee. Sometimes coffee costs Bill 20 cents and Al nothing, sometimes vice versa. Joe's cost for coffee is 10 cents per coffee break. What can be said about Bill's and Al's costs? Here there is no problem. Both common opinion and probability theory would put the cost for each of them at 10 cents per coffee break also, unless, of course, it is suspected for some reason that the odds between them are indeed not even. In this latter event, the average cost for each of them would be that fraction of 20 cents believed to represent the actual proportion of times each of them is expected to end up paying. For example, Bill may be so much more fascinated than Al by matching for his coffee that he will give favorable odds to entice Al to participate. Suppose Bill has a standing agreement that he wins only if both coins come up heads; otherwise Al wins. Since there are four possibilities at each matching session (H,H; H,T; T,H; T,T), and only one of these wins for Bill, Al will be expected to win three fourths of the times and Bill will be expected to win one fourth of the times. Thus, Bill's coffee will cost him an average of 15 cents per coffee break whereas Al's coffee will cost him an average of only 5 cents per coffee break. These average costs (10 cents per coffee break when the odds are even and 15 cents and 5 cents when the odds favor Al) are called "actuarial values" and are used to measure uncertain costs.

But if the full picture is to be seen, benefits as well as costs must be considered. Tangible benefits in the example are clear and certain. Joe, Bill, and Al each acquires the same thing: a cup of coffee at coffee-break time. But Bill and Al acquire something else as well—that "bit of fun" for their money. Risk assumption for them increases the utility received from a given outlay. With odds at 50-50 they both receive a 10-cent cup of coffee each time *plus* the gambling thrill, both for no more, on the average, than the cost of the coffee—an obviously efficient operation. For Joe, however, matching for his coffee would be inefficient, for it would produce a *net* disutility. The average cost of Joe's coffee over a period of time would be 10 cents whether he matched for it or paid for his own. Unlike Bill and Al, Joe does not find fun in chance taking. Instead, he finds it disagreeable. Therefore, if Joe matches for his coffee, he must subtract from the value of the coffee the cost of the disutility associated with risk taking. Joe is then left with benefits of less than 10 cents to match his average outlay of 10 cents per break, an obviously inefficient operation.[18] Just so, to the extent that business owners or managers are disturbed by particular instances of risk taking, risk management policies that remove or mitigate the risk produce a value.

In static risks the incidence of benefits is often uncertain. The insured under a windstorm insurance policy, for example, receives not only a bene-

---

[18] Of course, if Joe had no feelings one way or the other about risk taking on this scale, both methods of obtaining his coffee would be equally efficient.

fit in the form of relief from worry about possible losses from tornadoes or hurricanes but also a cash benefit if losses are incurred. How is the value of these *cash benefits* to be measured in advance? Although by now the general nature of the answer to this question should be clear, it is easy to overlook some important details.

One important detail often missed is that the after-loss benefits obtained from a risk management device may be considerably greater than the resources made available to offset that loss. Note that the discussion up to this point has been concerned with the amount of resources needed to save the *going-concern value* of the business. The *value saved* by having the right amount of resources available at the right time following a loss frequently is more than the value of the resources needed to preserve the business. Thus, the availability of a certain number of dollars either from a risk transferee or from a creditor, or even from segregated contingency funds within the business, may spell the difference between liquidation and continuation of the business. These dollars, by providing the marginal amount of cash required to preserve the business, protect the amount by which the going-concern value of an operating business exceeds the salvage value of a damaged one. More specifically, a $100,000 claims check may produce $200,000 in benefit by making it possible to change $50,000 worth of "smoking ruins" back into an operating business worth $250,000. Gains such as this one often are overlooked by risk managers when they measure benefits against costs in evaluating a risk-bearing device. When this elusive benefit is weighed along with the more apparent ones, the scales are often tipped in favor of the risk-bearing device.

How might this benefit figure in a decision to purchase insurance? Insurance companies, obviously, must try to see that premiums are actuarially sound from their point of view, that is, the premiums charged must be sufficient to cover expenses and claims payments. The loading for expenses lifts the premium charged the insured to more than the average cost of his losses. Thus, if indemnity were all that the insured purchased with his premium dollar, then the purchase of insurance would never be "actuarially sound" for him. He would always have to pay more than the actuarial cost of his loss. But the insurance buyer expects other benefits when he purchases insurance, and these other benefits are presumed to be sufficient to offset the expense loading in the premium.[19] As already pointed out, one of these benefits is freedom from worry. The feeling of security is worth something to those who seek it.[20]

---

[19] The term "expense loading" is used here in its broad sense to include funds for contingency reserves and profits.

[20] An individual who has insured in a company that fails to pay him his legitimate claim upon a loss has received something for his money, although not everything he has purchased. Similarly, one who purchases a policy that falls short of the coverage he thought he had bought will get more than he paid for, especially if he never suffers the loss and never becomes the wiser. (No morals are intended in these observations.)

But would a management that admits to no "worries" or "regrets"[21] about a risk find profit in insuring against it? If the amount of loss to be saved is greater than the dollars of claims to be paid, the answer would be in the affirmative. When, as suggested in the illustration given above, $100,000 of insurance can save a $200,000 loss, the risk manager can pay more than the actuarial value of his claims and still profit from the transaction. The same insurance policy can paradoxically be "actuarially sound" for both its seller and its buyer.

In summary, many additional benefits may be found in various risk devices, particularly in insurance. Even if use of the device (purchase of the insurance, for example) does *not* produce a gain on a purely monetary basis, the device may be worthwhile because of its benefits in reducing worry, eliminating regret, aiding in loss prevention, greater efficiency in claims investigation and settlement, and other auxiliary or collateral benefits.[22]

Play with the Odds. The full rationale of the rule "play with the odds" has now been investigated. In the form of "maximize your expectancy" it has turned out to be the fundamental rule. As will be seen in detail below, even the more commonly reported rule of "avoid disastrous losses" is dependent upon it.[23] A detailed statement of this fundamental rule follows.

The net value of a risk management device is measured by comparing the estimated value of the benefits it produces with the estimated value of the costs it generates. The benefits and costs are made up of both contingent and non-contingent values. Contingent values arise only if damage or loss occurs; non-contingent values arise regardless of the occurrence of loss or damage. The net value of a risk management device is the difference between the composite of contingent and non-contingent benefits and the composite of contingent and non-contingent costs.

The contingent benefit of a risk management device is its ability to reduce the size of the loss potential. Non-contingent benefits include in varying degrees such gains as reduction of worry, savings in administrative or operating costs, and improvement in credit standing. Contingent costs include losses which the business itself will absorb plus the auxiliary costs associated with loss absorption, such as interest on borrowed money and loss of profits when operations are curtailed by depleted working capital or by an impaired credit standing. Non-contingent costs include such items as fixed premiums for insurance, administrative and operating costs incurred in implementing the risk management device, and lower earnings arising

---

[21] Regret occurs after a loss takes place—a feeling of repentance for not having been insured.

[22] These auxiliary benefits were discussed in chap. 5.

[23] That another commonly reported rule, "loss prevention is the first rule of risk management," is also dependent upon the "odds"—a comparison of benefits with costs —has already been noted. See chap. 2.

from the conservative use of capital when, for example, the risk management device requires investment in safe, easily liquidated securities.

Monetary evaluation of contingent benefits and costs requires two estimates: (1) the dollars involved if a loss should occur,[24] and (2) the probability that loss or damage will occur. An estimated actuarial value of these contingent costs and benefits is determined in each instance by multiplying estimate 1 by estimate 2. In short, estimated probabilities are applied to the estimated amounts of dollars involved to determine which risk management devices are indicated by "playing with the odds."

The Role of Large Losses. A "large loss" in any given situation has been defined as a loss that is "financially disastrous." Since "financial disaster" must imply loss of operating effectiveness in the business, a large loss, by definition, will involve many indirect losses—loss of earnings, loss of goodwill, loss of contract rights, loss of credit standing, and so on. It is the avoidance of these indirect losses that very often raises the value of a risk management device to a figure far beyond the amount of money that the device must furnish to accomplish its goal. And, as has been shown, this difference can of itself make the purchase of insurance actuarially sound despite the premium loading against the insured. It follows, therefore, that, wherever a "large loss" can occur, it is likely to be profitable to pay something (such as an insurance premium) to avoid the risk. Therefore, the simple rule, "avoid those losses which might be ruinous," is commonly correct and in accordance with the basic objective, "play with the odds" (or, "maximize expectancy").

"Commonly correct and in accordance with the basic objective" is not the same thing as always correct and in accordance with the basic objective. There are some exceptions.

In the first place, when there is little difference between the value of the benefits received and the number of dollars required to offset the loss, the rules "avoid large losses" and "play with the odds," may be in conflict. If a business has little going-concern value (can lose little in the way of future profits, market position, or goodwill), it cannot unconditionally justify the payment of premiums much above its probable loss. Under these conditions, decisions to pay for risk avoidance or transfer are not at all automatic. The non-contingent benefits (freedom from worry, etc.) will have to be considered carefully in reaching a decision.

Another exception is found when loss probability is very high. An extreme example of this exception is seen when loss probability is so high that expected losses plus the operating costs of the risk transferee exceed the insured's maximum claim. A simple example is life insurance on a man aged ninety-eight. By a recent mortality table, the probability of his death with-

---

[24] On the "benefits" side, these dollars are the dollars saved by use of the risk management device. On the "costs" side they are the costs that the business itself will absorb plus the auxiliary costs discussed above.

in one year is 66.82 per cent; within two years, it is 100.00 per cent. If $1,000 of single-premium whole life insurance were to be issued on the basis of this mortality table and an assumption of 2½ per cent interest, a premium of over $967 would be required to pay for death claims alone. The addition of a loading to cover anything like usual life insurance expenses would run the total premium well beyond $1,000. However large the death loss might be to the insured or his family, risk transference cannot be advisable at such a premium! Even if the premium were slightly under $1,000, it is difficult to imagine a real gain in the transaction for any man to whom the mortality table applied (that is, for a man who has no reason to believe his personal chance of death is significantly higher than the rate indicated by the mortality table).[25]

Still a third exception is apparent when the risk transferee sets an exceptionally high fee for risk acceptance. In most property and liability insurance, the "markup" for the insurance service is 40-50 per cent—that is, of each dollar of premium charged, 40-50 cents goes to cover the insurance company's expenses and to provide a profit. Consider a median figure of 45 per cent; then the fee for the risk tranference service averages nine elevenths of the losses transferred. The difference between the benefits received from insurance and the dollar value of claims received must be sufficient to cover this nine elevenths if purchase of insurance is to be justified. This requires that the benefits be at least twenty elevenths (about 182 per cent) as large as the claims for the insurance purchase to be actuarially justified. Suppose the markup were 70 per cent; benefits would have to be ten thirds (about 333 per cent) of the claims for actuarial justification.[26] Even "large" losses do not automatically develop such a high ratio of benefits to dollars received.

Unusually high markups in premiums generally come from one or more of the following causes: extremely low loss frequency, lack of predictability in losses, rating methods that do not take account of a particular insured's good loss experience, and cost of auxiliary services furnished by the insurance company. If the cause of the high markup is the fourth —cost of auxiliary services furnished—the value of the auxiliary benefits helps justify paying the higher premium, of course, and this value added to the benefits received from claims payments may make the insurance worthwhile. The other causes do not produce such extra benefits.

Extremely low loss frequency may cause an increase in the percentage markup in premiums for one or two reasons. In the first place, oper-

---

[25] More than likely anyone who is insurable will have a death rate lower than that indicated in the mortality table used because these tables are "loaded" to include a safety factor.

[26] These figures assume that the prospective insurance purchaser estimates the loss probability facing him at the same rate used by the insurer—he is neither more pessimistic nor more optimistic (not a truly realistic assumption, by the way).

ating costs cannot always be reduced in proportion to sales price. Home office costs are not proportional to sales dollars, and a certain minimal marketing effort (and hence cost) is necessary to produce a sale, no matter how little gross revenue is involved. Thus, a minimal premium of $5, $10, or sometimes more, is generally felt to be necessary to cover policy-handling costs. If the premium necessary to cover losses alone is, say, $2, and the minimum premium is $10, benefits received by the insured must be five times claims to make purchase of the insurance worthwhile on an actuarial basis.

In the second place, low loss frequency is generally associated with lack of predictability in losses. This is particularly true if "predictability" is measured by percentage variation of losses from the expected average. If, from a given number of exposures, the expected loss frequency is ten, a variation of one loss up or down involves an amount of money equal to only 10 per cent of the average. However, if the expected frequency is two, a variation of one loss involves money equal to 50 per cent of the average rate. And the percentage of average loss is exactly what is at issue here. When loss predictability is poor, insurance companies naturally desire to increase their premium markup to provide themselves an additional margin for error. The *percentage* increase in premium to cover an extra loss or two clearly has to be greater when loss frequency is low than when loss frequency is high.

Lack of predictability in losses can be caused by factors other than loss frequency. The requisites of an insurable risk are necessary for predictability.[27] Failure to approach any one or more of the requisites impairs predictability. Possibility of catastrophic loss, for example, makes it easy for the loss experience in any given period to be far above the predicted (average) rate. If losses are not sufficiently fortuitous, loss rates can go up or down in response to conscious activities of insureds rather than merely in response to random variations, and this impairs predictability. Lack of sufficiently large number of homogeneous exposure units on which to base a rate also impairs predictability. And so on, through the entire list of requisites.

Finally, extra high markups *for particular insureds* can result from rating methods that base rates solely on averages over a variety of exposures. Those insureds with loss rates continuously lower than the group average are faced with higher markups than are other insureds in the group.

Improving the Odds.   When the markup in the insurance premium is too high to make insurance worthwhile, insertion of a deductible in the policy sometimes improves the situation. This is particularly true when the cause of the problem is high loss frequency. High loss frequency

---

[27] These requisites were discussed in chap. 5.

typically results from frequent small losses. If there can also be frequent large losses,[28] insurance is desired but may be too expensive. A deductible clause, which provides that the insurer will be called upon for resources only when one of the infrequent large losses occurs, can circumvent the high frequency problem.

Insurance buyers, however, sometimes find deductibles unattractive. Risk managers have complained that deductibles do not always bring the premium reductions that the managers think appropriate.[29] The reasons that insurers advance in answer to this criticism are among those already described: Large deductibles reduce claims frequency, sometimes to a point low enough to produce the difficulties mentioned above; insurance companies have had little experience with large deductibles; few businesses (which is to say, few exposure units) can or wish to employ them; and the amount of insurance coverage desired beyond large deductibles is so great as to raise the specter of a potential catastrophic loss. In short, the insurers believe that predictability of losses under policies with large deductibles leaves much to be desired!

One is led to suspect that, given the problems of the insureds *and* those of the insurers, compromises involving deductibles of an "intermediate" size may be the most practical and economical solution.

"Open End" Losses. An important problem in risk management is the "open end" loss. Perils that can cause losses without readily visible outside limits are embezzlement, forgery, and disability. Also in tort liability there is no fixed outside amount limiting the need for resources to offset losses. Another person or two, a few more items of property, always can be involved in the next accident to help set a new record for liability losses.

How are the benefits and costs of a risk management device balanced when this device is used for an "open end" loss exposure? The problem can be illustrated with reference to a given bodily injury liability exposure using the following assumptions: The probability that in a given year a loss in excess of $1 million will occur is unknown but is guessed to be about one one hundredth of 1 per cent. The cost of increasing the limits on the bodily injury liability insurance from $1 million to $2 million is $500. The effect of an uninsured loss in excess of $1 million is the loss of the business itself, which has a going-concern value of $500,000.

The actuarial value of the benefit of a second million dollars of bodily

[28] However, "frequent large losses" is almost a contradiction in terms. A "large" loss is one that has serious effects on the finances of the business. If such losses are frequent, the business must either be able to cover them—in which case they can hardly be said to threaten its financial standing—or it will go under. If the first, second, or third such loss causes it to go under, there is a definite limit on how frequent these "frequent" losses can be!

[29] For one way to solve the problem see Frederick M. Reiss, "Corporations and the Captive Insurer," *Proceedings of the Twelfth Annual Insurance Conference* (Columbus: Ohio State University, 1961), pp. 15–21.

injury liability insurance limits in the foregoing case is calculated by multiplying the maximum potential loss of $500,000 by the loss probability of 0.0001. This gives an actuarial value of $50, one tenth of the $500 premium. Note that with an "open end" loss the situation discussed earlier, in which $100,000 of insurance prevented a $200,000 loss, is reversed: insurance of much more than the $500,000 actually exposed to loss may be required if the $500,000 value is to be saved. It appears that the "worry" factor or fear of total destruction may have to be great if benefits are to compare favorably with costs, unless there is some other offsetting value.

The problem of open end losses is not limited entirely to liability and to the other exposures mentioned earlier. In one way any serious catastrophe might be considered capable of producing an open end loss. Failure of a business enterprise can cause losses in excess of the going-concern value of the business. Going-concern value essentially is a market concept expressing the price at which ownership interest in a successfully operating business can be sold. But failure of a business causes losses not included in going-concern value. Management and employees are out of jobs; their personal economic patterns, and those of the owners, may suffer important dislocation; and even family relationships may be disrupted. Consideration of these effects could make any type of major loss "open ended" in amount. Suppose this complication is added to the problem of bodily injury liability insurance discussed in the preceding paragraph. The most practical approach is the following.

The premium for the second million of liability coverage is $500. The probability of having to use it is put at 0.0001. If this expenditure is to be justified, the benefits of relief from worry plus 0.0001 times the loss saved must reach $500. The value placed on "worry relief" must be arbitrarily set by management.[30] Suppose management feels "disturbed" about this risk to the extent of $200.[31] If 0.0001 times the loss to be saved is to amount to a minimum of $300 (the difference between the $200 in worry and the $500 in premium), that loss must not be less than $3 million. Since the value of the business is only $500,000, the value assigned to the personal and family dislocation aspects of the loss must amount to $2.5 million. Unless this figure seems reasonable, the extra million of coverage is still not worthwhile.

---

[30] A sophisticated and thoroughly logical way of obtaining this value is suggested in Robert Schlaifer, *Probability and Statistics for Business Decisions* (New York: McGraw-Hill Book Co., Inc., 1959), chap. 2. A tentative adaptation of this method to the specific problem of deciding on liability insurance limits appears in Bob A. Hedges, "Adequate Liability Insurance Limits—A Problem in Decision-Making under Uncertainty," *Journal of Insurance*, Vol. XXVIII, No. 2 (June, 1961), pp. 71–76.

[31] In insurance marketing, particularly in the life and health field, emphasis is placed in the sales pitch on motivating the "prospect" to purchase by attempting to disturb or worry him enough to cause him to place a high value on the elimination of that worry.

Problems in Reaching the Risk Management Objective

In the management of static risks, as in management generally, some important decisions ultimately must be made on inadequate information and personal judgment, however arbitrary! Some techniques of analysis, however, are useful in management even if all they do is present the problem for decision in a form that clarifies, not only what is to be decided, but also the implications of alternative decisions. It is for this reason that the technique described is useful: It shows that a decision to buy the extra liability coverage implies not only that the disutility of the risk involved is worth something like $200, but also that the personal costs involved are worth at least $2.5 million. The assuredness that the risk manager feels about the truth or falsity of this last proposition is likely to be a lot greater than any confidence he may feel about his ability to face up directly to the original question: Should an additional $500 be spent on an additional $1 million of bodily injury liability coverage?

Attainability of the Objective. Is the restatement of the objective of risk management an improvement over the earlier statement? Is the maximization of productive efficiency an attainable standard? From an absolute or omniscient viewpoint, the answer would have to be in the negative, but from the viewpoint of the best information available, an affirmative answer is in order. And that is an improvement over the un-adorned objective, "preserve the business enterprise," which is clearly non-attainable even with respect to what is known, much less with respect to what is unknown. As long as the business exists, it must take risks, including some static risks involving potentially severe loss.[32] It is folly to pretend otherwise.

Nevertheless, in most situations the best risk management policy *is* to avoid or transfer all risks that expose the business to losses potentially large enough to wreck its finances. This rule is particularly applicable to those commonly insurable hazards and exposures which confront many individuals and businesses.

The Gray Area. Whenever two objectives are sought simultaneously, conflicts between them are possible. Now, with only a single risk management objective—to maximize productive efficiency—possible conflict between objectives is eliminated. The elimination of possible conflict, however, does not reduce the risk manager's task of achieving his objective to a simple problem in black and white. Much gray remains to challenge his gray matter. Ambiguity may result from (*a*) possible ties among the

---

[32] In this there is a significant difference between risk taking in business and playing poker, a difference that is pungently brought out in an article intriguingly (and appropriately) entitled "Theory of the Reluctant Duelist," by Daniel Ellsberg, in the *American Economic Review*, Vol. XLVI, No. 5 (December, 1956), pp. 909–23.

values of different alternatives and (*b*) unwillingness of the risk manager to make the necessary estimates, even guesses, on which to reach a decision.

The first of these obstacles is factitious and, if necessary, can be resolved by flipping a coin or consulting a table of random numbers. The second obstacle can be real. The only sure way around it is to change uncertainty to certainty, an unfortunately fruitless endeavor in most cases.

Persons bothered about the second obstacle prefer a set of arbitrary rules to get them around it, but unfortunately no satisfactory set exists. "Avoid large losses" is the rule usually cited for such cases, but it solves few really knotty problems (such as the one, "How much liability insurance?"). Not many risk managers will accept this rule blindly. They want to temper it with the accompanying rule "play with the odds." And, when the question of "odds" enters the picture, it raises exactly the same problems of benefit-cost estimations as presented by the "maximize--the-productive-efficiency" objective. The most promising path around the unwillingness-to-estimate obstacle is Schlaifer's method for establishing betting odds,[33] an extension of the approach described above in the discussion of "open end" losses. Schlaifer explores further the set of assumptions necessary to make a particular decision appear to be the best one. For example: if, in the illustration developed above, management were in doubt about whether personal and family dislocation costs would come to more or less than $2.5 million,[34] it could consider instead what a decision not to insure would mean. If the loss from dislocation were indeed $2.5 million or more, a decision not to buy the additional insurance would represent an assumption that the probability of a large liability loss was less than one one hundredth of 1 per cent. Then the question becomes how good an assumption that appears to be. This probability may be subject to some rough statistical checking, and for that reason this new question may be helpful in the decision making process. Similar computations may be made using different assumptions about the size of the dislocation loss.

The important point is that the original problem, "Should $500 be paid for an additional million of liability insurance?" can be converted into several other problems, each taking the form, "What must be true about condition *X* for a decision (to buy) (not to buy) to be the more efficient choice?" The purpose of making such a conversion is to base the end decision on the best estimate of the facts possible. Since a decision has to be made regardless of a lack of knowledge about the underlying facts, the aim of the technique is to deal with the problem in such a way that only a minimum of estimation has to be made about these facts. Instead

---

[33] Schlaifer, *loc. cit.*

[34] If management is unable to decide whether these dislocation costs should be included at all, study of sociology, history, and philosophy rather than of decision making is the remedy indicated.

of requiring estimates that the cost, value, and probability are each "thus and so," the technique requires estimates only that these quantities are "more" or "less" than a given break-even figure.

Because different assumptions about each pertinent quantity give different break-even figures for the other quantities, many estimation problems are possible. The trick is to select from all these possibilities those particular estimation problems which will decide the issue while minimizing the estimation difficulties. On most occasions some judicious searching will turn the trick. For example, in the illustration already used, it seems likely that in a business with an ownership interest worth $500,000 there will be no difficulty whatsoever in deciding that the personal and family dislocation costs from shutdown cannot possibly reach a figure of $2.5 million. If so, this estimation problem was a good one to pose, and the original problem is plainly solved.

SUMMARY

This is the first of two chapters dealing with risk management decisions. Its emphasis is on principles, and its concern is with the core of the risk management problem: How much and what kind of resources should be available to offset potential losses?

The amount of resources needed to offset losses is determined by the outlays required for preservation of the business organization and its market position. If these outlays equalled the amount of loss that would be suffered without them, the equality would be sheer coincidence. The difference is important. In measuring costs and benefits of a risk-bearing device, the cost is related to the amount of the outlays; the benefit is related to the loss that would be suffered if the outlays were not made.

Three sources of resources are available to cover a loss: the business itself (including its owners), credit, and claims arising out of the loss. Once the risk manager determines how much resources he needs to offset potential losses, his problem is to decide what (if anything) should be done about it. What arrangement should be made to provide this amount? What should be done to reduce the amount required?

The criteria for measuring the desirability of a resource are adequacy, reliability, and cost. Adequacy in a resource means simply that it can provide the amount of money needed. Reliability in a resource is a function of the ability and willingness of its source to perform as specified plus clarity as to what the specifications of performance are. A source is reliable if (and only if) it can and will provide the funds when expected. Uncertainty as to either (a) whether the requisite funds will be due or (b) whether they will in fact be forthcoming when due is sufficient to disqualify the resource as to reliability.

Risk management *is* management, and its basic purpose is the same as that of other management operation: to maximize productive efficiency.

The phrase "productive efficiency" is broad enough to include whatever costs and benefits are appropriate to be included in evaluating a management decision. It is also broad enough to include the benefit, "the business survives," but, unlike the "large loss principle," the objective of maximizing productive efficiency does not insist that business survival is the sole, overriding benefit in all cases.

One problem in determining efficiency is deciding what costs and benefits should be included in measuring it. The present text is entirely flexible here; it is not even wedded to the concept of "disutility of risk" as a necessary ingredient in costs. The management practitioner must, as indeed he will, make his own final determinations of what are costs and what are benefits. However, throughout this book, various costs (such as the onerousness of risk) and benefits (such as survival of the business) appear recurrently in discussions and illustrations because of their general usefulness in determining the productive efficiency of risk management operations.

Another problem in determining efficiency is uncertainty as to what costs and benefits actually will appear. The logical way of dealing with uncertain quantities is to take their actuarial values, that is, the product of the probability of their appearance times their expected values if they do appear. Costs and benefits that are certain should then be added to the actuarial values of those which are uncertain.

Reliance on measurement of costs and benefits raises fundamental problems of estimating a variety of intangible costs and benefits. The particular problem presented by the "open end" loss, and a technique for reducing some of the problems of estimation, are noted in this chapter.

One approach to solution of the problem of "open end" losses is outlined. In one form it reads: Consider the costs. Calculate what benefits must accrue if the costs are to be worthwhile. In this form, the solution requires that the probability of receipt of benefits (or, in some contexts, of incurrence of costs) be satisfactorily estimated. Since this may be the most difficult estimate to make, an alternative form of approach is suggested: Given estimates of benefits received from and costs incurred for a given risk management device, what would the frequency of the event have to be to make the benefits greater than the costs? Finally, since estimation of more than one of the three quantities involved (costs, benefits, and probabilities) may be difficult, a set of hypothetical questions may be posed, each based on a different set of assumptions. Sometimes (after enough estimates have been made to make the approach useful) it will develop that the ultimate decision remains the same over a fairly wide range of estimates, and determination of the reasonableness of this entire range as a proper description of actual facts is all that is necessary to produce a final decision.

REVIEW AND DISCUSSION QUESTIONS

1. Recast the rules of risk management in terms of profit and loss potential. What information must the risk manager have in order to apply these rules of risk management?

2. What consideration should be given to the time factor and the kind of loss suffered in judging what constitutes a "large loss"?

3. "The ability to cover the needs for actual cash outlay at least allows the organization to maintain its previous financial position, and this *may* be enough to ensure its survival." Explain the choice of the word *may* rather than *will* in the above sentence.

4. Can the amount of resources required to recover from a loss be *more* than the amount of the loss? Can it be *less?* Explain your answers.

5. Explain the following statement: "Risk managers, like other financial managers, cannot afford to limit their attention to balance sheets and income statements; they must realize that cash flows and cash budgets can be even more significant."

6. Evaluate *each* of the basic sources of funds to offset losses. What are the virtues and defects, benefits and costs, of each?

7. What are the reasons for, and extent of, the risk manager's interest in the financial plan of his business before a loss occurs? To what extent should he be involved in planning the regular finances of a business before a loss occurs?

8. If the purchase of new equipment after a loss improves both the net earnings and cash position of the business, then why wait for a loss to make the change?

9. The term "contingent liability" is used in this chapter to describe one potential source of funds to offset losses. In what other context is this term used by insurers and risk managers?

10. What risks are involved in the use of risk transference as a risk management device? How can the risk manager control these risks?

11. How can loss control serve as an alternative resource for meeting losses?

12. A stated but unattainable objective of risk management is to preserve the business against the adverse effects of loss as economically as possible. What are the limitations involved in applying the rules of risk management (discussed in Chapter 1) to achieve this objective? Evaluate as an attainable objective of risk management the maximization of productive efficiency.

13. Explain why the following statement is true: "The post-loss benefits obtained from a risk management device may be considerably greater than the resources made available to offset that loss." Explain why this statement supports the following conclusion: "The same insurance policy can paradoxically be actuarially sound for both its seller and its buyer."

14. Suppose the first statement in question 13 were not true, would the purchase of insurance ever be worthwhile? Explain in detail.

15. Explain why "play with the odds" may be said to be the fundamental rule of risk management upon which the other rules depend.

16. Under what specific conditions would the rules "avoid large losses" and "play with the odds" be in conflict? Then what does the risk manager do? Why?

17. The benefits and costs of a risk management device are made up of both contingent and non-contingent values. Describe the nature of the contingent and non-contingent benefits and costs. How is the net value of a risk management device measured?

18. Explain why a risk manager who would not purchase insurance against loss from a falling meteorite would *not* ask that this coverage be endorsed out of an all risk policy covering physical damage losses to his property.

19. What factors can account for unusually high mark-ups in premiums? Explain.

20. The insurance companies, like the risk managers, have to consider the rules of risk management before accepting a risk. Explain how these considerations affect the availability of insurance covers attractive to the risk manager. Explain why "deductibles" can make some of these less attractive covers more attractive. What factors might limit this potentiality of deductibles?

21. What are "open end" losses and what type of problem do they create for the risk manager?

22. An important problem in reaching the objective of "maximizing productive efficiency" is the unwillingness of the risk manager to make the necessary estimates, or even guesses, on which to reach a decision. What suggestions can you make to help solve this problem? What happens if no solution becomes apparent? What is the practical significance of this result?

Chapter 11

RISK MANAGEMENT DECISIONS:
APPLICATIONS

Management, being an art rather than a science, is devoted to solving particular problems rather than general ones. And the most practical and informative method of describing how particular problems are solved is the use of actual problem-solving case examples. This practical and informative instructional technique, however, is not without its drawbacks, especially in an introductory textbook. Three important limitations follow: (1) Of all the myriad variety of problems actually requiring solution, only a tiny fraction can be presented. (2) Although each real problem actually has several equally acceptable solutions, only one or two of them can be explained.[1] (3) The problems and solutions that are considered must be sufficiently limited in scope and circumscribed in effect to allow the reader who is not yet an expert in the field to recognize the heart of each problem and to see how the solution or solutions offered flow directly from it. Of course, solving "play like " problems is a long way from making real decisions under real circumstances, but it is a beginning step in that direction.

THE ART OF PROBLEM SOLVING

The purpose of problem solving in actual situations is to arrive at satisfactory solutions. In problems that the would-be problem solver finds either strange or complex, much patient, step-by-step unraveling is necessary. The steps to be taken in solving risk management problems were listed in chapter 10. But, in less complex or more familiar situations, reasonable answers may become apparent with little or no analysis. Intuition or

---

[1] Some "students" seem to confuse the statement, "There is more than one equally good solution," with the statement, "All solutions are equally good." Readers of this text are therefore warned to notice that there is a great deal of difference between the two statements—in this case, the difference between a man who knows what constitutes good handling of static risks and a man who does not know anything about them.

analogy may shorten the solution time considerably. Proper use of intuition and analogy are the heart of the art of problem solving.

Three risk management problems are presented in this chapter. The first two, while reasonable facsimiles of real situations, are deliberately limited in scope. In the first of these, the intuition of the student is likely to suggest a probably satisfactory solution with little step-by-step analysis. However, he will have to check the proposed intuitive solution against the previously established standards for an acceptable solution and to consider whether some variation might be even better. The second problem, although also limited in scope, is likely to be beyond the novice's ability to "see through" without a step-by-step analysis. The third problem, much more comprehensive in scope, will present most students with a situation in which they can immediately see parts of the ultimate solution but must work out the rest step by step. Thus a variety of ways to practice the art of solving risk management problems will (it is hoped) have been presented.

PROBLEM 1. LIMITED LOSS:
FREQUENT SHIPMENTS OF SMALL VALUE

Many businesses ship packages by parcel post or express. These packages are usually of small to moderate intrinsic value (say, $5-$500) but, in addition, involve some indirect values. If packages fail to arrive on time and in good condition, customers are irritated. Sometimes the loss of a given package, although of small intrinsic value itself, causes a much larger loss. Failure of just one mechanical part to arrive may hold up operations of a whole machine and even of an entire department for days. Important losses also may follow from failure of delivery of patterns, chemicals, or other aids or supplements to production.

A Specific Case

Consider, as a simple shipping exposure example, the problems of a specialty foods retailer who does a large volume of mail order business, particularly for gifts and particularly at Christmas time. The indirect loss costs here are clearly those of customer goodwill. Frequent failures to make deliveries safely and promptly would wreck this mail order business. On the other hand, to expect no losses at all would be unreasonable, and occasional complaints, therefore, will be assumed to have no significant effect on the reputation of the business. Estimation of the amount of goodwill lost by various delivery failure rates between "frequent" and "occasional" is one of those difficult problems in estimation mentioned in chapter 10. If management is asked to evaluate this goodwill exposure, an answer somewhat like the following may be given:

The loss rate we have been experiencing for the past two years has been perfectly satisfactory; loss of goodwill has been negligible. But, of course, there is the possibility that the loss rate during some period, the Christmas season for example, might jump significantly above the recent rate, and that possibility worries us considerably, for then the goodwill loss could be very serious.

Probable Solution. The foregoing observation clearly suggests a practical solution to this risk problem. Certain characteristics of this solution are obvious. Risk assumption is surely going to be the method for dealing with those losses which are at or below the level of the past two years. Some positive action, however, may need to be taken about the possible rise in the loss rate, even if the increase is likely to be only temporary. In this connection it appears that the first device to consider is loss prevention. Finally, since the amount of damage inflicted on goodwill by a rise in the loss rate is difficult to estimate, it may be well to follow the course of action suggested in chapter 10 for such situations: Make the easiest estimations first, then see just how much really needs to be known about those quantities which are the most difficult to estimate.

Now that hypotheses have been formulated about solutions, the next step is to check them.

Handling the Low Loss Rate

The first hypothesis to be checked is that simple risk assumption is appropriate to the recently experienced low loss rate.

Resources Needed. What resources are needed to deal with the loss when a package is not delivered in good condition? If goodwill is to be protected, either the missing or damaged merchandise must be replaced or the purchase price must be refunded. Assume that the cost of the first alternative is less and is therefore used whenever it is acceptable to the customer. Suppose that a review of past experience indicates the following information about the costs of replacement and refund. When the merchandise is replaced, the direct cost is 85 per cent of the purchase price; the average purchase is $15.00; replacement is used as the settlement for 60 per cent of all claims; the administrative and clerical cost of handling each claim, whether settled by replacement or by refund, is $3.50. Thus the average outlay per claim is $17.15, computed as follows: 60 per cent of 0.85 times $15, plus 40 per cent of $15, plus $3.50.

Resources Available. Each of these claims started as a sale—on the average, a $15.00 sale. It was one of many sales, most of which did not result in claims for loss or damage. In fact, statistics show that over the past two years the ratio of claims to the number of sales for this retailer has been 1 per cent. Thus 100 sales would be expected to bring in $1,500 in gross revenue and produce $17.15 in claims. Assume that all other costs (cost of goods, sales, overhead, etc.) connected with the 100 sales amount to $1,320. Obviously, in these circumstances, where $17.15 is the total loss cost (goodwill loss cost is "negligible"), simple risk assumption is feasible.

Productive Efficiency. If losses can safely be assumed without worry, and without special financial preparation, or any extra costs associated with unprepared-for losses, the cost of the *risk* of such losses is zero (chap. 4). The only costs are those of the losses themselves. Their reduction is a matter of loss prevention. In the present situation, a stipulation is that a low loss rate causes management no worry; analysis has shown that no special financial preparation is necessary to offset the loss, and there is no extra cost arising from lack of preparation for the losses. Therefore, it follows that assumption of the risk is the best (feasible and cheapest) method for dealing with these losses as long as their rate is low. The only remaining question is whether there should be additional effort at loss prevention. Loss prevention will be the first risk management device considered in dealing with the risk of possible high loss rates.

The Risk of a High Loss Rate

Before considering possible ways of dealing with the risk of high loss rates, it would be well to measure the extent of this risk.

Estimation of Probabilities. The average frequency of loss has been 1 per cent over the past two years. If there were no change in underlying conditions, this rate would be expected to continue with only random fluctuations. The risk manager who is not trained in statistics will need to consult a statistician to learn the probabilities of these random variations.

Suppose the past two years' experience has been based on 12,000 packages, with observations recorded on a monthly basis. In the two years, the smallest number of shipments in a month was 300, the highest, 1,000. It is believed that excessive loss rates will cause damage to goodwill if they prevail over a period of one month. Thus, the possibilities for any one month's loss experience must be determined. The amount of observed data is large enough for there to be little chance that the 1 per cent loss rate is far from the actual underlying probability. Therefore, it is accepted as closely indicative of the true rate.

The probability that the loss rate in a given month will exceed 2 per cent, then, is about 0.041 if there are 300 shipments and about 0.00076 if there are 1,000 shipments.[2] There is less than 0.0001 probability that the loss rate will exceed 3.1 per cent on 300 shipments and that it will exceed 2.2 per cent on 1,000 shipments.

Loss Prevention Proposed. Suppose the average loss rate could be cut by one fifth, reducing it to 0.8 per cent by spending $2,500 a year for stronger packaging materials and for more extensive checking of order forms and shipping labels. With these innovations, the probability of exceeding a 2 per cent loss rate on 300 shipments would be cut to about 0.010; on 1,000 shipments it would be less than 0.00001.

---

[2] These and the other probabilities in this section are based on the normal approximation to a binomial distribution. See glossary at end of appendix to chap. 4.

If loss prevention is to be worthwhile, the annual cost of $2,500 must produce benefits worth at least that much. Benefits will come from several sources. Each claim prevented saves $17.15 in loss costs. Furthermore, loss prevention reduces the probability that claims will be high enough to affect goodwill adversely. Also, since the managers of the business were quoted as saying that "the possibility that the loss rate during some period . . . might jump significantly above the recent rate . . . worries us considerably," loss prevention could produce benefit by reducing worry.

If every month in the year had only 300 shipments, the benefits of loss prevention, aside from the reduction of worry, would be a reduction in the average number of losses per month from 3.0 to 2.4. The average annual saving on immediate costs would be $123.48 (0.6 times 12 times $17.15). The probability that the claims rate in any month would be 2 or more per cent would be reduced from 0.041 to 0.010. The probability that the ratio will be *less* than 2 per cent, therefore, would be 0.959. If there were 300 shipments every month, the probability of having an entire year in which no month had an excessive claims ratio would be 0.959 to the twelfth power, written 0.959^{12}, that is, about 0.605. With a probability of only 0.010 that the claims ratio in any one month will reach 2 per cent or more, the probability of a year with no excessive claims ratio is 0.990^{12}, about 0.886.

If a year consisted of twelve months with 1,000 shipments per month, a loss prevention effort that reduced the average claims rate from 1 per cent to 0.8 per cent would reduce direct cost of claims by $411.60. The probability that the claims ratio in any one month would be 2 or more per cent would be reduced from 0.00070 to 0.00001. For a year with 1,000 shipments in each month, the probability of no month with an excessive claims rate would be just under 0.9917 without the suggested loss prevention and nearly 0.9999 with the suggested loss prevention.

Similar calculations can be made for any number of shipments in a month and for any combination of monthly shipments (not necessarily the same for each month) in a year. Thus, the expected results for a typical year of shipments could be calculated. Suppose a typical year consisted of two months with 300 shipments each, two months with 401 shipments each, seven months with 514 shipments each, and one month with 1,000 shipments (total, 6,000). If the long-run claims ratio were 1 per cent, then, according to the statistician, the probability that this typical year would not have a month in which the claims ratio was 2 or more per cent would be 0.812. If the long-run claims ratio were only 0.8 per cent, the probability that this typical year would not have a single month with claims ratio at 2 or more per cent would be 0.966.

In this typical year, a reduction of the average claims rate from 1 per cent to 0.8 per cent would produce an average saving on direct costs of $205.80. (Reduction is 0.2 per cent of 6,000 shipments, at a saving of $17.15

on each claim eliminated.) It follows that $205.80 of the annual $2,500 cost in loss prevention would be recouped by this reduction in direct loss, leaving over $2,294 to be justified by the reduction in indirect loss (goodwill, risk, and worry). Is such an expenditure justified?

Productive Efficiency of Prevention. Under present conditions, a year has a probability of 0.188 of producing a month with a shipping loss rate of 2 or more per cent.[3] The average cost per year of the possibility of such loss is 0.188 times the amount of the loss. The suggested loss prevention activity can reduce this average cost to 0.034 times the amount of the loss. For the loss prevention cost to be justified, this reduction must be worth at least $2,294. The reduction in probability is 0.154 (that is, 0.188 minus 0.034). If the cost of indirect loss is as much as $2,294 divided by 0.154— that is, if 0.154 times the cost of an indirect loss is as much as $2,294—the expense of the suggested loss prevention activity is justified. The quotient of $2,294/0.154 is approximately $14,896.

The question for management to answer now becomes: Would the goodwill (sales, profit) loss from a high claims rate amount to as much as $14,896? As was suggested in chapter 10, it may be easier to answer this question than to answer the question: How many dollars would the loss come to? If so, the application of a little ingenuity to the dabbling in statistics here has produced useful results.

Finally, if the cost of an excessive loss ratio were the "known" figure (that is, if it could be satisfactorily estimated), whereas the unknown factor were the point at which the shipping loss ratio became dangerously high, the technique could be applied to obviate the necessity of determining the exact crucial point of the ratio. The statistical manipulation is somewhat complicated and therefore not appropriate to development here, but the end result is a problem of the following type: Suppose the following were "known" (that is, acceptable estimates were available):

> Amount of loss to goodwill caused by excessive shipping claims is $10,000.
> Average direct cost per claim is $17.15.

---

[3] Does the reader note the implicit assumption here? In the situation under discussion, a "loss" is said to occur whenever the claims rate on shipments reaches or exceeds 2 per cent for any one month. And the only question under discussion is whether a "loss" of this type does or does not occur in any given year. The question of *how many* such "losses" there might be in the same year is ignored, implying that it is a matter of no importance. Thus, the criterion, "frequency of accuracy in forecasts," is actually being employed. (The only forecasts considered are "loss" and "no loss," and the question is the probability with which one of them is expected to be accurate, that is, how frequently will it be accurate?) Thus, the criterion is not treated as *completely* useless. In this instance, its use is based on the idea that, once a high claims rate occurs in a year, whatever goodwill can be destroyed by it is thereupon destroyed; nothing is left for subsequent high loss months to damage unless and until a new set of goodwill values is built up. The problem could be worked under other assumptions. Clearly the important point is to work on the basis of assumptions that seem closest to reality in the actual situation—which requires recognizing both what assumptions are being made and what the real conditions in the situation are.

Sales volume is 6,000 units for $90,000 in revenue and $9,780 in net profit.

Average claims rate presently is 1 per cent; the suggested loss prevention effort costing $2,500 per year would reduce it to 0.8 per cent.

The monthly shipments in a typical year are as given before.

The expected saving in direct loss, as indicated, is $205.80, leaving approximately $2,294 of expense to be justified. This $2,294 is 0.2294 times $10,000 (the amount of the assumed goodwill loss). The reduction in probability of occurrence of a goodwill loss must therefore be at least 0.2294 if the savings on direct cost ($17.15 per shipping claim) plus the prevention of the goodwill loss are to justify the annual expenditure of $2,500 on this program of loss prevention.

If the crucial claims rate is 2 per cent, the present probability that any year will produce a goodwill loss is only 0.188. Even a perfect loss prevention program (one that reduced the shipping claims rate to zero) could not get a reduction of 0.2294 from the present 0.188. Therefore, if the crucial point in the claims rate is at 2 *or more* per cent, the possibility of a $10,000 loss in goodwill is not sufficient reason to justify $2,500 annual expenditure on the suggested program of loss prevention. Of course, the higher the crucial claims rate, the lower the probability that it will be reached even without additional loss prevention. Investigation by trial and error reveals that the crucial point in the shipping claims rate must be something below 1.9 per cent for the $2,500 expenditure on prevention to be justified by the $10,000 value placed on goodwill. (If the crucial point is exactly 1.9 per cent, reduction of the average claims rate from 1.0 to 0.8 per cent produces an expected saving of $2,246 per year by the prevention of indirect loss.) So the question for judgment becomes: Is the crucial point in the shipping claims rate less than 1.9 per cent? If it is, the loss prevention proposal is justified on the basis of a saving in loss costs; if not, the proposal is not justified on this basis. (It may, however, be justified on the basis of management's aversion to or worry about risk.)

Other Risk Management Devices. There are, of course, other ways of dealing with a risk besides loss prevention and risk assumption. One is to create a fund to offset the loss. Can this risk management device be useful here? What would a fund accomplish? So far, the exact nature or content of the goodwill loss has not been made clear. If it means loss of profit on just one part of the business operations but not loss of the business itself, extra assets in liquid form would not be needed for business survival. As we examine what might be done, after a loss, with money from such a fund, we see that unless it will reduce the loss in some way it has no reason for existence.

Suppose an advertising and sales campaign, after the loss, costing $3,200, could reduce the goodwill loss by $6,000. Would advance funding for this $3,200 be worthwhile? With the present average claims rate of 1 per cent and the present rate of shipments, there is an 18.8 per cent probability that the fund would be used in any given year. If used, the net gain would be $2,800. (A $6,000 gross gain less the $3,200 spent to obtain it.) The annual actuarial value of the fund is therefore 0.188 times $2,800, or $526. Its cost is the annual income lost from the maintenance of a liquid fund of $3,200, and this must be less than $526 to justify the fund. The $526 is over 16 per cent of the $3,200 needed. If holding the $3,200 in liquid assets costs less than 16 per cent per year in income forgone, risk assumption with this fund is less expensive than is risk assumption without the fund.

However, even if the fund costs less than 16 per cent per year (as, of course, it most likely will), it may not be the cheapest way to get the $3,200. Suppose the $3,200 could be borrowed *for sure* after the loss, at a 6 per cent interest rate. The total cost of the borrowed fund would depend upon how long the money must be borrowed. Suppose this is three years. Eighteen (3 times 6) per cent of $3,200 is $576. There is only an 18.8 per cent chance of incurring this $576 cost in any given year, making the long-run average cost only 0.188 times $576, or about $108 per year. This last amount is approximately 3.4 per cent of $3,200. Therefore, unless the holding of $3,200 in liquid assets in advance of a loss costs less than 3.4 per cent in forgone income per year, advance funding of this after-loss expense is not economical (under the conditions described).

Risk transfer and insurance, also risk management devices, do not appear applicable here.

PROBLEM 2.   LIMITED LOSS:
TRANSIT EXPOSURE WITH LARGE VALUES

La Vie Moderne is a firm of interior decorators supplying not only a decorating service but also a complete line of high-quality domestic and imported furniture, wallpapers, fabrics, floor coverings, *objets d'art*, and other accoutrements of the finely appointed town or country house.

The Decision Problem

The hazards of transportation present one of the major static risk problems with this line of merchandise. Marring and scratching can cause declines in the market value of many of the items handled. Transportation companies of ordinary competence simply are not prepared to give the care required of this high value, specialty merchandise. On the other hand, the unit volume on such merchandise is so low that it would be unprofitable to use owned vehicles. These vehicles would stand idle much of the time, producing a waste of capital funds. An alternative is to hire vehicles with drivers as the occasion demands, using the decorating firm's own employees to do the loading and unloading.

The problem for decision has two parts. (1) Which trucking method to use? (2) What else, if anything, needs to be done about the risk?

Loss Size and Frequency. The starting point in dealing with any problem in risk management is losses. What is their potential size, nature, and probable distribution? In the case of La Vie Moderne, a single instance of bad marring or breakage on a large piece of furniture or *objet d'art* could produce a direct loss of $5,000. On the other hand, routine transit damage, such as rubbing or slight scratching and marring, which can be masked by an expert cabinetmaker, represents a cost of only $100-$200. So there is a large variation in direct loss costs from time to time.

Customers of high-priced interior decorators regularly are confronted with the problem of having to wait for "just the right piece" to be made (by skilled hand labor) or found (by patient search through a highly inefficient market). Either process is a slow one. Therefore, ordinary delays for repairs of minor damage are not particularly important. But once "just the right piece" has finally been made or found and has safely reached the shop of the interior decorator, then, if it is damaged irreparably by the decorator's employees or by his transportation agency (the customer is unlikely to distinguish—they are all "the decorator's men"), the customer is likely to be very dissatisfied: " 'I'm *not* going to go through all that again,' the lady said." Such indirect loss in this illustration is estimated to equal the direct damage cost.

Suppose that major damage to van loads handled by an outside trucker occurs, on the average, eight times in ten years. Two of the eight instances are caused by accident to the truck, the other six by mishandling of the contents. When the trucks and drivers are hired and the decorator's men handle the merchandise, the results are four major losses in ten years, two of them involving accidents to the vehicles themselves. On owned vehicles, the drivers are less experienced and receive less training in safety. The loss rate on owned vehicles is three major losses from damage to vehicles and one from other causes, making a total of four. The ten-year frequencies for reparable losses are 180 for outside truckers, 90 for supervised trucks, and 70 for owned trucks.[4]

Major damage averages $3,000 for direct loss and $3,000 for indirect loss. Reparable damage losses average $150.

The Decision

The two parts of the problem to be decided will be considered in order: first, selecting the trucking method (a problem in risk transference) and, second, determining the need to employ additional devices in the management of this risk. Finally, the first decision will be re-examined in the light of the second. In the final analysis, of course, the decision will

---

[4] These, like many of the "experience" figures used in this book, do not pretend to be figures from anyone's actual experience. They have been created for purposes of simple illustration.

hinge on comparative costs, comparative results, and the desire to reduce the probability of financial disaster.

Risk Transference. The estimated cost (excluding losses) of operating a sufficient number of owned vans to prevent excessive delays at peak times is $16,000 per year. The fees of a public delivery company would come to $9,000. The rental cost of chauffeur-driven vehicles with employees of La Vie Moderne controlling the operations would cost $12,500 exclusive of losses.

In view of the difficulties involved in handling this kind of cargo, the public delivery company will accept liability only for damage caused by accident to their vehicle, and then for only the direct loss.[5] The average annual total cost of using such carriers is therefore $9,000 (for the service) plus $2,700 (for annual reparable damage) plus $600 (annual indirect loss on major damage when trucker pays direct loss) plus $3,600 (total annual loss on major damage not involving accident to vehicle), a grand total of $15,900. When truck and driver are hired and their operations supervised, the truck owner accepts no liability for damage to cargo. Costs are therefore $12,500 plus $1,350 (reparable damage) plus $2,400 (major damage), total $16,250. On owned vehicles, losses include damage to the vehicles themselves plus liability arising out of their operation. Suppose the cost of these losses (including any insurance) averages $350 per year. When this $350 is added to the $16,000 cost of operating a fleet of owned vehicles, the cost reaches $16,350, and this is in addition to any cargo losses. Use of owned vehicles, therefore, is clearly an uneconomical alternative. If the decorating firm can handle the foregoing itemized costs and losses without either a special fund or the benefit of insurance, then the most economical way of handling this risk is independent contract trucking. (Note that this result is obtained because with independent contract trucking some of the risk is transferred.)

The Maximum Loss Problem. The next question must be: Would a fund or other cash source be necessary or desirable to offset losses? The answer to this question depends on the maximum, not the average, loss. Estimating the maximum loss potential requires further consultation with the statistician. He says that major variations in the small loss experience are most unlikely (given no change in underlying conditions). But he says that, for 99.9 per cent certainty of absorbing major losses in stride, preparation must be made to handle at least three losses in any one year if hired trucks and drivers are used and at least four if contract trucking is used. However, with contract trucking, knowledge of the division of the four losses between vehicular accidents and other causes is needed because the costs associated with each of these types are not the same. Another

---

[5] Metropolitan area delivery firms engaged in this kind of work are usually contract, not common, carriers, so are not subject to the statutory rules on absolute liability for losses.

look at the statistics reveals that for 99.9 per cent certainty of handling major losses without strain, preparation must be made for as many as four losses not involving accidents to the contract trucker's vehicles. If, for these four particular accidents, the losses average the same as for all major losses, they will total $24,000—$12,000 in cash, and $12,000 in goodwill. Three losses a year would amount to $18,000, similarly divided half in cash and half in goodwill. That losses may involve more or less than the long-run average value is always possible, of course.

The management of La Vie Moderne may decide that these amounts of loss are too large to be handled by risk assumption alone. In view of all the other risks that the firm must assume, including the dynamic ones, the transit risk may be manageable only if a separate source of funds large enough to cover at least the cash loss is maintained. La Vie Moderne, however, is in a business dominated by personal tastes, fads, and fashions. It is organized as a partnership, and its value depends almost entirely upon the effectiveness of the personal talents of the partners, both as decorators and as salesmen. While high-cost merchandise is sold, little of it is carried in inventory as a tangible base for borrowing. Also, no real property is owned. In short, the business neither has $12,000 to spare nor can it count on continuous credit lines to raise such a sum. Clearly, the purchase of insurance is the solution to its transit exposure.

Ordinary transit policies, unfortunately, cover little more than the risks that the contract carrier is willing to accept, that is, those involving accidents to the vehicle. Transit insurance coverage usually excludes damage by marring, scratching, or breakage unless the vehicle is upset or in collision. Here the firm needs the services of a good agent or broker. Policies do exist that might be fitted to the needs of this business. The Department Store Transit policy covers goods being delivered to customers (also goods coming in from suppliers) against loss "from any external hazard" (i.e., external to the commodity shipped). Some companies write a merchandise floater covering against "all risks of loss or damage" except as specifically excluded. The recently established Commercial Property Program of most companies also provides "all risks" coverage and may be applicable, but the rule book interdicts use of it for businesses that are principally sellers of service rather than of merchandise. Is La Vie Moderne principally a seller of service or of merchandise? Practically all the transit forms exclude "breakage of glass, glassware, statuary, marbles, bric-a-brac, porcelains . . ." Some of these excluded items can be insured as "fine arts," and perhaps a Fine Arts floater is a possibility for merchandise of the nature and quality handled by La Vie Moderne. The point is that risks similar to those of La Vie Moderne are written in one policy or another. Since the loss rate to be insured is moderate, and coverage for frequent, routine losses is not sought, it seems reasonable to believe that the risk can be underwritten. Negotiations, however, may be necessary to obtain the coverage actually desired. For these negotiations, La Vie Moderne needs an agent or broker who understands and appreciates the position and problems of both the insurance buyer and the home office underwriter, who knows what can be done beyond the rule book, and whose underwriting ability commands the respect of the insurance companies.

Risk Transfers Reconsidered. Suppose the required insurance coverage is made available. The underwriter will want a ratio of claims payments to premiums of no more than 55 per cent. Taking only the major damage and considering only direct costs,[6] the insurance premium charged when independent carriers are used would be $3,273 (55 per cent of $3,273 is $1,800, the amount of the direct loss from major damage not reimbursed by the carriers); with hired trucks, the premium would be $2,182 (55 per cent is $1,200, the amount of direct loss from major damage). The comparative annual costs are as follows:

	Independent Contract Carrier	Rented Truck, Driver
Payment to trucker...................	$ 9,000	$12,500
Indirect loss costs, major damage......	2,400	1,200
Loss costs, minor damage............	2,700	1,350
Insurance, direct costs, major damage..	3,273	2,182
	$17,373	$17,232

Consideration of the maximum loss problem, therefore, changes the picture. Use of independent contract carriers, instead of being more economical, now becomes slightly more expensive. A difference of $141 on a base of over $17,000 is less than 1 per cent, too small to be the sole determining factor in making a choice. A small error in overestimating the cost of indirect losses would wipe out this difference, or even reverse it. Therefore, additional exercise of judgment is in order. Do the owners of La Vie Moderne prefer to retain the responsibility for loss prevention in their own hands? Do they think that they might have underestimated the goodwill loss? If the answers to these questions are "yes," then hired trucks and drivers certainly ought to be used. If the management of loss prevention is, in the opinion of the decorators, a "headache," and if the original estimate of the goodwill loss was stated something like this: "The average value of this part of the loss would be $3,000 *at the most*"—then it would be proper to ignore the small difference in cost and transfer to others as much of the risk as possible. In this case, the transfer should be made to both contract truckers and commercial insurers. (If common carriers were available, even more of the risk could be transferred by using them.)

---

[6] La Vie Moderne is seeking coverage for the direct loss only. It is most unlikely that an underwriter would insure against the indirect loss—it is much too "indefinite in amount."

Conclusion

The student may feel let down and even annoyed by the somewhat indeterminate conclusion given above. But risk management is no different from any other kind of management in that facts and figures are invaluable aids to judgment but never a complete substitute for it. If all decisions could be made by administrative, technical, or clerical assistants through the application of a set of quotable rules to the results of some arithmetic processes, then, even if the arithmetic happened to require the use of a high-speed electronic computer, executive management would have no justification for its existence (or for its income level). Opinion without facts can be dangerous, but facts without opinion are useless.

DAMAGE DIRECTLY AFFECTING THE ENTIRE BUSINESS

The most difficult problems in risk management are those in which only *one of several* interrelated major operating units is severely damaged. In such situations the difficulties in (1) determining the effects of the indirect loss at the related, undamaged units and (2) giving adequate consideration to the various possible ways in which loss at each different major unit may be overcome (by shifting operations around, by contracting for some processing by outsiders, or by buying or selling semifinished goods) make for a truly complex problem in risk management. When there is only *one* major operating unit, the problem of determining risk management policy with respect to the potential destruction of this unit is the simplest type of problem in risk management, with the exception of the "limited effect" type of problem.

Consider a hypothetical drugstore, Central Avenue Pharmacy. As a single location merchandising operation, it represents a common type of risk management situation. A fire, explosion, tornado or hurricane, flood, or other major peril can reduce the value of the firm's physical assets to near or below zero. (If the property is sufficiently damaged, razing of the remains and removal of debris can cost more than the salvage value of remains. When this happens, the value of property after the loss is "below zero.")

Central Avenue Pharmacy is assumed to be reasonably typical of its class. Drugs are only the beginning of its inventory. Cosmetics and health aids, toys, stationery and office supplies, "quick lunch" foods and beverages, tobacco products, magazines and paperbound books, household electrical equipment, and a few small appliances—all are found here. In the event of major physical damage at the single operating location, essentially all these items can be damaged or desroyed. The only assets not directly affected would be cash and other liquid assets held in a depository, property in transit, and vehicles and other property away from the premises. Since the druggist keeps a set of accounts receivable records at the office of an outside bookkeeping firm, the principal part of these records would not ordinarily be affected by physical damage at the store. (A windstorm or earthquake could, of course, involve both the store and the office of the outside bookkeeping firm. Under some circumstances, so could a flood, conflagration, or explosion. A judgment decision has been made here that the circumstances warrant ignoring such possibilities.)

Prevention and Control of Asset Losses

As always, the starting point is the loss potential. It is convenient to begin, this time, by considering whether the loss potential is greater than it needs to be. Can the maximum loss potential be reduced? What about the loss frequency? Is it as low as it can profitably be? The major factors governing the answers to these questions will be examined first.

Amount and Location of Asset Values. In general, loss control by reducing asset values owned or by housing some significant portion of them away from the main premises is not likely to be a practical risk management device in the small to moderately sized retail store. Considerations of good merchandising practice and capital cost will necessarily dominate the selection of the kind and quantity of merchandise. The general location of assets is also determined by operating conditions. For example, the best place to keep bookkeeping records is where the bookkeeping is done, and that is determined on the basis of general operating efficiency. Storage of merchandise off the premises is also typically a purely operating question in the usual retail store. And so on.

However, while determination of the specific locations of particular items within the store is also a question of operating efficiency and sales effectiveness, what is "best" for these purposes is not at all hard and fast, and risk management considerations can and should play a part in the decisions. No questions of operating or sales efficiency require that inflammable fluids or plastics be displayed close to cooking equipment at the lunch counter. Neither do questions of operating or sales efficiency require that merchandise be located in such a way as to block needed exits or to obscure stairways or other hazards. If the objectives of good merchandising have not led management to have clear, well-lit aisles (which do help move goods and make for efficiency in handling stock), risk management considerations should provide the incentive.

Risk management considerations should lead to the proper use of available "fire-tight" compartments in determining the internal location of property. The type of fire-tight compartment most likely to be found in a retail store is a fireproof safe. (In a pharmacy, of course, some kind of safe must be present, and if it is adequate for protecting registered narcotics, it will bear some rating as "fire resistive.") If records that are held on the premises, particularly those of accounts receivable, are kept in the safe when not in use, the loss from most physical perils usually will be reduced (and premiums for accounts receivable insurance will be lower).

In some retail stores, a basement suggests some additional internal location problems. An important consideration is for the central heating plant to be kept isolated and segregated insofar as possible. The storing of property in the furnace room does not represent segregation of assets as much as it (1) represents additional exposure to loss from furnace fires and explosions and (2) provides ready fuel for the spread of fire following a severe malfunction in the furnace. Basement storage presents further difficulties—basement fires are often hard to locate, then cannot be selectively fought but must instead be drowned. Furthermore, water used to fight a fire on the main floor will flow down, thoroughly soaking items in the basement, thus increasing the loss. Finally, basement storage commonly makes the movement of stock more difficult and increases the hazard of strains and severe falls for stock handlers who must move items up and down. Attic storage has some of the same problems as basement storage, with electrical wiring and flues often substituting for the furnace as the special fire hazard.

Housekeeping. Consideration of basement and attic storage leads directly to another area of loss prevention and control: eliminating what fire insurance rate makers call "faults of management." Unlike those managerial decisions adverse to risk management which deal with the amount and location of assets, these "faults of management" add nothing to operating efficiency but, indeed, are likely to subtract from it. And they definitely increase the chance of loss. Included in a list of "management or housekeeping faults" are storage areas cluttered with inflammables (e.g., boxes, papers, rags, cleaning fluids), improper containers for oily or volatile substances, use of matches and smoking materials in inclosed areas containing flammables, storage at floor level of merchandise highly subject to water damage, and other practices that, in general, represent ignorance or failure to think rather than studied operating policy.

Damage Control. The installation of "first aid" fire-fighting devices and procedures, such as appropriate hand-operated fire extinguishers,[7] buckets of sand or water, instruction of employees in how (and when: immediately!) to call the fire department, do cost something, but so little that "operating efficiency" cannot be a real reason for doing without them.

Finally come those prevention devices which, although not interfering with good merchandising or the way in which operations are performed, do cost considerable sums of money. Here the question is that of achieving a balance between the cost of prevention and the potential saving of persons and property against injury or destruction. It is difficult to put dollar

---

[7] Note the word "appropriate." The extinguisher that puts out a fire in the cardboard-filled stock room may easily cause the sudden spread of a fire around the grease-laden grill of the lunch counter.

values on human injury and death; the risk manager can only follow some rule of thumb or mind that will produce high dollar figures for these losses. (At issue here are the intrinsic rather than the legal liability values of human health and life.) Among the loss control devices to consider are automatic sprinkler systems, fire detection and alarm mechanisms, masonry dividing walls (as around the furnace room or between the storage and public areas of the store) with automatic fire-door protection, and various other installations involving considerable work and at least some professional guidance. Some of these loss control devices reduce fire insurance rates significantly; some do not. When the insurance rate is not reduced, the value and economy of the installation are likely to be questioned. Management should not forget, however, that even the best insurance programs cover only part of all the losses suffered. This is particularly true of the personal life and health insurance coverage, under which important losses cannot even begin to be touched by cash reimbursements in any amount.

Prevention and Control of Income Losses

Let us suppose that the Central Avenue Pharmacy now has gone as far as it will at present in physical loss control.[8] The next areas to consider are those of the "indirect losses." These will be classified under three headings: net operating income, liability, and personal injury. On their face, these three areas overlap, but they will be sorted out as follows: Under "net operating income" these losses of net profit that flow directly from inability to use damaged property will be considered; under "liability" will come these legally enforceable claims for money on account of damage or injury to persons, property, or reputation of others; and under "personal injury" attention will be given to these losses, other than legal liability, that the owners incur because of injury to themselves or their employees. In the present discussion, however, the concern with these three categories of losses is not with the losses themselves but with their position as parts of a larger loss: the totality of the loss that results from physical damage to the assets at the major operating location of the business.

Income Losses in General.   As net operating income loss has been defined here, it is intimately connected with the physical damage loss. Although claims adjusters and underwriters have noted exceptions to the general rule

---

[8] Once again the student of risk management should realize that, while he does not need to be a thoroughly trained loss prevention specialist, he must have more than a bare acquaintance with the subject. This means more knowledge than can possibly be presented in a book (such as this one) in which loss prevention itself is not the central subject. Attention is directed to the books on loss prevention recommended for study by persons preparing for Part II of the examinations for the CPCU (Chartered Property and Casualty Underwriter) designation: Charles C. Dominge and Walter O. Lincoln, *Building Construction as Applied to Fire Insurance* (4th ed.; Philadelphia: Spectator, 1949); National Board of Fire Underwriters, *Building Codes, Their Scope and Aims* (New York: the Board, 1957); Harry R. DeSilva, *Why We Have Automobile Accidents* (New York: John Wiley & Sons, Inc., 1942); H. W. Heinrich, *Industrial Accident Prevention* (4th ed., New York: McGraw-Hill Book Co., Inc., 1959).

that "the greater the physical damage loss, the greater the net income loss,"[9] still, in a given business this relationship *is* the general rule. Control of the net income loss can be approached in various ways, but always central is the aim to preserve the going-concern value of the business—to have again, as soon as possible, a business just as firmly established and as profitable as before. This means that customer shopping habits and goodwill must be preserved. Three principal means toward this end are to (1) minimize the time over which a complete shutdown is necessary, (2) provide customer service on an interim basis from the date of damage to the date of full recovery, and (3) be sure that the customers know the first two are being done.

These means cost something of course, and the costs of the means should commonly be compared with the benefits of the ends. However, when one compares (*a*) the profit potential over the lifetime of the business if it does succeed in recovering its business position with (*b*) the costs that it might incur during the recovery period in an attempt to restore that position, costs that have a reasonable expectation of achieving the desired end should not be measured by any closely calculated standard of benefit. Making close calculations here is akin to pausing, while one's house is burning, to calculate the relative benefits and costs to be obtained from using particular quantities of water to try to put the fire out. There *is* some point beyond which use of water does no good (and will even cause harm, by increasing water damage), but niceties of calculation of the exact location of that point are hardly in order while the fire is raging. Similarly, too much expenditure on efforts to get business operations back to a normal rate can cause harm by weakening a company's subsequent cash position or credit standing. But the benefits of restoration are generally so great, and the means available for accomplishing restoration are usually so small, that it is mere foolishness to be picayunish about whether some particular portion of the available means should be expended in the attempt to re-establish the normal rate of operations.

Of course, when the means are limited, wisdom does require careful consideration of where among various alternatives the means can be best applied in order to maximize the probability of a favorable result. The firefighting householder who wisely does not stop to ponder *whether* he should expend more water does properly give considerable attention to *where* he should expend that water in order to have the best chance of putting out his fire. He does not, however, turn off the hose while he is trying to figure out the best direction in which to aim it! A business standing idle *is* like a house on fire; it loses more value with every passing moment, and comes closer and closer to total destruction.

Income Loss Exposure at Central Avenue Pharmacy. What plans can be

---

[9] Prentiss B. Reed, *Adjustment of Property Losses* (2d ed.; New York: McGraw-Hill Book Co., Inc., 1953), pp. 482–83, 502; cf. pp. 485–87. Henry C. Klein, *Business Interruption Insurance* (4th ed.; Indianapolis: Rough Notes Co., 1960), pp. 227–37.

laid for the Central Avenue Pharmacy for preserving or restoring its operations following major physical damage to its assets? Ability to lay such plans depends heavily upon knowledge of the precise characteristics of both the business in question and the market in which it operates. A quite possible set of characteristics for this neighborhood drugstore are the following:

From the standpoint of the local market conditions the store's operations can be divided into three parts: (1) the lunch counter and the "convenience" merchandise (e.g., tobacco products and commonly used, low-price brand-name cosmetics, health aids, and medicines), (2) prescription filling, and (3) all other sources of revenue.

"Convenience goods are those for which people do not shop and which they prefer to buy at places that are most accessible and that stock the desired goods at satisfactory prices. . . . If the price is the same at all stores, the purchase is made in the most convenient store."[10] The "convenience" category includes many restaurants and most lunch counters. It also includes most goods that are standard in quality (packaged, brand-name items), particularly if their unit price is low. Sales of convenience goods and services create a large proportion of the gross revenue of Central Avenue Pharmacy and a smaller but still important proportion of the net revenue. Insofar as net income is dependent on sales of convenience goods, the principal key to regaining normal operations is to ensure control of a good location. Normally, this means retaining the same location as was occupied before the loss. However, because most communities have more than one good retail location, a new location may provide a satisfactory solution. Ownership of the premises or the holding of a long-term lease that is not cancelled by damage to the property are obvious means toward preventing loss of location. But, to preserve these means, the business must have the resources to pay its bills during the period following the occurrence of physical damage and the restoration of operations. Thus, prevention of loss subsequent to a shutdown requires that some cash be available during the shutdown.

The service of filling prescriptions falls partly under the "convenience" category—many people go to the most easily reached pharmacist, having no other criteria for making a selection. However, once relations with a pharmacist have been established, some customer loyalty is often developed. The personality of the pharmacist; the promptness with which he produces the remedy needed to relieve pain, discomfort, and worry; his willingness to work off-hours for emergencies; success with his recommendations of non-prescription remedies—factors such as these take prescriptions and related drugs out of the "convenience" category. In addition,

---

[10] Converse, Huegy, and Mitchell, *Elements of Marketing* (6th ed.; Englewood Cliffs, N.J.: Prentice-Hall, Inc., 1958), pp. 130–31.

there are prescription refills. It is much easier and sometimes cheaper to call the druggist and ask for "a refill of prescription number 66247" than to call the doctor for a copy of the prescription form to take to a new druggist. Thus, loss prevention plans for the prescription business must consider preservation of two quite different values: the value of a personal service pleasingly, promptly, and effectively rendered and the value of being the only pharmacy in town that knows what Mrs. Angelino's prescription number 66247 contains. While these values are distinguishable, they are related. It does not do the Central Avenue Pharmacy much good to know the contents of particular prescriptions if it can do nothing about them; the services of compounding and delivering the prescriptions must still be provided if there is to be a sale or a satisfied customer.

Controlling Income Loss at Central Avenue Pharmacy. That there are *two* services—compounding and delivering (including "delivering" by simply handing the item to the customer on the other side of the counter)—suggests one line of solution—both customer relationships and the usefulness of old prescription files can be preserved if the "compounding" is farmed out and the "delivering" service is maintained. If the Central Avenue store can arrange for the temporary use of someone else's pharmaceutical facilities and compound the prescriptions themselves (or use other registered practitioners), delivery can still be made. Promptness will undoubtedly be sacrificed and emergency service may become impractical, but, in the face of obvious efforts of Central Avenue Pharmacy to care for its customers, most of them will make allowances (for a while). Three things are necessary for this solution: available alternative facilities, a practical method for getting the customers and the alternative facilities together, and the preservation or reconstruction of the prescription files.

Planning for alternative facilities in advance has some clear virtues; no time is lost in finding them after the loss, negotiations under stress are avoided, and *quid pro quo* is easier to provide ("If you are burned out, come to me; if I am burned out, I will come to you"). There are also some drawbacks; the exact conditions of the loss and the problems to be solved may not be foreseen, the desirability and availability of the particular alternative may change between the time the agreement is made and the time the loss takes place, it may be more difficult to interest other parties in a "might-be" situation than in an actual hard case, and agreements bargained for in advance may even be less, not more, favorable than arrangements made under the influence of a charitable feeling toward a victim of sudden disaster. Only personal knowledge of the actual fellow practitioners can finally determine the best approach, but agreement in advance would appear to be the safer alternative and the one more likely to minimize hiatus following severe physical damage.

The most important loss prevention advice for the maintenance of prescription files obviously is to store them in a safe with a high rating for fire resistance. Keeping copies away from the premises is a possibility, but probably an uneconomical one. When a pharmacy suffers severe physical damage, doctors, when they can, often are willing to give a pharmacist a rereading of still usable prescriptions for patients who are customers of the pharmacist. In most communities, a complete canvass of the medical profession for this purpose is completely infeasible. Any doctors who operate principally in the pharmacist's neighborhood might be canvassed. Recovery of old prescriptions from doctors can be on an *ad hoc* basis, but this works satisfactorily only during the hours when the doctors' offices are open. The evening hours, however, are the most important period for many neighborhood pharmacies. Probably a better approach is for the pharmacist to ask his known regular customers for a description of the prescriptions that they may need refilled and the name of the prescribing physician. Again, when the druggist suffers a major physical destruction of his store, cooperation from doctors' offices is quite possible. However, when many prescriptions are needed from a single office, the pharmacist may have to send someone to the office to copy the records—doctors' assistants and employees are busy, too. As usual, when what needs to be done if particular damage occurs is pointed out, the value in preventing the damage in the first place becomes apparent; preservation of the records is definitely simpler than reconstruction of them.

Once the prescription records are available (whether by preservation or re-creation) and temporary substitute pharmaceutical facilities are provided (whether by arrangement before or after the loss), the next step is to transmit word to the customers that the usual prescription services are available. The customer must be informed of how and where to get the service. The operating details and sales promotion angles must be worked out, and important time can be saved if they are worked out in advance. However, since these are operational and marketing problems, and since their solution depends on the specific difficulties to be overcome in a particular case, there is no need to work them out here.

The third category of operations, "everything else"—all revenue sources other than prescription filling and convenience goods—is to a considerable degree dependent on the other two. Many people first come into the store simply because it is convenient or because of the prescription service; either then or subsequently they buy other merchandise because they have seen it or because they know about the store and want something they expect a drugstore to have. Occasional sales promotions by the store or its suppliers and some shopping by persons actively seeking a place to buy general drugstore merchandise bring other customers, but few persons will pass up Drugstore A and Hardware Store B to get to Drugstore C to buy a small appliance, and few will go to a neighborhood drugstore rather than downtown or to an important shopping center when they have a full-fledged shopping list. In short, if the value of the prescription service and the convenience of location can be saved, then a normal rate of operations can probably be re-established rather quickly when (and if) physical facilities can be restored. Re-establishment may, in fact, be possible even after the prescription service has been totally interrupted, but maintenance of the service has two valuable functions: It provides some cash receipts and possible net revenue during a shutdown, and, in terms of the previous analogy, it is "more water on the fire"—a logical, useful, and even mildly spectacular[11] way to increase the probability that restoration of operations subsequent to the severe property damage actually will be accomplished.

Prevention and Control of Liability Losses

Damage from fire or explosion is not necessarily limited to single premises. Either peril can cause loss to neighboring property. And most perils capable of destroying property can cause bodily injury as well. As was explained in greater detail in chapter 7, if either the onset of the peril or its spread can be attributed to negligence (or failure to perform a statutory duty), tort claims can be expected to follow. Thus, if a fire starts in a dirty flue at Central Avenue Pharmacy and spreads to neighboring stores and houses, the owners of the pharmacy may have the problem, not only of restoring their own premises, but also of covering the costs of being defendants (successful or unsuccessful) in liability suits. The same is true if the fire has an innocent start (as, say, by lightning), but its spread to neighboring premises results from some fault in the operation of the pharmacy or in the maintenance of the premises—for example, if the spread of the fire is caused by quantities of inflammable trash that employees of the pharmacy have allowed to accumulate in the open space between the pharmacy building and a neighboring one.

In addition to liability on account of negligence or statutory duty, there may also be liability on account of contract. The Central Avenue Pharmacy is unlikely to have a contractual liability exposure on its premises, but, if the business were a tenant instead of the owner of the premises, it would probably have some contractual liability in its lease. Other possibilities of contractual liability for various operations were described at length in chapter 3.

Treatment of Liability Losses in Analysis. In most businesses it is more convenient in the management of risks to consider losses from liability for bodily injury (including workmen's compensation claims) as a separate "limited" category apart from physical damage. However, the two must be considered jointly when there is a possibility that the losses from each, separately considered, will not be larger than the business itself can handle.

---

[11] The authors know of one case in which publicity about the efforts to maintain operations actually increased sales volume. Another case with the same result is reported in *Fire, Casualty and Surety Bulletins* (monthly), Consequential Epb-1 to 3 (Cincinnati: National Underwriter Co.).

Since both physical damage and liability for bodily injury can easily arise out of the same event, management must be careful not to assume both on the basis of their separate effects alone. However, in most businesses neither the major physical damage nor the liability losses can be borne without help, even when separately considered. In such cases, analyzing them separately does no harm and does simplify the processes of risk analysis and selection of risk management policies.

Liability for physical damage is different. Some of it, of course, occurs apart from physical damage to the insured's own premises and is most efficiently considered separately; examples include liability for physical damage on account of vehicles, products, or operations whenever any of these are away from the business' own premises. But one of the most important categories of liability for physical damage is that for damage arising out of events occurring on the premises. An on-premises event that damages neighboring property will usually damage the premises of origin, too. (That events causing severe bodily injury do not typically have the same effect is one reason why separate consideration of bodily injury exposures is both practical and advisable.) Therefore, most loss and risk control devices that affect one part of the result affect the other. In the case of the Central Avenue Pharmacy, then, an estimate for liability for damage to property of others must be added to the maximum loss estimate on owned property. (The two parts of the loss do not have the same probability of occurrence, of course, just as major on-premises loss does not have the same probability of occurrence as does a minor on-premises loss.)

Loss Prevention and Control. In a consideration of loss prevention, attention must be given to containing a fire, that is, eliminating or reducing the possibility of its spread. This is in addition to the considerations already discussed in connection with the prevention of damage to the business' own assets. Besides keeping open areas clean, protection against the spread of fire is principally a matter of establishing fire blocks. A fire block is, generally, a solid wall—preferably with no openings, but if openings do appear they must be protected by special devices, such as wired glass or automatic fire doors or shutters. The creation of fire blocks in an already standing and occupied building is likely to cost more than management is willing to spend. An exception may be found, however, when the building has masonry walls with only a few unprotected openings of moderate or small size (e.g., *not* display windows). Installing protection over these openings may not be very expensive. All too often where there are fire blocks, the protected openings have been allowed to become, or have been deliberately caused to be, ineffective; self-closing fire doors are kept from closing, windows and doors with wired glass are left open, or holes are cut in the metal of protective shutters or doors. Since fire may spread in either of two directions—in from neighboring premises or out to them—effective fire blocks are doubly important, and interference with their operation should be avoided.

Of course, standard fire stops are not designed to stop explosive forces, and even fires will be held in check only up to a point. Therefore, presence of a fire block does not mean that potential liability for spread of damage may be ignored, any more than presence of fire extinguishers or automatic sprinklers means that potential on-premises damage from fire may be ignored.

Losses of Key Personnel

The final phase of loss potential resulting from severe physical damage at the major operating location of the business is the possible loss from physical injury to owners or employees apart from the legal liability for the injury. If the store manager or senior pharmacist is lost through death or injury, the operating efficiency or sales effectiveness of the business may suffer. The description of what should be done to preserve the existence of the business over a period of shutdown certainly has indicated how crucial the presence of effective managerial talent at this time can be. If the talent is suddenly impaired at this juncture, the business will probably be beyond saving. However, as with bodily injury liability, the risk of sudden loss of key management personnel is also important on its own, apart from any physical damage to the premises. Furthermore, again, as with losses from bodily injury liability claims, losses from death or disability of key personnel most frequently occur without any major physical damage to the business' premises. Finally—and this time *unlike* major claims for bodily injury, which are rather infrequent—losses from death or disability of key persons are the most frequent of the serious losses in small to moderate-sized businesses. For all these reasons and also because risk management techniques and devices for handling the loss-of-personnel problem have their own peculiar characteristics, this phase of the loss problem is better treated entirely separately and on its own.

Risk Avoidance and Transfer

All Central Avenue Pharmacy's principal loss problems connected with severe physical damage at its premises have now been reviewed, but with only one risk management device in mind: loss prevention and control. The usual and proper order of march is to consider what the losses would be and whether there are any obviously useful ways of reducing them. The next move is to consider what loss potential is left after the obvious steps to reduce this potential have been taken.

It is most unlikely that a single-location merchandising or manufacturing business will be able to bear its own risk of severe physical damage at its single major location. Central Avenue Pharmacy, it is assumed, is no exception. The question, then, is in what ways risks can be avoided or transferred.

Available Devices for Avoidance or Transfer. The only real way for the owners of the pharmacy to avoid the risk of physical damage to owned property is to give up ownership. They might give up ownership of the building by means of sale and lease-back, but that is about as far as they can go and stay in the drugstore business. That leaves the option of risk transfer. To whom, other than insurance companies, might the risk be transferred? No candidates other than insurers appear available. If some parts of the physical damage risk are not acceptable to commercial insurers, either these parts will have to be assumed or the nature of the business will have to be changed.

For present purposes it will be assumed that Central Avenue Pharmacy is already cleanly and safely operated, so it has no opportunities to improve on its current acceptability to underwriters. Its relation to insurance purchased, therefore, can be considered under the following categories:

I. Standard forms of insurance are readily available.
   A. Their purchase is advisable without question.
   B. Many businessmen have some question about the advisability of their purchase.
II. Standard forms of insurance are not readily available.
   A. Non-standard forms may be obtained in the special coverage markets.
   B. No coverage is obtainable.

Insurance Commonly Purchased. Such coverages as fire, explosion (steam or otherwise), and windstorm insurance on the store building, merchandise, and fixtures, furnishings, and equipment can be placed in Category IA above: Any one of these three perils could devastate the premises, standard insurance coverages are readily available, and there surely can be no real debate over the advisability of their purchase. Only the amount of the coverage can be debated, and even here the question is limited. In view of all the other losses that will be suffered simultaneously with the physical damage itself, the amount of physical damage insurance should be no less than the maximum potential physical damage: inventory value, machinery, furnishings, fixtures, supplies, plus all the real property value not either embodied in the land itself or deeply buried in it (e.g., site value, foundation footings, drains below the basement floor, surveying costs). These latter values are particularly minimal with respect to explosion: explosions of boilers or fuel lines in basements can indeed cause severe damage to underground piping and conduit and have, on occasion, even cracked or shifted building footings.

What are the perils that could demolish the premises? Mentioned have been fire, explosion (including explosion of steam boiler, if one is present), and windstorm (including tornado and hurricane). In addition, there can be falling aircraft, war, lightning, flood, earthquake, landslide, land subsidence and collapse, and collapse of structural members of the building from any causes not already mentioned, such as termites, rot or corrosion, bad building design, shoddy or defective work in construction, weight of ice or snow on the roof, damage by vehicles or heavy machinery. Additional possible causes are falling of meteors or satellites, demolition by order of civil authority, criminal wrecking, and "cause unknown." The most economical way to purchase fire, explosion (*excluding* explosion of on-premises steam boiler), and windstorm insurance is in the combination form known as "fire and extended coverage." This form also includes insurance against loss caused by lightning, falling aircraft (which the courts may or may not interpret to include satellites and rockets), vehicles, and riot and civil commotion (one form of "criminal wrecking"). Left, then, are (1) the other possible causes listed above and (2) losses by fire, windstorm, explosion, etc., which fall under the exclusions in "fire," "windstorm," "explosion," etc., insurance policies. (For example: Insurance policies of all kinds contain exclusion for warlike hostilities, and all but special atomic energy and irradiation forms exclude damage resulting directly or indirectly from atomic fission or fusion. "Damage by vehicle" forms available for businesses generally exclude damage caused by the insured's own vehicles, and explosion coverages provide that "concussion" is not explosion.[12]

In the first category ("readily available and should be bought"), then, are fire and extended coverage insurance plus, if appropriate, insurance against steam boiler explosion, on owned assets. The reader may agree with the authors that some other exposures, notably property damage liability, should be on the list of coverages automatically considered necessary.[13] But many businessmen do not carry insurance against liability for property damage caused by their general business operations, and a large proportion of those who do have such coverage carry inadequate amounts. Therefore, the need for such coverage is clearly *not* "beyond debate" and must be considered and discussed.

Other Insurance against Physical Damage. In the category, "insurance coverage is readily available, but the need to purchase it requires consideration," is a variable list of coverages. The list is variable because (1) there are some differences among premises as to the perils to which they are exposed and (2) the insurance industry is in the midst of many changes, and what was unavailable or purely specialty coverage one month may be standard coverage and readily available the next. Organization of a listing is further complicated because broader coverages are available for personal property in business than for business buildings.

The following is a list of coverages that can be called "generally avail-

---

[12] As a matter of scientific definition, concussion actually is not explosion. But some persons, including several judges, have thought that it was, so one more excluding phrase has been written into the policies.

[13] The reader is reminded that consideration of personal injury coverages has been specifically stated to be outside the scope of the present discussion.

able" and that apply to perils that might cause severe damage to the building:[14]

> Vandalism and malicious mischief
> Collapse of roof tanks
> "Explosion" or violent rupture of pressure equipment (other than steam boilers) or of machinery (particularly of heavy, rotating parts)
> Damage by burglars
> Earthquake

The list requires some comment. If one of the perils listed above causes a fire or explosion, the ensuing fire or explosion damage is covered by the fire or explosion policy. Furthermore, if the causation is reversed and a peril in the present list (other than criminal acts) appears as a direct result of a fire or explosion, then the entire loss is chargeable to the fire or explosion policy. For example, suppose a flywheel disintegrates and a piece of it cuts an electrical line, causing first sparks then fire. Fire insurance policies apply to the *fire part* of the loss. On the other hand, if a fire occurs and causes the flywheel to disintegrate and do further damage, then, if the original fire damage comes under the coverage of the fire policy, so does the damage caused by the hurtling pieces of the flywheel.

In part, that is the reason why the purchase of coverages in this second listing is debatable. How might burglars or vandals, for instance, cause severe damage to the building unless it be by fire or explosion? If loss by collapse of roof tanks is already insured when the cause is fire, windstorm, or explosion, what else is needed? Cannot collapse by the most likely other cause—rust and corrosion—be better handled by exercise of due care in loss prevention? Except for earthquake, a need for coverages against the perils in the foregoing list is not evident on the basis of their ability to cause severe damage to the real property of most businesses.

The peril of earthquake presents a different problem. The amount of damage to the building depends not only on the severity of the quake but also on the type and quality of the building's construction and the nature of the geologic foundation on which it is footed. In moderately destructive quakes, ordinary masonry buildings not footed on solid homogeneous rock are likely to crack; buildings footed on alluvium or other loose soil suffer severe damage. On the other hand, fire-resistive and reinforced masonry buildings based on solid rock suffered little quake (as distinguished from fire) damage in the severe earthquakes in San Francisco (1906) and Tokyo (1923).[15] However, the reason that earthquake insurance is omitted from

---

[14] The reader whose experience and knowledge in insurance are principally in the coverages for homes and families is warned that policies available for businesses do not always give as broad coverage as those available for dwellings, particularly for damage to real property—or at least that is true as of the time this note is written.

[15] Longwell, Knopf, and Flint, *A Textbook of Geology* (2d ed.; New York: John Wiley & Sons, Inc., 1944), Part I, p. 3366; and James T. Wilson, "Earthquake," *Collier's Encyclopedia* (New York: P. F. Collier & Son, 1954).

the list of undebatable coverages for purchase is, not the lack of loss severity, but the low loss frequency. In this country, outside of the far western states, there have been very few recorded earthquakes of sufficient intensity to cause severe damage. But there have been some, including a severe quake at Charleston, South Carolina (1886); a particularly widespread series of shocks, which covered hundreds of square miles on both sides of the Mississippi River, with their center near the site of New Madrid, Missouri, just south of the mouth of the Ohio (1811, 1812); and a severe quake centered near Cambridge, Massachusetts (1755).[16]

The Problem of Low Frequency in Losses. For the vast majority of American businessmen whose property is not in the western states, there is no "problem" of earthquake insurance. Most of them never think of it, and nearly all the rest dismiss it as totally unnecessary. Yet there is a standard form of coverage (Earthquake and Volcanic Eruption insurance) available in the parts of the country not regularly subject to quakes, as well as forms for use in those states in which losses are fairly common. Who, if anyone, should buy it? Should Central Avenue Pharmacy? What do the risk management principles say? Given the potential size of loss for ordinary buildings, the "large loss principle" indicates "buy." How about the "maximum profit" principle? "Play with the odds"—but what *are* the odds? About three major disturbances in all the United States east of the Rocky Mountains in some two to three hundred years. What does that mean to the neighborhood drugstore in, say, Springfield (Massachusetts, Illinois, Ohio, Missouri, or Florida)?

Consider again the bases for decisions to buy insurance:

I. Cost of insurance and cost of loss:
   A. Suppose—
      1. The insurance costs X dollars.
      2. On a loss it will pay Y dollars, which will prevent the insured from losing Z dollars.
      3. The probability of a claim of Y dollars is p.
   B. In the long run, it will pay to follow consistently the decision rule: "Choose the lesser amount of X and pZ"—that is, buy the insurance and pay the premium, X, if that is smaller; take the chance of loss, estimated at pZ, if that is smaller.
II. Disutility of (aversion to) risk:
   A. When risk is undertaken without transfer or insurance, there may be a direct disutility of worry or discomfort about the possibility of loss. Suppose a measure, call it U, can be put on this worry.
   B. Then the purchase of insurance is indicated whenever $X < pZ + U$.

Both these bases depend upon making some estimation of p. Many say that such estimation should not even be attempted when so little is known —such as the probability of earthquake damage in a given area of the central or eastern United States. But such a position is impossible for a risk

---

[16] Longwell *et al.*, *op. cit.*, pp. 358 f.; Wilson, *op. cit.*

manager. He cannot avoid a decision; he either buys earthquake insurance or he does not. Either way, he is making some kind of assumption about the probability of earthquake loss vis-à-vis the cost of earthquake insurance. It appears better to recognize this fact and try to decide whether his assumption about earthquake probability is reasonable. But what assumption about earthquake probability is reasonable? Here, indeed, is a question! (And the need for an answer to it constitutes one small example of the usefulness of statistical training in business management, not just static risk management, for all managers deal with risks and probabilities of one kind or another.) One way out is via an approach already described: Leave the toughest estimation to the last and then see what has to be estimated. Thus, suppose earthquake insurance would cost 15 cents per $100 of face amount (a realistic rate). Now the potential size of the uninsured loss must be estimated and the amount of insurance needed to reduce this loss to manageable size determined. Suppose, at Central Avenue Pharmacy, the loss without insurance was estimated at $200,000, while the uninsured portion of a loss suffered with $100,000 of earthquake insurance in force was estimated at $20,000. Is the premium less than the value of the insurance, that is, does either of the following inequalities hold?

$$(1) \quad (0.15)\$100,000/100 < p\$180,000,$$

or

$$(2) \quad (0.15)\$100,000/100 < p\$180,000 + U.$$

The premium is $150. If inequality 1 is to hold, p must be greater than 0.00083—one earthquake in every 120 years.[17] In inequality 2, p may be smaller, according to the value of U. What is required here is that p be no less than 0.00083 minus $U/180,000$. But how is U to be estimated? It was suggested in chapter 10 that a useful approach was to adjust Z so that it included all the potential losses that caused the worry about risk assumption. If this can be and is done, then inequality 1 serves the purpose (decision making about insurance).

Now the risk manager can ask himself (and others) whether it seems reasonable to expect that earthquake frequency in the area will be at least as great as once every 120 years.[18]

When there is an especially small chance of loss from a given peril, it is

---

[17] This simple calculation implicitly assumes that the only earthquakes to be counted are ones that cause severe damage and that every earthquake will cause severe damage. If the one earthquake in 120 years was expected to cause little damage, the insurance purchase would not be justified. On the other hand, if, in addition to severe quakes of a given frequency, smaller ones were expected occasionally to do some damage, the value of the insurance would be increased to the extent of the smaller loss payments.

[18] By one rational approach (too complicated and requiring too much mathematics for explanation here), a good estimate for average frequency is given by the formula, $f = (n + 1)/T$, where f is the expected average frequency and n is the number of damaging earthquakes known to have occurred in historical period T. T is taken, of course, as the maximum continuous period for which the area's earthquake history is available. Thus, around St. Louis, the continuous historical records go back about 200 years, with one known damaging quake (the New Madrid shocks). By the formula, the

generally cheaper to buy coverage against that peril in a package combined with other coverage than to purchase it separately. Therefore, insurance protection available as part of a package may be bought sometimes when the same protection offered separately would be by-passed. Also, of course, much of the other coverage in the package may be so desirable that the less desirable part is accepted in the package in order to get what is wanted. (The desired element is not always separately available.) Furthermore, if the chance of loss on the unwanted coverage is extremely small, its presence adds little to the total cost of the package.

In sum, it is not the sheer remoteness of the earthquake loss possibility that reduces the attractiveness of insurance protection against it; the cause is that insurers charge high premiums relative to the chance of loss. However, if Central Avenue Pharmacy is located in central Illinois and 1/100 is accepted as expected average frequency of damaging earthquakes in that territory, then it follows that Central Avenue Pharmacy should carry earthquake insurance if the previously computed 1/120 is indeed the lowest frequency for which the purchase of earthquake insurance would be economical for this pharmacy.

Property Income and Extra Expense Coverage. The purchase of income, liability, or other indirect loss covers might also be debated. Foremost among these covers in a consideration of severe physical damage loss at Central Avenue Pharmacy are business interruption and related covers and property damage liability insurance.[19] The criteria for determining the need for these covers have already been illustrated. Let us apply them to Central Avenue Pharmacy.

Consider first the subject matter of business interruption insurance and related covers: net income lost during and following a shutdown. It has already been determined that, in the event of a shutdown, the loss is minimized if prescription filling service is continued by use of other facilities and the business reopens as soon as reasonably possible at its previous site. Since the Central Avenue Pharmacy owns its site, the only assurance needed is that it will be able to pay all legitimate claims against the property coming due before full resumption of operations and that it has the financial or credit resources to fund the cost of rebuilding, repairing, and replacing the physical assets without delay. This requires the ability to satisfy previous creditors whose claims mature during the period and also to convince those who rebuild and replace that they too will be paid in proper time. Assume that the amount of the fire, extended coverage, and other physical damage insurance carried by the pharmacy is at least equal to the before-loss value

---

indicated *average* frequency for damaging quakes in this area is therefore 2/200, or one every 100 years. (However, the probability that there will be *no* earthquakes in any particular 100 years is indicated to be 44.4 per cent, and this is the modal value in this distribution: "none" is the number of earthquakes most commonly expected actually to occur in any given century.)

[19] To repeat, bodily injury liability (including workmen's compensation) and health and life insurance covers are arbitrarily considered to be another and separate topic.

of that part of the damaged property covered by these policies. Assume also that Central Avenue Pharmacy will have no damage to property *not* covered except as specifically mentioned in subsequent discussion. (This last assumption is made because the analysis, although of a "simple" situation, grows long, and omission of all complications not directly useful to the discussion is necessary if conclusions are to be reached within the space of one chapter!) Now what other protection should be purchased?

Assume that the exposure has been evaluated as discussed in Part III of the text, producing the following figures:

Cash resources needed

To carry on business organization during shutdown:

Debts already incurred and coming due	$ 2,500	
Minimum payroll	3,500	
Cost of continuing the prescription service (including drugs used)	4,800	
Reconstruction of prescription records	600	
Other costs to preserve customer and supplier goodwill	1,800	

To restore operations at old site:

Expenses to assess damage, handle salvage, and handle new merchandise	1,600	
Repair building	45,000	
Repair and replace fixtures and equipment	35,000	
Replace merchandise	40,000	
Funds for financing further operations	20,000	

To cover contingent claims:

Property damage liability	100,000	
Margins for errors in cost estimates	5,000	
Totals: Estimated for expenses		$154,800
Contingencies		105,000
Grand total		$259,800

Known resources

In the business:

Cash in bank	$ 17,500	
Recovery on receivables	1,250	
Revenue from continuing a prescription service	5,200	23,950

Physical damage insurance:

Merchandise	$ 40,000	
Fixtures and equipment	21,000*	
Building	40,000†	101,000

Trade credit:

New merchandise	$ 10,000	
Fixtures and equipment	17,500	27,500
Total resources		$152,450

Shortage in resources as compared to need

For estimated expenses, repairs, replacement	$ 2,350	
For all items, including contingencies	107,350	

° Amount of insurance claim assumed here to be limited to cash value of old assets, which is less than cost of new.

† This assumes that replacements and repairs of some of the components of the building involve betterments. The insurance payment is less than the repair and replacement cost to the extent that such betterment (improvement in value) occurs.

It becomes immediately clear that property damage liability insurance, covering use and ownership of the business premises, is essential coverage. Given $100,000 recovery from such insurance protection, the following questions remain:

1. What about profits? The computations as made relate to cash requirements for the business only; no specific provision was made for any cash needs of the owners and their families. However, the $3,500 item for "minimum payroll" contemplates continuing the salaries of all key personnel. This certainly includes the owners. If additional money is needed for income to the owners, the figures for shortages in resources should be adjusted accordingly.

2. What is the best way to make up the $7,350 potential shortage in resources still remaining after $100,000 is received from property damage liability insurance? Assuming that additional use of credit is undesirable on the grounds of expense, uncertainty of its availability, or the general desire to avoid more debt, two sources are available: (1) contingency fund held by the business and (2) additional insurance coverage. Costs of these two sources need to be compared. The needed additional amount of money from insurance may be made available in various ways, and their costs differ. The business could carry *replacement cost* coverage on its building; it might carry *extra expense* insurance on the temporary prescription filling service; it might carry *business interruption* insurance. In a comparison of these alternatives, the following observations should be noted:

a) "Extra expense insurance" pays only the difference between the cost of conducting operations on a temporary basis and the cost of regular operations. Since the gross cost of the temporary service for filling prescriptions is estimated as $4,800, including the cost of drugs used, and $600 more is needed to reconstruct the records to use, the amount of money received under extra expense coverage might cover the $2,350 deficit in resources as compared to estimated needs, but it would be less than the $7,350 needed if the margin for error is to be provided.[20]

b) Business interruption insurance, in addition to covering unearned net profit, provides payment for continuing expenses, such as necessary payroll, necessary outlays for services and supplies, and continuing accruals (e.g., taxes and interest). It pays for extra expenses of continuing operations only to the extent that they represent a saving on the interruption claim, and the saving is taken as credit against the interruption claim. For example, if the temporary prescription service were not provided, costs would go down, but by no more than $5,400 ($4,800 plus the $600 cost of reconstructing the records). Since this expenditure produces only $5,200 of revenue *during the shutdown*, the insurer would not be willing to pay any part of the

---

[20] Note the excellent example in this case of how detailed knowledge of insurance coverages and detailed knowledge of an insured's particular operations and needs must be brought together to reach a proper solution of an insurance purchasing problem.

necessary $5,400 directly. However, the regular profit on prescription services under normal conditions would be part of the business interruption claim. Let that claim be estimated as follows:

Minimum payroll ....$ 3,500
Other costs that *continue* (not *extra* costs to preserve goodwill)* .. 1,000
Stock handling during shutdown 600
Profits lost 6,000

Total business interruption claim $11,100

* Also excluded are bills incurred prior to shutdown; these are not "continuing expenses during interruption."

c) The amount by which replacement cost insurance reduces the deficit in resources depends entirely on the excess of the cost of building reconstruction or repair over the insurance payment made under the "actual cash value" limitation in regular physical damage insurance.[21] In the illustration this amount is $5,000, which is more than the estimated deficit in resources but less than the sum of that deficit plus the allowance for estimating error. Of course, if replacement cost does not exceed the claim under actual cash value insurance, replacement cost coverage pays nothing—but the total deficit is also accordingly smaller.

d) Not all the forms of coverage described are available against all important perils. Nor are the coverages that have been described the only ones that might be used to reduce the deficit in resources. Rental value coverage, for example, would provide some proceeds on the loss.

e) The rates charged per $100 of insurance are all different on the forms that have been described, but the lowest rate does not necessarily produce the smallest premium. While the *rate* per $100 of insurance may be lower for one form of coverage than for another, the operation of coinsurance and other minimum coverage requirements in the forms may necessitate the purchase of a larger *amount* of insurance under the form with the lower rate. Hence *premiums* and not rates must be compared.

First Set of Recommendations. At this point the conclusion is that from the "insurance coverages readily available," Central Avenue Pharmacy should carry physical damage coverage against the perils of fire, explosion, windstorm, damage by aircraft, and, if there is a boiler on the premises, boiler explosion. The amount of the insurance should equal the actual cash value of the maximum potential damage. The most economical form for these coverages, other than boiler explosion, is the extended coverage en-

---

[21] Replacement cost insurance, when it is written, applies to coverage on the *building*. Practically never is it available for personal property. (Of course, inventory value is not commonly subject to deduction for depreciation anyway, so this leaves only fixtures, equipment, machinery, and other "personal property in use" subject to the problem of the discrepancy between the outlay for replacement and the insurance recovery for "actual cash value" of the old property.)

dorsement, which also includes protection against riot, damage by vehicles, and "smoke." In addition, property damage liability insurance is necessary on premises and operations, with limits at or beyond the amount of the foreseeable damage from the spread of fire or explosion. Finally, enough additional coverage to bring the insurance proceeds up to the level necessary to offset the full cost of replacing assets and continuing operations should be considered. It can be provided by any of several different forms; the choice depends on the relative premiums, the extent of the need or desire for coverage on lost profits, and, of course, any other considerations (such as amount of claims payments on less than catastrophic losses) that management thinks pertinent to its selection.

The reader is reminded that this list is not intended to represent a *complete* insurance program for this store. Not only have all losses involving personal injury or death been excluded, but so have all losses that do not involve severe physical damage to the business premises, such as the crime losses. Some few of these (e.g., dishonesty of employees) can ruin a business just as effectively as a fire, windstorm, or explosion. Furthermore, the possibilities of severe physical damage from some perils, notably collapse of water storage tanks and leakage from sprinkler systems, have been assumed not to be present *in this particular store.*

Insurance Coverages Not Readily Available. The next category to be considered is that of insurance coverages not readily available. Whether any of these coverages should be purchased if they *are* available presents no new question. The problem is no different from that of deciding whether a readily available coverage should or should not be purchased. Hard-to-get coverages, however, exhibit a greater tendency to cost more than they are worth to the insured. Therefore, they are more likely to be uneconomical and for that reason avoided. However, the risk manager must keep in mind that the value produced by an insurance policy is generally much greater than the face amount of the contract. Thus, in the event of a large loss, the value of having sufficient cash available is much greater than the amount of the cash itself because other important values (such as customer goodwill) can be saved with it. Still other benefits beyond the face amount of the policy are the auxiliary benefits described in Part II (claims handling, loss prevention services, etc.). In liability insurance an important benefit is the company's experience in defending against claims as well as its agreement to pay the costs incurred in investigating and defending them. These costs are paid "in addition to the applicable limit of liability of [the] policy."[22]

Their expense and the difficulty of getting them are not the only problems associated with non-standard and hard-to-get forms. The risk manager

---

[22] The quotation is from a standard form of liability insurance. The reader is warned, however, that some non-standard liability coverages have similar provisions and some do not. In some, the *total* of the costs of investigation and defense *plus* any sums paid to third-party claimants is subject to the policy face as a limit.

has the additional problem of determining just which of these policies to seek. When the insurance buyer is considering potential causes of serious losses to a business, it is much easier for him to run down the list of known insurance coverages and check them off as needed or not needed than it is for him to survey the premises and study the accounting records and then try to create out of his own imagination and experience a comprehensive list of important perils. This latter procedure, indeed, adds another risk to be faced: the risk of unanticipated loss through oversight, mistake, or simple lack of sufficient background and experience. Here is a real problem in problem solving. Two of the fundamental techniques for reaching solutions are to (1) ask the right questions and (2) organize the field to be covered so that it may be searched systematically. However, the immediate subject matter is deciding what to do about particular, known causes of potentially severe damage at business premises when standard forms of insurance protection are not available for them. Suppose that at Central Avenue Pharmacy the loss potentials falling in this category are those resulting from the perils of rising water, ground water, sideslip, subsidence, and war. What should be done about these perils?

If the management of this business has reason to believe that protection may be needed against the first four of these five, it probably will be unable to get insurance coverage at any price, let alone at an economical one. An exploration of other possibilities is therefore in order. Possible action includes the following: move the business to a new location; improve the footings, foundations, and drainage at the present location; lay plans for controlling flood losses (along the lines suggested in chapter 1 for a waterfront warehouse, for example); maintain a stronger cash position against uninsured losses in general; initiate or support movements to get improvements in public drainage and flood control measures. Clearly, the specific and immediate facts (or best estimates or considered guesses) will be determinant of the choice. By the rules advocated here, the best choice is the one that produces the smallest index of probability times value foregone. (Refer again to the case of the waterfront warehouse, for one specific example.) In any event, potential losses from the water and earth movements perils must be kept in mind whenever the risk manager considers how much of the *insurable* loss potential to leave uninsured. In other words, in the determination of the maximum sum of losses (over a year or other period) that is to be left uninsured, non-insurance through necessity as well as choice should be considered.

The next peril on the list for Central Avenue Pharmacy is war. Without getting involved in questions of politics, long-range forecasting, or fundamental attitudes of optimism or pessimism with regard to the ultimate effects of atomic-age warfare, an important fundamental point can be illustrated about risk management by considering the war peril. The question here has consistently been "How can we save the business?" So far, it has been a valid question. But it is not always so; sometimes the business cannot be saved, at least not by any arrangements that its management can make. In a war involving major damage in the continental United States, whether the business is to be continued following severe loss will not be up to the owners or managers of the business itself. If a choice exists, its determination will be a matter of "public policy"; whether some of the limited amount of still usable national resources should be used for the restoration of all or a part of a particular economic unit will then be a decision made and carried out by whatever authority has effective control over the police power at the time. No financial preparation that business management can now make is likely to be effective. Some loss prevention (e.g., stockpiling of essential items in underground vaults or remote areas) is theoretically possible but uneconomical unless one puts a high probability on the occurrence of a major war in the next few years.

If other perils besides war also would cause losses from which the business could not be expected to recover, then again the question "How can the business be preserved?" is the wrong question. Death and major disability of a man or woman whose personality is the principal asset of a business operation are such perils. Loss of the use of a site in an area in which the business cannot be re-established because of current zoning laws can be another example.[23] ("*Can* be" rather than "is" such an example because in some cases the business can be preserved by re-establishing operations at a different site.) In such instances, in general, the questions to be asked shift from focus on the finances of the business entity to focus on the financial positions of the individuals and families who depend on the business for their livelihood. Unfortunately, there is not room here to discuss questions of this second type.

Unrecognized Risks and Hazards

One of the banes of risk management is the "unknown hazard" or "unknown risk."[24] The meaning of the word "unknown" in these phrases shifts with context, however. At least three distinct meanings have been given to

---

[23] When areas are first zoned or when zoning rules are changed so as to be more restrictive, it is customary to allow already established operations to continue at their old sites even when they are not in conformance with the new rules. However, it is also usual to provide that if a non-conforming operation is discontinued for a specified length of time *or if the structure containing it is physically damaged beyond a certain degree*, then the non-conforming operation may *not* subsequently be re-established in the area zoned against it.

[24] As "risk" and "hazard" are not synonymous in this text, so "unknown risk" and "unknown hazard" are not synonymous. But whether the unknown fact consists of the existence of an underlying causative factor for loss (i.e., of a hazard) or the presence of a particular type of loss potential (i.e., a kind of risk), the effect and problem are the same. The difference is that the phrase "unknown hazard" suggests a need to uncover overlooked causes, while "unknown risk" tends to emphasize the need to deal with unthought-of effects.

it in practice. A hazard or risk may be said to be "unknown" if (1) it is not discernible to the mind unskilled in risk and hazard analysis; (2) it is discernible to the skilled analyst but, for one reason or another, is in fact overlooked; (3) no system of analysis is known that would necessarily cause it to be discovered even by the skilled risk analyst.

In situations such as the one under discussion—the potential of severe physical damage at Central Avenue Pharmacy—the possibility of liability for property damaged by spread of fire is a common example of an "unknown risk" of the first type. Failure to remember to consider any of the facets of risk that have been discussed (e.g., preservation of the goodwill associated with prescription filling or the finding of a source of funds to cover the difference between present value and the cost of replacement of the building) would represent an example of the second type. However, just as soon as a risk of the third type is named, it ceases to be unknown and is no longer an actual example. Nevertheless, the following true case suggests what kinds of perils may be in the third type.

A furniture store had an air vent that would not close completely. While the store was closed for a weekend, a swarm of bees entered through this vent and sometime during or after their entry their queen was killed. Loss of the queen causes a violent reaction among swarming bees. They emit a substance much like beeswax, but more viscous and sticky. The furniture on display, the fixtures and equipment, and the store interior were covered with this substance. Most of the store contents were damaged to the point where they had to be thrown away or completely rebuilt and refinished; cleaning of the building interior was a slow and expensive job. The final loss came to thousands of dollars.

Here is an example of a totally unanticipated, sizable loss that did occur. And of what aid in risk analysis is knowledge of this loss? What does it teach us with respect to risk management policy at Central Avenue Pharmacy? Only that vents should be closable and closed and that there *are* potential causes of loss that cannot be dreamed of! These causes represent the truly *unknown* hazards, create the truly unknown risks.

Dealing with Unknown Risks and Hazards. What is to be done about the truly unknown risks and hazards? The best approach to this problem is not to try to solve it but to avoid it. This means one should try to deal with risks and hazards, not on a basis of named causes or subject matter, but on the basis of over-all effect. The problem is not "If fire causes a major loss, then how are we going to recover?" but " When a major loss occurs, how are we going to recover?" How, indeed? Here is an advantage in being able to assume one's own risks, to cover one's own losses without outside help; the internal fund can be called upon without having to name in advance the cause of the call. If the furniture store in the example given above could have withstood, financially, a major loss from fire or explosion, it could have withstood the loss by bees. The principal difficulty is that immediately after the bees the fire loss may still occur. Indeed, in the factual case, in the same year as the invasion by the bees the same store suffered a major water-damage loss from defective plumbing. The ability to bear major losses depends not only upon the size of such losses but also upon their repetitiveness. Their repetitiveness depends, in part, upon the particular nature of the hazards and can be ascertained only if the hazards themselves are known. Again and again it is clear that avoidance or transfer of as many serious risks as possible is commonly essential if the *remaining* (unavoided and non-transferred) risks are to be kept within the ability of the business to bear them.

Insurance for the Unknown Risks and Hazards. Recent developments in the insurance business have broadened the possibility of risk transfer. New forms are available that, in part, do not identify the risks transferred but the risks *not* transferred. The nature of contracts of this type (generally called "all risks" but sometimes named "comprehensive" coverages) are discussed in Part V on pages 491–92. What needs to be noted here is that the rules for buying "broad form" or "all risks" or "comprehensive" coverage are no different from the rules for buying any other kind of coverage. Does the broader form provide any coverage for losses that may be large? Is the extra cost of the broader form justified for the insured? The procedure is the same as the one used in the discussion of earthquake insurance, with the following additional notes.

Broader forms often provide payment for many more small losses than large ones. This runs the cost up faster than the benefits. But benefits do increase. Suppose a particular broad form costs 55 cents additional per $100 of insurance. Claims payments on small losses will reduce the net cost of the coverage of large losses. It is difficult to tell how much, but typically most of the premium will be for smaller losses. Assume 90 per cent, or 49.5 cents of the 55 cents. At a loss-to-premium ratio of 50 per cent (this ratio is lower for small losses than for large ones), 24.75 cents of the 55 cents will be returned, "in the long run," on small claims if the insured is "average." If the insured is careful of his property or if he does not file all his small claims, the figure will be smaller. On the grounds that risk managers who are informed enough to make such calculations are also informed enough not to have a large number of small claims against their insurance, the 24.75-cent figure can be cut, say, to 20 cents. This leaves a cost of 35 cents per $100 that must be justified by the important losses. If every dollar paid on large losses saves 2 dollars of business values, the frequency rate of large claims must be at least equal to the ratio of 35 cents to 50 dollars (or 7/1,000) to justify the additional premium for the broader coverage. Considering that the frequency of major fires is only about 3/1,000, a figure of 7/1,000 is not a low frequency rate for large losses. Therefore, large losses that are covered only by the broader forms ought to be of types with which many existing businesses have had experience. Water damage may be one of such perils; insurance companies and their representatives should be able to furnish other examples relevant to a particular insurance policy.

It is worth noting again that there is a risk of being unable to name all the possibilities, and this risk has its own disutility. Broader insurance forms should reduce this risk.

Finally, the reader is reminded that a major purpose of intelligent risk management is to get (and keep) static risks under regular administrative control so that top operating management can be left free to concentrate on problems that offer profit potential, that is, on the speculative risks. Purchase of insurance protection against some of the unknown (unidentifiable) hazards should further this purpose *if* there is a possibility that the broader protection may be called upon to pay for losses of significant size.

SUMMARY

This has been a chapter on "how to," by examples. In the beginning, the point was made that adequate generalization about specific, practical actions to be taken in specific, real cases is difficult, if not impossible. It follows that this is also true of summarization. However, specifics in particular instances can be reviewed and the points they illustrate brought again to mind.

Two Limited Loss Examples

Two examples of problems in physical damage loss involving goods in transportation were presented. Since these goods were away from the main business premises, physical damage to them would not commonly involve physical damage to the other property of the business, and in that sense these losses could be considered limited. However, since these physical damage losses could cause damage to the goodwill of the business, in another sense these losses would not be limited and could become important enough to be of concern.

In each example, the first things considered were the dimensions of the problem: loss frequency and the effect of the loss. Immediate consideration was given to the question whether these were as small as they should be. Could either size or frequency be reduced, and, if so, was reduction worthwhile? Answering these questions required estimation of the ultimate loss effect before and after additional effort was expended at loss prevention (the difference in effect was called "value saved") and the estimation of the probability that this loss would in fact occur. The value saved times the probability of the loss was then compared with the cost of achieving the saving. Important to the measurement of the ultimate loss effect was a comparison of the size of the dollar outlay required after a loss with the amount of resources available to the business after the loss. As the required outlay grew in relation to resources available, the significance of the loss became greater and greater—and this independently of the probability of the loss.

In one example (the decorating firm), risk transference was a major question, and the general process of reaching a decision was the same: the effect of loss times the probability of loss, compared with the related cost of the operation (transference or non-transference).

In each example, management's attitude toward risk entered the picture, but only as a guide toward solution. In one case, it was the means to uncovering the problem (management was worried about risk of a high loss rate in its mail shipments); in the other, it was introduced as a guide toward making a decision when other means did not clearly indicate a particular solution.

Major Loss

When a problem in major loss was considered, the first steps were the same in general but considerably different in detail. It was assumed—implicitly but realistically—that minimization of the loss called for re-establishment of the business rather than its demise. Other possibilities of loss prevention or reduction were noted more explicitly. The final loss figure was compared with resources in order to find the size of the problem.

To shorten the discussion and eliminate unnecessary exposition, the resources were assumed initially to include the kinds of physical damage insurance most businesses already carry. (But the *amounts* assumed to be carried—100 per cent of present insurable value—were higher than most businesses actually carry.) From there the discussion went on to consider what other resources were available and whether they should be used.

Finally, the problem of "he who knows not his hazards, and knows not that he knows them not" was touched upon. Three suggestions were made with respect to it: (1) Organize the study of the exposure as well as possible. (2) Try, as far as possible, to have a program of insurance (or, for that matter, of any and all risk management devices) arranged so as to minimize the need for knowledge of the specifics of risk exposures. (3) In planning non-insurance, remember the possibilities of the unknown and the uninsurable risks as well as the voluntarily uninsured ones.

REVIEW AND DISCUSSION QUESTIONS

1. Change the figures given in the text for the shipping exposure of the specialty foods retailer to the following:
   (a) The cost of replacing merchandise is 75 per cent of sales price.
   (b) Replacement of merchandise is used as settlement for 45 per cent of all claims; refunds for the rest.
   (c) The cost of handling each claim is $4.50.
   (d) The average sale is $25.00, and all costs except loss and risk costs connected with the sale (cost of goods, sales, overhead, etc.) average $23.00.
   (e) Ratio of claims to number of sales over the past two years has been 1.5

per cent, based on shipments totaling 30,000 packages, with observations taken on a monthly basis. The smallest number of shipments in any one month was 400, and the highest was 1,800 distributed as follows:

No. Times in Two Years	No. Shipments in Month	Probability That Loss Rate Would Reach or Exceed 2% with This No. of Shipments
Two months...............	400	.2062
Four months...............	800	.1230
Sixteen months	1400	.06178
Two months...............	1800	.04006

(*f*) Goodwill loss cost at a 1.5 per cent claims rate is too small to worry about but the possibility that the loss rate during some period (a month or more) might jump significantly above this rate does worry management.

(*g*) The average loss rate could be cut by a third by spending $4,000 a year on loss prevention. (When average rate is 1 per cent, the probability that the loss rate on 400 shipments would reach or exceed 2 per cent is .02222; on 800 shipments, this probability is .002256; on 1,400 shipments, the figure is .00008842; on 1,800 shipments, .00001022.)

Using the above figures show (*a*) whether the shipping exposure risk should be assumed by the specialty foods retailer and (*b*) whether the $4,000 expenditure should be undertaken for loss prevention.

2. Suppose that an after-the-loss advertising campaign, costing $4,000, could reduce the goodwill loss by $10,000 for the specialty foods retailer. What plans, if any, should he make to have this $4,000 available? Explain precisely how you reached your conclusions.

3. A local chain of specialty dress shops has five locations, one in the downtown shopping area and four in neighborhood shopping centers. These shops each have four show windows. What information should the risk manager have in order to reach a decision on whether to insure the glass panes against loss or damage? Assume a set of facts that would suggest that the risk be insured. What set of facts would suggest that the risk be assumed?

4. In the case of *La Vie Moderne*, a decision had to be made on the trucking method to be employed in the transportation of its furniture for delivery. What considerations other than those of risk management are involved in reaching a final decision? What formula would you use in weighing these considerations in arriving at a decision?

5. Change the figures given in the text for the delivery exposure of the *La Vie Moderne* interior decorators to read as follows:

(*a*) *Major* damage to van-loads handled by outside truckers occurs on the average of 18 times in 10 years of which 2 of the times the damage is a result of accident to the truck. The other 16 result from mishandling of contents. The 10-year frequency for reparable losses is 250.

(*b*) When the trucks and drivers are hired and the decorator's men handle the merchandise the results are 10 *major* losses in 10 years of which only 2 result from the mishandling of the contents. The 10-year frequency for reparable losses is 300.

(*c*) The loss rate on owned vehicle is 6 *major* losses in 10 years of which only 2 result from the mishandling of contents. The 10-year frequency for reparable losses is 50.

(*d*) Major damage averages $5,000 for direct loss and $10,000 for indirect loss. Reparable damage losses average $275.

(*e*) The fees of a public delivery company would be $9,500 a year.

(*f*) The estimated cost (excluding losses) of operating a sufficient number of owned vans is $12,000 a year.

(*g*) The rental cost of chauffeur-driven vehicles with employees of *La Vie Moderne* controlling operations would be $11,000 a year.

Using the above figures along with the other assumptions given in the text, select the trucking method that should be used.

6. What is the *maximum* loss potential per year when the trucking method selected in question 5 is used? What is the significance of this figure (or, if it has no significance, why not)?

7. Why is insurance part of the best solution to *La Vie Moderne*'s transit risk? Why is it particularly important that *La Vie Moderne* have an *especially* qualified agent or broker to arrange this insurance?

8. When the cost of insurance against major damage (direct costs only) is included in the calculations made in question 5, would the results affect the decisions made there?

9. Explain the importance of the following statement to risk management decision making: "Opinion without facts can be dangerous, but facts without opinions are useless."

10. How can a peril reduce the value of a firm's physical assets to below zero?

11. "A windstorm or earthquake could, of course, involve both the store and the office of the outside bookkeeping firm. . . . A judgment decision has been made here that the circumstances warrant ignoring such possibilities." What factors do you think were considered (or at least should have been considered) in making the judgment decision referred to in the above quotation?

12. How might questions of operating or sales efficiency be resolved in a way that will lead to a reduction of risk management efficiency? How might risk management efficiency improve operating and sales efficiency?

13. The Bickley Cleaners operate a local dry cleaning establishment with its plant and office located in a building on the edge of a major shopping center. The company does a cash and carry business, a pick up and delivery business, and operates a few coin do-it-yourself dry cleaning machines at its one location. What plans can the Bickley Cleaners lay to preserve customer shopping habits and goodwill following a major physical damage to the company's assets? In making decisions among alternative plans, or between a plan and no plan at all, what factors should the Bickley Cleaners take into consideration?

14. To what extent can the same perils which cause major physical damage to the assets of the Bickley Cleaners also cause the Bickley Cleaners to be a defendant in a liability suit for damage to property of others? How should this possibility affect risk management activities of Bickley Cleaners?

15. To what extent can the same perils which cause major physical damage to the assets of the Bickley Cleaners also cause the Bickley Cleaners to suffer losses of key personnel? What effect should this possibility have on this company's risk management activities?

16. In discussing the Central Avenue Pharmacy case, the text says: ". . . it will be assumed that Central Avenue Pharmacy is already cleanly and safely operated so that it has no opportunities to improve its current acceptability

to underwriters." Do you consider this assumption to be commonly valid? Explain your answer.

17. The text discusses exposures in relation to insurance covers under the following categories:

    I. Standard forms of insurance readily available
       A. Their purchase is advisable without question.
       B. Many businessmen have some question about the advisability of their purchase.
    II. Standard forms of insurance are not readily available
       A. Non-standard forms may be obtained in the special coverage markets.
       B. No coverage is obtainable.

    With respect to the exposures of the Bickley Cleaners, what insurance covers would you classify in each of the above categories? Why?

18. How would you arrive at the amounts of insurance to be purchased under those forms of insurance falling in Class I A (see question 17)?

19. Show how the Bickley Cleaners can use the formula $X < pZ + U$ to determine whether it should purchase earthquake insurance.

20. Explain by use of an illustration how detailed knowledge of insurance coverages, rates and premiums, and an insured's particular operations and needs can be brought together to reach a proper solution of an insurance purchasing problem. In answering this question, be sure to indicate the nature of the insurance purchasing problem posed.

21. What problems do risk managers have in dealing with non-standard and hard-to-get forms? What techniques are available for handling these problems?

22. What role should non-insurance through necessity play in reaching a decision on non-insurance through choice?

23. With reference to the Bickley Cleaners, illustrate three meanings of the word "unknown" when used in conection with an "unknown risk or hazard." What can the risk manager do about the *truly* unknown hazards and risks?

24. What factors should the risk manager consider in reaching a decision on whether to purchase broad forms of insurance protection?

PART V

Insurance and Risk Management

Commercial insurance coverage frequently is the appropriate device for managing risks. Risk managers, therefore, must gain sufficient understanding of the business of insurance to purchase insurance intelligently. This requires study of the insurance product and of the companies that underwrite it. Part V includes six chapters. Four are devoted to the insurance product, and two to insurance companies and their sales organizations. These six chapters present the absolute minimum insurance knowledge required of the risk manager if he is to show some degree of sophistication in his dealings with insurance salesmen, agents, and brokers.

Chapter 12

THE FIELDS OF INSURANCE

The *Agent's and Buyer's Guide*[1] names and describes over six hundred insurance coverages, starting with the abattoir bond and ending with yacht and motor boat insurance. After each coverage, the *Guide* inserts one or more of the following initials: F, C, M, IM, S, L, or A & H. These indicate the branch of the insurance business to which the coverage commonly belongs. The branches represented by the initials are fire, casualty, marine, inland marine, surety, life, and accident and health. Coverages that are considered multiple line are followed by the letters ML. Some coverages, like automobile collision and accounts receivable, are followed by more than one letter to indicate that they may be written by more than one branch.

The more than six hundred coverages listed in the *Agent's and Buyer's Guide* are classified in the Insurance Law of New York into twenty specific kinds of insurance. These coverages, as shown in Figure 12–1, are grouped into three fields of insurance: life, fire, and casualty. Until July 1, 1949, fire insurers doing business in New York State were authorized to write only fire and marine insurance; casualty insurers could write only casualty and surety insurance; and life insurers could write only life and health insurance. Beginning with July 1, 1949, fire and casualty insurers writing in New York were allowed multiple line underwriting powers, which meant that all forms of insurance except life could be issued by one insurer if that insurer satisfied the minimum capital and surplus requirements established for multiple line insurers in that state.

However, while the general privilege to use full multiple line underwriting powers is now well over a decade old, exploitation of the privilege is still in the exploration state. Monoline forms of behavior and habits of thought were too thoroughly ingrained in insurance company operations for much revolution. Furthermore, practical insurance operation rests on the use of past experience to estimate the future, and there was, of course, little multiple line experience on which to base estimations of premium

---

[1] An annual yearbook published by the National Underwriter Company, Cincinnati, Ohio.

needs and underwriting requirements for truly multiple line insurance protection. Therefore, not only are the old monoline policy forms still a prominent feature of the insurance scene, but the newer multiple line experiments are strongly grounded on and modeled after the familiar monoline approaches. It follows that risk managers, along with other students of insurance, need to be well acquainted with and to understand the old monoline tradition as well as the recent changes in it.

SEPARATION OF UNDERWRITING POWERS

The great New York fire of 1835 is credited (or charged) with furnishing the impetus that ultimately led to the principle of separation of underwriting powers. This fire, which continued for three days, eliminated the 648 buildings forming the major portion of the business district of New York City. Under the impact of the loss, which was estimated at $18 million, all but 3 of the 26 insurance companies in New York State were thrown into bankruptcy. The great Chicago fire of 1871, which destroyed two thirds of the city's buildings, created more supporters for the philosophy of the separation of underwriting powers. In a barn located in the area that nearly a century later was to house the University of Illinois at Congress Circle, Chicago, Cow O'Leary allegedly kicked over a lamp that started a fire responsible for $190 million in property losses, of which about $100 million was insured by 202 fire insurance companies. Only 51 of these companies were able to pay their claims in full; 83 were successful in negotiating partial settlements; and 68 experienced bankruptcy.

The Rationale

The rationale of the separation of underwriting powers was based in part on the notion that "life insurance particularly is a specialty; and the accumulated funds which are held by a company for a life-time as a savings bank, in sacred trust for the widow and orphan, should never be liable to be swept away by a storm at sea or a conflagration on land."[2] Furthermore, the regulatory authorities and the companies themselves considered the combination of unlike covers by a single company a threat to the safe underwriting of the old and proved lines of insurance. They feared, for example, that the security purchased by fire insurance policyholders (and the investment made by stockholders) would be endangered by company experiments in new and untried lines. It was generally agreed that the interests of both the insuring and the investing public could best be served by restricting companies to specific lines of insurance so that these companies could grow skillful in handling their specialized lines. Separation of underwriting powers was believed necessary, also, to keep the insurance business from becom-

---

[2] *First Annual Report of the Insurance Department of the State of New York*, March 1, 1860.

FIGURE 12–1

CLASSIFICATION OF INSURERS AND INSURANCE COVERAGES IN NEW YORK*

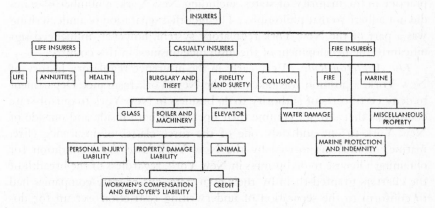

* In addition to these coverages, the New York law makes provisions for title insurance and property depreciation insurance (see n. 13).

ing concentrated in a few giant corporations, and this was thought to be in the general public interest. It was further argued that state regulation of insurance is simplified by the system of monoline underwriting.

The Opposition. The rationale of monoline underwriting did not go unchallenged. Many arguments were advanced for multiple line underwriting, not the least of which was its success abroad. Multiple line companies were able to offer the insurance buyer the protection he needed without impairing the safety of the companies; diversified activity decreased rather than increased the risk because a poor loss record in one line could be offset by good experience in other lines. Furthermore, multiple line companies were able to operate more efficiently; overhead costs could be spread over more coverages. As for state regulation, advocates of multiple line underwriting did not accept the argument that a workable solution to the complicated regulatory problems associated with multiple line could not be found. In fact, several suggested solutions were made, such as increasing the capital and surplus requirements, adding a contingency reserve requirement, and changing the annual form upon which companies are required to report their financial condition to the states. The forms could be made to include whatever additional information the regulators needed to perform their jobs.

Monoline insurance is strictly American: born, bred, and dead. The history of the rise and fall of monoline underwriting provides important background for the understanding of the American insurance industry. For reasons soon to become apparent, our brief historical excursion will be confined to the state of New York.

Separation of Underwriting Powers in New York

While for many years the separation of underwriting powers was the practice in the majority of states, including New York, a number of states did not adhere to that philosophy. The fact that separation of underwriting was a part of the New York regulatory system, however, influenced significantly the development of the insurance business in this country.

The Appleton Rule. Very early in the insurance regulatory history of New York, a position was taken by the New York Insurance Department to deny certificates of authority to do business in New York to out-of-state companies that did not confine their operations both inside and outside of New York to one and only one of the three classes of insurance (fire, marine, or life) authorized by the New York law.[3] As a condition for obtaining a license to do business in New York, regardless of the breadth of the charters granted them by their own state, out-of-state companies had to conform to the separation of underwriting restrictions set up for domestic insurance companies. This position, taken in 1860 by the superintendent of insurance in New York, was the forerunner of what was later to become the "Appleton Rule," named after Henry D. Appleton, deputy superintendent (later acting superintendent) of insurance in New York. At the turn of the century, Appleton ruled that the New York insurance law was extra-territorial in its application. New York companies must abide by the New York insurance code in their operations outside New York, and out-of-state insurance companies licensed in New York must accept the underwriting restrictions placed on New York companies wherever they operated. The Appleton Rule eventually was written into the statute and now appears as paragraphs 3, 4, and 5 of section 42 of the 1940 New York Insurance Code.[4]

Paragraph 5 of section 42 is further evidence of the impact that the New York Insurance Law could have on the insurance business in this country. It reads:

Except as otherwise specifically provided in this chapter no foreign insurer and no United States branch of an alien insurer shall be or continue to be authorized to do an insurance business in this state if it fails to comply substantially with any requirement or limitation of this chapter, applicable to similar domestic in-

---

[3] Circular No. 4 issued by the New York Superintendent of Insurance in 1860.

[4] The Appleton Rule was solely an administrative ruling until legislative action was taken in 1939 to put it into the 1940 insurance code. Before that time only an 1862 law made reference to out-of-state companies on the question of multiple line writings. That law read: "No company, partnership, or association, organized or incorporated by or under the laws of this *or any foreign government* transacting the business of life insurance in this state, shall be permitted or allowed to take any other kind of risks except those connecting with or appertaining to making insurance on life . . ." (italics added). (*New York Laws of 1862*, chap. 300). It should be noted that, in state law, other states of the United States are "foreign." Governments outside the United States are referred to as "alien."

surers hereafter to be organized, which in the judgment of the superintendent is reasonably necessary to protect the interests of the people of this state.

Thus, what was considered good (or bad) for domestic companies in their New York operations also was considered good (or bad) for them in their out-of-state operations. And, what was considered good (or bad) for foreign and alien corporations in their operations in New York State was also considered good (or bad) for them in their operations elsewhere. Since many of the important companies organized outside New York wished to operate in the big New York market, even at the expense of giving up some of the rights granted to them under their domestic charters, the importance of the New York code in shaping the American insurance scene is apparent.

All Lines to Monolines. Until about the middle of the nineteenth century, insurance companies in New York were incorporated directly by the state legislature under special charters. A number of individual companies were issued charters to write all lines of insurance then written (life, fire, and marine), but many of these companies restricted their writings to one line. In 1849 a general insurance act was passed under which companies could be chartered to write fire and marine insurance, either or both, but not life and health insurance. This act also provided for the chartering of companies to write life and health insurance, either or both, but not fire and marine insurance. Thus no company could be chartered to combine fire and marine insurance with life and health insurance. The insurance business in New York, therefore, became separated by law into two mutually exclusive classes.

A further separation of underwriting powers came in 1853 with the enactment of the Fire Insurance Companies Act and the Life and Health Insurance Companies Act. Under the Fire Insurance Companies Act, the fire insurance companies were restricted to the writing of fire insurance and insurance on inland navigation. They were not allowed to write ocean marine insurance. The Life and Health Insurance Act restricted the writings of these companies either to (*a*) life insurance and annuities or to (*b*) health insurance on individuals and insurance on the lives of livestock, but not both (*a*) and (*b*). As a result of the Acts of 1853, the insurance business in New York became separated into four mutually exclusive classes: fire and inland marine, ocean marine, life, and health.

The Genesis of New Coverages. The General Insurance Act of 1849 and the Fire Insurance Companies and Life and Health Insurance Companies Acts of 1853 made provisions for the then existing types of insurance written in this country. When additional types of coverages were demanded by the public to offset newly discovered risks, the laws had to be amended to grant underwriting powers to companies to meet the legitimate needs. In some cases, the underwriting powers of fire insurance companies were broadened to include more perils, property, and losses. Many of these new coverages came to be known as "allied lines" or "inland marine lines."

In other cases, in which the legislature (and in some instances the companies themselves) believed the new exposures to be too foreign to the fields of fire and inland marine insurance, the Life and Health Insurance Companies Act was expanded to allow for these coverages. These new coverages came to be known as casualty and surety forms, and the term "casualty" eventually was added to the title of the Life and Health Insurance Companies Act as another separate class of insurance covered under the act.

From Monoline to Multiple Line. New York moved from all lines underwriting to multiple line underwriting in 1849 and from multiple line to monoline in 1853. From 1853 to 1949 the slow trek back to multiple line underwriting was made, with intermediate stops in 1892, to reunite life and health insurance, and in 1910, to give fire insurers marine underwriting powers.[5] Along the way, casualty insurance was picked up as a new traveling companion, eventually producing the "traditional" threesome.[6] The threesome became a twosome in 1949, when the urge to merge fire and casualty underwriting was sufficiently importunate. The next step in the completion of the long journey home is to all lines underwriting. At the present time, however, it seems that this journey will have to be taken over heavily mined roads, at least in New York. The next few pages narrate the story in miniature of the emergence of new coverages and of the rebirth of multiple line underwriting as told to us by the insurance laws of New York.

The Fire Insurance Companies Act. The Fire Insurance Companies Act of 1853 allowed fire insurance companies "to make insurance on dwelling houses, stores, and all kinds of buildings, and upon household furniture and other property, against loss or damage by fire, and the risks of inland navigation and transportation." The act was amended a number of times to add additional property, perils, and losses. The list of subjects insurable against the risks of inland navigation and transportation was expanded in 1861 to include vessels, boats, cargoes, goods, merchandise, other property, and freights.[7] Automobiles and aircraft were later added in 1908 and 1919, respectively. The list of insurable perils was gradually lengthened throughout the years to include lightning (1880); windstorm and tornado (1882); earthquake (1907); water damage, sprinkler leakage, and ocean marine perils (1910); cyclone, hail, frost, snow, and explosion (1913); invasion, insurrection, riot, civil war, commotion, usurped power, and bombardment (1917); vandalism and malicious mischief, weather or climatic conditions, including excess or deficiency of moisture, flood, rain or drought, rising of the waters of the ocean or its tributaries, and loss or damage by insects or disease to farm crops or products (1920); loss by aircraft (1930); loss by

---

[5] In 1888, life insurers were given accident insurance powers. Not until 1917 were fire underwriting powers given to marine insurance companies.

[6] Life (including health), fire (including marine), and casualty (including surety).

[7] In marine terminology, "freight" is the charge for carriage, not the property being carried.

vehicles and smoke and smudge damage (1932); and, finally, at long last, volcanic eruption (1938).[8]

The types of losses mentioned in the Fire Insurance Companies Act also expanded. Fire insurance companies were given the right in 1911 to insure against legal liability for damage to property resulting from the maintenance or use of automobiles. Coverage against loss from inability to use or occupy premises was specifically provided for in 1913. The right to insure against legal liability for property damage arising from the maintenance or use of aircraft was granted in 1919. (Note that fire insurance companies could provide protection against liability for property damage caused by automobiles or aircraft, but not for bodily injury caused by them.) Loss of rental value of land used in producing farm crops or other products that have been lost or damaged by insects or disease was included in 1920. With the recodification of the insurance law in 1939, the authority to write consequential loss was spelled out carefully. That law stated: "The power to do any kind of insurance against loss of or damage to property shall include the power to insure all lawful interests in such property and to insure against loss of use and occupancy, rents and profits resulting therefrom but no kind of insurance shall be deemed to include . . . insurance against legal liability for personal injury or death unless specified therein."

With but few exceptions, the expanding list of perils, property, and losses insurable by fire insurers was not considered to be a trend toward multiple line underwriting because all of these new coverages were "fire" lines. Not until 1910 was there any move in the direction of multiple line underwriting with respect to fire insurance. It will be recalled that marine insurance and fire insurance were disunited in 1853, with the thought that never the twain should meet. A reunion of the twain was made possible, however, in 1910, when fire insurers were given ocean marine underwriting powers. Another multiple line underwriting mark was made in 1917 when marine insurance companies were given fire underwriting powers.

The Life, Health, and Casualty Act. Under the Life and Health Insurance Companies Act of 1853, underwriting powers were divided into two departments: *first*, "to make insurance upon the lives of individuals and every insurance appertaining thereto or connected therewith, and to grant, purchase, or dispose of annuities" and, *second*, "to make insurance upon the health of individuals, and upon the lives of horses, cattle, and other livestock." The 1853 act allowed companies to write insurance in either department, but not in both. Amendments to the act involved principally the second department. In 1865 that department was broadened to include "guaranteeing the fidelity of persons holding places of public or private trust" and "loss, damage or liability arising from any unknown or con-

---

[8] The fact that insurance against a peril is permitted does not mean that it will actually be written, of course.

tingent event whatever which may be the subject of legal insurance except the perils and risks included within the departments of fire, marine, and life insurance."

As mentioned, the term "casualty insurance" was added to the title of the act in 1879, and the underwriting powers under the second department were again amended. Companies operating under this department (casualty) could "make any of the following kinds of insurance: First, upon the health of persons; second, against injury, disablement or death of persons resulting from traveling or general accidents by land or water; third, guaranteeing the fidelity of persons holding places of public or private trust; fourth, upon the lives of horses, cattle and other livestock; fifth, upon plate glass against breakage; sixth, upon steam boilers against explosion,[9] and against loss or damage to life or property resulting therefrom; seventh, against loss by burglary or theft or both." The heterogeneity of the coverages included in the second department is similar to the hodgepodge written by fire insurance companies. Some of the coverages are classified as to peril (sickness, accident, crime, and steam boiler explosion), whereas others are based on property (horses, livestock, and plate glass).

The 1879 amendment retained the segregation of underwriting powers between the first department (life and annuities) and the second department. In addition, underwriting powers were further segregated in the second department. No company organized after the effective date of the act was allowed to "undertake to do more than one of the several kinds of insurance mentioned in the second department." Thus, a monoline approach was taken with respect to the individual coverages within the life, casualty, and surety branches of the business. A breach in this thinking took place in 1888, when life insurance companies were allowed to write accident insurance, and again in 1892, when the first and second departments as such were discarded and replaced by a list of coverages. This list included eight subdivisions:

1. Life, health, and annuities
2. Accidental injury, disablement, or death
3. Employer's and bodily injury liability
4. Fidelity and surety
5. Burglary and theft
6. Plate glass
7. Boiler and machinery (physical damage, liability, and inspection)
8. Any other casualty specified in the charter which may lawfully be the subject of insurance

Under the 1892 law, companies writing insurance in subdivision 1 were allowed to write the kinds of insurance specified in subdivisions 2 and 3. Companies not writing in subdivision 1 were allowed to write in any or all of the remaining seven subdivisions (2–8).

---

[9] Pipes, engines, and machines were added by an amendment in 1889. Also added in that year was the making of inspections.

Thus, in 1888 and 1892 two moves toward multiple line underwriting were taken; life insurers were given accident and then sickness and certain liability underwriting powers, and "general writing" casualty companies again could be chartered. The 1892 law made no progress toward multiple line policies, however, because it prohibited companies from combining in one policy coverages from more than one subdivision, with one exception —policies could be issued combining coverage in subdivisions 2 and 3.

Amendments to the Life, Health, and Casualty Insurance Companies Act were frequent until the recodification of the insurance law in 1939. These amendments expanded the list of perils, property, losses, and hazards that casualty insurers could be chartered to underwrite. Perils added were sickness (1901),[10] damage by flywheels (1910), damage by accidental discharge of sprinkler systems and fire extinguishing apparatus (1912), and forgery (1913). Property added included automobile collision (1907), theft of livestock and horses (1911), damage to sprinkler equipment and elevators (1914), damage to aircraft (1919), and all-perils coverage for merchandise owned by or held by jewelers (1925).[11] Types of losses expanded were credit (1899),[12] use and occupancy for boiler and machinery insurance (1910), and use and occupancy for sprinkler leakage insurance (1914). The types of hazards added were automobile liability (1907), horse and horse and wagon liability (1910), elevator liability (1914), comprehensive crime coverage for banks (1915), aircraft liability (1919), and professional liability (1926).

Insurance Law of 1939: Recodification. The insurance law of New York was recodified in 1939. The kinds of insurance that could be authorized in the state were enumerated and defined in section 46. In other sections of the code, special laws were set up for life insurers, fire and marine insurers, and casualty and surety insurers.[13] The list of coverages contained in

---

[10] Until 1879, health insurance could be included in the charters of general writing casualty insurers. From 1879 to 1892 only monoline health insurance companies could be chartered for this coverage. Between 1892 and 1901, only life insurers (or monoline insurers) could be chartered to underwrite health insurance. Since 1901, health insurance could be included in the charters of life, general writing casualty, or monoline companies.

[11] The Jeweler's Block policy is discussed later in this chapter. Coverage could be offered not only for physical damage but also for loss of use and liability. Casualty companies, however, left the Jeweler's Block to the fire and marine insurance companies.

[12] The law was amended in 1906 to prohibit granting charters to new general writing casualty companies to write credit insurance. Only monoline credit insurance companies could be chartered after that date until the law was again revised, returning these powers to general writing companies.

[13] Special laws were set up also for title insurers and property depreciation insurance. Title insurance is defined in the law as the insuring against loss by reason of defective titles to real property and against encumbrances thereon. In practice, title insurers provide an investigational service, principally, and guarantee the correctness of the research. Property depreciation insurance is defined as insurance against total or partial depreciation of buildings and machinery (including loss of use) existing at the expiration of the term of insurance or occurring prior to the expiration of the term of the insurance if

section 46 included the nineteen kinds of insurance outlined in Figure 12–1. Figure 12–1 also shows what types of insurance could be underwritten by life insurers, casualty insurers, and fire insurers. The following overlaps are easily noted: health insurance could be written by both life and casualty companies, and water damage and collision insurance were authorized to be written by both casualty and fire insurers. At noted, these nineteen kinds of insurance were defined specifically in the law. A review of a few of these definitions will reveal other areas in which the underwriting powers of fire and casualty insurance companies overlapped. "Motor vehicle and aircraft insurance" is listed as a fire coverage, but its definition includes "legal liability of the insured for loss or damage to the property of another." This overlaps with "property damage liability insurance," which is a casualty coverage. Included in the definition of "miscellaneous property insurance," a group of coverages authorized for fire insurers, are vandalism and malicious mischief. These perils are also included under the definition of burglary and theft insurance, which is a field authorized for casualty insurers. In addition, the miscellaneous property class includes steam boiler insurance to be written on a restricted basis. This overlaps with boiler and machinery insurance, a class restricted to casualty insurers. These overlaps were not a direct result of the 1939 law but developed as the original 1853 acts were amended throughout the years. The 1939 law made no changes in who could write what; it simply rearranged the written form of the law. All kinds of insurance were named in one section, and other sections were written to define the underwriting powers of life and health insurance companies, casualty and surety insurance companies, and fire and marine insurance companies.

The Diemand Committee. Separation of underwriting powers never met universal acceptance among the American insurance cognoscenti. Among those speaking out against it were prominent people in insurance regulation, management, and education.[14] Of course, others equally prominent defended the monoline concept and were for many years predominant. But finally their arguments became overworked and worn out. In face of sound arguments for change, those who seek to preserve the status quo eventually find their positions untenable. And that is precisely the story of the life of the monoliners.

In 1943 Charles Harrington was president of the National Association

---

resulting from sinking; subsoil water; dry-rot fungus; dampness of rooms; cracks in ceilings, supporting walls, or pillars; leakage in roofing or bursting of water pipes caused by deterioration; or by damage to the buildings resulting from causes other than those insurable by fire and casualty insurance companies. This coverage is called "property life insurance." Although provided for in the New York insurance code, it has never been written in the United States.

[14] A review of the names in the multiple line development can be found in D. L. Bickelhaupt, *Transition to Multiple Line Insurance Companies* (Homewood, Illinois: Richard D. Irwin, Inc., 1961), pp. 18–41.

of Insurance Commissioners. He appointed a new subcommittee of the Laws and Legislation Committee. This Subcommittee on Multiple Line Underwriting marked the beginning of the end of the monoline underwriting system. It was an eight-man committee composed of representatives of fire, casualty, and marine insurance companies, charged with the responsibility of investigating whether the public interest would best be served by extending fire and marine underwriting powers to casualty insurers and casualty underwriting powers to fire and marine insurers. The president of the Insurance Company of North America, John A. Diemand, an ardent supporter of multiple line underwriting, was made chairman of the committee. The committee is known either as the Harrington committee or, by its sparkling name, the Diemand committee.

Since the issue before the committee was controversial and the interests involved transcended those of the public, a great deal of compromising took place. This is indicated by both the unanimity in the 1944 report and the contents of that report. The report, like all products of compromise, did not fully satisfy either the monoliners or the multiple-liners. For each side, it was a tie ballgame.

The committee recommended the granting of only partial multiple line underwriting powers, advising the following extensions: Multiple line underwriting should be authorized on all business written outside the country and on *all* reinsurance business accepted, companies should be allowed to combine fire and casualty underwriting powers with respect to automobile and aircraft insurance so that the physical damage and bodily injury liability coverage could be written in one company, and multiple line underwriting should be permitted in the insuring of all non-business personal property so that the personal property floater could be written by either fire or casualty companies. An improved competitive position for American companies in foreign markets, expansion of the American reinsurance market, and better facilities for serving automobile, aircraft, and non-business personal property owners were offered as support for the recommendations. The recommendations stopped short of correcting what New York's superintendent of insurance twenty years earlier had believed was a "tendency on the part of those responsible for the laws to tell business interests what kinds of insurance coverages they may have rather than to provide the kinds of insurance that legitimate business needs."[15]

The recommendations of the Diemand Committee were eventually adopted in New York. Multiple line reinsurance and the multiple line personal property floater were sanctioned in 1946, whereas multiple line international business and multiple line automobile and aircraft coverages were authorized in 1947, effective January 1, 1948.

---

[15] *New York Insurance Report*, 1923, Part I, p. 15.

The Diemand committee was discharged in 1948, but in the year prior to dismissal the committee had recommended that both fire and casualty insurers be given multiple line underwriting powers to issue to home-owners policies uniting fire, theft, and liability coverages in one policy. The National Association of Insurance Commissioners agreed to study this suggestion.

Chapter 667, Laws of 1949. On July 1, 1949, fire, marine, and casualty insurers were authorized in New York to write all kinds of insurance except life, annuities, property depreciation, and title insurance. Whether a company can take advantage of multiple line underwriting depends upon its financial position. To acquire multiple line powers, a capital stock company was required to have a minimum capital and surplus of $3,550,000 and to maintain a continuing capital and surplus of $2,200,000.[16] The New York requirements are the severest, with those of New Jersey ($3,000,000) running a close second. The minimum capital and surplus requirements run all the way down to the $100,000 established in Ohio and Vermont.[17]

All Lines Underwriting. The legal wall between fire and casualty insurance crumbled with the passage of multiple line underwriting legislation. Only the partition between life insurance and non-life insurance remains.[18] Whether this wall eventually will tumble depends upon the amount of pressure put on it by insurers and insureds, especially by those who can convince the legislators that the public interest would best be served by granting all lines underwriting power to a single insurer under a single charter. Some leaders in both insurance company administration and insurance education expect this last major partition to be removed. For example, we find a company forecasting that eligible companies ultimately will be given all lines underwriting powers[19] and an educator foreseeing that personal insurance contracts issued a few years hence will include not only fire and casualty coverages but also health and life cover-

---

[16] In New York, stock companies wishing to restrict their business to casualty and surety coverages were required to have a minimum capital and surplus of $2,700,000 upon authorization (with only $1.8 million required for continuing in business after establishment). Stock companies organized to do a fire and marine insurance business were required to have a minimum capital and surplus of $1 million ($500,000 continuing). Specialty stock companies organized to write just one kind of casualty, workmen's compensation, for example, were required to have an initial capital and surplus of $375,-000 ($250,000 continuing) or $725,000 ($450,000 continuing) for fidelity and surety. A stock company organized to write *only* fire insurance coverages or only marine insurance coverages required a minimum initial capital and surplus of $500,000 (continuing $250,000).

[17] Professor D. L. Bickelhaupt has prepared a summary of the financial requirements set forth in the fifty states, the District of Columbia, and Puerto Rico for full multiple line stock insurance companies. See *op. cit.*, Appendix A, pp. 169–75.

[18] At the time of this writing, all lines underwriting (the writing of life, fire, and casualty insurance in one company) is permitted in thirteen states: Alabama, Alaska, Connecticut, Delaware, Georgia, Maine, Mississippi, North Dakota, Oregon, Rhode Island, South Carolina, Tennessee, and Wisconsin.

[19] Insurance Company of North America, *166th Annual Report*, 1957, p. 7.

ages.[20] The pressure is more likely to come from the insurers than from the insured, and for the purpose of improving the insurance product designed for personal rather than for business use. Once all lines underwriting is extended, however, all lines policies may be developed for business as well as for personal use, particularly in the mass markets. On this point Dr. Robert A. Rennie, vice-president in charge of research at the Nationwide Insurance Companies, stated: "I predict that [those companies] which have blazed new trails in the development of all-lines insurance for the personal market will provide much of the future leadership in the all-lines commercial markets."[21]

MULTIPLE LINE AND ALL LINES INSURANCE

In any discussion of multiple line and all lines insurance, there is more to review than simply underwriting authority. Long before multiple line underwriting powers were granted to fire and casualty insurers, there was a great deal of multiple line activity in the insurance world. Furthermore, there is a growing amount of all lines activity today, even though all lines underwriting powers have not generally been granted.

Buyers

First of all, insurance buyers have had to be multiple line and all lines operators in order to build an adequate insurance program for their families and businesses. The buyers in business, however, frequently are multiple line rather than all lines purchasers. In the first place, the use of life insurance to protect business assets and income has not been as widespread as the use of fire and casualty coverages.[22] In the second place, the most frequent use of life insurance in business is to fund death benefits and pension plans for employees. In a number of cases these plans are purchased and administered by persons not associated with the purchase and administration of multiple line insurance.

Agents

Multiple line insurance agencies also have long been the rule. The sales and service activities of the property insurance agent have not been confined to fire or to casualty insurance, one or the other.[23] The typical in-

---

[20] Laurence J. Ackerman, before the Casualty and Surety Club of Hartford, October 3, 1955.

[21] *Proceedings of the Twelfth Annual Insurance Conferences* (Ohio State University, 1961), p. 6.

[22] Casualty insurance coverages have not been used as widely as fire insurance coverages, thus leaving some monoline insurance buyers.

[23] An important exception is the part-time agent who writes only fire insurance coverages on mortgaged dwellings in connection with his principal business of lending money.

dependent agent represents several insurance companies, among which are both fire an casualty insurers.[24] The bulk of the life insurance, however, is sold by monoline agents wedded to one company.[25] Writing about all lines agents, Milton W. Mays, vice-president of the "Continental" group (a multiple line group), says:

> Agents have long had it within their power to make one-stop service for all lines insurance a reality for their customers. Some have actually developed this approach to their own advantage and profit. This has not come about on a large scale, perhaps because competition has not forced it, perhaps because the agents were not adequately trained for one-stop selling, or perhaps because a good enough living could be earned by the fire and casualty insurance agents without going into the life insurance business, and vice versa. When the economics of the insurance agency business is such that agents must adapt their operations to the all lines insurance approach to survive, then this change will promptly come about. Until then and for the foreseeable future, it is likely that fire and casualty insurance agents will continue to sell the bulk of fire and casualty insurance and life insurance agents will continue to sell the bulk of life insurance and the public will be served accordingly.[26]

But the movement toward all lines agents is likely to continue, with the major impetus coming from the independent local property insurance agent and the controlled agents of the exclusive agency all lines groups rather than from the agents who are specializing in the writing of life insurance. The independent local property insurance agent in some cases may be pushed into the life insurance business to offset loss of commissions resulting from inroads made on his premium volume by the price-conscious, highly competitive direct writers and exclusive agency companies.[27] Since many life insurance agents tend to emphasize the non-insurance aspects of their products (savings and investment), sometimes even to the point of de-emphasizing the insurance aspect, property insurance agents who are accustomed to the business of insurance might, if they become all lines agents, find themselves suddenly in a business foreign to their interests, aptitudes, and abilities. Whether the buyer of life insurance can expect better advice and service from a former multiple line agent than from an

---

[24] Some fire and casualty insurers use exclusive agents (sometimes called "captive" or "controlled" agents to distinguish them from other independent agents) to market insurance. These same agents market life insurance also if their insurer has an affiliated life company.

[25] Occasionally a monoline life agent steps out on his company and sells (brokers) a property insurance policy to pick up a few extra dollars. According to Kenneth Force, executive editor of the *National Underwriter*, "forty per cent of life agents sell some property insurance."

[26] Mays, "Critique of All Lines Insurance," *All Lines Insurance* (Homewood, Illinois: Richard D. Irwin, Inc., 1960), pp. 193–94.

[27] "Direct writers" are insurers using salaried representatives as marketing outlets rather than using the independent agency system or the exclusive agency system. (See chap 17.)

exclusive life agent could depend, to some extent, upon whether the buyer is interested in an insurance product or in a savings medium.[28] Because of his preoccupation with the investment uses of life insurance, the life insurance agent is likely to be more concerned with competition from mutual fund salesmen than from multiple line insurance agents.[29] Therefore, if he takes on another product, that product is more likely to be mutual fund shares than property and liability insurance. Already, there is some activity along these lines.

Insurance Groups

Multiple line insurance groups were in existence many years before multiple line companies were authorized. And, although all lines companies are not yet generally permitted in this country, in 1959 there were 84 all lines groups. These groups owned $23 billion in assets and wrote $8.6 billion in premiums.[30] These groups are growing both in number and in asset and premium volume.

An insurance group (or fleet) is composed of two or more separate companies under common ownership, management, or control. If the group is to be "multiple line," at least one company must be a fire company and one must be a casualty company. A group composed of only fire companies would be a monoline group. A group including a fire insurer, a casualty insurer,[31] and a life insurer would be an all lines group. Such, for example, is the Hartford Insurance Group. The Hartford Fire Insurance Company was organized in 1810. In 1913, when the Hartford Accident and Indemnity Insurance Company was organized as a companion company to write casualty insurance, Hartford became a multiple line group. In 1959, when the Hartford Fire Insurance Company acquired sufficient shares of the outstanding stock of the Columbian National Life Insurance Company,[32] Hartford became an all lines group.[33] The Hartford Accident and Indemnity Company became a multiple line company in 1950.

---

[28] This observation assumes that the multiple line agent has not revolutionized his thinking about the fundamental purpose of insurance: a device for reducing risk and sharing losses.

[29] Mutual fund salesmen point out the vulnerability of life insurance cash values to inflation and contend that mutual fund shares meet the challenge of inflation.

[30] *The Spectator*, November, 1960.

[31] Instead of a fire insurer and a casualty insurer, a multiple line insurer would be sufficient.

[32] The name of the life company was changed in 1960 to the Hartford Life Insurance Co.

[33] Other members of the Hartford Group include the Hartford Live Stock Insurance Company (organized in 1916), the Citizens Insurance Company of New Jersey (organized in 1929), the New York Underwriters Insurance Company (acquired in 1925), the Twin City Fire Insurance Company (acquired in 1921), and the London-Canada Insurance Company (acquired in 1921).

Policies

Policies combining fire and casualty coverages were common before modern multiple line underwriting was authorized. Combination automobile insurance policies, for example, were issued jointly by companies in a multiple line group; the fire company would write the physical damage coverage and the casualty company would write the public liability coverage. Similar arrangements were found in aircraft insurance. Even today, the Hartford Fire Insurance Company, for example, still issues combination automobile policies with the Hartford Accident and Indemnity Insurance Company.

All lines insurance policies are not yet written, but there is no reason to believe that they will not be introduced into the picture. As greater numbers of all lines groups are formed and as insurance executives and regulatory authorities widen their vision, new package policies will appear on the scene combining life and property coverages. This might be the prelude to all lines underwriting, just as multiple line policies were to multiple line underwriting.

Insurers

While multiple line underwriting is permitted, it has not been completely accepted in the industry or "even by multiple line insurers. Many companies still specialize in a few kinds of protection; separate their company organization and primary functions of sales, underwriting, rating and claim adjustment on the basis of departments in each kind of insurance; belong to rating bureaus separated 'by line'; issue many policies limited to coverage of either fire, or casualty, perils, or maintain separate affiliates for property, or casualty insurance."[34]

CLASSIFICATION OF INSURANCE COVERAGES

The development of insurance on a monoline basis has resulted in an inconsistent and awkward system of classifying insurance coverages. The effect has been to develop a number of different rating procedures and underwriting criteria[35] for the various types of policies issued. A close look at the array of policies available from insurance companies reveals five basic methods by which contracts are classified: perils, property, hazards, losses, and customers to be insured. That there is some overlapping in classification will become apparent as the discussion progresses.

Perils

Peril may be defined as the active cause of a loss. Typical perils are fire, windstorm, burglary, robbery, theft, forgery, collision, accident, sickness,

---

[34] Bickelhaupt, *op. cit.*, p. 161.
[35] The factors considered by the insurance company in making the decisions whether to insure a given applicant are called "underwriting criteria."

and death. A host of covers are classified according to the perils that are insured against in the policy. Examples among the policies written by fire insurance companies are fire and lightning insurance, optional perils coverage (explosion, riot and civil commotion, vandalism and malicious mischief, aircraft and vehicle damage), and rain insurance. Casualty policies classified according to perils include such coverages as mercantile robbery insurance, mercantile open stock burglary insurance, forgery and alterations insurance, personal theft insurance, accident insurance, and sickness insurance.[36]

The first modern insurance policies issued more than six centuries ago insured interests in vessels and cargo against all "Perils, Losses, and Misfortunes that have or shall come to the Hurt, Detriment, or Damage of the said Goods and Merchandises and Ship." Thus, the original purpose of modern insurance was to offer financial protection to the insured for *any accidental* loss of or damage to his property regardless of the cause. It has continued to be the custom in marine insurance to write policies designed primarily to cover losses with only limited concern for the cause of the loss.

It was with the writing of insurance on dwellings and other buildings that the philosophy of specified perils coverage was born. On Friday, September 2, 1666, an oven in the king's bakeshop became overheated and caused a fire that could not be contained. Before the blaze ran its course of five days, much of the city of London was engulfed in flames. The great financial losses caused by the conflagration made people aware of fire as a threat to their financial security and kindled a desire among them to do something about it.

In 1667 or 1681, Dr. Nicholas Barbon,[37] an ex-physician known for his building speculations, opened an office to write insurance against loss to dwellings by fire. Soon afterward other companies were formed and coverage was offered on business buildings. Later, contents were also insured.

---

[36] It is apparent that some of these policies are also classified according to the type of customer to be insured, e.g., *mercantile* robbery and *personal* (i.e., residential, not business) theft insurance.

[37] An alteration; the baptismal name of this remarkable entrepreneur was either "Christ-came-into-the-world-to-save Barebones" or "If-Christ-had-not-died-thou-hadst-been-born-damned Barebones." These were the names of the two sons of Praise-God Barebones (of Cromwell's "Barebones Parliament"), and Doctor "Nicholas Barbon" was one of them. The record as to which he was is not clear, but persons who participated in various of Nick's money-raising schemes reportedly used the shortened form, "Damned Barbon," in referring to him, rather than anything based on the other name. For some of the story, see Francis Boyer Relton, *An Account of the Fire Insurance Companies* . . . (London: Swan Sonnenschein & Co., 1893), pp. 19–22, and P. G. M. Dickson, *The Sun Insurance Office 1710–1960* (London: Oxford University Press, 1960), pp. 7–9. Relton, following earlier sources, places the opening of Barbon's first insurance office in 1667, but Dickson says that this date "appears to be unsupported by any evidence" and places the beginning year as 1681, when Barbon was certainly connected with "the Fire Office at the backside of the Royal Exchange."

In those days, fire was the only peril covered by insurance contracts issued on buildings and their contents. Although coverages against a multitude of other perils were offered, they seem not to have caught on. In general, it was only with the development of the industrial revolution, particularly with respect to inland transportation, that sufficient demand for protection against other perils developed to make writing insurance against them sensible or profitable. And the growth was principally peril by peril.

Property

Property covered seems to be the principal basis for classifying marine insurance. Cargo and hull insurance are two of the most important ocean marine coverages, and among the portfolio of inland marine insurers are many policies distinguishable by the nature of the property covered. Examples are accounts receivable insurance, contractors' equipment floater, fine arts insurance, physicians' and surgeons' equipment floater, neon sign floater, and salesmen's samples floater, to name only a few!

Even though perils covered are the principal basis for classifying fire and allied lines coverage, even some of these are catalogued according to property covered. Examples are aircraft hull insurance, automobile physical damage insurance, yacht and inboard hull coverages, and improvements and betterments insurance. Among the property-based classes of casualty contracts are the money and securities broad form and comprehensive glass insurance.

Policies whose identity is based on the type of property covered usually (but not always) cover perils comprehensively. The specified property commonly is insured against loss or damage per se and not against loss or damage from a few of the perils that threaten it. This result is accomplished either by specifying the covered perils in a very comprehensive way or, more often, by covering all perils except those specifically excluded. The excluded (or not included) perils usually are those that are believed to be uninsurable, that require special underwriting and rating, or that are not eligible to be underwritten by the insurer offering the policy.[38]

Hazard

Hazard can be defined as a condition that creates or increases the chance of loss arising from given perils. In the various fields of insurance a number of policies are identified on the basis of the hazard insured. In marine insurance, for example, several policies are written to cover the transporta-

---

[38] In some cases, glass insurance, for example, a peril (fire) may be excluded because the insured is likely to have that peril covered under some other policy.

tion hazard: annual transit floater, first class mail floater, parcel post insurance, registered mail insurance, and blanket motor cargo insurance. These policies either are comprehensive as to the perils covered or specify a set of perils commonly associated with transportation exposures.

In health insurance, a number of specified hazard contracts are written as limited policies. Among the accident coverages, for example, are automobile accident policies, travel ticket policies, and a host of what are called "special risk" accident policies covering professional athletes, "human guinea pigs," and workers concerned with atomic and hydrogen bomb experiments. Among the sickness insurance coverages are the dread disease policies (covering only a few specified diseases, such as poliomyelitis, encephalitis, diphtheria, tetanus, scarlet fever, and spinal meningitis), non-occupational health insurance policies, and occupational accident and disease coverage, written usually in conjunction with workmen's compensation insurance.

In casualty insurance the outstanding examples of hazard-classed policies are found among the liability coverages. The principal peril covered under a liability policy is negligence, or alleged negligence, on the part of the insured that results in bodily injury or property damage caused by accident (or sometimes by occurrence). The activities engaged in by the insured affect materially his chances of becoming involved in (or being accused of) such a negligent act. The liability exposure is greater for those who own or operate automobiles than it is for those who are not exposed to the automobile liability hazard. The same can be said for those who own or operate aircraft, elevators, or watercraft. The manufacture, sale, or distribution of goods exposes businessmen to the products liability hazard; the performance of a professional service (legal, medical, dental, insurance, or accounting, for example) exposes the professional man to the malpractice liability hazard. Persons or organizations engaged in the business of manufacturing, selling, or distributing alcoholic beverages, and owners or lessors of property used for these purposes, are exposed to a special liability hazard created by dramshop or liquor control laws on the books of a number of states. Persons or organizations entering into agreements under which they assume the liability of others expose themselves to what is known as the contractual liability hazard. Businesses owning, operating, or using nuclear facilities are exposed to a very special liability hazard. All these hazards are in addition to those resulting from the ownership, maintenance, or use of premises and from any business operations incidental to the use of the premises. Aside from the basic premises and operations forms, liability policies classified according to hazards therefore include automobile liability, aircraft liability, elevator liability, watercraft liability, products liability, professional liability, liquor liability, contractual liability, and nuclear energy liability insurance, and several others.

Losses

A peril can cause several types of losses: (1) loss of property, (2) loss of income, and (3) loss through the creation of additional expenses. Some insurance policies are classified according to the type of loss incurred rather than the type of property, hazard, or peril involved. Prominent examples in the field of fire insurance are business interruption insurance (loss of earnings resulting from the suspension of business because of physical damage to property by an insured peril), extra expense insurance (to cover the additional expenses of doing business caused by damage to the premises of the insured), leasehold interest insurance (to cover the loss of a favorable rent differential suffered when an attractive lease is canceled after a fire), profits and commissions insurance (to cover, among other things, loss of profits to the manufacturer resulting from the damage of finished products caused by perils insured against), and rent insurance (to cover loss of rental income or the rental value of property damaged or destroyed by an insured peril).

In health insurance, policies are frequently classified as to the loss insured. Classified in this way are disability income policies, hospital expense policies, surgical expense policies, and medical expense contracts. Most policies classified on the basis of the property covered also may be said to be classified according to loss because the loss of that property is the subject of the insurance. In these cases, with few exceptions, the loss covered is restricted to the loss of the property itself and does not extend to the loss of use of that property or to any extra expenses incurred as a consequence of that loss.

Customers

In recent years the greatest changes in the insurance product have been in packaging. Several covers have been put together to meet the needs of certain types of customers. The current activity along the lines has been the result principally of multiple line underwriting legislation. However, long before multiple line underwriting powers were granted, certain policies developed on a single line basis for the use of specific types of customers became available and are currently in wide use. Typical ones offered by fire insurers have been the garage keepers legal liability policy, the hangar keepers legal liability policy, and tuition fees insurance. Typical of those offered by marine insurers are the block policies,[39] the first of which was the jewelers block policy originally issued just before the turn of the present century by the underwriters at Lloyd's of London. Lloyd's fulfilled the jewelers block demand in this country until the end of World

---

[39] The term "block" is believed to be derived from the French *en bloc*, i.e., "all together."

War I. Following that, a stepped-up crime rate stimulated the jewelers' interest in the coverage, but dampened the interest of the underwriters at Lloyd's. The result was a gap in the market that could be filled only if the laws of many states were changed to allow the jewelers block to be written in the American market. Changes in the law were necessary because the jewelers block policy combined fire and casualty protection in the same contract. Fire insurers were allowed to write theft coverage only when a transportation hazard was involved, and, while casualty companies could write the theft coverage, they were not authorized to write the rest of the jewelers block protection. Therefore, before the jewelers block could be written, the laws in a number of states had to be amended. Both the fire and the casualty laws were amended for that purpose.[40]

The underwriting authority of marine insurance companies was to insure "against all kinds of loss of or damage to . . . goods . . . merchandise, effects, . . . and all other kinds of property . . . in connection with any and all risks or perils of . . . transportation . . . on land . . . or while being . . . prepared for shipment or while awaiting the same or during . . . storage, . . . or reshipment incident thereto. . . ."[41] Operating under this authority, marine underwriters went "wild" in the 1920's and wrote a number of contracts as "transportation risks," to the dismay of fire and casualty underwriters, who complained of the invasion of their fields by the marine companies. Since there was no definition of the term "transportation risks," marine underwriters placed the broadest possible interpretation on their powers. For example, they wrote "all risk" coverage on merchandise for chain stores under the theory that because this merchandise moved from warehouse to store to customer, it was logical to insure it as a transportation risk. Other stocks of goods principally situated at factories and warehouses were insured as transportation risks because they eventually would be moved when sold. Fire and casualty underwriters soon began to lose business to marine underwriters, who were not restricted by rules of rating bureaus as to the forms that could be used or as to rates that could be charged. Marine underwriters in a number of cases could tailor the coverage to meet the needs of the customer and proceed to offer it at a lower rate than the fire underwriters were required to charge for the fire coverage alone.[42] Fire and casualty underwriters believed that much of this business should be insured on fixed location forms and that the marine

---

[40] The New York law was amended in 1925. Although the casualty companies were given broader powers (they could include liability coverage in their contract), these companies left the jewelers block to the inland marine underwriters, who were experienced in "all risk" insurance.

[41] Laws of New York, 1904, chap. 33, sec. 150, as amended by Laws of New York, 1923, chap. 437.

[42] This is not to say that the lower rate was always justified, but it is not to say that it never was, either.

underwriters were exceeding their authority. The battle lines were drawn.[43] Efforts to resolve the conflict finally ended with the adoption by the National Association of Insurance Commissioners on June 2, 1933, of the *Nation-wide Definition and Interpretation of the Insuring Powers of Marine and Transportation Underwriters*. By either legislative or administrative action the *Nation-wide Definition* soon became the law in most states, and marine underwriters were forced to curb their imaginations. In many cases, this curb was to the disadvantage of the insurance buyer, who was denied the right to purchase policies tailored exactly to his needs. He had to mark time until mid-century, when multiple line underwriting was reintroduced.

The *Nation-wide Definition* included the jewelers block policy as a "marine coverage" but excluded block policies for dealers in other types of merchandise except fine arts and antiques. Permission was granted to write block coverage for stamp and coin dealers, although authorization was not specifically included in the 1933 definition. After the full-scale return of multiple line underwriting in the 1950's, marine underwriters once again turned their talents toward the writing of block coverages for storekeepers, who had been denied these coverages by the *Nation-wide Definition*. Inland marine underwriting now includes block policies for furriers, dealers in agricultural equipment, dealers in construction equipment, musical instrument dealers, and camera dealers. These block policies became permitted types of inland marine coverages in a revised *Nation-wide Definition* adopted in 1953. Because multiple line underwriting had been extended, the revised definition is for purposes of classification only and no longer serves to restrict underwriting powers.

In the casualty insurance field, liability coverages classified according to customers include lawyers liability insurance; druggists liability insurance; hospital liability insurance; physicians, surgeons, and dentists liability insurance; contractors protective liability insurance; garage liability insurance; and storekeepers liability insurance. Among the many crime policies classified according to customers are the bankers blanket bond and similar special "bonds" for other financial institutions,[44] bank burglary and robbery insurance, and the storekeeper's burglary and robbery policy.

Among the relatively new multiple line coverages are several contracts designed specifically for certain types of business activity. A special policy for businesses engaged principally in the buying and selling of merchan-

---

[43] Although fire companies were authorized to write marine insurance, some restricted their operations to fire coverages only, whereas others with fire and marine operations in the same company kept them as separate departments. The result was intracompany skirmishes, or desk-to-desk fighting.

[44] Although called "bonds," these contracts are actually comprehensive crime insurance policies.

dise (wholesale, retail, and kindred operations) was first made available through the mercantile block policy, later called commercial property coverage. For manufacturers, a manufacturers output policy has been developed, and for the business or professional office, the office contents special form is available. These are "all risk" forms with respect to perils, but with respect to losses they restrict coverage to direct loss of the property itself. No loss-of-use or liability protection is included. The recent industrial property policy program and the public and institutional property program have been developed principally as named perils forms.

A broader program designed to meet a wider range of the needs of particular customers is the special multi-peril policy program under which a package policy is issued to include both property and liability insurance. This program began some years ago with special policies for homeowners. The first form developed for businesses has been the special motel package policy in which the coverage is written on a specified perils rather than on an all risk basis. A number of endorsements are available so that eligible businessmen can cover most of their insurable exposures (property, perils, hazards, and losses) in one package. With the endorsements, the insured can cover (1) practically all his property against a number of specified perils (with some property protected on an "all risk" basis), (2) his business interruption losses when caused by one of a shorter list of insured perils, and (3) his liability for bodily injury and property damage. The special multi-peril package policy program has been expanded to include policies for a number of different types of customers. Such development greatly simplifies the insurance problems of many buyers and offers them the economy of combining nearly all their coverages in one policy (see chap. 14).

THE EFFECT OF THE INSURANCE CLASSIFICATION SYSTEM ON THE INSURANCE BUYER: A SUMMARY

The awkward system of classifying insurance coverages has had a pronounced effect on the problem of insurance buying. For one thing, it has limited the availability in the American market of the broad type of coverage sought by a number of insurance purchasers. For another, the awkwardness of the system has contributed to a number of mistakes in insurance buying, particularly those of oversight in omitting important coverages in the planning of insurance programs, and sometimes in the duplication of other coverages.

Limitations on the Market

The traditional division of insurance coverages in the United States into specific lines has limited the development of insurance coverages to the disadvantage of insurance buyers. Policies that some buyers would have found advantageous to own and that some insurance companies would have been willing to write could not be made available in the American market. In general, property owners were restricted to insurance coverages against named losses resulting from named perils. For example, insurance against loss by fire or windstorm could be purchased only from fire insurance companies, and insurance against loss by burglary or robbery could be purchased only from casualty insurance companies. With few exceptions, no policies were available under which a property owner could insure himself against loss of his property without having to speculate as to what would cause that loss. He had to name the perils to be insured. Several policies were necessary if all the major perils were to be insured.

Only marine insurance companies were allowed by their charters to write all perils coverage (erroneously called "all risk" coverage in the insurance trade). These companies, however, for the most part were restricted to the writing of insurance on property in transit or on property connected with transportation and communication. Coverage for property at fixed locations was available at first only to dealers in jewelry, fine arts, and stamp and coin collections. Later, furs, cameras, musical instruments, and agricultural and contractors' equipment were added. These contracts, even though they provide comprehensive property and perils coverage for eligible insureds, do not provide comprehensive loss coverage; coverage is restricted to direct loss of the property itself for its actual cash value plus the cost of protecting it, or trying to protect it, against further loss.

The reintroduction of multiple line underwriting in this country, however, is bringing about a significant change in the American insurance market. As mentioned earlier, new policy forms have been introduced to make it possible for homeowners, farmowners, and certain businessmen to insure most, if not all, of their important exposures under one policy. Significant strides have been made under these multi-peril and multi-loss policies. Some of the multiple line contracts have developed on an "all risk" basis, whereas others have developed as named perils coverages.

Mistakes in Insurance Buying

The task of insurance buying has been complicated by the separation of the American insurance industry into life, fire, and casualty companies. The development of insurance contracts on a monoline basis with separate policies covering each exposure individually has needlessly complicated the job of insurance buying. Adding to the difficulty is the multi-system of classifying the various insurance coverages, with some classified as to peril, some as to losses, others as to property, and still others as to hazard. The insurance buyer is faced with the monumental task of organizing his exposures to conform with the traditional grouping of coverages found in the insurance industry. If he is an unskilled buyer and his insurance adviser is less than professionally competent—an all too common combination of circumstances—he is likely to find himself exposed to losses that not only could have been covered but also should have been insured.

For one simple example, consider the ownership of a professional office building. Life for the insurance buyer would be simple if all he had to do was purchase one policy that would insure him against all insurable financial losses he might suffer because of the building. With the traditional insurance coverages, however, such simplicity has not been his lot. First, he has had to classify his exposure on the building as to the perils involved. A number of these perils can be covered under a fire insurance policy with an endorsement written to extend the coverage to windstorm, hail, explosion, riot and civil commotion, smoke, and damage by aircraft and vehicles. Vandalism and malicious mischief insurance can be added to the fire policy by endorsement and, in several states, so may earthquake insurance. Loss caused by an explosion of a steam boiler located on the premises (or of one owned or operated by the insured) has to be covered under a separate boiler and machinery insurance policy. Damage by water also must be covered under a special policy. Liability insurance to protect the building owner against the cost of lawsuits for bodily injury and property damage and to pay the judgment rendered against him in such suits, has to be purchased as a separate policy (with several endorsements, if it is to be complete). If the building is damaged or destroyed, the owner stands to lose his rental income until the building is restored; a separate rent insurance cover is necessary to provide coverage for this. And so it goes (for this is not the end of the list)!

With all the possible loss exposures to think of and with the haphazard method of classifying insurance coverages, it is no wonder that some important peril, loss, property, or hazard may be overlooked by the lay or even professional insurance buyer. Special policies packaged for each major type of customer appear to be the sensible answer to the insurance buyer's problem. The insurance industry now recognizes this need. With the recently acquired multiple line underwriting powers and a newly found aggressive, competitive spirit, the industry is now moving at an accelerated rate in the direction of simplifying the insurance buyer's problem, through package policies with combinations of coverages including various optional features to give both comprehensiveness and flexibility to insurance protection.

REVIEW AND DISCUSSION QUESTIONS

1. In the United States in the latter half of the nineteenth century, "the regulatory authorities and the [insurance] companies themselves considered the combination of unlike covers by a single company a threat to the safe underwriting of the old and proven lines of insurance." Today, however, multiple line companies dominate the property and liability insurance fields. Has this change represented (*a*) substitution of a right view for a wrong one, (*b*) substitution of a wrong view for a right one, or (*c*) a change in what con-

stitutes the right view because of changes in the scene being viewed? Justify your answer, using as many facts and principles of insurance and finance as possible. And if your choice of answers is (*a*) or (*b*), how do you account for adoption of an erroneous view by leaders in insurance practice and regulation? If your answer is (*b*) or (*c*), how do you account for the fact that multiple line underwriting has been standard practice outside the United States in both the 1800's and 1900's?

2. In view of the commonly recognized good standard of insurance regulation in New York, is the New York practice of giving its rules an extraterritorial effect a good thing or bad? Do you consider the nature and widespread effect of New York's regulatory actions to support argument for or against (or irrelevant to) proposals for uniform regulation of insurance on a nationwide basis by the national government?

3. Why has union of life insurance underwriting with property and liability underwriting not been accomplished in this country even though fire and casualty underwriting have been brought together? Do you consider these reasons valid, either as of the past, the present, or the future? Explain.

4. Would you designate the legislative history of underwriting powers in New York from 1849 to 1949 as "The Century of Progress"? Justify your position.

5. How can the history of hodgepodge accretion of additional lines of insurance to both fire and casualty underwriting powers be explained?

6. Would either progress or financial safety in insurance be (or have been) significantly affected if insurance statutes stated underwriting powers in broad, general terms, rather than by means of lists authorizing specified kinds of insurance? Explain.

7. When the text says of the study by the Diemand committee that "the interests involved transcended those of the public," what is meant? Do you agree with what is meant? Why or why not?

8. The pressure for all lines coverage in a single policy "is more likely to come from insurers rather than the insured, and for the purpose of improving the insurance product designed for personal rather than for business use." What reasons can be advanced to support this prognostication? Do you find these reasons convincing? If not, why not?

9. Would it be better if all insurance covers were written in such fashion that they could be classified by just one or perhaps two classificatory principles (e.g., according to perils insured again, and (or) types of losses covered)? If so, what one or two principles would you select, and what would the classes be? If not, why not?

10. Does the increase in "package" policies suggest that the need for highly trained buyers and sellers of insurance is growing, or declining? Justify your conclusion.

11. "The awkward system of classifying insurance covers has had a pronounced effect on the problem of insurance buying." What have these effects been, and why? Have there been any beneficial effects for the buyer? If so, what effects? If not, why was a system with no such effects developed by the companies and encouraged by responsible public officials?

12. What classification system of present insurance covers would you recommend if you were asked to prepare a classification system "from scratch"? What arguments would you use to defend this system against attack? What difficulties would you face in an attempt to get this system adopted?

Chapter 13

THE INSURANCE POLICY

An insurance policy is a document containing the term of the agreement between the insurer and the insured. It sets forth both the rights and the duties of all parties to the agreement. To be legally enforceable, however, the agreement must comply with the common-law requisites of a valid contract.[1]

FORMATION OF AN INSURANCE CONTRACT

The formation of an insurance contract is governed by the same general requirements applicable to the formation of any other valid contract: mutual assent by competent parties for the performance of a legal act for a valuable consideration. However, because of the quasi public nature of the insurance business and its accompanying statutory control, contract law in its application to insurance has been modified. Special rules have been developed that make some aspects of insurance law unrecognizable to the student of general contract law.

Mutual Assent

Mutual assent is manifested when the terms offered by one party are accepted by another within a reasonable time. The intentions of the parties to enter a binding contract must be evident from their words or actions. Preliminary negotiations must not be mistaken either as an offer or as an acceptance.

Customary procedures for the formation of contracts have been de-

---

[1] The term "common law" originates in England and was used in its nascent form to mean those principles of law that were common to all England as distinguished from those applying only in certain localities. Today the term has a more technical meaning. In the United States, the common law in any jurisdiction is composed of (1) the body of rules evidenced by appellate court decisions and (2) that part of English law not contrary to the public policy of the jurisdiction in which it is applied. Common law is distinguishable from statutory law and is sometimes referred to as the unwritten law. For the most part, contract law was created in the common law.

veloped in the insurance business. The procedures followed in the formation of life insurance contracts are different from those practiced in most other fields of insurance. The restricted authority given to life insurance agents accounts for much of the difference. With rare exceptions, life insurance agents do not have the authority to bind their principals unconditionally to insurance contracts.[2] The job of distinguishing good and bad risks requires technical ability beyond that possessed by the typical life insurance agent. Because life insurance contracts may not be cancelled by the insurer, once an underwriting mistake is made it cannot be corrected. The insurer, consequently, will delegate the authority to make underwriting decisions only to those specially trained for this purpose.

Agents for property and liability insurers may be given contract-writing powers. Since most property and liability insurance policies have provisions for cancellation, poor underwriting judgment on the part of agents can be corrected in the home office by the simple process of cancelling the policy (after giving the insured the minimum number of days' notice specified in the contract).

Since no agreement can be legally binding until an offer is made and accepted, it is important for the risk manager to know what constitute offer and acceptance in the formation of a contract of insurance. Only then will he know the effective date of his coverage.

Offer and Acceptance in Life Insurance. A completed application for key man or other life insurance may be an acceptance, an offer, or an invitation for the insurer to make an offer, depending on the circumstances.[3]

If the risk manager (acting for the business) gives the agent a check for the first premium along with the completed application, the business is accepting a conditional offer of a contract from the insurer. The written evidence of this contract is often called a "binding receipt," but "conditional receipt" is the correct term in most instances. The condition is that the life to be insured be "insurable," that is, that it meet the underwriting standards of the insurer, *as of the date of the completed application.* When this condition has been met (as determined by later review of the application by a home office underwriter), then the contract begins as of application and premium payment date. The insurer, through its sales agent, offered to insure. The terms of its offer, as shown in the conditional receipt, were that acceptance could be made only on behalf of an acceptable life, and only by completing an application in proper form (including medical examination, if required) and paying the initial premium. When

---

[2] Janice E. Greider and William T. Beadles found two life companies in North America that permit their agents to issue unconditional binders for temporary coverage pending home office action on the application. *Law and the Life Insurance Contract* (Homewood, Illinois: Richard D. Irwin, Inc., 1960), pp. 87 ff.

[3] This analysis is based on Greider and Beadles, *op. cit.*, pp. 82 ff. Their analysis differs in some respects from that found in most textbooks on insurance but is in accord with current life insurance practice and recent court decisions.

these acts were performed with respect to an insurable life, the insurance contract came into being.[4]

If the key man dies in an accident before the application is reviewed, the insurer is obligated to pay the face amount.

If the risk manager had submitted the application without tendering the first premium, then the insurance company was being invited to make an offer to write the insurance. The company would review the application, and, if the subject were found insurable, the policy would be issued and forwarded to the agent for delivery to the risk manager. Agents as a rule do not have the authority to deliver the policy unless the subject of the insurance is still in good health at time of delivery. Delivery of the policy by the agent is then the offer. When the risk manager indicates acceptance of the offer by paying the first premium, the insurance becomes effective.

Occasionally, a completed application and prepaid premium will be tendered without the issuance of a conditional receipt. In these instances, the application and premium constitute an offer to buy. This offer is accepted, and the insurance contract becomes effective, when (and if) the home office underwriting department decides that the application is acceptable.

In some cases the insurer will find a particular proposal (premium, amount of insurance, policy form) unacceptable and will issue a policy on terms different from those specified in the application. If the risk manager has not paid the first premium with his application, this action on the part of the company creates no special problem. The company is simply making an offer different from the one it was invited to make. The risk manager can accept or reject this offer as he sees fit. But if the risk manager had made the company an offer by tendering the first premium with his application, this action on the part of the company results in a counter-offer, which the risk manager must *specifically* accept before the contract becomes effective, even though the company retains the amount paid by the risk manager as payment (or part payment) of the first premium on the contract offered under the counterproposal.

Offer and Acceptance in Property and Liability Insurance. In property and liability insurance the common procedure is for the risk manager to make the offer to the insurer to purchase the desired coverage. Rarely does the insurer make a formal offer to sell the risk manager a particular coverage. This is true in spite of the obvious efforts of insurance salesmen to peddle their wares. What the insurance agents and brokers are trying to sell the risk manager is the idea that insurance coverage is needed and that it be applied for through them.

Applications for property and liability insurance are usually oral in form, although for some types of coverages written applications are re-

---

[4] The actual provisions in conditional receipts vary some from company to company, but the majority practice is described here. *Ibid.*, p. 88.

quired. The application must provide the insurer with sufficient information to identify, underwrite, and rate the exposure. Upon receipt of the risk manager's application, the insurer or his agent will review it. If it is acceptable, the policy will be issued. But all this may take time, and the risk manager cannot afford to be patient. What if a loss should occur between the submission of the application and the issuance of the policy? To take care of the unavoidable time lag, the agent frequently issues a "binder." This is a memorandum evidencing that the insurance has been granted for a limited period of time ranging from 15 to 60 days. The binder specifies the day and the hour that the coverage commences. It is a valid contract if all the other requisites have been satisfied.

Although binders may be oral, risk managers should insist on written confirmation of all binders; the existence of an oral agreement is difficult to prove. Furthermore, when the insurance transaction is negotiated through an agent or broker, as it is in the majority of cases, the risk manager must satisfy himself that such intermediary has binding powers. The power and authority of agents is such an important consideration for the risk manager that this subject is handled later in this chapter under a separate section. As a general rule, property and liability agents have the power to bind their companies on insurance contracts, but there are several exceptions.

The properly prepared binder will include the name of the insurer or insurers bound to the contract. Because the typical independent insurance agent represents more than one company, it is important that the "bound" insurers be identified. Unless there is a "meeting of the minds," there cannot be a valid contract. The binder is usually cancellable by the insured immediately and by the insurer after giving a specified minimum number of days' notice. The risk manager must pay the customary premium for the insurance for the period that the binder is effective if the policy is not issued or accepted. When a policy is issued and accepted by the risk manager, the binder becomes null and void. The premium to be paid is then for the policy period as originally proposed. The binder imposes upon the insurer the obligations and terms assumed under contracts ordinarily written for the proposed coverages unless otherwise stated.

Thus, in the formation of a property or liability insurance contract, the insurance is effective as soon as the agent tells the risk manager, "O.K., you are covered." This is usually immediately after the risk manager says that he wants the coverage, and some days or weeks before the policy is written. If the insurer, after making an underwriting investigation, decides not to continue the coverage, the binder or policy can be cancelled in accordance with the terms of the contract.

Competent Parties

To be legally competent to contract, a natural person must be of legal age and of sound mind; a corporation must be acting within the scope of the powers granted in its charter or articles of incorporation. These are the general rules of contract law on this subject, but notable exceptions are to be found, particularly in the formation of insurance contracts. When one party to an agreement does not have the capacity to contract, the agreement has been held void in some circumstances, voidable by the incompetent party in others, and valid in still others. Of course, the decisions will vary among the jurisdictions on a given set of facts, particularly with reference to agreements made by legally competent insureds with legally incompetent insurers.

Capacity of the Risk Manager To Contract. If the risk manager is representing adult, sane, natural persons (proprietorship or partnership), there is no question of his legal competency to enter into a contract of insurance, assuming, of course, that he has the authority to act for his principals in this capacity. Furthermore, the legal capacity of a corporation to contract for insurance to protect its assets and income against loss cannot be successfully challenged. Such power is implied even if not specifically expressed in the charter. Questions have sometimes been raised about the power of a non-insurance corporation to buy insurance from cooperative insurers. Some persons (usually representatives of stock insurance companies) have suggested that such purchases may be *ultra vires* on the grounds that they constitute engaging in the insurance business. Insureds in interinsurance exchanges insure each other, at least technically if not actually. In mutuals, the insureds "control" the company in the same way and to the same extent as stockholders "control" a stock corporation —they vote for members of the boards of directors and on such major changes in operations as amendments to a charter or by-laws. However, the uniform legal holding has been that purchase of insurance protection from a cooperative insurer is just as much a part of a corporation's implied powers as the purchase of protection from a proprietary type of insurer. The risk manager, therefore, need not be concerned about the capacity of his company to enter into insurance contracts.

Capacity of the Insurer To Contract. To be legally competent to issue insurance contracts, the insurer must be given the authority by its charter or articles of incorporation and must have satisfied the requirements for engaging in the insurance business in its home state and in the state where the contract is written.

State statutes set forth in detail financial and other requirements for the organization and licensing of insurance companies. The requirements are stricter than those usually imposed on other business concerns so as to give the public some protection against poorly financed insurers and dishonest and incompetent managements. The articles of incorporation specify the types of insurance that the insurer is authorized to write: life, health, and annuities, fire and marine, casualty and surety, or multiple lines (all except life and annuities).

Not only must the insurer organize according to the statutes of the state, it must also obtain a license to do an insurance business. The license is an official certification that the insurer has complied with the state laws and is authorized to write the types of insurance specified. Although the states collect revenue in the form of license fees, the licensing power is used chiefly as an instrument for controlling insurers. An insurer must obtain a license from each state in which it does business, subject to an exception to be noted later.

With respect to the business that an insurer does in the state of its incorporation, it is called a domestic insurer; with respect to business that it transacts in another state, it is called a foreign insurer; and with respect to business that it does in different nations, it is called an alien insurer. Insurers (domestic, foreign, and alien) licensed to do business in a state are called "admitted" or "authorized" insurers in that state, and as long as they are writing the kinds of insurance specified in their articles of incorporation and for which they are licensed, they have the legal capacity to contract.

Unauthorized Insurers. But what about the legal capacity of an insurer to contract when it is writing unauthorized coverages or when it is not admitted to do an insurance business in the state? Should the risk manager be concerned about the power of his prospective insurer to make a valid contract? The courts in most jurisdictions will uphold the insured's rights in an agreement with an insurer that is legally incompetent to contract if the agreement was made in good faith and without the insured's knowledge of the incompetency.[5] The courts reason that the insured cannot be expected to look into the organization and operation of his insurer to see whether it has complied with all the rules and regulations necessary to give it the legal capacity to write the insurance. Thus, if an insurance agent binds his company to a type of insurance coverage that it is not authorized to write, the courts will generally uphold the agreement under the theory that the insured may assume that the insurer is legally competent to write the policy.[6]

But what if the risk manager knowingly purchases insurance from an unauthorized insurer? The risk manager may be unable to obtain the coverage he needs from the authorized insurance market and may have to look to the unadmitted market, particularly the market abroad. For one thing, the capacity of the admitted market is limited. If the values to be

---

[5] In some states, agreements made with legally incompetent insurers are void by statute. In these jurisdictions the insurance company officers or agents who attempt to bind the insurer to unauthorized contracts can be held personally liable under these contracts. The insurance company will be held liable only for a return of the premiums collected under the policies.

[6] In this case, the agent would no doubt be acting outside the scope of his actual authority and would therefore be liable to the insurer for any losses paid under the contract. The agent would also be subject to whatever penalties are assessed for violating the law: fine or imprisonment or both. If the insurer issues the policy, it might also be subject to penalties.

insured are extremely large or concentrated in one location, the authorized market may be unable or unwilling to handle all the insurance required. In the second place, the risk manager may be seeking a type of coverage or form not offered by duly licensed insurers. Authorized insurers may not write the coverage because the type of risk is unique or rare and one with which they have had little or no experience. Or they may, from their viewpoint, have had too much experience with it: Either the particular risk or the general underwriting class to which it belongs may have been so unprofitable that the admitted insurers now desire to avoid it. Furthermore, because unauthorized insurers are not subject to the state's regulatory practices, the risk manager has more freedom in negotiating manuscript policies[7] with them to meet his specific needs.

Typical of the coverages for which unadmitted insurers play an important role in this country are insurance on major bridges and tunnels, aircraft liability, excess fire insurance in which large deductibles are involved, public liability insurance in which limits exceed several million dollars, water damage legal liability, malpractice insurance for doctors and nurses, personal accident insurance on hazardous travel and work abroad, errors and omissions (liability) insurance on many classes of risks, liability imposed by dram shop acts, public liability on oil-well drilling both on and offshore, warehousemen's legal liability insurance for the operators of commercial warehouses, and insurance for liabilities under the Jones Act (applying to disability of masters and members of the crews of ships under American jurisdiction).

Most states recognize some of the risk manager's need to purchase insurance in the unauthorized market and have adopted laws providing for the regulation of dealings with unadmitted insurers. These laws, known as "surplus lines" or "excess lines" laws, are by no means uniform among the states, although the National Association of Insurance Commissioners is working on a model Uniform Non-admitted Insurance Act through its Committee on Unauthorized Insurance.[8]

In general, the laws provide that a broker or agent must obtain a special license (known as a surplus or excess lines broker's or agent's license) before he can legally place insurance with an unauthorized insurer. Most surplus lines brokers and agents are specialists in this area, and a number of them do no other type of business. The general writing agent or broker frequently will purchase surplus lines coverage for the risk manager through these licensed specialists. Surplus lines laws generally provide that

---

[7] Definition: "manuscript— . . . a written or typewritten document of any kind as distinguished from a printed copy." *Webster's New Collegiate Dictionary* (2d ed.; Springfield, Massachusetts: G. & C. Merriam Co., 1951). Standardized forms in insurance, designed for use by many insureds, are printed, of course.

[8] For a state-by-state summary of surplus lines legislation see the *Agent's and Buyer's Guide* (annual) (Cincinnati: National Underwriter Co.).

domestic agents or brokers may not arrange for insurance from unauthorized insurers unless the admitted market has insufficient capacity or unless the coverage sought is not written in the admitted market. The surplus lines laws generally require the agent or broker to post a bond, to pay license fees, and to accept responsibility to pay the premium taxes on business placed with unadmitted insurers.

The objective of surplus lines laws is to give some measure of protection to buyers of insurance from insurers not otherwise regulated by the state and to provide for the collection of the state premium tax from unauthorized insurers.[9] The Illinois surplus lines law, for example, prohibits the surplus lines agent or broker from placing business in an unauthorized insurer unless (1) it makes a deposit of cash or securities in Illinois (the required minimum being the same as for a domestic company) or satisfies the Illinois department that it has a deposit in another state or has established a trust fund in the United States in like amount, (2) it appoints the director of insurance as attorney for service of process and consents to the jurisdiction of the Illinois courts, (3) the insurer is qualified by its charter to write the class of business it proposes to write, and (4) it fulfills the requirement for filing policy or certificate forms and financial statements.

There are some notable variations in surplus line laws. For example, Florida and Massachusetts issue lists of approved companies for surplus line business, and business may be placed only with companies shown on this list. In New Jersey and Missouri, transactions are permitted only with insurers declared eligible by the commissioner. In California, responsibility for the soundness of nonadmitted insurers lies with the surplus lines broker, and the commissioner assumes that the broker has not fulfilled that responsibility unless the insurer meets the financial requirements for admission to California. The Alabama Code makes no provision for surplus line business but does provide that agents placing business with unlicensed companies are to be held personally responsible for losses sustained on those contracts.

Florida and New Jersey publish a list of automatically "exportable" lines (revised annually) on which no affidavit of unavailability is required. For example, on a recent Florida list were interruption insurance, cemetery malpractice liability, contingent commissions (casualty only), broad form engineers professional liability, false arrest liability, health club liability, livestock mortality, masseurs liability, motorcycle and motor scooter coverages, nursing homes professional liability, twin insurance, workmen's compensation excess loss, stop loss for workmen's compensation self in-

---

[9] The laws of 24 states require the insured to pay the premium tax if he obtains coverage directly from an unadmitted insurer, that is, if he does not purchase through an agent or a broker. The laws of two states prohibit an insured from purchasing insurance directly, but the constitutionality of these laws is questioned. In addition to the state premium tax, a 4 per cent tax on premiums is levied by the federal government in the form of a stamp tax.

surers, and workmen's compensation restrospective penalty premium indemnity.

"Doing Business" in the State. What constitutes "doing business" in a state presents an interesting question. When the insurer operates through agents in a state for either soliciting insurance, investigating the risk, or paying the claim, it is deemed to be "doing business" in the state. And unauthorized companies can be controlled through controlling their agents. But what about business conducted entirely through the mails? The United States Supreme Court, on June 5, 1950, upheld the state of Virginia's power to issue a cease-and-desist order against solicitation of insurance by an out-of-state mail order insurer.[10] However, if a risk manager initiates the contact with a non-admitted foreign or alien insurer for the purchase of insurance, and all arrangements relating to the insurance are conducted outside the state, the unauthorized insurer cannot be said to be doing an insurance business in the risk manager's state. Sophisticated risk managers are able to select well-financed and well-managed unauthorized insurers who have well-established international reputations for settling losses fairly and promptly. They do not need the added protection of state regulation for comfort as might less astute buyers of insurance. As a matter of fact, the overseas unauthorized insurance market has had an enviable financial record, one that compares favorably with that of admitted insurers. In recognition of the financial stability of these unauthorized insurers, American insurers buy a large part of their reinsurance protection from these same foreign and alien insurers,[11] thus showing the confidence the admitted market has in this segment of the non-admitted market.

To help the risk manager avoid the expense, inconvenience, and confusion of having to bring action for legal remedy in the courts of the state or country of the insurer's domicile, most states have enacted the Unauthorized Insurer's Service of Process Act, a model law drafted by an all-industry committee working with the National Association of Insurance Commissioners. Under this legislation, unauthorized insurers doing business in the state are made subject to the jurisdiction of the courts of that state. The act designates the insurance commissioner as the agent of the unauthorized insurer to receive the service of notice of suit. The act is designed principally to protect insureds against companies that do business by mail or who have moved away from the state. Judgments obtained by the insured in his own state court against the insurer must be given "full faith and credit" by the courts of the states where assets of the insurer are held.

Thus a risk manager may make a legal contract of insurance with (*a*)

---

[10] *Travelers Health Association* v. *Commonwealth of Virginia*, 339 U.S. 643 (1950), 70 S. Ct. 927, 94 L. Ed., 1154.

[11] Reinsurance is the insurance of insurance. Reinsurance as it affects the risk manager is discussed in chap. 16. Additional discussion of unauthorized insurers also appears in that chapter.

authorized insurers through licensed agents and brokers or direct or with (*b*) unauthorized insurers through surplus lines agents or brokers licensed in the risk manager's state or by direct dealing with the insurer in a state or country where it is licensed. In dealing with unauthorized insurers, the buyer is given the protection of the Insurer's Service of Process Act in most states.

A Legal Act

For a contract to be valid, it must be for a legal purpose. The courts will not enforce agreements that require the performance of illegal or immoral acts or that tend to promote results against public policy. Public policy holds that no person may lawfully do anything that tends to injure the public or public good. The courts differ widely both as to what this statement actually means and as to what contracts are in violation of any particular meaning.

Several questions relating to public policy in connection with insurance contracts have been adjudicated. The question was once raised as to whether liability insurance was contrary to public policy because it would reduce the financial incentive for the insured to act in a careful manner, thus endangering the lives and property of others. Public policy was held not to be outraged by liability insurance. Life insurance policies on the lives of key men and others generally require the consent of the subject of the insurance; otherwise the contract is invalid. (This "consent" requirement has been made statutory in some states.) In other states, insurance issued on the life of any adult without his consent is against public policy.

Wagering or gambling agreements are illegal in most American jurisdictions. How does this ruling affect contracts of insurance? A wagering agreement is "one in which the parties stipulate that they shall gain or lose, upon the happening of an uncertain event in which they have no interest except that arising from the possibility of such gain or loss."[12] Note the phraseology, "no interest except. . . ." An insurance agreement would be a wagering agreement, and hence in violation of public policy, if the insured did not have an "insurable interest" in the subject matter (life or property) of the insurance. Insurance written without an insurable interest is an outrage of public policy not only because it becomes a wagering contract but also because it tempts persons seeking gain from these policies to destroy lives or property. As Professor Kimball so ably puts it: "Use of the insurance contract as a gambling device was not unknown in the twentieth century, but was relatively uncommon. By then costs of operations were so substantial and actuarial knowledge so advanced, that the gambler

---

[12] *Black's Law Dictionary* (St. Paul, Minnesota: West Publishing Co.), "Wagering Contracts."

had no reasonable chance unless he ceased to gamble and deliberately brought about the loss."[13]

Insurable Interest. Broadly viewed, one has an insurable interest in life or property "when he stands in such relation to it that he will be benefited by its continued existence and damnified by its destruction."[14] In discussing this broad view of insurable interest Vance raises an important question: "Must the expected benefit have such a legal basis that its conferring could be compelled by law, or the loss be such as would entitle the insured to damages against a tort-feasor causing it? . . . In answering this question a sharp distinction must be made between . . . property insurance and . . . life insurance."[15] Other questions also require a sharp distinction between insurable interest in property and life insurance: When must the insurable interest exist, and how much insurable interest is required? These questions will be discussed only to the extent that they are of concern to the risk manager.

What Constitutes an Insurable Interest? For *property insurance*, ownership of property gives the business an insurable interest in it. A legal or equitable title to property, however, is not necessary. An expectation of benefit from the continued existence of the property is sufficient to support an insurable interest if this expectation is based on a legal right. For example, both the stockholders and employees of a corporation may expect to benefit from the continued existence of the corporation's assets, but neither owns these assets. They belong to the corporation. Yet the stockholders have an insurable interest in these assets because of their legal right to share in the profits of the corporation and in its assets if the corporation is dissolved. The employees have no such legal rights, and therefore they have no insurable interest in the assets of their employer. Similarly, a mortgagee has an insurable interest in the mortgaged property, whereas a general creditor may not have an insurable interest in the assets of his debtor.[16] A business may stand to lose if a supplier's or customer's property is damaged, but the business does not generally have an insurable interest in the assets of its suppliers and customers. Nevertheless, it does have an insurable interest in its own profits, and these may be lost through damage to this non-owned property. A tenant does not have an insurable interest in the property of his landlord, but the rental agreement may be the basis of several

---

[13] Spencer L. Kimball, *Insurance and Public Policy* (Madison: University of Wisconsin Press, 1960), p. 32.

[14] William R. Vance, *Handbook on the Law of Insurance* (3d ed.; St. Paul, Minnesota: West Publishing Co., 1951), p. 157.

[15] *Ibid.*

[16] "May not" rather than "does not" is used here because a general creditor could be construed to have an insurable interest in the only income-producing asset of an infirm debtor. See Edwin W. Patterson, *Essentials of Insurance Law* (2d ed.; New York: McGraw-Hill Book Co., Inc., 1957), p. 116.

insurable interests: usufruct interest in improvements, leasehold interest, responsibility for returning the property to the landlord in the same condition as received, rent expense when the lease requires the tenant to continue paying rent during a period during which the property is untenantable, and responsibility for liability claims to third parties for bodily injury or property damage arising out of the use of the premises.

The important point for the risk manager to remember is that he must insure the correct interest. A usufruct interest is distinct from a property interest, and the interest insured as well as the person or persons who have the interest should be clearly spelled out in the contract.

In *life insurance*, the expectation of benefit from the continuation of the life insured need not have a legal basis. "An insurable interest exists whenever the relation between the assured and insured, whether by blood, marriage, or commercial intercourse, is such that the assured has a reasonable expectation of deriving benefit from the continuation of the life insured, or of suffering detriment or incurring liability through its termination. . . . The benefit must, however, be valuable and not merely sentimental."[17] Thus an employer has an insurable interest in the lives of his *key* employees but by definition does not have an insurable interest in the lives of "ordinary" employees. A partner has an insurable interest in the lives of his copartners. A stockholder has an insurable interest in the lives of his co-stockholders, and a corporation in the lives of its stockholders when the purpose of the insurance is to fund a stock purchase or retirement plan intended to prevent the forced sale of the deceased's share in the business. A creditor has an insurable interest in the life of his debtor.

When Must the Insurable Interest Exist? In *property insurance* the insurable interest need exist only at the time of the loss. It is not necessary to require an insurable interest at the inception of he policy because a property insurance contract is a contract of indemnity, that is, it is an agreement to reimburse the insured for losses actually sustained. The law will not allow the insured to collect unless he has an insurable interest. Thus, the lack of an insurable interest at the time the policy is purchased should not create a temptation to bring about the loss, nor does it create a wagering contract. To require that there be an insurable interest in the property when the contract is written would unnecessarily restrict the insurance companies in their efforts to develop forms to meet the needs of business. Reporting forms on variable inventories, builders risk forms, annual transit forms, and many other useful coverages promise insurance protection on property that the insured will not acquire or have responsibility for until some later date.

In *life insurance* the insurable interest must exist only when the policy is

---

[17] Vance, *op. cit.*, p. 190. As the context shows, Vance uses "assured" to designate the owner of the policy, "insured" to designate the person whose death is insured against.

purchased. A life insurance policy is not a contract of indemnity. It is a contract to pay the beneficiary a given amount of money upon the death of the subject. No proof that a monetary loss has been suffered is necessary.

The ruling that an insurable interest in life insurance need not exist at the time of loss arose originally from conditions that are no longer present. Life insurance policies in the early days had no provision for cash surrender values. To rule these policies unenforceable if no insurable interest were present at the time of the loss would work an economic injustice on the policy owners. They would not be allowed to realize the value of these policies by selling them in a free market; if the incipient insurable interest upon which the policy was issued ceased to exist, the policy would have to be sold to someone who had an interest. The market would be severely limited, and the seller would be at a distinct disadvantage.

But today's level-premium life insurance policies provide for cash values. This leads Patterson to conclude: "If the question were to be decided today, without regard to precedent, a just solution would be to allow the insured, whose interest has become extinguished, only the cash-surrender value (if any) of that date, together with premiums paid thereafter in mistaken reliance on the contract."[18] Yet this does not seem to be a just solution. A policy may easily be worth more than its guaranteed cash value. Suppose a policy has been carried on the life of a key man who has been retired early because of ill health. Should the employer be denied the speculative value of this policy because he no longer holds an insurable interest in the subject of the insurance?

Under the rules as they stand at present, a life insurance policy on a key man remains valid when a key man leaves the company's employment. The risk manager therefore must decide whether to continue the policy or to dispose of it. Perhaps the policy should be kept as a good investment. The decision should be made only after consultation with the financial manager of the company. A similar question may have to be answered when a closely held corporation goes public or when a partnership incorporates into a public held corporation.

How Much Insurable Interest Is Required? In *propery insurance* the amount of insurable interest is one of the limits fixing the maximum amount the insured can collect for a loss.[19] This rule also arises out of the principles

---

[18] Patterson, *op. cit.,* p. 164. Two or three states do require existence of insurable interest at death.

[19] An exception to this rule is the valued policy under which the face of the policy is agreed to be the amount of the loss in the event of a total loss, and to furnish the basis for loss settlement in the event of a partial loss. Even here, however, if the values agreed upon are excessive, the insured may be guilty of fraud, which will make the contract unenforceable. More than 40 per cent of the states have laws that make some policies valued with respect to total losses. Nearly all these statutes apply to insurance on real property only, and they apply to losses by fire or certain other perils only. (For a good historical and philosophical discussion of the pioneering Wisconsin valued-policy law see Kimball, *op. cit.,* pp. 240–49.)

of indemnity. One factor complicating the application of the rule is that of placing a value on the interest. That this can be a significant problem has already been indicated (chaps. 8 and 9).

In *life insurance* the amount of insurable interest is of no importance, since it ordinarily does not control the amount payable under the policy.[20] The risk manager, therefore, does not have to prove the amount of his loss in order to collect the full face amount under a key-man life insurance policy. This is indeed fortunate because, except in a limited number of key-man situations, who can tell what the key man really was worth to the business?

Valuable Consideration

In an executory contract,[21] such as a contract of insurance, consideration consists in a benefit accruing to the promissor or a detriment suffered by the promissee. Ordinarily both parties to the contract receive a benefit and suffer a detriment. Insurance contracts often state that the consideration of the insured consists of "the provisions and stipulations herein and of the premium specified." In most property insurance contracts, the promise to pay the premium is sufficient consideration, whereas in life insurance the first premium must actually be paid before the contract becomes effective. The insurer's consideration is the promise to make payments upon the occurrence of stipulated events. Thus, the detriment to the insured is the premium that he pays or obligates himself to pay and the conditions to which he agrees, and the detriment to the insurer is the chance that it will have to pay out a sum of money in excess of the premium received. The benefit to the insured is the promise of reimbursement for his losses to the extent agreed upon in the contract, whereas the benefit to the insurer is the premium paid.

Agency in Contract Formation

In its strict sense, the term "agency" means a relationship between two parties in which one (the agent) has the authority to create or modify contracts on behalf of the other (the principal). Most insurers are corporations, that is, artificial persons created by law with the authority to act in their own name but without the human ability to do so. They must, therefore, act through natural persons. These natural persons are agents of the corporation and in an insurance company include its officers, operating personnel, and local sales force. In the language of the street, however,

---

[20] The exception is found when the insurable interest is based on a debtor-creditor relationship. In most jurisdictions the face amount of the policy must bear a reasonable relationship to the debt *at the time the policy is written.*

[21] Executory contracts are distinguished from executed contracts. A contract is executory as long as one of the parties has a promise outstanding. Insurance contracts are executory, since the insurer, in exchange for the premium, makes a promise to pay the insured if he suffers a covered loss.

only the sales personnel are referred to as "agents." Most of the questions involving agency in insurance contract formation revolve around the power and authority of the local agent to bind the insurer.[22] These questions are decided on the basis of whether the risk manager had reasonable grounds for assuming that the authority had been granted.

Life Insurance Agents. Life insurance companies do not grant their sales agents the authority to accept an application for insurance and unconditionally bind the insurer. They give the authority to bind the company conditionally, as mentioned earlier, but only under the terms of the printed receipt issued in exchange for the first premium. The risk manager is put on notice of the limitation on the authority of the agent by a clause in the application blank stating, to quote one version:

No one except the president, a vice-president, the secretary, or an assistant secretary has the power on behalf of the company to make, modify, or discharge contracts, or to waive any of the company's rights or requirements (and in writing only), and these powers will not be delegated; that notice or knowledge of the soliciting agent or the medical examiner, if any, is not notice to or knowledge of the company; and that neither the soliciting agent nor the medical examiner is authorized to accept risks or to pass upon insurability.

In general, limitations on the contract-making authority of the agent, communicated to the insured through the application form, have been upheld by the courts. However, many courts refuse to honor the stipulation that knowledge of the soliciting agent is not knowledge of the company. These courts hold these stipulations to be inequitable and therefore against public policy.

Property Insurance Agents. Sales agents of property and liability insurers generally are given the authority to pass on risks and to bind the companies unconditionally to many kinds of insurance contracts. They are usually provided with some blank policies, which they sign and issue to the insured. If the insurer objects to any policy issued by one of its agents, it can cancel the policy in accordance with its terms. The insurer usually restricts the types of coverages or exposures that the agent is empowered to write, but these restrictions are not necessarily binding on the buyer, particularly if he could not reasonably be expected to know of these limitations on the agent's authority. What is reasonable for the risk manager to believe in any dispute is, of course, a matter for decision by the court. Custom of the trade plays its part in the deliberations of the courts, along with the question of what constitutes proper communication to the buyer.

The power of the local agent to bind the insurer to a contract is illustrated in the following case. The risk manager purchased a fire insurance

---

[22] An important distinction exists between the power and the authority of an agent. The law will give the agent the power to bind the insurer under certain circumstances even though the agent has not been given the express or implied authority by the insurer to act on its behalf in these circumstances. The discussion here will be concerned mainly with the agent's powers.

policy covering equipment at three locations for a total sum of $76,000, with a limit of $35,000 at location A, $1,000 at location B, and $40,000 at location C. A fire destroyed $60,000 of equipment at location A. The risk manager believed that he was entitled to collect $60,000, whereas the insurer believed that its liability was only $35,000. The risk manager's contention was based on an alleged conversation with the agent after the policy was delivered. The agent was said to have told the risk manager that, despite the location limit shown in the policy, any loss would be adjusted on the basis of the valuation shown at any one location in the monthly report upon which the premium was based and paid. The monthly report prior to the fire showed a valuation of $60,000 at the location where the fire occurred. The court held for the risk manager.[23]

The court said that it is well-settled law that an oral agreement cannot vary the terms and provisions of a written contract. It is also well settled that a policy provision to the effect that an agent is not empowered to alter the terms of a policy contract is binding. But, by an interesting argument, the court insisted that neither of these rules applied in this case. As a general agent of the insurer, the agent had authority to issue oral binders. His statement to the risk manager constituted an oral binder; hence a new contract was brought into existence and the suit was under the new contract.

Risk managers, however, should not depend upon ingenious reasoning by courts for their reimbursement. They should insist that all oral communications by the agent be reduced to writing and made a part of the policy. In the first place, it is not always so easy to prove an oral agreement. In the second place, not all courts are as ingenious as the one just described —nor does their ingenuity, when exercised, always redound to the benefit of the insured. And, finally, it is wise practice to be careful and exacting about the content and form of all contracts so that costly, inconvenient, and annoying law suits can be avoided.

Brokers.   Risk managers frequently arrange some or all of their coverage through insurance brokers. An insurance broker is a middleman between the insured and the insurers. In some ways he is much like the agent, but there are differences. One important difference is that, although brokers solicit insurance from the public, they technically are not representatives of insurance companies. Their business is that of buying for their customers, from insurers, insurance that either the brokers or the customers select. Therefore, a broker is an agent of the risk manager for the purpose of procuring insurance, even though insurance brokerage commissions are customarily paid by the insurers, not by the insureds.[24] Brokers, unless they

---

[23] *Federated Mutual Improvement and Hardware Insurance Company* v. *Fairfax Equipment Company*, 261 E. 2d 207, U.S. App., 10th Cir., Oklahoma.

[24] The insureds pay the brokers' fees indirectly, of course, since premiums are set to cover this as well as other expenses incurred by the insurers.

happen also to be insurance agents, do not have the power to make oral contracts of insurance on behalf of insurers. Brokers must place their business either through insurance agencies or directly with the insurance companies.[25] Of course, the agency with which the broker deals can bind the insurer to the coverage proposed by the broker, and the broker may be authorized to bind the insured to the contract offered.

Other important differences between the legal status of agents and brokers will become apparent as the discussion develops. Additional discussion of the subject appears in chapter 17.

RULES OF INTERPRETATION OF INSURANCE CONTRACTS

When a difference of opinion arises concerning the intentions of the parties to the contract, it may be necessary to resort to the courts for interpretation. Contract construction, that is, construing what the parties presumably had in mind, is a function of the courts in the event of disagreement. Various rules have been developed by the courts in resolving such disputes.

Conflicts between Policies and Endorsements

Most basic insurance contracts are standardized into uniform policies. In order to adapt these contracts to the differing needs of different insureds, certain alterations have to be made. For example, standard forms may have to be endorsed to broaden the coverage to include additional perils, property, persons, locations, hazards, and losses. Endorsements may also be required to reduce the coverage from that offered by the uniform policy, to complete the statement of coverage, to increase or decrease the amount of insurance, to adjust a rate, to correct an error subsequently discovered, or to record a change of address, among other things.

An important rule of policy construction is that the terms of an endorsement take precedence over the terms of the basic policy. Furthermore, it is important that the effective date of each endorsement be made clear because later endorsements take precedence over earlier ones.

Uniform printed endorsements are frequently available, so the agent has only to fill in the blanks with the information relating to the change. When printed endorsements are not available, the agent or risk manager will have to draft one and type it in its entirety. Another important rule of contract construction is that, when typed or written words are in conflict with printed words, the typed or written wording will govern. It is assumed, quite logically, that, since the specially written word was added by the

---

[25] Statutes in some states make anyone who assists in creating insurance contracts an agent of the insurer for some purposes, particularly premium collection. These laws do not make the broker an agent *only* of the insurer; he is still an agent of the insured for some purposes, while being an agent of the insurer for others.

parties to the printed form, the written words express more exactly the intent of the parties.

Another rule of construction is especially important when disputes arise over manuscript policies. No inaccuracy in the use of language or grammar, or omission of words or phrases intended to be inserted, will defeat the intent of the parties if that intent is clearly manifested. The court will not be precise in following the rules of grammatical construction.

An important condition of most insurance contracts is that no provision shall be waived or altered except by written endorsement attached to the policy. Some oral changes made by authorized agents may be upheld on the ground that they constitute a new contract, as demonstrated in the Fairfax Equipment Company case discussed earlier. This particular ruling, however, would apply when the change involved the subject matter or the amount of the insurance but not the printed contract terms or conditions.

Standardized Provisions

Insurance contracts, for the most part, are contracts of adhesion. That is, when the risk manager purchases an insurance contract, he ordinarily has to adhere to the terms prescribed by others. He has no bargaining position in the transaction.

Prescription by Law. Insurance is a technical business and subject to the use of unfair and deceptive policy provisions. To protect insureds against unscrupulous insurers, the states in various ways control the terms of insurance policies. The basic fire insurance policy, for example, is prescribed in statutes or administrative regulations, and insurers must use the exact language specified. But endorsements are added to standard fire policies to adapt them to the various risks to be insured. Most endorsements are drafted by rating organizations and are used uniformly by the insurers. Many of these uniform endorsements extend the coverage beyond that prescribed in the standard form. Because the forms are changed from time to time, frequently liberalizing the coverage, they include a clause granting each insured the benefit of any free liberalization that takes place while the policy is in force.

In some forms of insurance a set of standard provisions rather than an entire form is prescribed; this is the case in life and health insurance. The exact language of these provisions is left to the insurer. He may be more liberal in his treatment of the insured than the law requires. Thus the required provisions give an insured certain minimum protection. (Various other provisions that insurers have used in the past to weaken the protection are prohibited.)

An important rule of contract interpretation is that terms prescribed by statute cannot be bargained away and must be regarded as contractual terms, even if they are not written in the policy. Also certain terms cannot be bargained into the contract and must be ignored when they are found in the policy. Furthermore, accepted common law rules are to be read into the policy even though they are contrary to the intentions of the parties.

Prescription by Company Agreement. Many policy forms have been standardized by intercompany agreement in order to give the rating bureaus a stable basis for developing rates. Rate filings without the filing of policy forms are useless. Rates cannot be judged independently of coverage.

Thus insurers offer the risk manager policies that have been developed for the public at large rather than for him individually. The forms are drafted by the insurers (and in some cases dictated by the states), and the risk manager's autonomy in relation to them is reduced to that of deciding only whether he wants to enter into these standardized mass-produced contracts.[26]

Ambiguous Provisions

An important rule of policy interpretation is that, in case the meaning of the policy is not clear, it will be strongly construed against the insurer. The burden of achieving clarity falls on the party who draws up the contract and not on the party who simply adheres to it. Because the words used in the policy are the insurer's words, he should pay the penalty for their ambiguity. Of course, a policy is not ambiguous solely because the risk manager's impression of what it means is different from the insurer's impression. Courts are inclined to assign the usual meaning to words unless the words have specialized meanings that should be apparent to both the insurer and the risk manager. If it is unlikely that the risk manager would be familiar with what the insurer insists is the customary usage of a term, the courts will interpret the words to mean what a reasonable man would expect them to mean.

Finding or Creating Ambiguity. Many cases involving the question of ambiguity may be found in the court records. In some of them decisions are rendered which reasonable men would find difficult to accept as representing the intention of either party to the contract. Is it reasonable to suspect that a person intends his automobile liability policy to cover for bodily injury accidentally inflicted on a hunting companion when a bullet shot from a gun resting on the automobile misses its target? A court thought so.

Another interesting case in which the insured claimed ambiguity is illustrated in the following dispute over a personal liability policy.[27] In May,

---

[26] Professor Patterson (*op. cit.*, p. 83) points out that "the movement to *standardize* insurance contracts was begun and promoted by insurers as well as by prospective insureds, and standard forms were voluntarily adopted by marine insurers and fire insurers long before legal requirements were enacted." These circumstances provide an additional argument to show the need for regulation of policy forms to prevent conditions adverse to public policy and morality from being developed and imposed en masse on the insureds.

[27] *Farm Bureau Mutual (Nationwide) Insurance Company* v. *Greist et al.*, 251 F. 2d 85, U.S. App., 2d Cir., Vermont.

Richard Greist's parents were guests in his home. During the visit, Richard's mother fell and broke her hip. The insured knew of this at the time but did not report it to Nationwide, his insurer, until ten months later, when he received a letter from a law firm advising him that his mother was taking steps to enforce a claim against him. The policy in question was written on an "occurrence" basis,[28] and required notice from the insured "as soon as practicable." The district court found that the word "occurrence" was ambiguous and created an ambiguity in the policy in that it could be interpreted to mean, not only the accident upon which the insured's liability was based, but also the receipt by the insured of a claim against him. The court applied the rule of ambiguity—that when an ambiguity exists it must be construed favorably to an insured—and rendered judgment adverse to Nationwide.

Nationwide appealed the case and won. The U.S. Court of Appeals, second circuit, did not agree that the use of the word "occurrence" created an ambiguity in the notice provisions of the policy. The court pointed out that the terms of an insurance contract are to be given a reasonable construction, dependent upon the common understanding of their meanings and the context in which they appear. To construe "occurrence" as the receipt of a claim would render meaningless the sentence in the notice condition, "Such notice shall contain reasonably obtainable information respecting the time, place and circumstance of the occurrence. . . ." The court concluded: " We hold that the word 'occurrence' . . . relates to the event upon which the insured's liability is alleged to exist, which in this case is the accident . . . in May. . . ."

Mutual Mistakes in Policies

Sometimes a policy will not reflect what was agreed upon by the risk manager and the agent. The risk manager not only should be aware that mistakes can be made in the writing of policies, but should also take the necessary steps to guard against such errors. The best time to correct a policy error is before, not after, a loss. But if the risk manager slips up (risk managers are human), and his insurer insists on applying the terms of the contract as written, the courts may provide a remedy. When the proof is conclusive that the agreement reached between the risk manager and the agent does not appear in the written contract because of either a mistake on both sides or a mistake on one and fraud on the other, the courts will correct the mistake by reforming the contract to express the original intention of both parties. A basic rule of interpretation is that a contract should be construed to give effect to the intention of the parties. And this intention is to be ascertained not only from the language of the contract but also from the facts and circumstances surrounding the making of the contract.

---

[28] Policies written on an occurrence basis do not require the injury to be caused by accident.

For example, one E. F. Ball contracted with a private trucker, M. M. Dickerson, Jr., for transportation of $11,000 worth of tires from Dallas to Brownsville. Mr. Ball then asked an agent of the Gulf Insurance Company to insure the shipment under a trip transit policy in the sum of $8,910. In typing the policy, the agent showed the amount of insurance as $891 and named Dickerson instead of Ball as the insured. Ball called these errors to the agent's attention, and he promised to correct them but failed to do so. In the meantime the truck was forced off the highway. While Dickerson was in Kingsville looking for a mechanic and a wrecker, the truck caught fire from an unknown cause and the load of tires was completely destroyed. Ball entered his claim, which the insurer denied on several grounds. Among them were the contentions that the amount of insurance was only $891 and that Ball was not the insured. (The insurer had other grounds for denying liability to Dickerson.) The district court entered judgment in favor of Ball for $8,910, finding that there was a contract of insurance between Ball and the insurer's agent for that amount. The appellate court affirmed the decision, holding that the testimony of the agent established the contract of insurance.[29]

PERFORMANCE UNDER THE CONTRACT

Insurers are obligated legally as well as morally to perform under valid contracts of insurance. But disputes do arise from time to time as to the validity of insurance contracts under various sets of circumstances. For example, the insurer may contend that because of a mistake on the part of the risk manager in describing the property there was no mutual assent and thus no contract. For reformation, the mistake must be mutual or fraudulent. Thus, if the risk manager intends to insure a warehouse located on East Lake road but by mistake insures a warehouse located on West Lake road, the insurer is not obligated to perform under the agreement, since there was never any meeting of minds as to the piece of property covered. However, if the agent knew the precise property that the risk manager intended to insure, there would have been mutual assent regardless of the mistake in the policy, and the courts, if not the insurer, would reform the policy to obligate the insurer.

Another reason for an insurer's denial of liability under the contract may be his contention that the risk manager has made false warranties or false representations to the agent, or that material facts have been fraudulently concealed. The insurer, furthermore, may claim that some condition of the policy has been violated (for example, the notice provision mentioned in the Greist case discussed above) and on this basis deny liability.

The risk manager may admit to the facts presented by the insurer but

---

29 *Gulf Insurance Company* v. *Ball*, 324 S.W. 2d 605—C.C.A., Amarillo.

contend that, because of additional facts relating to the conduct of the insurer or its agent, the insurer has waived his defense or is estopped from using it.

The law with respect to these various possible contentions by insurer and insured now needs to be considered.

Warranties and Representations

A warranty is a statement in, or implied to be in, the policy relating to the nature of the risk insured. A warranty may relate to some fact now existing, with no reference to what might be expected in the future; it is then called an *affirmative* warranty. If the statement indicates that something is true now and will continue to be true in the future, or that some action will be taken in the future, the warranty is *promissory*. Courts construe a warranty to be affirmative if there is no clear proof that it was intended to be promissory. Thus the statement "Smoking is not allowed on the premises" was held by the United States Supreme Court to be an affirmative warranty. Therefore, smoking on the premises after the contract had been made did not render the warranty false if in fact smoking was not allowed at the time the contract was made.[30] For the warranty to have been promissory, the insurance company would have had to make it clear in the contract that smoking was to have been forbidden during the entire term of the contract.

Implied warranties are exceptions to the usual rule that warranties must be written or printed and made a part of the policy. Implied warranties are found only in marine insurance and apply only to contracts insuring hulls (ships). The insured under a hull policy impliedly warrants that the vessel is seaworthy, that the ship will move on the customary and usual course between the ports named (no deviation),[31] and that the vessel will not be used in any illegal enterprise or for the transportation of contraband.

A representation is a statement made by the risk manager to the insurer as an inducement to write the policy. Under common law rules, a representation differs from a warranty in that it is not a part of the policy itself and may be made orally.

The Common Law Doctrines of Warranty and Representation. Under the common law, noncompliance with a warranty, or the making of a falsely warranted statement, furnishes grounds for the insurer to avoid the contract.[32] A warranty is presumed to be material, that is, to deal with subject matter crucial to the terms of the contract. Furthermore, a claim that

---

[30] *Hosford* v. *Germania Fire Insurance Company*, 127 U.S. 399 (1888), 8 S. Ct. 1199, 32 L. Ed. 196.

[31] Deviation is permitted only to avoid storms or for errands of mercy.

[32] A voidable contract is one that may be disaffirmed. Until disaffirmation takes place, the contract is valid. It is only when the agreement is not binding on either party that it is properly called void rather than voidable. Many insurance policies use the word "void" where "voidable" is the correct term.

breach of a warranty was unintended is no defense. All the insurer needs to do to avoid the contract is to prove that a warranty was violated.

For an insurer to avoid a policy for a false representation, it must prove that the representation was material. And, when the representation dealt with a matter of opinion or belief rather than of past or present fact, the insurer must prove not only that the representation was material and false but also that it was fraudulently made, that is, made with the intent to deceive.

When the insurer is allowed to rescind a contract on the grounds of misrepresentation, it must return the premium to the insured. But avoidance brought about by a breach of warranty does not entitle the insured to a return of premium unless the breach took place before the effective date of the insurance.

Judicial Modifications of the Common Law. The rules expressed above are the common law doctrines of warranty and representation. Except in marine insurance, the American courts as a rule do not follow the strict English common law here.

One modification of the common law doctrine of warranty has been created by the refusal of courts to treat as warranties any *immaterial* statements not specifically warranted. In addition, an increasing number of courts, though not yet the majority, apply the doctrine of beneficent interpretation to warranties. Interpretation of warranties by the American courts has been, variously, literal, functional, or equitable. Under literal interpretation a warranty must be complied with strictly, but under a functional or equitable interpretation some leeway is allowed. A functional construction interprets the warranty in relation to its purpose, whereas an equitable construction "is guided by sentiments of mercy rather than by the *literal* meaning, or even the *functional* meaning, of the words in the contract."[33]

By way of illustration, suppose the risk manager promised, in connection with his burglary insurance, to keep two watchmen recording hourly rounds on a watchmen's clock while the premises were closed for business. Before the policy expired and without notice to the insurer, the business installed a new protection system calling for one watchman to signal an outside central station hourly. This altered system is considered to be as effective as the old one, if not more effective. Under a literal interpretation of the warranty, the change would constitute a breach, whereas under a functional interpretation there would have been no breach. Now suppose that, before the change, one of the watchmen had left the premises for a little while, thus breaking the company rules. A literal or functional interpretation of the warranty would find a breach, whereas an equitable interpretation would find no breach if the court concluded that the insured

---

[33] Patterson, *op. cit.*, p. 314.

had done all that could be reasonably expected of him by selecting what had seemed to be a reliable watchman.

A third type of judicial modification of the common law doctrine of misrepresentations and warranties consists of the refusal of a number of courts to distinguish sharply between misrepresentations of opinion and misrepresentations of fact. These courts have held that the applicant for insurance was not guilty of false representations if the representations were made "to the best of his knowledge and belief." This rule has been used particularly with respect to applications for life insurance.

Statutory Modifications.   Finally, the harsh aspects of the common law doctrines of warranty and representation have been softened by statutory modification. Many states have statutes that prevent the insurer from using false representations as grounds for avoiding a contract unless these representations have been made in writing and included in the contract. Most of these statutes apply only to life insurance or life and health insurance.

Whenever statements made by the applicant are put in writing and incorporated into the policy, they may become warranties rather than representations. But over half the states (again, with respect to life insurance or life and health insurance) require that statements made by the insured in his application be deemed representations and not warranties, thus requiring the insurer to prove the materiality of these statements if the policy is to be avoided.

In a few states the common law has undergone statutory modification so that a false warranty or false representation by an insured must actually cause or contribute to the loss in order for the insurer to have grounds for rescinding the contract.[34] Under these statutes, it is not enough to prove that the warranty or representation was material; the breach itself must be shown to have been material to the loss. A few statutes require a slightly less stiff test and provide only that the breach increase the chance of loss. No causal relationship need be shown between the breach and the loss itself, but it must be shown that the breach increased the chance of loss. For example, in the burglary insurance illustration presented earlier, the change in the protection system constituted a breach of a material warranty. Under the "warranties shall be deemed representation" statutes, this violation would be sufficient to avoid the policy in a court that construed the warranty literally. Under the "contribute to the loss" statutes, the breach would not be sufficient to defeat the policy unless the breach itself was material to the loss. And under the "increase the chance of loss" statutes,

---

[34] In all but one of these states (Iowa) the burden of proof of a causal relationship between the loss and the breach is on the insurer. In only one state (Nebraska) does the statute apply to all forms of insurance, but here it applies only to warranties. In another state (Texas) the statute is limited to fire insurance, whereas, among the remaining six states with such a statute, three (Kansas, Missouri, and Rhode Island) apply it only to life insurance, one (Oklahoma) only to industrial life and health insurance, and two (Iowa and New Hampshire) to all forms of insurance other than life.

the violation would not defeat the policy if the new system could be shown to be at least as effective as the old one in reducing the hazard. In fact, the "increase the chance of loss" statutes force on the courts a functional interpretation of warranties.

Concealment

In insurance, "concealment" means the failure of the insured to volunteer information of a nature material to the insurer. In marine insurance the English common law is applied in the United States—if the insured knows something material about the risk that the insurer does not know, he had better tell him or take his chances that the insurer will use this non-disclosure as grounds for avoiding the contract. All the insurer need prove to defeat the policy is that the insured knew the fact at the time the contract was written, that the fact was material, and that the insurer did not know this fact at that time. In other forms of insurance the common law of concealment has been softened. The courts insist upon several additional qualifying conditions before they will allow the insurer to avoid a policy on the grounds of concealment: the insured must have been aware both that the fact in question was material and that the insurer had no knowledge of it, and the failure to disclose must be motivated by an intent to defraud the insurer. The burden of proof of these stipulations rests with the insurer.

In California the common law of concealment has been modified by a statute that allows *unintentional* concealment to be a ground for avoidance of the contract.

Waiver and Estoppel

Technically, a waiver is the voluntary relinquishment of a known right; an estoppel is a bar or impediment raised by the law to prevent a person from asserting that which he previously denied by his words or his conduct, or from denying that which he previously asserted. In insurance, the defenses of waiver and estoppel produce the same results. It does not matter to the insured, therefore, whether the conduct of the insurer or its agent will be considered by the court to have constituted a waiver or to have set up an estoppel. The effect either way is to eliminate what would have been a good defense for the insurer and to require it to perform under the contract.

The workings of the legal doctrines of waiver and estoppel can be seen best (indeed, can almost be seen *only*) through the use of illustrative examples. White owned a 17-foot boat; he decided to cover its hull with fiberglass. While this work was in process, he purchased insurance on the boat. Subsequently, he claimed that the following event occurred. While he was operating the boat on the Lake of the Ozarks, it struck some "unknown object." The craft began to take in water and soon sank. White sought to collect from his insurer, which then investigated the claim. The boat was raised and the insurer's inspector found that the fiberglass coating of the hull was split and had pulled loose from the hull. He concluded that the fiberglass had been applied without application of calking to the seams and cracks between the planking; that moisture from inside the boat had seeped through the uncalked seams and gotten between the hull and the fiberglass, loosening the bonding, so that, when the fiberglass was split and ripped, water could flow into the hull. The insurer, relying on the implied warranty of seaworthiness, denied liability.

White took his case to court and won a verdict, which was upheld in the appeals court.[35] The court held that the insurer was estopped from asserting the defense of seaworthiness. The insurer's agent saw the boat at least three times while the fiberglass was being applied to the hull. If the work was not being done properly, it was open and obvious to the agent, but he issued the policy anyway and collected the premium. An insurer is charged with the same knowledge as its agent and is bound by his acts within the scope of his authority. Therefore the company could not complain, after the loss, of a condition of which it had earlier impliedly approved (through the action and inaction of its agent).

Liability policies usually include the following clause: "The insured shall cooperate with the company and, upon the company's request, attend hearings and trials and assist in making settlements, securing and giving evidence. . . ." In spite of receiving several letters and a telegram from the insurance company, the insured failed to appear at the trial of the suits against him. The insurer defended the action without the insured's presence but refused to pay the judgments rendered against the insured on the ground that he had abrogated his coverage by violation of the cooperation clause of the policy. The judgment creditors of the insured took legal action against the insurer to compel payment of their claims. The district court held for the insurer, stating that the insured's failure to cooperate voided the policy. But the case was appealed and the district court was reversed.[36] The higher court held that when the insurance company conducted a defense of the action against its insured, with knowledge of his failure and refusal to attend the trial and without taking a reservation of rights or non-waiver agreement, the company by its behavior waived its right to deny liability on ground of violation of the cooperation clause.

ANATOMY OF AN INSURANCE POLICY

An insurance policy usually contains four major sections: declarations, insuring agreements, exclusions, and conditions. Some policies include a

---

[35] *White v. Citizens Insurance Company of New Jersey*, 355 S.W. 2d 421 (1962), Mo. App., Kansas City, Missouri.

[36] *Beam et al.* v. *State Farm Mutual Automobile Insurance Company*, 269 F. 2d 151 U.S. App., 6th Cir., Kentucky.

separate section on definitions. Endorsements or riders are frequently attached to the policy to extend, restrict, modify, or complete the coverage. The bulk of these policies and endorsements are standardized by custom, law, or intercompany agreement. It is necessary to refer to specimen policies in connection with the study of the remainder of this chapter.[37]

Declarations

Declarations are statements about the subject of the insurance and the insured. In some lines of insurance, the declarations are included in the application and made a part of the policy. In other lines, where no written application is required, the declarations are usually typed in on the first page of the policy. Typical items contained in declarations are the name of the insured, location of the exposure, type of business insured, previous experience of the applicant with respect to cancellation or declination of insurance by another insurer, inception and expiration dates, and amount of insurance in the present policy. Various other matters pertinent to the underwriting and rating of the exposure, such as any warranties or promises made by the insured regarding the nature and control of the hazard, can also be included.

Insuring Agreements

The insuring agreements define broadly the coverage afforded under the contract. For example, the insuring agreements in the standard scheduled automobile liability policy describe two coverages: bodily injury liability and property damage liability. These agreements provide for these coverages with respect to three classes of hazards: owned automobiles, hired automobiles, and non-owned automobiles.[38] In addition, several service and indemnity agreements are included relating to defense of suits and payment of premiums on bonds. The insuring agreements in this policy also define the meanings of a number of the terms used. While definitions are found in other policies, they are not always a part of the insuring agreements.

Exclusions

The insuring agreements are modified by exclusions. For a number of reasons, insurers find it necessary to restrict the coverage through the use of

---

[37] Specimen policy kits are available from the American Mutual Insurance Alliance, 20 North Wacker Drive, Chicago 6, Illinois, or from the Insurance Information Institute, 60 John Street, New York 38, New York.

[38] Policies may be written on either a scheduled form or a blanket form. Under a scheduled form the hazards, perils, losses, or pieces of property covered are listed, with limits and premiums assigned to each scheduled item. Under the blanket form, a single limit and premium applies to all hazards, perils, losses, or pieces of property covered. The policy described in the text is called "scheduled" primarily because of its schedule treatment of the three classes of hazards mentioned in the text. In addition, however, most forms used with this policy require scheduling of each individual vehicle whose operation is to be considered a covered hazard within the one general class, "owned automobiles."

exclusions. The major reasons are (1) to eliminate uninsurable risks, (2) to eliminate coverages of a specialized nature requiring special rating and underwriting, (3) to facilitate the management of the moral hazard, (4) to eliminate coverage that would duplicate that of other policies that the insured is likely to carry, (5) to eliminate coverages that, though important to some risk managers, are not needed by the typical insured, and (6) to hold premium rates within reasonable levels. A review of the exclusions in any policy will usually reveal the reason or reasons why each exclusion is used.

Conditions

Operating rules regarding the coverage are set forth in the conditions. These rules impose definite obligations on the insured if he wishes to collect under his policy. They also impose some obligations on the insurer. In addition, they give both parties certain rights. Some of the more common conditions may be briefly summarized here. They are discussed further in chapter 15. In any case, the risk manager must read his policies carefully to familiarize himself with all the conditions.

Subrogation. Most insurance contracts are contracts of indemnity. To permit the insured to recover fully for his loss under his insurance policy and also collect from the person responsible for the loss would be in violation of the principle of indemnity. Neither is it sound public policy to permit the person responsible for the loss to escape liability. The law resolves this problem by allowing the insurance company, after it has paid the loss, to substitute itself for the insured in maintaining action against the wrongdoer. The insurer is allowed to retain an amount equal to the loss paid plus the costs of the action. Of course, if because of deductibles or inadequate limits the insurance proceeds are insufficient fully to indemnify the insured, he retains the right of action against the wrongdoer for this deficiency. If the insured signs away his right to collect from the responsible party, then the insurer will have no right of action, because the equitable right of subrogation gives the insurer only those rights held by the insured.

To preserve the value of its right of subrogation, the insurer inserts a subrogation clause as a condition of the policy. Under this condition the insured is obligated to cooperate with the insurer in maintaining this right and must do nothing to prejudice the insurer's rights. Thus, if the insured waives his rights against a third party, he also waives his rights to collect under his insurance unless the right of subrogation has been waived by the insurer. In most current policy forms, this provision applies only to waivers made *after the loss*. In older forms, however, waiver of rights *any time during the policy period* is prohibited. Therefore, when a business agrees to hold others harmless for losses for which they might be liable, the risk manager should check his policies to see whether their subrogation clauses are being violated.

Cancellation. Most insurance policies allow for cancellation by either party. The insurer must give the insured a minimum number of days' notice before the cancellation becomes effective. The number of days' notice and the method of giving this notice vary among policies. The insured is entitled to a pro rata return of his premium when his insurer initiates the cancellation.

The insured may cancel his policy immediately upon notifying the company. However, the amount of his return premium is based on a short rate table under which the refund is less than a pro rata amount. For example, if the insurer cancels a one-year policy after it has been in force for 91 days, the insured will receive a refund of 75 per cent of the premium. If the cancellation is initiated by the insured, the refund will be less than this—65 per cent under most policies. The penalty is charged to offset the initial cost of writing the policy and to discourage selection against the company. It is also designed to discourage cancellation and switching of policies. Life insurance policies and a growing number of health insurance policies are not cancellable by the insurer.

Assignment. Most insurance contracts are personal contracts. It is common to speak of the property as being insured, but technically the person having the insurable interest is the insured. Insurance policies have been described as contracts of the utmost good faith (*uberrimae fidei*), and the insurer and insured consider (or should consider) seriously the character, conduct, and credit of each other before entering into the agreement. The insurance policy, being a personal contract, does not go with the property when the property is transferred to a new owner. Consent of the insurer usually is required to assign the policy, and the conditions of the policy set forth this requirement.

Since life and health insurance policies are not considered personal contracts, they may be assigned without the consent of the insurer, but notice of the assignment is required or the insurer will not be bound by it. The insurer refuses to assume any responsibility for the validity of the assignment.

Waiver and Change. Insurance policies generally incorporate "waiver" or "change" clauses as protection against overly generous agents who may orally promise coverage not contemplated by the policy. These clauses specify that no terms of the policy may be waived or changed unless expressed in writing and added to the policy. Furthermore, they specify that "notice to any agent or knowledge possessed by any agent or by any other person shall not effect a waiver or a change in any part of this policy or estop the Company from asserting any right under the terms of the policy."

Most courts uphold the requirement that the waiver must be in writing, but some courts have allowed verbal waivers in spite of the policy provision to the contrary. These courts have held that, since the agent has the authority to waive certain provisions, he can waive the waiver clause. As to the stipulation that the insurer shall not be charged with the knowledge of his agent, Vance has this to say: "That the insurer shall not be charged with knowledge acquired by agent . . . according to many courts, essays to set aside a settled rule of law, and is therefore contrary to public policy; but under what now appears to be the majority view such limitations will be enforced."[39]

The risk manager, therefore, will do well to consider these clauses as an indication of the limited authority of the agents and proceed cautiously. However, if a loss has occurred, and the insurer uses these conditions as grounds for denying liability, the risk manager can take another look, throw caution to the wind, and proceed full steam ahead to what may well be a sympathetic court.

Inspection and Audit. In workmen's compensation, liability, and boiler and machinery insurance, the insurer's inspection service could be of great importance to the risk manager in uncovering hazardous conditions. Inspection is equally important to the insurer as a means of controlling losses. The inspection clause gives the insurer the right to inspect the premises of the insured as they relate to the subject matter of the insurance, but, unfortunately for the risk manager, the clause does not give him the converse right to demand inspection from the insurer. As mentioned, amounts and types of loss prevention services offered by insurers vary among the companies and agencies, and even the same agency and insurer do not offer the same services to all their insureds. These factors should be considered by the risk manager when he settles down to the business of choosing his agent or insurer.

In some policies, the premiums are based on some fluctuating unit, such as sales, payroll, or admissions. In other policies, the amount of insurance fluctuates in accordance with the value of the exposure, and the premiums are based on the values insured. To obtain the information necessary for an accurate rating of exposures, the insurer reserves the right to examine and audit the insured's books and records so far as they relate to the premiums due the insurer.

Loss Adjustment Conditions. Insurance policies contain a number of provisions relating to what the insured should and should not do after a loss. While these provisions are considered at some length in chapter 15, the following introductory notes about them are appropriate here.

One set of provisions deals with notice of loss. These provisions state when the insured is to notify the insurer of a loss, and what the form of the notice should be. Another subject is proof of loss. The proof is a sworn (notarized) statement by the insured containing all the facts necessary to justify issuance of a check for his claim. The facts necessary for this pur-

---

[39] Vance, *op. cit.*, p. 453.

pose are listed in detail in some policies, notably the 1943 New York Standard Fire Insurance policy.

Another group of provisions deals with protection of the property at and after a loss and with the insured's obligation to aid and cooperate with the insurer in determining the nature and extent of the loss or in defending against claims made by third parties.

Property insurance policies generally have an appraisal clause to be used in resolving disagreement over the amount of the insurer's liability. These clauses are of value to the risk manager as well as to the insurer because they help to keep these differences out of court—expensive litigation may be eliminated and the loss adjustment process may be faster.[40]

In property insurance policies other than ocean marine, the insured cannot abandon the property to the insurer after a loss and claim a total loss. A no abandonment condition is written into some policies and read into the others by the courts. In marine insurance, the insured can, under certain conditions, abandon the property to the insurer and claim a constructive total loss. A typical condition appearing in marine insurance policies is "No recovery for a Constructive Total Loss shall be had hereunder unless the property insured is reasonably abandoned on account of its actual total loss appearing to be unavoidable, or because it cannot be preserved from actual total loss without an expenditure which would exceed its value when the expenditure had been incurred."

A repair-or-replace option is found in a large number of property insurance contracts. The insurer rarely if ever uses this option under most policies, but in Plate Glass insurance the usual practice is for the insurer to replace the broken glass. Good working relations between insurers and glass companies produce fast service and discount prices—both of which benefit the risk manager.

An important set of loss adjustment conditions deals with the relations of the insurer with third parties who have an interest in the claim. Under some types of insurance, Bailees' Customers and Furriers' Customers forms, for example,[41] the contracts provide that at the insurer's option the claim may be adjusted with and paid directly to the insured's customer. This makes it possible to reach an agreement with less delay and, as a result, helps to retain good customer relations. Under other coverages, Accounts

---

[40] In some jurisdictions it has been strangely held that only the insurer can force the use of the appraisal clause. We say "strangely" because the provision at issue has been that of the 1943 Standard Fire Insurance policy, worded as follows: "In case the insured and this Company shall fail to agree as to . . . the amount . . . , then, *on the written demand of either*, each shall select . . . [an] appraiser . . . ," etc. The part here italicized seems to the authors to leave no room for even an issue as to whether the clause applies equally to *either* party's demand. Sometimes the workings of the judicial mind, or else its understanding of the English language, really are beyond the comprehension of the rest of us.

[41] These are policies under which commercial bailees (such as dry cleaners, launderers, or fur stores) insure against loss on customers' property.

Receivable insurance, for example, the insurer is not permitted to approach the insured's customers. In this way the insured can protect in his own way the customer relationships he has developed over the years. Professional Malpractice policies prohibit the insurer from settling any third-party claim or suit without the written consent of the insured. An important purpose of the Professional Malpractice policy is to pay the cost of defending the good name of the insured, and in many cases the insured is not willing to settle out of court. He is afraid that this would be interpreted as an admission of guilt.

Still other loss adjustment conditions are those dealing with the time limit for paying claims and for bringing suits.

Definitions. In life, fire, and marine insurance, terms generally are not defined in the contract. The risk manager has to rely on statutes or a body of court decisions for definitions. On the other hand, in casualty insurance, terms are usually defined in the policy. Sometimes they are defined in the insuring agreements (Automobile and Workmen's Compensation), sometimes in a separate section labeled definitions (Comprehensive 3-D and Mercantile Safe Burglary), and sometimes as a part of the policy conditions (Manufacturers' and Contractors' Liability and Mercantile Open Stock). Among the terms defined in the Workmen's Compensation policy are "workmen's compensation laws," "state," "bodily injury by accident," "bodily injury by disease," and "assault and battery." Among the terms defined in the Comprehensive 3-D policy are "money," "securities," "employee," "premises," "banking premises," "messenger," "custodian," "robbery," "safe burglary," and "loss." The Mercantile Safe Burglary policy, in addition, defines the term "property." The Manufacturers' and Contractors' Liability policy defines "elevators," "automobiles," and "assault and battery," and the Mercantile Open Stock policy defines "premises," "burglary," "robbery of a watchman," "loss," and "jewelry."

Conditions Affecting the Limits of Liability. A number of conditions affecting the amount payable by the insurer are included in most insurance contracts. These conditions and the other limitations on amounts recoverable by the risk manager under insurance contracts are discussed in chapter 15.

Endorsements

Much has already been said about endorsements and riders in this chapter. Flexibility in standard forms is achieved through the use of endorsements.

Forms. Some standard policies (the Standard Fire policy, the Annual Transit policy, and the Schedule Property floater, for example) are incomplete documents and require an endorsement (commonly called a "form") to complete the contract. These forms describe the subject matter of the insurance.

The basic fire policy, for example, insures against direct loss by fire or lightning. The risk manager, however, may need protection not only against direct loss of his property but also against loss of income while the damage is being repaired. Furthermore, he may need protection against perils other than fire and lightning, such as explosion, riot, earthquake, and windstorm, to name a few. The fire insurance companies write these coverages and many more under the Standard Fire policy. Over one hundred forms are available in most territories to be used with this standard policy. They describe the nature and location of the property to be insured (Building and Contents form), extend the standard policy to cover additional perils (the Earthquake Damage Assumption endorsement), and extend the standard form to cover other losses (business interruption forms). Endorsements also provide for fluctuating amounts of insurance (reporting forms) and for variable locations of the insured property (multiple location forms).

Some writers prefer to make a distinction between the terms "form" and "endorsements." William H. Rodda writes that "the term 'form' is used to describe the piece of paper that contains the principal modifications to the policy contract. The term 'endorsement' is used to describe other additions to the policy further modifying its terms."[42] He goes on to say that this distinction is not universal, although he believes it to be common and proper. However, for all practical purpose, there is little to be gained by insisting on technical distinctions between endorsements, forms, and riders. They all amount to the same thing: completion or modification of the terms of the basic policy.

SUMMARY

The insurance policy is a document containing the contract of insurance. For the agreement to be a valid contract, it must comply with the common law: mutual assent by competent parties for performance of a legal act for a valuable consideration. Mutual assent is manifested when the terms offered by one party (in insurance, usually the insured) are accepted by another within a reasonable time. The risk manager needs to be familiar with what constitutes an offer and an acceptance so that he will know when his insurance coverage becomes effective.

The risk manager, when acting within the authority granted him by his employer, may be assumed to be legally competent to contract for insurance. Authorized insurers (those licensed to do business in the insured's state) have the legal capacity to contract in that state either directly or through licensed agents or brokers. Unauthorized insurers have the legal capacity to contract in the insured's state through licensed surplus lines agents or brokers or directly in their own states or countries or in any state or country where they are authorized.

---

[42] Rodda, *Fire and Property Insurance* (Englewood Cliffs, New Jersey: Prentice-Hall, Inc., 1956), p. 63.

For the contract to be valid it must be for a legal purpose. Thus, an insurable interest is required so that the policy will not be a wagering contract or endanger life or property of others by providing an incentive to bring about the event against which the insurance is written.

The consideration supporting an insurance contract is the premium paid or to be paid by the insured and the contract conditions to which he agrees. The insurer's consideration is the promise to indemnify the insured under the conditions agreed upon in the policy.

Agents play an important role in the formation of insurance contracts. Life insurance agents do not have the power to bind their companies unconditionally. However, as a rule, they can bind their companies conditionally, that is, subject to the findings that the life to be insured is insurable. On the other hand, property and liability insurance agents usually are given the authority to bind the insurers. Brokers also serve as middlemen between the insurer and risk manager, but they are agents of the insured unless otherwise provided by law.

Several rules of contract interpretation have evolved. One rule of policy construction is that the terms of the endorsement take precedence over the terms of the policy. Another rule is that when typed or written words are in conflict with printed words, the typed or written words will govern. Furthermore, no inaccuracy in the use of language or grammar, or omission of words or phrases intended to be inserted, will defeat the intent of the parties if the intent is clear. Terms prescribed by statute or accepted common law cannot be bargained away, nor can prohibited provisions be allowed to remain, regardless of the intentions of the parties. In case the meaning of the policy is not clear, it will be strongly construed against the insurer. Policies will be reformed by the courts to correct mutual mistakes.

Insurers are legally as well as morally obligated to perform under valid contracts of insurance. The insurer, however, is not legally obligated to perform when there is no mutual assent, or when the insured has made false warranties or false representations of material facts, or when the insured has fraudulently concealed material facts. Nor is he obligated to perform when the insured violates some condition of the policy. The insurer, however, may be denied his defense if the court concludes that a waiver or estoppel situation has been created.

An insurance policy usually consists of four major sections: declarations, insuring agreements, exclusions, and conditions. Sometimes a separate section on definitions is included, but, more often, when the policy defines terms these definitions are a part of the insuring agreements or conditions. Conditions common to most policies are those relating to subrogation, cancellation, assignment, waiver and change, inspection and audit, loss adjustment, and limits of liability. Endorsements are necessary to complete or modify the terms of the basic policy.

REVIEW AND DISCUSSION QUESTIONS

1. In what way do practices with respect to offer and acceptance differ in life insurance from other forms of insurance? What is the actual significance of these differences to the insurance buyer?

2. To what extent, if any, is the competency of parties to contract a concern of the buyer of insurance?

3. Of what use to the risk manager are unauthorized insurers? Would they be any less useful if they were authorized? If so, why? If not, why do they not seek authorization?

4. What are the rules of your state with respect to unauthorized insurers (including surplus line regulation)? What changes would you like to see in these rules? Why?

5. Why must "sharp distinction" be made between property insurance and life insurance with respect to the legal basis for an insurable interest? What distinctions are made? Do they appear reasonable to you? Why or why not?

6. What is the basis for insurable interest in liability insurance? What is the basis in bailee's insurance, under which a bailee can insure property of customers without regard to his liability for damage thereto?

7. Suppose a policy has been carried on the life of a key man who has been retired early because of ill health. Should the employer be denied the speculative value of this policy because he no longer holds an insurable interest in the subject of the insurance? What *non*-speculative value exists here which the employer should not be denied? Explain.

8. What is meant by the "authority" of an agent, and how does this differ from his "power"? What significance, if any, does this difference have for a risk manager? Explain.

9. The authority usually granted to agents of property-liability insurers differs from that granted to agents of life insurers. Is it reasonable that there should be this difference? Justify your position.

10. In your state, is an insurance broker ever considered an agent of the insurer? If so, under what circumstances or for what purposes?

11. In law in general, a buyer's broker who accepts payment from the seller from whom he buys is considered to have violated his agency relationship with his original principal (the buyer). Why should not this rule be applied in insurance? (Or, if it should be applied, why is it not?)

12. The 1943 New York Standard Fire Insurance "policy" states, "This policy shall not cover accounts, bills, currency, deeds, evidences of debt, money or securities" (lines 7-9). This standard fire policy appears in its entirety in Homeowners policies. In one of the early versions of these policies, the following is the *only* other specific reference to these same kinds of property:

LIMITATIONS OF COVERAGE

Under Coverage C or D, this company shall not be liable:

c) for more than $100 on money, including numismatic property;

d) for more than $500 on notes, securities, stamps, including philatelic property, accounts, bills, deeds, evidences of debt, letters of credit, passports, documents and railroad or other tickets; . . .

What is the status of coverage on these types of property as the result of the presence of all these provisions in the same policy? State specifically how the rules of contract interpretation apply in determining the answer to this question.

13. What protection, if any, does the risk manager get from state supervision of policy forms? Is this protection necessary? Justify your position.

14. Under what circumstances does an insurance policy mean something other than what it says? How can one know what it does mean then?

15. Distinguish between warranties and representations; between misrepresentations and concealments. What are the various possible effects of breaches of warranties, of misrepresentations, and of concealments?

16. American courts and legislatures have "liberalized" the old common law rules of warranty and misrepresentation. What effects should this liberalization have on the behavior of insurance buyers? Why?

17. What effect should the doctrines of waiver and estoppel have on the behavior of insurance buyers? Why?

18. Why do insurance policies contain (*a*) assignment, (*b*) subrogation clauses? What are their effects?

19. What is the relation of the waiver clause in a policy to the general legal doctrine of waiver? What do the waiver and estoppel cases reported in the text suggest about waiver clauses in policies? Is this the general rule for waiver clauses in (*a*) life insurance, (*b*) other forms of insurance?

20. What are the functions of endorsements and riders? Would it not be better to print up an entirely different policy for each different situation covered by a standard form, rather than have just one policy with a multiplicity of forms which may be attached to it? Why, or why not?

Chapter 14

INSURANCE COVERS

The purchase and the administration of insurance occupy much of the time of the risk manager, in fact so much of his time that he calls his national organization the American Society of Insurance Management, Inc. The society in turn calls its official bimonthly publication the *National Insurance Buyer* and has as a slogan "An informed buyer is a better buyer."[1] A perusal of the articles published in this magazine indicates that its editors believe that for the risk manager to be a better insurance buyer he must be informed on insurance covers and insurance markets. This means, broadly, that the risk manager must know what is available and where to get it.

What is available involves not only knowledge of the types of policies written but also an understanding of the coverage that is or can be included in these policies. Furthermore it requires an awareness of what is not covered by "standard" insurance policies and what apparently cannot be covered by any policy.[2] *Where to get it* includes, in general, what insurers and what distributors (independent agents, brokers, company salesmen) to patronize. These questions in turn require consideration of costs, service, underwriting capacity, and financial responsibility.

What is available is the subject of this and the following chapter; where to get it is the subject of chapters 16 and 17.

---

[1] The editorial office of the *National Insurance Buyer* is at 8 West Fortieth Street, New York 18, New York.

[2] In the early days of insurance, there was no uniformity among insurance policies. One insurer's contract was likely to be different from the other. Policy competition among the companies worked a hardship not only on the companies themselves but also among the buyers. The need for some form of standardization was apparent. Today, insurance policies are standardized by three methods: custom, statute, and intercompany agreement. For example, ocean marine covers are standardized by custom, fire covers are standardized by statute, and automobile covers are standardized by intercompany agreement. A standard policy may be defined as one that, for a given cover, is substantially like that written by the majority of insurers in the field. Of course, not all policies are standardized, and even when standard policies are available the risk manager does not necessarily have to purchase the standard form. He may negotiate with the insurer and tailor his own form to meet his need.

461

INSURANCE POLICIES

The insurance industry is in the midst of a policy revolution incited by the activities of companies seeking to take advantage of opportunities offered by multiple-line insurance legislation (chapter 12), and fed by a new-found aggressive competitive spirit. The revolution has progressed along three fronts: the broadening of specified perils policies, the introduction of new "all risks" contracts, and the development of the package policy.[3]

Dwelling Covers

The testing ground for this revolution was in the field of dwelling covers. In the fall of 1954 the Interregional Insurance Conference[4] recommended the Dwelling and Contents Broad form (a specified perils form), and in June of the same year it recommended the Dwelling Buildings Special form (an "all risks" form).[5] About two years earlier (September, 1952), the Multiple Peril Insurance Rating Organization[6] had introduced the Homeowners policy, a package policy combining fire and related covers, personal theft, and personal liability. The prototype Homeowners package, however, was written in September of 1950 by a large, aggressive eastern company.[7] The prototype "all risks" policy on dwellings was introduced independently in California as early as 1951, and the Pacific Fire Rating Bureau had approved a broad form specified perils policy for dwellings in December, 1952.

---

[3] Significant changes or developments of an evolutionary nature involving both the broadening of coverage and the packaging concept had taken place on limited fronts during the prerevolution days. However, these changes, to be discussed presently, were made within the confines of the monoline insurance legislation then in effect.

[4] The Interregional Insurance Conference was formed in 1954 to coordinate at the national level the work of the regional fire insurance rating bureaus operating on behalf of the capital stock insurers.

[5] The Dwelling Buildings Special form was originally called the Dwelling Buildings All Physical Loss form, but the name was changed because of a feeling that the term "all physical loss" was misleading.

[6] The Multiple Peril Insurance Rating Organization was created to devise forms and promulgate rates for multiple line policies on an individual basis, that is, to develop one premium for the package rather than separate premiums for each coverage included in the policy. Another organization, the Interbureau Insurance Advisory Group, had as its function the coordination of the work of the various rating bureaus operating on behalf of the stock companies in the development of package policies. The forms and rates for each of the coverages in the package were developed independently by the rating bureaus having jurisdiction, and the Interbureau established the over-all policy discount. The Multiple Peril Insurance Rating Organization and the Interbureau Insurance Advisory Group were consolidated into the Multiple Peril Insurance Conference in May, 1957.

[7] As early as 1943 a few fire and casualty insurers (usually members of a single company group) were joining together to write "combination policies" for householders, under which fire and casualty coverages were combined in one document but were rated and underwritten separately by the respective fire insurer and casualty insurer. The premiums, however, offered no savings to the policyholders.

The standard Dwelling and Contents Broad form currently available covers houses and household contents against nineteen specified perils. The current edition of the standard Dwelling Buildings Special form covers real property, equipment pertaining to its service, and materials intended for use in its construction, alteration, or repair. Coverage is written against all risks of direct physical loss except when caused by earth movements, some water disturbances, nuclear reactions, wear and tear, deterioration, rust, rot, mold, insects, mechanical breakdown, settling, cracking, shrinkage, expansion, contamination, smog, and smoke from agricultural smudging or industrial operations. The Homeowners policy program in current use offers the buyer five forms, of which the most popular is Form 2. This form covers the dwelling building, private structures, and personal property against the nineteen perils included in the Dwelling Buildings and Contents Broad form and includes additional living expenses arising from any of these perils, plus comprehensive personal liability insurance including medical payments cover, fire legal liability cover, and coverage for physical damage to property of others.[8]

Broadened Forms for Business

In the homeowners' field, the package policy has met with far more success than have the broadened forms. In fact, package policies have revolutionized the dwelling insurance business. In the commercial or business insurance field, developments were concentrated on broadened forms until 1960, when the first package policy was issued for motels.

Mercantile Covers. The Jeweler's Block policy was the first of the broad forms of insurance written for commercial risks by American insurers (chapter 12). Inland marine insurers began writing this "all risks" coverage in the 1920's but were not permitted to offer similar coverage to other merchants, except dealers in fine arts, coins and stamps, until the late 1940's and early 1950's. Then equivalent broad coverage was made available to dealers in furs, musical instruments, camera, office machinery, household appliances, sporting goods, marine supplies, heating and air-conditioning equipment, scientific and professional instruments, and industrial machinery and tools.

Until the Interregional Insurance Conference, the National Bureau of Casualty Underwriters, and the Inland Marine Insurance Bureau[9] jointly

---

[8] For the specific details of these covers and those offered by the four other Homeowners forms see the National Underwriter Company, *Fire, Casualty, and Surety Bulletins* (monthly), "Dwellings" (Cincinnati: National Underwriter Co.), pp. Ga–1 to 4, H–1 to 20, J–1 to 15.

[9] The National Bureau of Casualty Underwriters develops premiums for automobile liability insurance, general liability insurance, burglary insurance, and various other casualty lines. The "National Bureau," as it is called, operates in general on behalf of stock casualty insurers. The Mutual Insurance Rating Bureau operates in general on behalf of mutual casualty insurers.

introduced the Mercantile Block policy in 1954, all "block" covers were considered inland marine insurance rather than multiple line. Rates were therefore filed by the Inland Marine Insurance Bureau or the Transportation Insurance Rating Bureau.[10] The Mercantile Block policy, however, was viewed as a multiple line contract, and its rates were filed jointly by the fire insurance rating bureaus, the National Bureau of Casualty Underwriters (or the Mutual Insurance Rating Bureau), and the Inland Marine Insurance Bureau (or the Transportation Rating Bureau). When the Interregional Insurance Conference revised the standard "all risks" coverage for mercantile risks in 1957, the appellation "Commercial Property Coverage" was substituted for "Mercantile Block."

Industrial Covers. Multiple line coverage for manufacturing risks was pioneered during the late 1940's by a few large insurance companies and was later adopted by the Multiple Peril Insurance Rating Organization. The prototype policy was designed for automobile manufacturers, but a similar cover, called the Manufacturers Output policy, was soon made available to a large number of other specified classes of manufacturers. The policy provides "all risks" protection but applies principally to non-manufacturing locations.

A standard multiple line insurance for manufacturing risks devised by the Interbureau Insurance Advisory Group was introduced in 1957 and called the Industrial Property policy program. This program and the Manufacturers Output policy were brought under the jurisdiction of the Multi-Peril Insurance Conference in May of 1957, when the Interbureau group and the Multiple Peril Insurance Rating Organization were consolidated. Though broad in scope, the Industrial Property policy program offers specified perils coverage only, except for an optional Special Personal Property endorsement, which may be used to add the "all risks" protection found in the Manufacturers Output policy and "all risks" coverage on finished stocks while at the factory.

Office Covers. The Interregional Insurance Conference designed a multiple line policy for offices not operated in connection with a store or manufacturing concern or used by a physician or dentist. The policy, first issued in 1956, provides "all risks" coverage.

Public and Institutional Property. The Interregional Insurance Conference introduced a multiple line Public and Institutional Property program in 1960. The coverage under this program is written on a specified perils basis.

Package Policies for Business

Like the broadened "all risks" and specified perils policies developed for dwellings, the broadened coverage offered under the Commercial

---

[10] In general, the Transportation Insurance Rating Bureau operates on behalf of mutual insurance companies, the Inland Marine Bureau for stock companies.

Property program, the Industrial Property program, the Public and Institutional Property program, the Manufacturers Output policy, and the Office Contents form have attracted insurance buyers. But the broadened forms have not had the success in their respective fields that the package policies have had in the homeowners' field. If experience in the business field turns out to be the same as that in the homeowners' field, the development of package policies for business can be expected to revolutionize business covers and make relics of forms currently being used.

The Standard Multi-Peril Policy Program. The Interregional Insurance Conference introduced its standard Special Multi-Peril policy program in late 1960. The prototype forms, rules, and rating methods were developed for motels. The program was later extended to include forms, rules, and rating methods for apartment houses, offices, and retail stores. The next steps probably will be the development of forms, rules, and rating methods for other service firms, manufacturers, and wholesalers, so as to make the program applicable to virtually all types of business enterprise.[11]

The Special Multi-Peril policy program is a package multiple line insurance program combining fire and allied lines, marine, casualty, and surety covers in one policy. Some of the covers are mandatory; a number of others are optional. Because the specific forms and rules developed under the Special Multi-Peril policy program are designed separately for each class of eligible risks, variations will be found among the mandatory covers and among the optional features available for each type of insured. The retail stores form requires insurance of stock, fixtures, equipment, improvements, and other business personal property against the perils of fire, lightning, windstorm, hail, explosion, riot, civil commotion, smoke, falling aircraft, and vehicle collision, which are the traditional fire and extended coverage perils. Broader coverage is optional and may be arranged by an "all risks" form similar to the Commercial Property coverage forms. The basic mandatory property coverage for motels, apartment houses, and offices, however, includes more than the minimum fire and extended coverage perils required for retail-store owners. Bodily injury and property damage liability insurance is required in the package for insureds of all classes.[12] Medical payments cover (insurance to cover the medical expenses of members of the public who sustain bodily injury caused by an accident arising out of the ownership or use of the premises or operations necessary or inci-

---

[11] A number of companies had developed and filed forms, rules, and rating methods for commercial multi-peril package policies before the Interregional Insurance Conference made its filings. Not only were independent versions of motel, apartment, and store owners packages made available, but also independent packages were developed for launderers and dry cleaners, funeral directors, and wholesalers. Independent filings of other packages are likely to take place before the Interregional Insurance Conference completes its standard program.

[12] Not all liability hazards are required to be insured, however. Some of the liability covers are optional, and some, notably automobile, are not included in these policies at all.

dental thereto) is mandatory on the basic retail stores form but is optional for motels, apartment houses, and offices.

The optional covers available under the Special Multi-Peril policy program are extensive. Some of them are included in the basic form but can be endorsed out if the risk manager does not want them. Others may be added by endorsements. Among the optional covers written with the retailers package are an Additional Coverage endorsement extending the insurance on property to include a number of other perils; Business Interruption cover (insurance against loss of earning resulting from the interruption of business when caused by damage to property on the premises by an insured peril); Comprehensive Glass cover; All Risks Neon Signs cover; Improvements and Betterments coverage against the perils insured; Rent insurance; Elevator Collision cover; Personal Injury Liability insurance covering false arrest, detention, imprisonment, malicious prosecution, libel, slander, defamation of character, invasion of privacy, wrongful eviction, or wrongful entry; Comprehensive Personal Liability insurance for an owner or manager who lives on the premises; Comprehensive Crime cover providing employee dishonesty coverage and Money and Securities Broad Form coverage; and cover to protect against a loss resulting from an accident in a specified boiler, machine, refrigerating and air conditioning system, or similar specified object.

All the covers mentioned in the preceding paragraph will be discussed later in this chapter. At this point they are mentioned only to illustrate how few gaps are left in the coverage available in a complete package written under the Special Multi-Peril policy program. For example, the only major covers missing in the retailers' package are automobile, Workmen's Compensation and Employer's Liability, Valuable Papers and Records, Extra Expense, Leasehold Interest, surety bonds (other than fidelity), and life and health. Eventually most, if not all, of these covers will be optionally available. Some of them are available in the other packages. For example, Extra Expense and Valuable Papers and Records covers are written for limited amounts as extensions on the apartment house and the office forms.

Should a Package Policy Be Purchased? The principal attraction of the package policy to the risk manager is the opportunity to purchase combined covers at a discount. The Retailers package policy, for example, offers a premium discount of 15 per cent from the cost of covers individually purchased. The discount for the property covers in the Apartment Owners and the Office package policy is 20 per cent and in the Motel package, 25 per cent. Reduced costs of writing and handling several covers in one policy are only partly responsible for the ability of the insurer to offer these discounts. Other factors contributing to lower costs are mandatory cover requirements, strict underwriting rules, and restricted eligibility standards.

Mandatory covers help to reduce adverse selection against the insurer. Minimum amounts of coverage are specified to guard against the problem of underinsurance and so produce an adequate premium volume for the exposure. Underwriting rules generally require an authorized inspection of the "risk" and strict compliance with any resulting engineering recommendations. If the eligibility of a given type of occupancy is considered questionable by the insurer, it will not qualify for a package policy. No "accommodation business" is accepted at package policy rates, that is, no business will qualify just because it is submitted by an agent who has placed a large premium volume with the insurer or because the applicant has insured other exposures with the insurer. The insurer's underwriting standards must be met in every case.

Eligibility rules for package policies usually are detailed. Aside from specifying the general types of business activity that are eligible for a given package, the rules set forth certain lines of business that are specifically excluded. For example, among the many types of business ineligible for the retailer's package are bailees, automobile dealers, service stations, restaurants, pet shops, pawnbrokers, drugstores, and supermarkets. These types of business are excluded because they present significantly different underwriting problems, have significantly different coverage needs, or require special rating.

If the risk manager decides that he does not want all the mandatory covers, the discount may not be sufficient to warrant purchasing the package. Strict underwriting rules and restricted eligibility requirements will eliminate package policies from consideration in a number of instances. In these instances, the covers would have to be purchased separately or in groups of special policies designed for these special instances.

INSURANCE COVERS

The types of insurance covers needed by business will vary both as to the type of enterprise and as to the risk management policy set up for the firm. Viewed broadly, insurance covers may be classified into eight groups: physical damage, consequential loss, marine, crime, liability, life, health, and surety. Each of these classifications may be subdivided into specific types of covers.

Physical Damage Covers

The basic physical damage cover is fire insurance. It is usually written with an Extended Coverage endorsement to indemnify the business for direct loss to its buildings, stock, furniture, and equipment when caused by fire, lightning, windstorm, hail, explosion, smoke, riot and civil commotion, or damage by aircraft or vehicles. The fire policy also may be endorsed to cover against vandalism and malicious mischief. Water damage, sprinkler leakage, and earthquake exposures may be covered on a fire form or by special policies. Boiler and machinery and glass are examples of other physical damage covers. Also available for some exposures are broad physical damage forms covering many perils or "all risk" physical damage forms with a limited number of excluded perils.

The insured's interest in improvements and betterments can be covered against physical damage by fire and other perils. Improvements and Betterments cover provides that (1) if the landlord restores the improvements, no indemnity is payable; (2) if the tenant restores the improvements, he is entitled to recover the cost of restoration less depreciation; and (3) if the improvements are not restored, the tenant is reimbursed for that portion of his investment in improvements that the unexpired term of the lease bears to the time from installation of the improvements to the expiration of the present lease. When feasible, a better insurance solution to the improvements and betterments exposure is to have the insurance on the building written in the name of the landlord and tenant jointly, thereby insuring both interests with one premium.

Valuable papers (written, printed, or otherwise inscribed documents and records, including books, maps, films, drawings, abstracts, deeds, mortgages, and manuscripts) may be covered against "all risks," either under a schedule providing a specific amount of insurance on each item, or, if the items are replaceable, on a blanket basis for their actual cash value. Valuable papers may require separate cover because of the limited coverage afforded them under the usual standard physical damage forms.

Consequential Loss Covers

Physical damage insurance indemnifies the business only for *direct* loss to property and not for consequential loss. This means that the loss must be the *direct* result of one of the covered perils. Where the line is drawn between a direct and an indirect result is not always clear. Conflicting court decisions involving this question can be found. Food in a freezer was spoiled when a windstorm idled a utility substation some distance away. Was the food spoilage a direct or an indirect result of the windstorm? General Insurance Company said that it was an indirect result, but Lipschultz, the insured, insisted that it was a direct result and sued for recovery under his direct loss policy. The court, being unable to find any intervening causes, agreed with Lipschultz and found windstorm to be the proximate cause of the loss.[13] It is both unwise and unnecessary for either the insurer or the risk manager to leave questions of this kind to the courts. The insurer should state unequivocally in the contract what it means to cover (or, as is customary, what it does not mean to cover) under the term "direct loss." The risk manager can then purchase the kinds of direct and conse-

---

[13] *Lipschultz* v. *General Insurance Co.*, 9 C.C.H. (Fire and Casualty) 1064.

quential (indirect) loss covers he wants to include in his insurance program by carefully spelling them out in his policies.

Consequential loss covers can be classified into two kinds: those involving a time element and those not involving a time element. They are usually written in endorsements to be attached to the standard fire policy.

Time Element Covers. Time element covers are those consequential loss forms in which the measure of loss is related to the length of time over which damaged property is totally or partially withdrawn from use. The most widely purchased business time element cover is *Business Interruption insurance,* designed to offset the loss of earnings resulting when described property is damaged by a covered peril and the business operation is necessarily curtailed or suspended until the property can be restored. When the described property is the plant of an important supplier or customer, the cover is called *Contingent Business Interruption insurance.* If management deems it unwise to suspend operations while the damaged property is being restored, *Extra Expense insurance* may be available to pay the additional cost of operating at a temporary location.

Important time element covers written with the *Boiler and Machinery* policy are *Use and Occupancy* and *Outage.* Boiler and Machinery insurance essentially is physical damage and property damage liability insurance covering damage to property belonging to the insured or for which the insured may be liable, when that damage is caused by a covered accident to the boiler or machinery. A Use and Occupancy endorsement provides insurance against partial or total suspension of business caused by a covered accident to a designated boiler or machine. Outage insurance pays a specified amount for each hour a described boiler or machine is out of operation, regardless of whether the business is interrupted. Outage insurance is designed to pay the cost of substitute facilities and therefore is similar to Extra Expense insurance. Insurance cover against the failure of public utility to supply power because of an accident to the utility's physical equipment is available under a *Power Interruption* policy.

Rent Insurance covers are available to indemnify (1) a tenant who must continue to pay rent even though the leased premises become untenantable because of damage by fire or other covered peril or (2) the owner for the loss of rents if he was not fortunate enough to shift this risk to the tenant. When the premises are owner-occupied, *Rental Value insurance* may be purchased by the owner to protect himself against the loss of use of these premises during time required to restore them after damage by a covered peril.

Consequential Loss Covers without Time Element. If the measure of an indirect loss is not related to elapsed time, it may be covered by a non-time element consequential loss insurance contract, of which there are several.

Leasehold Interest insurance is available to protect a tenant against loss of a valuable lease through cancellation following damage caused by a covered peril to the leased premises. The measure of recovery is the difference between the current rental value of similar premises and the rent payable under the lease. This amount is discounted (usually at 4 per cent) for the unexpired period of the lease. Leasehold interest forms are also available to protect tenants against loss of prepaid rent or other funds sunk into the premises (such as the cost of renovating the property prior to its use).

Accounts Receivable insurance provides "all risks" coverage against inability of the insured to collect outstanding accounts following destruction of his account records. In addition, it covers interest charges on loans incurred to offset an impaired cash position pending eventual collection of such funds, also extra expenses of collection, and any reasonable expenses incurred in re-establishing the accounts receivable records.

If a business is exposed to spoilage or other damage to property because of fire or other accident to heating, refrigerating, humidifying, and similar equipment, a *Consequential Loss clause* may be included in the physical damage forms to cover this loss, usually without additional cost if the equipment is located on the same premises. If the equipment is located off the premises, an extra charge is made for the coverage. One of the covered perils, however, must *physically* damage the equipment for the loss to be covered. Riot and vandalism usually are excluded from this cover unless added by the *Consequential Riot and Vandalism Loss Assumption endorsement*. Consequential damage cover may also be written as an endorsement to the boiler and machinery policy but requires an additional premium and covers not only the insured's property but the spoilage of any property for which he is legally liable. Consequential loss and damage assumption clauses also are available for garment manufacturers to offset loss in the value of the remainder of a suit if a separate part of it is damaged by a covered peril.

If the business owns a building of outlawed construction,[14] it must be demolished rather than rebuilt if it is severely damaged (usually to the extent of 50 per cent or more). Physical damage policies cover only the actual cash value of the damage itself, leaving uncovered both the value of the undamaged portion and the cost of its demolition. Furthermore, any increased cost of replacement necessary to comply with building or zoning laws is not covered under physical damage forms. These exposures, however, may be protected under endorsements to the physical damage contract. In the eastern states, for example, a combination of a *Demolition endorsement* and an *Increased Cost of Construction endorsement* will be sufficient to cover the entire contingent liability from action of the build-

---

14 Building or zoning laws that set standards of construction in particular areas are frequently encountered. If a structure already present does not measure up to the prescribed standards, it is allowed to remain. Such a building is known as one of "outlawed construction."

ing laws if the physical damage insurance is written on a replacement cost basis and a sufficient amount of insurance is purchased. *Replacement Cost insurance* provides that a loss will be settled on the basis of the cost of replacement without deduction for depreciation. It is written only on buildings, generally as an endorsement to physical damage forms.

If fire or some other peril destroys a manufacturer's finished goods, his physical damage insurance normally will pay only for the cost of restoring these goods. It will not pay for the loss of anticipated profits on these goods. This "profits" exposure may be protected by including a *Market Value* or *Selling Price clause* in the physical damage form.

Business firms (called brokers, factors, or selling agants) who contract to sell part or all of a manufacturer's output for an agreed-upon commission can lose all or part of this commission if the manufacturer's plant or his finished goods are damaged. These selling agents can cover this exposure with *Commissions of Selling Agents insurance*, a cover that combines contingent business interruption insurance with profits and commissions insurance, since it indemnifies the selling agent for loss resulting both from the destruction of finished products of the manufacturer and from the inability of the manufacturer to produce the finished product for sale. The damage, of course, must be caused by a covered peril.

If the success of a business venture depends upon favorable weather, the business has a rain, hail, snow, or sleet exposure that can be covered with a *Rain insurance* policy. Rain insurance covers are written to protect the insured against loss of income or extra expense due to rain, hail, snow, or sleet. Some forms require a fixed minimum amount of precipitation, whereas others require only that there be precipitation during some specified period. Threatening weather is not sufficient to give rise to a claim even if such weather causes the insured a loss.

Another consequential loss cover, found in the Boiler and Machinery policy, is *Expediting Expense*. This pays the reasonable cost of temporary repairs and the cost of expediting permanent repairs. Overtime and the extra costs of rapid transportation are paid. Glass insurance also provides a consequential loss cover in paying the cost of installing temporary plates or boarding up openings when there is an unavoidable delay in replacing the glass.

Marine Covers

The physical damage and consequential loss covers discussed up to this point primarily are written on property at fixed locations. Conveyances (automobiles, aircraft, watercraft, bicycles, motorcycles, horses and wagons, etc.) and property being conveyed (foreign and domestic shipments) are covered under marine forms. Also covered under marine forms are instrumentalities of transportation (bridges, tunnels, piers, pipelines, etc.); instrumentalities of communication (television and radio towers, signs, telephone lines, etc.); the interest of bailees in property entrusted to their care (an interest resting on the bailees' legal liability for loss of their customers' property or on their desire to preserve customer goodwill by indemnifying bailors for loss even though no liability exists); and the "on location" as well as the transportation exposures of movable property not permanently located in one place (stocks of merchandise, scientific instruments, and equipment belonging to contractors, farmers, morticians, physicians, and actors, etc.). The last two types of covers are called "floaters," that is the cover floats (moves) with the property in its different locations. Marine forms include not only physical damage coverage but also, in some cases, limited consequential loss insurance and liability coverage.

Conveyances. The ownership or use of automobiles, aircraft, and watercraft presents the business with an exposure that requires separate handling in arranging insurance covers. General physical damage covers on building and personal property usually exclude or severely restrict coverage on automobiles (broadly defined), aircraft, and watercraft. Likewise general liability covers exclude or severely restrict coverage for liability arising out of the ownership or use of these conveyances.

The broadest protection available for direct damage to a covered automobile may be purchased by combining the *Collision* and *Comprehensive Automobile Physical Damage* covers. In addition to providing virtually all risk physical damage protection, this combination offers some consequential loss cover. Comprehensive Automobile Physical Damage insurance gives limited loss-of-use coverage for stolen automobiles and pays general average charges for which the insured becomes legally liable.[15]

The broadest liability cover for automobiles is *Comprehensive Automobile Liability insurance,* under which the insured is protected for liability arising out of the ownership, maintenance, or use of any automobile, regardless of ownership. *Automobile Medical Payments* cover is available to pay the medical expenses of anyone injured and the funeral expenses of anyone killed while riding in a covered automobile. Because medical payments is accident rather than liability cover, medical expenses are paid without regard to liability.

Unlike automobile insurance, aircraft insurance policies are not standardized. The broadest physical damage protection available for aircraft is *All Risks Ground and Flight* cover. Limited forms of aircraft hull insurance also are offered. The broadest aircraft liability insurance protection may be purchased through an insuring agreement combining basic aircraft liability insurance with passenger liability cover and endorsed with *Non-Ownership Liability insurance* to include rented or borrowed aircraft. Aircraft medical payments cover is available. A form of compensation

---

[15] General average is discussed on pp. 000.

insurance may be written to pay a fixed sum on behalf of guests who are killed or dismembered if the claimant agrees not to sue for damage. This cover is known as *Voluntary Settlement* or *Passenger Admitted Liability insurance.*

Insurance policies on watercraft, like those on aircraft, are not standardized. Ocean marine forms are used to cover all boats with inboard power, whereas inland marine forms are usually used to cover boats with outboard motors. The two types of forms are significantly different. The broadest protection for inboard vessels includes four covers: *Hull insurance* providing specified perils coverage against physical damage to the boat and its equipment and general average charges, plus property damage liability for collision with other ships; *Protection and Indemnity insurance* covering general liability to public and employees; *Longshoremen's and Harbor Workers' Compensation insurance* covering the insured's liability under that federal statute; and *Medical Payments insurance*. All four of these covers are offered under the *Yacht insurance* policy, the name given the policy regardless of the type of inboard craft that it covers.

The broadest physical damage protection covering outboard motors and boats is written on an "all risks" form with the usual inland marine exclusions (wear and tear, gradual deterioration, mechanical breakdown, moths, vermin, inherent vice, latent defect, etc.). The broadest liability insurance available is the *Broad Form Watercraft Liability insurance* endorsement covering bodily injury and property damage liability arising from the use not only of the named boat but also of any private pleasure boat rented or loaned to an insured. The endorsement includes three additional covers: medical payments; Federal Longshoremen's and Harbor Workers' Compensation insurance; and Workmen's Compensation indemnity insurance (indemnifies the insured for workmen's compensation benefits that he is required to pay).

Motorcycles may be covered on automobile insurance forms. For businesses owning bicycles, physical damage cover is available under a *Bicycle floater*. The liability exposure is usually insured under public liability insurance covering premises and operations. Business concerns using horses and wagons for delivery conveyances may obtain specified perils coverage for physical damage through the *Horse and Wagon floater*. The liability exposure can be covered by a *Teams endorsement* to the premises and operations liability cover when the basic public liability insurance written for the business excludes liability from "draft or saddle animals, vehicles for use therewith, and vehicles from which merchandise is sold."[16]

Property Being Conveyed. Nearly every business is exposed to the

---

[16] The standard Owners, Landlords, and Tenants Liability policy incorporates the exclusion quoted above. The Manufacturers and Contractors Liability form and the Comprehensive General Liability form have no such exclusion.

hazards of transportation on incoming or outgoing goods or on both. Some are exposed to the hazards of foreign shipment, whereas others are exposed to the hazards of domestic shipment only.

The *Open Cargo* policy offers the broadest physical damage insurance for ocean transportation. It covers all shipments made over an indefinite period. The insured under this policy reports his shipments to the insurer as they are made and pays a monthly premium on the basis of the actual amount. The cover is effective until the policy is canceled by either the insurer or the insured. Consequential loss cover for general average charges is included in the physical damage form. The insurer, however, is not liable for loss of market or deterioration arising from delay in arrival of the goods unless such liability is expressly assumed in writing and made a part of the contract. Coverage is often on an "all risks" basis, subject to an exclusion of small losses.

Various types of transportation covers are available for domestic shippers. These covers may be classified according to the mode of shipping. For incoming or outgoing shipments by railroad, railway express, and coast-wise steamers, the *Annual Transit* policy offers broad physical damage coverage on a named perils basis. A *Trip Transit* form is also available. in which each shipment is separately specified. A *Railway Express* form offering even broader coverage is available for those who ship only by railway express, and this form may be endorsed to cover shipments by air express. *Contingent Transit* cover is available for business firms set up to collect their own claims from the transportation carrier. The functions of transportation insurance are (1) to assure prompt payment for losses, even though the carrier is finally found liable, (2) to cover losses in excess of the carriers liability,[17] and (3) to provide indemnity for losses (those caused by "acts of God") when no liability is imposed upon the carrier. Only the second and third functions are completely fulfilled by contingent transit cover. Payment of indemnity by the insurer when the carrier is found liable is made only after the insured has made every possible effort to collect from his transportation carrier.

The *Blanket Motor Cargo* policy, written for those who use public trucks as their principal means of shipment, provides physical damage cover against named perils.[18] For those who haul their merchandise on their own or leased trucks, a *Motor Cargo Insurance Owners* form is available.

Air Cargo insurance, written on an "all risks" basis, is available for

---

[17] Goods frequently are shipped under a released-value bill of lading under which the carrier is released from damage claims in excess of the value stated in the bill of lading. This happens when the tariff filed by the carrier fixes a maximum valuation less than the goods are worth. It is usually cheaper to assign a low value on the bill of lading and cover the excess with insurance.

[18] The Blanket Motor Cargo insurance form is also used by truckmen to cover against liability to shippers for damage to their goods.

those who transport their goods by air. In addition to physical loss cover, the insurance includes protection against general average charges. The airlines usually can procure the insurance for the shipper. When air shipments are infrequent and time is so important, as it must be when air shipments are involved, the services of the airline in arranging for the insurance can be a valuable one.

Three covers are available for postal shippers: *Parcel Post, Registered Mail,* and *First Class Mail.* Parcel Post insurance provides "all risks" physical loss coverage for packages while in the custody of the United States Post Office. Registered Mail insurance covers shipments of such property as securities, stamps, currency, coupons, negotiable paper, jewelry, gold, and silver on an "all risks" basis and is written only for fiduciary firms (banks, investment companies, insurance companies, securities brokers, and trust companies). When ordinary first class mail is used to ship these items (except checks, currency, precious metals, and jewelry), the fiduciary firm may insure the exposure on an "all risks" basis with First Class Mail insurance.

When a shipment fails to arrive or arrives in an unusable condition, the consignee may lose production time or sales volume. *Transportation Contingent Use and Occupancy insurance* is sometimes written to cover this exposure.

Instrumentalities of Transportation and Communication. While it is true that conveyances are instrumentalities of transportation, the general classification here refers principally to immovable structures that aid in transportation and communication. The principal covers in this class are either multi-peril or "all risks" physical damage insurance and, in many cases, use and occupancy insurance on bridges, tunnels, dry docks, outdoor cranes and loading bridges, marine railways, piers, wharves, docks, slips, pipelines, transmission lines, and radio and television transmitting equipment. Very few risk managers are faced with any of these exposures. The covers ars not standard so are tailored to meet the needs of the individual buyer and tempered by the underwriting philosophy of the insurer. One instrumentality of communication frequently found among the exposures of a business is a neon or electric sign. "All risks" physical damage cover is available for this exposure.

Bailee Covers. Two kinds of bailee covers are written: *Bailee Liability insurance* and *Bailees' Customers insurance.* The principal difference between the two is that the first one is purely a liability cover whereas the other is a physical damage cover. The standard *Warehousemen's Liability* policy, an example of bailee liability insurance, protects the insured against his liability for loss of property from any cause except fire and sprinkler leakage. The various *Bailees' Customers floaters* written for laundries, dry cleaners, rug and furniture cleaners, upholsterers, cold storage and locker plants, and other establishments handling customers' goods are examples of bailees' customers insurance. These policies provide named perils coverage on property of the customer while it is on the bailee's premises or in transit between the bailee and his customer. The coverage does not depend upon the bailee's common law liability for the loss. A form of consequential loss cover may be written under these policies to insure the bailee against loss of processing and storage fees if his customer refuses to pay these charges because his goods are lost or damaged. Bailees' customer forms are not standardized.

Other Floater Policies. Some stocks of merchandise and other "floating" property (property not permanently located) may be insured under forms offering "floating" protection. Floater policies usually cover the property at regular locations and always cover the transit exposure and temporary locations not owned or controlled by the insured. Examples of floater policies already mentioned are the Dealers' forms (jewelers, musical instruments, furriers, cameras, fine arts, industrial machinery and tools, appliances, etc.), Commercial Property forms, Manufacturer's Output forms, Industrial Property forms, Institutional Property forms, and Office Contents forms. In addition, a large number of other floater policies are available based on the type of property covered. Examples of these are the *Salesman's floater*, written on a specified perils or an all risks form to cover loss of salesmen's samples away from the premises; the *Contractor's Equipment floater*, usually written on a named perils basis; the *Conditional* or *Installment Sales floater*, also written on a specified perils basis; *Installation floater*, covering on a specified perils basis the physical damage exposure of machinery and equipment while being transported to and installed on the customer's premises; and the *Pattern floater*, covering loss of patterns, dies, molds, etc., away from the insured's premises and arising from named perils.

Crime Covers

The principal differences among the major crime covers are in the crimes insured against, the type of property protected, the locations covered, and the status of the criminal in relation to the insured. Crimes covered by one or more of the various forms include burglary (forcible entry to premises), robbery (forcible taking from a person), theft or larceny (felonious taking-away of property), forgery (false making or alteration of a document), embezzlement (fraudulent appropriation of property), and other dishonest or fraudulent acts. Property covered by one or more of the various forms include merchandise, furniture, fixtures, equipment, money, and securities. Damage done to real as well as to personal property usually is covered if caused by a successful or attempted crime insured against in the policy. Crime forms may cover on-premises losses only, off-premises losses, or both. Crime covers that protect against criminal acts of the general public usually do not insure against fraudulent or dishonest acts of employees, and those that protect against the criminal acts of employees do not cover those of the general public.

Covers Not Involving Employees. The *Mercantile Open Stock Burglary* form covers direct loss of merchandise, furniture, fixtures, and equipment caused by burglary. Robbery of a watchman also is covered. Theft insurance may be added to the cover by endorsement. *Mercantile Safe Burglary insurance* covers direct loss of any property, including money and securities, when taken by forcible entry into vaults or safes. Coverage for burglary, robbery, and theft losses from cash registers, cash drawers, and key-locked safes may be added. *Mercantile Robbery insurance* covers loss of money, securities, and other property from within the premises caused by robbery or attempted robbery and loss away from the premises caused by holdup while the property is being conveyed by a messenger. The insured may purchase inside cover alone if he wishes.

A *Burglary Special Coverage* policy is available for combining covers, such as the Mercantile Safe Burglary and the Mercantile Robbery covers. Other crime covers are written on forms designed for use with the special coverage policy. For example, *Paymaster Robbery insurance* is written on a form to be used with the Burglary Special Coverage policy. This form covers robbery of the payroll of the insured from the time it is drawn from the bank until the workers are paid. Pay in the hands of employees is covered if employees are robbed on the premises on payday in conjunction with a robbery or attempted robbery of a messenger or custodian. A *Paymaster Broad Form* is available to cover the payroll against loss by destruction, disappearance, or wrongful abstraction. *Money and Securities Destruction insurance* against loss of money and securities (or securities only) from within the premises while the premises are open for business or from within a locked safe or vault is written on a form to be attached to the special coverage policy.

The broadest cover on money and securities is offered by the *Money and Securities Broad Form* policy. Insurance under this form may be purchased to cover the premises exposure, the outside exposure, or both. The premises cover protects the insured against loss of money and securities from within the premises, or from within the premises of a bank or other recognized safe place of deposit, caused by destruction, disappearance, or wrongful abstraction. Loss of merchandise and equipment is covered if caused by robbers or safe burglars. The outside cover protects the insured against the destruction, disappearance, or wrongful abstraction of money and securities while being conveyed by a messenger or an armored car company, or while within the living quarters of a messenger. Loss of merchandise and equipment is covered against robbery or attempted robbery while such property is being conveyed, and against theft from the living quarters of a messenger.

Depositors' Forgery insurance covers losses caused by the forgery of outgoing and incoming checks, drafts, notes, and similar instruments. Protection may be purchased for outgoing paper only if the insured does not want cover for incoming paper.

A package *Storekeeper's Burglary and Robbery* policy combining inside and outside robbery cover, safe burglary, and mercantile open stock cover is written for small shopkeepers. The minimum coverage is $250, and the maximum is $1,000, for each of the seven separate insuring agreements in the policy. (The same amount always applies to each of the seven.)

Employee Dishonesty Covers. Financial protection against the dishonesty of employees is purchased through a fidelity bond. A fidelity bond is often said not to be "insurance" if that term is strictly interpreted. Through a fidelity bond, the bonding company (the surety or guarantor) guarantees the employer (the obligee) against loss caused by dishonesty of his employee (the principal or obligor). The obligor is liable to the surety for losses paid. Modern practices and forms in fidelity bonding have created fidelity insurance.[19] When blanket fidelity forms are used, the employer deals directly with the surety (insurer), from whom he obtains a straight promise of indemnity for loss caused by dishonesty of employees. The surety groups this exposure with many others and so produces an insurance operation. The right of the surety to collect from defaulting employees is no different in effect from the general right of insurers to collect from other tort feasors who have caused insured losses. However, insurance or not, fidelity covers are called "bonds."

Fidelity bonds are written on an *individual, schedule,* or *blanket* basis. When the bond is written on an individual basis, the bond names the individual to be bonded. When the bond is written on a scheduled basis, it may name either the *individuals* to be covered or the *positions* to be covered. The broadest fidelity cover is the blanket bond, of which two types are written for general business firms.[20] The *Commercial Blanket* bond covers the dishonesty of *all* employees up to the penalty (amount) of the bond. The *Blanket Position* bond guarantees against the dishonesty of *each* employee up to the penalty of the bond. Neither blanket form names individuals or positions. The difference between the Commercial Blanket and the Blanket Position is in the maximum liability of the bonding company. Under the Blanket Position bond, the maximum liability assumed by the bonding company for any one loss is the product of the number of employees involved in the crime multiplied by the penalty of the bond. Under the Commercial Blanket bond, the maximum liability assumed by the bonding company is the penalty of the bond regardless of the number of employees involved in the crime.

---

[19] "Fidelity" insurance pays for losses caused by *in*fidelity just as "life" and "health" insurance pay for losses caused by lack of life or health.

[20] Special forms have been devised for various types of financial institutions.

Comprehensive Crime Covers. Comprehensive crime protection is offered on a scheduled basis by the *Comprehensive Dishonesty, Destruction, and Disappearance* policy (called the Comprehensive 3-D) and on a package basis by the *Broad Form Storekeeper's* policy and the *Blanket Crime* policy.

The 3-D form schedules five covers on the basic form: (1) either the Commercial Blanket bond or the Blanket Position bond, (2) Money and Securities Broad Form protection on premises, (3) Money and Securities Broad Form protection off premises, (4) Money Orders and Counterfeit Paper Currency cover protecting against loss resulting from accepting worthless money orders or counterfeit United States or Canadian paper money, and (5) Depositors' Forgery insurance (outgoing paper only). The insured may purchase various combinations of these covers under the 3-D form. At least eleven additional covers may be added to this form by endorsement; among these are Incoming Check Forgery cover, Mercantile Open Stock Burglary or Theft cover, and Broad Form Payroll cover.

The Broad Form Storekeeper's policy written for store owners having no more than four employees combines into a package the covers available under a blanket fidelity bond, Money and Securities Broad Form, Mercantile Open Stock Burglary, Depositors' Forgery, Money Orders and Counterfeit Paper, and physical damage by vandalism and malicious mischief. The maximum coverage available is $1,000 per cover. The minimum is $250.

The Blanket Crime policy is a package policy that contains several major crime covers written with a single over-all limit of liability. The covers are the Commercial Blanket bond, Money and Securities Broad Form, Money Orders and Counterfeit Paper, and Depositors' Forgery. Other crime covers may be endorsed on the policy.

Liability Covers

Based on the hazards involved, liability covers for business are of five major types: automobile (and water and aircraft), general, professional, employers, and personal injury. Automobile, water, and aircraft liability covers have already been discussed. Off-premises automobile and watercraft and all aircraft liability hazards are excluded in the general liability forms.

General Liability Covers. General liability forms for business are of four types: scheduled, comprehensive, broad form, and specific. The basic differences among the forms are in the hazards that are covered and in the manner of defining the coverage.

Two scheduled general liability forms are written: the *Owners, Landlords, and Tenants* (OL&T) and the *Manufacturers and Contractors* (M&C). As the name suggests, the M&C form is used for insuring the public liability exposures of manufacturers and contractors, whereas the OL&T

form is used to insure the liability exposures of other types of business operations. Both forms schedule four "hazards." Each hazard is rated separately, and the insured need not purchase all of them. The Premises and Operations, Elevators, and Products and Completed Operations hazards are scheduled on both forms. The OL&T also schedules the Structural Alterations, New Construction, and Demolition hazard, whereas the M&C schedules the Independent Contractors hazard.[21] The premises and operations coverage written on the M&C form is in some ways broader than the coverage on the OL&T form. Only designated premises, and operations incidental to these premises, are covered by the OL&T policy, whereas all operations at any location are covered under the M&C form.

Both the OL&T and the M&C forms schedule four "insuring agreements": bodily injury liability, property damage liability, medical payments, and Contractual Liability.[22] (Actually, despite the policy terminology, Contractual Liability is a fifth hazard, and the policy provides for bodily injury and property damage but not medical payments coverage under it.) These "insuring agreements," like the four recognized "hazards," are rated separately and may be purchased individually. Bodily injury and property damage liability covers are similar to the covers offered in the automobile liability policy. The medical payments cover is less broad, in that it does not cover the insured. The Contractual Liability insuring agreement covers liability assumed under a sidetrack agreement, an easement agreement in connection with a railroad grade crossing, and an agreement required by municipal ordinance in connection with work for the municipality. Other contractual liability exposures may be covered by endorsement to the scheduled liability policy. Because the bodily injury exposure and the property damage exposure for contractual liability are separately rated, the insured may purchase one without the other.

A *Comprehensive General Liability* policy is available to cover all hazards that are scheduled on the OL&T and M&C forms. Products liability

---

[21] The insured's liability arising from the hazard of normal maintenance, repairs, and structural operations that do not change the size of or move the building is covered under the Premises and Operations division of both the OL&T and the M&C policies regardless of whether the work is done by an employee or an independent contractor. The hazard of more extensive operations is covered under the Premises and Operations section of the M&C form if the work is done by employees but not if it is done by an independent contractor. The Independent Contractors division provides the coverage for this hazard. The hazard of more extensive structural operations is not covered under the Premises and Operations section of the OL&T policy no matter who does the work. The Structural Alterations, New Construction, and Demolition division provides the coverage for this exposure.

[22] Some coverage against contractual liability is offered under the Premises and Operations division of both the OL&T and M&C policies. The Premises and Operations division of these forms covers liability assumed by the insured under any easement agreement except in connection with a railroad grade crossing; under any agreement required by municipal ordinance, except in connection with work for the municipality; or under a lease of premises agreement. Liability assumed under an elevator or escalator maintenance agreement is covered under the Elevator division.

and contractual liability covers can be removed by endorsement. Medical payments cover can be added by endorsement. Property damage liability cover may be eliminated as in the scheduled form simply by not including the exposure in the premium. The Comprehensive General Liability policy may be written in combination with the Comprehensive Automobile Liability policy.

A *Storekeeper's Liability* policy offers broad form liability protection for the operators of most kinds of retail stores. It contains only one insuring agreement and one policy limit to cover both the bodily injury and the property damage liability exposure. The policy covers the premises and operations hazard and most of the products and completed operations hazard. The elevator hazard may be covered by endorsement. Medical payments cover is written as a part of the contract.

Broad form liability covers are used in the special Multi-Peril policy programs discussed earlier in this chapter. The Retailers package policy includes liability protection similar to that of the Storekeeper's Liability policy. The Motel package contains even broader liability protection; the liability cover in this package is written on an *occurrence* basis, that is, it is not limited to injury and damage *caused by accident* as is customary in standard liability insurance policies written for businesses.[23]

The meaning of the term "caused by accident" has been blurred by conflicting court decisions.[24] The confusion seems to result from the different ways in which the courts apply the traditional tests for determining what constitutes an accident. The generally accepted tests have been: (1) the cause of the damage must be both definite and unintentional, and (2) the exact time and place that the damage occurs must be clear.

What about bodily injuries or property damage resulting from repeated exposures to some given condition? Are they caused by accident? The answer is "No," according to those courts that attach importance to the impossibility of pinpointing the exact time of occurrence of gradually developing damage. These courts reason that, for an event to be accidental, it must be sudden, not gradual. Life with the "caused by accident" restriction would not be so complicated if all courts accepted this reasoning. But the term "accident" does not mean the same thing to all courts, and, even if it did, all courts would not reach the same conclusions in applying the definition to the facts of a given case. Thus, it has been held that bodily injuries and property damage resulting from a series of distinctive events are caused by accident, regardless of whether these events and the accom-

---

[23] The liability cover in the Homeowners package and in the Family Automobile policy also are written on an occurrence basis.

[24] Cf. *United States Fidelity and Guaranty Co.* v. *Briscoe*, 239 Pac. (2d) 754, and *Canadian Radium and Uranium Corp.* v. *Indemnity Insurance Co. of North America*, 104 N.E. (2d) 250. Also *M. Schnoll and Son* v. *Standard Accident Insurance Co.*, 154 Atl. (2d) 431 and *Rex Roofing Co.* v. *Lumber Mutual Casualty Insurance Co.*, 116 N.Y. Sup. (2d) 876.

panying damage were noted at the time they occurred. These courts reason that the establishment of a specific time of occurrence is not necessary to support a conclusion that an injury was caused by accident if the facts show that the injury could only have been accidentally caused, that is, could not have been foreseen.

What about damage when it is the natural result of the action taken? Is this damage caused by accident? The answer is "Yes," according to some courts, if the damage was not intentionally inflicted. These courts reason that failure to use precaution to prevent damage from an intended act does not prove that the damage itself was intended. According to some courts, the answer is "No" if the damage could not have been prevented by the use of precaution or if no attempt was made to use precaution when precaution could have been effective.

The insurer's interpretation of the words "caused by accident" may not be as liberal as that of the courts. The risk manager, of course, should try to avoid having to depend on the courts rather than on the insurer for a liberal interpretation of policy language. In the present case, he can accomplish this objective by having the "caused by accident" restriction eliminated from his liability insurance policy and the word "occurrence" substituted in its stead. Insurers are prepared to make this substitution in the bodily injury liability cover but usually have been reluctant to do so for property damage liability cover. The substitution is made by endorsement on the general liability forms for which there is an additional charge.

Meanwhile, "back at the motel": in the Motel package, both bodily injury and property damage liability insurance are written on an occurrence basis, in one insuring clause, subject to one limit. The term "occurrence" is defined as "an event, or a continuous or repeated exposure to conditions, which causes bodily injury or property damage during the policy period that is neither expected nor intended by the insured. All such exposure to substantially the same general conditions existing at or emanating from each premises shall be deemed one occurrence." Liability for injuries intentionally inflicted by or at the direction of the insured, however, are not covered. The *Apartment House* package and the *Office* package also include single limits for bodily injury and property damage liability cover on an occurrence basis.

In addition to scheduled, comprehensive, and broad form liability covers there are several important specific liability policies. Any liability that is specifically imposed on liquor dealers or their landlords under liquor control laws is excluded under the general liability forms. *Liquor Liability insurance* is written to cover this hazard. Other special liability policies written are *Nuclear-Energy Liability*, *Sprinkler Leakage Liability*, *Water Damage Liability*, and *Fire Legal Liability* (liability for property damage caused by spread of fire or, sometimes, explosion).

Professional Liability Covers. A number of *professional liability insur-*

ance forms are written to provide protection for doctors, druggists, nurses, lawyers, insurance agents, accountants, and others against claims arising out of alleged malpractice, error, or mistake in rendering or failure to render professional service. Professional liability cover for insurance agents, accountants, lawyers, and others outside the medical profession is frequently called *Errors and Omissions insurance*, whereas covers concerned with the healing professions are sometimes called *Malpractice insurance*.

Professional liability insurance is written on an occurrence rather than on an accident basis and includes only one principal insuring clause. Wherever applicable, the insuring clause will include not only bodily injury and property damage liability but also liability for mental suffering, invasion of privacy, slander, and other intentional torts. An important attribute of most forms of professional liability insurance is the provision prohibiting the insurer from settling claims out of court without the written consent of the insured. The insured's reputation is at stake in a malpractice case, and he has the right to his day in court for defense regardless of whether the insurer thinks that it would be less expensive to settle the case quietly out of court.

Professional liability insurance restricts coverage to liability arising from professional service only and does not cover the premises hazard. One of the general liability forms is needed to protect against this hazard. The general liability forms, on the other hand, do not cover liability arising from the rendering of any professional service. Thus, when there is a professional liability exposure, the insured will need both a general liability policy and a professional liability policy.

Employer's Liability Cover. Employer's liability cover is usually written in conjunction with workmen's compensation insurance on the *Workmen's Compensation and Employer's Liability* policy.[25] Under Coverage A of the standard form, the insurer assumes the insured's liability under the workmen's compensation laws specifically designated in the policy declarations. Under Coverage B, the insurer agrees to protect the insured against his common law liability for bodily injury caused by accident or disease sustained by employees and arising out of or in the course of their employment. The employer's liability hazard, like the automobile and professional liability hazard, is excluded in the general liability form.

Personal Injury Liability Covers. The general liability forms cover only claims involving bodily injury and property damage caused by accident or, when written on an occurrence basis, caused unintentionally. They do not cover claims alleging personal injury arising from intentional torts. Several personal injury liability forms have been developed to handle these exposures. *False Arrest Liability insurance* covers claims for damages in which

---

[25] In states where workmen's compensation insurance funds are maintained, private insurers write employer's liability insurance separately for those insureds who cover their compensation exposure in state funds.

false arrest, false imprisonment, detention or malicious prosecution is alleged. Coverage for assault and battery may be added to the form.[26] A *Libel* policy is written to protect the insured against claims alleging libel, slander, invasion of privacy, plagiarism, piracy, and violation of copyright.[27] A liability policy covering claims alleging *wrongful eviction* or *wrongful entry* may also be purchased. These personal injury liability covers are available as an endorsement to the package policies issued under the Special Multi-Peril policy program.

Life Insurance Covers

Life insurance covers may be classified on the basis of the insurer's obligation under the policy and on the basis of the insured's obligation. If the insurer is obligated to pay a benefit only if the subject dies within a given period, the policy is called *Term insurance*. If, in addition, the insurer obligates itself to pay a benefit if the subject outlives the death protection period, the policy is called *Endowment insurance*. If the insurer promises to pay a death benefit regardless of when the subject dies, the policy is called *Whole Life insurance*. If, in Term insurance, the insurer allows the insured to continue the insurance in force for one or more additional periods without submitting evidence of insurability, the policy is called *Renewable Term*. And, if the insured without evidence of insurability is allowed to exchange a Term policy for a Whole Life or Endowment policy before the term expires, the policy is called *Convertible Term*.

If the insured agrees to pay for the insurance in equal periodic payments over the life of the policy, the insurance is called *Continuous Premium*. If the insured agrees to pay for the insurance in equal installments over a period shorter than the term of the policy, the insurance is called *Limited Payment* (for example 20-Payment Life). And, if the insured agrees to pay for the protection in advance all in one sum, the policy is called *Single Premium*.

Thus, with three types of policies based on the insurer's obligation to pay claims and three types of policies based on the insured's obligation to pay premiums, nine basic combinations of life insurance policies are available.

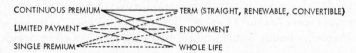

Some of these combinations are uncommon, however.

Yearly Renewable Term insurance offers the insured the opportunity to purchase life insurance protection on a "natural premium" basis, that is, for

---

[26] A false arrest rider may be attached to a *Bankers Blanket* bond.

[27] The authors of this text have not purchased this cover. We do not know whether our publisher has.

a premium that reflects the insurance cost for the year covered. In the foregoing classification, yearly renewable term insurance would be Single Premium Renewable term. This form of cover might be used to insure against loss caused by the death of a key man when the business finds no net appeal in building cash balances through life insurance policies.[28] It may be used in other business life insurance situations in which low initial costs are more appealing than the accumulation of cash values in spite of the realization that the annual premium will increase each year as the subject of the insurance advances in age.

A form of cash value life insurance may be necessary to accomplish the business objective for which the insurance is purchased. For example, when the employer wants to use life insurance to attract and retain key men, he might find the *split-dollar plan* a useful device. The split-dollar plan by its nature requires the use of cash value life insurance. Under this plan, the policy is purchased by the employer on the life of the key employee. The premium is shared by the employer and the employee. The maximum amount paid by the employer each year is that amount by which the cash value of the policy will increase during the year. The employee pays the balance. The absolute amount of increase in the cash value of the policy will grow from year to year until eventually the amount of the increase will exceed the annual premium. The employee's share of the cost, therefore, will decrease each year and finally reach zero. The employer will never have put more into the policy than its cash value. The employment agreement provides that, upon the death of the employee, the employer will be paid from the policy proceeds an amount equal to the predeath cash value of the policy. The remainder is paid to the employee's beneficiary. The one-year term dividend option under which policy dividends may be used to purchase one-year term insurance for an amount not to exceed the cash value of the policy can be used to keep the employee's share of the policy proceeds at least equal to the face amount of the policy during a large part of the life of the policy.[29]

The business uses of life insurance are many and varied. Some call for the use of Yearly Renewable Term insurance (Group Life insurance, for example), whereas others call for Level Premium or Limited Payment Whole Life or Endowment policies (individual policies to fund pension trusts, for example).

An *Annuity* is a type of life insurance that pays a periodic income to the insured until he dies. The principal use of the Annuity in business is to fund insured pension plans, and for this purpose it is written on a group basis.[30]

---

[28] For an explanation of the source of cash value in a life insurance policy see Robert I. Mehr and Robert W. Osler, *Modern Life Insurance* (3d ed.; New York: Macmillan Co., 1961), pp. 8–20.

[29] *Ibid.*, p. 433.

[30] *Ibid.*, pp. 319–27.

Health Insurance Covers

Broadly classified, health insurance covers are of two types: income replacement and medical expense.

Income Replacement. Health insurance forms covering income replacement may be classified according to (1) the perils covered and (2) the continuation privileges granted to the insured. Forms covering loss of time may provide benefits for disabilities caused either by accident or by sickness, or benefits may be restricted to disabilities caused by accident only. Limited accident policies are written to cover only travel accidents, vacation accidents, or accidents while engaging in some sport, for example. If the purpose of the disability income insurance is to indemnify the business for the loss of the services of a key man or to attract a key man by giving him a *Disability Income* policy as a fringe benefit, the perils of both accident and illness should be covered as broadly as possible. When the cover is given under a group plan, however, it is customary to exclude occupational injuries because they are covered under workmen's compensation insurance.

As to continuation provisions, the principal consideration is whether the insured has the right to renew the cover. If both the right to renew and the premium are guaranteed, the policy is called *"Non-Can"* (from "noncancellable"). If the right to renew is guaranteed, but the insurer reserves the right to increase premiums for whole classes of insureds (*not* just individual insureds), the policy is called *Guranteed Renewable, Adjustable Premium* (or *G.R.*). Policies on which renewal may be refused by the insurer and those which may be cancelled by the insurer at any time are at the other extreme in the scale of continuation provisions and have no generally accepted class name. In the middle, and also nameless, are policies issued with restricted termination rights, under which the insurer cannot deny renewal unless renewal is denied on all policies of the same class.

Expense Reimbursement. Among the health expense reimbursement covers are *Hospital insurance, Surgical Expense insurance, Basic Medical Expenses insurance* (for doctors' bills), and *Major Medical Expense insurance* (for physicians' and surgeons' bills, hospital expenses, nursing care, etc.). Major Medical Expense insurance is written to exclude the first few dollars of medical bills and frequently requires the insured to pay 20–25 per cent of the covered expenses. Health expense covers may be purchased by the business on an individual basis for specific key employees, or they may be purchased on a group basis to cover all employees. The expense covers may be written broadly enough to include expenses incurred on behalf of members of the insured's family.

Surety Covers

Certain business situations require one party to furnish a guarantee to another that indemnity will be paid in the event of failure to perform some act. A *surety bond* is a means of providing this guarantee. The surety (bonding company) agrees to fulfill the obligor's promise in the event of a default. For example, when a contractor bids on a construction job he may be required to furnish a *Bid bond* guaranteeing that he will sign the construction contract if his bid is accepted and that he will furnish a *Construction bond* guaranteeing that he will erect the building according to contract. A *Completion bond* may be required of a borrower guaranteeing that the money will be used for the purposes for which it was borrowed and that the work will be completed.

When a manufacturer agrees to furnish semifinished manufactured products to a finisher, the finisher may require a *Supply bond* to guarantee that, if the products do not flow as agreed upon, he will be compensated for the interruption in his production schedule.

The foregoing bonds are contract bonds. Fidelity bonds have already been discussed. In addition, businessmen may be required to post bonds in court actions guaranteeing the payment of any damages or expenses involved in an appeal case or in an unjustified attachment of property. These bonds are called *Litigation bonds*. If a business or businessman should have occasion to manage money or other property for others under court supervision (as receiver for a bankrupt, for example), a *Fiduciary bond* will ordinarily be required. Finally, a business may be required to post a *License or Permit bond* before it can get government permission to engage in certain kinds of activities.

A final type of cover, one that may be classed as a surety cover, is *Credit insurance*. This form of insurance is written for manufacturers, jobbers, and wholesalers to protect them against losses in excess of the normal rate of bad debts arising from the insolvency of customers or from the delinquency of accounts.

CONCLUSION

These few pages represent only a brief cataloguing of covers written by insurers. The classification system used in this catalogue is one that reflects product organization within the insurance industry. It is not necessarily the best one for educating a given risk manager in matching covers to his exposures. Rather than looking at physical damage, time element, marine, crime, liability, life, health, and surety covers he may find it more rewarding to consider the assets and the personnel of the business in the light of the perils that can reduce their usefulness and the ways in which the resulting losses will be manifested. Armed with this information, he can comb the catalogue of insurance forms trying to find the combination of covers that offers the protection he wants. Or, if he is big enough and smart enough, he might even design from scratch the covers he needs and invite insurers to stray from their catalogues.

The process can be illustrated with cash, the first item on the balance sheet. Several perils can cause loss of cash; it may be physically destroyed, be wrongfully abstracted, or just plain disappear. Because cash is readily replaceable, there will be no business interruption loss if the asset loss itself is cared for. The Money and Securities Broad Form policy will cover loss of the money from virtually any cause on or off premises except when caused by embezzlement by an employee or when voluntarily surrendered. Fidelity and forgery covers are necessary to fill out the insurance against loss of cash.

Now consider the factory building. This asset can be damaged or destroyed by fire, lightning, the extended coverage perils, vandalism and malicious mischief, snow and ice, earthquake, explosion of a steam boiler, and other causes. Because it takes time to restore a building to use after serious physical damage, a business interruption loss exposure exists. And, because members of the public and employees can be injured on the premises, a liability exposure inheres in the ownership, maintenance, and use of the building. A whole set of covers is necessary for maximum insurance protection against these exposures. One possible set would include an Industrial Property policy, Earthquake insurance, Boiler and Machinery insurance, Business Interruption insurance, Manufacturers and Contractors Public Liability insurance (covering premises and operations plus elevators, if any), and Workmen's Compensation and Employer's Liability insurance. If the building were leased instead of owned, Leasehold Interest, Improvements and Betterments, and Fire Legal Liability covers might be needed, but physical damage covers on the building might be unnecessary.

And so on, through all the exposures and covers!

REVIEW AND DISCUSSION QUESTIONS

1. Before 1953 "all risks" coverage on stocks of merchandise was available only to jewelers and fine arts dealers. In 1953 the list of acceptable types of business was broadened to include dealers in cameras, musical instruments, and a few other products. In 1954 the allowed list was broadened a great deal more. How may these limitations and the changes in them be logically explained?

2. Distinguish between "package policy," " 'all risks' coverage," and "multiple line cover." To what extent do these three forms of protection overlap?

3. Do the new broader covers make the risk manager's job easier or more difficult? Explain.

4. Suppose you were the risk manager for a single location retail store dealing in some form or forms of apparel. Write the insurance policy you would like to buy (and do not forget the cost factor).

5. Suppose you were the underwriter asked to issue the policy drawn up in response to question 4, above. What changes would you want to make in this cover before issuing it? Why? (If no changes, explain why the cover detailed in question 4 is not in fact generally available to such stores today.)

6. In the view of insurers, what feature or features distinguish "consequential loss" from "direct loss"? Why would they wish to make such a distinction? Is such a classification also useful to the risk manager? Explain.

7. What explanation can be advanced for the distinctions between property subject to marine insurance covers and property subject to fire and allied lines or casualty physical damage insurance covers? Are these distinctions useful to the risk manager? Explain.

8. What are the major divisions among crime insurance covers? Is division of crime insurance coverage in this particular way useful to risk managers? Explain.

9. Do you consider the way in which insurers have divided liability insurance protection among the various liability covers a useful division from the viewpoint of insurance buyers? Why or why not?

10. What do you believe the phrase "caused by accident" ought to mean in insurance policies? How about the phrase "accidental loss or damage"? In what cases would it help if your definitions were written into policies which use these phrases?

11. It seems unlikely that persons who have not studied the subject (meaning nearly all insureds) are aware of the difference between "bodily injury" and "personal injury." Do you think anything should be done about this? If so, what? If not, why not?

12. Which type of life insurance policy is generally best to use when insuring the business against loss from the premature death of a key man? Explain your answer.

13. Which type of health insurance policy is generally best to use when insuring the business against loss from the disability of a key man? Explain your answer.

14. Which type of health insurance policy is generally best to use when insuring employees' medical expenses? Explain your answer.

15. How are surety covers classified? Is this classification system useful to the risk manager? Explain.

Chapter 15

INSURANCE COVERAGE

The risk manager needs to know a great deal more about a cover than its name and catalogue description. He needs to be able to define precisely the coverage afforded by the policy. Only then will he know that he has purchased all the protection intended, and only then will he be able to avoid the expense of unnecessary duplication of covers.

REASONS FOR LIMITATIONS ON COVERAGE

All insurance policies limit coverage, and these limits have eight dimensions: perils, property, losses, hazards, persons, places, period, and amount. Even though limitations on coverage complicate the job of the insurance buyer, they are necessary to the efficient operation of an insurance service. Limitations on coverage help contain premium rates within reasonable levels by facilitating management of the moral and morale hazards and by reducing the possibility that the insured will have duplicate coverage in some other policy. Limitations on coverage help give the insured an equitable rate by eliminating the cost of coverage needed by only a minority of those who purchase the policy. Insurers also limit coverage to eliminate uninsurable exposures and to exclude covers that require special underwriting and rating techniques more conveniently handled under a separate policy or endorsement. Every limitation on coverage can be explained in terms of the foregoing reasons.

ANALYZING COVERAGE IN INSURANCE CONTRACTS

It would be helpful to refer to specimen policy forms[1] when studying this chapter. In order to illustrate points, use will be made of various policies. No effort will be made to analyze any cover in detail except in the

---

[1] Policy kits may be obtained from the American Mutual Insurance Alliance, 20 North Wacker Drive, Chicago 6, Illinois, or from the Insurance Information Institute, 60 John Street, New York 38, New York.

summary of the chapter, where one simple policy will be analyzed in full. A *procedure* for analyzing the coverage in a policy, not the details about any one cover, is the objective of the following discussion.

What Perils Are Covered?

Insurance policies restrict the perils insured against, either by naming the perils that are covered or by naming those that are excluded. When the covered perils are named, the policy is called a *specified perils* policy. When all perils are covered except those specifically excluded, the contract is called an *"all risks"* policy or a *comprehensive* policy.

Physical damage insurance on a store building, for example, may be written as specified perils cover or as "all risks" cover; either way, the Standard Fire insurance policy and an appropriate descriptive form (the Building and Contents form, for example) would be used.[2] To broaden the specified perils cover, the *Extended Coverage endorsement* can be used. Fire and lightning are covered under the standard fire policy and the perils of windstorm, hail, explosion, riot attending a strike, civil commotion, aircraft, vehicles, and smoke are covered by the extended coverage endorsement. For "all risks" cover the *Special Extended Coverage endorsement* is available; under it the policy is "extended to insure against all other risks of direct physical loss, except as hereinafter provided." The words *"except as hereinafter provided"* are the key words in the insuring clause, and they are the words that make "all risks" cover not really all risks cover.

Among the exclusions in the Special Extended Coverage endorsement are those usually found in "all risks" physical damage forms; not covered are losses caused by wear and tear, deterioration, rust or corrosion, mould, wet or dry rot; inherent or latent defect; smog; smoke, vapor, or gas from agricultural or industrial operations; mechanical breakdown, including rupture or bursting caused by centrifugal force; settling, cracking, shrinkage, bulging, or expansion of pavements, foundations, walls, floors, roofs, or ceilings; or animals, birds, vermin, termites, or other insects.

The endorsement also excludes all earth movements, such as earthquake, volcanic eruption, and landslides. A water exclusion applies to flood, surface water, waves, tidal water or tidal wave, overflow of streams or other bodies of water, or spray from any of the foregoing, all whether driven by wind or not; water which backs up through sewers or drains; and water below the surface of the ground, including that which exerts pressure on or flows, seeps, or leaks through sidewalks, driveways, foundations, walls, basement

---

[2] The Standard Fire policy is not in itself a valid insurance contract. This document states the name of the insured, the location of the property, the types of insurance purchased, and the maximum loss payable for each type of property covered. To complete the contract, a form describing the physical nature of the property and the terms under which this property is covered must be endorsed on the standard policy. Further endorsements may be used to extend the coverage to additional perils, locations, and losses.

or other floors, or through doors, windows, or any other openings in such sidewalks, driveways, foundations, walls, or floors.

Unexplained or mysterious disappearance of any property or shortage disclosed on taking inventory, or caused by any wilful or dishonest act or omission of the Insured or any associate, employee, or agent of any insured is excluded along with theft of any property not an integral part of the building at the time of the loss. Also not covered are losses occasioned directly or indirectly by enforcement of any local or state ordinance or law regulating the construction, repair, or demolition of buildings or structures. Nor does this form insure against loss by explosion of steam boilers, steam pipes, steam turbines, or steam engines when owned, leased, or operated by the insured. A war clause excludes liability for loss caused directly or indirectly by hostile or warlike action in time of peace or war, including action in hindering, combating, or defending against an actual or expected attack; or caused by insurrection, rebellion, revolution, civil war, usurped power, or action taken by governmental authority in hindering, combating, or defending against such an occurrence. Finally, loss by nuclear reaction or nuclear radiation or radioactive contamination, all whether controlled or uncontrolled, is not covered.

These seemingly inexhaustible exclusions may shock the reader into questioning whether the Special Extended Coverage endorsement leaves any worthwhile coverage for the policyholder. But when he directs his attention to the even more apparently inexhaustible list of perils that can threaten property, he will realize that far more coverage is left for the policyholder than is taken away. Furthermore, when he views these exclusions thoughtfully he will readily understand that they are necessary to provide attractive and equitable premiums for the insured as well as to protect the solvency of the insurer.

Limitations on Covered Perils. Sometimes a peril may be covered, but only to a limited extent. When this is the case, the form must specify what part of the peril is covered or what part is not covered. For example, a health insurance policy covering the peril of sickness may be restricted to a list of specified "dread" diseases. On the other hand, the policy may cover the peril of sickness broadly; then any illness is covered unless otherwise excluded. Sickness policies specifying the part of the peril not covered sometimes exclude mental illness, veneral disease, or pregnancy, childbirth, and miscarriage.

Definition of Covered Perils. Various words are used in insurance policies to indicate the perils covered, and these words do not always have the same meaning in insurance language as they do in everyday language. Sometimes the policy contains definitions of key words. For example, the *Mercantile Open Stock Burglary* policy defines burglary as "the felonious abstraction of insured property (1) from within the premises by a person making felonious entry therein by actual force and violence as evidenced by visible marks made by tools, explosives, electricity, or chemicals upon, or physical damage to, the exterior of the premises at the place of such entry, or (2) from within a showcase or show window outside the premises by a person making felonious entry into such showcase or show window by actual force and violence, of which force and violence there are visible marks thereon." Robbery of a watchman is defined as "the felonious taking of insured property by violence or threat of violence inflicted upon a private watchman employed exclusively by the insured and while such watchman is on duty within the premises."

What can be used for a definition when the policy does not contain its own dictionary? For example, the Standard Fire insurance policy does not define *fire*. A line of court decisions arising out of disputes over the interpretation of the term "fire" has established its insurance meaning to include two requisites: (1) a combustion rapid enough to produce both heat *and* light and (2) the combustion, if started for a useful purpose, must have escaped from the receptacle or area normally intended for it. Thus a combustion not sufficiently rapid to cause ignition (decay, rust, scorch) is not a fire under the terms of a fire insurance policy. And a combustion rapid enough to produce a flame or glow is not covered under a fire insurance policy unless the combustion is unfriendly or hostile. A *friendly fire* is a combustion that is started for a useful purpose and that remains in its normal confines; a fire in a fireplace is an example of a friendly fire. A *hostile fire* is a combustion that was started for a useful purpose but later escaped from its intended location or one resulting from arson or accident. A flame caused by a spark from defective wires is an example of a hostile or unfriendly fire.

Some perils are defined in state statutes; an example is the peril of riot. Riots mean different things in different states. In Illinois "if two or more persons actually do an unlawful act with force or violence against the person or property of another with or without a common cause of quarrel, or even do a lawful act in a violent or tumultuous manner, the persons so offending shall be deemed guilty of a riot." Most other states require at least three persons to be involved before there can be a riot. Some states restrict the definition of riot to unlawful acts only. Courts must interpret the statutes, of course. The burden of proof that there has been a riot (or whatever specified peril is claimed) is on the insured.[3]

Courts are frequently called upon to decide the meaning of a peril covered or excluded in the policy. When the officers and crews of seven ocean-going vessels owned by the Republic of China defected to the Communist government and delivered the vessels to the Communists, their action was held to be barratry within the terms of the ocean marine policy, and not

---

[3] For a case involving peril of riot under the Illinois statute, see *Walter* v. *Northern Insurance Co.*, 18 N.E. (2d) 906.

"capture or seizure," which is excluded from coverage.[4] A hospital expense policy excluding hospitalization for nervous or mental disorders or rest cure was held to cover arteriosclerosis and cerebral atrophy because these are pathological conditions that affect motor and physical functions, not just mental activities, and so are functional and organic, not "nervous."[5]

The term "accident," as was mentioned earlier, has been and still is subject to much litigation. When a contractor was reroofing a house, a half an inch of rain fell and did over $4,000 damage to the house and its contents. The liability insurer denied liability under the Manufacturers' and Contractors' Liability policy on the grounds that the loss was not the result of an accident. The court argued that, since the word "accident" is not defined in the policy, it must be interpreted in its usual, ordinary, and popular sense. It concluded that because showers do not often occur in Albuquerque in October, and the weather bureau did not foresee rain (the contractor had checked with the weather bureau), the rainstorm must be considered an "accident" within the meaning of the policy.[6]

"When I use a word" Humpty Dumpty said in a rather scornful tone, "it means just what I choose it to mean, neither more nor less." "The question is," said Alice, "whether you can make words mean so many different things." "The question is," said Humpty Dumpty, "which is the master, that's all."

But, as has already been pointed out, when an insurance company uses a word, it means what the court chooses it to mean. And the courts follow the principle that when there is ambiguity the words are to be construed strongly against those who write them. An insured under automobile medical payments cover was held to have "been struck by an automobile" when he collided with a parked automobile while riding his bicycle. The court reasoned that "being struck" means the striking together of two objects even though one may be stationary. The policy said nothing to the effect that the insured must be struck by a *moving* automobile![7]

Even when the policy defines the peril, as is done in the Robbery and Safe Burglary policy, questions of interpretation may arise. In the definition of robbery, coverage is granted for the felonious taking of insured property "from within a show window in the premises while regularly open for business, by a person who has broken the glass thereof from outside the premises, or by an accomplice of such person." The money-handling operations of a hotel insured under this policy were carried on in a glassed-in office visible from the lobby. There were two external windows

---

[4] *National Union Fire Insurance Co.* v. *Republic of China et al.*, 254 E. 2d 177—U.S. App. 4th Cir.

[5] *Reserve Life Insurance Co.* v. *Jansen*, 357 S.W. 2d 770.

[6] *O'Rourke* v. *New Amsterdam Casualty Co.*, 362 Pac. 2d 790—Sup. Court, New Mexico.

[7] *Houston Fire and Casualty Co.* v. *Kahn*, 355 S.W. 2d 221. One wonders whether, when A's moving fist contacts B's stationary nose, A may now complain of having "been struck by" B.

in the back wall of the office. While the employees were out for lunch and the office was locked, one of the external windows was broken by a large rock and the windows raised. The office was burglarized. When the insurer's adjuster issued a draft in payment of a claim under the policy, the insurer refused to honor the draft on the grounds that the policy did not cover the loss. The insured brought suit to enforce payment of the draft. The court held for the insured, stating that if the adjuster considered the office a show window, then the loss was covered and the adjuster had the authority to settle the claim. The court reasoned that, since the words "show window" are undefined in the policy and their intended meaning is doubtful, it would be reasonable to interpret them in such manner as to provide indemnity. That common usage and standard dictionaries define a "show window" as "a display window in a store" did not influence the court. Whether the court would have upheld the insured's claim if the adjuster had denied it is another matter, for in the case at hand the court said its function was, not to determine the meaning of the words "show window," but to decide whether the insured had acted in good faith in asserting his claim. This decision depended on whether the claim had an appearance of merit sufficient to raise a possible doubt in his favor.[8]

Thus, in determining what perils are covered, the insured must look to the contract for a listing of those perils that are covered and of those that are not covered. He must also check the policy for any limitations on covered perils and for definitions of covered perils. He must look to the courts for interpretations of statutory definitions of perils and for interpretations of perils either defined or undefined in the policy. The multitude of court cases dealing with disputes involving the question of what perils are covered under an insurance policy suggests that the answer is not always simple. Therefore, great care is necessary in the phrasing and organization of insurance forms.

What Property Is Covered?

Property, like perils, may be covered on a named property basis or on an "all except" basis. The Comprehensive Glass policy is an example of the named basis for covering property. This policy covers damage to the glass described in the declarations and to the lettering and ornamentation separately described. The word "comprehensive" in the policy title refers to the perils covered and not to the property covered.

The Standard Store Owner's policy provides an example of the "all except" basis for covering property. Personal property covered is defined broadly in this policy as consisting principally of (1) stock of merchandise, supplies, and materials; (2) furniture and fixtures, machinery and equipment; and (3) personal property of others usual or incidental to the in-

---

[8] *Weinberg et al. v. Globe Indemnity Co.*, 355 S.W. 2d 341.

sured's business while in the care, custody, or control of the insured and for which the insured is liable. The policy also covers, at the option of the insured, personal effects not usual or incidental to the insured's business, while at the premises, for an amount not exceeding $1,000, but not against the perils of vandalism and malicious mischief. The cost of reproduction of valuable papers and records pertaining to the insured property is covered for an amount not exceeding $1,000.

Specifically excluded are automobiles, motor trucks, trailers (except trailers held for sale and designed for use with private passenger vehicles for general utility purposes or carrying boats), and similar vehicles; motor-cycles, motor scooters, and similar vehicles, all while licensed for highway use; aircraft; watercraft (including motors, equipment, and accessories) while afloat; and money and securities. "Money" is defined as "currency, coin, bank notes, and bullion; and travelers checks, register checks, and money orders held for sale to the public." "Securities" are defined as "all negotiable and non-negotiable instruments or contracts representing either money or other property and includes revenue or other stamps in current use, tokens, and tickets," but not including money. "Valuable papers and records" are defined as "written, printed, or otherwise inscribed documents and records pertaining to the insured's business, including books, maps, drawings, abstracts, deeds, mortgages, and manuscripts," but not money or securities, films or electronic recordings, or property held as samples or for sale or for delivery after sale.

Liability insurance offers the insured protection against claims arising out of damage to property belonging to others. Liability claims for damage to certain property may be excluded in these policies. The automobile liability policy, for example, does not apply to "injury to or destruction of property owned or transported by the insured, or property rented to or in charge of the insured other than a residence or private garage" injured or destoyed by a private passenger automobile covered by the policy. This is one version of the "care, custody, or control" exclusion found in most prop-erty damage liability insurance policies.[9] Some liability policies exclude damage to property if the insured is exercising physical control over it, regardless of whether he has the right to exercise that control. Unless the policy specifically uses the words "is exercising physical control" (the general liability forms do; the automobile liability forms do not), the courts do not apply the exclusion when the insured exercises physical control but does not have the right to do so.

Importance of Knowing What Property Is Covered. The risk manager must understand fully what property is covered under a given form and what property is excluded. Aside from checking to see that he has covered

---

[9] For a discussion of court cases involving "care, custody, and control" see the *Fire, Casualty, and Surety Bulletins* (monthly) (Cincinnati: National Underwriter Com-pany), Casualty and Surety Volume, Public Liability, Dpc 1-8.

all the property that he decides should be covered, he must check to see that no property is covered that he does not intend to cover. This is necessary because in fixing the value for coinsurance purposes all property covered by the form is included. Thus, if the insured misses some covered property in calculating the amount of insurance necessary to satisfy the coinsurance requirement, he may incur a coinsurance deficiency and have to bear part of his loss.[10]

What Losses Are Covered?

Insurance policies are written to cover three kinds of losses: loss of the physical asset, loss of earning power, and loss through unexpected extra expenses. *Property* insurance may be written to cover one or more of these types of losses. *Health and life* insurance are written to cover loss of earning power and expenses associated with accident, sickness, and death. *Liability* insurance is written to cover extra-expense losses arising from claims against the insured.

In analyzing the coverage under any policy, therefore, attention should be given to the nature of the losses covered because more than one type of loss may be covered. The *Gross Earnings Business Interruption* form, for example, covers income loss directly resulting from the necessary interruption of business caused by damage to, or destruction of, real or personal property by the perils insured against. Also covered are such expenses as are necessarily incurred for the purpose of reducing any loss under the policy (except expense to extinguish a fire, for which separate cover is available). The *Comprehensive Automobile Physical Damage* form includes, along with the physical damage and crime cover, limited protection against loss-of-use following theft. *Transportation* insurance forms usually do not cover loss occasioned by a delay in shipment but only the loss of the goods themselves and any general average, salvage and sue-and-labor charges.[11]

More losses are covered by *liability* insurance policies than the typical insured realizes. Aside from paying damages that the insured becomes legally obligated to pay, the insurer will defend the insured against suits alleging injury and claiming damages if the insurance covers the insured's potential liability for the loss. The insurer also agrees to pay all premiums on bonds to release attachments and all premiums on appeal bonds re-

---

[10] A coinsurance clause requires the insured to maintain insurance at or above a given percentage of the value of covered property if he wishes to collect the full amount of his loss up to the face amount of the policy. Coinsurance will be discussed later in this chapter.

[11] General average charges were explained in an earlier chapter (see Index for reference). Sue-and-labor charges arise out of the policy condition requiring the insured to "sue, labor, and travel for, in and about the defense, safeguard, and recovery of the property insured. . . ." The sue-and-labor clause requires the insured to take the necessary steps to eliminate or reduce a loss covered by the insurance and obligates the insurer to reimburse the insured for the costs involved regardless of whether the effort is successful.

quired in any such defended suit. In addition, the insurer will pay all expenses incurred by the insurer, all costs taxed against the insured in any such suit, and all interest accruing after entry of judgment until the insurer has paid or tendered or deposited in court such part of the judgment as does not exceed the insurer's liability. Expenses incurred by the insured for such immediate medical and surgical relief to others as shall be imperative at the time of the accident will be paid by the insurer, and so will all reasonable expenses, other than loss of earnings, incurred by the insured at the insurer's request. In automobile liability insurance, the insurer also agrees to pay premiums on bail bonds.

What Hazards Are Covered?

A hazard may be defined as any condition that increases the chance of loss from a given peril or set of perils. In order to control the risk, insurers place certain restrictions in the policy which limit coverage under hazardous conditions.

For example, the *Standard Fire* insurance policy suspends coverage "while the hazard is increased by any means within the control or knowledge of the insured," or "while the building, whether intended for occupancy by owner or tenant, is vacant or unoccupied beyond a period of sixty consecutive days unless otherwise provided in writing and endorsed on the policy." The *Building and Contents* form designed for use with this policy contains a *Work and Materials* clause that grants permission to the insured to use the premises in any way usual or incidental to the occupancy described in the policy without fear of violation of the increase in hazard clause. An *Alterations and Repairs* clause is also included in the form, giving the insured permission to make alterations and repairs and to construct additions to the building. (If the building is protected by automatic sprinklers, special permission must be obtained from the insurer for reconstruction or enlargement of the building.)

The *Mercantile Open Stock Burglary* policy is suspended "while there is any change in the condition of the risk or during a fire in the premises." The *Annual Transit* policy usually excludes the hazard of illicit trade. *Group health insurance* policies usually exclude the occupational hazard: on-the-job injuries are not covered.

The hazards covered (and those not covered) commonly are the distinguishing feature between one kind of liability policy and another. Automobile liability policies are an example. The ownership, maintenance, or use of an automobile clearly constitutes a liability hazard. This is the hazard specified as insured against in automobile liability policies. On the other hand, most of this particular hazard is excluded from coverage under the majority of other kinds of liability policies.

Schedule liability policies list and describe the hazards to which they may be applied. For example, the Manufacturer's and Contractor's Schedule Liability policy lists five hazards, as noted in the preceding chapter: premises and operations, elevators, independent contractors, products and completed operations, and contractual liability of specified types (sidetrack agreement, easement agreement in connection with a railroad grade crossing, and an agreement required by municipal ordinance in connection with work for the municipality). Each hazard is rated separately, and the insured may choose to cover only the premises and operations hazard if he wishes. He may also select all, none, or any one of the other hazards for cover.

If only the premises and operations exposure is covered on the schedule, then the following hazards are excluded from coverage: (1) watercraft away from premises owned by, rented to, or controlled by the named insured, unless specifically covered in the declarations; (2) automobiles away from such premises or the ways immediately adjoining; (3) aircraft; (4) elevators; (5) independent contractors; (6) products and completed operations; (7) liability assumed under any contract or agreement *except* written easement agreements (other than those in connection with a railroad grade crossing), written agreements required by municipal ordinance (other than those in connection with work for the municipality), and a written lease of premises; (8) liability hazards under dramshop acts; and (9) liability toward employees arising out of the employer-employee relationship.

In addition, one exclusion in the Manufacturer's and Contractor's form illustrates the distinction between a *peril* exclusion and a *hazard* exclusion. This exclusion (which is not applicable to all insureds) denies coverage for damage to underground conduits, wires, pipes, or similar property when *caused by* and *during the use of* mechanical equipment for grading, paving, drilling, or excavating. The phrase "caused by" makes a peril exclusion; the phrase "during the use of" creates a hazard exclusion. In one case, a bulldozer was driven over a pipeline. Although its blade had been raised, a digging tooth still struck and damaged an underground pipeline. There was no question but that the *peril* part of the exclusion was satisfied, but what about the *hazard* portion?[12] The court split on this question. The majority held that even though the bulldozer's blade was up at the time of the accident (hence no grading was going on at the moment), the movement involved was an essential and integral part of grading operations, so the accident did occur "during the use of mechanical equipment for the purpose of grading land."[13] On the other hand, an occasion could arise in which a loss occurred during the use of mechanical equipment for grading, paving, etc., so that the excluded hazard was present, yet not responsible

---

[12] Note that in this particular exclusion both the peril *and* the hazard portions must apply before coverage is denied. More often, exclusions are connected by an *or*—if *either* the peril specified *or* the hazard named is involved, coverage is denied.

[13] *Texaco-Cities Service Pipe Line Co.* v. *Aetna Casualty & Surety Co.*, 10 C.C.H. (Fire & Casualty) 598.

for the loss. Thus, a boundary stake might be pounded in at a corner of a plot while an excavation was being made in the center of it. If the stake punctured a gas line, that would not appear to be a loss caused by the use of mechanical equipment for excavating. Therefore, even though the excluded hazard were present, the peril coupled with it in this particular exclusion would not be the cause of the loss. Liability for this damage, therefore, would be covered.

Many of the hazards (and perils) that are excluded in Premises-Operations liability cover can be covered by use of other parts of the schedule liability policies, by endorsement to such policies, or by purchase of separate policies. Most of the liability hazards of a business may be covered by switching from schedule liability policies, in which covered hazards are listed and described, to comprehensive liability policies, in which only *uncovered* hazards are listed and described.

What Persons Are Covered?

Insurance policies may cover losses sustained by the named insured only, or they may provide coverage for others as well. The *Annual Transit* policy, for example, covers the named insured only. When the goods are no longer at the risk of the named insured, the coverage for those goods terminates. The *Building and Contents* form used with the Standard Fire insurance policy covers the named insured, his legal representatives, and the mortgagee if a mortgage clause is used. Personal property of employees and officers of the insured may be covered by endorsement if the policy is written with at least an 80 per cent coinsurance clause.

The *Owners', Landlords', and Tenants' Schedule Liability* policy covers the named insured plus partners, or stockholders and executive officers while acting officially in that capacity. It also covers organizations acting as real estate managers for the named insured. The *Mercantile Open Stock Burglary* policy covers the named insured and, at his option, property of others in his possession. Health insurance policies written for loss-of-income benefits cover the named insured only, but, when written to pay medical expenses, eligible members of the insured's family may be included.

The *Schedule Automobile Liability* policy defines the insured as the named insured and, for owned and hired automobiles, any person while using the automobile and any person or organization legally responsible for its use, provided that (1) this other insured does not own the automobile and (2) its actual use is by the named insured or with his permission. For the non-owned automobile hazard, the policy covers only the named insured and any executive officers thereof.[14]

---

[14] The policy contains certain hazard exclusions that apply to persons or organizations other than the named insured. Other hazard exclusions, of course, apply to the named insured also.

Most insurance policies have provisions governing the assignment of the contract before a loss. The 1943 New York Standard Fire Insurance policy, for example, states that "assignment of this policy shall not be valid except with the written consent of the insurer." Life and health insurance policies usually state that no assignment shall be binding upon the insurer unless and until the original or a duplicate is filed at the insurer's home office. Ocean marine cargo policies, however, are freely assignable, and often no reference to assignment appears in the policy. Credit insurance policies, on the other hand, are not assignable under any circumstance.

What Places Are Covered?

Some insurance policies limit coverage to one or more specified sets of premises, whereas others provide coverage over an entire territory, such as the United States and Canada or the Western Hemisphere, or place no territorial limitation at all.

The *Building and Contents* form written with the Standard Fire policy covers property attached to or contained in the building named in the policy and personal property in the open or on vehicles or railway cars within 100 feet of the building. Screens and storm windows and doors are covered while located in other buildings on the premises. If contents have to be moved for safekeeping because the premises are threatened by a covered peril, the moved property is covered at its new location for up to five days.

Annual Transit policies may limit the coverage to continental United States and Canada. Some restrict coverage to land shipments only, whereas others allow Atlantic coastal shipments. Coverage on export shipments terminates at shipboard. The *Mercantile Open Stock* policy covers the interior of designated premises (all premises of the insured if coverage is written blanket), plus showcases and show windows used by the insured outside the premises but inside the building line. *Life and health insurance* policies usually cover anywhere in the world. The *Schedule Automobile Liability* policy applies only to accidents occurring within the United States, its territories or possessions, or Canada, or while being transported between ports thereof.

If the policy does not specify premises or territorial limits, then the coverage is world-wide.

What Period Is Covered?

Insurance policies may be written for a period of a year, less than a year, more than a year, or for an indefinite period. The *Standard Fire* policy is written from noon standard time on the day the policy is effective until noon standard time, usually one, three, or five years later, when the policy expires. However, coverage can be cancelled by the company at any time upon giving five days' notice to the insured (ten days' notice to a mortgagee). The insured may cancel the policy immediately upon giving notice to the insurer.

The *Annual Transit* policy covers the insured from noon standard time at the place of issuance and terminates one year later unless previously cancelled by the insurer (15 days' notice required) or the insured. Note that the time governing commencement and the expiration of coverage is the time at the place the policy is issued and not the time at the place the property is lost or damaged. The *Owners', Landlords', and Tenants' Liability* policy is written from 12:01 A.M. standard time at the address of the named insured and terminates at the same hour one or three years later. The insured can cancel the policy immediately upon giving notice, whereas the insurer must give ten days' notice before cancellation.

The *Comprehensive Dishonesty, Disappearance, and Destruction* policy is written for an indefinite period. The contract states that the policy period is from noon on a given month, day, and year to noon on the effective date of the cancellation or termination of the policy, standard time at the principal address of the insured as stated on the policy. Fifteen days' notice is required for cancellation by the insurer. The insured may cancel immediately upon giving notice.

When must the loss take place before it is covered by the policy? The incident causing the loss must arise during the policy period. If the loss extends beyond that period, the insurer continues to pay. For example, Business Interruption Insurance policies state that the insurer will pay the actual loss sustained directly resulting from the interruption of business for only such length of time as would be required with the exercise of due diligence and dispatch to rebuild, repair, or replace the damaged property commencing with the date of such damage or destruction and *not limited by the date of expiration of the policy*. Weekly indemnity benefits payable for disability under a health insurance policy will continue beyond the policy period provided that the disability commences while the policy is in force.

Some health policies provide that no benefits will be payable for sickness unless the illness commences after the first fifteen days from the date of the policy. On the other hand, some policies pay for loss or injury suffered before the policy became effective. For example, embezzlement of funds by an employee may not be discovered until many years after embezzlement has begun. A *Discovery* form of fidelity bond pays for losses if it is in effect when they are discovered. Marine hull policies commonly insure the vessel "lost or not lost" as of the original date of the policy. And health insurance policies issued today provide that disabilities suffered while the policy has been continuously in force for two or more years are covered even if their origin antedates the policy.

With respect to losses incurred during the policy period but not discovered until after it has expired or been canceled, standard fidelity bonds provide for a "discovery period," which runs after a bond has been terminated; a loss discovered and reported to the surety during this period is covered if it occurred while the bond was in force. The discovery period is one year in some bonds, two years in others. To provide continuing coverage after an employer changes sureties, each new surety agrees to pay for losses that would have been covered by the old bond except for the expiration of its discovery period. Forgery bonds and a few other crime policies have similar provisions.

What Amounts Are Covered?

Limitations on the insurer's liability under an insurance policy are related to (1) the principle of indemnity, (2) the amount of insurance, (3) the total value of all property insured under the policy, (4) the variation between the amounts of insurance on different perils, and (5) the use of deductibles.

The Principle of Indemnity. The Standard Fire Insurance policy, along with many other policies, limits the liability of the insurer to the actual cash value of the property at the time of the loss, and, if less, to the interest of the insured. The purpose of these limitations (actual cash value and insurable interest) is to preserve the insurance contract as a contract of indemnity. If the insured were allowed to collect more from his insurance than his actual loss, the contract would become a gambling contract and could create a moral and morale hazard. In certain types of insurance, when the insured is allowed to collect more than the amount of his loss, insurers are faced with insurance-induced losses. For example, in the area of medical care, in which the insured may have coverage under two group policies (his own employer's and that of his spouse's, for example), each paying full benefits without regard to the other, hospital stays can become profitable to the insured. Such opportunity for profit can encourage overutilization of hospital services. Insurance-induced losses are obviously against public policy, although some situations that encourage them are not themselves always held to be contrary to public policy. (Statutes that make valued policies of all fire policies on real property are an example of such a situation—see below.)

Fire insurance forms covering buildings may be endorsed to change the basis of recovery from actual cash value to replacement cost. Whether an insurance policy that provides for the full replacement cost of a damaged building is in violation of the indemnity principle and whether it creates a moral hazard are much debated questions. Both insurance buyers and sellers realize, however, that, if the insured is forced to provide the resources necessary to offset the difference between the replacement cost and the actual cash value of his property after a loss, he may be hard pressed to do so, especially if the "new" is not expected to be any more productive than the "old." Replacement cost insurance requires the insured to rebuild the same type building on the same site and for the same type of occupancy, thus reducing the moral hazard.

Some policies are written on a valued basis, that is, the insurer and the insured agree in advance on the value of the covered property. In the event of a total loss, the insurer will pay the agreed-upon value. Art objects and other property likely to be subject to wide variations in appraisal after a loss usually are insured under a valued form. A few states require insurers to treat every total loss of real property from fire as though the policy were written on a valued basis. If the agreed-upon values are sound values, valued policies do not violate the principle of indemnity.

The amount of insurable interest does not affect the amount payable under a life insurance policy except in cases involving a debtor-creditor relationship. The amount of insurance held by a creditor in the life of the debtor must have a reasonable relationship to the amount of actual dollar interest involved. In no other relationship, however, is a life insurance policy considered to be a contract of indemnity.

Also arising out of the principle of indemnity are the *other-insurance clauses* found in most insurance policies. In contracts of indemnity, an insured is not allowed to collect the full amount of his loss from each of several insurers. Existence of other insurance may affect an insurer's liability in one of several ways. In some policies, each insurer agrees to contribute with the other insurer on a pro rata basis. The Manufacturer's and Contractor's Liability policy, for example, states that "if the insured has other insurance against a loss covered by this policy the company shall not be liable . . . for a greater proportion of such loss than the applicable limit of liability stated in the declarations bears to the total applicable limit of liability of all valid and collectible insurance against such loss."[15]

The type of clause just described is known as a "pro rata liability" type of other-insurance clause. Many policies provide a different rule for allocation of a loss among the several insurers who are to share in it. This rule is known variously as the "limit of liability" or the "joint loss apportionment" rule. Under it, each insurer's share of a loss depends on what each insurer would have paid on the loss had no other insurance existed. For example, take three policies applicable to a $10,000 loss:

Policy	Face Amount
A	$ 5,000
B	15,000
C	30,000
Total	$50,000

---

[15] The Standard Fire insurance policy has a similar clause but makes the insurance contributing insurance with other insurance, *whether collectible or not.*

Amount each policy would have paid if it had been the only policy applicable:

Policy	Limit of Liability
A	$ 5,000
B	10,000
C	10,000
Total	$25,000

The amount each company would have paid if it had been the only insurer is called its "limit of liability." (This limit can be less than the loss, of course, for any of several reasons, such as a coinsurance deficiency—see below). Under the limit of liability rule, losses are shared in proportion to the limits of liability. This may be compared with results under the pro rata liability rule (sharing according to face amount of insurance):

Policy	Share of Loss under Limit of Liability Rule	Share of Loss under Pro Rata Liability Rule
A	5/25 of $10,000 = $ 2,000	5/50 of $10,000 = $ 1,000
B	10/25 of 10,000 = 4,000	15/50 of 10,000 = 3,000
C	10/25 of 10,000 = 4,000	30/50 of 10,000 = 6,000
Total.............	$10,000	$10,000

Joint loss apportionment clauses appear in Boiler and Machinery policies and Extended Coverage endorsements. In Boiler and Machinery policies, joint loss apportionment applies if the "other insurance" contains a similar clause; otherwise, an apportionment provision peculiar to the Boiler and Machinery policy (which gives the boiler and machinery insurer a much smaller share of most losses) is provided. Extended coverage provides that apportionment is under pro rata liability when the "other insurance" is either windstorm insurance or fire insurance policies (with or without Extended Coverage); otherwise, joint loss apportionment is used.

Some policies contain a clause providing that their coverage becomes excess insurance in case there is other insurance on the same exposure. The Mercantile Open Stock policy, for example, provides that "if there is any other valid and collectible insurance which would apply in the absence of this policy, the insurance under this policy shall apply only as excess insurance over such other insurance." A policy may make its coverage contributing with other insurance on some part of the exposure and excess on the other part. For example, under the Schedule Automobile Liability policy, the insurance is contributory with other insurance for the owned car hazard and excess for the hired and the non-owned automobile hazards. When two or more policies each provides that it shall be excess over all other insurance, all are treated as co-insurers and share any applicable loss among themselves. (If no basis for such sharing is provided in the policies themselves—the usual case—then either the insurers must agree on a basis of allocation or the insured can get a court to pick a basis of allocation for them.)

In ocean marine insurance, the insurance purchased first is primary cover, and regular insurance bought subsequently is void up to the amount of the prior policy. All insurance having the same attaching date is deemed simultaneous and each insurer will be liable for a ratable contribution to the loss or damage in proportion to the amount for which each company would otherwise have been liable without the other insurance. The following example illustrates how this unique type of other-insurance clause works.

Assume that Heriberto Purcell purchases $10,000 of cargo insurance to attach on November 1. Jorge Lora, his agent, also purchases $12,000 of insurance for the same cargo, to be effective November 2. On November 20, the cargo is completely destroyed by a covered peril. The insurer on the policy Purcell purchased will pay $10,000, and the insurer on the policy Lora purchased, will pay $2,000. If Lora had purchased $10,000 of insurance or less, that insurance would be completely void. As it is, he has purchased $2,000 of valid insurance and is entitled to a refund of the premium for the $10,000 of void insurance. Suppose Purcell's purchase and Lora's purchase were simultaneous (i.e., the policies had the same attachment date), then the Purcell policy would be liable for $10/22$ of the loss and the Lora policy would be liable for $12/22$. Since the maximum liability of the two insurers combined would be $12,000, the Purcell insurer would have a maximum liability of $5,455, whereas the Lora insurer would have a maximum liability of $6,545. The Purcell insurer would be required to refund the premium on the $4,545 of void insurance, and the Lora insurer would have to refund the premium on the $5,455 of void insurance. Refunds of premiums for excess insurance are not usually found in other lines of insurance, however.

In some policies, other insurance is not permitted. For example, the Retailers' Package policy provides that "other insurance covering the property insured is not permitted, except against losses not insured against under this policy or unless this policy is otherwise endorsed." The policy becomes excess when other insurance is permitted by endorsement.

In life insurance policies and many health insurance policies, other insurance does not affect the liability of any insurer. These contracts are not considered to be contracts of indemnity. Overinsurance does not create as serious a problem in life insurance as it does in health insurance because the amount of insurance payable rarely induces loss. In health insurance, however, the lack of other-insurance clauses has created a moral hazard. In group health insurance, the risk manager might well consider inclusion of provisions to avoid overinsurance, especially in medical expense covers. With the large number of working wives, it is possible, as mentioned, for the employee and his family to be overinsured if they are covered under both his and his wife's group benefits.

The Amount of Insurance. The amount of insurance available under the policy to cover each loss is expressed in various ways. Some policies are written without face amounts. The insurer simply promises to indemnify the insured for the actual cash value of his loss. These forms may contain sublimits covering certain use or expense losses in connection with the property loss. For example, the basic Comprehensive Automobile Physical Damage cover is written without an over-all dollar limit; the insurer assumes liability for damage to the car up to its actual cash value. In case of theft of the automobile, the insurer will pay, in addition, the actual expenses incurred in the rental of a substitute automobile, including taxicabs, after the elapse of 72 hours following the reporting of the loss to the insurer and the police and continuing until the automobile is paid for or its whereabouts becomes known. This loss-of-use cover, however, is subject to a limit of $5 per day and an over-all maximum of $150.[16]

The Comprehensive Glass policy also is written without an over-all policy limit. The liability of the insurer is limited to the actual cash value of the property at the time of the loss, or what it would then cost to repair or replace the damaged property with other of the nearest obtainable kind and quality. A $75 limit with respect to loss resulting from any one occurrence at any location, however, is applied to each of the following: (1) the cost of repairing or replacing frames immediately encasing and contiguous to such glass when necessary because of such damage, (2) the cost of installing temporary plates in or boarding up openings containing such glass when necessary because of unavoidable delay in repairing or replacing such damaged glass, and (3) removing or replacing any obstructions, other than window displays, when necessary in replacing such damaged glass, lettering, or ornamentation.

Normally, however, policies are written with over-all face amounts. For example, on the Retailers' Package policy, separate limits of liability are written for each of the five covers in the basic package: personal property, improvements and betterments, business interruption, store-owners' liability, and store-owners' medical payments.

Sometimes a policy will be written blanket, that is, it will cover a particular class of property in several locations or different classes of property at the same location. A blanket policy, unlike divided cover, is written with

---

[16] Private passenger cars owned by sole proprietors and husband and wife partnerships may be covered under the broader *Family Automobile* policy. This form covers loss-of-use after 48 hours, and the maximum per day is $10 with an over-all maximum of $300. Included under the cover are all transportation expenses, not merely substitute automobiles or taxis. And the expense reimbursement continues until the automobile is returned to use or the company pays the loss.

only one over-all limit. When a blanket policy is used, a *pro rata distribution clause* may be required. An example of this clause is the following: "This policy shall attach in each building or location in the proportion that the value in each bears to the value in all." Assume that a $100,000 policy is written blanket to cover three locations (or three classes of property). The total value involved is $150,000 distributed as follows: A, $30,000; B, $75,000; and C, $45,000. The pro rata distribution clause will distribute the $100,000 of insurance as follows:

Item or Location	Value	Proportion of Total Value	Insurance Applicable
A	$ 30,000	30/150	$20,000
B	75,000	75/150	50,000
C	45,000	45/150	30,000

If the value of (or at) B should increase to $100,000 while the values of (or at) A and C are reduced to 25,000 and 40,000, the insurance would be redistributed as follows:

Item or Location	Value	Proportion of Total Value	Insurance Applicable
A	$ 25,000	25/165	$15,151.50
B	100,000	100/165	60,606.10
C	40,000	40/165	24,242.40

Thus, if an insured has fairly stable total values (such as total investment in raw materials, goods in process, and inventory), but the locations containing these values change (from raw materials warehouse to factory to various distribution centers, for example), a single policy can be written so that the distribution of its coverage changes automatically as the location of the values insured changes.

The Boiler and Machinery policy covers physical damage, expediting and temporary repairs, property damage liability, and bodily injury liability all under one policy limit applicable to each accident. Indemnity for expediting and temporary repairs is available, however, only if any insurance is left over after payment of physical damage losses. Payment of property damage liability claims has third priority, whereas payment of bodily injury liability claims is residual. This order of priority gives preference to losses not covered under other policies. Property damage and bodily injury liability claims are covered under general liability policies.

Many kinds of sublimits exist. For example, the Retailers' Package policy places a special limit of $1,000 on coverage for personal effects not usual or incidental to the insured's business. A separate limit of $1,000 is also set for expenses necessarily incurred by the insured for the reproduction of valuable papers and records pertaining to the insured property. The

Boiler and Machinery insurance policy limits payment on expediting expenses to $1,000 or an amount equal to the loss paid for damage to property of the insured, whichever is the lesser amount. The Mercantile Open Stock Burglary policy has the following sublimits: $100 for loss of the contents of any showcase or show window not opening directly into the interior of the premises and $50 for any one article of jewelry. A Major Medical policy may place a limit on the daily hospital room-and-board rate or other services. The Building and Contents form used with the Standard Fire policy places a limit of 1 per cent of the amount of the insurance on the building for coverage of personal property pertaining to the sole use or service of the building. Business Interruption forms limit the coverage to a period of two consecutive weeks when, as a result of a peril insured against, access to the premises described is prohibited by order of civil authority. These sublimits do not grant insurance in addition to the face amount of the policy; they are subject to the over-all face amount of the policy.

Some policies include sublimits that do add to the amount of the insurance, or they provide for extra benefits beyond the face of the policy. For example, the disability income benefits written with life insurance policies are not charged against the face amount of the policy, although this has not always been the case. Earlier disability income clauses provided for a reduction in the face amount of the policy with each periodic disability income payment, and clauses of this type are still found among some group life insurance policies.

Liability insurance policies usually contain two limits for bodily injury and one for property damage, although some forms are written with a single limit covering both bodily injury and property damage. An automobile liability policy might show, for example, $100,000 for each person and $300,000 for each accident as bodily injury liability limits. This means that no more than $100,000 will be paid to any injured person or more than $300,000 for all persons injured in one accident. The policy might show $100,000 for each accident as the property damage liability limit. The Storekeepers' Liability policy will show only one limit, for example, $100,000. This limit is a "per accident" limit and applies to both bodily injury and property damage claims. A third limit called an "aggregate limit" is found in some liability covers (product liability, for example), which sets the insurer's *maximum total liability for all claims incurred in a policy year.*

The costs of defense, premiums on appeal and other court bonds, and expenses for immediate and imperative medical and surgical relief to others at the time of an accident are paid in addition to the applicable policy limits in most liability insurance. Automobile liability policies cover premiums on bail bonds required of insureds in the event of accidents but restrict the amount to $100 per bond.

Medical payments cover written with automobile liability insurance has just one limit, a limit per person as a result of any one accident. Medical payments cover written with the general liability policies includes a limit not only per person but also per accident.[17]

An important consideration in analyzing policy limits is whether the amount of insurance is restored after a loss. Physical damage insurance forms usually contain a loss clause stating that any loss under the policy shall not reduce the amount of the insurance. Crime forms usually restore the insurance after the loss. The Mercantile Open Stock Burglary policy, for example, states that the occurrence of a loss reduces the applicable limit of insurance until the premises are restored to at least the same condition of safety as prior to the loss. If the insured maintains a watchman, then the reduction shall not apply to loss occurring subsequent to the receipt of notice of loss. The Robbery and Safe Burglary policy provides that upon the payment of any loss the amount of insurance will be reduced but that the amount of such reduction shall be restored automatically with respect to loss occurring thereafter.[18]

Some major medical insurance plans have aggregate lifetime limits, but the insured usually is allowed to reinstate the aggregate limit after he has drawn a given amount of benefit, provided, of course, that he is insurable at that time. The amount of insurance under the Extra Expense form in fire insurance is reduced by payment of a loss without automatic reinstatement.

Total Value of All Property Insured. In order to discourage underinsurance and to help achieve equity in rates, insurers use coinsurance provisions in some insurance contracts.[19] A coinsurance clause requires the insured to have insurance at the time of the loss for an amount no less than a stated percentage of the value of the property covered. If the insured fails to meet the coinsurance requirement, then, and only then, must he bear a portion of the loss (coinsure). When there is a coinsurance deficiency, the insurer's liability is then for only a portion of any loss. The insurer shares the loss in proportion as the amount of insurance purchased comes up to the amount of insurance necessary to meet the "coinsurance

---

[17] Personal liability forms, as with the automobile forms, have only the per person limit.

[18] The insured is required to pay an additional premium for the amount of insurance restored unless he has purchased an endorsement waiving this premium.

[19] Since the chance of loss by fire of the first 50 per cent of the value of property is far greater than the chance of loss of the last 50 per cent, the cost of insurance for a total loss should be considerably less than twice the cost of insurance for only a 50 per cent loss. A level rate for each $100 of insurance, therefore, would produce an inequitable premium unless a discount in this rate were given to the insured for accepting an agreement either to purchase a minimum percentage of insurance to value or to become a coinsurer of his own loss. Compare the discussion in chap. 17 on the question of equity in premiums.

requirement." Thus, if $100,000 of insurance is written on a $200,000 building and an 80 per cent coinsurance clause is used, the insured has come up to $^{100}\!/_{160}$ of requirement: He is carrying $100,000; he has agreed to carry $160,000 (80 per cent of $200,000). On an $80,000 loss, the insurer owes as follows:

Value of building at time of loss $200,000
   × coinsurance percentage 80%

   = amount of insurance required $160,000

Amount of insurance purchased $100,000
   ÷ amount of insurance required 160,000

   = 5/8, the insurer's share of loss

5/8 × $80,000 loss = $50,000 (claim)

If the insured had purchased $160,000 (or more) of insurance as required, the insurer would have been liable for the full $80,000 loss, as would be seen by substituting $160,000 for $100,000 in the equation given above.

Variations in coinsurance requirements are found among policies, with some few requiring 100 per cent coinsurance. Although no coinsurance clause is written into ocean marine policies, 100 per cent coinsurance is assumed by custom; thus underinsurance always results in the insured's bearing part of his loss.

In Mercantile Open Stock Burglary insurance there are two coinsurance limits: a coinsurance percentage and a coinsurance amount. The percentage varies with the location of the insured's business, whereas the amount depends on his type of business. For example, the percentage figure is 40 per cent in most of Illinois but 60 per cent in Chicago. For a pawnbroker, the amount limit is $20,000, but for dealers in organs and pianos the amount is only $1,000. (The greater the susceptibility of the merchandise to burglary, the higher the coinsurance amount.) The policy provides that, as between the percentage and the amount limits, the one that produces the lower dollar amount is the one that applies. Thus a Chicago pawnbroker with an inventory of $100,000 would need to have $20,000 of burglary insurance to satisfy the coinsurance requirement, whereas one with an inventory of $30,000 would need burglary insurance of $18,000 to meet the requirement.

The term "coinsurance" is used in health insurance and in credit insurance, but in these lines the word is used in a purer sense—the insured "coinsures" with the insurer on all losses as a matter of planned underwriting policy, not merely as a penalty for failure to live up to part of his agreement. In major medical expense insurance, the typical arrangement is for a deductible to be applied to the loss first, then for the insured and the insurer to share the loss in excess of the deductible on some basis such as 20 per cent for the insured and 80 per cent for the insurer (up to the insurer's maximum payment, of course). The arrangement in credit insurance is similar but not identical. In credit insurance, the total loss up to the amount of insurance available per account is first shared (with the insured typically paying 10 per cent of this amount); *then* the general deductible in the policy (called the "primary amount") is subtracted *from the insurer's share of the loss only*. Clearly, the coinsurance requirements in these policies are simply additional deductibles against claims and are not the kind of underwriting or rating device that other coinsurance provisions are.

Variation in the Amounts of Insurance on Different Perils. An apportionment clause is used with the Extended Coverage endorsement written with fire insurance. Under this clause, the insurer's liability for an extended coverage loss is restricted to the proportion of the loss that the amount of insurance written with Extended Coverage bears to the whole amount of fire insurance covering the property. Thus, if an insured purchases Extended Coverage in connection with one $50,000 fire policy but not with another $50,000 fire policy covering the same property, then only one half of any loss caused by an Extended Coverage peril will be paid (up to a maximum payment of $50,000, of course). The rate charged for Extended Coverage protection is computed on the assumption that the insured will purchase as much Extended Coverage as fire insurance.

The Use of Deductibles. Insurers may eliminate liability for small losses by including deductible clauses in their policies. Deductibles are optional in some covers and mandatory in others. Deductible clauses are of several types. The *straight deductible*, under which the insurer excludes coverage for the first few dollars of loss, is the most common. An example is found in the automobile collision policy that offers coverage "only for the amount of each such loss in excess of the deductible amount stated in the declarations. . . ."

The straight deductible in some policies may apply to some perils but not to others, or to some losses but not to others. For example, the special Personal Property endorsement written to extend the basic Industrial Property coverage to an "all risk" basis requires the use of a $100 deductible. This deductible, however, does not apply to fire or Extended Coverage perils (except it does apply to damage by windstorm and hail to property outside the building), vandalism, malicious mischief, sprinkler leakage, burglary or robbery, or some transportation exposures. A Major Medical policy may not apply the deductible to hospital room-and-board charges or to hospital extras.

Ocean marine insurance policies often contain what is known as a *franchise clause*. A franchise clause is essentially a deductible clause. One form states that the insurance is "free of particular average amounting to less than 3 per cent of the value." The term "average" in marine talk means "partial loss," and the word "particular" is used to distinguish this loss from *general* average.[20] Therefore, under this franchise clause, if the loss is less than 3 per cent of the value of the property, the insurer will not be liable for any of it. But if the loss is in excess of 3 per cent, the insurer is liable for all of it (subject, of course, to other applicable limitations in the policy).

A *disappearing deductible* is one in which the deductible reduces to zero as the loss increases. Disappearing deductibles combine the features of straight deductibles and a franchise clause. The Motel Package policy, for example, has a diminishing deductible. For all losses $50 and under, a straight $50 deductible is used. For losses between $51 and $499, the insurer is liable for 110 per cent of the amount of loss in excess of $50. For losses over $500, the deductible disappears entirely and the insurer is liable for the full loss, subject to the other limitations on liability. This deductible applies only to the physical damage covers and is usually mandatory for windstorm and hail damage to building, structures, and personal property situated in the open. A deductible clause applying to all perils except fire and lightning is optional.

Waiting periods are a type of deductible found in disability income coverage written under life or health insurance policies. Permanent and total disability income benefits under a disability income rider attached to a life insurance contract usually require a waiting period of six months, that is, income payments do not commence until after the disability has lasted six months. Health insurance policies may require a waiting period of 7, 14, 30, 60, or 90 days before disability income payments begin. A policy may require a waiting period if the disability is caused by sickness but pay benefits immediately if the disability is caused by accident. It is possible to find policies that use the franchise principle for waiting periods, that is, if the insured is disabled for a period in excess of a given period, he becomes entitled to collect the benefits for the waiting period retroactively.

OTHER IMPORTANT POLICY PROVISIONS

Insurance policies generally have four parts: declarations, insuring agreements, exclusions, and conditions. To determine the perils, property, persons, losses, hazards, places, period, and amounts covered, reference will have to be made to all four parts. Aside from the details of defining coverage insurance policies, particularly in their conditions, contain a number of other provisions of importance to the risk manager. Most of these deal with loss adjustment.

---

[20] The term "general average" has been explained in chap. 4. Under particular average, the loss or damage is to a particular portion of the cargo or vessel, not an assessment against the interest to cover general average charges.

Loss Adjustment Provisions

Since the right to collect a claim under an insurance policy becomes one of the insured's most important assets at the time of a covered loss, the conditions of claim collection as set forth in the policy are of major concern. A number of these conditions are written into the policy and the risk manager should familiarize himself with them.

Notice of Loss. Insurance policies usually say when, to whom, and sometimes how notice is to be given of knowledge of a loss or of an occurrence that may give rise to a claim. The Standard Fire insurance policy requires that the insured give *immediate written* notice to the insurer. Most other policies require that the insured give notice "as soon as practicable" to the company or to one of its authorized agents. Courts read the requirement of "immediate" notice as meaning "as soon as practicable." Some policies place time limits for the giving of notice: hail insurance, 48 hours; windstorm insurance, 10 days; and health insurance, 20 days, for example.

Most policies do not require written notice. Some crime policies, however, require telegraphic notice, and the hail policy requires that notice be given by registered mail to the hail department of the company. In addition to notice to the insurer, crime policies require that notice be given to the police.

Liability insurance policies require the insured to given written notice to the insurer or to any of its authorized agents as soon as practicable after an accident or occurrence. In addition, if a claim is made or a suit is brought against the insured, he must immediately forward to the insurer every demand, notice, summons, or other process that he receives.

When it is impossible for the insured to comply with the policy requirements, the company (or the courts, if necessary) will waive them. When it is possible to comply, the insured, to be on the safe side, should do so in order to avoid possible friction with his insurer or the cost of court action and, most of all, to protect the validity of the insurance that he purchased. A number of cases are on record in which the insured lost his protection by failing to comply with the notice provision. One interesting case involves a declaratory judgment action on a Garage Liability policy to determine whether the insurer is obligated to defend and to pay judgment rendered in a suit against the insured when notice of accident was delayed nearly two years.

An automobile dealer, when asked to furnish automobiles for an American Legion parade, refused to provide company cars but offered the use of his own car. Several of his salesmen also agreed to drive their own cars, which they used as demonstrators. While taking part in the parade held on June 23, 1956, a part-time non-salaried salesman for the automobile agency ran into a pedestrian, breaking his leg. The automobile dealer heard of the accident three days later and was told that a report had been made to the salesman's insurer. The dealer's insurer, however, was not notified of the accident. The salesman's insurer later paid the injured party $14,000 under a covenant not to sue.

On April 30, 1958, the postman brought the automobile dealer a letter from the injured man's attorney threatening suit. The letter was sent on to the dealer's insurance agent. On June 20, 1958, the dealer was sued as the salesman's principal. The insurer disclaimed liability on the grounds of failure to give notice as soon as practicable and initiated action for declaratory judgment. The district court held for the insurer and the insured appealed.

The appeals court affirmed the ruling of the district court.

A review of the authorities indicates that what may be a reasonable time depends upon the circumstances involved in each respective case. Here there was a delay of almost two years in making report of accident. Lochmandy (the insured) made its own decision that it was not liable because Miller (the salesman) was not its agent and because Miller carried his own insurance. Had Miller not carried insurance would Lochmandy have acted in the same way? We do not think so. . . . Lochmandy did not act as a reasonable prudent person under the circumstances. Appellant also contends that the notice was timely because Hartford (the insurer) was in no way prejudiced by the delay . . . the better rule and most recent cases hold that where "delay of notice was unreasonable in itself" a presumption of prejudice arises, and where that presumption is not rebutted, prejudice will be deemed to exist. Here that presumption was not rebutted.[21]

It should be pointed out that reputable insurers seldom try to avoid a policy on a technicality unless the infraction is flagrant or the company is suspicious of the circumstances surrounding the loss.

Proof of Loss. The insurance policy frequently specifies when and how "proof of loss" must be filed. Some policies have more elaborate requirements than others. For example, the Standard Fire policy has elaborate proof-of-loss requirements. Proof of loss must be filed within 60 days after the loss, and must be signed and sworn to by the insured, stating the knowledge and belief of the insured as to each of the following: (1) the time and origin of the loss; (2) the interest of the insured and of all others in the property; (3) the actual cash value of each item and the amount of the loss; (4) all encumbrances on the property; (5) all other contracts of insurance; (6) any changes in the title, use, occupation, location, possession, or exposures of said property since the policy was issued; (7) by whom and for what purposes the building was occupied at the time of loss; and (8) whether the building was on leased grounds. The reasons for requiring all this information should be obvious after reviewing the limitations on coverage in a fire policy.

Most policies have far less elaborate proof-of-loss provisions. The Automobile Physical Damage policy, for example, requires that the insured

[21] *Hartford Accident and Indemnity Co.* v. *Lochmandy Buick Sales*, 302 F. 2d 565 (1962).

"file with the company, within 91 days after loss, his sworn proof of loss in such form and including such information as the company may reasonably require." Even simpler is the provision in the Mercantile Open Stock Policy that requires the insured to "file detailed proof of loss, duly sworn to, with the company within sixty days after the discovery of loss."

The insurer generally will provide the insured with proof-of-loss forms, and the adjuster frequently will help the insured complete these forms. To avoid costly litigation, the insured should be careful to state the facts correctly. However, if he should make a mistake in his facts the courts will protect him unless the insurer can prove not only that the facts were material but also that they were fraudulently misstated. In one case, the insured put in a claim for over $78,000 on a list of 532 items. It developed that 78 of the items were rifles more than fifty years old, but the insured had claimed for them at the wholesale price of new rifles, for a total of nearly $5,000 for the 78. Representatives of the manufacturers, testifying as expert witnesses for the insurers, valued the 78 at no more than $800, total, saying they were so badly worn or damaged that they had little value even as collectors' items. The appeals court held that the statements made by the insured with respect to these guns in his sworn proof of loss were so far from the truth as to constitute intentional false swearing as a matter of law (that is, the opinion of a jury or trial judge as to the *fraudulent intent* of the party making the statement is immaterial). Therefore, because of false swearing with respect to this part of the covered property, the insured had violated his policy conditions and could not collect for his loss on *any* of the property insured under the same policies.[22]

A misstatement of material facts in the insurer's favor will be set aside in the light of new evidence.

Loss Protection.   Insurance policies covering property often impose an obligation on the insured to help hold the loss to a minimum. The Standard Fire policy, for example, requires the insured to protect the property from further damage. If the insured fails to comply with this provision, the insurer is relieved of liability for the additional loss caused by this negligence. Here again, the adjuster often helps the insured fulfill his obligation to prevent further loss. Reasonable expenses incurred in saving property from loss threatened by a peril insured against are covered by the policy, subject to its limits.

Marine insurance policies contain the sue-and-labor clause mentioned earlier. This clause differs from the "protect-the-property" clauses in other physical damage covers in that the insured is reimbursed for his expenditures in protecting and saving the property (at and after a loss) even if such reimbursement means that he is paid more than the value of the property or the face amount of the policy.

---

[22] *Tenore et al.* v. *American and Foreign Insurance Company et al.*, 256 F. 2d 791.

Other loss protection clauses are found in various forms. For example, the insured must make a reasonable effort to reduce loss under the Accounts Receivable policy by trying to collect the amounts due him; the insurer will pay the extra costs involved in making such collections. The Parcel Post policy requires that the insured file a tracer with the post office if a package does not arrive at its destination. The Robbery and Safe Burglary policy requires the insured to take all reasonable means to prevent the negotiation, sale, or retirement of all stolen securities. The risk manager needs to check each of his policies to find out whether he has any specific duties to perform relating to loss protection.

Assistance in Third Party Dealings. Liability insurance policies usually include provisions requiring the insured to cooperate with the insurer in dealing with third parties. The various liability forms state that

the insured shall cooperate with the insurer and, upon the insurer's request, shall attend hearings and trials and shall assist in effecting settlement, securing and giving evidence, obtaining the attendance of witnesses, and in the conduct of suits. The insured shall not, except at his own cost, voluntarily make any payment, assume any obligation or incur any expense other than for such immediate medical and surgical relief to others as shall be imperative at the time of accident.

Other Loss Adjustment Provisions. Various other loss adjustment provisions have been mentioned earlier (notably in chap. 13); they should always be noted, of course. Some policies may fix a maximum time limit for paying claims. As a rule, however, reliable insurers pay their claims promptly. Maximum or minimum (sometimes both) time limits may be placed in the policy for bringing suit under the policy. Options may be found in the policy giving the insurer the right to repair or replace the damaged property. Some policies give the insured the right to select optional settlements, particularly in life and health insurance.

Provisions may be found in some policies giving the insurer the right to deal directly with third parties (Bailees' Customers' policies, for example). In others, the insurer may be prohibited from dealing with third parties (Accounts Receivable policies, for example, and professional liability policies for members of the learned professions). "Evidence" clauses are found in various policies requiring the insured to submit to examination of books and records (fire insurance, for example) or to examination of his person (health insurance, for example). The honest insured, however, need not worry about these clauses.

Subrogation Clauses

The right of the insurer to subrogation of the insured's claims against anyone who is responsible for the loss arises from the principle of indemnity. To protect the value of this right, the insurer will include a subrogation clause in his policy. A typical subrogation clause states: "In the event of any payment under this policy, the insurer shall be subrogated to all the insured's rights of recovery thereof against any person or organization and the insured shall execute and deliver instruments and papers and do whatever else is necessary to secure such rights. The insured shall do nothing after loss to prejudice such rights." Some policies have an additional clause that reads "No loss shall be paid hereunder if the insured has collected the same from others." If the insurance is for less than the amount of the loss (inadequate policy limits or an applicable deductible amount) the insurer usually is entitled to participate in any recovery from third parties only after the insured has been fully indemnified. (See discussion below under *"Recovery Clauses."*)

Benefit of Bailee or Carrier. Inland Marine forms usually include the following provision: "This insurance shall not inure directly or indirectly to the benefit of any carrier, bailee, or other party, by stipulation in the bill of lading. . . ." Insurers use this clause to protect their subrogation rights against bailees or transportation carriers who include in their contracts a provision abrogating liability to customers if they are insured against the loss. When the insured has a loss, the insurance company will proceed against the bailee or transportation company on behalf of the insured. The insurer will lend the shipper the money to offset his loss in the meantime. If the insurer is unsuccessful in collecting the money from the bailee or carrier, the loan is cancelled. If the insurer is successful, the shipper can use the money to pay off the loan received from the insurer.

Subrogation clauses are not found in contracts that are not contracts of indemnity.

Recovery Clauses

Many crime policies have recovery clauses similar to the following in the Robbery and Safe Burglary policy.

In case of recovery, from any source other than insurance or indemnity, on account of any loss covered by this policy, the net amount of such recovery, after deducting the actual cost and expense of making such recovery, shall be applied to reimburse the insured to the extent, if any, that the loss exceeds the total amount of all valid and collectible insurance and indemnity, and the balance, if any, shall be applied to reduce the liability of, or to reimburse, the company. If the loss does not exceed the total amount of all valid and collectible insurance and indemnity, such net recovery shall be applied to reduce the liability of, or to reimburse, the company.

Change Clauses

Most policies include a clause that reads as follows:

Notice to any agent or knowledge possessed by any agent or by any other person shall not effect a waiver or a change in any part of this policy or estop the insurer from asserting any right under the terms of this policy, nor shall the terms of this policy be waived or changed except by endorsement issued to form a part of this policy, signed by a duly authorized officer or representative of the insurer.

As discussed in chapter 13, the legal interpretation of the change clause indicates that it may not accomplish its stated effect.

SUMMARY

A systematic analysis of an insurance policy involves, first, an analysis of the coverage afforded by the policy and, next, a review of the obligations of the insured after a loss. This chapter has set forth a procedure for policy analysis. This procedure can now be applied to one policy by way of a summary illustration. Since the procedure itself, and not the complicated aspects of coverage, is the principal objective of the chapter, a simple policy has been selected for analysis: the *Comprehensive Glass* policy.

An Analysis of the Comprehensive Glass Policy

The Comprehensive Glass policy may be analyzed according to the method developed in this chapter.

What Perils Are Covered? The policy covers breakage and damage by chemicals. Breakage need not be accidental, but damage by chemicals is restricted to chemicals accidentally or maliciously applied. Certain perils are excluded: fire, declared and undeclared war, civil war, insurrection, rebellion, and revolution. Since the policy covers only for breakage and damage by chemicals, scratching and other disfigurements are not covered. The policy also contains the nuclear energy exclusion common to nearly all property insurance policies.

What Property Is Covered? The policy covers only the glass items described in the declarations and the lettering and ornamentation separately described in the declarations. It also covers frames immediately encasing and contiguous to such glass when damaged along with a covered glass loss.

What Losses Are Covered? The policy covers physical damage loss and the expense of installing temporary plates or boarding up openings when necessary because of unavoidable delay in repairing or replacing damaged glass. It also applies to the cost of removing or replacing any obstructions, other than window displays, when necessary in replacing damaged glass, lettering, or ornamentation.

What Hazards Are Covered? The war and nuclear energy exclusions might be viewed as hazard exclusions as well as peril exclusions because they apply to "any act or condition incident to" the excluded perils as well as to the perils themselves.

In addition, the policy declarations provide that the described covered glass "is plain flat glass with all edges set in frames, unless otherwise stated herein." Glass with one or more exposed edges, or clamped instead of framed, presents a greater hazard (greater probability of loss). Also, curved glass and glass under tension or pressure are more hazardous than plain flat glass. Since glass policies insure for actual cash value of the glass, there is also greater hazard (*dollar* loss rates are higher) if the glass is "fancy" (e.g., plate, engraved, etc.) rather than plain. These hazards are not intended to be covered unbeknown to the underwriter, and the stated wording suggests a hazard limitation here. There is every chance, however, that this limitation would be effaced by estoppel against its use, for the insurer's agent could easily have noted most violations by one quick look at the property if he had considered the matter of any importance.

Insurance on damaged glass is sometimes written. Then the hazard of extension of the original damage is excluded.

What Persons Are Covered? The policy covers the named insured and contains an assignment clause that requires the insurer's consent. If the insured dies, or is adjudged bankrupt or insolvent, and written notice is given to the insurer within 60 days after such adjudication, the policy will cover the insured's legal representative.

What Places Are Covered? The policy covers glass while located as described in the declarations.

What Period Is Covered? The policy usually is written for a period of one year only and from 12:01 A.M. standard time at the address of the insured. The rules of some states permit three-year policies. The policy contains a cancellation clause under which the insured has the right of immediate cancellation, whereas the insurer must give not less than ten days' notice of cancellation.

What Amounts Are Covered? The limit of the insurer's liability is the actual cash value of the insured glass, ornamentation, or lettering at the time of the loss but in no event more than the cost to replace the glass with other glass of the nearest obtainable kind and quality. Special limits of $75 for any one occurrence at any one location are applied to each of the three covered extra expense items: the cost of repairing or replacing frames, the cost of installing temporary plates in or boarding up openings, and the cost of removing or replacing obstructions. The policy includes an "other-insurance clause" of the "limit of liability" type, and the application is to valid and collectible insurance. Many specialty insurers write glass policies with aggregate deductibles: the deductible amount applies once to the sum of all the losses in a year.

Loss Adjustment Provisions. Upon knowledge of loss, the insured is required to give notice as soon as practicable to the insurer or any of its authorized agents. Upon the insurer's request, the insured must file proof of loss, under oath if required, on forms provided by the insurer. The insured may take no action against the company unless he has complied fully with all terms of the policy and 30 days have elapsed since proof of loss has been filed with the insurer. The insurer has the option of paying for the loss in money or of replacing the property. (The insurer generally selects the option to replace the property, although this option is not widely used in most other covers.) The salvage belongs to the insurer when he pays for the loss or replaces the property.

Subrogation. The policy incorporates the typical subrogation clause.

Changes. The typical clause with reference to changes is found in the glass policy.

REVIEW AND DISCUSSION QUESTIONS

1. Define each of the following terms as it is used in this chapter: perils, property, types of loss, hazards, persons, places, period, and amount.

2. Why do insurance covers contain limitations on coverage?

3. Distinguish between "specified perils" cover and "all risks" cover. To what extent are the other limitations on coverage subject to analogous dichotomies in form?

4. What appear to be the purpose or purposes behind each of the peril limitations in the Special Extended Coverage endorsement?

5. Show that the Special Extended Coverage endorsement is indeed broader in coverage than fire with regular Extended Coverage endorsement by describing several claims which would be covered by one but not the other.

6. The meaning of the word "fire" in fire insurance is found neither in policies nor in dictionaries. A similar situation exists for some other terms and phrases in insurance. (*a*) How can a risk manager know what these terms and phrases are *before* he has a loss affected by them. (*b*) Applying the method you suggest, find at least two other words or phrases used in insurance which the courts *regularly* interpret in a way neither defined in the policy nor found in a dictionary.

7. When the attorney for a particular insured persuades a court in a particular case that the dictionary definition of a policy term should be ignored, is the job of professional risk management thereby simplified, complicated, or neither one? Explain.

8. What appear to be the reasons for each of the property exclusions in the Standard Store Owner's policy?

9. Why must the risk manager know what property is covered under his policy? (Don't stop with a surface answer.)

10. Many liability policies provide that when the injured individual is an employee of the insured, the claim is not covered by the policy. Under which of the "eight dimensions" of limitation should this particular limitation be classified? Why? (Be careful—consider first the following question: When John Jones sues both Mike Kelly and the ABC Construction Company for bodily injury suffered by Jones, who need to be the "*persons* covered" in the applicable liability policies?)

11. Consider a standard fire policy containing any particular one of the standard forms available for insuring inventory, fixtures, and tenant's interest in improvement and betterments. When a business buys coverage on these classes of property under this particular form, what coverage does it automatically acquire for *loss of earning power* and *loss through unexpected extra expenses?*

12. In some states, the provision about "increase of hazard within the knowledge or control of the insured," found in standard fire policies, is interpreted as a *peril* exclusion rather than a *hazard* exclusion. What difference does *this* make? Explain with an example.

13. What reasons can be adduced for allowing marine cargo policies to be freely assigned before loss while marine hull policies and inland marine floater policies (e.g., contractor's equipment floater, fine arts floater) are not?

14. A "discovery period" provision is written into fidelity bonds and a few other covers. What is the effect of omission of such provision from policies in (*a*) fire insurance, (*b*) burglary insurance, (*c*) health insurance? What is the effect of a change in insurers on continuity of coverage under these three kinds of policies?

15. What is "indemnity"? Why is it so fundamental to insurance and risk management? How is it related to "insurable interest"?

16. The text mentions some situations in which policy provisions or state statutes ignore, or even override, the principle of indemnity. Why would insurers deliberately write such policies and legislators deliberately pass such statutes? (If the public policy objective of avoiding insurance-induced losses is violated in such cases, what public policy objective is served by them?)

17. What are the strong points on each side in the debate over whether replacement cost covers can be said to violate the principle of indemnity? What is your conclusion, and why?

18. "The best way to state the limit or amount of insurance under any policy insuring against damage to, or loss of, property is 'actual cash value of the property insured.'" What benefits would be gained from such an arrangement? What problems or undesirable features do you see in it? What is your conclusion?

19. Although pro rata distribution clauses (see discussion under "Blanket Insurance") and coinsurance provisions appear in this chapter because they may or do set a limit on the dollar amount of coverage in a policy, the purpose of these clauses is to preserve rating equity among insureds. Explain how these provisions aid in achieving equity of insurance cost between different insureds.

20. Mike Newman had $27,000 of blanket cover on inventory at two locations. On October 1, the value of covered property at location "A" was $10,000, with $20,000 at "B." The following February 1 the values were, respectively, $10,000 and $25,000. Consider separately each of the following losses:
    a) $5,000 at location "A," October 1.
    b) $10,000 at location "A," October 1.
    c) $5,000 at location "A," February 1.
    d) $10,000 at location "A," February 1.
State the amount Newman should collect from his insurer for each of these losses under each of the following policy provisions separately considered:
    a) Pro rata distribution clause.
    b) 80 per cent coinsurance clause applicable against the total value of property insured.

21. Mark Greene was insured under two policies. Policy A was for $20,000, Policy B for $40,000. His property suffered $10,000 damage covered by both policies. If both policies were fire and extended coverage, how much should each pay? If Policy A was a boiler insurance policy and Policy B was fire

and extended coverage, how much should each pay? Suppose the loss had been $30,000? $50,000?

22. Some risk managers believe that the use of a deductible in automobile property liability insurance is just as logical as the use of a deductible in automobile collision insurance. Others feel that deductibles in liability covers are not as desirable as in covers on owned property. What reasons can you see for this second point of view? What is your own opinion, and why?

23. Occasionally, underinsurance under a coinsurance clause represents a deliberate plan to introduce a "deductible" into the coverage. Majority opinion considers this an undesirable practice, however. Supposing that, in general, deductibles are desirable in insurance, what arguments may still be advanced against this use of the coinsurance clause penalty to create a deductible?

24. What is the similarity between the coinsurance feature in major medical expense insurance and the deliberate underinsurance procedure described in the previous question? In view of this, do you consider the form of coinsurance used in major medical insurance desirable, useful or necessary? Explain.

25. Discuss the relative merits of (*a*) straight deductible, (*b*) franchise type of deductible, (*c*) "disappearing deductible."

26. Requirement that notice of loss be written is undoubtedly the most frequently waived provision in insurance. Why? How can the insured tell when this requirement has been waived? Of what significance is all of this to the professional risk manager?

27. Consider the duties of an insured at and after a loss under an automobile physical damage insurance policy. Are the provisions here more like those in a fire insurance policy or those in a policy of marine insurance? Why?

28. Compare the duties and responsibilities at and after a loss of an insured under liability insurance with those of insureds under physical damage insurance. How many differences are there? How may these differences be explained?

29. In what ways do the various loss and claim provisions in policies help maintain the principle of indemnity? Be specific.

30. Using the analysis of the Comprehensive Glass Policy as a model, analyze some other policy or cover.

Chapter 16

THE INSURANCE MARKET:
SERVICES AVAILABLE

A market consists of buyers and sellers. In most markets in America, buyers can successfully wait for the sellers to make themselves known. Personal selling, advertising, and other aggressive marketing activities are typical of operations in the American economy, so a buyer needs only to select among those sellers who make themselves known to him. Among the familiar stereotypes is the omnipresent insurance salesman, always knocking on doors, always asking, even insisting, that people buy the services he offers. Although this stereotype is more commonly applied to life insurance sellers, some of it is expected to apply to purveyors of other types of insurance protection. As is the usual case with stereotypes, some of what this picture suggests is true. But, as is even more often true, most of the stereotype picture is false.

Sellers useful to the insurance buyer do not always knock unbidden on his door; some of them must be sought out. And, of course, whether the sellers call on him or he calls on them, the buyer needs information that will help him select intelligently among all the various sources of supply available to him. Much of this needed information may be had from the sellers themselves, but they do not always volunteer it; the right questions must be asked of them. Some few important pieces of information, however, must be sought out from other sources. These last two chapters in Part V survey the facts that are pertinent to the insurance buyer in finding and selecting from among possible suppliers of insurance services, and they also touch on a few myths that are sometimes taken for facts about the insurance market. The present chapter deals with insurers and their services. The next chapter deals with the costs of these services.

TYPES OF COMMERCIAL INSURERS

Selection of sources of supply for insurance services involves the making of choices at two points in the line of supply: choice of the immediate sales representative with whom one does business, that is, the "retailer" of the service; and choice of the insurance company or other organization that makes and stands behind the promises that are the heart of the insurance policy, that is, the "manufacturer" of the service.[1] Sometimes selection of one is selection of both. When an insurance company is represented in the market only by salaried or semi-salaried employees, selection of the company as insurer generally means selection of the particular sales representative who is assigned to the contact; conversely, selection of one of the sales representatives of such a company automatically means selection of the particular insuring organization (or set of jointly operated organizations) that he represents. But many times the two selections (of sales representatives and of insurance company) are not always tied together; given one, some range of choice remains available for the other.

Explanation of the nature and significance of the choices available is easier if the various types of insuring organizations are considered first. These organizations may be classified in several ways, but several of the best known and most used classifications are not particularly useful to the insurance buyer. Allegations of the importance of these non-useful ways are among the myths of the insurance market that need to be cleared up and put out of the way so that they do not interfere with judgment of more important material.

Statutory Classifications of Insurers

Over the whole range of law, statutory classifications of subject matter are generally intended to simplify or clarify application of the law, to provide equity in the impact of the law on different cases, or, in reverse, to provide special benefits (not equity) for selected groups that the legislators consider to be uniquely worthy of benevolent attention. Classifications for these purposes are not necessarily useful for other purposes, and many of the statutory classifications for these purposes are not particularly useful for the purposes of insurance buyers. However, some of these classifications do have significance for insurance buyers, and those which do not are talked about and sometimes have had spurious significance attached to them. Therefore, the professional risk manager should know and understand these statutory classifications.

Forms of Organization. A major type of statutory classification of insurers is by legal form of organization. In business in general, the principal forms are sole proprietorship, general partnership, and general corporation,

---

[1] The analogies "retailer" and "manufacturer" are true only in a restricted sense. In the insurance business the sales representative is often called a "producer," which indeed he is. The insurance "product" comes into being when and only when a sale is consumated; the sale itself produces the contract, which might be considered the "product" of the insurance company. However, if the performance called for under the contract, that is, payment of claims, is considered the insurance "product," then the insurance company stands rather clearly in the role of "manufacturer."

supplemented by a variety of limited partnerships, joint ventures, and trusts. In addition, there are various "not for profit" corporations and associations, some of which carry on commercial transactions or otherwise deal in services for the public (e.g., consumers' and producers' cooperatives, hospitals, schools, community improvement groups, and a wide variety of others). Most of these forms have counterparts in insurance, and these counterparts are generally like the forms used in other business.

Forms of insuring organizations may be divided first into two major groups: *proprietary* and *cooperative*. Proprietary insurance organizations are owned by persons who have invested in the operations avowedly for purposes of profit. Insurance cooperatives are consumers' cooperatives in form and technically are "not for profit" organizations. A few special forms of organization in insurance do not fit neatly into these two main classes. The best-known exceptions are the dozens of organizations operating under the trade names "Blue Cross" and "Blue Shield." Most of these organizations are like producers' cooperatives in form (hospitals and doctors are the "producers"), but a few operate under forms like those of other insurers.

The proprietary and cooperative forms may be cross-classified as *incorporated* and *unincorporated*. Incorporated proprietary forms are called stock companies; incorporated cooperative forms are called mutual companies or simply "mutuals." The unincorporated proprietary forms have borrowed luster by naming themselves after the one famous member of their group; they are referred to as Lloyds-type, or simply Lloyds organizations. Unincorporated cooperatives are interchangeably called interinsurance exchanges, reciprocal exchanges, or reciprocals. Not all the cooperative forms can be readily classified as incorporated or not incorporated. The statutes provide for some very special types of insurance cooperatives, such as fraternal benefit organizations and burial societies, which are difficult to classify either as incorporated or not incorporated; in some ways these organizations have legal identities separate from their membership, and in other ways they do not. However, a professional risk manager is most unlikely to do business with these organizations (although he may occasionally be called upon to advise employees or colleagues with respect to them).

In past years, a great to-do was made about the differences among the various statutory forms of insuring organizations, and echoes of the old debates and imbroglios occasionally are heard today. The fact of the matter is, however, that any legal form of insuring organization can be as sound, efficient, or service-providing as any other. The quality of the individual insurer, not the organizational class to which it belongs, ultimately determines whether the buyer should look to it for his insurance. Statutory forms of organization have this bearing on the matter: In judging quality, some of the peculiar features of each form of organization must be taken into consideration. What these peculiar features are will be discussed later in this chapter, as each major factor that makes for good (or poor) quality in any insurer is considered.

However, the peculiar features of certain forms of insuring organizations will not be discussed because these organizations are unlikely to be used by a professional risk manager in a business situation. Besides fraternal life insurance organizations and burial societies, local farm mutual fire, wind, or hail insurance companies are in this list.[2] Businesses are unlikely to have use for, indeed often will not even be eligible for, the insuring services provided by organizations of these special types.

Lines of Insurance Written. As was discussed at length in chapter 12, insurers are divided according to the types or lines of insurance they write. Under present multiple line conditions, an insurer that writes life insurance or annuities will not be licensed to write other lines except health insurance. An insurer that writes any line of insurance other than life (and annuities) and health will not be licensed to write life insurance (although it may have a license for health insurance). However, not all insurers are licensed to write all the lines that the statutes allow, and, even when licensed to write a line, an insurer may not necessarily do so. In addition, quite a few insurers prefer to be specialists in certain lines, even though they are licensed to, and do on occasion, write other lines. For example, there are several large insurance companies (mostly mutuals) whose primary interest is in writing workmen's compensation insurance and who accept other lines principally as a means of getting workmen's compensation business.

Some lines of insurance are supplied wholly or in large part by companies that specialize in them. These lines are credit insurance, title insurance, animal mortality insurance, aviation insurance, and boiler and machinery (also called power plant) insurance. In credit and title insurance, single line (or monoline) companies write nearly all the coverage. In animal mortality, a monoline company and one multiple line company dominate the native market. In boiler and machinery insurance, two monoline companies write well over half the American business (and provide extensive amounts of reinsurance for the rest).

Two considerations appear most important in weighing whether to use specialty insurers. In general, the specialists offer the most service and capacity for their specialty lines.[3] This advantage is accompanied by the

---

[2] Note that the description here is "*local* farm mutual . . . companies." These are companies organized under special statutory rules, which provide, among other things, that their activities are to be limited to only one or a few townships or counties within their home state. Many organizations that have the words "farm mutual" in their name and others that are primarily farmer organized and operated, are regular mutuals in form and operation and are competitive in some or all of the general insurance market. These organizations are blanketed under the various discussions of the features of mutual insurers in general.

[3] "Capacity" in insurance means, as might be guessed, the amount of insurance that an insurer can and will write, particularly for an individual exposure unit or a set of exposures in a single catastrophe area.

disadvantage of little or no service or capacity in other lines, which immediately raises the issue of accommodations. In insurance, an accommodation is a willingness to write a cover that the underwriter does not want in return for having the opportunity to write a cover that the underwriter does want.

Clearly, many types of accommodation cannot be offered by specialty insurers. However, this disadvantage is markedly tempered by the fact that specialty insurers operate principally in lines of insurance that general writing insurers do not usually like to write. Indeed, this is one of the principal secrets of success in specialty underwriting: the ability to make money in a line that other insurers find generally unprofitable. Thus the specialist is guaranteed a market that competitors are unlikely to be able to share without also becoming specialists. Because the natural limits of the particular market often indicate insufficient support for more than a few specialists, the first entrants into a specialty line may find themselves with a kind of natural monopoly or oligopoly. Of course, as the market widens, this natural defense disappears. Also, after specialists have pioneered in a line, it may turn out that their techniques are adaptable by general insurers. In that case, each competitor's share of the market for this line does not have to be large enough to support his entire insuring organization, and the line passes into the general competitive field. Nearly all lines of insurance began as specialty operations, and most have since passed into the hands of general writing insurers. Undoubtedly this same process will be repeated in the future.

Domicile of an Insurer. As discussed in chapter 13, companies in each state can be classified according to whether they are chartered in that particular state, in some other state of the United States, or by an authority in some other nation. These classifications are called, respectively, domestic, foreign, and alien. The classifications themselves are not of much interest to a risk manager, but the particular place of chartering or, in the case of an alien company, the port of entry into the United States may be of interest.[4] In the immediately following discussion, references to "state of domicile" apply both to state of charter of an American insurer and to state of entry of an alien insurer.

The risk manager will have an interest in the state of domicile of his insurer for several reasons. In the first place, the requirements for chartering and initial licensing vary greatly from one state to another. Even more important, most of the regulation of a company is done by the state in which it is domiciled, and the efficiency of this regulation also varies widely

---

[4] The port of entry of an alien company is the place where it first meets the laws of an American state for entry into American operations. Not all states provide ports of entry. Illinois, for example, requires that an alien insurer newly seeking an Illinois license must first meet the laws of some other state for entry of an alien insurer. As one might expect, New York is the state most favored as a port of entry. California is also popular.

from state to state and—to make the risk manager's life even more difficult —may even vary from time to time in the same state. Some few states are widely known for the thoroughness of their supervision of their home companies;[5] several states are known for their laxity; most lie at varying points between these extremes. Finally, taxes levied on domestic insurers may be lower than those required of foreign and alien insurers, and these tax savings may be passed along to the insured through cost-plus rating formulas.

Admitted and Nonadmitted Insurers. As was noted in chapter 13, an insurer must be licensed in each state in which it "does business." It is said to be "admitted" in a state only for the lines of insurance for which it is licensed. For all other lines it is "nonadmitted" (or "unauthorized"). To be licensed in another state for a given line of insurance, a company must, first, be licensed for the same kind of insurance in its domiciliary state and second, must meet any other requirements imposed on foreign or alien insurers.

Some requirements for admission clearly have the purpose of protecting the citizens of the licensing state from undesirable foreign and alien insurers. Insurers domiciled in a state with weak regulation have been kept out of states with more stringent regulation. Other times, however, inability to get a license in a particular state is due to mere technicalities in the laws. Thus, a Wisconsin company engaged in writing insurance that protected mortgagees against loss from default on mortgage payments was classified and licensed as a title insurance company under Wisconsin statutes; it was unable to obtain a license in states that classified this cover as credit insurance. Some licensing statutes are purposely rigged against out-of-state insurers. Thus, the Robertson Law of Texas requires out-of-state life insurers to invest in the securities and debt instruments of Texas individuals, businesses, and governmental units an amount equal to at least 75 per cent of the reserves behind policies on lives of Texas residents. A large number of life insurers considered this law offensive and withdrew from the state. Although most of these companies have since returned (good investment can be found in Texas), this law is an example of regulation that may keep foreign and alien insurers out without regard to their financial soundness or commercial honesty. Finally and unfortunately, it appears that on some occasions companies have been refused licenses because they would not pay the political blackmail required to get favorable action from the regulatory authorities in charge in the state at that time.

A common recommendation to an insurance buyer is to purchase insurance only from insurers licensed to do business in his home state. Chief among the reasons given for this recommendation are (1) protection given

---

[5] Some companies have two "homes"—place of charter and place of operating headquarters. Generally, the regulatory authorities of both places will be equally interested in the affairs of such insurers.

by home-state licensing laws, (2) greater ease of enforcement of disputed claims, and (3) greater amount of claims and other service that can be provided by an insurer operating in the insured's own territory. Reason number one has been discussed. It remains now to examine the second and third reasons.

In order to enter suit, a person must find a court having jurisdiction over both the subject matter and the defendant. When the subject matter is a claim under an insurance contract, jurisdiction can be established on the basis of where the loss occurred or where the contract was made. But suppose the insured and the site of the loss are in, say, California, and agents, offices, and property of the insurer can be found only in Illinois. How is notice of process to be served? A federal court can be found in whose district property or representatives of the company are located, but pressing suit at long distance generally is cumbersome and expensive.

As stated in chapter 13, most states have adopted an Unauthorized Insurers' Service of Process Act, which provides that service of process on the domestic commissioner of insurance constitutes effective process on an insurer of property or persons within the state. The commissioner normally forwards the notice to the insurer's office, of course, but whether the insurer responds is immaterial under this law.

Of course, once process has been obtained, the suit must still be won. And after a suit is won there is still the problem of enforcing the claim. Under the "full faith and credit" provision of the United States Constitution, a judgment at law obtained in one state is to be enforced in all other states. With the judgment of a domestic court in hand, the insured, through attorneys, may go to a court in any state in which the insurer can be found and get an enforceable order against the insurer. But the process is slow and cumbersome, even more so than the usual procedures at law—which makes it very cumbersome and slow indeed!

What about disputes short of suits at law? When an insured believes that he is not getting fair treatment from his insurer, he may write his insurance commissioner. If the commissioner agrees that action is appropriate, he has many ways of bringing pressure to bear on an admitted insurer.[6] As to a nonadmitted insurer, all he can do is disapprove its status as a "surplus lines" insurer and request its home state commissioner to exert pressure to bring it into line. Since few states make provision for official approval or disapproval of particular insurers for "surplus lines" business,[7] the disappointed insured may get no satisfaction here. Whether the commissioner of an in-

---

[6] For the ways, see Edwin W. Patterson, *The Insurance Commissioner in the United States* (Cambridge, Massachusetts: Harvard University Press, 1927), pp. 347–440, 491–510.

[7] Some provisions dealing with "surplus lines" insurance were described in chap. 13. Other aspects are discussed later in the present chap.

surer's state of domicile will respond to a suggestion that he crack down on one of his domestic insurers will depend upon such variables as the nature of his relationships with the complaining commissioner, his previous experience with the insurer in question, and the general strength of his office as a regulatory agency.

As to services offered by a nonadmitted insurer, the definition of "doing business" is so broad that unlicensed insurers can have essentially no representation of any kind within the insured's state except through licensed "surplus line" brokers. Nonetheless, such a generally unauthorized organization as the Underwriters at Lloyd's, London,[8] maintains representation in all major ports of the United States, as well as the rest of the world, so that immediate service on ocean marine claims may be had around the globe. It is difficult for an insurance commissioner to insist, after a resident of his state has legally procured insurance from a nonadmitted insurer, that this resident (voter and taxpayer) cannot have a representative of that insurer come into the state to expedite collection of a claim covered by a legally contracted policy. Insured, insurer, and enforcement authorities are in an irregular position under these circumstances.

Why a buyer might nevertheless purchase coverage from a nonadmitted insurer was explained in chapter 13. Also explained was the statutory device by which the transaction may be regularized: placement of the contract through a licensed "surplus lines" broker under prescribed conditions. This device appears to be a method for regularizing a set of useful transactions while protecting the tax revenue of the state (the broker and the insured are responsible for payment of the premium tax) and the competitive positions of domestic insurers and others who behave like them.[9] In addition, however, the whole treatment of unauthorized insurers puts up a protective barrier between the general run of insureds and most of those insurers who are unable, as well as those who simply do not choose, to meet the local state's licensing requirements. This barrier reduces the number of insureds who get trapped by outside insurers of questionable ethics or financial stability. However, use of the United States mails allows circumvention of this barrier, and among those who work hardest at such circumvention are, naturally enough, the very insurers who have made the barrier desirable.[10]

For the professional risk manager, the best protection against undesirable

---

[8] London Lloyd's underwriters are licensed in the United States only in Illinois and Kentucky, and some of their insurance on American exposures is contracted directly from London by mail and not subject to American licensing at all.

[9] "Surplus lines" markets are legally usable only when licensed insurers will not provide the coverage, *not* when the same coverage is available in the domestic market but only at a higher price, and also probably not when the domestic coverage is generally the same but differs as to details.

[10] For example, see George H. Kline, *Regulation of Mail Order Health Insurance* (New York: State of New York Insurance Department, 1949).

insurers is found in careful study and selection of the insurers themselves, not in reliance on the licensing authority of any particular state. Factors to consider in such study and selection are discussed later in this chapter.

Market Classifications of Insurers

Insurers may be classified by their behavior in competing for position in the market place. There are several standard ways of trying to reach insurance buyers and each of these ways has important effects on the over-all behavior of the insurers who use it.

Marketing Channels.   Although insurance men are fond of noting how different their problems are from those of other businesses, all insurance marketing problems have their counterparts in various other fields of commerce, and some of these counterparts are distinguishable from insurance problems only in technical detail. Given the same problems, insurance men have evolved the same types of answers as have other businessmen. The principal difference seems to be a somewhat stronger tendency in insurance to cling to older methods of distribution. This affinity may be explained by the lack of change in the nature of the insurance product or its usage over a long period of time. But, given that insurance selling is insurance production, the lack of change in selling methods and the lack of change in the product undoubtedly have been mutually reinforcing inertias.

Methods of Sales Contacts with Buyers.   Insurance marketing features are usually and most usefully classified according to the method by which sales contacts are made with buyers. These methods can be categorized according to some of the usual marketing classifications. Four major methods are used: brokers, independent retailers, direct sales representatives (à la manufacturers' sales representatives), and direct sale. The methods are not mutually exclusive. In particular, brokers may be employed in connection with any of the other three. In general, the independent retailers accept business generated by brokers. However, some important employers of direct sales representatives or direct selling refuse to accept business through brokers.

The relative importance of the methods and their particular places in the insurance market are summarized below.

Independent Retailers.   Independent retailing has been the predominant method of marketing property and liability insurance in the United States from the beginning. This long and successful history, together with the fact that independent retailing distinguished insurance marketing in the United States from the methods used in Europe, caused (and allowed) this form of marketing structure to become known as "the American agency system" (or even, as written by some, "The American Agency System"). Naturally, this appelation has been used by some persons to imply that a different marketing method is somehow "the *un*American agency (or whatever) system." In recent years, however, the predominance of the independent retailer or independent agency system has been reduced so that now it produces little more than a mere majority of the dollar sales by American property and liability insurers (native organizations and American offices of alien organizations). This reduction in importance has not been the same in all segments of the market, however; the independent agents have apparently retained a larger share of sales to businesses, governments, and institutions than to families and individuals.

The actual selling effort through independent agencies may be put forth by the agents themselves, by hired solicitors, or by brokers. The mix of efforts through any particular agency will depend on such factors as its size, the nature of its clientele, the talents and predilections of its owner-managers, and the customs of the local market.

Regular contact between an independent agent and the companies whose services he sells (and whom he represents in a variable number of other ways) is maintained by salaried, traveling representatives of each company-group. These representatives are technically known by various titles with varying meanings, but all of them are commonly called and recognized in the trade by the generic term, "field men." (That is, they spend most of their time "out in the field," specifically the sales field, as distinguished from usually remaining in a home, branch, or other office.) Field men initiate the creation and termination of agency appointments, assist appointed agents in their work (particularly selling), and otherwise forward the interests of their employing companies by communicating with, encouraging, cautioning, and appropriately "wining and dining" the agents. One major function is "field underwriting"—educating agents in the ascertainable differences between profitable and unprofitable underwriting situations and leading or directing them to devote their selling efforts toward the former and not the latter.

Sometimes the independent retailers are serviced through independent wholesalers, called "general agents." A general agency provides the marketing function in a particular territory for one or more insurers. When the general agency is used, the general agent employs and directs the field men who call on the retailing agents.

Direct Sales Representatives. Selling through exclusive direct sales representatives is the fastest-growing method of marketing property and liability insurance. It is, with some variation, the traditional method for marketing life insurance. (Paradoxically, the independent retailing method has recently had some new success in life insurance, even as it was losing considerable ground elsewhere to the direct marketing methods that still account for 90 or more per cent of life insurance sales.)

So far, the greatest successes with direct sales representation in the property and liability insurance market have been at opposite ends of the buyer spectrum: with the multitudinous customers in the mass markets for automobile and household insurance and with the comparatively limited number of businesses and institutions that individually spend many thousands or even millions of dollars on premiums for one or more lines of insurance, particularly workmen's compensation and public liability insurance. (There are interesting similarities here to life insurance markets: on the one hand, the usual market for individual policies; on the other hand, the market for big group insurance and pension-plan contracts.)

Direct Selling. Many have tried but few have succeeded in establishing successful insurance operations on a direct selling basis, that is, without an organization of resident sales agents (independent or otherwise) scattered over a wide territory. With rare exceptions, the successes that have occurred have been in limited markets. The limitation may be geographic, as with farm mutuals of the assessment type or with the perpetual mutuals in fire insurance;[11] it may be with respect to type of insured, as is the case with the factory mutuals, which write only superior industrial exposures; or it may be as to line of insurance, as in ocean marine insurance.

Direct writers are generally of two kinds: mail order and direct transaction. A very few insurers have managed to establish an operable mail order business dealing with the general public. Most direct writers, including direct writing marine insurers (such as the underwriters at Lloyd's, London), have many face-to-face transactions with brokers representing the buyers. The direct writing insurers whose services are desired by professional risk managers will almost always be of this kind. With these insurers, the best approach for most risk managers is through a broker (often a "surplus lines" broker).

Insurance Brokers. Those who say that "insurance is different" from other businesses with respect to marketing problems and practices have one indisputably good basis for their opinion—brokerage operations in insurance are indeed "different." With respect to contract negotiations, insurance brokers are universally understood and adjudged to be representatives of the *buyers*. Yet these same brokers are also generally counted as part of the *sales* force in the insurance market and are (with rare exceptions) paid their commissions by the *sellers*, not the buyers, of insurance! Many buyers are therefore totally unaware of the differences between insurance agents and brokers—and indeed never have any occasion to discover any difference.

Besides the lack of power to bind an insurer to a contract, the important characteristic of a broker is his ability to search the insurance market on behalf of a prospective buyer. But some brokers are in fact no freer than agents; in practice they deal only with a limited list of insurers. (Some brokers are known as "house brokers" because their operations are housed in

---

11 There are six "perpetual mutuals" in the United States. Each limits its writings to dwellings in one or two counties. A single deposit premium provides insurance in perpetuity, the investment earnings paying the claims, operating expenses, and some dividends. Naturally, this premium is of considerable size.

the office of the agency or insurer with whom they place most, if not all, of their business.) Other brokers have wide contacts in the insurance market and place business wherever proposals of insurers seem most attractive. "Attractiveness" is measured, of course, in terms of the broker's business of attracting and satisfying his customers while providing an acceptable profit to himself. The need for a profit puts some limit on his range, of course.

Insurers who refuse to pay brokerage fees will not ordinarily be reached through brokers, but this is not likely to create a problem—insurers that refuse brokerage deals are seldom needed by professional risk managers. More serious are differences among commission rates paid by those insurers which do accept brokerage business; such differences may affect a broker's choices to the detriment of his customers. (The same problem exists with agents, of course; their choices of companies to represent and of companies in which to place particular business can easily be affected by differences in commission dollars.)

Companies and Market Organization. In the past there was some identification in property and liability insurance between forms of company organization and types of marketing organization. Stock companies generally utilized independent agents, while direct sales representatives almost always worked for mutuals or reciprocals, and most direct writers were mutuals. Even in those days, however, some important mutuals used independent agents (although typically at a lower "mark-up" [i.e., commission] than allowed by the stock insurers). Today the identification is even less strong.

In the past decade stock insurers have suffered operating losses from a combination of causes: inflation, inability to get governmental approval for rate increases, and increased competition with respect to prices. The increased competition has come principally from newly growing insurers with direct representation. These insurers have shown marked gains in market shares, primarily at the expense of the independent agency stock companies. The stock companies have tried to cope with these problems by creating new "products" (covers), by reducing overhead expenses, and by changing some of their marketing practices. In the last category, they have tried, with varying success, to bring commissions down (producing similarity with the independent agency mutuals) and to tie their agents more closely to them (somewhat approaching direct representation). Agents' resistance to these moves, coupled with strong competitive pressures from companies using other marketing systems, have led to a shift from the former emphasis on the distinction, "stocks" versus "mutuals," to a new dichotomy, "independent agent" versus "direct representative." And, while most independent agency representation is of stock companies, with some mutuals and an occasional reciprocal thrown in, the insurers on the other side of the division include a miscellany of legal types of organization. Although the older directly represented mutuals are still the most numerous group in the direct representative class, the greatest gain in market share has been experienced by four company-groups, in which two of the parent organizations are mutuals, one is a stock company, and one is a reciprocal—and each of the mutuals has at least one stock company subsidiary! Furthermore, another fast-growing operation that has only recently reached the "big time" is headed by a stock company that combines some direct representation with an unusually successful direct-writing campaign.

COVERS OFFERED BY INSURERS

In appraising insurers, risk managers will need to investigate four features: covers offered, financial soundness, nature and quality of claims and other services, and cost. Consider first the covers offered.

Lines Offered

The subject of lines of insurance and insurers has already been discussed, both in chapter 12 and earlier in the present chapter. Not all insurers offer all lines. Some lines are offered only or principally by specialty insurers. These facts naturally limit choice of insurers for particular forms of coverage. But even when an insurer does deal in a particular line of insurance it may not offer a particular individual or business the cover it needs or desires.

Standard and Special Forms

As has been noted in earlier chapters, particularly chapter 14, many insurance covers are standardized, with identical forms used by many companies. These forms exist because they are economical for insurers, provide the coverage wanted by most insureds, and reduce uncertainties as to what the contracts mean and, hence, how much they should cost. Risk managers should use standard forms whenever they will provide the coverage needed at an acceptable price. And, since there are hundreds, even thousands, of standard forms, a wide variety of risk situations can be adequately accommodated.

Limitations on Standard Forms. No set of forms can be completely adaptable to every possible situation and still remain standardized. The contents of standard forms are controlled by the demand from a reasonably large number of buyers and the willingness of a sufficient number of insurers to participate in the underwriting.

However, the actual effects that the demands of buyers have on forms of cover are subject to such obfuscating factors as the understanding that buyers have of their own needs and the notions that policy draftsmen have of what buyers want.

The necessity of attracting sufficient insurers to participate in the underwriting generally leads to the production of forms that are conservative and cumbersome. A standard form must be acceptable to many underwriters, which means it must be acceptable to the most cautious of the necessary number. This perpetuates conservatism. However, because differing experiences of different underwriters often lead them to be cautious about different things, several points of view about caution must be satisfied. This promotes cumbersomeness in forms.

Overlying the other factors is the need to satisfy insurers' legal counsels. Their different estimations of the expected judicial interpretation of a given form lead to further modification and, usually, complication, if not limitation, of the coverage provided.

In view of all the foregoing, a risk manager who has a good understanding of what his particular insurance needs are may have difficulty in handling them under standard forms. Two types of difficulty are possible. The more common one is deciding exactly how a standard form relates to a particular risk situation. The other type occurs when it is clear that the standard forms have not been designed to deal with the particular risk problem at hand.

Problems in Interpretation. An example of a problem of interpretation was given in chapter 14 when the problem of distinguishing between "direct" and "indirect" losses from a given peril was discussed. Another example can be given to illustrate both the difficulty of interpretation and the problem of no coverage under standard forms.

Most standard forms in liability insurance do not cover for damage to "property in the care, custody or control of the insured," or, alternatively, to property in "charge of the insured." The meaning of this exclusion in particular cases is often in doubt. Thus, an insured garage owner was working on a customer's car, and fire damaged the car. One court (Illinois) held the loss to be covered, whereas another court (California) in a similar case held the exclusion to apply.[12] Interpretation of the meaning of the policy after the loss is inevitable in some instances, but the risk manager wants to avoid the juridical risk as far as possible, particularly with respect to large-loss potentials. Therefore, if he has a possibility of large losses that might or might not be considered to fall under the "care, custody or control" exclusion, he will want a clarification of its application to them. This clarification might be obtained by way of an official interpretation of the application of the exclusion to the kinds of losses in question, such interpretation to be in writing signed by an executive officer of the insuring organization. Insurers are notably reluctant to issue such binding interpretations in advance of losses, however, and the desirability of using an insurer

---

[12] The cases are, respectively, *Welborn* v. *Illinois National Casualty Company*, 347 Ill. App. 65 (106 N.E. 2d 142) and *Guidici* v. *Pacific Auto Insurance Company*, 79 Cal. App. 2d 128 (179 Pac. 2d 337).

may be based in part on its willingness to establish interpretations of covers before, instead of only after, losses have occurred.

Special Forms. Of course, when coverage of some potentially large losses is not provided in standard forms, then special forms will have to be used. One criterion for selection of an insurer will necessarily be its willingness to write the coverage. Thus, for many years it was necessary for some insureds—particularly building and other contractors—to do business with issuers of non-standard forms if they were to obtain liability covers that clearly included protection against suits for damage to property or premises on which they were working.[13] Today, a standard endorsement is available that deals adequately with the problem for some insureds but not for others. Some must still purchase special coverage, usually in the "surplus lines" market.

Underwriting Standards

Any insurer will refuse some applicants and accept others. Furthermore, while some applicants may be rejected by most underwriters, others may be acceptable to all but a minority of insurers. Many insurers announce themselves as dealing with "preferred" or "superior" risks only; a somewhat smaller number do in fact limit their underwriting to such risks. Most companies are uneven in their standards of acceptance, with immediate decision hinging upon current estimates of recent experience, and hence anticipated results, on the kind of business offered. Anticipation of results is generally considered to be affected by the following features of the proposed contract: the line of insurance and the particular form or cover desired within that line; the location of the exposure; the agency or brokerage house through which the offer has come; the general nature of the applicant's business, and various specific features of its management, operations, finances, and economic prospects; the amount and kinds of other insurance the applicant carries or is willing to carry with the same insurer; the financial terms (amount of insurance and the premium and rate to be charged) proposed or obtainable; and the possibility and probable cost of reinsurance protection.[14] Some of these factors are general, pertaining to an entire class of exposures of which the applicant is only one instance; other factors are particular and apply to the applicant individually. Some factors are subject to control or change by the insured; others are not (unless he changes the entire nature of his operations).

---

[13] For a summary of the problems faced and solutions formerly available see the collection of articles by members of the Northern California Chapter of the Society of C.P.C.U., published under the general heading, "The Problems of Care, Custody or Control," *Annals of the Society of Chartered Property and Casualty Underwriters*, Vol. VIII, No. 1 (February, 1956), pp. 15–38.

[14] "Reinsurance" is insurance obtained by an insurer to protect itself against untoward loss under the policies it has issued to the general public. See the discussion later in the present chapter under the heading "Financial Soundness."

Obtaining Accommodation Covers. The general factor most likely to be subject to control by the insured is the influence of the agent or broker. First, he may exercise his freedom of choice by selecting an agent or broker who is able to influence underwriters favorably. The amount of influence that an agent or broker can exert on underwriters is conditioned by (1) the profitability and (2) the total volume of the insurance business he brings (or could or would bring) to these underwriters. Having selected a potentially influential channel to the underwriter, the buyer's second step is to get himself in a position to take advantage of this influence. The best way is to supply a good quality and quantity of other business to the same agent or broker. In short, the most common way to get undesirable exposures insured is by what insurance men call "agency accommodation"—the underwriter accommodates the dollar-producing sales organization, and the sales organization accommodates the dollar-producing insurance buyer as a goodwill gesture to keep the desired dollars (in sales volume and profit) coming.

The amount of pressure that can be put forth to get an accommodation depends upon ability to suggest an effective "or else"; the buyer must be in a position to say, "Take my undesirable exposures or else I will take my good ones elsewhere," and have the statement mean something; there must be somewhere else he can go and be welcomed. Similarly with the agent or broker; he must have a real possibility of shifting to other suppliers *and taking his customers with him.* Such a shift is usually possible for the independent agent or free-lance broker. For one thing, he "owns his expirations," as the trade jargon puts it. This means that when the independent agent or broker brings in business to an insurer, the insurer is prohibited (by contract) from soliciting new or renewal business from those insureds, either then or later. The right to solicit these accounts belongs strictly to the agent or broker (and his heirs or assigns). In addition, most persons who buy insurance through independent agents or brokers identify their source of supply as that agent or broker. They pay little or no attention to the name of the insurer with whom the agent or broker places the business and are seldom even aware of any changes in insurers that may be made from time to time. As a result of this control over the allocation of his premium volume among insurers, the independent agent has leverage (up to a point) in obtaining accommodations from his insurers. Few insureds can exert the same amount of leverage directly against an insurer but may be able to exert it to some degree against a particular agency or brokerage firm.

Salesmen who are direct representatives of insurers typically do not own their expirations; rights to solicit renewals belong to their employers, who are commonly more clearly identified in the transaction than are the insurers used by an independent agent or broker. This means that if a direct representative wishes to change insurers, he can take customers with him only by the sheer force of his personality and highly superior sales ability

—requirements seldom possessed in a degree necessary to get the job done. This leaves the direct representative with little leverage against his company. Accommodation writings, therefore, are not usual among insurers using direct sales representatives, and even more unusual among direct-writing insurers. The principal exceptions to this rule are found among insurers who specialize in writing certain kinds of insurance for large businesses. Thus, the big specialists in workmen's compensation insurance offer other lines of coverage in order to help them get the workmen's compensation lines they desire, and the factory mutuals, which specialize in fire insurance and allied lines for superior industrial property, own a subsidiary company to write the miscellany of ordinary property owned by insureds who also possess the big superior exposures.

Improving Acceptability. Of course, the risk manager should consider improvement of the particular features that make his operations undesired by good underwriters. Sometimes these underwriters will name the particular features to which they object. Other times only vague, general explanations will be offered for a declination: "We are sorry, but this particular risk does not happen to meet our underwriting standards." Then it is up to the risk manager to know or to learn enough about underwriting practices, underwriting principles, and loss prevention to uncover the specific difficulties for himself. He may then work to remove them, or he may decide that the rejection was unjustified and seek to change the minds of the rejecting underwriters or to find underwriters who see his exposures as he does.

Underwriting Standards and Selection of Insurers. What are the risk manager's interests in insurer's underwriting standards? One major interest is in their effect on premiums. Another interest is in their possible effects on insurers' financial soundness. Both these matters are considered later. Given a particular cost of insurance protection and service and a set of financially sound insurers who are willing to undertake the risks, of what further interest are underwriting standards? The only further interest appears to be in the possibility of becoming unacceptable to an insurer in event of a bad run of losses or a visible increase in the hazard offered. *Other things being equal*, it would appear desirable to select underwriters with low standards because a margin for underwriting error or deteriorating hazard would then exist. (But note the cautions against *too* low underwriting standards given in the next section!)

FINANCIAL SOUNDNESS IN INSURERS

For an insurer to be useful to any risk manager, two qualities are essential. It must offer coverage wanted, and it must be financially able to pay claims when they become due. No other qualities are as important as these, and neither one of these is useful without the other.

Forecasts on the financial future of any type of operation are fraught with uncertainties. Fortunately for risk managers, however, these uncertainties are significantly fewer when the forecasts are made for insurers because (1) each insurer is required to file an extensive annual report with the regulatory authorities, a report backed up by periodic full inspection of the insurer's books and operations by the same regulatory authorities, and (2) insurance is a risk-reducing device, and insurers' finances can benefit from this fact. Not that insurers cannot go broke; they have, they do, and they will. One report states that in the period from 1930 to 1962, 384 property and liability insurers failed to meet their obligations; this was 6.9 per cent of "insurance companies active in the U.S. at some time during the period."[15] In addition, some hundreds of other insurers were closed out with some delay of weeks, months, and occasionally years before they paid 100 cents on each dollar of their obligations. But the careful risk manager would not have been insured in most of these organizations, particularly by the time their difficulties became serious. Nearly always, clear warning signs are visible to those who know where and how to look.[16]

Solvency of Insurers

It is customary, in financial analysis, to distinguish between liquidity and solvency and to discuss the significance of each. If liquidity is defined as "ability to pay obligations as they become due," this is all that interests the risk manager. And his only interest in solvency is in its effect on this liquidity.

Solvency Requirements. The importance of solvency in insurers with American licenses is established by state regulation. An insurer whose assets (as measured under the regulations) do not exceed its liabilities (as measured under the regulations) is not permitted to continue in business. The amount by which assets must exceed liabilities will vary among types of insurers and lines of insurance written. In a capital stock company the excess must be at least equal to the stated value of the capital stock, but requirements above this minimum amount vary. In some states the statutes set minimum surplus requirements, according to the nature and number of the lines written. In the other states the statutes set no fixed minimum for the surplus of an already established (as distinguished from a newly created) company. In all states the commissioner at his discretion may refuse to license an insurer if he thinks that it is in an unsafe financial condition— a thought that he should have before the insurer's stated surplus declines to the statutory minimum.

Some commissioners use a rule of thumb in determining when a surplus

---

[15] "Surety and Stability," *Journal of American Insurance*, Vol. XXXVIII, No. 11 (November, 1962), pp. 16–17.

[16] The principal exception to this rule is loss caused by fraud on the part of the insurer's management.

is approaching a dangerous position. In order to avoid meaningless distinctions between proprietary and cooperative insurers, this rule is stated in terms of the excess of "admitted" assets (assets as measured by the rules and regulations) over "statutory" liabilities (same measure). In usual business finance this margin is called the "equity." In insurance finance it is called "policyholders' surplus."[17] The rule is that the unearned premium reserve in a fire insurer should not exceed the policyholders' surplus; the unearned premium reserve in a casualty company should not exceed twice its policyholders' surplus. The most explicit exponent of this rule is Roger Kenney, insurance editor and columnist of *United States Investor*. He expounds on this rule on various occasions in his column and explains the application of the rule and its limitations in his book, *Fundamentals of Fire and Casualty Insurance Strength*.[18] One major difficulty with any simple rule is that regardless of how its expert exponents may attempt to hedge it with necessary adjustments and exceptions, it is the rule and not the exceptions that get bruited about.

Mr. Kenney, in one column, praised a Missouri commissioner of insurance for his campaign to strengthen the financial position of Missouri insurers of substandard automobile risks, but added that in his view the commissioner's announced goal of holding premium writings to no more than *four* times policyholders' surplus was much too "venturesome," particularly in view of the general unprofitableness of substandard automobile insurance underwriting. He concluded by castigating "the all too common practice of resorting to stop-gap gauges of the rule of thumb variety which disregard the fact that the answer to the question whether a company is 'coming or going' can only be found in *intelligent analysis of the operating account in connection with the balance sheet*."[19]

Much more important than the exact level of the ratio of premiums to policyholders' surplus are the factors that determine how high this ratio can

---

[17] Some object to this version; they insist that the reference should be to "surplus as regards policyholders." Their objection is to the possessive form, "policyholders'." They point out that when the insurer is incorporated, everything in the corporation belongs to the corporation. Furthermore, in a stock insurer, the equitable interest belongs to the stockholders, not the policyholders. The present authors note that all statements are wrong when they imply that the "surplus" is subject to ownership by anyone, whether a real person or a corporate body. The "surplus" involved here is an accounting concept, not a piece of property or a property right. Ownership exists with respect to the assets of a business, and it exists with respect to all its assets, not merely the portion or proportion of them that happens to be equal to the dollar value of the equity or to the equity ratio. But, in English, possessive forms of nouns and pronouns are not limited in usage to the relationships of possession: the collection, "John's home," "John's wife," and "John's boss," indicate a variety of relationships, only one of which is the relationship of possession. "Policyholders' surplus" is as legitimate a construction for "surplus as regards policyholders" as "our neighbors" is for "persons who are neighbors with respect to us."

[18] 3d ed.; Dedham, Massachusetts: The Kenney Insurance Studies, 1957.

[19] "Regulating for Solvency Calls for Stern Action by Insurance Commissioners!" *United States Investor*, Vol. LXXVIII, No. 42 (October 15, 1962), pp. 3017–22. Quotation is from page 3022; italics as in the original.

safely be. These factors have a bearing in two ways: In the first place, they actually help determine what the absolute size of the premiums and the policyholders' surplus will be; second, they suggest what the ratio between their sizes can safely be.

Causes of Insolvency. There is a saying in insurance finance that underwriting problems get property and liability insurers into trouble, whereas investing problems get life insurers into trouble.

Since the passing of the old-style fraternal life insurance organizations (in which membership fees were not graduated according to ages and, usually, premium income was obtained only by assessments), life insurers have found it difficult to get into trouble on account of underwriting losses. Such a feat requires an unusually persistent refusal to observe the elementary rules of life underwriting. Life company failures in the past half-century have been caused by misuse of assets, usually brought on by the attempt of some executive or owner to increase his personal profits.

Property and liability insurers, on the other hand, probably get into trouble more often from the underwriting side than from the investment side of their business. The investment side does cause trouble, however. Chicanery and self-seeking occur among managers and owners of property and liability insurers, as they do everywhere else. In addition, whereas life insurers invest almost all their assets in debt instruments, property insurers invest a large part of their assets in equity issues, which makes it easier for even honest managements to get into investment trouble.

When asset values decline faster than liabilities, or liabilities rise faster than asset values, surplus is reduced. Surplus needs to have been sufficiently large before the reduction in order to leave the company solvent and viable afterward.

Changes in Assets vs. Changes in Liability. Changes in asset values in any business can be associated with changes in the actual quantity of assets or with changes in the worth of an unchanged quantity of assets. Cash that an insurer held yesterday may be gone today because it was needed to pay a claim. The one hundred shares of Du Pont stock that the insurer held yesterday, while still present today, may be worth $100 less because the market has dropped a point.

However, the use of cash to pay a claim did not affect the insurer's surplus. The claim payment was already owed, and, when it was paid, the transaction decreased liabilities by the same amount as assets, leaving surplus unchanged. It was when the claim sprang into being that the insurer's surplus was reduced.

And so it is for most other changes in the quantity of assets held. Seldom are assets given up on other than a *quid pro quo* basis, either to extinguish a debt in the same amount or to acquire another asset of the same apparent value. The two exceptions are involuntary conversions and the payment of dividends to equity holders.

Therefore, in trying to anticipate the amount of policyholders' surplus that will be needed to keep an insurer solvent, the main interest in asset changes lies in potential changes in the value of a given stock of assets, with only secondary reference to the possibilities of physical loss or destruction of assets and of overgenerosity in dividend policy.

The remaining potential for decline in policyholders' surplus lies in possible increases in liabilities without accompanying increases in assets, discussed a little later.

Asset Values in Insurance. Not all the assets owned by insurers may be counted in official financial statements. Certain investments, such as loans to officers and second mortgages, are classified as "nonadmitted" for purposes of official statements. Personal property used by the insurer (e.g., furnishings, supplies) also is "nonadmitted."

Assets admitted to the statements are stated at values determined in accordance with statutes and regulations. In general, debt instruments that are not in default as to principal or interest are carried at amortized values; other securities and notes are carried at market; owned real property is variously valued at cost-less-depreciation or at market value. (There are strict limitations on how much real estate may be held, and for what purposes.)

The difficulties arise from the items valued at market and, potentially, from the defaults on debt instruments held at amortized values. Clearly, the need for surplus is related to (1) the distribution of the investment portfolio between assets carried at market and other assets, (2) the current degree of inflation in the market for the assets valued at market, and (3) the potentiality of default on securities carried at amortization values.

In view of the usual behavior of the markets and the economy, the foregoing analysis suggests the following pragmatic approach. "When production levels in the economy are high or growing, the amount of policyholders' surplus needed to cushion against possible shrinkage in asset values is determined principally by the amount of stocks held by the insurer; when the economy is depressed, the soundness of the debt instruments held becomes more important in determining the need for surplus. A proviso, however: the foregoing presumes that in periods when production is up, there is little chance of default on the debt instruments an insurer holds. This should be the case, but the quality of the portfolio must be examined to see whether it is indeed the case. If it is not, no amount of surplus the insurer is likely to hold would seem to be sufficient to overcome the loss potential inherent in the simultaneous presence of inflated values in the assets carried at market and shaky values in the assets carried on an amortization basis.

Liability Accounts in Insurance. The liability accounts of property and casualty insurers may be considered in three categories: unearned premium reserves, claims reserves, and ordinary liabilities.

"Ordinary liabilities" are those any business could have—open-account debts to suppliers of services and materials (e.g., stationery, office equipment); accruals for various obligations, such as rents and taxes; sums owed for borrowed money (rare in insurance), and so on. Ordinary liabilities are of minor consequence in the balance sheet of an insurance company.

When there has been an occurrence that will or can lead to a claims payment under an insurance policy, the insurer has an actual or potential liability. This liability is *estimated* in the claims or loss reserve of a property or liability insurer[20] and in the reserve for supplementary contracts of a life insurer.

(In life insurance, the average length of time from loss to payment of lump-sum benefits is so short that liability for unpaid lump-sum claims is an insignificant factor. However, the insured or beneficiary may exercise his option to have the policy proceeds held at interest by the company, to be paid out later in agreed installments or on call; the terms settled on are called a "supplemental contract." The policy reserve is then eliminated, and a reserve for liability under the supplemental contract is set up instead. This new reserve, however, is indeed a claims reserve, just like the reserve that a workmen's compensation insurer sets up for its obligation to keep up weekly payments during the disability of an already injured workman, or a health insurer sets up for its obligation to continue regular installment payments to a disabled insured.)

When an insurer issues a policy it takes on a considerable future financial obligation of an unknown amount. This obligation is *recognized*, but its extent is *not measured* by the unearned premium reserve account of a property or liability insurer. In life insurance this obligation is recognized in the policy reserve account; this account does purport to estimate, but in fact systematically overestimates, the dollar amount of the insurer's obligations under its policies in force.

The liabilities of an insurer consist principally, then, of two classes of "reserve" accounts—in a property or liability insurer, the unearned premium reserve and claims reserves; in a life insurer, the policy reserve and, to a much less extent, the reserve for supplementary contracts. In addition, life insurers frequently show one additional liability account of some, but not great, significance: policyholders' funds left on deposit with the company. These consist partly of advance payments of premiums, but mostly of policyholders' dividends left on deposit at interest with the company. And all insurers have some, but except in brand-new insurers not a significant amount, of the ordinary kinds of liabilities found in businesses of any kind.

---

[20] Insurance adjusters speak of occurrences to which liability covers are applicable as "third party claims," or simply "claims." Occurrences to which other covers are applicable are "losses" (and the insurance is referred to as "first party insurance"). The words are used interchangeably in this text, however.

Growth in the liabilities of insurers without accompanying growth in assets is a function of the underwriting operations—of sales of new policies and of claims under existent ones. Since growth is an operational function, it is best considered in connection with discussion of items found in operational statements rather than in balance sheets.

Profitability and Liquidity of Insurers

The theory of business finance that is here being applied to insurance organizations is essentially the following: A business that continuously takes in more assets than it has to pay out will not get into trouble. If its present financial position is poor, it will become good; if its present financial position is good, it will get better. On the other hand, a business that continues to pay out more assets than it takes in must, sooner or later, get into trouble. All that its present financial condition can indicate is whether that trouble will arrive sooner or later.

In many lines of business, two applications of the rule are necessary—it must be applied both to cash flow and to the flow of all values. It must be applied to cash flow because a business may have enough assets to cover its debts but not enough cash to make actual payment; such a business is technically solvent but not liquid—and its lack of liquidity may easily destroy its solvency. The rule needs to be applied to the flow of total values because cash can sometimes be built up by the expedient of not meeting obligations; then there can be a large quantity of money on hand but an even larger collection of claims against it.

Cash Flow in Insurance. It is accepted and provable dogma that life insurers achieve liquidity from the continual nature of their cash flows. Most policies on the books of a life insurer produce a continuing inflow of cash from premiums. The invested assets produce a continuing inflow of cash from interest (and some rents and dividends) and from maturities and calls of securities. It is indeed a rare month when a seasoned life insurer (an active insurer at least ten, perhaps only five, years old) does not take in, merely by continuing in business, more money than it is required to pay out. Indeed, this feature is so strong that it has allowed hidden chicanery or other maloperation in certain life insurers for many, many months. A company can be looted of a goodly share of its invested assets and continue to meet its claims and other bills promptly and in cash, particularly if its sales force continues to be active and successful.

The same is not considered to be true generally of insurers in other lines. For one thing, continuance of premiums on past sales is not so automatic. There is no investment, or cash value, feature in property and liability insurance policies for policyholders to protect by continuing premium payments. In addition, as economic conditions weaken and deflation sets in, property values decline, and so does the amount of insurance on them. (It has been often observed that very little decline of this sort occurs in life insurance, in which marked underinsurance is the usual rule.) Moreover, when insurance is marketed through independent agents, a given insurer can quickly lose its renewal premiums by losing its agents.

Furthermore, in property insurance the needs to raise cash for payouts are said to be very irregular. Even though cash flows to insurers are, as they must be, favorable over time, claims for conflagrations, windstorms, and other catastrophes may be bunched so that cash needs within a particular space of time exceed the regular cash receipts in the same period.

Nevertheless, insurers whose exposures are spread over a wide territory seldom find their cash needs exceeding their normal cash inflow for any appreciable period. As the investment officer for one multiple line insurance group described it, "We keep our funds in bank deposits until the deposits exceed a certain figure, when we invest a certain amount. Then we wait until our bank accounts get excessive again, and we make new investment again." It is difficult to find an operating property insurer that has sold investments in the past twenty, thirty, or even forty years in order to pay claims or other bills. Occasionally, the proceeds from maturities or calls have not been reinvested. And, also rarely, short-term loans have been used to get over a temporary shortage of cash. But sales of securities forced by needs for operating funds have become very, very unusual except for insurers with little or no diversification as to area or type of business insured, and except for insurers whose continuing unprofitability has brought them to technical or factual insolvency.

Of course, it is exactly for safety in the "very, very unusual" cases that liquidity in assets is necessary. An examination of some of these cases[21] has suggested that, even here, little asset liquidity is necessary—much less than is commonly stated by the few published works on the subject. The best statement appears to be that profitably operated insurers (considering investment as well as underwriting profit) whose exposures are diversified and whose dividends allow for asset growth have sufficient liquidity in their ordinary cash flow, including normal turnover of investments, for liquidity in their investments to be "frosting on the cake."

Accounting for Operating Expenses in Insurance. Reading financial statements of property and liability insurers is a shocking experience for persons familiar with normal rules and procedures in modern accounting. Therefore, some explanation of their reporting methods is necessary before the significance of their reports can be understood. All that will be attempted here is explanation; justification (real or alleged) is too long a story.

Suppose a three-year fire insurance policy is sold for a total premium of $300. At the time of the sale, this amount of premium is said to be "written." Let the agent's commission be 20 per cent, the premium tax be 2 per cent,

---

[21] Robert A. Hedges, "The 'Capacity' Problem in American Fire and Casualty Insurance Companies" (Master's thesis, University of Illinois, 1950).

with the other costs incurred because of this particular sale at 5 per cent of premium. Assuming these costs are reflected as of date of sale, the *changes* in the insurer's balance sheet will be as follows:

Asset	Change	Liability	Change
Accounts receivable	+$300	Accrued tax	+$ 6
		Commission due	+ 60
		Other accrued expenses	+ 15
		Unearned premium reserve	+ 300
		Equity	
		Surplus	−$ 81
Total	+$300	Total	+$300

These changes reflect the fact that the agent has not remitted the premium. They also reflect the fact that the "unearned premium" liability is based on the total premium charged the insured. In usual accounting terms, this is a deferred income account—it recognizes the fact that an advance payment has been received (in this case, by the company's agent) for services that have not been rendered (insurance protection over the time covered by the policy). In usual accounting procedures, when income is deferred, any directly associated expenses (here, the agents' commission plus $21 in other immediate expenses) are also deferred. But in property and liability insurance such deferral of expenses is neither customary nor allowed by the regulatory authorities. So the associated expenses are entered above as fully charged costs.

Now look at the *additional* changes over the next year during which this policy is on the books. Suppose no bills other than agent's commission have yet been paid. Assume that $12 is assigned to this policy as its share of overhead during the 12 months, and that the claims ratio on this policy is some average figure, say 56 per cent, and expense of handling these claims is 4 per cent, of the earned premium. The "earned premium" is the amount of (gross) income that is released from the unearned premium reserve (deferred income account) because some of the services paid for (insurance protection over time) *have* been rendered. In one year, one third of the promised protection time has been provided, so one third of the original $300 payment has become earned premium (gross income). In order to keep a record of these changes in the balance sheet, all operations are assumed to be on credit. Then—

Asset	Additional Change	Liability	Additional Change
No payments in or out—all items shown as incurred only		Accrued overhead	+$ 12
		Claims reserves	+ 56
		Accrued claims adjustment expense	+ 4
		Unearned premium reserve	− 100
		Equity	
		Surplus	+$ 28
Total	$ 0	Total	$ 0

If overhead, claims, and claims expense accrue at the same rate as before, the changes over each of the next two years will be the same as over the first year. For the entire three years, the over-all change then would be the sum of the change at time of sale plus three times the additional change shown above for the first year thereafter. The net result, still keeping all transactions as credit transactions, is as follows:

Asset	Change	Liability	Change
Accounts receivable	+$300	Accruals:	
		Tax	+$ 6
		Sales expense (incl. commission)	+ 75
		Overhead	+ 36
		Claims adjustment	+ 12
		Claims reserves	+ 168
		Unearned premium reserve ..	0
		Equity	
		Surplus	+$ 3
Total	+$300	Total	+$300

During any accounting period while this policy is on the books *after* its inception date, the insurer's statements will show a profit at the rate of $28 for each year the policy remains in force. However, for the accounting period in which the sale is recorded, $81 will be charged against the surplus, producing an apparent loss for the first accounting period. Neither the recorded gain of $28 per policy year nor the recorded loss in the year of sale represents the insurer's actual experience of an average profit of $1 per year over the three-year life of the policy.

This unusual method of accounting for income vis-à-vis expenses means that a property or liability insurer's profitability cannot be judged directly from its official statements. The most widely accepted method of adjustment for this accounting peculiarity proceeds from the following reasoning:

1. Some expenses are incurred in the process of putting a policy on the books. These expenses generally vary with the dollar volume of sales, called "premiums written."

2. Other charges, such as claims and overhead, are incurred over the life of the policy. Now if premiums are properly set (adequate but not excessive), they will fluctuate directly with claims and underwriting expenses. Insurers generally aim at maintaining certain ratios between premiums and the sum of expenses and claims. Therefore, when a company earns $200 rather than $100 in premiums, the assumption is that its claims, claims expense, and overhead costs will also be about twice as much.

Given assumptions 1 and 2, and using the expenses and ratios in the earlier balance sheet illustrations, the analysis proceeds as follows:

When this company makes a sale—obtains some written premium—it immediately incurs a cost of about 27 per cent of that premium (20 per cent for commission, 2 per cent for taxes, 5 per cent for other expenses). As that policy moves toward its expiration date, additional expenses equal to about 72 per cent of the policy premium (12 per cent for overhead, 60 per cent for claims and adjustment costs) will be incurred. This leaves a 1 per cent margin for profit.

The question is, what are these ratios for each company? They can be estimated for current activities by making the following calculations from the company's report. First note the dollar amount of expenses incurred on account of sales and compare these with amount of sales (written premiums). Then note the dollar amount of other expenses and claims incurred and compare these with the earned premiums.

Return to the example of the $300 premium in the earlier balance sheet exhibits and consider what the insured's books would show on this policy at the close of the calendar year (the closing date for all insurance company annual statements) if the policy had been written on July 1 of that year. The given sales costs would have been incurred in the year plus one-half (we assume) of all the other first-year costs. The written premium would have been $300; the earned premium would have been $50 (one sixth of $300). The $81 of expenses incurred at time of sale is 27 per cent of $300. The remaining incurred expense of $36 (one half of $12-plus-$56-plus-$4) is 72 per cent of $50. These add to 99 per cent, and the forecast is that the remaining 1 per cent of premium would eventually show up in surplus as underwriting profit. These figures contrast with the company's official report of $81 plus $36, or $117, as incurred expenses in this period against an earned premium income of $50, for an underwriting loss of $67.

In the jargon of the trade, the indicated loss of $67 is called the "statutory" result from underwriting, because it is produced by the application of governmental rules to the company's underwriting operations. Application of the indicated profit margin of 1 per cent of premium income to the premium income earned during the year—$50—gives a current profit of 50 cents. This figure is called the "trade profit" in underwriting, and the indicated 1 per cent margin is called the company's "trade position" with respect to underwriting.

Not all analysts use this method in exactly the same way. Two versions are most frequent. In one version, all underwriting expenses other than claims and claims adjustment expense are measured against written premiums, with claims and claims expense compared to earned premiums. This method is the more common one and is the one used by the Alfred M. Best Company. Best's reports are the mostly widely read and probably the most highly regarded of financial reports on insurers. The second important method adds overhead (the official categroy is "general" expenses) to claims and claims adjustment expense for comparison against earned premiums and takes only sales (called "acquisition") expenses and "taxes, licenses and fees" against written premiums.[22] This method is the

---

[22] *Income* taxes are not included anywhere in any of these ratios. That is, these analyses are always of "before [income] tax" positions.

one used here and the one used by the superintendent of insurance of New York in his reports. An intensive study of the relative merits of the two positions, based on data from the years 1944–52, indicated that in fire insurance the overhead or "general" expenses category varied slightly more with earned premiums than with written, without being closely tied to either one.[23]

In life insurance, the regulations allow considerable deferral of charges into policy years after the first one. However, some large insurers with comfortable surpluses do not choose to take advantage of this allowance; they prefer not to make their current surpluses look any bigger.

Accounting for Claims. The most important expense in insurance consists of claims for covered losses. In property insurance, relatively little time elapses from the claim itself to its payment. Hence, this expense may be accounted for relatively easily. The same is true for lump-sum payments in life insurance. When life insurance proceeds are payable under a life annuity option, the liability may be underestimated; lengthening of the average life span increases the liability of insurers under annuity agreements, and, over time, original estimates have proved markedly inadequate. Therefore, the long-run profitability of a life insurer with a large number of present and potential liabilities under annuity agreements (either through annuity contracts or through life annuity settlement options in life insurance contracts) may be less than is indicated by current estimates of the liability under these contracts. So far, however, this potential underestimate is too small relative to total results to mean much in the over-all safety of a life insurer with the usual preponderance of life policies over annuity contracts, and the usual conservatism in making actuarial estimates.

In liability and disability income insurance (including workmen's compensation), this rapidity of passage from claim to payment in full does not always appear. Claims that involve expensive, protracted disabilities take years to settle or pay off. In the meantime, the insurer has the problem of estimating the dollar value of its liability with respect to them.

When a claim arises under a long-term disability cover (health or workmen's compensation), an estimate must be made of the likely term of disability. (A disability may be terminated by either recovery or death.) For many of the permanent disabilities, mortality tables based on experience with different disabilities are available and usually are referred to in setting the claim reserve. But the medical expense factor (important in workmen's compensation in many states) seldom abides by past experience.

In liability claims the term involved is shorter—the 3-to-7 years to court settlement rather than the lifetime of the disability—but other difficulties

---

[23] Robert A. Hedges, "Principles of Financial Analysis of Underwriting Expenses in Property Insurance" (doctoral dissertation, University of Illinois, 1954).

arise. The actual fact of any liability has yet to be established in many cases, and the amount is at issue in most of them. Furthermore, the ultimate cost of the claim will depend not only on the medical facts of the disability (which may not be entirely known to the liability insurer) but also on the litigious circumstances—the capabilities of the plaintiff's attorney, the plaintiff's versus the defendant's ability to arouse the sympathy of a jury, the forum or forums in which the case will or may be heard, the changing reliability of witnesses' memories wth the passage of time, and other imponderable but crucial factors.

The question is, how can the outsider, studying the insurer's reports, make any estimation of the ability and willingness of a particular insurer's management to reflect all these factors in its claims reserves? To the reader's surprise, perhaps, there *is* a way to do so with fair, albeit a little belated, accuracy. The details of the method will not be retailed here,[24] but the general approach is as follows:

From certain schedules in the insurer's annual statements, the reader can get the following information: (1) the insurer's estimation of its incurred but unpaid claims liabilities for each policy year[25] and (2) the actual payments made on these same claims in each calendar year, starting with the year the policy was written.[26] Thus, as the calendar years roll by, the reader can compare the company's estimates with its subsequent actual payments on the same claims. In this way he can tell whether the insurer has previously been charging accurately for claims reserves.

Of course, as was said, this is a little belated. As a practical matter, it takes about three calendar years to get a good idea of how the reserves originally set up in the first year have actually "developed" (to use the trade jargon in this connection). Nevertheless, this information is considerably better than no information at all, and a management that has consistently overestimated or underestimated its need for reserves should certainly be presumed to be continuing to do the same until there is proof to the contrary. Furthermore, explanation is required whenever a company reports a sudden shift in either (1) the average amount of its dollar reserve per claim outstanding or (2) its ratio between dollars reserved and premiums earned.

Profitability in Investment. In many years large numbers of property and liability insurance companies of all ages and sizes have increased their earned surpluses despite underwriting losses. This has been because of gains and profits on investments. In profitable underwriting years, invest-

---

[24] More detail may be found in Roger Kenney, *op. cit.*

[25] "Claims liabilities for each policy year" means the liabilities for claims incurred under all the policies written in a given calendar year.

[26] However, the estimates and claims payments for policy years more than five calendar years back are reported in a single aggregate figure, not on a policy-year-by-policy-year basis.

ment gains and profits augment asset and surplus growth, of course. And, in some years, net losses on investments may reduce or eliminate surplus gains created by underwriting profits or augment surplus declines caused by underwriting losses.

Gains and profits from investment should be divided into three categories: "current earnings" (rent, interest, and dividends accrued plus net changes in values by amortization), "capital gains realized," and "capital gains not realized." (Capital "gains" of either kind may be negative, of course.) Which of these three parts may be generally relied upon to continue and which represent real flows of values are self-evident.

The Total Picture. Naturally, the ability of an insurer to maintain the profitability and cash flow necessary to a sound financial position is a function of over-all results; a dollar of cash or other real value contributed from the investment side is neither more nor less valuable for meeting obligations than a dollar contributed from the underwriting side, and the same goes for each dollar drained out by costs or losses. The one significant difference lies in implications for the future—past capital gains and losses tell little about the future. But current earnings on investments are a source of funds and profits and are more stable than are underwriting results.

Probably the best single guide to the financial future of an insurer is found in the history of the following quantity: the sum of (1) current earnings on investment, plus (2) trade profit on underwriting (adjusted for known distortion in liability and disability claims reserves), less (3) cash dividends (and any other cash outlays that have been charged directly against surplus rather than against either investment or underwriting results). The important aspects of this figure are (1) its absolute amount together with its size relative to incurred expenses and claims, (2) any trends in its amount or relative size, and (3) the stability of the amount and relative size. The last of these three—stability—unfortunately has been more desired than observed for the past several years in property and liability insurance. For large segments of the industry, the secular trends have been down for some time, with only intermittent and short-lived relief. It seems clear that lower margins of profit are the new order in property and liability insurance. This naturally makes stability of results even more important.

Other Factors. The previous discussion is, of course, a bare introduction to the subject of insurers' finances. There are other important factors.

Major changes in management naturally lead to doubt that a company's past is a direct guide to its future. The past behavior of the management is likely to be more important than the past behavior of the company managed. (This assumes the company is in a position to have a future, of course.)

Diversification of the loss exposures by geography and by line has already been mentioned as an important factor. Akin to diversification (or spread) of exposure, and partially a substitute for it, is the reinsurance carried. Reinsurance is insurance purchased by an insurance company against claims under policies it has issued. An insurer with loss potential equal to, say, 30 per cent of its assets concentrated in the area of a single possible catastrophe (such as conflagration, hurricane or tornado, or major explosion) lacks dispersion or diversification of exposure. If it can buy re-insurance sufficient to cut that potential to less than 10 per cent of its assets (still a pretty large figure), it has accomplished the same result with respect to spread as though it had written only the lesser amount in the first place (assuming, of course, that its reinsurance agreements—called "treaties"—are soundly conceived and placed with reliable insurers). Although matters of concentration and spread of exposure and of reinsurance arrangements are of prime importance in the financial soundness of any insurer, they are also matters about which useful information is seldom readily available. Indeed, useful information of this kind is sometimes not even "un-readily" available; it simply is not to be had.

Another factor important to the future of an insurer is the state of its marketing force. The assumption throughout this chapter is that the insured wants only a going concern as his insurer. It is this assumption that produces most of the difference between the financial analysis that appears in this text and traditional analysis. But a going concern cannot keep going unless it continues to be reasonably successful in marketing its services. The viability of an insurer's marketing force is not always evident; the inertia of past effort has on occasion carried a moribund insurer through a rather prolonged marasmus. How is a buyer to know whether the marketing "force" of an insurer is actually a force or merely a presence? Often he cannot know.

Summary. The best key to the financial soundness of an insurer appears to be past profitability, together with ability to maintain a flow of incoming cash. The difficulties in ascertaining and measuring the other important factors plus the assumption that the interest is in a going, not a defunct, insurer produce this conclusion: The "proof of the pudding" cooked by any particular management lies in having achieved success in the past. Such success presumably arose from ability to handle all the relevant factors, measurable and immeasurable. While there is truth in Edmund Burke's statement, "You can never plan the future by the past," there is equal truth in the remark of his contemporary, Patrick Henry, that "I know of no way of judging of the future but by the past."[27] The past is the only, however imperfect, guide to the future, and risk managers, like everyone else, must make their judgments and lay their plans accordingly.

---

[27] From, respectively, a letter by Burke to a member of the National Assembly, and a speech by Henry in the Virginia Convention.

SERVICES FROM INSURERS

The values received in return for insurance premiums are in the services supplied by insurers and their representatives. These services may be classified into two types: insurance service and auxiliary services. Insurance service consists of providing indemnity plus some essential related services. All other services offered by insurance organizations are (here called) auxiliary.

Insurance Service

Provision of indemnity for an insured's losses means adjusting as well as paying claims. When the Big Valley Construction Company receives notice that Mary Lamb tore her hose and cut her leg as she passed by a pile of concrete reinforcing rods on the premises of her employer, immediate action should be taken to ascertain whether the Big Valley Company should make prompt settlement for a particular number of dollars, delay commitment pending further developments and detailed investigation, or deny all responsibility. Deciding or helping to decide on a course of action, implementing it, and paying for it (subject to the limits of insurance carried) constitute insurance service.

When Mack Brown, Wyoming sales representative for the Bonny Dee Manufacturing Corporation, is involved in a collision while passing through Bitter Creek, he becomes subject to various expectations. He may be expected to satisfy the owner of the other car and the local authorities that they will be able to enforce claims or charges against him if any arise from the accident. And, if the accident causes property damage in excess of a certain amount or any bodily injury, the state authorities will want a written report in proper form, together with proof of financial responsibility. Automobile liability insurance policies provide that the insurer will pay "all premiums on bonds to release attachments not in excess of the limit of liability of this policy" (this deals with the problem of surety to protect the owner of the other car) and "the cost of bail bonds required of the insured in the event of accident or traffic law violation during the policy period, not to exceed $100 per bail bond" (which deals with the charges by the local authorities).[28] In addition, although the policy provides no specific promise to do so, the insurer or its representative will usually take care of filing the accident report with the state,

---

[28] The quotations are from a standard form. Perhaps it should be noted that the policy goes on to say, "without any obligation [on the part of the insurer] to apply for or furnish any such bonds." However, superior claims service would include assisting the insured to obtain such bonds. Other kinds of liability insurance do *not* include the promise to pay premiums on *bail* bonds.

together with a certificate of insurance coverage as proof of Brown's (and/or his employer's) financial responsibility.[29] Payments of premiums for bonds are indemnity and are part of the insurance service; the filing of an accident report and proof of financial responsibility represent auxiliary service.

Claims Service. For most insureds, claims payment is the most important service in insurance. Given that an insurer is financially able to pay, the important questions are whether it is willing to pay and whether it has the administrative machinery for paying promptly.

As was described in chapter 5, the claims service of an insurer may have usefulness beyond coverage for the loss insured against. In some businesses there is a distinct advantage in having third-party claimants deal with representatives of an insurer rather than with the insured himself. Any resulting frictions may then redound to the detriment of the "public image" of the insurer rather than of the insured. This may apply to claims by customers, by employees, or by members of the general public.

Willingness To Pay. What the insured wants, of course, is an insurer willing to pay for losses of the kinds and amounts that he intended to have covered under his policy, no more and certainly no less. Such an ideal result presumably would minimize premium costs, obviate the need for special understandings with the underwriters, and simplify loss adjustments. The principle obstacles to reaching this ideal situation are three:

1. Only a few buyers are big enough to have special forms written to fit their particular needs. Most buyers are insured under standard forms designed to apply to a variety of situations. Use of standard forms for many insureds is necessary because the costs of creating and handling special forms are high and because uniformity of coverage over a large number of independent units is needed for application of the law of large numbers in rate making.
2. The buyer cannot foresee all the kinds of losses he will want covered. The form that is ideal *post hoc* in all events cannot be drawn up in advance because of the inability to anticipate all the kinds of loss-causing events.
3. Language is an imperfect means of communication. Even if every insurance form were specially drawn for a particular insured and even if every type of possible loss event could be anticipated, the translation of the buyer's desires and intentions into coverage could be no more precise than the language. Policy draftsmen know only too well that when they thought they had written "black," insureds, juries, and judges may read "green" or "purple" or even, on occasion, "white."

Therefore, forms must frequently be interpreted with respect to their application to given losses. The amount of coincidence between the intent of the insurance buyer and the insurer's interpretation of the cover is a variable that affects the buyer's loyalty to an insurer.

---

[29] To be accepted as proof of financial responsibility, a policy must be in sufficient amount and be issued by an insurer licensed to do business in either the state in which the filing is made or in the state where the automobile is ordinarily kept.

Some buyers mistakenly believe that the insurer with the broadest interpretation of the coverage afforded is necessarily the best in this respect. But the insureds, as a group, must pay for the losses covered by this interpretation if the insurer is to remain financially sound; a discriminating buyer will not be willing to contribute toward the costs of all forms of loose interpretation. To repeat, what the buyer wants is an insurer whose interpretation of the cover coincides as nearly as possible with his interpretation. This is possible, of course, only if the buyer's interpretation is realistic and in accord with necessary underwriting considerations—which means an interpretation consonant both with the general nature of the particular policy and with basic insurance theory. The requisites of an insurable risk are quite relevant here: The buyer should not expect the insurer to be willing to pay losses that are not fortuitous, might expose the insurer to catatrophic loss situations, involve disproportionately high operating costs (as in the case of small but frequent losses), and so on. In fact, insurers that are willing to pay losses of these kinds should usually be avoided as either being too expensive or having a doubtful financial future.

When a buyer has had satisfactory experience with the contract interpretation of a particular insurer, he should be most loath to change. It is difficult to tell in advance of direct experience what the intepretive practices of a particular insurer may be. Reliable information from other insureds may be useful if it can be obtained. But few insurers treat all insureds exactly alike. Some of the variation depends on the attitudes and practices of the insureds themselves. Risk managers who consistently try to overreach their insurers, to squeeze each and every possible dollar out of their insurance contracts, must expect to encounter resistance and countermeasures. It certainly does not follow that no pressure should ever be brought to bear on an insurer for broader interpretation of contract coverage or of measures of indemnity. But pressure should be selectively used, being reserved for those occasions on which there is both reasonable theoretical ground (in insurance theory and in law) and practical reason (meaning, principally, importance of the loss) for seeking a broader interpretation.

An insurer that consistently puts a narrow interpretation on its covers is unlikely to be desirable. Insurance policies contain various provisions designed to protect underwriters from overly grasping, including purely dishonest, insureds. It has long been a deplored feature of insurance law that these same provisions can sometimes be used to defeat insureds of ordinary or even superior honesty. A. F. O'Shea, in his 1962 presidential address before the Insurance Institute of London, said of policy restrictions: "Unfortunately, the frailty of human nature prohibits the removal of all safeguards, but let us not fall into the error of holding them to be as immutable as the laws of the Medes and Persians. They are our shield against the dishonest man, the near-dishonest or the smart Alec; not a sword with which to strike the honest majority."[30] Insurers that make the most of such provisions are unlikely to provide the reliable protection the risk manager is seeking.

Claims Adjustment Organization. The delay or difficulty that an insured may encounter in getting his claims paid may not be because of unwillingness to pay. Sometimes delay and difficulties are inherent to the loss situation itself—essential information may be hard to get after the loss, or, in a liability claim, the third-party claimant may be uncooperative or may appear unreasonable in his requirements for settlement. The difficulty also may lie in the inability of the insurer's claims adjustment organization to carry through the mechanics of adjustment smoothly and quickly. This inability may be caused by a shortage of either quality or quantity of personnel.

With respect to quality, the personnel may be inherently lacking in the intelligence, integrity, and energy required for the job; they may be suffering from inadequate supervision and training; or the organization may be so staffed and arranged that men with willingness and authority to make decisions may be too far up in the hierarchy and too centralized in location for quick results. The good claims man is quickly promoted to an inside job, often leaving the field barren. How is the risk manager to tell? Apart from his own experience with a particular adjusting organization, he may try to converse with others about their experiences and he may, on occasion, try to get acquainted with some of the relevant claims personnel and attempt to make some judgments himself. A broker or independent agent who is providing real service in connection with the selection of insurers has a collection of experiences and impressions about the claims-handling techniques of some number of insurers.

Since a large number of insurers use the same claims adjustment organizations—particularly the General Adjustment Bureau and the Underwriters Adjustment and Inspection Company—there is no organizational difference among these companies in the field. However, the independent judgment and decision making allowed the field adjuster may vary from one of these insurers to another, as may the interpretation of some points of coverage. The adjuster who works for a single company can have the advantage of knowing his company's philosophy, practices, and rules very well; this can speed up settlement. On the other hand, it is difficult or impossible for a single company using its own adjusters to cover all territories as thoroughly or to operate with as much flexibility as to location as can be achieved by adjustment organizations representing the pooled efforts of many companies.

The extent of the territory covered by the insurer's claims adjustment organization—especially the nearness of an adjuster to any place where

---

[30] *The Review* (London), Vol. XCIII, No. 4111 (October, 1962), p. 1123.

the insured may need claims adjustment service—is the quantity factor in the claims adjustment service. This factor is more easily checked than is quality. The problem of quantity is both alleviated and complicated, however, by the existence of independent, or free lance, adjusters who may be used by an insurer to supplement the regular staff. Thus, an insurer can have claims representation even in places where it otherwise conducts no business. The complicating feature is that the quality of the work of these independent adjusters cannot be estimated in advance, nor is the quantity of their services always subject to good estimation.

Loss Reduction Service. Assistance in loss reduction can be an important service to an insured; sometimes, to an extremely large insured, loss reduction is even more important than risk transfer. Insurers' loss reduction services were discussed at length in chapters 2 and 5. Here the reader is reminded that loss reduction services from insurers can take several forms. Most obvious is advice and guidance in safety engineering and planning loss control. Less often considered are the services of claims adjusters and other agents of insurers in reducing losses through salvage and subrogation. One risk manager reported the following experience: On a fleet of 1,400 vehicles scattered over the United States and Canada, the owning corporation could pay the collision losses without any danger to its financial position. But about 40 per cent of the collision losses involved claims against others for the damage they caused. The average value of these claims was under $300. There were not enough claims in any one place to keep an attorney on a retainer to handle them there, and their value was too small to interest attorneys in handling them occasionally on a contingency fee. Collision insurance was purchased because the insurer could charge for losses net of collections under subrogation rights, and it could effectuate subrogation because, with many insureds, it could afford to keep regular claims representation in many cities scattered through the vast territory involved.

Another loss prevention advantage held by insurers with widespread exposure is in recognizing and discouraging fraudulent claims. Fraudulent claims are often brought to light only because the same claimant appears time after time. Insurers and their organizations are much more likely to experience and spot this repetition than is a single business organization that handles only its own claims.

Risk Management Advice. Bringing an outside interest into contact with the static risk management problems of a business can be useful if the outside interest is competent and is allowed and encouraged to help. Many times, however, outside help obtained from insurers or their representatives is less than competent. In some cases, agents' and insurers' self-interests interfere with the soundness of their advice. On other occasions, the advice is turned away or ignored because it is unsettling, increases expenditures on premiums, is not understood, or is disbelieved. Insurance agents who work at giving sound advice tell of cases in which serious defects were found in a buyer's insurance program, only to have the buyer either remain undisturbed or turn and call "good old Joe" (the agent who made the mistake) and tell him to "fix it up." Of course, experienced buyers and other informed observers of insurance markets can tell even more numerous stories, not only about the time "good old Joe" made that egregious mistake, but also about how no one else ever caught it until it was brought forcefully to everyone's attention *after the loss.*

This is not to say that the best buyer working with the best advice will never make a mistake in his insurance program. But it is likely that the better the buyer and the better the advice, the fewer and probably the less costly the mistakes. Therefore, "Seek first a good agent, broker, or other adviser for your insurance program, and all else that can be will be added to you" is good advice for most insurance buyers.

In some few cases, the adviser may be a home office official of the insurer, but most buyers will never see anyone but field personnel. Besides sales personnel, this group contains claims adjusters, loss prevention specialists, auditors (to check on premiums due under variable premium policies), rating engineers, and the special agents who back up the sales force. Of all these, only the sales personnel and the special agents are expected to consider the efficacy of the insured's collection of policies. If they do not, it is exceptional for anyone else on the insurer's side to do so.

Common conversation has it that some risk managers are burdened with doing business with "captive agencies"—agencies in which the managers of the insured business have a financial, kinship, or simply friendly interest. A risk manager in this position appears to have five alternatives: shut up and relax, try to get another job with the same employer, try to change employers, work harder to carry his own burden and try to get the best out of the given agency, or try to sell the boss on using better insurance service. If his choice is the first or second alternative, he will not have read this far into this book, of course. For others who have this problem, personal competence in the risk management job will clearly be of help in the event of choice of the fourth alternative (and some risk managers have elected it successfully), and it should be of help if the choice is the third or fifth alternative. For those who are reading this, the authors naturally hope that they have found some useful guidelines toward the necessary competence.

The importance of sound buying advice naturally suggests that the reverse situation—*no* established relationships with agents, brokers, or other representation—can be detrimental, too. Jumping from insurer to insurer, from agent to agent, diminishes the interest that an insurer or agent has in the problems of the buyer. Therefore, the more free lance are the buyer's operations, the more capable he must be of handling them wholly out of the resources of his own personnel plus such free good advice as he picks up in his contacts with many insurers and agents. Surprising as it may seem, the last item mentioned can be of considerable importance; good advice can be had in many places in the insurance market at little or no cost. Insurance men like to talk about their business on any, or even no provocation. The problem, of course, is distinguishing the free good advice from the equally free bad advice.

The risk manager has several sources for potential self-education in the matter. Trade associations for insurance buyers in particular (e.g., American Society for Insurance Management and the Insurance Division of the American Management Association) and for management in general (i.e., many of the thousands of associations for business in particular lines of trade) provide publications, short courses, and seminars devoted to or including problems of static risk and insurance management. While some of the meetings are expensive for small businesses, some are inexpensive, and many individual publications may be purchased out of pocket money. In addition, among the uncounted publications and bulletin services available to insurance men for their own information and edification, many are very useful to the buyer.[31]

SUMMARY

When the supply side of the insurance market is being analyzed, two points in the line of supply must be considered: the retail outlet with which direct contact is made and the insurer that the outlet represents.

Insurers may be classified according to their *legal characteristics*: according to their legal form of organization (stock, mutual, reciprocal, Lloyds-type, etc.) or according to the jurisdictions in which they are chartered and licensed. They also may be classified according to the types of insurance that they are licensed to write.

Marketing methods provide another basis for classifying insurers. The major classes are independent agency, direct representative, and direct sales systems. Brokers may be used by buyers with any of these systems, but not all sellers accept business through brokers.

The most important bases for classifying insurers are according to the *services provided* and their costs. The paramount questions involving services offered by an insurer are the insurance covers it makes available and its ability to pay any claims that may arise under these covers. Unless an insurer is willing and able to provide *coverage the buyer desires*, other questions about it are a waste of time. There are several reasons for restrictions on the covers an insurer will offer a buyer; these reasons are associated with restrictions on use of special forms and the need to avoid underwriting losses. In general, nonadmitted insurers have a freer hand with forms

---

[31] For a list designed for insurance agency or brokerage offices of ordinary size see Bob A. Hedges *et al.*, "Bibliography on Real Estate and Insurance," Small Business Bulletin No. 65 (Washington: Small Business Administration, 1962).

of cover. And independent agents or brokers provide more help in getting undesirable lines accepted than do representatives of other systems, although here the insured may be able to help himself by reducing his hazards.

Financial soundness in insurers is primarily a matter of over-all (not merely underwriting) profitability. Technical solvency is essential because of licensing regulations, and here, given operating profitability, the possible decline in market value of assets compared to the size of net surplus is the key factor. The actual profitability of an insurer cannot be ascertained directly from its official statements, for these are joggled by the custom-become-law that income but not expenses shall be deferred in the official accounts. Hence the sum of two ratios—one to earned premiums, the other to written premiums—is used to determine an insurer's "trade position," or expected long-run profitability from underwriting, as distinguished from its "statutory" or officially reported underwriting profit. To this, current earnings from investments should be added to obtain the final estimate of the ability of the insurer to maintain its financial integrity.

Aside from outright fraud in the statement (which fraud may or may not be detectable in the statement itself), the principal source of concealed trouble in an insurer's official financial reports lies in the loss reserves for bodily injury claims (in liability, workmen's compensation, and health insurance). However, schedules in the statement allow comparison of past reserves against subsequent development of actual payments on the same policies; this gives a valuable clue to a management's propensity to charge the profit statement with too little (or too much) for current incurred-but-unpaid claims.

Indeed, in the end an insurer must be judged by the past effectiveness of its management in producing profitable results and reporting them fairly. But judgment enters; allowance must be made for the possibility that past results may not be repeated in the future. Management may have changed; the underwriting practices may have left the company unduly exposed to the effects of bad loss experience in a particular area, line of trade, or type of insurance cover, and this exposure may not be properly reinsured; or the marketing organization may not be holding its own in the market place and so possibly threatening an inability to maintain the necessary flow of cash income and required diversity of loss exposures.

Given financial soundness, the next important characteristics of an insurer are *willingness and promptness in claims payment*. Some insurance forms are better drawn for the purposes of the insured than are others, but interpretation is always necessary. The willingness of the insurer to interpret in accordance with the insured's sound needs for insurance protection is an important service. Speedy payment of claims is another desideratum and depends on the quality and quantity of the insurer's claim forces.

Loss reduction is another important service. In addition to the engineering service discussed in earlier chapters, it includes the handling of claims in a way that will hold down their net costs.

The final service to consider is *advice in static risk management*. Insurer's sales representatives are the primary source of this service, when it is provided. However, many sales representatives are not willing and able to provide such service, and insurance buyers are not always receptive to it when it is available. Of course, the risk manager's office should itself be continually growing in competence in this area.

REVIEW AND DISCUSSION QUESTIONS

1. To what extent is it true that "the two selections (of sales representative and of insurance company) are not tied together; given one, some range of choice remains available for the other"? When is it not true?

2. What considerations bear specifically on the particular problem of deciding whether a given line of insurance should be purchased from a specialty insurer or a general writing insurer?

3. Explain why the risk manager has an interest in the state of domicile of his insurer. How do you think risk managers regard insurers domiciled in your home state? If you are unfamiliar with the information needed to provide an answer to this question, how could you find an answer?

4. What is the reasoning behind the advice to purchase insurance only from insurers licensed to do business in the home state of the insured? In spite of these arguments, why do some risk managers purchase coverage from nonadmitted inurers?

5. In what ways do the various marketing systems used in the insurance business parallel those in the clothing business? Discuss the effectiveness of each insurance marketing system in terms of (*a*) premium volume, (*b*) segments of the market in which they operate, and (*c*) their current rate of growth.

6. In what respects are brokerage operations in insurance different from those in other businesses? In what respects are they similar? (Be especially careful on this one!)

7. To what extent should the risk manager concern himself with the ownership, organizational structure, and the marketing system of his prospective insurer?

8. When should risk managers use standard forms of insurance? What are some of the problems associated with the development of standard forms? What are some of the difficulties faced by risk managers in handling insurance needs with standard forms?

9. What can a risk manager do to make an otherwise unacceptable risk acceptable to a given underwriter? What underwriting factors are outside of the control of the risk manager? Why might one insurer accept a risk that another might reject?

10. Explain the following statement: "Accommodation writings . . . are not usual among insurers using direct sales representatives, and even more unusual among direct writing insurers." Are there exceptions to this statement?

11. How does the risk manager prepare himself for an opportunity to take advantage of accommodation writings should the need arise? Does the prepara-

tion for such an opportunity cost the risk manager anything? If so, is the opportunity worth the cost? Discuss.

12. If the risk manager finds that the insurer is willing to undertake his risk, what further interests should the risk manager have in his insurer's underwriting standards? Where is he likely to get the information to satisfy these interests?

13. To what extent is state supervision of insurance companies helpful to the risk manager in his effort to evaluate the financial soundness of a prospective insurer?

14. How are the number and timing of financial failures among insurance companies affected by state regulation of insurance company affairs?

15. How important to the risk manager are the rules of thumb that (*a*) premiums written in a year by a fire insurer should not exceed policyholders' surplus and (*b*) premiums written in a year by a casualty insurer should not exceed twice its policyholders' surplus? The text presented no rule of thumb for life insurers. Why?

16. How can the amount of surplus needed to assure the financial solvency of an insurer be measured? What information must the risk manager have about the insurer and what technical knowledge about insurance accounting and finance does he need to have to appraise the financial condition of his insurer? Where and how can he get this information and technical knowledge?

17. Are the reserves maintained by life insurers more reliable than those of property and liability insurers in measuring the solvency of the insurer? Explain your answer.

18. How important is the concept of "cash flow" in measuring the financial soundness of an insurer?

19. How does insurance accounting differ from the normal rules and procedures in modern accounting? Distinguish between an insurer's statutory profit (or loss) and its trade profit (or loss) from underwriting. How do the Best's reports differ from those used by the Superintendent of Insurance of New York? Which version is the more useful for the risk manager?

20. Why do you suppose the regulations (state) allow considerable deferral of charges in life insurance accounting but not in property and liability insurance accounting? How is this deferral accomplished? Why do some life insurers fail to take advantage of this allowance, i.e., why do they want to hold down the size of their surplus?

21. The adequacy of a liability insurer's claim reserve depends upon the ability and willingness of the insurer's management to allow all of the pertinent factors to be reflected in this reserve. What are these pertinent factors, and how can the risk manager judge the insurer's performance in this regard?

22. What is the best *single* guide to the financial future of an insurer? What other factors are important?

23. Aside from a guide to the financial solvency of his insurer, can you see any other reason why the risk manager might be interested in the claims' reserve practices of his insurer?

24. Aside from the underwriting practices and the financial soundness of prospective inurers, the risk manager is interested in how these insurers measure up in terms of services provided. What are the dimensions to be measured in this regard? How can the risk manager get the information necessary to measure these dimensions?

25. What is encompassed in the idea of "insurance service" offered by an insurer? What are the controlling factors on this service?

26. Are differences between the coverage which the buyer desired and the coverage which his insurance cover provides inevitable? Why? (Are there any reasons beyond those mentioned in this chapter?)

27. The difference between the coverage intended under marine insurance policies issued by underwriters at Lloyd's, London, and the coverage actually provided by these policies is considered to be the smallest difference of this kind found anywhere in the insurance world. How has this result been achieved? At what cost has it been achieved?

28. What are the arguments behind the assertion, "What the insured wants, of course, is an insurer willing to pay for losses of the kinds and amounts which he intended to have covered under his policy, no more, and certainly no less"?

29. Some paragraphs after the statement quoted in question 28, the following appears: "To repeat, what the buyer wants is an insurer whose interpretation of the cover coincides as nearly as possible with his interpretation." (*a*) Is this actually in the nature of a "repetition" of the earlier statement, or does the second sentence say something different than the first one? Explain. (*b*) In any event, what must the buyer do to achieve consonance between his and his insurer's understanding of the nature of the coverage he has purchased?

30. Which would you consider more important from the buyer's point of view: That his insurers agree with his interpretation of his covers, or that the courts do? Explain.

31. Why might an insurer that is willing to pay a claim yet delay in paying it? What should the risk manager do about this problem? Can it always be overcome?

32. "The good claims man is quickly promoted to an inside job, leaving the field barren." Is this a good policy on the part of management in claims adjustment organizations? Why or why not?

33. Would you rather have your claims adjusted by an employee of the insurer, by an employee of an adjustment company controlled by many insurers, or by an independent or free-lance adjuster—or by a combination of these? Explain.

34. " 'Seek first a good agent, broker, or other adviser for your insurance program, and all else that can be will be added to you,' is good advice for most insurance buyers." (*a*) Why is this good advice? (*b*) What are the things which can *not* "be added to you," even with good advisers? (*c*) The statement refers to "most" insurance buyers. Should this read "all"? Why or why not?

35. Summarize the qualities of an insuring organization which determine its desirability as an insurer.

Chapter 17

THE INSURANCE MARKET:
PRICING AND COSTS

The services obtained in the insurance market must be paid for. If, in the long run and over the mass of insureds, they are not paid for in full, they cannot continue to be delivered. But this is *not* to say that every insurance buyer gets just what he pays for, even in the long run. The same set of services does not necessarily cost the same from different insurers. And even when identical services are purchased from the same insurer, net costs of providing them may be different for different insureds— differences in the charged premiums do not always equal differences in the average costs of rendering the same services to different insureds. The buyer's objective is, of course, to obtain maximum service at minimum cost, but what does *that* mean?

RATES AND PREMIUMS

State laws require that insurance rates shall be adequate, not excessive, and not unfairly discriminatory. Such a statement misdirects attention because it is actually the premiums that should be adequate, not excessive, and equitable (not unfairly discriminatory). Rates are merely a means to an end. What the insurance buyer pays and what the insurance company receives is a premium. Premiums, therefore, constitute the cost to the buyers and the income to the company.

Equity

Premiums are expected to be "equitable," that is, each insured is expected to contribute to the premium income of the insurer roughly in proportion as his exposures contribute to the claims and underwriting expenses (on an "average" or "long-run" basis) of the insurer.

Premiums are commonly determined by multiplying the rate times a quantity called the rate base, so both the rate and the rate base affect the premium. This leads to difficulties and inequities in pricing insurance. Some few premiums are developed without applying a rate to a rate base. This is essentially true of the premiums for automobile liability insurance. Premiums for the minimum amounts of insurance offered are reached directly from loss statistics and are not "per" anything. Premiums for additional amounts of insurance are also determined directly, not by multiplying a rate times anything. When this direct method is used, the problem becomes one of arriving at equitable (and adequate and non-excessive) premiums directly, but this approach is just about as difficult as using rates and rate bases. Some premiums are established by using a combination of both methods, with the difficulties inherent in each.

Rate Bases. The most familiar type of rate base is the amount of insurance. Premiums in life insurance and fire insurance traditionally have been quoted as "so much per $X of insurance." The usual value of this X in life insurance is 1,000; in fire insurance it is 100.

More recently, life insurers have adopted pricing methods that vary the rate per $1,000 according to the number of thousands purchased. One major reason for this innovation has been that contracts of medium size have not lapsed as readily as contracts of smaller size. Since the major expenses other than claims are incurred when a policy is initiated, the longer the insurance stays in force, the smaller will be the portion of total premium income allocated to pay these expenses.

For years, fire insurers have had to devise rating systems to deal with even more difficult problems relating to the quantity of insurance purchased. Consider the following: In a certain territory, the windstorm insurance per $100 of insurance is 19 cents. In the very same area, the rate for the Extended Coverage endorsement to a fire policy is 17 cents per $100 of insurance. But the Extended Coverage endorsement covers all the same losses as windstorm insurance and covers most losses by explosion, riot, aircraft, and a few other perils besides!

Can these *rates* be said to be equitable? Their rationale lies in the equity of the *premiums* they produce. Typically, householders who bought windstorm insurance bought face amounts of from $2,000 to $5,000—paying, at the 19-cent annual rate, from $3.80 to $9.50. But the underwriting rules make it necessary to buy Extended Coverage insurance in an amount equal to the fire insurance on the same property (or settle for only partial payment on losses, large or small). Since the same householders typically bought fire insurance in amounts like $12,000–$18,000, their Extended Coverage premium, at the 17-cent rate, was $20.40–$30.60.

This *higher premium* has made it equitable to offer more coverage at a *lower rate.* But, of course, the premiums as well as the rates would be inequitable for the man who bought $15,000 of fire and windstorm insurance rather than $15,000 of fire and Extended Coverage insurance. Any buyer would be foolish to do so, but (1) most insurance buyers would not know about the rate differential and not *every* agent would tell them about it, and (2) while the error here, in this elementary situation, is patent to most persons with any acquaintance with insurance, there are more complicated situations in which exactly the same type of error occurs repeatedly. Indeed, hundreds of agents and consultants can report having seen a failure to use the reduced rate contribution (or coinsurance) clause in insurance programs that met the requirements of the clause; the cost of such failure commonly runs from 20 to 40 per cent of the total fire and Extended Coverage premium. And to most persons with a modicum of knowledge of insurance covers for business, this error is almost as inexcusable as the purchase of a large amount of windstorm insurance instead of the Extended Coverage endorsement. Beyond these errors are others that can be discovered only after considerable search by persons thoroughly familiar with insurance covers, markets, and rate-making techniques.

Judgment in Rating. In the previous section some rate differentials were explained on logical bases that are supportable by statistics. But no rate or premium is ever based on statistics alone. Even life insurance rates, which have the most statistically reliable base of all insurance rates, contain several judgment factors. Actual mortality experience does not increase smoothly from year to year as the ages of the persons observed increase, so actuaries' judgments as to proper methods of "smoothing the curve" have been employed; furthermore, as a matter of caution and to eliminate some technical difficulties in setting up reserves, actual experience is "loaded" (that is, estimations of claims rates are stepped up) before being published in official mortality tables; finally, life insurance rates actually charged must allow not only for mortality but also for lapses and surrenders, investment earnings (interest rates), and company operating expenses, each for many years into the future. Clearly, judgment factors enter into life insurance rates!

In other lines of insurance, judgment plays an even greater part in rate making. Of course, the shorter time periods covered in contracts issued in other lines of insurance (excluding noncancellable, guaranteed renewable health insurance) make it generally unnecessary for their rate makers to peer so far into the future. But claims statistics in these lines provide much less reliable bases than are found in life insurance. Hence, judgment must enter into property and liability insurance rate making at every step— from selection of the classification systems used in recording claims, through determination of the amount of reliance to place on yearly variations in claims experience, to final promulgation of the rate with one eye on assumed level of operating costs and the other on premiums that competitors are changing.

Finally, in rating schemes applied to insurance buyers with many exposures to cover and much money to spend, judgment factors are specifically built in; these systems provide for modification of rates according to the insured's own loss experience—past *and prospective.*

Statistics in Rate Making. Outside life insurance, the principal role of statistics in insurance rate making is in setting rate levels. If an entire class of insurance in a particular territory has been producing inadequate or excessive profits over a period of time, the entire set of rates is likely to be moved up or down; this is a change in the rate *level.* Usually such a change is based primarily on statistics, but a judgment factor may be introduced to allow for trends or for obvious changes in clearly relevant exogenous factors. (Among exogenous factors that have been used are legislative changes in benefits provided under workmen's compensation laws and the introduction of automobile gasoline rationing after America's entry into World War II.) Except in fire and allied lines insurance, a change in rate level is usually accompanied by a restudy and readjustment in the relationships between individual rates. In fire and allied lines insurance, the determination of relationships between individual rates is handled by methods different from those used in the determination of rate levels. Next to life insurance, statistics have the most effect on rate making in the two major forms of disability insurance (health insurance and workmen's compensation) and in crop insurance, followed by liability insurance, particularly automobile liability, and then by other lines of casualty insurance. Statistics have the least effect on rates in those lines in which few policies are written or, if a large number of policies are written, in which the exposures protected have little homogeneity. (Examples are found among the inland marine covers, most surety forms, and fire and allied lines policies for business and industrial insureds.)

Merit vs. Class Rates. Rating methods are often categorized according to whether they produce "class" (or "manual") rates or "merit" rates. The distinction is according to whether activities or conditions within the control of or peculiar to the individual insured can directly affect his individual rate. A classic example of a class rate is the windstorm insurance rate for dwellings. All one- to four-family dwellings in a single rating territory ordinarily have the same rate for windstorm (and usually also for Extended Coverage) insurance. The "cost plus" premium available to some workmen's compensation insureds provides a classic example of merit rating. In this case, a large business can elect to have its premium determined under "retrospective rating" under which it is charged for the actual losses plus a stated rate for the insurer's operating expenses and an insurance charge to reflect both the credibility of the insured's experience and the maximum limits on losses chargeable to the insured.

Between these two extremes are the varying degrees of influence that the hazards faced by an individual insured have on his individual rate for insurance. A kind of semantic game is sometimes played by professional students of insurance, in which one challenges another to state whether a particular rating method produces "class" or "merit" rates. "Schedule" rating causes the most uncertainty. For example, an insured who installs a burglar alarm of approved type pays a lower premium for his Open Stock Burglary insurance than does an insured whose exposure is the same except for the burglar alarm. Query: Do the discounts for approved burglar alarms represent recognition of individual loss prevention effort (and hence constitute merit rating), or is this rating differential merely a refinement of class rating that differentiates "stores with burglar alarms" as one class and "stores without burglar alarms" as another class, just as class rating in fire insurance distinguishes between "frame dwellings" and "brick dwellings"?

This taxonomic problem is of little direct interest to practicing risk managers, but its existence indicates that the rates for each risk manager's business are in varying degrees dependent on loss experience or conditions within that individual business, with conversely varying degrees of dependence on conditions outside that business. Clearly, the insurance premiums that a particular business has to pay will vary according to both hazards within the business and those within a class of businesses and in accordance with the extent to which each set of hazards is relied upon in the development of the rates. This suggests again that there may be differences in rates that are not a matter of "he who pays less, gets less, and he who gets more, pays more."

Adequacy (and Non-excessiveness)

The conclusion just drawn—that there is not necessarily a direct relation between benefits and costs, which is to say, that there are varying margins between what insurers receive and what they pay out—clearly implies that the sophisticated risk manager will try to take some advantage of these differences. And so he will. But it is best to condition this point with a reminder of a statement made in the preceding chapter: an insured who consistently gets more from an insurer than he pays for will sooner or later either have to start paying more (sometimes considerably more) or be without an insurer. Of course, an insured who consistently overpays an insurer for benefits received should eventually either be paying less or see to it that insurers who overcharge him will have to get along without him among their insureds.

Adequacy over Time. Generally accepted axioms of sound competitive underwriting include the following: An underwriter should never expect to recoup past losses from future premiums. The rule is that each policy period is expected to stand on its own; bad experience may indicate that future premiums should be higher so that the future periods can produce an adequate profit level *for themselves,* but not for the past periods as well. If underwriters are to be expected to apply this rule when there are underwriting losses during a given period, then the insureds surely should expect the rule to be applied also when there are underwriting profits for a given period—future underwriting losses should not be planned to balance past underwriting gains.

One exception may appear to apply to this rule, but the appearance is deceiving. Exceptionally large losses (the official term in fire and allied lines insurance is "catastrophes") are too irregular in occurrence and too important in effect to be charged solely to the year (or sometimes even the two- or three-year period) in which they happen to occur. To preserve some degree of stability in rates (a necessary feature if insureds are to be able to plan their future expense and cash budgets ahead), the cost of extremely large losses must be spread out over several policy periods, that is, over several successive premiums. But the allowance set up in each premium to cover catastrophic losses should itself not be unduly affected by individual catastrophes either. It should respond rather to estimates of the general level of catastrophes expected to be encountered over the span of several or many policy periods. In other words, the rule with respect to premium allowances for irregularly spaced large losses is the same as for regularly experienced losses except that it is to be applied to units of time containing more than one policy period and premium payment. In either case, each future time span is to be expected to stand on its own and not make up for past mistakes; the difference is in the length of time over which this result is expected to be achieved.

Adequacy in Amount. What constitutes an "adequate but not excessive" level of rates and premiums is, naturally, a subject of much dispute.[1] Many factors must be considered, of course: the extent that underwriting income is needed to attract additional outside capital or to provide funds to plow back into the growth of the insurer, the level and behavior of underwriting expenses and claims, the competitive situation in the insurance market, the public welfare (since these rates are state regulated, presumably for public benefit), and historical levels of profit. In negotiations between underwriter and risk manager, however, probably three of these factors are controlling: the expected level and behavior of underwriting expenses and claims, the competitive situation in the insurance market, and historical levels of profit.

If the underwriter sees a prospect of matching historical levels of profit,

---

[1] At one time (1921) a profit margin of 4–6 per cent in fire insurance rates gained recognition as a proper measure of adequacy without excessiveness. This margin, which has always been more of an ideal than a working principle, has since been subjected to considerable attack and some modification. The story is too long to relate here, but its principal ingredients are found in the *Proceedings of the National Convention of Insurance Commissioners, 1922,* pp. 19–29 of the section on Adjourned Session of the 1921 meeting; and *Proceedings of the National Association of Insurance Commissioners, 1946,* p. 411, and *1949,* pp. 258–90. (The "Convention" and the "Association" are the same organization. The name was changed in December, 1935.) No comparable consensus on margins in other lines has ever been reached.

he will nearly always be satisfied that the rate and premium are adequate (and not excessive). Pressure from competition may make him willing to accept less. His expectations as to his underwriting expenses and claims generally establish the floor on what he is willing to accept, of course, although that floor is not necessarily set exactly at the level of this expectation. Depending on competitive conditions, this floor may be above, or sometimes even slightly below, his expectation as to *total* costs and claims on the transaction in question; coverage of *marginal* costs (including claims) may be sufficient.

Governmental Regulation

Rates in all lines of insurance except life and marine are generally regulated by the states. In nearly all the states this means that either the rate or the system for determining it (as in experience rating) must be approved by the insurance commissioner's office before it is used.[2]

Effects of Regulation. Rate regulation naturally puts considerable restriction on the ability of the risk manager to negotiate for lower rates and premiums. However, the restriction is not always so great as would appear at first glance. For one thing, there is the non-admitted, and hence unregulated market. For another, there are those judgment factors which are built into some approved rating systems. And sometimes there are varying ways to interpret the rules on how a rate is to be applied. Although these modifying factors are principally of benefit to larger businesses, sometimes moderate-sized businesses may also benefit from them; again, much depends on the competitive situation and the desirability of the business to the underwriter (which latter means, principally, his expectation as to costs and claims on it).

Although rates are regulated, this does not mean that rates of all insurers are identical. In most states, insurers who have reasonable prospects of lower costs or claims than others can get approval for lower rates. The risk manager, however, should watch for two things: differences in premiums as distinguished from differences in rates and differences in services received for differences in premiums paid. (While he is at it, he should also keep his eyes open for the converse situations, which appear with even greater frequency: differences in premiums without differences in rates; and differences in services received without differences in premiums paid.)

Buyers' Effect on Regulation. No affected citizen should always take

---

[2] At the time this is written, this approach to rate regulation, known as "prior approval," is under attack by several important segments of the insurance industry. Other segments of the industry and the relevant committee of the National Association of Insurance Commissioners (which is merely a consultative and advisory body) defend the present system. The change proposed is to the system known as "subsequent disapproval," which is used in California. Under this system, rates may be used immediately upon filing with the commissioner's office (or, perhaps, shortly thereafter) unless and until they are disapproved.

laws and governmental regulations for granted. Risk managers have the usual citizen's (and taxpayer's) privilege and obligation to study, comment upon, and attempt to get improvement in the efficiency and actions of public officeholders. The rules of a democratic government are not an irrevocable *faite accompli*. Of course, the active citizens in a democratic society also have the serious obligation not to harm society as a whole by their actions, successful or otherwise. ("What is good for us is good for the country," is equally fallacious reasoning whether that "us" is *small* or *large*. One person, a hundred and fifty million persons, or any other fraction of the whole citizenry, can wreak social damage by setting its own interests paramount over those of the rest of us.)

A special obligation of those who seek changes in the way technical matters are handled is to start with some understanding of the techniques and technical problems involved. Two simple examples from rate making in automobile liability insurance illustrate the point:

1. Citizens, particularly newspaper editors, in Miami, Florida, complained about high auto liability insurance rates in their county. One of their arguments was that Miami was getting charged for "all those accidents" caused by "tourists" and other visitors, of whom their city had (fortunately for its income!) a great many. It was not until later that the complainants learned that liability claims are charged against the experience of the territory where the insured auto is principally garaged, not the territory in which the accident occurs.

2. Periodically, someone proposes that auto rates be based, at least in part, on mileage driven during the policy period. This certainly appears a rational basis for measuring relative exposures to collision and liability loss. The difficulty is how insurers can distinguish honest mileage reports from dishonest ones. (Mileage indicators are not tamper proof.) For a short space of time some decades ago, rates were dependent in part on whether the car was driven more or less than 7,500 miles a year. Experience quickly showed that, according to the statements of buyers of automobile insurance, practically no one in the United States drove more than 7,500 miles a year—despite the fact that this distance was then believed by highway, traffic, and other experts to be only slightly more than the national average for private passenger cars. This mileage classification system was quickly dropped.

BENEFITS VS. PREMIUMS

Yes, rates and premiums may vary; the question still remains: Do benefits vary with them? And suppose a higher premium means greater benefits; are the benefits sufficiently greater to justify the difference in premium?

Benefit Factors in Premiums

What does or can an insurer do with premium money that may provide a direct benefit for an insured? Three ways in which an insurer may use premium money will be considered: He may use it (1) to indemnify in-

sureds for losses, (2) to pay other operating expenses of the insurer, or
(3) to build a margin for profit and contingencies. In the terminology of
insurance accounting these three are, respectively, claims, claims and adjustment expense and underwriting expenses, and underwriting profit. The
standard major categories of underwriting expenses are acquisition expense (which may be translated as marketing expense); taxes, licenses,
and fees (exclusive of income taxes); and general expenses (but again excluding income taxes).

Claims. The benefits that an insured receives by having his losses indemnified by an insurer have been a major topic of many chapters of this
book. The concern here, however, is with one additional feature of these
benefits, a feature that can be identified as follows: It is assumed that, other
things being equal, the risk manager desires his indemnity benefits to be
as large as possible in relation to premiums paid. Put another way, he prefers
that the insurer's mark-up over dollars delivered in claims be as low as
possible.

Claims Adjustment Expense. In identifying the direct benefits provided
to an insured by the insurer's expenditures for claims adjustment, a separation immediately needs to be made between third-party claims and first-
party claims.

Liability and workmen's compensation insurance deal with third-party
claims, that is, with claims for losses by persons who are not one of the
two parties to the insurance contract. When a liability or workmen's compensation claim is brought against an individual or organization, certain
costs are incurred in dealing with it. When an insurer takes care of any of
these costs (whether in cash or in kind), the insured receives a direct
benefit.

In losses in which insurance claims adjustment is strictly between the
insured and his insurer, claims adjustment costs that would not be present
in an uninsured situation are added. Communication between the insured
and his insurer, and record keeping by the insurer, are net additions over
the cost of the uninsured loss and provide no direct benefit to the insured.

On the other hand, as has been noted previously, some loss reduction
benefits can arise from claims adjustment activities of an insurer. To the
extent that these activities reduce uninsured loss that the insured otherwise
would have borne himself, a direct benefit clearly is involved.[3]

Acquisition Expense. The key to any direct benefit that an insured may
receive from his insurer's expenditure on acquisition (i.e., sales or marketing) expense is found in a statement made in the preceding chapter: "Only
the sales personnel and the special agents are expected to consider the efficiency of the insured's collection of policies. If they do not, it is exceptional

---

[3] If loss reduction to the insurer produces lower premiums to the insured, that is a
direct benefit, of course. But it is a benefit recognized in cost comparisons, as discussed
earlier in the chapter, rather than in benefit comparisons, the present subject.

for anyone else on the insurer's side to do so." The proposition that the cost of services that sales representatives provide for their customers must be covered by remuneration received (and so must in some way be limited by that remuneration) is sufficiently axiomatic to serve as the basis for a generalization: More risk management advice should be available from sales representatives who make more money per sale. Three important limitations, however, are imposed on this proposition.

First, as has been noted before, not every sales representative who is paid enough to cover the cost of this service is willing or even able to provide it.

Second, not all expenditures on acquisition expense are available to cover customer service of this kind. Part of the commission paid to independent agents is intended and needed to cover the cost of clerical work: policy writing, billing and collecting, and keeping of agency accounts. To the extent that an insurer's higher acquisition costs are used to cover these expenses, no direct benefit accrues to the insured.

Third, *some* risk management advice is on occasion given by insurance personnel other than sales representatives.

It should also be noted that a sales representative may assist in claims adjustments between the insured and the insurer. This assistance may take the form of actual claims settlement by the agent, of agency assistance in getting claims paid in cases of debate as to amount or coverage, or of agency action as a simple channel of communication between the claimant insured and the insurer or claims adjuster.

Some sales representatives also provide loss prevention advice, particularly on preventive activities that have a direct and immediate effect on an insured's premiums (such as installation of approved burglar alarm or appropriate types of fire extinguishers).

Taxes and General Expenses. Expenditures on taxes, licenses, and fees provide no direct benefit to an insured. General underwriting expenses include provision for loss reduction activities. To some extent, any of the services discussed in the previous chapter may appear in this group of expenses.

Balancing Benefits and Premiums

The chain from specific premiums paid by a particular insured to expenditures on specific benefits received by that same insured is at best tenuous. Premiums as a whole are used for claims and expenses as a whole. The first question is, What is the total allocation of these expenditures to finance services of direct benefit to insureds? The next question is, What portion of these total expenditures can be expected to be available to provide these services to a particular insured? Then, to what extent will the availability of money for services be translated into services actually rendered? Finally, to what extent are the rendered services of actual value to this particular insured?

Claims. Company A has an over-all claims ratio (ratio of claims incurred to premiums earned) of 67 per cent; the ratio for Company B is 53 per cent. What does this mean? Nothing, if A and B are writing different lines of insurance. Typical claims ratios in workmen's compensation are 63–68 per cent; in fire insurance, typical ratios are 50–55 per cent; in fidelity bonding, they are 32–37 per cent.

Suppose attention is directed to a single line—say, workmen's compensation insurance. Suppose Company C has a 62 per cent ratio, Company D a ratio of 69 per cent. Does this give any more information? Perhaps not. It is a well-known phenomenon in workmen's compensation that small businesses, particularly service businesses and small manufacturers, have, as a class, a poorer work injury record than do large businesses. Consider further what happens in retrospective rating (used by the larger insureds). Each insured pays for his own losses (usually up to some maximum figure) plus a fee for the insurer's overhead—a "cost plus" type of contract. What happens if the insurer provides an effective loss prevention service? Claims go down, and premiums do too—but the fee for overhead does not. The insurer's claims ratio goes down!

Nonetheless, useful information sometimes can be obtained from comparisons of claims ratios. Consider two real insurance companies, which we shall call X and Y. First, we have the general information that X writes workmen's compensation on a wide variety of businesses, large and small; Y specializes in writing this cover for large employers, and its principal sales pitch is how it reduces premium costs by providing efficient loss prevention engineering service. Then we discover that the workmen's compensation claims ratio for X regularly runs around 62 per cent; for Y, around 68 per cent. Now Y offers to write our workmen's compensation insurance at a premium 15 per cent below the premium of X.

To come out at its own average claims ratios, X would need to have 62 cents in losses per $1.00 of premium. On the same exposure, Y is asking for only 85 cents in premium; 68 per cent of this is approximately 58 cents in claims, that is, the loss prevention aid received from Y must reduce compensation payments to our employees by about 6 per cent to meet Y's usual ratio. Unless we already have a phenomenally good record, this much improvement is easily feasible. This is reassuring, because it indicates that Y could stick to its bargain (not cancelling or rewriting the contract in mid-term) without having to resort to such practices as tightening up on claims payments or battling continually with our production managers over bigger improvements in our loss prevention measures. Put another way, the indication is that Y is making a *bona fide* offer, not a "teaser" or "loss leader" aimed solely at getting our name on the books with the hope of recouping later for initial losses. (Note the assumption, however, that the offer from X was itself reasonable and *bona fide;* the reasoning has been purely by comparison between the two. If, on the contrary, X's offer represented pure fishing for business, "any business," then Y's was even more so.)

More difficult is the following situation, also based on real companies. Company R writes its fire insurance in some territories at standard rates with a policyholders' dividend at the end of the policy year, and in others at an originally discounted rate. This company's claims ratio on premiums before policyholders' dividends runs around 38 per cent. When premiums after policyholders' dividends are considered, this ratio jumps to about 42 per cent. Company S does not issue participating policies, and its claims ratio runs around 51 per cent. The fire rates of Company R, net after dividends, run about 10 per cent less than the rates of Company S. Both companies have been clearing a net margin in fire insurance ranging from 1 to 4 per cent of premiums (figuring on a "trade" basis[4] and, in Company R, on premiums after policyholders' dividends).

The claims ratios and relative rate levels of the two companies suggest that for every $1.00 that Company R pays in claims, Company S (which charges about 11 per cent more) pays $1.52. This at least raises a question about the bargain offered in the discounted rates. The question is, of course, are Company S's higher claims payments made to businesses like that of the risk manager's? Perhaps these higher payments are accounted for by claims paid on hazardous tenements, rundown factories, and ancient hotels, or perhaps they are paid on a multitude of small losses reported by insureds who believe that an insurance policy should be regularly milked, like a cow. In short, the question is: Is the higher claims ratio to be accounted for on the basis of a liberal claims policy or of loose underwriting?

Since S's claims ratio is actually a little lower than that of most fire insurers, and S has avoided net losses on its fire underwriting (trade basis), the hypothesis of loose underwriting is unsupported. It therefore appears that R's claims policy or its underwriting practice is strict; either way, its lower premiums indicate that it is giving something less in services to some insurance buyers.[5]

In general, claims ratios must first be adjusted for reductions in premiums by policyholders' dividends. After this adjustment, it is usually more desirable that an insurer have a high claims ratio than a low one—or, more accurately, that the mark-up in premium to cover expenses and profit be small rather than large. This is true, however, only to the extent that the

---

[4] See chap. 16.

[5] The conclusion given above is presented for illustrative purposes only. Actually another possible explanation would have to be checked out before this conclusion could properly be drawn: Were R's writings heavily concentrated in lines that all insurers found highly profitable? In fire insurance, this would mean insurance on dwellings, for they constitute the only class that would have produced both a nice underwriting profit and a premium volume sufficient to sustain a large fire insurance operation. (R and S each earned around $25 million a year in fire insurance premiums during the years in question.)

mark-up is sufficient to cover expenses—so that the insurer's financial position is protected. And direct comparison between two companies must take into consideration differences between the kinds of insurance and the types of insureds they write.

Expenses in General.[6] One might suppose that an unusually low expense ratio would indicate that the insurer could not be providing much in auxiliary services, while higher ratios would be characteristic of insurers who provided large amounts of auxiliary benefits.[7] These conclusions would presumably be true, "other things being equal." But "other things" of consequence are so seldom "equal" that different expense ratios rarely indicate anything about relative expenditures on auxiliary benefits. The effects of two of these unequal factors provide an illustration of what can happen.

First, reinsurance transactions change both the total expense ratio and the relative size of the ratios for particular expense categories. The nature of these changes varies according to the type of reinsurance agreement.[8] However, just a single example will illustrate some of the changes that can occur. The type of agreement used here is known as an "excess line" treaty. Under an excess line treaty, the company that originates the business (that is, writes insurance protection for a member of the non-insurance public) shares its larger policies with one or more other companies, the reinsurers. In each treaty the size of each reinsurer's share varies with the size of the original policy. Claims, claims expense, and premiums are all divided according to the established share.[9]

Because reinsurers want to encourage originating insurers to do business with them, they allow a commission on reinsured business. On desirable business the commission is set to provide the originating insurer some profit over its expenses (such as sales commissions and premium taxes). This allowance is entered as "Commissions and Brokerage expense" by both the reinsurer and the reinsured. For the reinsured, the amount is entered as an offsetting, or negative, item against its other expenses, of course. Compare two cases. In each instance the originating insurers shows $1,000 in "net" premiums written, that is, in premiums that are *not* reinsured.[10] But Com-

---

[6] Claims payments are not usually termed "expenses" in insurance finance. And the term "underwriting expenses" is applied to "expenses" of the insuring operations, except claims adjustment expenses.

[7] Note that the text does *not* say that higher ratios would *indicate* insurers who provided larger amounts of auxiliary benefits.

[8] Reinsurance agreements are called "treaties," presumably because they were originally contracts between insurers in different countries.

[9] The insured under the original policy is not a party to the reinsurance agreement, however. The only contract he can enforce is his policy with the originating insurer, which remains fully responsible to the insured for fulfilment of its promises in that policy.

[10] Business that is not reinsured is said to be "retained by the company for [or, on] its own account."

pany A has written an additional $250 of reinsured premium, while Company B has written an additional $1,000. In each case the following assumptions are used. (The figures are realistic for many companies.)

1. Acquisition expenses (principally commissions and brokerage) incurred on sales to the general public are 30 per cent of all premiums written.
2. Taxes, licenses, and fees (principally premium taxes) for all business written for the general public equal 2 per cent of all premiums written.
3. The general costs of an organization large enough to manage $1,000 of premiums on its own account are a flat $130.
4. Each dollar of reinsured premium handled by an originating insurer costs an additional 4 cents in underwriting expense beyond the costs listed above.
5. Commission paid by reinsurers is 40 per cent.

COMPANY A	PREMIUMS	COMPANY B
$1,250	Gross premiums	$2,000
250	Reinsurance ceded	1,000
$1,000 (100.0%)	Net premiums	$1,000 (100.0%)
	EXPENSES	
	Acquisition expenses incurred	
$ 375	Gross	$ 600
100	Commission received	400
$ 275 (27.5%)	Net	$ 200 (20.0%)
25 (2.5%)	Taxes, licenses, and fees	40 (4.0%)
140 (13.5%)	Other underwriting expenses	170 (15.0%)
$ 440 (44.0%)	Total underwriting expenses	$ 410 (41.0%)

Note both the difference in total expense ratio (44 versus 41 per cent) and in the ratios for particular expense categories, particularly acquisition expense. Then consider the result if an insurer should, under the assumption given, write $15,000 in premiums, ceding $14,000. Acquisition expense would become a negative figure ($4,500 gross minus $5,600 commission received); taxes, licenses, and fees would be $300; "other" expenses would be $690; and total "expenses" would be shown as *minus* $110! Many small insurers do achieve a negative "expense" figure in this way. Such insurers are simply acting as sales agencies for their reinsurers, and, as is expected in any well-run independent sales agency, their commissions received exceed their total operating expenses. But since these particular agencies are organized and licensed as insurance companies, the commissions they receive are recorded as offsets to expense rather than as income received. Clearly, their net expense ratios literally mean "less than nothing at all."

A second illustration of factors affecting expense ratios can be derived from the results achieved by insurers who are able to cut the number of dollars needed to produce and handle a given amount of insurance protection and cut premiums accordingly. Suppose an insurer has the following outlays for each $100 in premiums: claims $53, claims expense $10, acquisition $25, taxes $1, general expenses $9; leaving a profit margin of $2. Then suppose it transfers some record keeping, policy writing, and billing operations from agency responsibility to home office operation. Let the cost of the transferred operations be $5 when performed on a typewriter in an agency office but only $2 when done by electronic equipment in the home office. The premium needed to provide the same net return to both the agent and the insurer is found by adding $63 for claims and claims expense plus $20 for acquisition plus $1 for taxes[11] plus $11 for general expenses plus $2 for the insurer's profit margin. The new premium is $97.[12] Formerly, total underwriting expenses came to 35 per cent of premium. Now they amount to just under 33 per cent and are distributed differently among the categories.

It should also be noted that, despite the adoption of regulations for uniform accounting in insurers' official reports, differences in cost accounting procedures as well as differences in organization of operations can cause costs to be assigned to different categories.[13] When the difference is purely a matter of cost allocation, the total expense ratio should not be affected, of course. But when the cost assignment involves allocation of a portion of home office expenses to the cost of claims adjustment, ratios for "*underwriting* expenses" are affected, for these are defined as excluding both claims and claims expense.

Claims Expense. With regard to the specific category, claims (or adjustment) expenses, the ratio of a particular insurer tells nothing worthwhile about the extent of its adjustment services. Claims expenses ratios run considerably higher when there are third-party claimants than when claims are confined to those of the insureds alone. But a claim expense ratio that is unusual for the type of insurance involved will probably be due either to reinsurance arrangements or to organizational peculiarities of the insurer. Many insurers write or cede reinsurance under treaties in which claims expenses are not shared proportionately with premiums. Some insurers have many claims settled by agents, whose payment comes under commissions and brokerage expense; some insurers regularly employ independent

---

[11] The small reduction in premium taxes resulting from the reduction in premium is ignored here for convenience.

[12] The reader is warned that this is not the way in which rating bureaus arrive at rates or premiums except, perhaps, for some workmen's compensation premiums. The method used in the text is justified because it deals with expense behavior in the instant case, something the bureau methods do not do.

[13] *Proceedings of the National Association of Insurance Commissioners, 1949*, pp. 42–125; *1950*, pp. 28, 68–91, 503, 512; *1951*, pp. 205–7, 423–39; *1952*, pp. 329, 801.

adjusters, whose charges for adjustment include overhead expenses which may be charged to the general expense category by insurers that do their own adjusting.

Acquisition Expenses. Of all the ratios for expenses, the acquisition cost ratio contains the most interest for the buyer. The initial assumption is that a higher acquisition expense ratio means greater service potential from the sales representative, and vice versa.

As has been seen, the net ratio of acquisition expenses to premiums, taken after commissions for reinsurance transactions have been recorded, can be quite different from the ratio in which the risk manager is interested: commissions paid to agents who sell to the general public taken as a ratio of premiums charged the general public. Fortunately, this latter ratio is computed by insurers and published in public sources.[14] The ratios are generally called the "ratios on direct premiums" because they relate to business done directly with the general public rather than to intercompany transactions. Typically, acquisition ratios on direct premiums are highest when sales are made through independent agents, not as high when direct representatives are used, and lowest when selling is direct from home or branch office to customer.[15] This differentiation accords in general with the natural assumption that availability of service from a sales force will vary roughly with the income-per-sale received by the force. Thus, when there is no local sales force, service would appear necessarily limited and acquisition costs are in fact lowest. Knowledge of the actual nature of some direct representation forces in property and liability insurance—of their organization and training, and of the bases of their income—strongly indicates an intent that these people are hired to *sell*. In particular, payment of little or no commission on renewal premiums shows that the representatives are expected to spend little effort on servicing policies already in force (except, of course, as it may lead to more new sales). On the other hand, contracts between insurers and independent agencies typically provide that commission percentages paid on renewals are the same as on new business. While the prime reason for this feature is that the insurers do not want agents to switch old business from one insurer to another just to get a "new" business commission, a potentially valuable by-result is that the agent can afford to spend considerable time taking care of old customers rather than looking for new ones. Indeed, a recurrent complaint in home offices is that in many agencies there comes a time when nearly all the effort is spent on

---

[14] Such as *Best's Fire and Casualty Aggregates and Averages* (annual) (New York: Alfred M. Best Co., Inc.).

[15] *Ibid.* Note however that Best's follows the usage common among insurance men, which is to apply the phrase, "direct writer" to any insurer that sells by *either* the direct representation or the direct sales method. "Direct writing" then refers to any system in which the insurer reaches the buying public through its own, rather than independent, oganizations or agencies.

conservation rather than expansion of business. Another result of level commissions is the higher acquisition expense ratio for insurers who use independent agents.

Of course, not every purchase from an agent makes the same contribution toward his ability to pay for services to insurers. Clearly, the size of the premium paid is an important factor. In addition, commission percentages vary—not all insurers pay the same percentage, and, even with a given insurer, the percentage varies with the line of insurance sold, the type of agency,[16] and the amount of underwriting profits that the insurer makes on business received through the agency. Nevertheless, when a buyer spends considerable premium money with an agency, and this premium money is more than he would have had to spend for a similar cover obtained elsewhere, equivalent useful services (beyond what he could get from the lower cost source) should be available from the agent.

Suppose these useful services *are* available. The next question is whether they would be worth their additional cost if they were received. No universal answer is possible: sometimes they are; sometimes they are not. One major factor to consider is the buyer's own sophistication in insurance, his ability to fend for himself. This, of course, is a relative, not an absolute, matter. Simple problems take simple solutions, and a little sophistication suffices. With extremely complex problems, even a very sophisticated buyer can make good use of outside advice for best results. The quality and quantity of aid needed naturally depend on the size of the gap between the buyer's knowledge and the complexity of his problems. Aid from less than the most expensive type of agency operation may be adequate when this gap is not large.

Ability of the buying organization to command attention at an insurer's home or branch office is another factor to consider. A buyer of sufficient importance can take his problems directly to an insurer's executives and administrators without an agency intermediary. Several direct-selling specialists in workmen's compensation insurance have been successful at making this approach work.

However, with some important buyers, a reverse effect appears. An experienced risk manager who works for an important buyer of insurance may wish to confer with the home office officials of his insurers, not to seek advice, but to explain to them what he wants. But so few American home offices are accustomed to providing underwriting services on a custom basis that he may have trouble getting the coverage he desires. Then the services of a sales intermediary, particularly a large agency or brokerage

---

[16] Some agency types are general agency, recording agency, and survey agent. Officially, a general agent obtains and writes business through subagents; a recording agent has no subagents but writes policies; a survey agent merely "surveys" risks and takes applications for insurance thereon, and the policies are written up in the insurer's own office. In practice, recording agents have often collected general agency commissions and survey agents have been paid as though they were "recording" and writing policies.

firm, may be worthwhile. Large intermediaries are familiar with custom covers and with the markets for them. Their premium volume makes these intermediaries highly influential in these markets, and their experience teaches them how to use this influence most effectively.[17]

To summarize, there does not appear to be a need for the services and costs of a sophisticated intermediary when (1) the insurance sophistication of the buyer is adequate to handle his problems and (2) the regular market is adequate to supply his needs.[18] If the disparity between the buyer's knowledge and problems is not great, some help is needed, but help that does not add much to premium cost may be sufficient. This help may be provided by lower-paid sales representatives or by occasional contacts with home office personnel. When there is considerable disparity between knowledge and problems, highly competent assistance is worth paying for. Underlying all these conclusions is one assumption, of course—that the buyer is always sophisticated enough to recognize how big the disparity between his knowledge and his problems is! And even to estimate this with some accuracy calls for a fair degree of knowledge about insurance and his business.

An additional note should be added for managers of small to medium-sized businesses. In these businesses, attempts by management to learn enough about insurance and static risk management to make outside advisers unnecessary are unlikely to be worthwhile. The profits lost because management time and attention are taken away from dynamic risks will ordinarily be greater than the premium costs that can be saved by dispensing with outside aid in static risk management.

Now suppose that the services which a good agent could provide are known to be worth their cost to a given business organization. One important question still remains: Will these services in fact be received? The difficulty is that not every agent (or other outside adviser) is "good" in the sense at issue here; indeed, the agents competent to plan and carry through a sound risk management program for a business are in the minority.

Six ingredients are necessary to effective receipt of good risk management service. Three of these ingredients must be supplied by the advising agency: knowledge of insurance, an organization adapted to processing information and producing recommendations, and willingness to spend the time and effort required. The other three ingredients must be provided by the buyer: knowledge of the business to be insured, willingness to provide the adviser with all the information he needs, and willingness to pay the price for advice. These mean that the buyer must have confidence in,

---

[17] Repeated use of their influence has made at least some of these intermediaries decidedly unpopular with many insurers. Thus they exemplify a little-recognized fact: being popular and having influence are not necessarily the same thing!

[18] Or he does not spend enough premium money to warrant the costs of a search beyond the regular market.

and spend time in conference with, the adviser. Inquiry among intelligent buyers of insurance, talks with likely candidates for the job of insurance adviser (agent, broker, or consultant), and even experimentation with the actual use of different advisers are the usual means of finding the right sources of outside help in static risk management.

A final note: While many of the more expensive agents do not deliver as much service as the buyer is paying for, some of the less expensive agents deliver more service than might ordinarily be expected from them in view of the commissions that they are being paid. Indeed, there appears to be a trend toward improving agency efficiency with some resulting premium savings for the insureds. These improvements are most often produced by a reduction in the amount of paperwork handled in agencies. This can be accomplished either by completely eliminating some operations (as happens when a single package policy replaces several formerly separate forms) or by transferring their site of performance from agencies to home offices (usually accompanied by a changeover from typewriter and [perhaps] bookkeeping machine operation to electronic data processing). Many independent agents oppose these changes, however, as reports from most of their Association meetings show. Much of their opposition arises from fear that their independence will be impaired—that their companies will acquire control, first over renewals and then over other dealings with insureds. Some of the opposition arises, however, from experience that the new arrangements may not reduce agency costs as much as agency commissions are reduced. Good management requires that agents keep many records about their insureds and about their own businesses, no matter what the companies do. Some increased bookkeeping by the companies can therefore represent duplication, rather than transfer, of paperwork, and so represent increased rather than decreased total operating cost.

Taxes and General Underwriting Expenses. The ratio of taxes, licenses, and fees to premiums is of no direct interest to insurance buyers. It is determined primarily by the premium taxes in the states in which the insurer operates and the relative amounts of reinsurance written and ceded. There are no direct benefits to the insured.

Two matters of interest about the category "general underwriting expenses": One is that most of the insurer's expenditures on loss prevention are assigned to this category. The other is that there is often a complementary relationship between these "general" expenses and the acquisition expenses.

One cannot tell from the published expense figures whether an insurer is spending much or little on loss prevention service. And if one could, the question of how much loss prevention service a particular insured could expect would remain unanswered. The only really significant point is this: In the few cases in which loss prevention expense is a particularly important item among an insurer's total expenditures, claims should be reduced. This combination of expenditure and prevention reduces the insurer's claims ratio and increases its ratio for general expenses. The classic example of this effect is found in the ratios of specialists in boiler and machinery insurance. General expense ratios on this line commonly exceed 30 per cent, compared with the 12 per cent figure that is usual for property and liability insurance in general. So, when loss prevention is a major part of the service rendered, a high ratio for general expenses may result, and it should not necessarily be considered disadvantageous.

The complementary relationship between general expenses and acquisition expense has already been noted several times. Salaried personnel in or from home or branch offices may be substituted for advice from agents; costs for paperwork may be transferred (preferably with a reduction) between agencies and company offices. The buyer is interested in the effects of these transfers on total costs and services. Total costs interest him in two ways—in their effect on his premiums and in their effect on the insurer's financial soundness; both these effects have already been discussed. The effects on services received have also been mentioned previously. Two distinct conditions may be identified. (1) The transfer of expenses from the acquisition to the general category represents only a transfer of mechanical functions, such as recordkeeping. (2) The transfer represents reduction or elimination of agency services, with servicing as well as recordkeeping transferred into the company office. Neither condition appears in a pure form very often, of course.

An example of the various relationships between the acquisition and the general expense ratios can be found by looking at the figures for different stock companies writing automobile bodily injury liability insurance. Table 17–1 shows one year's underwriting ratios for three different stock company groups. (A "company-group" is a collection of companies under one management. If the largest company is a stock company, the group is then a "stock company group.") These three groups were selected as follows: All the stock company groups were classified according to whether they marketed their services primarily through independent agents, through direct representatives, or by direct selling. In each marketing class, the company-group writing the largest volume of automobile bodily injury liability insurance was selected. Comparison of various expense ratios for these different groups shows both transfer of some costs between the acquisition and the general category and entire elimination of some costs. When studying the ratios in the table, the reader should remember that the *premium levels* of the companies in Groups II and III are lower than those of the companies in Group I. That is, the companies in Groups II and III generally charge less than the companies in Group I for the same, or approximately the same, cover. Therefore, the differences in *dollars* of underwriting expenses charged against a particular cover are not indicated directly by the *ratios* shown in Table 17–1. The same thing applies to claims dollars and claims ratios, of course. These are shown in Table 17-2, which also includes trade position ratios (sums of ratios in Tables 17-1 and 17-2). The figures in both tables show the wide variation that can be found among different companies, particularly when there are large differences in the amounts and kinds of work done by the field sales forces.

TABLE 17-1

RATIOS OF UNDERWRITING EXPENSES TO WRITTEN PREMIUMS

	Company-Group I (Independent Agents)	Company-Group II (Direct Representation)	Company-Group III (Direct Writing)
Commissions and Brokerage	15%	8%	½%
Other acquisition	5	10	5
Total acquisition	20%	18%	5½%
General	3½	5	4½
Taxes, licenses, and fees.	3½	3	3
Total underwriting expense	27%	26%	13 %

TABLE 17-2

RATIOS OF CLAIMS FIGURES TO EARNED PREMIUMS AND TRADE POSITION RATIOS
(See Also Table 17-1)

	Company-Group I	Company-Group II	Company-Group III
Claims incurred	70%	56%	59%
Adjustment expense ...	9	15½	13½
Total claims	79%	71½%	72½%
Sum of claims and underwriting expenses.	106%	97½%	85½%

Conclusion: Costs and Auxiliary Benefits. Clearly, expense ratios by categories are only modest aids in studying auxiliary benefits offered or received. But when these ratios are unusual, they are of some aid, principally in suggesting points to investigate. Surely the risk manager would want to know just what service an insurer with low ratios in all underwriting expense categories can afford to offer. A common question is whether the services offered by independent agents (or brokers) would be worth their extra cost (as illustrated by a comparison between the figures of the first two companies in the preceding paragraph, where the higher agents' commission rate was applied to the higher premium charge). In the end, whether any kind of auxiliary benefits actually will be received must be checked by direct investigation. The payment to cover the costs thereof will ordinarily follow and probably be reflected in the expense ratios of the insurer. Of course, a buyer who considers himself unable (or who, being able, is unwilling) to check services and costs for himself needs at least the service of advice in selection of companies and therefore should be willing to pay for at least this much service. Furthermore, such a buyer seems most unlikely to be able (or willing) to deal with the further problems of selection of particular policies and forms, so probably needs further service in these matters. In short, such a buyer seems a proper customer for full-line, rather than supermarket, insurance service. Depending on the complexity of his problems, this means varying degrees of service from a good agent (or broker) or a skilled direct representative.

SUMMARY

Presumably, a buyer desires to get maximum service at minimum cost. The insurance buyer trying to reach this objective finds his way beset with several obstacles of particular importance in insurance.

The freedom of insurance buyers and sellers to set their own prices is restricted by governmental regulation. Over the long run and for insureds as a whole, insurance premiums are supposed to be adequate to protect the financial soundness of the insurer yet also be equitable as between buyers and not excessive for buyers as a whole. Among the factors that produce variations in premiums are the nature and behavior of rate bases, judgment factors in rating, claims experience of all insureds of a given class, and hazards and loss prevention activities of particular insureds. Buyers should not necessarily be content with the way in which these factors are applied.

Differences in premiums may or may not be accompanied by differences in services received by an insured. Therefore, premium differences must always be compared against service differences. The services that an insurer (or its sales representatives) may provide can be considered according to the accounts against which the insurer charges its costs:

Accounts	Services
Claims	The indemnity benefit itself
Claims adjustment expense	The service of dealing with the claims of others; also, loss reduction through salvage and subrogation
Acquisition expense	Agents' services: risk management advice; aid in claims collection
Taxes and general expenses	Loss prevention; possibly some claims adjustment work or risk management advice

The relative amount of premiums earned (net of dividends) that goes to claims incurred can be significant as a guide to an insurer's behavior. A high claims ratio may lead to a change in underwriting practices, premiums charged, or coverage offered. A persistently low ratio suggests an overly strict claims policy or unusually tight underwriting.

The relative amount of premium money that goes to each of the expense categories is, with few exceptions, a weak guide to the quantity and quality of services that the premium payer will receive. Expense ratios are strongly affected by factors having nothing to do with the quantity or quality of service offered by one insurer as compared with another. Among these factors are lines of insurance written, types of insureds, reinsurance written and ceded, and methods of dividing functions and costs among various parts of the organization.

Most of whatever useful information is available in underwriting expense ratios lies in the acquisition expense ratio, particularly in its commissions and brokerage expense component. The ratio for this component can be determined free of the immediate effects of reinsurance transactions because commissions and brokerage expense ratios for original transactions and reinsurance transactions are published separately as well as on a combined basis. The commission rate for sales representatives suggests how much time and effort they can afford to spend in service to customers.

Agency services—risk management advice, some aid in claims settlement, possibly some reduction in premiums through advice on loss prevention—may be supplied to some extent by an insurer's home or branch office personnel. But there are two types of insureds who are likely to need more risk management aid and advice than they can get from office personnel. One type consists of businesses whose regular operations (management of dynamic risks) require the full- or nearly full-time attention of all members of management. The other type consists of businesses that have large, complex operations and sophisticated managers of static risks; such businesses are likely to need help in finding sound insurers who will write the special covers these risk managers want. When the static risk management problems are not too complex, and the business's management has some sophistication in insurance, less expensive risk management advisers may be adequate.

That there is no simple relationship between contribution to agency costs and benefits from agency service is a major problem in the service of risk management advice. Often more is paid for than is received; sometimes the happy reverse occurs. Transfers of record keeping and other paperwork from agency office to home office may reduce the amount of money the agent needs to cover the cost of direct services to insureds and, when it does, usually reduces total underwriting expenses as well.

Delivery and receipt of good risk management service require ability and willingness on the part of the adviser *and* confidence and cooperation on the part of the insured.

The claims adjustment ratio and the ratio for taxes, licenses, and fees convey no information about services available.

With respect to the ratio for the general expense category, two things can be said: (1) It usually is complementary to the acquisition expense ratio. (2) When a particularly large amount of auxiliary service (such as loss prevention) is provided from an insurer's offices, the general expense ratio can be expected to be high (although the converse does not hold).

The net result of all expense ratio analysis is that it is no substitute for direct check of what services are in fact delivered to the insured. Buyers who do not make such checks for services in general are in particular need of good risk management advice, so certainly should make sure that they get at least that one service in addition to claims payments.

REVIEW AND DISCUSSION QUESTIONS

1. What role should the premium charged for insurance play in the risk manager's deliberations in selecting an insurer?

2. What is the difference between saying insurance *rates* must be equitable and insurance *premiums* must be equitable? Illustrate your explanation with examples. Why is it important for the risk manager to keep this distinction in mind?

3. Explain why you agree or disagree with the statement that *no* rate or premium is ever based on statistics alone. What is the principle role of statistics in insurance rate making? Explain why statistics play a greater role in the making of rates in some lines of insurance than in other lines. Why is this information important to risk managers?

4. Explain how both "class" rates and "merit" rates are designed to achieve rate equity. Explain why neither class rates nor merit rates can guarantee that "he who pays less, gets less, and he who gets more, pays more." Why is the realization of the above statement important to the risk manager?

5. Of what importance to the risk manager is the statement that an underwriter should never expect to recoup past losses from future premiums? Do you agree with the statement? Explain your position.

6. In negotiations between underwriter and risk manager what factors are controlling in deciding upon a rate or premium which is adequate and not excessive? What effect does state regulation of rates have upon rate negotiations between the risk manager and insurers?

7. What are the limitations imposed on the proposition that more risk management advice should be available from insurance sales representatives who make more money per sale? Of what importance are these limitations to the risk manager?

8. Some insurers charge higher premiums than others for the same coverage. Among those who charge a higher premium are those insurer that give additional services. For some risk managers these additional benefits are worth the additional cost. For others, the additional benefits do not justify the difference in premium. What is the nature of these additional benefits? How can the risk manager measure whether these additional benefits may be worth the cost with one insurer but not with another? Explain your answer.

9. Other things remaining the same, is it wiser for the risk manager to purchase insurance in the company that has a high claims ratio than one that has a low claims ratio? What are these *other things* that are assumed to remain the same?

10. Do you agree with the statement that higher ratios would indicate insurers who provided larger amounts of auxiliary benefits? Explain your position.

11. How can an insurer have "negative" expenses? What kinds of insurance company operations are most likely to have "negative expenses? Why?

12. What factors should the risk manager consider in determining whether the services which a *good* agent *could* provide are worth their cost to him? How can the risk manager tell whether a given agent is in fact both capable and willing to provide these services?

13. What must the insurance buyer contribute toward the receipt of good advice from his outside advisers? Why are so many buyers unwilling to contribute this?

14. Consider the figures presented in tables 17–1 and 17–2 in the text. How can you account for the size of each figure and for the variations among the companies? Of what value are these tables to the risk manager, that is what do they tell him that will make him a better risk manager?

PART VI

Cases in Risk Management

This part contains two chapters: "Cases in Risk Analysis" and "Cases in Financial Analysis of Insurers." Arthur Stone Dewing has written that "cases should be used with the clear consciousness that the purpose of business education is not to teach truths . . . but to teach men to think in the presence of new situations." In other words, the virtues of case study lie in the practice of analysis—of identification of the problem to be solved, of selection of principles to be used in solving it, and of adaptation of these principles to the always imperfect and incomplete set of facts which are all that life ever makes available.

Chapter 18

CASES IN RISK ANALYSIS

In studying problems in decisions, practice in actually making decisions is indispensible, even if it be done only in simulation. The cases in this chapter provide a basis for analysis and simulated decision making. Although there are only three cases here, they were selected to present variety as to complexity and nature of problems to be solved. Bryan's Shoe Stores is the simplest case of the three. The Wholesale Company case contains much financial detail and can be dealt with after the fashion used in the text for the Central Avenue Pharmacy (Chapter 11). The problem of the "C" Dairy Corporation was designed as an exercise in the proper selection of insurance covers, and contains the most physical detail.

Obviousy, it is impossible to describe any situation in all the detail which a risk manager could reasonably use. In any extensive use of these or other cases, therefore, assumptions may have to be added to cover additional information required for the particular type of decisions the teacher or the student has in mind. All the assumptions which the authors, as teachers, have found it necessary to give their classes in assignments using these problems have already been included in the cases as presented here. Beyond this, they have told their classes, "Make any assumptions which are necessary and reasonable."

BRYAN'S SHOE STORES

James Bryan owns and operates two shoe stores—one in each of two adjacent county seats in northern Illinois. Both stores handle products primarily in the middle price range and handle men's, women's, and children's shoes plus a small line of sox and hose and shoe accessories. Mr. Bryan himself actively manages one store. The other is managed by Peter Mariano, who has been with Bryan ever since graduating from high school 23 years ago and has been manager of the second store since it was opened 8 years ago. Mariano has lately taken over primary responsibility for the buying for both stores while Bryan has become, in effect, chief financial and accounting officer for the entire operation. Each man has ultimate responsibility for sales, advertising, and personnel for the store which he individually manages. Each man draws a $10,000 "salary" from his own operation. Profits beyond that are shared as follows:

Store #1, managed by Bryan: 85% to Bryan

15% to Mariano

Store #2, managed by Mariano: 75% to Mariano

25% to Bryan

Store #1 is in a building owned by Bryan. The shoe store occupies the full first floor, plus all of the basement not needed for building maintenance facilities (heating equipment, janitor's supplies, etc.). The second floor is rented to others: a dentist's office, an insurance agency, and a manufacturer's representative. (Mariano does not share in the building profits, and a fair rental value, fixed in advance for each year, is subtracted from the Store #1 income before Mariano's share is calculated.)

Store #2 occupies leased premises. Byran is the lessee and paid for the improvements. Bryan owns all of the equipment and inventory in both stores, and is personally liable for all debts.

Store #1 employs four full-time salesmen and one stenographer-bookkeeper. The stenographer-bookkeeper does the clerical work and keeps records for Store #1 and for the business as a whole. Store #2 employs three full-time and one part-time salesmen. Mariano does clerical and bookkeeping work pertaining directly to Store #2. The business engages the services of an accountant on a part-time basis.

It can be seen that the shoe sale business is operated much like a partnership, although it is not one in fact (and creditors clearly understand this). Bryan is 63 years old, Mariano is 41. Bryan plans to retire in the next five or six years. He expects to keep an investment share in the business, with Mariano taking over management control and an ownership share. The only formal movement toward this end so far has been leaving some of Mariano's profit share in the business. This amount is understood by both men to be a legal claim by Mariano against Bryan, but it is shown as an "equity" item in the accounts because it is present to help Mariano acquire a true ownership interest when Bryan retires. (There is no present intention that Mariano will acquire an interest in the building.)

Assets

Store #1		
Cash		$ 8,100
Accounts receivable	$ 4,250	
For bad debts	128	
Net		4,122
Inventory		80,200

Equipment and furnishings .... $ 37,100
    Depreciation 11,130

     Net 25,970

    Total, Store #1 .... $118,392

Store #2
  Cash 4,200
  Accounts receivable .... $ 2,100
    For bad debts 63

     Net 2,037
  Inventory 66,100
  Equipment and furnishings .... $ 24,500
    Depreciation 11,760

     Net 12,740
  Improvements and betterments .... $ 6,400
    Amortized 2,560

     Net 3,840
  Advance rent 400

    Total, Store #2 .... $ 89,317

General
  Cash 1,200
  Office equipment and furnishings .... $ 1,700
    Depreciation 680

     Net 1,020

  Total, All Parts $209,929

Liabilities

Store #1
  Current accounts (merchandise) .... $ 21,000
  Accrued personal property tax 350
  Bills accrued 520
  Installment payments
    Current 2,500
    More than 1 year 13,500

  Total, Store #1 .... $ 37,870

Store #2
  Current accounts (merchandise) 16,600
  Accrued personal property tax 300
  Bills accrued 350
  Installment payments
    Current 1,700
    More than 1 year 1,700

  Total, Store #2 .... $ 20,650

General
  Miscellaneous accruals 450

  Total, All Liabilities .... $ 58,970

Net Worth

Mariano's interest in undistributed profits .... $ 30,000
Net worth to Bryan 120,959

Total Balance $209,929

Statement of Bryan's Building Interest

Assets		Liabilities	
Cash .... $ 2,000		Property taxes accrued. $ 2,400	
Real estate (cost).. $45,000		Other accruals 300	
Depreciation .. 15,000		Reserve for repairs 650	
Net 30,000			$ 3,350
Unconsumed		*Net Worth*	
supplies 400	Bryan 29,050		
$32,400			$ 32,400

Statement of Income (12 months)

Store #1
Net sales $160,500
Cost of goods sold 103,000

Gross margin .... $ 57,500
Operating expenses
Salesmen's salaries and commissions .... $ 20,000
Bryan's salary 10,000
Rent 6,000
Electricity and water 1,200
Memberships and donations 700
Personal property tax 350
Advertising 1,720
Depreciation 2,226
Miscellaneous 1,100

Total Operating Expenses 43,396
Share of overhead
Stenographer-bookkeeper, salary (75%) ... $ 2,250
Other overhead (60%) 480

Total Share of Overhead 2,730

Net, Store #1 .... $ 11,374

Store #2
Net sales $128,700
Cost of goods sold 85,060

Gross margin 43,640
Operating expenses
Salesmen's salaries and commissions .... $ 15,500
Mariano's salary 10,000
Rent 4,800
Electricity and water 900
Memberships and donations 400
Personal property tax 300
Advertising 1,300
Depreciation 1,470

Amortization (Improvements)	512	
Miscellaneous	718	
Total Operating Expenses		35,900
Share of overhead		
Stenographer-bookkeeper, salary (25%) ... $	750	
Other overhead (40%)	320	
Total Share of Overhead		1,070
Net, Store #2		$ 6,670
Total Net before Taxes and Apportionment		$ 18,044
Profit sharing		
(beyond $10,000 salaries and before income taxes)		
Mariano		
75%, Store #2 .... $	5,002	
15%, Store #1	1,706	
Total		$ 6,708
Bryan		
85%, Store #1 .... $	9,668	
25%, Store #2	1,668	
Total		$ 11,336
Bryan's income from building		
Rental income		
Shoe store .... $	6,000	
J. J. Jones, D.D.S.	1,200	
B-B-B Insurance Agency	1,500	
Joe Doakes, manufacturers' representative..	900	
Total Income		$ 9,600
Building operating expenses		
Janitorial service and supplies .... $	2,000	
Heat, power, water	1,450	
Repairs and maintenance	800	
Depreciation	1,000	
Property taxes	1,200	
Total Expenses		6,450
Net from Building		$ 3,150

Expectations of events following severe damage to either store are as follows:

1. That part of the sales operation would be shut down until the quarters were repaired or replaced. (Office operations would be conducted from Bryan's home in event of severe damage at Store #1.)
2. Salesmen would not be retained for shutdowns lasting more than five weeks.
3. In event of a constructive total loss* to the building containing Store #1, it would be replaced with a smaller structure on the same site, a structure sufficient to house the store only. Such a building would cost about $40,000

---

* A constructive total loss is incurred when the cost to repair the property is greater than the value of the property after it is repaired.

if constructed on unimproved land. (Current value of the land on which this building stands is estimated as $25,000. Actual cash value of the present building is estimated at $30,000, of which $26,600 is "insurable" value. Cost of constructing a new, similar building on unimproved land is estimated at $55,000.) Construction of the proposed smaller building would take about four months.

4. In event of loss of use of the premises at Store #2 for more than one month, the lease is automatically canceled. New quarters would be sought immediately upon event of severe damage at Store #2. Presently, such quarters are available and could be prepared for occupancy (cost, $35,000, including equipment and furnishings) in five weeks. Rental rate would be about $5,100 for a ten-year lease. (Present lease has two years to run.)

5. Replacement of furnishings and equipment at Store #1 would cost $40,000.

6. Bryan would be willing to put an additional $25,000 in the business in event of loss, but Mariano has no personal resources of consequence.

This case is particularly useful for possibilities of discussion of its risk management policy in general and of its risk assumption, risk reduction, and risk transfer devices in particular. Sufficient data are presented to make discussion of most of its insurance program practical also.

THE LOZADA WHOLESALE COMPANY, INC.

The Lozada Wholesale Company, Inc., is a wholesale grocery house which operates through a voluntary chain of independent retailers in the states of Ohio and Indiana. The corporation handles about 1,500 ordinary grocery items stocked by the ordinary grocery store, including frozen foods and produce, but excluding fresh meat. Some 600 of the 1,500 items sold bear a private brand name belonging to the Lozada Company.

The merchandise is obtained either directly from producers or in large lots from brokers. Regular orders from customer stores are received weekly and are filled from inventory. There are about 225 regular customers, 60 of whom provide over half of Lozada's total sales.

The most recent balance sheet and profit history of the Lozada Company are presented below. The Company's cash position is weak because it recently had to purchase land and build a new warehouse in Indianapolis, one of its three distributing locations. Its home office and principal warehouse are in Cleveland; land and building there are owned by the Company. In Cincinnati it occupies a warehouse under a ten-year lease which has four years to run. It is seeking land to buy in this area, and hopes to build its own warehouse there as soon as feasible. At Indianapolis it has excess warehouse capacity, so has rented part of the space to a tenant under a two-year lease signed when the warehouse was first occupied three months ago.

Shown here for the Lozada Company are the following: two latest annual balance sheets, each taken at the end of a fiscal year (when inventory is low and cash is up); income statements for the past two fiscal years; current actual cash value and replacement cost figures for assets; and estimated operating results following severe physical damage at each location.

This case is particularly adapted for consideration of the kinds and amounts of insurance the Lozada Wholesale Company should carry for protection loss on account of severe physical damage to its assets.

BALANCE SHEETS, END OF TWO LATEST FISCAL YEARS

(Add 000)

Cash	Next to Latest Year	Latest Year
In banks	$ 56	$ 31
On hand	4	4
U.S. Bonds	12	—
Receivable (net)	125	190
Inventory		
On hand	400	560
In transit	15	15
Parts and supplies	6	9
Unexpired insurance	5	9
Deferred charges	1	10
Furniture and fixtures (net)	28	40
Delivery equipment (net)	66	63
Real estate (net)	168	463
Totals	$ 876	$1,394
Payable (current)	133	190
Accruals	30	35
Mortgage		
Due within year	30	70
Long term	156	336
Convertible preferred stock (5¼%)	—	225
Common stock	450	450
Surplus	77	88
Totals	$ 876	$1,394

INCOME SUMMARY, TWO YEARS

(Add 000)
Last Year

	Total	Cleveland	Cincinnati	Indianapolis
Net sales	$3,500	$1,400	$ 875	$1,225
Cost of merchandise	3,096	1,238	774	1,084
Direct costs				
Wages	182	75	47	60
Other	21	8	5	8
Overhead (net)*	158	62	41	55*
Net before tax	$ 43	$ 17	$ 8	$ 18
Income tax	21			
Net after tax	$ 22			

Previous Year

Net sales	$3,377	$1,395	$ 870	$1,112
Cost of merchandise	2,989	1,235	770	984
Direct costs				
Wages	179	74	47	58
Other	19	8	5	6
Overhead	154	63	41	50
Net before tax	$ 36	$ 15	$ 7	$ 14
Income tax	18			
Net after tax	$ 18			

° Rent receipts of $4,500 at Indianapolis (3 months) have been netted against overhead charges there.

ACTUAL CASH VALUE AND REPLACEMENT COST FIGURES, BY LOCATIONS

(Add 000)

	Cleveland	Cincinnati	Indianapolis
Cash in bank			
Maximum	$ 31	—	—
Minimum	15	—	—
Cash on hand (including checks)			
Maximum	40	$ 5	$ 5
Minimum	2	1	1
Receivable (net)ª			
Maximum	92	58	80
Minimum	48	30	42
Inventory on handᵇ			
Maximum	240	150	210
Minimum	224	140	196
Parts and supplies	4	2	3
Unexpired insurance	6ᵉ	1	2
Deferred charges	1	1	8
Furniture and fixtures			
Cash value	16	10	17
Replacement cost new	25	14	19
Delivery equipmentᵈ			
Cash value	63	—	—
Replacement cost new	78	—	—
Real estate			
Land value	130	—	100
Improvements			
Cash value	210ᵉ	—	200ᶠ
Replacement costᵍ	340	—	200

ª Ledgers for all accounts are in the office at Cleveland. Each warehouse has copies of invoices from which ledger of receivables for customers served through that warehouse could be reconstructed at a cost of about ten cents for each dollar in the accounts.
ᵇ Maximum in-transit inventory at any one place is estimated at $8,000. Inventory in transit includes some incoming items by common carrier (rail or truck) as well as outgoing and some incoming items on owned trucks.
ᶜ Premiums on unexpired insurance not associated with specific locations (*e.g.*, all liability insurance, vehicle insurance, and blanket fidelity bonds) are included in Cleveland figures.
ᵈ Values of trucks are shown in "Cleveland" column solely for convenience. Actually the vehicles may be anywhere, and, for efficient loading and unloading, the Company tries *not* to have more than one at any warehouse at once. Cash values of individual

units range from $8,000 to $20,000. With full cargoes added, values range from $20,000 to $80,000.

e Approximately 15 per cent of this value represents property excluded from coverage in standard fire insurance forms on buildings because commonly considered "undamageable." (See any standard coinsurance or reduced rate contribution clause.)

f Approximately 20 per cent of this value is in property commonly considered "undamageable"—see preceding note.

g These estimates are for cost of converting from severely damaged old structure to new structure on the same site, not cost of a new structure on an unimproved and unimpaired site. Estimate of clearing and reconstruction time is eight months.

ANTICIPATED INCOME RESULTS IN EVENT OF SEVERE DAMAGE

Figures are for eight months following incidence of damage, which is estimated repair and reconstruction time. Results given are for the *entire Company* when the specified unit has been severely damaged.

	No Unit Is Damaged	Eight Months Expectation When: Severe Damage Occurs at:		
		Cleveland	Cincinnati	Indianapolis
Net sales	$2,667	$2,355	$2,479	$2,061
Cost of merchandise	2,360	2,102	2,199	1,839
Direct costs				
Wages	137	125	131	110
Other	16	14	15	12
Overhead (net)				
Depreciation	7	4	6	3
Other	112	118	103	104
Special costs[a]	—	13	5	5
Net before tax	$ 53	$ (21)	$ 20	$ (12)
Income tax	27	[b]	[b]	[b]
Net after tax	$ 26			

a These are costs which would be incurred to obtain temporary facilities and to notify customers (and suppliers) of continued operations. When the severe damage is at Cleveland, these costs include extra costs of acquisition and operation of temporary office facilities. These costs do not include replacement of any assets on a permanent basis. They *do* include reconstruction of records *other than* accounts receivable.

b The amount of income tax charge or credit when there is a loss depends not only on net before-tax income from operations, but also on the extent to which there is uninsured damage to assets which can be charged against taxable income. This amount in turn depends not only on the amount of insurance carried but also on the value of the property for income tax purposes. (If any reader is interested in such values, he may take them as equal to book values in this case.)

THE "C" (DAIRY) CORPORATION

NOTE: This case is from Part II of the examinations given by the American Institute for Property and Liability Underwriters, Inc. It appeared in the 1956 examinations. These examinations (in five parts) are taken by candidates for the professional designation of Chartered Property and Casualty Underwriter (C.P.C.U.). Each year, Part II contains details of a case such as this, and these cases are excellent practice material for students of risk management. Copies of past examinations (five years back, each part separately) may be obtained for a modest fee from the Institute, 270 Byrn Mawr Avenue, Bryn Mawr, Pennsylvania. Each year's examinations in Parts I and II are also reprinted in some trade publications, including *Best's Insurance News* and *The Local Agent*.

These cases are particularly designed as problems in making recommendations for complete programs of insurance and suggestions for loss prevention and control.

The "C" Corporation, which was originally formed to carry on a dairy business in a suburban community, expanded its deliveries to the city. Later it acquired a modern processing plant with pasteurizing and bottling equipment, a fleet of delivery vehicles, facilities for expediting city deliveries, an ice cream plant, and a roadside restaurant.

Principal Location

The principal location of the "C" Corporation is on a 14-acre tract on the south side of a secondary road. It consists of five buildings, the fronts of which face the public highway. The five buildings are separated from each other by 40-foot asphalt driveways. Between the highway and the buildings, a paved parking area for 20 cars has been provided for visitors, while extensive paved parking areas for employees' cars and for more than half of the company's vehicles are located behind the buildings. All parking spaces are clearly marked off and designated as to use.

Building #1, housing the principal offices, is located at the east end of the tract. It is of masonry construction, two stories in height, with a slate roof, and has a small 1½ story wing at the rear which contains the manager's office. Building #1 was originally a farm residence and has been extensively remodeled to serve its present purposes: accounting and clerical staff are housed on the first floor, while the secretary-treasurer's office and a conference room for board meetings are on the second floor as well as a space for storing records.

Immediately east of Building #1 and connected to it, although separated by an adequate firewall, is the boiler room which supplies heat for all plant buildings plus the copious quantities of steam and hot water required for sanitation. It is equipped with two oil-fired steam boilers, replacing an earlier coal-fired installation; there is a 45-foot brick smokestack; fuel oil storage tanks with a capacity of 10,000 gallons are buried under the adjoining driveway.

Across the driveway in a southwesterly direction from Building #1 is the main processing building (Building #2), which is a one-story brick structure 140 feet by 40 feet, divided into five sections. The front section, separated from the rest of the building by an adequate firewall with automatic self-closing doors, contains a visitors' lounge, a small room with refrigerated cases for display of the corporation's products, the telephone switchboard, and the plant foreman's office. Here also is the laboratory, including all necessary equipment for testing and quality control of the firm's dairy products. Behind this section are the pasteurizers and related equipment; then in the next section the bottling room, then the chill storage section, and finally the loading room and dock.

Building #3, directly west of Building #2, houses the purchasing and sales departments and plant maintenance shops. It is of one-story brick construction, approximately 25 by 55 feet. The shops are in the rear half, the front being devoted to office space including the cashier's cage where the driver-salesmen settle their accounts.

Across the next driveway to the west is Building #4, of cinder block construction, largely used for supply and miscellaneous storage, although a few of the roofed cubicles are used as garages. An end compartment of Building #4 is designated for acid storage; at the opposite end two compartments house fire-fighting equipment including a 250-gallon portable foam extinguisher, ladders, hooks, axes, etc.

Building #5 is one story in height, of fire-resistive construction and is directly west of Building #4. It is in two main sections: a parapeted firewall completely separates the automotive repair and servicing shop from the garages; the latter has three sections with capacity of three units each, housing the corporation's refrigerated tanktrucks. The repair and service shop has large overhead doors on the east and west sides and is adequately equipped to handle the regular servicing of the corporation's vehicles. Outside to the west and south are the paved areas where most of the delivery fleet is stored.

Two gasoline delivery pumps and an oiling rack are installed adjacent to the west door of the service shop. The gasoline pumps are served from tanks with a total capacity of 15,000 gallons buried under the parking area.

The 14 acres at this principal location are extensively landscaped but not fenced.

"D" Company—Ice Cream Plant

One mile away the Ice Cream Plant is operated by "D" Company, a wholly owned subsidiary of "C". The plant includes a substantially constructed frame barn on a one-story foundation set back 150 yards from the highway, and is used for storage of supplies. On the south side of the barn a cinderblock one-story structure has been added for the offices of the plant foreman and the clerical staff, and a completely enclosed boiler room with an oil-fired boiler for heat and hot water. Beyond this one-story structure but attached to it is a large one-story fire-resistive building in which are located all the ice cream making machinery, refrigerated space, and loading dock.

"E" Roadside Restaurant

The "E" Roadside Restaurant, another wholly owned subsidiary of the "C" Corporation is located on an adjoining property and is about 200 yards from the ice cream plant. The Roadside Restaurant is a frame 1½ story building approximately 50 by 40 feet in area with paved parking space for 40 cars. In addition to the restaurant and fountain service, it provides a retail sales location for the products of "C" and "D". A modern kitchen uses propane gas for actual cooking but the other equipment is electrically operated. The dining space seats 70 at tables and in booths; there is a soda bar with eight stools. Two large refrigerated cases are used for the display of the dairy products to be retailed.

"C's" City Depot

To facilitate and expedite retail deliveries to its customers, "C" owns and operates a City Depot. It is a one-story brick building, 30 years old, with a flat asphalt and gravel roof, located in a light industrial area of the city, not far from the city limits. There are no serious exposures.

Operations

In summary form "C's" operations consist of: the processing of milk and cream (at the principal location), the distribution of the resulting dairy products at wholesale and retail, the purchase and resale of related products, the manufacture and distribution of ice cream through the "D" Company, and the operation of the "E" Roadside Restaurant. "C" sells milk and cream in all grades, buttermilk, chocolate milk (where permitted by local ordinance), egg nog, butter, cottage cheese, eggs, orange concentrate and orangeade. "E" also retails these products at the restaurant.

The raw milk processed at the principal location is supplied under contract with 38 farms and is hauled to the plant by "R", a contract trucker who owns and maintains for the purpose a fleet of two tank trucks with 3,000 gallons capacity and six stake-body trucks which pick up the raw milk in 20-gallon cans and bring it to the main plant.

"C" Corporation purchases, on an annual contract basis, its requirements for other retail items (eggs, butter, orange concentrate and orangeade) from distributors in the nearby city.

"C" Corporation distributes almost 95 per cent of its milk products directly to homes, restaurants, and retail stores in the city and suburban area. Only about 5 per cent of the business is through wholesalers. "D" Company's ice cream goes 50 per cent to retail sales, the other 50 per cent to stores and restaurants at wholesale.

"C" Corporation owns and maintains a fleet of 80 retail delivery trucks of the driver-step-down type; it has four refrigerated trucks to make wholesale deliveries and to shift product from the principal location to the city depot; three refrigerated trucks for ice cream deliveries; four business sedans for general use by employees, an emergency tow truck for road service, and one panel-type light delivery truck for utility use as well as a ½-ton pickup truck used by the maintenance staff. Joint use of the trucks and automobiles by "C", "D", and "E" is adjusted by appropriate bookkeeping with "C" Corporation having title to all the vehicles and "D" and "E" paying for use on a mileage-rental basis. Company sales personnel other than retail delivery men use their own cars on a mileage reimbursement plan.

Other Information

Other information regarding the "C" Corporation and its subsidiaries is as follows:

	"C" Principal Location	"C" City Depot	"D" Ice Cream	"E" Restaurant	
No. of employees					
Plant	35	5	11	Kitchen	4
Driver-salesmen	52	21	8	Waitresses	8
Office-clerical, inc. management	20	3	2	Managers	2
No. of retail routes served.......	42	15			
Annual payroll	$ 428,000	$126,000	$105,000	$ 42,000	
Gross sales	1,680,000	450,000	350,000	145,000	
Cost of raw materials	924,000	248,000	200,000	80,000	
Replacement value of buildings ..	350,000	51,000	58,000	22,000	
Replacement value of contents (excluding vehicles)	550,000	9,000	65,000	21,000	

The average value of the products carried by a driver-salesman in his retail delivery driver-step-down truck when he starts out on his route is between $60 and $70.

The "C" Corporation and the "D" Company have to secure both state and municipal licenses to deal in milk and milk products. "E" is required by local ordinance to secure a retail mercantile license.

At all locations, "C" Corporation, "D" Company, and "E" Roadside Restaurant use electric power supplied at usual commercial rates by the public utility corporation which serves the city and five western counties of the state.

Chapter 19

CASES IN FINANCIAL ANALYSIS
OF INSURERS

Yearbooks on insurance finance are full of figures which provide plenty of case material in insurance company finance. The annual reports to stockholders and even some copies of the official statements to insurance commissioners may also be obtained from the insurers themselves. However, for those who do not have more complete sources available, some bases for exercises in the financial analysis of insurers are presented here.

The figures in these cases were gleaned from *Best's Insurance Reports* (fire and casualty edition) and *Best's Fire and Casualty Aggregates and Averages*.[1] The figures extracted here are necessarily less complete than are given in the sources from which they were taken, but are full enough to provide material for much thought and analysis. The companies reported on were selected solely for the usefulness of their figures to the purposes at hand. For this reason, and to reduce bias or prejudice on the part of students to whom the actual names would carry a particular "corporate image," the name of the companies are omitted.

CASE I: TWO SPECIALTY COMPANIES

Consider two insurance companies which specialize in serving the same market. Each deals almost exclusively with retail stores of a certain type. These two insurers will be called Company I and Company II. (In all cases, the year "R" means the most recent year, "R − 1" the year before that, "R − 2" the year before that, and so on.)

Company I is a stock company represented by sixty agents in all but eleven states. The premiums it charges for fire and allied lines covers are 20 to 25 per cent less than standard, and in one territory it pays a 10 per cent dividend as well. Casualty lines are written at standard rates. The

---

[1] Both published annually at New York by Alfred M. Best Co., Inc.

maximum amount of insurance kept by the company on any one exposure ("maximum net retention") is $15,000. With its reinsurance treaties, this allows the writing of coverage of as much as $50,000 on any one exposure ("maximum gross line"). Its reinsurer is sound and experienced. The company is characterized by low acquisition costs and careful underwriting. In the most recent year it paid just under $250,000 in regular commission on nearly $1,371,000 of direct business. It ceded nearly $645,000 in premiums for which it received almost $293,000 in commissions. Since contingent commissions (paid or received) added over $15,000 to net expenses, the net figure for Company I's commissions and brokerage expense was *minus* $27,655 on $726,208 of net premium writings. The total picture for expense ratios in year "R" was:

Commissions and Brokerage	Taxes, etc.	Salaries	Other	Total
(−3.8)%	6.8%	12.0%	12.8%	27.8%

Company II is a mutual company licensed in only eleven states. Its policies are written at standard rates, from which policy dividends are paid. On fire and allied lines the dividends are 25 to 30 per cent; on automobile lines, 20 per cent is paid. Company II's maximum net retention on fire and allied lines is $12,500; automatic reinsurance coverage allows $50,000 maximum gross line, with special arrangements ("facultative treaty") available for larger amounts. For losses which involve more than one insured property at a time, there is a catastrophe reinsurance treaty covering after the first $20,000 up to $120,000. (That is, the treaty provides for $100,000 of insurance after the first $20,00 which Company II bears itself.) Automobile liability cover is 100 per cent reinsured; on other automobile covers, all losses over $5,000 are reinsured. The reinsurers are all large companies with excellent financing and reputations.

Company II's underwriting practices are just as conservative as Company I's. Company II's acquisition cost is also low for it pays no commissions on direct business. In the most recently completed year, this company wrote over $564,000 in direct premiums with zero commissions and brokerage expense thereon. In addition, readjustment of some reinsurance it had previously written produced a net "minus" amount of "reinsurance premiums written" figure (−$167); on this, Company II *recovered* $3,604 it had previously paid in commissions! Furthermore, cession of nearly $59,000 in reinsurance produced a commission income ("negative expense") of over $16,000. The net result for the year was commission and brokerage expense of *minus* $19,918 on $510,421 of net premiums written. The total underwriting expense picture was:

Commissions and Brokerage	Taxes, etc.	Salaries	Other	Total
(−3.9)%	2.3%	19.7%	18.2%	36.3%

Other figures from recent years appear in the following tables.

HISTORY OF OPERATING EXPERIENCE, FIVE YEARS

(All dollar figures in thousands.)

	Years	Assets	Policy-holder's Surplus	Premiums Written Direct	Premiums Written Net	Net Earned	Ratios Claims*	Ratios Underw. Expense†	Ratios Sum	Stat'y Underw. Profit	Investment Current Earning	Investment Capital Gain	Income Tax	Dividends Stock	Dividends Policy
COMPANY I	R	$4,187	$3,375	$1,371	$726	$ 706	43.3%	27.8%	71.1%	$ 190	$136	$ 3	$173	$ 90	$ 4
	R–1	4,077	3,305	1,252	673	671	39.5	27.9	67.4	219	140	5	136	90	4
	R–2	3,908	3,171	1,201	662	633	31.7	33.2	64.9	213	131	–7	160	90	5
	R–3	3,761	3,093	1,115	638	632	40.7	31.3	72.0	175	130	–17	136	90	4
	R–4	3,750	3,038	1,137	660	656	42.0	25.9	67.9	209	141	18	173	120	5
	5 years			$6,076	$3,359	$3,298	39.5%	29.2%	68.7%	$1,006	$678	$ 2	$502	$480	$ 22
COMPANY II	R	$1,181	$ 803	$ 564	$ 510	$ 500	26.2%	36.3%	62.7%	$ 183	$ 28	$13	$ 8	—	$129
	R–1	1,091	717	509	482	484	32.4	35.9	68.3	154	25	47	4	—	125
	R–2	978	619	484	477	462	36.2	28.3	74.5	112	23	–14	4	—	113
	R–3	952	617	451	453	451	29.6	37.9	67.5	146	21	–2	4	—	115
	R–4	982	573	533	458	466	44.5	35.4	79.9	88	24	5	5	—	126
	5 years			$2,541	$2,380	$2,363	33.6%	36.8%	70.4%	$ 683	$121	$49	$ 25	None	$608

* Claims (includes claims expense) ratios to earned premiums before policy dividends.

† Underwriting expense ratios to written premiums before policy dividends.

DISTRIBUTIONS OF BALANCE SHEET FIGURES, TWO YEARS

Company I Year:			Company II Year:	
R	R—1		R	R—1
		Assets		
12.8%	8.5%	Cash	9.1%	7.6%
		Bonds		
18.9	22.4	U.S. gov't	31.9	29.8
44.6	48.3	Other gov't	35.2	37.4
—	2.1	Other	—	2.3
—	4.0	Mortgages	—	1.2
4.6	10.5	Stocks	4.5	14.0
15.4	6.2	Real estate	13.0	6.9
3.7	1.0	Other	3.3	0.8
100.0%	100.0%		100.0%	100.0%
		Total Assets		
$4,187	$1,181	(000's of dollars)	$4,077	$1,091
		Liabilities		
1.3%	1.8%	Claims	0.8%	3.2%
12.0	25.5	Unearned premiums	11.8	26.7
5.0	1.8	Accruals	5.4	1.5
		Contingencies		
1.1	2.8	and miscellaneous	0.9	2.9
80.6	68.1	*Policyholder's surplus*	81.1	65.7
100.0%	100.0%		100.0%	100.0%

NET EARNED PREMIUMS AND OPERATING RATIOS BY LINE, YEAR "R"

Company I			Lines of Insurance	Company II		
Share of Total Net Earned Premiums‡	Claims° to Earned Premiums‡	Underwriting Expenses to Written Premiums‡		Share of Total Net Earned Premiums‡	Claims° to Earned Premiums‡	Underwriting Expenses to Written Premiums‡
92.1%	45.8%	28.3%	Fire & extended coverage	85.8%	22.1%	36.7%
1.6	32.1	34.9	Homeowners	7.6	41.8	36.8
—	—	—	Auto liability	†		
—	—	—	Other auto	5.6	41.2	33.8
2.9	29.1	35.6	Miscellaneous liability	—	—	—
3.4	24.1	35.6	Glass and theft	—	—	—
—	—	—	Other	1.00	17.7	19.1
100.0%				100.0%		
$706			Premium totals§	$500		
			Dividends to			
$ 4			policyholders§	$129		

° Including claims adjustment expenses.
† Some small amounts written but all reinsured.
‡ Ratios are based on premiums *before* dividends to policyholders.
§ In thousands of dollars.

DIRECT AND NET WRITTEN PREMIUMS, TWO YEARS

(Thousands of dollars)

Company I				Lines of insurance	Company II			
Year R		Year R—1			Year R		Year R—1	
Direct	Net*	Direct	Net*		Direct	Net*	Direct	Net*
				Fire and extended coverage				
$1,245	$656	$1,167	$626		$448	$433	$413	$419
35	16	22	11	Homeowners	84	81	32	31
—	—	—	—	Auto B.I. liability	27	—	23	—
—	—	—	—	Auto P.D. liability	12	—	11	—
—	—	—	—	Auto collision	16	16	16	16
—	—	—	—	Auto fire, etc.	12	12	11	11
59	23	40	15	Misc. B.I. liability	—	—	—	—
3	1	3	1	Misc. P.D. liability	—	—	—	—
14	14	9	9	Glass	—	—	—	—
16	16	11	11	Burglary-theft	—	—	—	—
—	—	—	—	Other lines†	3	5	3	5

° Net premiums equal direct written plus reinsurance written less reinsurance ceded.
† In "Net" column, "other lines" includes excess-of-loss reinsurance written (for other insurers).

Problems to Consider

The question is, would a business be wise to buy insurance protection from one of these companies, assuming they were willing to write it? For discussion purposes, this question may best be considered in two parts: (1) the wisdom of buying from a specialty company such as these rather than obtaining the same cover from a more general writing company; (2) assuming that one were going to buy from one of these two specialty companies, then from which one?

The student should begin by marshalling the advantages and disadvantages of dealing with specialists like these. The next question is, do these vices and virtues indicate a definite answer for all cases, or does the answer depend upon some particular characteristics in the busines to be insured? If so, what are these particular characteristics? When do they indicate use of specialty insurers, when the contrary? (If the student wishes to have some figures of general writing insurers for comparison, he can refer to the companies in Case II of this chapter, or, of course, to any selected companies in the published reports cited at the beginning of this chapter.

For further useful exercise in company analysis, the student should now assume (regardless of what was decided above) that insurance is to be purchased from one of the specialty companies reported on here. Suppose $40,000 of fire and extended coverage insurance on contents (in leased quarters) is to be purchased. (a) Which of these two companies would be preferred? (b) What additional covers written by that company should also be purchased from it? (Each answer should be supported by a statement of "why," of course.)

CASE II: TWO MODERATELY LARGE MULTIPLE LINE COMPANIES

Consider now two moderately large stock multiple line companies—Company A and Company B. These companies were selected for study because they have similarities and dissimilarities, and because they present certain interesting features for analysis. (What these features are is left for the student analyst to discover, of course.) To aid in analysis of these two companies, not only their figures, but average figures for companies of their same general type are also given.

Both Company A and Company B are licensed throughout the United States and in Canada and also write in other foreign countries. In the United States and Canada, both companies market exclusively through independent agents (except for sales of reinsurance, of course). Company A writes all its covers at standard rates. Most of Company B's sales are made at standard rates, but it has recently been writing an increasing percentage under independent filings as to rates and forms.

The largest net retention on any single exposure is $200,000 in Company A and $300,000 in Company B. The maximum gross amount which A writes on any line is not reported; the maximum gross line of B is $2,500,000. Both companies have extensive reinsurance protection in well-regarded insurers, here and abroad. Each company participates in several specialty underwriting pools, such as in ocean marine, aviation, grain processing and storage, oil processing and storage, nuclear energy, cotton transport, excess reinsurance, foreign operations, and some other types of high value property.

The younger of these two companies was over 80 years old in year "R." Neither had experienced any major changes in management in the several years before "R" but at the end of "R − 2" Company B made a change in its operational and reporting procedures. Starting with "R − 1," operations of B and its subsidiary companies were all pooled and reported on a consolidated basis. In year "R" and earlier the figures reported for B were for its own operations alone.[2] Company A also has subsidiary operations, but its reporting was put on a consolidated basis over two decades before year "R."

Major figures for Companies A and B appear in the several tables that follow.

Notes to table of "premium volume and operating ratios by line" (see also notes at bottom of the table):

All dollar figures are in thousands.

Claims ratios were taken against net earned premiums.

Claims adjustment expenses are included in the figures for "claims" in

---

2 The effects of this consolidation can best be seen in the table headed "premium volume and operating ratios, by line, three years."

History of Operating Results, Three Years

(All dollar figures are in thousands)

	Years	Net Premiums		Ratios*					Stat'y Underw. Profit	Investments		Income Tax	Dividends (Stock)
		Written	Earned	Claims	Commissions	Taxes	Other	Sum		Current Earning	Capital Gain		
Company A	R	$41,084	$39,992	62.2%	26.5%	3.1%	12.2%	103.0%	$−1,933	$2,168	$ 720	$ 83	$1,000
	R−1	37,999	36,627	62.1	27.9	2.9	13.3	106.2	−2,997	1,877	5,598	35	1,000
	R−2	35,386	33,002	64.8	27.5	2.8	13.2	108.3	−3,395	1,764	−4,744	−327	1,000
Company B	R	$46,068	$44,658	60.2%	24.1%	2.9%	11.6%	98.8%	$ 114	$1,662	$1,701	$496	$ 840
	R−1	41,780	40,055	63.7	25.1	2.8	12.2	103.7	−2,133	1,503	7,270	− 40	800
	R−2	33,108	23,958	57.4	21.6	2.1	12.3	93.4	− 863	1,110	−1,051	− 86	800
"Average Comp'y"†	R	$21,441	$20,786	58.5%	24.3%	2.9%	13.8%	99.5%	$− 121	$1,661	$1,330	$188	$ 934
	R−1	20,945	20,382	60.1	24.7	2.9	14.0	101.7	− 571	1,654	7,661	138	905
	R−2	20,175	19,283	63.4	24.8	2.8	14.7	105.7	−1,377	1,597	−3,257	− 88	913

* Ratios of claims (which includes claims expense) and "other" expenses are to earned premiums; ratios of commissions and taxes are to written premiums.

† "Average company" figures are based on sets of companies which had the following characteristics: stock companies doing a multiple line business but with fire and marine lines predominant. All business written at standard rates. The identity and number of these companies varied from year to year; each year's figures are averages for companies which had these characteristics that particular year.

workmen's compensation and liability insurance lines (miscellaneous, B.I., auto B.I., and auto P.D.) only; for all other lines, claims adjustment expenses are included in the "expenses" column. Either way, adjustment expenses are stated as percentages of net earned premiums.

All underwriting expenses are stated as percentages of net written premiums.

The lines individually mentioned in the table are all those which supplied one or more per cent of the net written premiums for either Company A or Company B in year "R."

The columns headed "average company" show average figures for sets of companies of the same general type as Companies A and B. For this particular table, a company was considered of the same general type as Companies A and B *with respect to the particular line under consideration* if it was a stock company in their same size class *for that line*. With only a few exceptions this was the largest size class for that line.

DISTRIBUTIONS OF BALANCE SHEET FIGURES, THREE YEARS

	Company A Year:			Company B Year:			"Average Company" Year:		
	R	R−1	R−2	R	R−1	R−2	R	R−1	R−2
Assets									
Cash	5.6%	6.8%	4.8%	3.2%	4.2%	2.7%	3.7%	4.3%	4.6%
Bonds									
U.S. gov't.	14.5	17.2	20.3	16.5	14.8	15.3	14.6	15.2	16.3
Other gov't	13.0	8.8	16.2	26.8	22.5	24.7	14.5	13.6	14.2
Other	17.3	11.3	0.1	0.1	—	0.2	2.3	2.1	1.1
Mortgages ..	—	—	—	—	—	—	—	—	0.1
Stock	32.6	37.7	41.1	36.0	38.9	37.3	53.6	53.8	52.5
Real estate..	—	—	—	2.4	2.4	2.9	1.1	1.1	0.1
Other	17.0	18.2	17.5	15.0	17.2	16.9	10.2	9.9	11.2
Total assets ...	100.0%	100.0%	100.0%	100.0%	100.0%	100.0%	100.0%	100.0%	100.0%
(000's) ...	$79,619	$75,943	$67,843	$87,012	$83,619	$71,494	$65,179	$64,821	$55,820
Liabilities									
Claims res'ves	20.6%	17.4%	16.2%	18.5%	16.9%	15.6%	11.2%	10.4%	10.9%
Unearn. prem.	38.4	38.8	41.4	36.1	35.8	39.5	28.8	29.3	31.7
Comm's, taxes	1.6	1.7	1.3	2.0	1.6	1.7	1.3	1.4	1.4
Contingencies and other.	9.3	9.9	10.5	10.6	13.8	13.6	2.9	3.1	3.5
Net Worth									
Stated capital	6.3	6.6	7.4	4.6	4.8	5.6	4.4	4.7	5.6
Surplus, surplus reserves...	23.8	25.6	23.2	28.2	27.1	24.0	51.4	51.1	46.9
	100.0%	100.0%	100.0%	100.0%	100.0%	100.0%	100.0%	100.0%	100.0%

Note: In this table, the "average company" figures again were taken from sets of companies with the following characteristics: multiple line stock companies with fire and marine lines dominant among their lines, all or most of the business being written at standard rates. Since the identity and number of such companies changed from year to year, the average figures given cannot be taken to represent the growth or evolution of any particular company or set of companies.

Premium Volume and Operating Ratios, by Line, Three Years

Line	Year	Premiums Written Direct		Premiums Written Net		Premiums Net Earned		Ratios Claims			Ratios Expenses		
		Co. A	Co. B	Co. A	Co. B	Co. A	Co. B	Co. A	Co. B	Aver. Co.	Co. A	Co. B	Aver. Co.
Fire	R	$16,624	$14,689	$12,974	$13,472	$13,042	$13,395	52.3%	49.1%	50.3%	51.8%	44.5%	48.3%
	R−1	15,851	13,166	12,557	12,680	12,903	12,954	56.5	56.0	51.3	53.1	47.8	49.2
	R−2	13,687	11,585	13,038	12,829	12,797	10,492	53.6	46.9	51.6	50.7	51.6	49.5
Ext'd Cov'r.	R	$4,593	$3,940	$4,068	$4,135	$4,111	$4,348	45.7%	43.5%	42.4%	53.3%	51.5%	53.4%
	R−1	4,517	3,805	4,119	4,412	4,213	4,555	39.2	40.3	39.8	51.8	53.0	53.7
	R−2	4,579	3,835	4,294	4,665	4,123	3,498	55.3	40.1	50.3	50.6	53.2	55.3
Homeowners	R	$2,097	$1,924	$2,493	$2,582	$1,819	$1,946	46.3%	43.2%	45.4%	50.1%	52.1%	45.5%
	R−1	1,320	1,195	1,499	1,601	1,169	1,291	50.6	47.6	50.5	52.3	52.6	46.9
	R−2	924	913	1,152	1,134	748	587	47.8	40.5	51.9	48.4	48.3	47.3
Allied Lines	R	$1,337	$1,542	$459	$323	$500	$343	55.5%	51.3%	48.1%	45.6%	35.0%	36.0%
	R−1	1,173	865	455	333	626	1,013	46.2	42.3	48.9	56.7	36.8	37.7
	R−2	373	N.A.	209	(126)*	442	N.A.	70.5	79.9	63.8	50.4	38.0	41.4
Ocean Marine	R	$3,966	$7,109	$2,469	$1,625	$2,480	$1,406	61.2%	73.1%	61.4%	30.2%	32.8%	34.6%
	R−1	4,120	6,867	2,658	1,227	2,753	1,255	77.7	70.2	62.5	31.5	38.5	35.0
	R−2	4,340	8,438	3,218	1,495	3,142	1,460	82.8	78.3	68.3	26.9	30.7	34.7
Inland Marine	R	$2,395	$1,814	$1,509	$1,915	$1,574	$2,121	46.8%	44.2%	51.1%	44.5%	55.0%	46.6%
	R−1	1,690	2,750	1,597	2,436	1,689	2,396	49.6	58.1	52.5	46.1	51.8	48.6
	R−2	1,744	2,579	1,672	2,258	1,760	1,942	58.1	55.8	57.7	44.2	49.8	39.3

		1	2	3	4	5	6	7	8	9	10	11	12
W'r'm'n Comp.	R	$ 2,026	$ 1,659	$ 2,389	$ 2,655	$ 2,203	$ 2,554	73.2%	72.6%	74.2%	38.6%	33.1%	25.3%
	R – 1	2,027	1,705	1,982	2,363	1,786	2,225	75.0	60.9	71.4	41.3	32.2	25.7
	R – 2	1,468	1,272	1,433	999	1,313	450	73.3	58.2	70.3	44.0	30.8	25.8
B.I. Misc.	R	$ 1,078	$ 1,166	$ 1,554	$ 1,908	$ 1,308	$ 1,799	61.0%	55.1%	58.0%	36.4%	36.4%	38.5%
	R – 1	1,023	965	1,167	1,694	949	1,453	41.8	69.6	60.8	41.3	39.1	39.1
	R – 2	638	643	751	1,080	506	299	62.6	34.8	58.8	41.5	37.5	39.6
B.I. Auto	R	$ 3,604	$ 2,519	$ 4,343	$ 6,307	$ 4,224	$ 6,074	75.2%	69.7%	74.6%	36.6%	31.8%	30.6%
	R – 1	3,379	2,397	3,695	5,456	3,158	4,918	71.3	79.8	78.5	40.8	32.5	31.6
	R – 2	2,440	1,688	2,623	2,257	2,145	843	80.9	72.1	82.0	39.8	30.8	32.7
P.D. Auto	R	$ 1,555	$ 1,115	$ 1,960	$ 2,795	$ 1,883	$ 2,688	80.4%	71.0%	65.8%	38.8%	36.5%	31.7%
	R – 1	1,462	1,091	1,596	2,337	1,364	2,086	87.4	86.3	68.1	42.1	35.3	33.1
	R – 2	1,006	709	1,089	946	860	358	100.1	71.6	70.4	40.0	31.7	34.3
Auto Phys.D.	R	$ 4,841	$ 3,189	$ 4,878	$ 5,111	$ 5,037	$ 4,996	59.0%	43.4%	51.6%	47.5%	50.7%	40.6%
	R – 1	4,457	3,468	4,983	4,583	4,765	4,250	53.3	53.1	53.0	53.0	49.8	43.3
	R – 2	4,026	3,156	4,541	3,451	4,364	2,881	55.0	55.1	58.6	50.8	53.0	42.9
Surety	R	N.A.	$ 488	$ (265)*	$ 696	$ (255)*	$ 616	81.2%	44.3%	46.2%	70.2%	68.9%	57.5%
	R – 1	N.A.	317	(263)*	579	(220)*	471	43.6	49.5	23.6	58.9	66.0	60.0
	R – 2	N.A.	295	(184)*	353	N.A.	166	N.A.	114.8	27.0	N.A.	60.8	61.4
Other	R	$ 2,330	$ 3,010	$ 1,988	$ 2,539	$ 1,811	$ 2,372	Not available					
	R – 1	2,146	2,046	1,691	2,079	1,493	1,921						
	R – 2	1,424	1,901	1,366	1,641	1,023	1,072						

N.A. Not available.

* Included in the "other" category at the end of the table.

Additional notes which should be read with this table appear on the next page.

The "other" lines written by Company *B* were commercial multiple peril, earthquake, individual and group health, miscellaneous property damage liability, fidelity, glass, burglary-theft, boiler and machinery, air physical damage, and growing crops. The list was the same for Company *A* with the following additions: surety, manufacturers output, industrial multiple peril, and nuclear energy. Each company also wrote some excess-of-loss reinsurance, which was included in the "other" lines figures.

Questions to Be Considered

Again, two sets of questions arise. One set deals with whether to purchase insurance from companies of the general type of *A* and *B*. The second set deals with selection among companies of the type.

The student should consider the question of what are the important characteristics of the "general type" of insurer of which Companies *A* and *B* are examples. What advantages and disadvantages do these characteristics offer the risk manager? Under what conditions, if any, do these advantages outweigh the disadvantages for the risk manager, and vice versa?

Then, whatever his answer to the last preceding question, the student should consider himself the risk manager of a business for whom the services of companies of the type under discussion *are* advantageous. Now a choice among *three* companies appears: Company *A*, Company *B*, and an "average company" of their general type.

Indexes

INDEX OF TOPICS

M

INDEX OF AUTHORS AND SOURCES CITED

647

This book has been set on the Linotype in 10 point Janson, leaded 2 points, and 9 point Janson, leaded 1 point. Part titles are in 24 point Janson italics; part numbers and chapter numbers and titles are in 18 point Janson italics. The size of the type page is 27 by 46 picas.